Intentional Conceptual Change

INTENTIONAL CONCEPTUAL CHANGE

Edited by

Gale M. Sinatra
University of Nevada, Las Vegas

Paul R. Pintrich
The University of Michigan

LEA LAWRENCE ERLBAUM ASSOCIATES, PUBLISHERS
2003 Mahwah, New Jersey London

Lawrence Erlbaum Associates, Inc., Publishers
10 Industrial Avenue
Mahwah, New Jersey 07430

Cover design by Kathryn Houghtaling Lacey

Library of Congress Cataloging-in-Publication Data

Intentional conceptual change / edited by Gale M. Sinatra and Paul R. Pintrich.
p. cm.
Includes bibliographical references and index.
ISBN 0-8058-3825-2 (alk. paper)
1. Concepts. 2. Change (Psychology). 3. Learning, Psychology of. 4. Intention. I. Sinatra, Gale M. II. Pintrich, Paul R.

BF443 .I58 2003
153.4—dc21 2002069344
CIP

Books published by Lawrence Erlbaum Associates are printed on acid-free paper, and their bindings are chosen for strength and durability.

Printed in the United States of America
10 9 8 7 6 5 4 3 2 1

Contents

Preface

The world we live in is a product of our thinking,
to change the world we must change our thinking.[1]

The idea of changing the world through changing our thoughts is a powerful one. Traditional views of knowledge reconstruction placed the impetus for thought change outside the learner's control. The teacher, instructional methods, materials and activities were identified as the seat of change. Recent perspectives on learning, however, suggest that the learner can play an active, indeed *intentional*, role in the process of knowledge restructuring (Bereiter & Schardamalia, 1989).

The purpose of the present volume is to explore the role of the learner's intentions in knowledge change. The idea of *intentional conceptual change* was inspired by Bereiter and Schardamalia's (1989) description of the intentional learner and Pintrich and his colleagues' perspective that there is more to conceptual change than "cold cognition" (Pintrich, Marx, & Boyle, 1993). At the intersection of these ideas is the notion that learners' intentions can determine the likelihood of knowledge change.

This volume assembles research by a group of international scholars from a variety of disciplines who have examined the role of intentional level cognition in conceptual change learning. These researchers draw on different perspectives to examine the influence of constructs such as epistemological stance, self-regulation, metacognition, and motivation on

[1]Paraphrase of a quote commonly attributed to Einstein.

learning. They seek to define when and how these constructs can be intentionally brought to bear on knowledge change.

The volume is intended for scholars studying knowledge acquisition and change. Such scholars would be from a broad array of disciplines including educational psychology, developmental psychology, science education, cognitive science, learning science, instructional psychology, and instructional and curriculum studies. We hope this book would also be used in graduate courses in education and psychology exploring topics such as conceptual change learning, knowledge acquisition, intentional learning, learning theory, and cognitive development.

The volume is organized in three parts. In the introductory chapter, we seek to explain our perspective that intentional conceptual change is characterized by *goal-directed and conscious initiation and regulation of cognitive, metacognitive, and motivational processes to bring about a change in knowledge* (Sinatra & Pintrich, chap. 1, this volume, p. 6).

Part I goes on to explore the role of cognitive and metacognitive processes in intentional conceptual change. Constructs such as self-regulation, self-explanation, and metacognitive control are considered as possible mechanisms of intentional knowledge change. A variety of challenging issues are explored, such as the difficulty of overcoming the incommensurability of ideas, the interaction of domain-specific knowledge with intentions, and the design of instruction to promote intentional conceptual change. These chapters provide theoretical groundwork, experimental research, and practical examples illustrating how learners regulate knowledge change.

Part II examines the role of epistemological, social, and motivational constructs in intentional conceptual change. In this section a broad array of intentional constructs are examined and empirical evidence is provided illustrating that beliefs, attitudes, emotions, goals, interests, and dispositions are determinants of the likelihood of change. Suggestions for how instruction can be designed to encourage students to bring their intentions to bear on restructuring their knowledge are also discussed.

Part III explores the prospects and problems for this new perspective. The question of whether and how much of conceptual change is intentional is examined. Intentional conceptual change may be a powerful, but much less common means of knowledge transformation than unintentional change. Finally, the concluding chapter highlights key themes in the volume and looks ahead to the work that must be done if this perspective is going to prove fruitful for researchers.

We are indebted to the authors for their willingness to take up the challenge of exploring the idea of intentional conceptual change. We are grateful that the contributors were willing to engage in thoughtful dialogue as we worked together to assure that each chapter contributed a unique perspective to our theme. This entailed an exchange of ideas that informed our thinking and broaden our perspective. It is our sincerest hope that the readers of this volume will have a similar experience that may result in a change in their thinking. The power of change in thought can be realized more readily when it is our goal and intention to change.

REFERENCES

Bereiter, C., & Scardamalia, M. (1989). Intentional learning as a goal of instruction. In L. B. Resnick (Ed.), *Knowing, learning and instruction: Essays in honour of Robert Glaser,* (pp. 361–392). Hillsdale, NJ: Lawrence Erlbaum Associates.

Pintrich, P. R., Marx, R. W., & Boyle, R. A. (1993). Beyond cold conceptual change: The role of motivational beliefs and classroom contextual factors in the process of conceptual change. *Review of Educational Research, 63,* 167–199.

1

The Role of Intentions in Conceptual Change Learning

Gale M. Sinatra
University of Nevada, Las Vegas

Paul R. Pintrich
The University of Michigan

Views of conceptual change that emerged during the cognitive revolution of the 1970s and 1980s described how students come to the learning situation with preconceived notions, naive conceptions, or misconceptions about the world around them. These existing conceptions can serve as scaffolds or as barriers when learning new concepts. Research on conceptual change from the science education and cognitive developmental psychology perspectives focused on detailing the structure of learners' existing knowledge representations, and the means by which teachers and instructional methods might facilitate change in those conceptions (see for example, Schnotz, Vosniadou, & Carretero, 1999).

Examining these two traditions of research reveals both tremendous contributions and some shortcomings. The early cognitive developmental literature provided a good description of the various internal cognitive processes that mediate conceptual change. More recently, there has been increased discussion of the related social and situational factors that might facilitate conceptual change (Pintrich, Marx, & Boyle, 1993; Saljo, 1999). The science education literature also has contributed extensively to our understanding of how external factors, such as the teacher, the format and content of the instruction, or the structure of the activities in which students engage can facilitate change.

Yet a common shortcoming of these approaches can be identified. Both perspectives suggest that if learners recognize and become aware of the conflict between their existing knowledge and the scientific conception, conceptual change is possible. They suggest that conceptual change pedagogy is a matter of placing students in circumstances that highlight points of conflict. However, we have argued that cognitive conflict and deep engagement are often insufficient to induce change (Dole & Sinatra, 1998; Pintrich et al., 1993). Change often does not occur, even in situations designed to promote knowledge restructuring, due to learner characteristics such as motivation (Pintrich, 1999), affective resistance (Linnenbrink & Pintrich, 2002), and learners' beliefs (Sinatra, Southerland, McConaughy, & Demastes, 2001). Although recently both traditions of conceptual change research have begun to acknowledge the role of these characteristics, both underemphasize the degree to which they are *controlling factors* in the change process.

Recently, Vosniadou (1999) called for increasing the ties between the cognitive developmental and science education perspectives on change. She suggested that integrating these perspectives would make the connections between the internal and external factors in change more explicit. We agree. We suggest, however, that attempts to integrate the two perspectives would be facilitated by an examination of the construct of the *intentional learner* (Bereiter & Scardamalia, 1989). The "value added" of intentional learning as a general mediating process between external factors and internal psychological processes is that *the impetus for change is placed within the learner's control*. Conceptual change depends, then, not only on cognitive factors such as the recognition of conflict, but on metacognitive, motivational, and affective processes that can be brought under the learner's conscious control and may determine the likelihood of change.

An examination of the psychological and educational literature of 1980s and 1990s reveals that views of learning shifted toward a greater emphasis on the role of the learner in the learning process (Boekaerts, Pintrich, & Zeidner, 2000). The view that emerged is that learners are not only active in their construction of meaning, but they can be *intentional* (Bereiter & Scardamalia, 1989). Learners cognitively engage in the learning process, but also monitor and regulate their learning in a metacognitive manner. Learners have motives, goals, and emotions that contribute to and even determine the learning outcome. Views of learning as a simple interaction of students' knowledge with the to-be-learned content are being replaced by perspectives depicting a complex interplay of learners' knowledge, intentions, and the environmental and social context (Dole & Sinatra, 1998; Linnenbrink & Pintrich, 2002; Pintrich et al., 1993).

Conceptual change researchers, like other cognitive psychologists, have been relatively slow to delve into the intentional and affective constructs of "hot cognition" (e.g., motivation, metacognition, affect, reflectivity; see Pintrich et al., 1993). Yet, a group of researchers has emerged whose perspective on conceptual change reflects that called for by Vosniadou (1999). Looking forward toward new theories of conceptual change, she noted, "motivational beliefs, beliefs about the self, goals and other variables . . . need to be brought into the picture as we move away from 'cold' cognition" (p. 11).

The theoretical accounts and empirical investigations of conceptual change contained in this volume explore the role of learners' intentions in the change process. With the consideration of intentional constructs such as epistemological stance, self-regulation, metacognition, motivation, and dispositions, the view of conceptual change presented in the following chapters is that of a complex interaction between internal cognitive processes and external environmental factors that *can* be intentionally initiated and controlled by the learner.

WHAT IS INTENTIONAL CONCEPTUAL CHANGE?

There is certainly more than one idea as to what constitutes *intentional conceptual change*. Indeed, each contributor to this volume weighs in on this matter in considerable depth, and the chapters represent a wide variety of definitions and perspectives. We provide an overview here of some of the issues related to developing models of intentional learning and conceptual change.

Most conceptions of *intentional cognition* describe the construct as a state of mind or a level of cognition that is to be distinguished from unconscious or automatic thoughts and/or behaviors (see Stanovich, 1999). This view takes into consideration the fundamental notion from cognitive science that the human cognitive processing system has a differentiated architecture (e.g., Anderson, 1990; Newell, 1990). Cognitive scientists assume that cognition is organized in a manner that allows information to be processed and represented in qualitatively different ways. For example, some processing occurs quickly, accurately, and almost effortlessly, such as the automatic recognition of a familiar word in a text or a familiar face in a picture. Processing that occurs automatically is said to involve the *algorithmic level* of cognition (Stanovich, 1999).

When the mind acts on information, it often does so without intent (Bargh & Chartrand, 1999). The learner does not necessarily plan to modify information in a specific way; rather, such constructions can and often do occur without the learner's awareness. Indeed, countless studies have revealed that learners can modify information in such a way as to construct a mental representation that differs from what was conveyed. For example, when young learners, who believe the earth is flat are told that the earth is round, they often construct the understanding that the world must be shaped like a pancake (Vosniadou & Brewer, 1992).

Knowledge construction that occurs at the algorithmic level is characterized as incidental or implicit. That is, deliberate effort and conscious attention are not necessary for learning to occur at this level. Rather, learning can occur simply from exposure and repetition. Incidental learning is not the only means of developing algorithmic-level knowledge, however. Much of what we learn through conscious effort can become automatic with experience. Strategies that we once applied deliberately to study and learn can become automatic with repeated use (O'Brien, 1995). Despite our subjective experience that we spend a considerable portion of our day in deliberate intentional thought, it has been argued that much, if not most, cognitive processing occurs at the algorithmic level (Bargh & Chartrand, 1999).

The features of intentional level cognition can best be understood in comparison to those of the algorithmic level. Unlike unintentional constructions of knowledge, intentional level processing is *goal-directed and under the learner's control*. Rather than learning from simple exposure, students' goals guide the learning process. For example, when studying, a reader may have a goal to learn certain information. Thus, she may deliberately spend more time processing some information than other information. If she is aware that her goal is not being met (the information is not yet learned), she can modify her learning strategy to better meet her goals (see Reynolds, 2000, for a review of empirical evidence of goal-directed text processing).

The learner initiates intentional, goal-directed processing. This type of processing does not occur simply in response to environmental events. That is, the information that is relevant to a student's learning goal does not automatically draw additional resources, produce differential strategy use, use more processing time, or generate motivated effort to learn in and of itself. Rather, the learner must decide which bits of information warrant additional attention and effort, and must allocate the processing resources accordingly. Reynolds (2000) made this point clear in his discussion of the role of executive control of attention in reading comprehension: "the genesis of this behavior seems to have been internal to the reader, rather than external" (p. 15).

Intentional level processing is not only initiated by the learner, it is under the learner's conscious control. Unlike automatic processes that cannot easily be overridden once learned, intentional processes in a learner's conscious awareness can be redirected or ceased at will. Intentional level processes such as awareness and regulation allow the learner to evaluate goal satisfaction and direct and redirect attention to particular information as needed. For the learner who is *not* engaged in intentional, goal-directed processing of information, processing resources are controlled by other factors (i.e., background knowledge, task difficulty, topic familiarity, etc.).

How does intentional level processing impact learning? Sinatra (2000) defined the intentional learner as "one who uses knowledge and beliefs to engage in internally-initiated, goal-directed action, in the service of knowledge or skill acquisition" (p. 15). Thus, intentional constructs are those that are evoked in the process of intentional learning, such as the deliberate use of knowledge and beliefs to achieve goals, an orientation toward goal-directed action, the self-regulation of cognitive processes, and certain cognitive dispositions toward thinking and learning.

Researchers extending theoretical accounts and empirical investigations of conceptual change are now exploring how intentional constructs play a significant role in the knowledge reconstruction process. For example, conceptual change researchers explored how conscious beliefs, attitudes, goals, motivations, dispositions, etc. contribute to (and sometimes impede) the change process (e.g., Pintrich, 1999; Pintrich et al., 1993; Venville & Treagust, 1998). Researchers also demonstrated that intentional constructs account for learning and change even after differences in traditional cognitive constructs (such as prior knowledge and reasoning ability) are taken into account (see Kardash & Scholes, 1996; Stanovich, 1999).

To understand how intentional level constructs come into play during conceptual change learning, consider the nature of the conceptual change process. The various models or accounts of the change process differ in detail but agree on the following: The change process involves the restructuring of existing conceptions to account for new information (Chi, 1992; Dole & Sinatra, 1998; Posner, Strike, Hewson, & Gertzog, 1982; Vosniadou, 1994). They also agree that in order for change to be possible, students must juxtapose their existing conceptions against new ideas and weigh the similarities and differences. Yet, even when these circumstances are met, change does not always occur (see Dole & Sinatra, 1998).

These basic elements of the change process can be enhanced by intentional cognition. Ferrari and Elik (chapter 2) describe the process thusly: "intentional conceptual change stems from perturbations to one's existing concepts that lead individuals to question their current understanding (mind-to-world fit), followed by deliberate efforts to account for those perturbations." In order to recognize a perturbation, one must first be aware of one's existing knowledge. Next, one must also be aware of a piece of anomalous data that leads to dissatisfaction with the existing conception (Chinn & Brewer, 1993). To question their current understanding, students must have a deliberate *goal orientation* (Pintrich, 2000a, 2000b, 2000c) to learn and understand the material. Attempts to resolve the perturbation may involve experimentation, questioning, discussion, or some other form of *high engagement* (Dole & Sinatra, 1998) that allows students to compare rival conceptions. Then, students must weigh the plausibility and fruitfulness of the prior conception in comparison with the new one (Posner et al., 1982). Ultimately, learners must be willing to engage in critical reflection which requires a disposition toward engaging thoughtfully with ideas (see Sinatra et al., 2001).

Laced throughout this description of the conceptual change process are internal initiations of cognitive and motivational processes and the intentional use of knowledge, epistemological beliefs, metacognitive processes, goals, and strategies. The learner can and does initiate, regulate, and control the use of these constructs intentionally to resolve disequilibrium and bring about understanding and conceptual change. Thus, we would characterize *intentional conceptual change* as the goal-directed and conscious initiation and regulation of cognitive, metacognitive, and motivational processes to bring about a change in knowledge.

It is important to note, however, that *not all conceptual change is intentional.* Several contributors to this volume explain how changes can occur without the learner's intentions. Ferrari and Elik note how "instances of unintentional conceptual change include discoveries that are made by chance or through serendipity." Vosniadou (chapter 13) explains how change can occur without the learner's awareness. In chapter 14, Hatano and Inagaki also question the degree to which intentions play a role in conceptual change. Indeed, unintentional conceptual change is not only possible, it may be more common in learning both in and out of school. Given the effort, skills, and dispositions needed to initiate and sustain change, learners often do not bother. However, an interesting and yet unresolved issue is the relative utility and quality of representations of knowledge that have been restructured *intentionally* compared to those that have been unintentionally reorganized. Another issue that warrants investigation is the relative permanence of intentionally versus unintentionally formed knowledge constructions. Furthermore, the goal of schooling and instruction is to facilitate change in children's conceptions. Accordingly, schooling is a context where intentional conceptual change should be fostered, as more deliberate student involvement in the change process may result in deeper, longer lasting change. Models and research on intentional conceptual change should explore these possibilities as they may help create a more effective conceptual change pedagogy.

TRADITIONAL MODELS OF CONCEPTUAL CHANGE

Why is there a need to consider the construct of intentional conceptual change? The simple answer is that traditional models of conceptual change do not fully account for learners' intentions in the change process.

As noted, two research traditions have greatly contributed to our understanding of conceptual change: science education research and cognitive developmental research (see Vosniadou, 1999 for an excellent overview of these perspectives).

The science education perspective emerged out of educators' and researchers' observations that students bring alternative conceptions about scientific phenomena to the learning experience. Turning to the history of science, researchers likened the change in individuals' conceptions to that experienced by a scientific community during a paradigm shift (Kuhn, 1970; Lakatos, 1970). Based on this perspective, Posner et al. (1982) identified four critical variables in the conceptual change process. First, individuals must become *dissatisfied* with their existing conceptions. Second, individuals must find the new conceptions *intelligible*. Third, students must regard the new conceptions to be *plausible*. Finally, students must find that the new conceptions are *fruitful*, that is, the new conceptions must lead to new insights.

The science education model for conceptual change has been a useful and productive one and has inspired both research and instructional interventions. However, the model has a number of limitations that many researchers recognize. First, the original model assumes the process of knowledge restructuring to be much more rational than is likely true of individual conceptual change (Strike & Posner, 1992). Second, the model assumes students' conceptual knowledge is more coherent than some researchers have suggested (diSessa, 1993). Third, some have questioned the assumption of revolutionary change or conceptual replacement in favor of a more evolutionary or gradual change view (Siegler, 1996; Smith, diSessa, & Roschelle, 1993).

These critiques notwithstanding, we believe a more serious concern is that conceptual change interventions inspired by Posner et al. focused mainly on the learning environment and what teachers can do to manipulate the context to support individuals' knowledge restructuring. What is lacking in the model and its related instructional techniques is a description of the role of the students' intentions in bringing about change.

Student intentions are certainly not ignored in the model. For students to become dissatisfied with their existing conceptions requires a level of awareness. For students to judge whether they find the new conception intelligible, fruitful, or plausible requires some reflection. However, the model does not explain how the four components of change may be either *initiated and/or controlled by the learner's intentional cognitive or motivational processes*.

The second approach to the study of change is that taken by cognitive developmentalists (e.g., Carey, 1985). According to this perspective, "initial conceptual structures undergo radical changes with development"

(Vosniadou, 1999, p. 5). Developmentalists trace the refinement of students' naïve theories or frameworks as they mature. Conceptual change requires not only the learning of new knowledge but also the acquisition of developmental capabilities (such as metacognitive awareness, theory of mind, and logical thought) that support knowledge restructuring. Much research in this area is aimed at understanding how young learners' conceptual structures are organized and represented (Wellman & Gelman, 1998). Other researchers focus on examining what cognitive processes are involved when naïve conceptions are transformed into more mature ones (Vosniadou & Brewer, 1992, 1994).

In contrast to science educators who focused mainly on the external context (such as social environment, curriculum interventions, teachers actions, etc.) needed to support conceptual change, cognitive developmentalists tended to focus more on the internal context. That is, they examined students' knowledge structures and the cognitive mechanisms and processes implicated in the change process, while largely ignoring the external context (Vosniadou, 1999; cf., however, diSessa, 1993, and Smith et al., 1993 for notable exceptions). From our point of view, a critical failing is that despite taking a more internal look at change, like science educators, developmentalists also largely ignored the motivational and intentional processes of learners and their role in knowledge restructuring.

The contributors to this volume recognize the need for greater understanding of students' intentions in the change process. Specifically, in the following chapters, contributors who are international scholars in the area of conceptual change explore the role students' knowledge, epistemological beliefs, motivations, metacognition, and self-regulation can play in bringing about knowledge restructuring.

The volume is organized into three sections. The first section explores cognitive and metacognitive aspects of intentional conceptual change. The second endeavors to explain how students' epistemological beliefs and motivations can intentionally be brought to bear on changing their conceptions. The third section questions how much and whether conceptual change is or needs to be intentional. The concluding chapter suggests where researchers may want to consider taking these ideas into the future.

COGNITION, METACOGNITION AND INTENTIONAL CONCEPTUAL CHANGE

Ferrari and Elik begin the first section by providing readers with a conceptual road map to the key constructs central to our theme: *intentions, concepts*, and *conceptual change*. They begin by tracing the philosophical roots of the terms *intention* and *intentionality*, and they explain how work in this volume speaks to the sense of "intrinsic intentionality" or mental states about "our perceptions, thoughts, beliefs, desires, and intentions in the everyday sense." They go on to clarify what psychologists mean by *concepts, conceptual stability*, and *conceptual change*. Bringing these ideas together, they explain that intentional conceptual change "involves a person's (or group's) deliberate attempt at radical change from one conceptual system to another. . . ." Ferrari and Elik go on to help us appreciate these abstract definitional nuances by providing a more concrete discussion of the change process. Here they discuss mediators of intentional conceptual change (the individual, social, and cultural contexts in which the change process is inextricably embedded) and moderators of intentional conceptual change (factors that facilitate or impede the process). Finally, they help us to understand when change is intentional and when it is not.

In Chapter 3, deLeeuw and Chi provide a clear illustration of how and when conceptual change learning can be intentional. Chi and her colleagues have investigated the "self-explanation" effect for some time (e.g., Chi, deLeeuw, Chiu, & LaVancher, 1994). As defined in their chapter, self-explanations are goal-directed attempts toward understanding a text or problem that require conscious thought and effort, and are therefore an "intentional strategy on the part of the reader." In the most intriguing aspect of their chapter, deLeeuw and Chi compare their view of *mental model revision* to Kintsch's view of building a situation model as described in his construction integration model (Kintsch, 1998). Both perspectives consider the role of background knowledge in the construction of text or problem understanding. Both describe situations that call for the reader to make conscious repairs of their mental model or situation model. In comparing and contrasting the role of automatic versus controlled processes in the two views, deLeeuw and Chi provide a rich context from which to consider the theoretical grounding of the construct of intentional conceptual change.

Thagard and Zhu (chapter 4) take a very different direction by tackling the issue of incommensurability of ideas across cultural groups. By examining Eastern and Western physicians' views on acupuncture, they explore whether these views are so different as to prohibit any rational comparison of the two perspectives. Through the explication of the linguistic, conceptual, referential, and explanatory differences between the two perspectives, they conclude that the two approaches are not as irreconcilable as one might assume. Thagard and Zhu go on to explain how the prospect of resolving the incommensurability of the two perspectives is enhanced when individuals have intentional goals and the disposition to consider alternative points of view. They explain, "the development of mutual understanding and the process of conceptual change depend in part on the intentions of people to take seriously conceptual systems that differ from the ones they currently hold." Their conclusion that these two extremely different viewpoints can be rationally compared suggests there is hope for students resolving the incommensureability of their ideas with scientific ones.

In chapter 5, Hennessey takes us from theory into practice by describing the process of intentional conceptual change as she observed it in her students. This chapter serves two objectives: First, it provides an in-depth look at the role of metacognition in the intentional conceptual change process, and second, it serves as a primer on how to adapt Bereiter's (1990) description of *intentional learners in inquiring classrooms* to conceptual change pedagogical practice.

Through her rich description of the classroom context, instructional methods, and students' resulting oral discourse and written products, we see the development of her students' conceptual thinking from an insider's perspective, rather than as distant observers. Central to the process of intentional learning and conceptual change from Hennessey's point of view is a very "sophisticated" level of metacognitive engagement. Based on findings from two longitudinal studies of her students' ability to represent and reflect on their own ideas, she concludes that even very young students are willing and able to engage in the high level of "evaluative" metacognitive processing necessary for intentional conceptual change.

This section concludes with a discussion of the role of domain-specific knowledge in intentional conceptual change. In chapter 6, Limón illustrates "the interaction between cognitive, metacognitive, and motivational factors and how they may influence intentional conceptual change" in different domains. She identifies three prerequisites for change: metacognitive awareness, volition, and self-regulation. Thus, her conceptualization of intentional conceptual change is consistent with several contributors to this volume. However, she explicitly describes the conditions under which someone might make the effort to achieve change, illustrating how intentional conceptual change is a special case of knowledge restructuring requiring greater demands of the learner. Those demands include time and motivated effort. She goes on to examine the role of affect and resistance to change and explains how emotions may serve to obstruct the change process. The unique contribution in this chapter is the explanation of how processes, not just the outcomes, of intentional conceptual change are affected by the level of expertise and knowledge. In particular, she notes that intentional conceptual change processes may require a certain level of prior knowledge in order to operate, as individuals with little prior knowledge are less likely to be aware that their conceptions are not adequate.

EPISTEMOLOGICAL AND SOCIAL/MOTIVATIONAL FACTORS IN INTENTIONAL CONCEPTUAL CHANGE

In the second section, the role of constructs such as epistemological beliefs, motivation, and interest and their interactions with cognitive constructs in conceptual change processes are explored. Andre and Windschitl begin chapter 7 by exploring how students' personal interests may influence conceptual change. By summarizing and reanalyzing a series of studies, they describe empirical evidence showing that, indeed, interest affects knowledge reconstruction. They go to explain how this relates to intentional conceptual change by proposing a tentative model whereby "interest influences intention to engage in the cognitive processing necessary for conceptual change."

Andre and Windschitl then demonstrate, through a series of studies involving students' learning about the cardiovascular system, how personal epistemological beliefs influenced the change process. They found that students who viewed knowledge as changing exhibited greater change in their own knowledge. Epistemological beliefs also interacted with the type of instruction students experienced. "Individuals with more sophisticated epistemological beliefs performed better when allowed to construct and test their own hypotheses, but individuals with less sophisticated beliefs did poorly when asked to do the same."

Finally, they describe how Windschitl explored some of these same notions with pre-service secondary science teachers learning about classroom inquiry. He found that prospective teachers' views about the nature of scientific inquiry influenced how they conducted their own inquiry projects and influenced whether they were likely to change their views about teaching inquiry to their future students. Andre and Windschitl explain, "epistemological beliefs in such a context would become both a mediator and an object of intentional intellectual activity."

In Chapter 8, Mason also examines how personal "beliefs about the nature of knowledge and knowing may facilitate or constrain intentional conceptual change." She begins by providing an overview of the research on epistemological belief development and learning. She then examines how epistemological beliefs impact conceptual change. Through case study analysis, we see how individual students' epistemological beliefs "act as thinking dispositions to guide students' efforts toward the goal of knowledge revision." We see how Guiliana's beliefs that science is constantly evolving and, therefore, that ideas are never certain lead her to approach learning as a problem-solving process. She intentionally sought to resolve two competing positions on whether the Egyptians built the pyramids by weighing and considering the conflicting evidence. However,

Valerio, who believed that knowledge is certain and stable, remained resolute in his opinions despite the presence of conflicting data. These case studies eloquently illustrate the power of students' beliefs and intentions in conceptual development and change.

In Chapter 9, diSessa, Elby, and Hammer also take a case study approach—or, more specifically, a "microcausal analysis"—to examine one student's epistemological stance while learning physics. This student (J) is interesting in that her epistemological views interfered with her ability to learn about physics concepts. diSessa et al. conclude that J's epistemology is complex and defies a straightforward global categorization scheme. In addition, her views were contextualized, suggesting that current views of epistemology as global traits or perspectives may be oversimplified. diSessa et al. go on to clarify the distinction between implicit and explicit knowledge of epistemology and, therefore, help to explain when and how explicit epistemological stances may be a factor in intentional conceptual change.

In Chapter 10, Hynd considers the process of intentional conceptual change that results from "motivated, metacognitive effort" put forth by learners processing a persuasive message. She reviews theory and research in attitude change and persuasion from the fields of educational psychology, social psychology, and communication, as well as her own research on conceptual change in physics, to illustrate the role of intentions in conceptual change. Likening the process of conceptual change to attitude change, Hynd explores the role of beliefs, affect, and dispositions in processing persuasive messages. Research in persuasion makes it clear that affect is central in determining whether or not conceptual change occurs and needs to be more fully accounted for in models of conceptual change.

One interesting finding from her work on persuasion is that central and peripheral routes can both be used to promote conceptual change. The central route is the path to persuasion that involves the careful consideration of ideas. The peripheral route involves the consideration of peripheral cues that are independent from the message itself but, according to Hynd, may play their own unique role in promoting conceptual change. Whether peripheral cues can lead to conceptual change seems to depend on the degree to which learners are aware and reflective, key aspects of intentional learning. In addition to the consideration of peripheral cues, intentions play another important role in the change process. An interesting aspect of Hynd's argument is that the change process requires not only the thoughtful consideration of new conceptions, but also the deliberate inhibition of old conceptions. This illustrates that intentions may be critical to the concerted effort required both to inhibit old concepts and to acquire new ones.

Chapter 11 presents what Southerland and Sinatra call a special case of intentional conceptual change: learning about biological evolution. In the past 15 years, a number of researchers investigated students' understandings of biological evolution (Bishop & Anderson, 1990; Demastes-Southerland, Good, & Peebles, 1996). Although some of this research focused on the intrinsic difficulties of the underlying science concepts, a great deal of the research attempted to tease out how students' beliefs impact the way they come to understand the topic (Demastes-Southerland et al., 1995; Lawson & Weser, 1990; Scharmann, 1990). Clearly, biological evolution is an area ripe for the investigation of how students' intentions help shape learning.

Southerland and Sinatra capitalize on this naturally occurring intersection of beliefs and knowledge to examine the relationship between students' conceptions of biological evolution and their personal epistemological views about the nature of science (NOS). Their research suggests that students who view knowledge as absolute reject evolutionary explanations of human origins because evolution is "just a theory." Alternatively, students who have a more flexible epistemological stance and are disposed to open-minded thinking are more likely to say they accept human evolution. Taking these findings into account, they argue that heightening students' awareness of their epistemological views and current conceptions of NOS promotes conceptual change—particularly for those students whose epistemological stances conflict with the view that evolution (indeed, all science) is in a continuous state of theoretical flux. Thus, the key to conceptual change in evolution education is the juxtaposition of personal and scientific epistemologies, which makes the study of evolution learning particularly useful for exploring intentional conceptual change.

Linnenbrink and Pintrich conclude the second section by discussing the role of achievement goals in intentional conceptual change. They begin chapter 12 by clearly explicating three criteria for intentional conceptual change. First, they explain why students must have a learning goal, as opposed to other types of goals. In doing so, they clarify what it means for conceptual change learning to be goal-directed. Second, they argue that students must be aware of their goals and conscious of their pursuit. This criterion explains why metacognitive awareness is a defining feature of intentional conceptual change. Finally, Linnenbrink and Pintrich's third criterion requires that "there must be some type of agency, control, volition, or self-regulation on the individual's part as he or she uses various strategies to obtain this goal of conceptual understanding." This third feature connects awareness with goal-directed action, completing the cycle of intentional learning.

Then, given the centrality of goals to their criteria, they explain implications for intentional conceptual change that emerge from achievement goal theory. Using specific examples from their own research and others', they explain why, specifically, mastery goals are key to intentional conceptual change. Their theoretical analysis of achievement goal theory in relation to prominent theoretical perspectives on conceptual change learning illustrates how the concept of intentional conceptual change might fit within and extend existing theory in conceptual change.

PROSPECTS AND PROBLEMS FOR MODELS OF INTENTIONAL CONCEPTUAL CHANGE

The third section takes a critical look at the promise of this new perspective. In chapter 13, Vosniadou shines a critical light on the construct of intentional conceptual change by questioning whether intentional learning is, indeed, needed to promote knowledge restructuring. She agrees with Bereiter and Scardamalia's (1989) view that "intentional learning is an achievement, not an automatic consequence of human intelligence" (p. 366). According to this perspective, intentional learning does not develop on its own and is not supported by traditional school tasks.

So, if intentional learning is rare, how does conceptual change occur? Vosniadou argues that much of it occurs without the learners' conscious awareness. Evidence for her point of view comes from the internal inconsistencies and lack of explanatory coherence in students' representations of the shape of the earth. She argues that the intentional learner "checks for and corrects the conceptual system for consistency," thus inconsistencies should be rare if learners are being intentional. However, one question arises: If students are not aware of the fragmented nature of their knowledge, could they still be intentional about their learning? Does lack of a coherent representation signal lack of intentions to learn? An interesting direction for research would be to distinguish between unintentional and intentional changes in knowledge and the quality of representations underlying both.

Finally, we do agree with Vosniadou that unintentional conceptual change is possible. However, we wonder whether it is optimal. Unintentional change may result in the type of "synthetic models" Vosniadou describes, a consequence of which is inconsistent and contradictory reasoning. These unintentional changes may also be less stable and more fleeting. Vosniadou acknowledges that there may be something "value-added" about change that occurs intentionally. Questioning whether and how conceptual change can be intended generates many issues for further investigation.

A cognitive-sociocultural view of intentional conceptual change is presented by Hatano and Inagaki in chapter 14. They agree with Vosniadou that intentional conceptual change is not necessarily a frequent occurrence. The effort necessary for intentional conceptual change, and the tendency for individuals to prefer their original conceptions, lead Hatano and Inagaki to "assume that a large scale revision of conceptual knowledge is induced only when there is no other choice." Like Vosniadou, they argue that teachers and peers, not individual students, are the more likely impetus for conceptual change. It is important to note, however, that they do acknowledge the key role students' motivation to comprehend plays in the change process. Within this framework, they explore a comprehension activity designed to promote conceptual change, whereby there is peer support and encouragement for conceptual change. Through their examination of students' classroom discourse while attempting to comprehend two alternative explanations of a phenomenon, Hatano and Inagaki describe the role of external influences on conceptual change, such as the teacher, peer support, the activity, external rewards, and the sociocultural context. While not denying the role of individual agency and intentions, Hatano and Inagaki raise the interesting question of whether sociocultural factors may ultimately play the more significant role in determining the likelihood of change.

Finally, in Chapter 15, we summarize the various themes raised by the different contributors to the volume. We describe the prospects and promises as well as the challenges facing researchers in this emerging field of study. Key themes highlighted include: (a) clarification of our constructs and models for intentional conceptual change; (b) specification of the structures and processes involved in intentional conceptual change, including a discussion of the issues of automaticity and unconscious processes that might impede or possibly facilitate conceptual change; (c) issues of domain specificity, such as consideration of the need for different models depending on the content domain under consideration (math, science, social science); (d) developmental differences or the potential need for different models for different age groups; (e) the measurement of intentional conceptual change, including what type of evidence is necessary to validate our models; (f) the role of contextual factors including classroom and peer interaction features that might facilitate or constrain conceptual change; and finally, (g) design principles, such as the potentially important design features of classrooms or other contexts that need to be used to facilitate conceptual change.

We hope that this volume inspires researchers to devote more attention to the role of the intentional learner in the conceptual change process. Specifically, we hope researchers can more accurately describe the processes and mechanisms of conceptual change that are and are not under the learner's control. In doing so, we hope to bring models of conceptual change into balance in terms of their emphasis on the internal and external factors controlling the change process. Finally, our hope for the intentional conceptual change perspective is to inform the development of a more effective conceptual change pedagogy by inviting students to control rather than resist the restructuring of their knowledge.

REFERENCES

Anderson, J. R. (1990). *The adaptive character of thought.* Hillsdale, NJ: Lawrence Erlbaum Associates.

Bargh, J. A., & Chartrand, T. L. (1999). The unbearable automaticity of being. *American Psychologist, 54(7),* 462–479.

Bereiter, C. (1990). Aspects of an educational learning theory. *Review of Educational Research, 60,* 603–624.

Bereiter, C., & Scardamalia, M. (1989). Intentional learning as a goal of instruction. In L. B. Resnick (Ed.), *Knowing, learning and instruction: Essays in honour of Robert Glaser* (pp. 361–392). Hillsdale, NJ: Lawrence Erlbaum Associates.

Bishop, B. A., & Anderson, C. W. (1990). Student conceptions of natural selection and its role in evolution. *Journal of Research in Science Teaching, 27,* 415–427.

Boekaerts, M., Pintrich, P. R., & Zeidner, M. (2000). *Handbook of self-regulation.* San Diego, CA: Academic Press.

Carey, S. (1985). *Conceptual change in childhood.* Cambridge, MA: MIT Press.

Chi, M. T. H. (1992). Conceptual change within and across ontological categories: Examples from learning and discovery in science. In R. N. Giere (Ed.), *Minnesota Studies in the Philosophy of Science: Vol. XV. Cognitive models of science* (pp. 129–186). Minneapolis, MN: University of Minnesota Press.

Chi, M. T. H., deLeeuw, N., Chiu, M. H., & LaVancher, C. (1994). Eliciting self explanations improves understanding. *Cognitive Science, 18*(3), 439–477.

Chinn, C. A., & Brewer, W. F. (1993). The role of anomalous data in knowledge acquisition: A theoretical framework and implications for science instruction. *Review of Educational Research, 63*(10), 1–49.

Demastes-Southerland, S., Good, R., & Peebles, P. (1995). Students' conceptual ecologies and the process of conceptual change in evolution. *Science Education, 79*(6), 637–666.

diSessa, A. (1993). Towards an epistemology of physics. *Cognition and Instruction, 10,* 105–225.

Dole, J. A., & Sinatra, G. M. (1998). Reconceptualizing change in the cognitive construction of knowledge. *Educational Psychologist, 33,* 109–128.

Kardash, C. M., & Scholes, R. J. (1996). Effects of preexisting beliefs, epistemological beliefs, and need for cognition on interpretation of controversial issues. *Journal of Educational Psychology, 88*(2), 260–271.

Kintsch, W. (1998). *Comprehension: A Paradigm for Cognition.* Cambridge: Cambridge University Press.

Kuhn, T. (1970). *The structure of scientific revolutions* (2nd ed.). Chicago: University of Chicago Press.

Lakatos, I. (1970). Falsification and the methodology of scientific research programs. In I. Lakatos & A. Musgrave (Eds.), *Criticism and the growth of knowledge* (pp. 91–196). Cambridge: Cambridge University Press.

Lawson, A. E., & Weser, J. (1990). The rejection of nonscientific beliefs about life: Effects of instruction and reasoning skills. *Journal of Research in Science Teaching, 27*(6), 589–606.

Linnenbrink, E. A., & Pintrich, P. R. (2002). The role of motivational beliefs in conceptual change. In M. Limón & L. Mason (Eds.), *Reconsidering conceptual change: Issues in theory and practice* (pp. 115–135). Dordrecht, The Netherlands: Kluwer Academic Publishers.

Newell, A. (1990). *Unified theories of cognition.* Cambridge, MA: Harvard University Press.

O'Brien, E. J. (1995). Automatic components of discourse comprehension. In R. F. Lorch & E. J. O'Brien (Eds.), *Sources of coherence in reading* (pp. 159–176). Hillsdale, NJ: Lawrence Erlbaum Associates.

Pintrich, P. R. (1999). Motivational beliefs as resources for and constraints on conceptual change. In W. Schnotz, S. Vosniadou, & M. Carretero (Eds.), *New perspectives on conceptual change* (pp. 33–50). Amsterdam, The Netherlands: Pergamon.

Pintrich, P. R. (2000a). An achievement goal theory perspective on issues in motivation terminology, theory, and research. *Contemporary Educational Psychology, 25,* 92–104.

Pintrich, P. R. (2000b). Multiple goals, multiple pathways: The role of goal orientation in learning and achievement. *Journal of Educational Psychology, 92,* 544–555.

Pintrich, P. R. (2000c). The role of goal orientation in self-regulated learning. In M. Boekaerts, P. R. Pintrich, & M. Zeidner (Eds.), *Handbook of self-regulation* (pp. 451–502). San Diego, CA: Academic Press.

Pintrich, P. R., Marx, R. W., & Boyle, R. A. (1993). Beyond cold conceptual change: The role of motivational beliefs and classroom contextual factors in the process of conceptual change. *Review of Educational Research, 63,* 167–199.

Posner, G. J., Strike, K. A., Hewson, P. W., & Gertzog, W. A. (1982). Accommodation of a scientific conception: Towards a theory of conceptual change. *Science Education, 67*(4), 489–508.

Reynolds, R. E. (2000). Attentional resource emancipation: Toward understanding the interaction of word identification and comprehension processes in reading. *Scientific Studies of Reading, 4*(3), 169–195.

Saljo, R. (1999). Concepts, cognition, and discourse: From mental structures to discursive tools. In W. Schnotz, S. Vosniadou, & M. Carretero (Eds.), *New perspectives on conceptual change* (pp. 81–90). Amsterdam, The Netherlands: Pergamon.

Scharmann, L. C. (1990). Enhancing an understanding of the premises of evolutionary theory: The influence of a diversified instructional strategy. *School Science and Mathematics, 90*(2), 91–100.

Schnotz, W., Vosniadou, S., & Carretero, M. (1999). *New perspectives on conceptual change.* Amsterdam, The Netherlands: Pergamon.

Siegler, R. S. (1996). *Emerging minds: The process of change in children's thinking.* New York: Oxford University Press.

Sinatra, G. M. (2000, April). From passive to active to intentional: Changing conceptions of the learner. In G. M. Sinatra (Chair), *What does it mean to be an intentional learner? Alternative perspectives.* Symposium presented at the American Educational Research Association Annual Meeting, New Orleans, LA.

Sinatra, G. M., Southerland, S., McConaughy, F., & Demastes, J. (2001, April). The role of intentions, beliefs, and knowledge in learning about evolution. In L. D. Bendixen (Chair), *Epistemological beliefs and learning: What do we know and how do we know it?* Symposium presented at the American Educational Research Association Annual Meeting, Seattle, WA.

Smith, J. P., diSessa, A., & Roschelle, J. (1993). Misconceptions reconceived: A constructivist analysis of knowledge in transition. *The Journal of the Learning Sciences, 3*(2), 115–163.

Stanovich, K. E. (1999). *Who is rational? Studies of individual differences in reasoning.* Mahwah, NJ: Lawrence Erlbaum Associates.

Strike, K. A., & Posner, G. J. (1992). A revisionist theory of conceptual change. In R. A. Duschl & R. J. Hamilton (Eds.), *Philosophy of science, cognitive psychology, and educational theory and practice* (pp. 147–176). Albany, NY: State University of New York Press.

Venville, G. J., & Treagust, D. F. (1998). Exploring conceptual change in genetics using a multidimensional interpretive framework. *Journal of Research in Science Teaching, 35,* 1031–1055.

Vosniadou, S. (1994). Capturing and modeling the process of conceptual change. *Learning and Instruction, 4,* 45–69.

Vosniadou, S. (1999). Conceptual change research: State of the art and future directions. In W. Schnotz, S. Vosniadou, & M. Carretero (Eds.), *New perspectives on conceptual change* (pp. 3–13). Amsterdam, The Netherlands: Pergamon.

Vosniadou, S., & Brewer, W. F. (1992). Mental models of the earth: A study of conceptual change in childhood. *Cognitive Psychology, 24,* 535–585.

Vosniadou, S., & Brewer, W. F. (1994). Mental models of the day/night cycle. *Cognitive Science, 18,* 123–183.

Wellman, H. M., & Gelman, S. A. (1998). Knowledge acquisition in foundational domains. In W. Damon (Series Ed.) and D. Kuhn & R. S. Siegler (Vol. Eds.), *Handbook of child psychology: Vol. 2. Cognition, perception, and language* (5th ed., pp. 523–573). New York: Wiley.

I

COGNITION, METACOGNITION, AND INTENTIONAL CONCEPTUAL CHANGE

2

Influences on Intentional Conceptual Change

Michel Ferrari
Nezihe Elik
Ontario Institute for Studies in Education
University of Toronto

Any discussion of intentional conceptual change must carefully consider what is meant by the term, as well as how such change actually occurs in individuals and among groups of people. In this chapter, we consider philosophical definitions of the terms *intention, concept,* and *change,* psychological theories and research on intentional conceptual change, and the pragmatics of it. We especially focus on *radical conceptual change,* in which foundational conceptions of a domain must be changed, such as when learning about evolution and other complex systems, or when our conception of self must be radically transformed in therapy. The first part of the chapter focuses on philosophical definitions; the second part is more psychological and discusses the research on the pragmatics of change in various sociocultural contexts. Finally, we briefly describe a model that aims to explain interactions between the variables that influence intentional conceptual change.

PERSONAL SELVES AND INTENTIONAL CONCEPTUAL CHANGE

Before we define concepts and intentionality, we need to answer the question: Where is the center or seat of intentional conceptual change? The answer to this question clarifies the focus of this chapter: interaction between intentional agents and their environment. We suggest that intentional conceptual change is only possible in a person who intends to change his or her conceptual understanding—a person, as Dennett (1995) reminded us, who is created through the dialectical synthesis of both a biological capacity to entertain intentions and the cultural objects and practices integral to their culture (i.e., memes) that shape their mental structures.[1]

Thus, the two principle sources of conceptual change identified by Saxe (1999), individual agency and culture, are inextricably intertwined. True, individuals are a source of concepts and intentional conceptual change through their ability to progressively construct an understanding of their material, personal, and social worlds; however, this understanding necessarily makes use of cultural symbol systems developed over generations (Baldwin, 1894/1968; Cole, 1996; Rogoff, 1998; Vygotsky, 1934/1986).

So, any comprehensive account of conceptual change must necessarily integrate both individual agency and culture in its analytical framework. Taylor (1985, 1995) provided such a framework in his conceptualization of what it means to be a person, a view very much like Dennett's (1995). Both suggested that the person is the seat of the ideas about him or her self—self-concepts and self-narratives—as well as biological experiences of pleasure, pain, pride, and shame. Taylor (1985) explained:

> A person is a being with a certain moral status, or a bearer of rights. But underlying the moral status, as its condition, are certain capacities. A person is a being who has a sense of self, has a notion of the future and the past, can hold values, make choices; in short, can adopt life plans. [. . .] A person must be a being with his own point of view on things. The life plan, the choices, the sense of self must be attributable to him as in some sense their point of origin. A person is a being who can be addressed, who can reply (p. 97).

The implications of this view are far-reaching because, given our current "historical consciousness" (Gadamer, 1958), to be a person in a culture no longer has a fixed meaning for us. For example, it may mean being a rational agent, a spark of the divine spirit, or many other things, depending on historical developments in a particular culture—a fact that has important implications for the ethical treatment that we accord others that we count as persons, and even the ethical relation we hold when caring for ourselves (Foucault, 1982/1988, 1994).

A person is not only a part of his or her culture at the macro level but is also part of the dynamics of relationships around him or her at the micro level. At this level, emotions are significant for intentional conceptual change. From the dynamic systems perspective, change can be achieved when feelings are so extreme that they disrupt the existing patterns (or frame) of relationships (Pepler, Craig, & O'Connell, 1998). However,

---

[1]This is what distinguishes persons from artifacts (books or computers) that have only derived intentionality (Dennett, 1995; Popper, 1994).

frames developed over a long period of time (e.g., parent–child relationships) are very stable, and it requires a lot energy to disrupt them (Pepler et al., 1998). Therefore, although persons are the seat of intentional conceptual change, the stability of the existing patterns may hinder them, and they may need support from another person to change (e.g., intervention of a psychologist to change the family dynamics).

The person, then, is composed of interactions between culture and biology. The result is an "observer" or "self" who is both a private agent and bound to a community of shared norms and values—a point also made by both Searle (2000) and Bruner (1990; Amsterdam & Bruner, 2000). Personal selves are one's narrative and affective center of gravity and experienced seat of will or agency (Dennett, 1995; Naipaul, 1984; Pascual-Leone, 1990; Pascual-Leone & Irwin, 1998; Searle, 2000). Persons are significant because they are the center of will and what Taylor (1995) called strong evaluation of experience. Strong evaluations are appraisals about actions that are a source of pride or shame to the individual; that is, actions that matter deeply because they are about the kind of person one is and the kind of world one helps to create (Lavalleee & Campbell, 1995; Taylor, 1989, 1995). It requires and promotes self-awareness and self-understanding. In contrast, weak evaluation refers to an evaluation of preferred outcomes, such as the relative merits of going on vacation in Hawaii or Florida that have no deep personal implications, even if they entail pragmatic ones. Intentional conceptual change occurs when persons intend to change their own or another's conceptual understanding. The question is then: What is the nature of this conceptual understanding? Now we turn to the definition of concepts and intentions, and their relationship.

CONCEPTS

Answering the question "What changes in conceptual change?" requires a good understanding of what a concept is (diSessa & Sherin, 1998). When considering intentional conceptual change, there is the further difficulty of understanding what we mean by intentions and how these relate to concepts. Inasmuch as both intentions and concepts are perennial notions in cognitive science and philosophy, we do not pretend to provide any ultimate definitions. Rather, we lay out some central issues and present what we consider the best current definitions.

What Is a Concept?

Standard conceptual change models often fail to explain what they mean by a concept (diSessa & Sherin, 1998), even though concepts are defined differently by different disciplines and within disciplines (Komatsu, 1992; Rey, 1998).

For logicians and formal semanticists they are the set of real and possible objects and functions defined over them, whereas for philosophers of mind they are properties, "senses," inferential rules, or discrimination abilities. For psychologists, concepts are typically considered internal representations (images, stereotypes) that are the vehicles for thought in the mind or brain (diSessa & Sherin, 1998; Komatsu, 1992; Rey, 1998).

Experimental studies of concepts and concept learning typically rely on some combinations of these different meanings. According to the standard experimental psychology account, concepts are categories defined by a list of features (i.e., properties or attributes of representations) that are necessary and sufficient to determine category membership (Bruner, Goodnow, & Austin, 1956; diSessa & Sherin, 1998; Medin, Lynch, & Solomon, 2000). A problem with this view, called the *typicality effect*, is that some instances of a category are considered to be better examples of that concept than are others. For example, a sparrow is typically considered a better example of the concept "bird" than is a penguin (diSessa & Sherin, 1998).

Probabilistic theories of concepts were developed in reaction to considering concepts as categories. One version of these theories, *prototype* theories, considers concepts to be represented by a prototype that is essentially an idealized mental representation of a set of objects (e.g., a robin is a prototypical bird; a penguin is not). A variation on this idea is *exemplar* theories, in which a concept is represented by a set of specific examples of the concept (the concept "bird" would be represented by robin, penguin, and other specific kinds of birds). Probabilistic models of concepts have their own problems; although probabilistic models explain the content of a concept, like categorical models, they do not explain why some exemplars are considered more typical than others.

Another group of thinkers (Lakoff, 1987; Putnam, 1975; Quine, 1990) proposed *theory-based* models of concepts as more elaborate mental structures than prototypes (diSessa & Sherin, 1998). According to these models, a concept is understood in relation to an idealized cognitive model (Lakoff, 1987) that is not divorced from knowledge of context and social structure. For example, priests and homosexuals are not typically called bachelors. According to the theory-based model approach, this typicality effect can be explained by the presence of a society in which a bachelor is someone potentially interested in heterosexual marriage (Lakoff, 1987), and a priest or homosexual is not. However, the theory-based model approach to concepts remains somewhat vague on the nature of the theories that constitute their core (diSessa & Sherin, 1998).

Relational theories try to circumvent this problem by proposing that concepts get their meaning by engaging in a web of relations with other concepts and sometimes consider concepts as *patterns of activation,* perhaps, in a neural net (diSessa & Sherin, 1998). Finally, according to *actional/situated perspectives* on concepts, concepts are not localized in individual minds (e.g., Magnusson, Templin, & Boyle, 1997); rather, they are abstractions that apply to people acting in social settings (diSessa & Sherin, 1998).

For our purposes, we think that Rey (1998) provided an elegant definition designed to straddle the many different meanings of the term *concept*:

> A concept is supposed to be a constituent of a thought (or "proposition") rather in the way that a word is a constituent of a sentence that typically expresses a thought. [. . .] Concepts seem essential to ordinary and scientific psychological explanation, [. . .] if psychologists are to describe shared patterns of thought across people, they need to advert to shared concepts.// Concepts also seem essential to categorizing the world, for example, recognizing a cow and classifying it as a mammal (p. 1).

Rey's definition concurs with our view of concepts. We agree that concepts are the constituents or the smallest units of thought and that they are shared among people in a society (and sometimes, around the world).

As will soon become clear, all of these approaches seem to presuppose an "intrinsic intentionality" to concepts, in that people are presumed to know them through experience and to understand their meaning, not merely to store and transmit them to others, as a book might do (Searle, 1998). Even so, it is not always easy to determine whether or not someone possesses a concept (diSessa & Sherin, 1998).

Two Factors in Concept Possession. Most traditional approaches to possession of a concept were concerned with *internal states*, mainly the beliefs of the conceptualizer. Quine (1960) raised a challenge for such an approach in his doctrine of confirmation holism, wherein a person's beliefs are fixed by what they find plausible overall. To him, the argument that beliefs define concepts is arbitrary, because people with different beliefs share the same concepts in actual practice. For example, we may have very different beliefs about cities (about whether they are centers of culture or sources of pollution) but still agree on attributes, prototypes, and even themes about the concept. An opposing view suggests that concepts are shared by virtue of their *external (social) environment*; for example, people have the concept of water by virtue of interacting with the substance called "water" in different ways (Rey, 1998).

A more synthetic and dialectic view, that we endorse, proposes what is called a *two-factor* theory (Rey, 1998). This theory includes both the internal component of a concept that plays a role in psychological explanation, and an external component that determines how the concept is applied in the world. We think that the two-factor theory is the best account of concept possession, as concepts are presumed to have two components: one in the head, consisting of an internal representation playing a certain psychological role, and the other in the environment that determines the real-world truth conditions of that concept (Jackson, Doster, Meadows, & Wood, 1995).

INTENTIONS

Intentionality is a hotly debated notion in contemporary philosophy. We focus on the work of Dennett and Searle, two leading contemporary thinkers in the long-running debate in philosophy about the nature of intentionality. A possible confusion exists between two meanings of *intentional*. The everyday sense of intentional is of something being done "on purpose." In the philosophical sense of intentionality, however, this is just a special case of a general feature of our mental lives, its "aboutness."[2] In other words, any mental act—whether of understanding or expressed through behavior—needs to be about something if it is to be considered intentional (Dennett, 1996; Searle, 1998). So, the object of our thoughts (real or not) is aimed at something in a particular way (i.e., the intentional object); that is, intentional phenomena are aimed at whatever they refer or allude to (e.g., perceptual states to perceptual content, emotional states to affective feelings, intentional actions to deliberate behavior). Dennett (1996) gave the example that if you perceive a horse, this is what your representation is about (i.e., horses), even though you might have been wrong and what you saw was really a zebra. Thus, the intentionality of a person's thought or action requires it to be about something, whether an object, a perception, a feeling, or a behavior.

Stances Toward the World

One way of approaching this philosophical sense of intentionality as aboutness is in terms of the stances we adopt toward any living being or artifact. According to Dennett (1981, 1996) there are three principle stances toward predicting activity: the physical stance, the design stance, and the intentional stance.

The *physical stance* is the method the physical sciences use to tell us about the physical makeup of things—for example, why water freezes or the laws of physics. For contemporary Western thinkers, this is the only stance available for things that are neither alive nor artifacts. The *design stance* applies to human artifacts that are designed for some purpose. For example, if I set my alarm clock to ring at 7 a.m., I predict that it will ring

[2]In a deep way these are related (Aquinas, 1266/1945; Freeman, 1999).

then because of the way the clock has been designed. This stance also works very well on "natural artifacts." So, we predict seeds will grow when planted under the right conditions. For Dennett (1996), the *intentional stance* is a special case of the design stance, in which the designed thing is some sort of agent. It applies when explaining people's actions, but also those of, say, a computer playing chess. Presupposing intentionality in all of your dealings with chess programs is easier than considering their physical or design characteristics; that is, thinking that they will consider the best legal move is a good way to predict their next action in the game. So it is not wrong to say Deep Blue is "trying to capture the center of the board." But such an attribution is limited to describing actions from an objective (third-person) perspective and it ignores a deep problem: The intentionality of current chess programs is not intrinsic to them, but is designed by some human agent.

Intrinsic and Derived Intentionality

What Dennett (1996) described as *intentional stance* can be considered in terms of either intrinsic (or original) or derived intentionality (Dennett, 1996; Searle, 1998). *Intrinsic intentionality* is the aboutness of mental states; that is, the aboutness of our perceptions, thoughts, beliefs, desires, and intentions in the everyday sense. *Derived intentionality* refers to "inferred aboutness" such as what we find in artifacts like words, books, maps, or computer programs. In the case of, say, a chess-playing program like Deep Blue, Searle suggested that although it does display intentionality when it considers pawns as different from the king or tries to capture the center of the board, it does so only because of the intentionality designed into it by human programmers. It has no intrinsic intentionality. Pawns, kings, and chess games have no intrinsic meaning to the machine, which merely follows a complex set of rules; it is all syntax and no semantics, as his famous example of "the Chinese room" was designed to show (Searle, 1990, 1998).[3]

Quine (cited in Dennett, 1996, p. 51) also gave a wonderful example of this distinction: "Our mothers bore us." Does this refer to a present boredom, or to our past birth? Only the person who wrote that sentence could say; there is nothing in the marks on paper that allows us to decide, so they clearly do not have intrinsic intentionality. And Dennett goes even further: Although our mental processes have intrinsic intentionality—in

[3]In the Chinese room example, a man follows a set of rules about how to deal with different sets of Chinese characters without understanding what they mean in his native language, meanings that Chinese speakers outside the room understand. This is a wonderful analogy to the way computers operate, and shows that they can achieve what appear to be intentions, without intrinsic understanding of their actions (Searle, 1990).

agreement with Searle—our thoughts themselves, whether as internal speech or as a "language of thought" do not. They are designed into our minds through the evolution of ideas within our culture. A central disagreement between Searle (1998) and Dennett (1995), however, is that Searle rejected Dennett's belief in the intentionality of designed biological objects. For example, Dennett (1996) suggested that viruses show us the birth of agency, in that these macromolecules are the first to have sufficient complexity to perform actions (self-replication instead of just having effects). Searle (1998) argued that it is absurd to talk of this as intentionality because then every lawful effect in the universe could be considered intentional. This debate proceeds unabated. For Dennett, it is much more useful, at the risk of anthromorphosizing, to consider intrinsic intentionality as a complexification of earlier forms of real intentionality. Dennett, thus, finds Searle's entire way of framing this discussion of intentionality somewhat problematic: How does one build up to the full-blown human version of intrinsic intentionality if not from complex macromolecules, like a virus? This disagreement is very hard to resolve, because they both seem to be making equally valid, if different, points. Computers and viruses do not have intrinsic intentionality (although viruses may indeed be precursors to our kinds of mind). In any case, only beings capable of intrinsic intentionality are capable of intentional conceptual change. Intrinsic intentionality as aboutness presupposes connection between intentions and the phenomena in the world. This connection was discussed by Searle (1998) as *directions of fit.*

Intentions and Direction of Fit

Different types of intentional states are different ways in which the contents of intention relate to the world (Searle, 1998). Regarding the structure of intentional states, Searle argued that the same content can be expressed through or presented in different intentional modes (be these perceptions, beliefs, or intended actions): One can *hope* it rains, *fear* it rains, *desire* it rain, *believe* it rains, or *intend* it to rain (by seeding clouds in a drought). Each such intention has *conditions of satisfaction,* specifically, truth conditions for belief, fulfillment conditions for desires, carrying out conditions for intentions (Searle, 1998). These different conditions of satisfaction have what Searle called different *directions of fit* (i.e., directions of relatedness between our minds and the world).

Mind-to-world fit requires organizing one's mind according to the reality of the world. Beliefs and hypotheses, perceptions and memories have a mind-to-world direction of fit because they are said to be true or false depending on whether the world really is the way they represent it (Searle,

1998). In all such cases, if our thoughts do not represent the way the world really is, then we change our conception of them to fit the world. For example, if we think electricity is like water, but it is really an equilibration process, then we need a radical change of our belief for our understanding of electricity to be true to how the world is (Chi, 1997).

World-to-mind fit requires that we organize or change the world to fit our minds. Desires and intentions (in the everyday sense) have a world-to-mind direction of fit because desires and intentions represent how we would like things to be, or how we plan to make them to be, rather than how they really are (Searle, 1998). If the desire or intention is not satisfied, the responsibility lies with the individual who has failed to make the world meet the content of the desire or intention. For example, if we desire a new political party in government, in a democracy, it is up to us to vote for that party and make the world change in that way. If we cannot do so in the usual way (e.g., because we are out of the country), it is our responsibility to take appropriate steps to vote through an embassy.[4]

To presage our later argument, a lot of potential confusion in discussions of intentional conceptual change, we believe, centers around the dynamic interplay between these two directions of intentional fit. When we change our understanding of concepts and frameworks to attain a better representation of the truth about something, we are concerned with a mind-to-world fit. But our desire or intention to improve this fit is itself an example of world-to-mind fit, directed toward changing the mental objects that inhabit the world of human culture expressed in abstract scientific and artistic objects, or what Popper called *World 3* (1990, 1994).[5]

To sum up, intentionality, in the broad sense, is foundational to human understanding because concepts are how we think about and act on the world. Concepts are intentional in the sense that they are the contents of what thought is about. Intentional conceptual change, if it is not an oxymoron, must refer to deliberate attempts to understand the intentional objects (i.e., concepts) that belong to Popper's "World 3."

With these hopefully not overzealous preliminary discussions of intentionality and concepts now in place, let us turn to the main concern of the chapter: intentional conceptual change, and how and when it can be intended.

[4]Searle (1998) introduced two complexifications into his story about direction of fit. First, not all intentional states have entire propositions as their contents (e.g., loving or hating someone or something may be general). Second, not all intentional states have one of these two directions of fit; instead, some presuppose that the fitting has already occurred (e.g., being sorry for insulting a friend, or glad the sun is shining). Such cases have a "null direction of fit" because they do not aim to be fulfilled even if they have propositional content.

[5]The other worlds are natural material objects (World 1) and our particular subjective experiences (World 2). Although Worlds 1 and 2 have the mediums needed to support and express World 3, the latter has an existence distinct from the other two.

CONCEPTUAL STABILITY VERSUS CONCEPTUAL CHANGE

Explanations of conceptual change must consider both conditions under which concepts change and those under which they do not. This insight is perhaps self-evident; indeed, it is critical to one of the oldest texts in human culture, the Chinese *Book of Changes* (see Wilhelm, 1971). We begin our discussion of this question by considering when conceptual systems and frameworks do not change, but remain stable.

Conceptual Stability

According to Eco (1998), when two cultures with different conceptual systems come in contact with each other at the cultural level, there are three possibilities that short circuit radical conceptual change.

First, there may be no communication between members of different groups. In this case, different groups or schools of thought do not interact with each other and they live in their own communities. Historically, examples include the civilizations of Europe and China that developed virtually independently of each other, with very little contact between them until the last few centuries. An example closer to home is the relative isolation of science and religion. Although each framework has numerous followers who subscribe jointly to the beliefs and values of each system, very few attempt to integrate these two systems of thought either socially or personally. So, typically they do not interact with each other except through "border skirmishes" concerning, for example, what can or cannot be taught about human origins in the schools (Gould, 1999).

A second mode of encounter that precludes conceptual change is what Eco (1998) called *conquest*. In such cases, the more powerful of two opposing groups considers the concepts of the other group as being of a lower status and, in the name of making them more civilized, forces them to adopt the conceptual system of the powerful group. It is politically correct to be appalled at such "colonial" practices, but it is important to remember that there are clear instances where certain cultural practices are almost universally reviled by contemporary Western citizens, and no objection would be heard if governments attempted to stamp them out (cannibalism and ritual sacrifice come to mind). A more mundane example is when teachers impose the curriculum on their students, with no discussion or regard for their personal understanding.

Finally, a dominant group may engage in what Eco (1998) called *pillaging*. In these instances, the powerful group sees the other group as having some special knowledge. Although they admire this knowledge, they do not assimilate it into their other systematic beliefs. The "exotic beliefs" are adopted by a few members of the group, but they do not change the general cultural climate, or the dominant political or cultural institutions. One example of this might be the practice of yoga in North America. Although some North Americans perceive yoga, with its complex system of "energy Chakras," as having special merits for developing health and character that they struggle to understand, yoga is rarely prescribed by hospitals or therapists. And the practice of yoga itself (and its associated conceptual system) does not adapt so as to become better integrated into other aspects of contemporary Western culture; in principle, it remains the same as it was developed and applied in the Far East.

Eco's (1998) ideas about conceptual stability at the cultural level can be adapted to individual conceptual stability (see Fig. 2.1). A person who does not want to change his or her view about an issue might either refuse to listen to any challenges to that view (no communication; Fig. 2.1., Panel Ia); might believe that what others are saying is wrong and useless (resistance to conquest; Fig. 2.1., Panel Ib); or might think that others' ideas are interesting but refuses to incorporate them into his or her system of thought in any deep way (pillaging; Fig. 2.1., Panel Ic).

Is conceptual stability intentional? It may or may not be. A relatively new approach to human development, called *dynamic systems* approach, helps explain dynamic stability. Dynamic systems theory proposes that "all developmental outcomes can be explained as the spontaneous emergence of coherent, higher-order forms through recursive interactions among simpler components" (Lewis, 2000, p. 36). Dynamic systems theory considers individual intentionality or will power to be part of a dynamic of relationships with forces that emerge spontaneously outside of one's control. It explains how roles and behavior patterns in a relationship become established through repeated interactions that reinforce and complement each other both cognitively and emotionally, and become more stable over time (Case, 1998; Lewis, 2000; Pepler, Craig, & O'Connell, 1998). For example, in an authoritarian family a child feels more secure and comfortable if he or she does not challenge parents. This pattern of relationship becomes established over time, so that challenging parents becomes increasingly difficult for the child. For instance, a mentor might support the child when his or her ideas contradict those of parents and thus help the child to challenge them. Ultimately this may alter the overall system of power relations and lead to a massive reorganization of this family system. Change can only occur when another element (e.g., a friend or therapist) is introduced that destabilizes the existing pattern, and thus, helps the child change (Pepler, Craig, & O'Connell, 1998).

Despite these many instances of conceptual stability, there are many occasions when we observe conceptual change. Let us now consider what supports conceptual change.

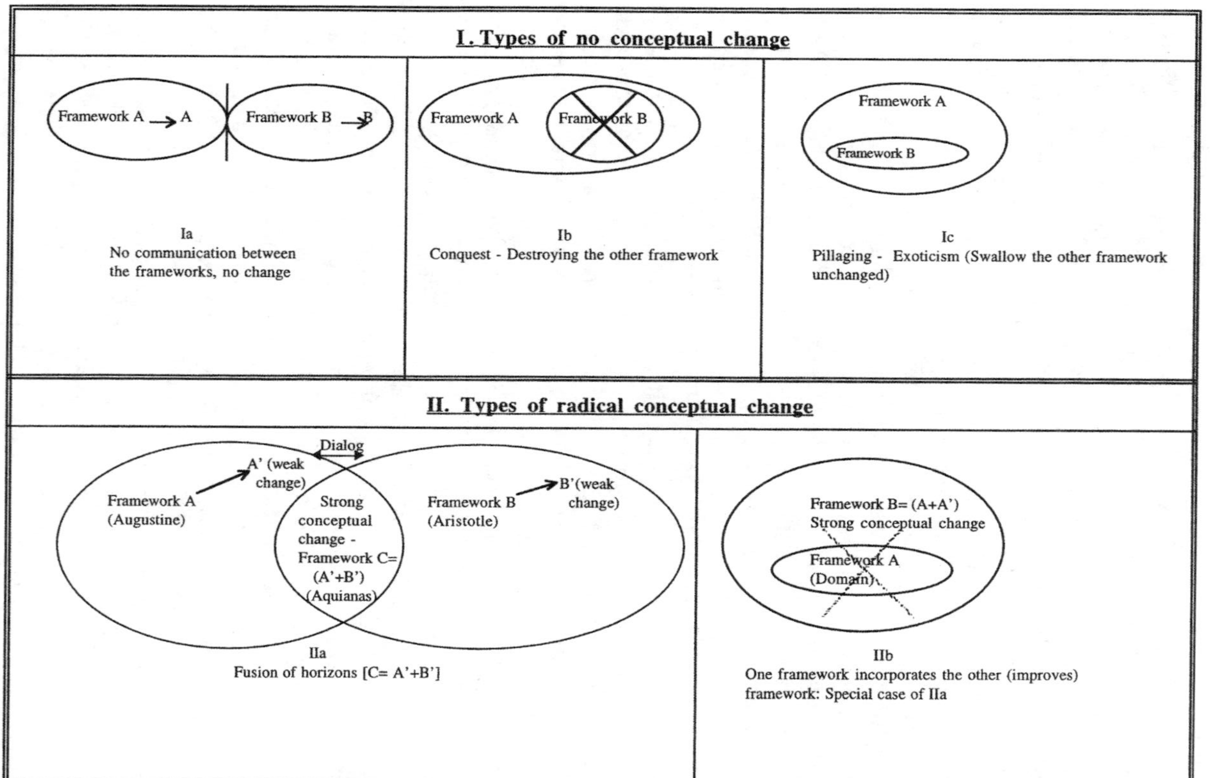

FIG. 2.1. Types of conceptual change (Domains/concepts that do or do not change).

Conceptual Change

The standard model of conceptual change in cognitive science (Carey, 1988; Gentner et al., 1997) was inspired by the history of science literature, particularly the work of Kuhn (1993, 1996). This tradition distinguishes between routine learning and deep or radical conceptual change (diSessa & Sherin, 1998). Kuhnian notions of "normal science" and "scientific revolution" are used as examples in describing the difference between regular learning and radical conceptual change. In regular learning, individuals or schools of thought do not change their framework, but rather add new knowledge into their existing framework. Thus, regular learning involves a mere articulation of an existing conceptual framework (Carey, 1991; Chi, 1992; Thagard, 1992), or what is sometimes called weak conceptual change.

Carey's (1988) work is a good example of standard conceptual change models. She defined regular learning as the change in the relationships between concepts (weak knowledge restructuring). Radical conceptual change in her account is the change in the ontology or essence of the concepts themselves (strong knowledge restructuring). Another example of the standard model is that of Gentner et al. (1997), who distinguish between belief revision (change in facts), theory change (change in global knowledge structure), and conceptual change (change in the fundamental concepts that compose the belief structure). One problem with the standard conceptual model is that it is not entirely clear whether conceptual change refers to the process or the end product of change (Chi, Slotta, & deLeeuw, 1994).

Standard models of conceptual change ignore an important point: Radical conceptual change, both personally and in science, can lead to better or worse mind-to-world fit (Piaget & Garcia, 1987).

Flawed Radical Change. Not all conceptual change is for the better; sometimes individual or group practices deteriorate, and inferior practices replace better ones. For example, when a previously tolerant person joins a religious cult group that advocates killing people in the name of religion, most not in that group would consider this a flawed radical conceptual change. To take a more mundane example, if a student abandons a Darwinian account of evolution to embrace a Lamarckian one for reasons that seem compelling to him or her, this is a flawed conceptual change from a scientific standpoint.

How can we avoid a complete relativism that says that all value judgments about which conceptual system is better or worse reflect current political and cultural views held by dominant groups, and that no system is intrinsically superior to the next? We follow Taylor (1995) in suggesting that flawed conceptual change reflects a lack of articulation (that is, lack of expression of or reflective thinking about one's behaviors and thoughts) that accepts ideas without rational questioning or strong evaluation.

Positive Radical Change. If possessing a concept has both a psychological component (internal representation) and an external (historical, real-world) component, then the effective real-world power of different conceptual systems of explanation can be compared. Even if systems are truly incommensurate, they can still be rationally evaluated ad hominem. In other words, an argument need not seek universal external points of reference in abstract principles, but rather one can compare traditions on their own merits, which includes their real-world effects or plausibility (Taylor, 1995).

The only reason that such ad hominem arguments are disparaged is because our modern intellectual culture emphasizes abstract knowledge over practical action. As Taylor (1995) suggested, "One of the most important roots of modern skepticism [is] that people will tend to despair of practical reason to the extent that they identify its mode of argument as apodictic (p. 38)."[6] People look for criteria on which they can agree. But this, as Kuhn (1996) famously showed, argues for the "incommensurability" of different scientific outlooks that followed each other historically. Indeed, their concepts cannot be intertranslated, and—more unsettling—they look to different features or considerations to test their truth. We are faced with a situation in which there seems to be no objective criteria for deciding between them (Taylor, 1995). But Taylor (1995) proposed three argument forms that increasingly deviate from foundationalist (apodictic) modes of thinking in evaluating the advantage gained in changing conceptual frameworks.

The first argument form involves a comparative judgment, in which two opposing positions can be evaluated against agreed-on facts. In such cases, the one that best explains the facts is judged as superior (Taylor, 1995). Importantly, here both incommensurate systems agree on the external criteria for successful explanation. For example, Lamarckians and Darwinians disagreed on the mechanism of phenotypic change in species, but they agreed that the real-world similarity and diversity among biological forms is what needed to be explained.

This first level is not strictly ad hominem, as it refers to external criteria for truth that both theories must agree on. Most studies of radical conceptual change in science education seem to be of this kind, which is not surprising because it is the most tractable. In essence, adopting the superior of two explanatory frameworks is what Chi (1992) proposed as the basic mechanism of radical conceptual change.

---

[6]Apodictic explanations appeal to a foundationalist model of knowledge that presupposes that we can establish truth independently of our own subjective perspective.

However, one may want a more powerful comparison of two conceptual frameworks. What about theories that involve two different frameworks that are incommensurable with each other and that do not agree on which criteria constitute evidence for their claims? Because the different theories operate in different paradigms of understanding, to which the criteria of the other theory do not apply, there is no rational justification for choosing one over the other. According to Taylor (1995), in this second form of argument, a superior theory makes explicit our "pre-understandings"—that is, "the understanding that we originally have prior to explicitation or scientific discovery" (p. 48) and extends our understanding of the underlying connections between our ideas that support our ability to deal with the world. This knowledge improves our practices and purposes, so the criterion for evaluating both theories is the extension of our practical capacities (Taylor, 1995). As a concrete example, ballistic technology developed by Galilean physics was more powerful than that developed under the Aristotelian view. In other words, one could fire more accurate projectiles using Galilean physics than its Aristotelian counterpart. Even those who disagreed with the type of scientific evidence presented in support of either theory shared the value of creating more powerful weapons and were forced to concede that the other conceptual system was more effective. So, the success of the two incommensurate systems is linked to people's shared values and ideas about what is better and more powerful practice.

Finally, a third form of argument is to show that the transition from conceptual framework A to framework B overcomes a contradiction or confusion, or acknowledges an ignored factor in the earlier theory. This level is free of any shared, external criteria and it is entirely ad hominem (Taylor, 1995). An example can be the transition from Cartesian view of mind and body as distinct substances to the Darwinian view of the mind as an expression of human biological life. The Cartesian view has the inherent and insurmountable difficulty of explaining how an immaterial mind can interact with a physical body, and vice versa. This is a problem that the Darwinian account simply does not encounter. However, it can explain why the Cartesian account was formulated (by considering individual psychic experience to be immaterial) and show that this is not an adequate formulation of the human mind.

Taylor (1995) pointed out that these competing claims can be evaluated by considering how each conceptual system deals with the facts at hand; the superior conceptualization explains the world better, avoiding certain problems associated with the other proposed conceptualization (so we might ask—as did even the early church fathers—what sort of a body could support an immaterial mind or soul; Ware, 1999). Now, in the religious claim that humans have an immortal soul versus the scientific claim that they do not, the stakes may be seen as so high and so central to our conception of what it means to be persons, neither side agrees to debate for or against their respective claims. In such cases, Taylor (1995) acknowledged that debate may be impossible if both sides refuse to engage the conversation.

INTENTIONAL AND UNINTENTIONAL CONCEPTUAL CHANGE

What then can we conclude about intentional conceptual change? We suggest that intentional conceptual change involves a person's (or group's) deliberate attempt at radical change from one conceptual system to another because they are captivated by the power of that new conceptual system (Bourdieu, 1991; Foucault, 1994/1997), or because they perceive some deep flaw in their current view (Kuhn, 1964/1981; Piaget, 1975, Piaget & Garcia, 1987).

This ad hominem approach to radical conceptual change is our answer to Carey (1999). She acknowledged the Piagetian notion of disequilibrium as source of change, but thought it insufficient for change, saying that inconsistent beliefs merely serve a motivational role leading one to deliberately reflect on limit cases or engage in analogical mapping (applying the conceptual structure of one domain to a new one; Carey, 1999). The dynamic systems view we propose agrees with this, but goes further to suggest that intentional conceptual change stems from perturbations to one's existing concepts that lead individuals to question their current understanding (mind-to-world fit), followed by deliberate efforts to account for those perturbations. In the case of radical conceptual change, a new framework or way of conceptualizing (i.e., a new cognitive structure) may be created to resolve these perturbations (Lewis, 2000), one that is more stable and more complex. Work by Case (Case & Okamato, 1996; Moss & Case, 1999), Karmiloff-Smith (1992) and Piaget and Garcia (1987) showed how intentional reworking of problems leads to more complex conceptual understanding.

DYNAMIC SYSTEMS THEORY AND CONCEPTUAL CHANGE

In sum, our view of intentional conceptual change is in line with the dynamic systems perspective and involves a destabilization of existing patterns of thought and behavior in individuals (thought and behavior that is shaped by parents, teachers, or others who embody the institutional reality and cultural capital of a particular society and culture). Our view is best explained by the theoretical model called *catastrophe theory*, originally proposed by Zeeman (1976) and revised by van der Maas and Molenaar (1996; also Case, 1998; Lewis, 2000; van der Maas, 1996; see Fig. 2.2). It is a version of dynamic systems theory that explains the dynamic reconfiguration of elements in a social or psychological system. In the figure, the X axis represents the available resources such as the knowledge or tools. On the Y axis, we have the individual's level of cognitive or conceptual development, that is, the capability of the individual to use the available resources. On the Z axis, we have the probability of conceptual change as a result of interaction of available resources and conceptual development. The surface of the figure represents the type of conceptual change, whether it is radical change or gradual transition (i.e., regular learning). In the case of radical change, the transition to a new framework is discontinuous; it is a jump or sudden change and requires extensive reorganization of the conceptual understanding. However, on the rear side, the surface is continuous and that represents a regular learning where the individual reorganizes his or her ideas in small steps. There is always a probability of going back to the old conceptualization in this model, but returning to old conceptions from a new un-

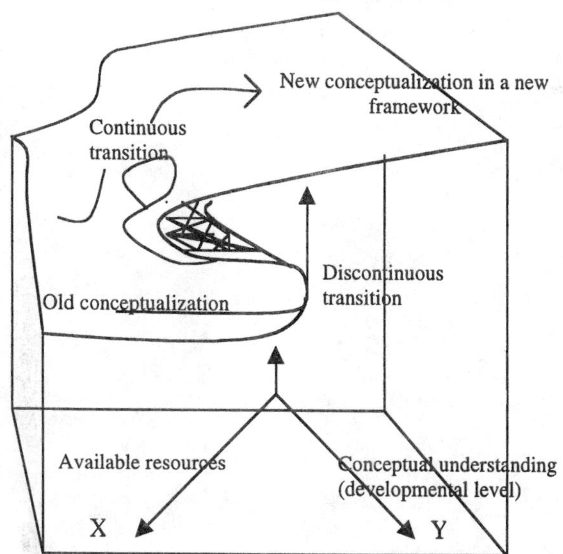

FIG. 2.2. Conceptual change as catastrophe theory (van der Maas & Molenaar, 1996). The two axes in the bottom of the figure indicate the two independent variables that determine one's position on the surface. These are real-time contextual constraints, such as available resources (Axis X) and developmental level of the individual (Axis Y). The Z axis indicates the probability of the conceptual change.

derstanding does not occur at the same point that the jump from old to the new conception occurred. This asymmetry is called *hysteresis* (Case, 1998), meaning that one needs to have extra degrees of illusion than his or her earlier illusion in order to regress to old conceptualization.

Intentional conceptual change, thus, involves a deliberate attempt to change frameworks and allows individuals to realize that some figures that were conceptualized as ground are really to be foregrounded. Figure 2.3 shows the famous gestalt figure that can be perceived either as two faces or a vase. A similar shift in the organization of an individual's ideas occurs when conceptual change is achieved. Therefore, radical conceptual change does not always involve a change in the concepts themselves or even abandoning one concept for another; rather, we propose that it is a change in the patterns of relationships and appreciation of some of the concepts that already existed as more significant. Such change requires a reinterpretation of the components of the whole picture or idea (Jackson, Doster, & Meadows, 1997; Jackson, Doster, Meadows, & Wood, 1995; Taylor, 1985). Acquiring this new organization of these competing concepts requires metaconscious appraisal and articulation of both. Likewise, in psychotherapy it is very difficult to change one's life patterns unless one deeply understands them cognitively and emotionally.

FIG. 2.3. Both the vase and the faces can be seen as figures, but not simultaneously.

RESULTS OF RADICAL CONCEPTUAL CHANGE

So, how do we define conceptual change? In our view there are two types of radical conceptual change (See Fig. 2.1, Panels IIa and IIb). In Taylor's (1995) terms, these are called *fusion of horizons* (Panel IIa) and *incorporation* (Panel IIb). Fusion of horizons is achieved through communication or interaction between two or more incommensurate conceptual systems or ideas, and results in a change in our evaluation of both or in the creation of a new framework (Taylor, 1995). *Incorporation* involves assimilation of the earlier theory into the structure of the more superior theory as a special case. Thus, the old theory adds perspective to the new one; however, the latter goes further and develops a new framework. A classic example of incorporation is the explanation of Newtonian physics as a special case of Einstein's theory of relativity.

INFLUENCES ON INTENTIONAL CONCEPTUAL CHANGE

Under real-world conditions, both old and new concepts are influenced by moderators and mediators of conceptual change (see Fig. 2.4). Mediators frame one's entire approach to a particular concept; moderators influence how easily or thoroughly one will attempt to change existing concepts. These influences necessarily expand on what has been called the "cold" model of conceptual change, in which scientific paradigms are driven only by logic and scientific findings. Real social conditions require developing "hot" models, in which radical conceptual change is also driven by historical, social, and motivational factors (Dole & Sinatra, 1998; Pintrich, Marx, & Boyle, 1993). We have space only to briefly mention some key issues associated with these pragmatic aspects of intentional conceptual change.

We consider cultural framework, social context, and ontological focus to be critical *mediators* of conceptual change (see Fig. 2.4). Cultural frameworks mediate conceptual change through canonical narratives and concepts, institutional norms and practices, and through producing physical artifacts (e.g., books and paintings) and language that generate an institutional and cultural reality that frame conceptual understanding (Bruner, 1990; Nelson, 1999; Searle, 1998; Taylor, 1989). Specific social contexts mediate conceptual change through the influence of other people.[7] Finally, concepts are always

[7]For a detailed discussion of social context and the peripheral cue (communication of an idea through a person who is interesting or important to others, so, people engage the idea), see Dole and Sinatra (1998).

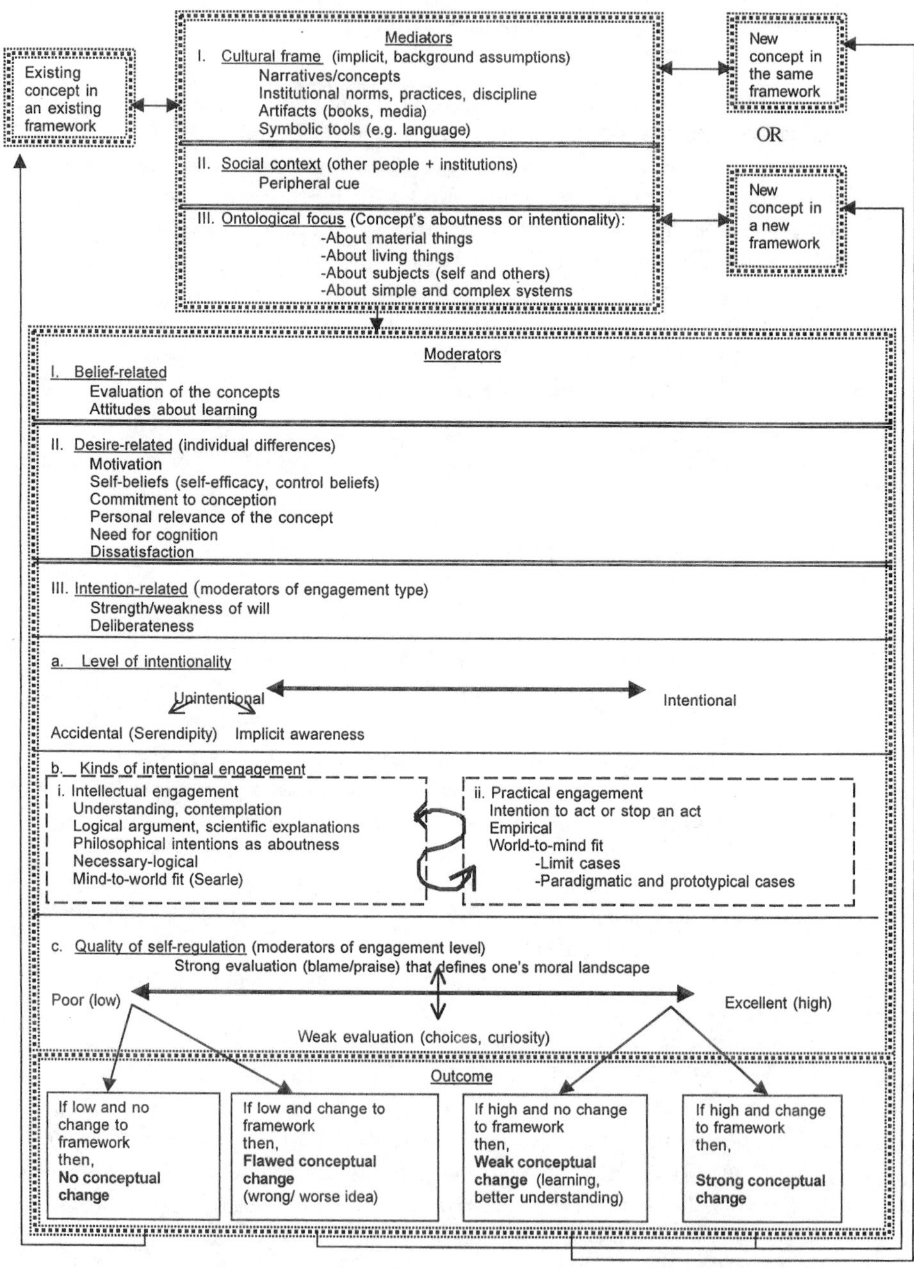

FIG. 2.4. Influences on intentional conceptual change.

understood within a broad ontological category (e.g., substance or process; mind or matter). *Ontological focus* influences how a concept is integrated into one's conceptual ecology, and if it is "misclassified" then it becomes very difficult to learn the new concept—that is, one's intentions will always be misdirected (Chi, 1992, 2000; Ferrari & Chi, 1998).

Searle (1998) introduced an important distinction between observer-dependent and observer-independent phenomena, where "observer" refers generally to anyone who has intrinsic intentionality. A chair, for example, is a material object that exists independent of any observer; however, its name and function as a chair depends on its being conceived as such by some observer (Searle, 1998). Or consider a very different sort of phenomenon: death. Nothing is more certain than our own death, so in one sense death is observer-independent. However, if one has a close relationship with a dying person, the meaning of his or her death will be very different from that of a person one does not know, so death here is observer-dependent. And how infinitely more is this true when considering the meaning of one's own death. The concept of death is unintelligible from a first-person perspective unless it is understood as observer-dependent (Nagel, 1986). So central are these ideas that one's understanding of death and any possible afterlife influences our observer-dependent experience of living and dying (Sogyal, 1992).

Concepts that implicate subjects have a different ontological focus from the ones about the world (see Fig. 2.4.). The self-concept is necessarily observer-dependent, comprising both cognitive and affective dimensions that influence how we live out our concepts and intentions. Concepts about self imply metaconscious self-appraisal as expressed through self-esteem, self-worth, or experiences of being authentic or inauthentic (Harter, 1999; Pinard, 1992; Taylor, 1989). Concepts about others include the evaluation of others' behaviors or the relationships with them and our feelings toward them.

Concepts about the world, on the other hand, are observer-independent; no matter how well or poorly we understand it, the world is a certain way. For example, the North American continent did exist, even if Columbus, on arriving here, thought he had reached India. He was wrong. Likewise, complex abstract systems, like eco-systems or the process of natural selection, although not unique physical objects, have a coherence that allows us to grasp their existence and appreciate their dynamics (or to be mistaken about them).

Moderators are factors that facilitate or impede intentional conceptual change. We propose three types of moderators: (a) belief-related moderators, including one's prior knowledge and expertise, (b) affect-related moderators, including emotional appraisal, motivation, and values, and (c) intention-related moderators, including will power and quality of self-regulation (see Fig. 2.4). The first two groups of moderators are explained in detail by leading researchers in this area (see Dole & Sinatra, 1998; Pintrich et al., 1993; and other chapters of this volume). Therefore, we refer the interested reader to those sources, and use our limited space for a detailed description of intention-related moderators.

Intention-Related Influences on Intentional Conceptual Change

This group of moderators concerns influences on the strength of intentions, specifically, on personal will power to undertake conceptual change, which we take to be synonymous with *volition* (Corno, 1993). Volition is moderated by one's degree of intention, type of intentional engagement, and quality of self-regulation (see Fig. 2.4).

Degree of intention exists along a continuum, where the low end is lack of any intention and the high end is extreme determination. One's level of intention is influenced by one's beliefs and emotions, including one's metacognitive knowledge and metadesires (i.e., desires about desires). Although no change is likely if individuals have little intention to change (unless forced to change), extreme determination to change should result in either flawed or positive radical conceptual change, depending on the quality of self-regulation (see Fig. 2.4).

Quality of self-regulation refers to how effectively one engages in intentional conceptual change, with low quality referring to poor self-regulation (e.g., poor planning, little monitoring or evaluation) and high quality referring to excellent self-regulation (careful planning, monitoring, and evaluation). Excellent self-regulation involves articulate evaluation and other forms metaconsciousness (i.e, metacognition and metadesire).

In other words, effective self-regulation requires strategic action, based on careful self-appraisal and self-management, that foster explanations in which both will and skill are interwoven (Paris & Winograd, 1990). Intentional self-management is particularly important because it is through one's self-management in novel contexts that one comes to modify one's understanding of the task and its requirements (Inhelder & Cellérier, 1992; Paris & Byrnes, 1989; Paris, Byrnes, & Paris, in press; Paris, Lipson, & Wixon, 1983). Strategic agents select actions to attain specific goals, which requires both intention and effort (not an accidental or obedient response).

Believing that one is capable of effectively self-regulating intentional conceptual change (i.e., high perceived self-efficacy about intentional conceptual change) should influence how effectively one is able to make the required conceptual change (Zimmerman, 2001). Effective self-regulation can involve "strong evaluation." Strong and weak evaluations are related to how effectively we self-regulate both desires and intentions; one can have a second-order (meta) desire (e.g., not to smoke, despite wanting a cigarette), and one's intention can align with this "higher" desire.

Metaconsciousness and Intentional Conceptual Change

We suggest, therefore, that the strongest form of intentional conceptual change relies on metaconscious transparency (Pinard, 1992). Metaconsciousness refers to taking an authentic "meta" stance toward one's own conscious experiences. In other words, it involves explicitly interpreting and mastering one's intentions in light of deeply held beliefs and values, and is a special case of metacognition (Amsterdam & Bruner, 2000; Pinard, 1992; Schooler, 2000) that requires active self-regulation. Metaconsciousness can assure that self-regulation effectively actualizes and implements intentions that one authentically judges most important. For example, a person going through therapy with the intention of learning about himself or herself requires metaconsciousness for achieving therapeutic reconceptualization and understanding of his or her current troubling experiences (Schooler, 2000).

Metaconsciousness is central to any "metacognitive experience" (Ferrari, 1996; Flavell, 1981, 1992; Pinard, 1992), that is, to internal dialogues and emotions that provide an explicit interpretation of the value and the efficacy of one's regulation of a task, and thus positively or negatively affect the outcome of one's activity (Flavell, 1981; Pinard, 1992). The more actively and deeply one seeks to comprehend, and thereby provoke metacognitive experiences, the more likely one will see inconsistencies that a more superficial processing would fail to discover (Flavell, 1981). Metacognitive experiences are provoked as the result of active reflection. Active reflection maximizes articulate interpretation by making critical predictions about the expected results of one's efforts. There is an obvious parallel between the notion of provoked metacognitive experience and the notions of self-diagnosis and perceived self-efficacy in the social learning model of self-regulation (Bandura, 1986, 1997).

Intention is also mediated by the type of intentional self-regulation one engages in. In general, intention can be directed toward *contemplation*, and hence at improving theoretical understanding (i.e., intellectual engagement with a task requires developing a theory or an explanation—a mind-to-world fit). Or intention can be *practically* oriented and aim to evaluate how to act in a specific situation under consideration to accomplish some action (a world-to-mind fit). Practical change thus requires choosing between courses of action, something that can involve considering paradigmatic, prototypical, or limit cases.

Finally, not all conceptual change is intentional, that is, deliberate or willed. Instances of unintentional conceptual change include discoveries that are made by chance or through serendipity (Eco, 1998; Roberts, 1989; Simonton, in press). For example, Columbus wanted to reach India but he found America. Often in such cases, though, "Chance favors the prepared mind," as Louis Pasteur famously said. Virtually all examples of serendipity in the history of science involved capitalizing on chance occurrences to solve long-standing problems, but were noticed by individuals with enough knowledge of a domain to appreciate the implications of unexpected results and enough will to intentionally pursue their implications (Ferrari, in press; Roberts, 1989; Dunbar, 1995).

A further distinction seems important here, that of levels of awareness with regard to deliberate intentions. People are sometimes not explicitly aware of their intentions. For example, they may have implicit tacit knowledge of how to act in a particular context that they are unable to describe, even though their performance is flawless (Tirosh, 1994; Torff & Sternberg, 1998).

Not all instances of explicit awareness are tied to intentional control (Bargh & Chartrand, 1999). Consider the neurotic self-consciousness of obsessive–compulsives. Such persons may intend to stop thinking unwanted thoughts or washing their hands frequently; however, they are unable to stop. This situation may result from the unconscious intentions to think or act in ways that the person is not aware of and that override their explicit intentions to stop. Of course, our intentions can also be overlapping, or sidetracked, leading to slips of intention either with regard to implementation or termination of one's intentions (Heckhausen & Beckmann, 1990). Also, Wegner and Wheatley (1999) discussed several studies in which individuals have the illusion of intentionally causing or willing some event to occur, but are mistaken. One of our favorites is their *I Spy* study, in which a confederate forces the participant to choose a particular object. If the confederate forced the subject to stop at a certain time soon after the participant had been primed with the word for that object, these subjects were significantly more likely to consider stopping on the object an act of their own will.[8]

CULTURAL AND INSTITUTIONAL REALITY

So far almost our entire discussion of intentionality has focused on the individual. But much of our lived intentional experience involves us in institutional or sociocultural reality (Foucault, 1994a; Taylor, 1989). For Searle

[8]Searle, in a recent discussion of these results (2000), correctly noted that such illusions of will no more undermine the concept of will than perceptual illusions undermine the reality of perception. However, they are instructive of the conditions under which we are mistaken in feeling that our actions are the result of acts of will.

(1998), institutional reality relies on three essential ingredients. The first is collective intentionality (or joint intentions), which is integral to feeling a part of social events like a college classroom, political rally, or even a conversation. Whenever people share thoughts or feelings, there exists collective intentionality. Indeed, even conflict requires some agreement about the need to argue (Searle, 1998).

The second building block is the *assignment of function* (by using something as a tool). Attributing a function presupposes that there exists some purpose, goal, or objective that can exist only relative to intentional agents (Searle, 1998). The third building block is the idea of *constitutive rules*. Unlike regulative rules that govern preexisting behavior (e.g., rule to drive on the right side of the road), constitutive rules make possible the forms of behavior they govern (e.g., the rules of chess). Searle's (1998) clearest sociocultural example of this is money: "The physics of money alone—unlike the physics of a knife or a bathtub—does not enable the performance of [its social] function." (p. 126).

With all of the preceeding discussion as a backdrop, let us now briefly consider some influences on how intentional conceptual change occurs, or does not occur, under various social conditions.

PRAGMATICS OF INTENTIONAL CONCEPTUAL CHANGE

In "real life" social contexts, intentional conceptual change takes place at four levels (see Fig. 2.5), ranging from change in individual concepts to change in the collective understanding of groups or entire disciplines.

Intentional conceptual change at the individual level (see Fig. 2.4, panel A) can refer, for example, to a child who changes his or her conceptualizations as he or she gains the capacity to understand increasingly complex and abstract concepts, perhaps through reflective abstraction (Case, 1998; Piaget, 1975). Or to a novice, like Bereiter's (1990) "intentional learner" who sees himself or herself as having some control over his or her learning and is motivated to resolve the conflict between prior and new knowledge. Finally, the individual can be a genius or extraordinary mind who is able to conceive of new conceptual structures, perhaps by seeing implications or gaps in a particular concept that were not appreciated by others. For example, Freud and Einstein were both critical to establishing the conceptual structures that shape our modern worldview (Gardner, 1993, 1997). The relationship between individuals and disciplines is never divorced from considerations of power, in that what counts as a fact in that discipline frames how one governs one's self or others (Bourdieu, 1997; Foucault, 1982/1988)—for example, psychiatrists can determine who is insane, and have them committed to asylum. Sometimes, individuals create concepts, like the concept of disability, that not only describe, but even prescribe who they refer to, so individuals who might have thought of themselves as very different (e.g., as blind, an amputee, or mentally slow) now all see themselves as a common marginal group of disabled persons (Bourdieu, 1991; Hacking, 1995).

The second level at which intentional conceptual change occurs is through one-to-one tutoring of an individual novice by an expert or peer (see Fig. 2.5, panel B1). At this level, the issue of collective intentionality becomes important for conceptual change. Both the student's intentions to learn and the expert's (teacher, parent, or therapist) intention to teach become two aspects of the same conceptual change process. Intrinsic intentions in the novice are often supported by the derived intentionality of cultural artifacts like books or computer simulations intended by their creators to help novices achieve conceptual change. For example, simulations were particularly useful in overcoming students' misconceptions about the cardiovascular system when these were used in a constructivist instrumental setting, as compared to using the simulation to confirm information (Ferrari, Taylor, & VanLehn, 1999; Windschitl & Andre, 1998).

Mentoring relationships also necessarily involve dynamics of power and ethical concern for the treatment of others (Foucault, 1994/1997). This is true both for one-to-one coaching (Ericsson, 1996, 2001; Zimmerman, 2001) and for cases in which adult support allows for optimal performance (Fisher & Bidell, 1998; Vygotsky, 1934/1986), including instances of individual therapy. It is by examining the dynamic interplay between teachers and students—especially in how students and teachers make use of opportunities for scaffolded instruction—that one can begin to dynamically assess conceptual change (Magnusson et al., 1997).

At the third level, we have regulation of groups of novices by one expert, as in the classroom or in group therapy (See Fig. 2.5, panel B2). In such cases, the intention of the expert to teach can have a major impact on novices' conceptual change because it sets the intentional tone for the group of learners. For example, whether teachers focus on deep or surface processing in educational contexts influences motivation and understanding of the subject by students in the classroom (Biggs, 1985, 1987, 1993; Marton & Säljö, 1976a, 1976b). When classroom dynamics place more importance on surface performance than on deep mastery of the subjects, student motivation and intentions adapt accordingly (Ames, 1992). The same principle applies to different approaches to group therapy. In cognitive therapy the therapist is usually more directive and focuses on behavioral and cognitive change. In gestalt therapy or psychodrama, on the other hand, the therapist is usually less directive and focuses on life patterns and emotions; thus the participants in each group differ in what they intend to change.

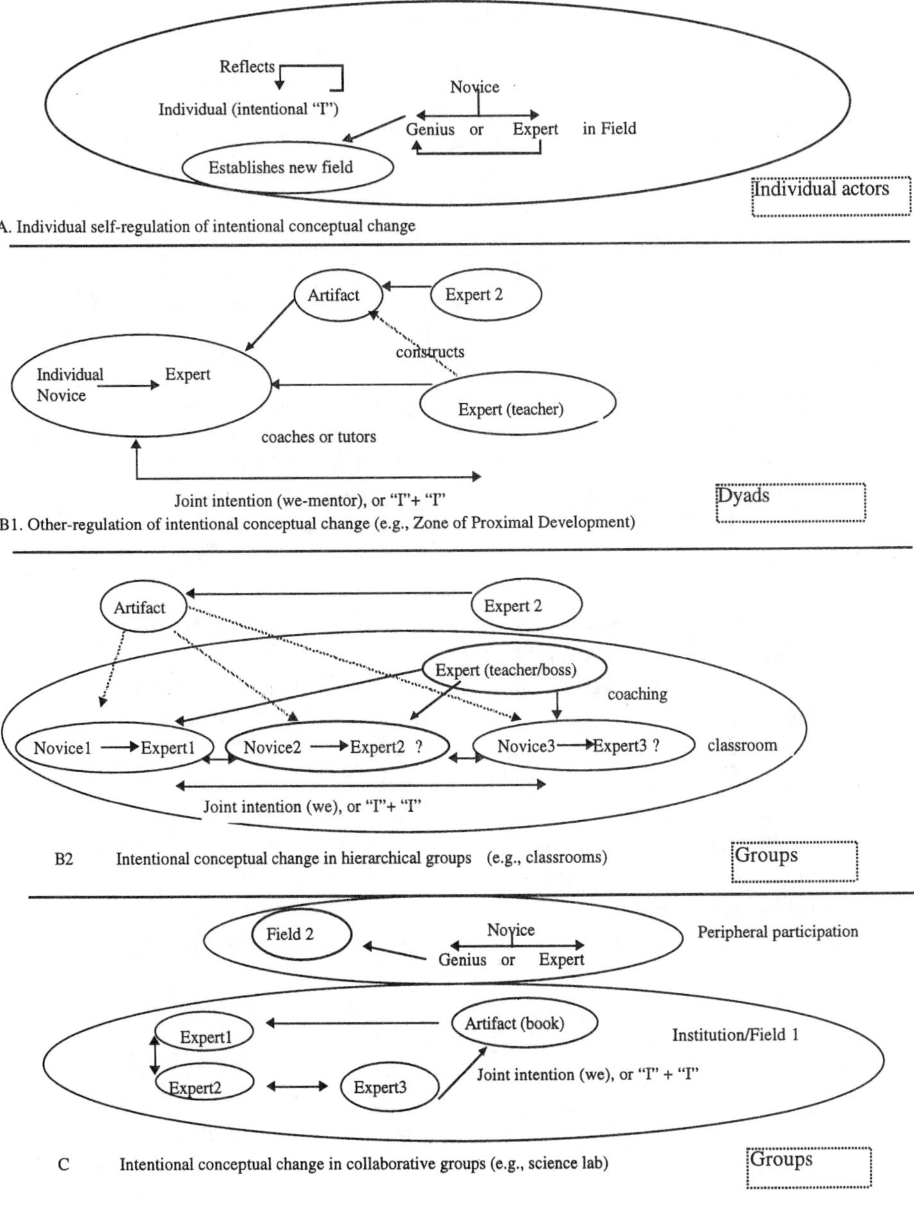

FIG. 2.5. Fields and intentionality in conceptual change.

Intentional conceptual change may also take place through collaboration among or within groups of experts, like a science lab (Dunbar, 1995), or, in the case of paradigm shifts, within the field as a whole (Kuhn, 1993, 1996; see Fig. 2.5, panel C). In effective expert groups, individuals pool different areas of expertise to tackle complex problems, for example by generating local analogies that throw new light on unexpected findings (Dunbar, 1995). However, in less effective groups, power struggles can result as individuals seek to dominate the group agenda.

Sometimes, conceptual change within groups involves what Engström (1999) called *interconnected activity systems*. In these cases participants are spurred to change by internal contradictions in the system that lead them to question existing standards of practice. This often results in a deep analysis of problematic cases within the system. For example, Engström (1999) described the restructuring of relations between a health center, a children's hospital, and the child-patient's family. Such systemic changes often engage broader cultural institutions in revising social contracts, including key legal decisions made by the courts (Amsterdam & Bruner, 2000).

Finally, to complete our circle, novices can intentionally strive to master the knowledge needed to become a full member of a collaborative group or culture, and this may require radical conceptual change—for example, when a student wants to become a biologist and to do so must master Darwin's theory of evolution (Ferrari & Mahalingam, 1998). Of course, unintentional conceptual change also takes place within groups, for example, when novices participating on the periphery of a well-organized group spontaneously move toward the center to become fully functioning members (Rogoff, 1998; see Fig. 2.5, panel C). There is an implicit expectation for change in cases of peripheral participation, which often involves acquiring tacit knowledge that is the hallmark of practical intelligence (Piaget, 1974a, 1974b; Torff & Sternberg, 1998). Likewise, but moving in the opposite direction, an extraordinary individual may decide to remain on the periphery (or be forced to the periphery) of existing groups because he or she has a unique vision. A wonderful example is Thagard's (1992) discussion of Lavoiser's radical reconceptualization of combustion, which took him over a decade of experimentation and theorizing.

If an entrepreneur or genius is able to persuade others of the power of his or her views, he or she may create or attract a following around his or her own innovative concepts and create a new discipline or subdiscipline within the imaginative space of a culture (Amsterdam & Bruner, 2000; Gardner, 1997; Simon, 2001).

Finally, to make a full circle, we suggest that persons engage radical conceptual change most often for concepts critical to important personal projects (i.e., concepts that have personal relevance to valued life pursuits, including projects involving professions or communities of which one is a member). The development of personally significant concepts leads to *personal cognitive development* (Ferrari, in press; Ferrari & Mahalingam, 1998); that is, development that fosters an intimate or "hot" relationship (rather than a distant or "cold" one) between persons and the concepts they develop. By providing the material and educational conditions that foster intentional conceptual change, we engage students and ourselves in learning that promotes personal cognitive development at the deepest, "hottest" levels.

CONCLUSION

Intentional conceptual change remains an enduring problem for philosophy and an exciting new direction for educational research. We hoped to show in this chapter how intentions and concepts work together in intentional conceptual change. This led us to a close examination of some problematic issues associated with notions of intentionality, conceptualization, and intentional conceptual change. We focused, in particular, on the difference between conceptual changes that involves mind-to-world fit (to attain a better representation of the truth about something) and world-to-mind fit (change one's own understanding of cultural and mental objects). We also briefly touched on pragmatic influences to whether and how effectively individuals and cultural groups engage in intentional conceptual change. Although this chapter makes no pretense at having explained the deep nature of intentional conceptual change, we hope we showed some of the fascinating complexities that surround this difficult idea.

REFERENCES

Ames, C. (1992). Classrooms: Goals, structures, and student motivation. *Journal of Educational Psychology, 84*(3), 261–271.

Amsterdam, A., & Bruner, J. (2000). *Minding the law*. New York: Harvard University Press.

Aquinas, St. T. (1945). *Introduction to St. Thomas Aquinas* (A. C. Pegis, Ed.). New York: Random House (The Modern Library). (Original work published 1266)

Baldwin, J. M. (1894/1968). *Mental development in the child and the race: Methods and processes*. New York: A. M. Kelley. (Original work published 1894)

Bandura, A. (1986). *Social foundations of thought and action: A social cognitive theory*. Englewood Cliffs, NJ: Prentice-Hall.

Bandura, A. (1997). *Self-efficacy: The exercise of control*. New York: Freeman

Bargh, J. A., & Chartrand, T. L. (1999). The unbearable automaticity of being. *American Psychologist, 54*(7), 462–479.

Bereiter, C. (1990). Aspects of educational learning theory. *Review of Educational Research, 60*(4), 603–624.

Biggs, J. B. (1985). The role of metalearning in study processes. *British Journal of Educational Psychology, 55*, 185–212.

Biggs, J. B. (1987). *Student approaches to learning and studying (Research monograph)*. Melbourne: Australian Council for Educational Research.

Biggs, J. B. (1993). What do inventories of students' learning processes really measure? A theoretical review and clarification. *British Journal of Educational Psychology, 63*, 3–19.

Bourdieu, P. (1991). *Language and symbolic power* (J. B. Thompson, Ed.). Cambridge, MA: Harvard University Press.

Bourdieu, P. (1997). *Méditiations pascaliennes (Pascalian meditations)*. Paris: Seuil

Bruner, J. (1990). *Acts of meaning*. Cambridge, MA: Harvard University Press.

Bruner, J. S., Goodnow, J., & Austin, G. A. (1956). *A study of thinking*. New York: Wiley.

Carey, S. (1988). Reorganization of knowledge in the course of acquisition. In S. Strauss (Ed.), *Human development: Vol. 2. Ontogeny, phylogeny, and historical development* (pp. 1–27). Norwood: Ablex.

Carey, S. (1991). Knowledge acquisition: Enrichment or conceptual change? In S. Carey & R. Gelman (Eds.), *The epigenesis of mind: Essays on biology and cognition* (pp. 257–291). Hillsdale, NJ: Lawrence Erlbaum Associates.

Carey, S. (1999). Sources of conceptual change. In E. K. Scholnick, K. Nelson, S. A. Gelman, & P. H. Miller (Eds.), *Conceptual development: Piaget's legacy* (pp. 293–326). Mahwah, NJ: Lawrence Erlbaum Associates.

Case, R. (1998). The development of conceptual structures. In W. Damon (Ed.-in-chief) and D. Kuhn & R. S. Siegler (Vol. Eds.), *Handbook of child psychology, Vol. 2: Cognition, perception, and language* (5th ed., pp. 745–800). New York: Wiley.

Case, R., & Okamato, Y. (1996). The role of central conceptual structures in the development of children's thought. *Monographs of the Society for Research in Child Development, 61*(1–2), Whole serial: 246.

Chi, M. T. H. (1992). Conceptual change within and across ontological categories: Examples from learning and discovery in science. In R. Giere (Ed.), *Cognitive models of science: Minnesota studies in the philosophy of science* (pp. 129–186). Minneapolis, MN: University of Minnesota Press.

Chi, M. T. H. (1997). Creativity: Shifting across ontological categories flexibly. In T. B. Ward, S. M. Smith, & J. Vaid (Eds.), *Creative Thought: An investigation of conceptual structures and processes* (pp. 209–234). Washington, DC: American Psychological Association.

Chi, M. T. H. (2000). Self-explaining expository texts: The dual processes of generating inferences and repairing mental models. In R. Glaser (Ed.), *Advances in instructional psychology, Vol. 5: Educational design and cognitive science*. Mahwah, NJ: Lawrence Erlbaum Associates.

Chi, M. T. H., Slotta, J. D., & de Leeuw, N. (1994). From things to processes: A theory of conceptual change for learning science concepts. *Learning and Instruction, 4*, 27–43.

Cole, M. (1996). *Cultural psychology: A once and future discipline*. Cambridge, MA: Belknap Press of Harvard University Press.

Corno, L. (1993). The best-laid plans: Modern conceptions of volition and educational research. *Educational Researcher, 22*(2), 14–22.

Dawkins, R. (1976). *The selfish gene*. Oxford: Oxford University Press.

Dennett, D. C. (1981). *Brainstorms: Philosophical essays on mind and psychology*. Cambridge, MA: MIT Press.

Dennett, D. C. (1991). *Consciousness explained*. Cambridge, MA: Bradford/MIT.

Dennett, D. C. (1995). *Darwin's dangerous idea: Evolution and the meanings of life*. New York: Simon & Schuster.

Dennett, D. C. (1996). *Kinds of minds: Toward an understanding of consciousness*. New York: Basic Books.

diSessa, A. A., & Sherin, B. L. (1998). What changes in conceptual change? *International Journal of Science Education, 20*(10), 1155–1191.

Dole, J. A., & Sinatra, G. M. (1998). Reconceptualizing change in the cognitive construction of knowledge. *Educational Psychologist, 33*(2/3), 109–128.

Dunbar, K. (1995). How scientists really reason: Scientific reasoning in real-world laboratories. In R. J. Sternberg & J. E. Davidson (Eds.), *The nature of insight* (pp. 365–395). Cambridge, MA: MIT Press.

Eco, U. (1998). *Serendipities: Language and lunacy*. New York: Columbia University Press.

Engström, Y. (1999). *Expansive learning at work: Toward an activity–theoretical reconceptualization*. Paper presented at CLWR 7th Annual International Conference on Post-compulsory Education and Training.

Ericsson, K. A. (2002). Attaining excellence through deliberate practice : Insights from the study of expert performance. In M. Ferrari (Ed.), *The pursuit of excellence through education* (pp. 21–55). Mahwah, NJ: Lawrence Erlbaum Associates.

Ericsson, K. A. (1996). The acquisition of expert performance: An introduction to some of the issues. In K. A. Ericsson (Ed.), *The road to excellence: The acquisition of expert performance in the arts and sciences, sports and games* (pp. 1–50). Mahwah, NJ: Lawrence Erlbaum Associates.

Ferrari, M. (1996). Observing the observer: Self-regulation in the observational learning of motor skills. *Developmental Review, 16*, 203–240.

Ferrari, M. (in press). Integration and conclusion: Educating selves to be creative and wise. In L.S. Shavinina & M. Ferrari (Eds.), *Beyond knowledge: Extracognive aspects of high ability*. Mahwah, NJ: Lawrence Erlbaum Associates.

Ferrari, M., & Chi, M. T. H. (1998). The nature of naive explanations of natural selection. *International Journal of Science Education, 20*(10), 1231–1256.

Ferrari, M., & Mahalingam, R. (1998). Personal cognitive development and its implications for teaching and learning. *Educational Psychologist, 33*, 35–44.

Ferrari, M., Taylor, R., & VanLehn, K. (1999). Adapting work simulations for school: Preparing students for tomorrow's workplace. *Journal of Educational Computing Research, 21*(1), 25–53.

Fisher, K. W., & Bidell, T. R. (1998). Dynamic development of psychological structures in action and thought. In W. Damon (Ed. in Chief) and R. M. Lerner (Vol Ed.), *Handbook of psychology (Vol. 1), Theoretical models of human development* (5th ed., pp. 467–562). New York: John Wiley & Sons.

Flavell, J. H. (1981). Cognitive monitoring. In W. P. Dickson (Ed.), *Children's oral communication skills* (pp. 35–60). New York: Academic Press.

Flavell, J. H. (1992). Cognitive development: Past, present, and future. *Developmental Psychology, 28*(6), 998–1005.

Foucault, M. (1988). Technologies of the self. In L. H. Martin, H. Gutman, & P. H. Hutton (Eds.), *Technologies of the self: A seminar with Michel Foucault* (pp. 16–49). Amherst: The University of Massachusetts Press. (Original work published 1982)

Foucault, M. (1994a). On the genealogy of ethics: An overview of work in progress. In P. Rabinow (Ed.), *The essential works of Michel Foucault 1954–1984, Vol. 1: Ethics: Subjectivity and truth* (pp. 253–280). New York: The New Press.

Foucault, M. (1997). *The essential works of Michel Foucault 1954–1984, Vol. 1: Ethics: Subjectivity and truth* (P. Rabinow, Ed.). New York: The New Press. (Original work published 1994)

Freeman, M. (1999, February). *Rethinking the fictive, reclaiming the real: Autobiography, narrative time, and the burden of truth*. Paper presented at the Narrative and Consciousness Conference. Texas Tech University, Lubak, Texas.

Gadamer, H. (1995). *Truth and method* (2nd revised ed.). New York: Continuum.

Gadamer, H. (1996). Le problème de la conscience historique. [The problem of historical consciousness]. Paris: Editions de Seuil. (Original work published 1963, based on lectures given in 1958)

Gardner, H. (1993). *Creating minds*. New York: Basic Books.

Gardner, H. (1997). *Extraordinary minds: Portraits of 4 exceptional individuals and an examination of our own extraordinariness*. New York: Basic Books.

Gentner, D., Brem, S., Ferguson, R. W., Markman, A. B., Levidow, B. B., Wolff, P., & Forbus, K. D. (1997). Analogical reasoning and conceptual change: A case study of Johannes Kepler. *Journal of the Learning Sciences, 6*(1), 3–40.

Gladd, J. (2000, May 27). Court orders treatment for sleepwalking stabber. *Globe & Mail*, p. A31.

Gould, S. J. (1999). *Rocks of ages: Science and religion in the fullness of life*. New York: Ballantine.

Hacking, I. (1995). *Rewriting the soul: multiple personality and the sciences of memory*. Princeton, NJ: Princeton University Press.

Harter, S. (1999). *The construction of the self: A developmental perspective*. New York: The Guilford Press.

Heckhausen, H., & Beckmann, J. (1990). Intentional action and action slips. *Psychological Review, 97*(1), 36–48.

Inhelder, B., & Cellérier, G. (1992). *Le cheminement des découvertes de l'enfant: Recherche sur les microgenèses cognitives*. [Children's pathways to discovery: Studies in cognitive microgenesis]. Neuhchâtel: Delachaux et Niestlé.

Jackson, D. F., Doster, E. C., & Meadows, L. (1997). Reply to "Hearts and minds in the science classroom: The education of a confirmed evolutionist revisited." *Journal of Research in Science Teaching, 34*(1), 93–94.

Jackson, D. F., Doster, E. C., Meadows, L., & Wood, T. (1995). Hearts and minds in the science classroom: The education of a confirmed evolutionist. *Journal of Research in Science Teaching, 32*(6), 585–611.

Karmiloff-Smith, A. (1992). *Beyond modularity: A developmental perspective on cognitive science*. Cambridge, MA: MIT Press.

Köhler, W. (1969). *The task of Gestalt psychology*. Princeton, NJ: Princeton University Press.

Komatsu, L. K. (1992). Recent views of conceptual structure. *Psychological Bulletin, 112*(3), 500–526.

Kuhn, T. (1993). *Thomas Kuhn and the nature of science* (P. Horwich, Ed.). Cambridge, Mass: MIT Press.

Kuhn, T. (1996). *Structure of scientific revolutions* (3rd ed.). Chicago: University of Chicago Press.

Kuhn, T. S. (1981). A function for thought experiments. In Ian Hacking (Ed.), *Scientific revolutions* (pp. 6–27) New York, NY: Oxford University Press. (Original work published 1964)

Lakoff, G. (1987). *Women, fire, and dangerous things: What categories reveal about the mind*. Chicago: University of Chicago Press.

Lavallee, L. F., & Campbell, J. D. (1995). Impact of personal goals on self-regulation processes elicited by daily negative events. *Journal of Personality and Social Psychology, 69*(2), 341–352.

Lewis, M. (2000). The promise of dynamic systems approaches for an integrated account of human development. *Child Development, 71*(1), 240–249.

Magnusson, S. J., Templin, M., & Boyle, R. A. (1997). Dynamic science assessment: A new approach for investigating conceptual change. *The Journal of the Learning Sciences, 6*(1), 91–142.

Marton, F., & Säljö, R. (1976a). On qualitative differences in learning. I. Outcome and process. *British Journal of Educational Psychology, 46*, 4–11.

Marton, F., & Säljö, R. (1976b). On qualitative differences in learning. II. Outcome as a function of the learner's conception of the task. *British Journal of Educational Psychology, 46*, 115–127.

Medin, D. L., Lynch, E. B., & Solomon, K. O. (2000). Are there kinds of concepts? *Annual Review of Psychology, 51*, 121–147.

Moss, J., & Case, R. (1999). Developing children's understanding of rational numbers: A new model and an experimental curriculum. *Journal of Research in Mathematics Education, 30*(2), 122–147.

Nagel, T. (1986). *The view from nowhere.* New York: Oxford University Press

Naipaul, V. S. (1984). *Finding the centre: Two narratives.* London: Andre-Deutsch.

Nelson, K. (1999). Levels and modes of representation: Issues for the theory of conceptual change and development. In E. K. Scholnick, K. Nelson, S. A. Gelman, & P. H. Miller (Eds.), *Conceptual development: Piaget's legacy* (pp. 269–291). Mahwah, NJ: Lawrence Erlbaum Associates.

Paris, S. G., & Byrnes, J. P. (1989). The constructivist approach to self-regulation and learning in the classroom. In B. J. Zimmerman & D. H. Schunk (Eds.), *Self-regulated learning and academic achievement: Theory, research, and practice* (pp. 169-200). New York: Springer-Verlag.

Paris, S. G., Byrnes, J. P., & Paris, A. H. (in press). Constructing theories, identities, and actions of self-regulated learners. In B. Zimmerman & D. Schunk (Eds.), *Self-regulated learning and academic achievement; Theoretical perspectives* (2nd ed.). Mahwah, NJ: Lawrence Erlbaum Associates.

Paris, S. G., Lipson, M. Y., & Wixon, K. K. (1983). Becoming a strategic reader. *Contemporary Educational Psychology, 8,* 293–316.

Paris, S. G., & Winograd, P. (1990). How metacognition can promote academic learning and instruction. In B. F. Jones & L. Idol (Eds.), *Dimension of thinking and cognitive instruction* (pp. 15–51). Hillsdale, NJ: Lawrence Erlbaum Associates.

Pascual-Leone, J. (1990). Emotions, development, and psychotherapy: A dialectical–constructivist perspective. In J. Safran & L. Greenberg (Eds.), *Emotion, psychotherapy, and change* (pp. 302–334). New York: Guilford.

Pascual-Leone, J., & Irwin, R. R. (1998). Abstraction, the will, the self, and modes of learning in adulthood. In M. C. Smith & T. Pourchot (Eds.), *Adult learning and development: Perspectives from educational psychology* (pp. 35–65). Mahwah, NJ: Lawrence Erlbaum Associates.

Pepler, D., Craig, W. M., & O'Connell, P. (1998). Understanding bullying from a dynamic systems perspective. In A. Slater & D. Muir (Eds.), *Developmental psychology* (pp. 440–451). Oxford, England: Blackwell.

Piaget, J. (1974a). *La prise de conscience* (Conscious realization). Paris: Pressess Universitaires de France.

Piaget, J. (1974b). *Réussir et comprendre* (Success and understanding). Paris: Pressess Universitaires de France.

Piaget, J. (1975). *Etudes d'épistémologie génétique: Vol. 33. L'équilibration des structures cognitives: Problème central du développement* [Studies in genetics epistemology: Vol. 33. Equilibration of cognitive structures: The central problem of development]. Paris: Presses Universitaires de France.

Piaget, J., & Garcia, R. (1987). *Psychogenesis and the history of science* (H. Feider, Trans.). New York: Columbia University Press. (Original French edition published 1983)

Pinard, A. (1992). Metaconscience et métacognition (Metaconsciousness and metacognition). *Canadian Psychology, 33*(1), 27–41.

Pintrich, P. R., Marx, R. W., & Boyle, R. A. (1993). Beyond cold conceptual change: The role of motivational beliefs and classroom contextual factors in the process of conceptual change. *Review of Educational Research, 63*(2), 167–199.

Popper, K. R. (1990). *A world of propensities.* Bristol: Thoemmes.

Popper, K. R. (1994). *Knowledge and the body–mind problem: In defence of interaction* (M. A. Notturno, Ed.). London & New York: Routledge.

Putnam, H. (1975). The meaning of "meaning." In Philosophical papers, Vol. 2, *Mind, language, and reality* (pp. 215–271). Cambridge: Cambridge University Press.

Quine, W. V. (1960). *Word and object.* Cambridge, MA: MIT Press.

Quine, W. V. (1990). *Pursuit of truth.* Cambridge, MA: Harvard University Press.

Rey, G. (1998). Concepts. *Routledge Encyclopedia of Philosophy,* CD-ROM, version, 1.0, Online.

Roberts, R. M.(1989). *Serendipity: Accidental discoveries in science.* New York: Wiley & Sons.

Rogoff, B. (1998). Cognition as a collaborative process. In W. Damon (Ed.-in-chief) and D. Kuhn & R. S. Siegler (Vol. Eds.), *Handbook of child psychology, Vol. 2: Cognition, perception, and language* (5th. ed., pp. 679–744). New York: Wiley.

Saxe, G. B. (1999). Sources of concepts: A cultural–developmental perspective. In E. K. Scholnick, K. Nelson, S. A. Gelman, & P. H. Miller (Eds.), *Conceptual development: Piaget's legacy* (pp. 253–267). Mahwah, New Jersey: Lawrence Erlbaum Associates.

Schooler, J. W. (2000). *Consciousness, meta-consciousness and the role of self-report.* Paper presented at the "Toward a Science of Consciousness 2000" conference, Tucson, Arizona.

Searle, J. R. (1990). Is the brain's mind a computer program? *Scientific American, January,* 26–37.

Searle, J. R. (1998). *Mind, language and society: Philosophy in the real world.* New York: Basic Books.

Searle, J. R. (2000). *Consciousness and free action.* Paper presented at the "Toward a Science of Consciousness 2000" conference, Tucson, Arizona.

Simon, H. (2001). Achieving excellence in institutions. In M. Ferrari (Ed.), *The pursuit of excellence through education* (pp. 181–194). Mahwah, NJ: Lawrence Erlbaum Associates.

Simonton, D. K. (in press). Exceptional creativity and chance: Creative thought as a stochastic combinatorial process. To appear in L. V. Shivanina & M. Ferrari (Eds.), *Beyond knowledge: Extracognitive facets in developing high ability.* Mahwah, NJ: Lawrence Erlbaum Associates.

Sogyal, R. (1992). *The Tibetan book of living and dying.* Calcutta: Rigpa & Co.

Taylor, C. (1985). *Human agency and language: Philosophical papers 1.* New York: Cambridge University Press.

Taylor, C. (1989). *Sources of the self: The making of modern identity.* Cambridge, MA: Harvard University Press.

Taylor, C. (1995). *Philosophical arguments.* Cambridge, MA: Harvard University Press.

Thagard, P. (1992). *Conceptual revolutions.* Princeton, NJ: Princeton University Press.

Tirosh, D. (1994). *Implicit and explicit knowledge: An educational approach.* In D. Tirosh (Ed.), *Human development, Vol. 6.* (pp. 111–130). Norwood, NJ: Ablex.

Torff, B., & Sternberg, R. J. (1998). Changing mind, changing world: Practical intelligence and tacit knowledge in adult learning. In M. C. Smith & T. Pourchot (Eds.), *Adult learning and development: Perspectives from educational psychology* (pp. 109–126). Mahwah, NJ: Lawrence Erlbaum Associates.

van der Maas, H. L. J. (1996). Beyond the metaphor? *Cognitive Development, 10,* 621–642.

van der Maas, H. L. J., & Molenaar, P. C. M. (1996). Catastrophe analysis of discontinuous development. In A. von Eye (Ed.), *Categorical variables in developmental research: Methods of analysis* (pp. 77–105). New York: Academic Press.

Vygotsky, L. S. (1986). *Thought and language.* Cambridge, MA: MIT Press. (Original work published in 1934)

Ware, K. (1999). The soul in Greek Christianity. In M. J. C. Crabbe (Ed.), *From soul to self* (pp. 49–69). London & New York: Routledge.

Wegner, D. M., & Wheatley, T. (1999). Apparent mental causation: Sources of the experience of will. *American Psychologist, 54*(7), 480–492.

Wilhelm, R. (1971). *The I ching; or book of changes* (3rd ed.). London: Routledge & K. Paul.

Windschitl, M., & Andre, T. (1998). Using computer simulations to enhance conceptual changes: The roles of constructivist instruction and student epistemological beliefs. *Journal of Research in Science Teaching, 35*(2), 145–160.

Zeeman, E. C. (1976). Catastrophe theory. *Scientific American, 234*(4), 65–83.

Zimmerman, B. J. (2001). Achieving academic excellence: A self-regulatory perspective. In M. Ferrari (Ed.), *The pursuit of excellence through education* (pp. 85–110). Mahwah, NJ: Lawrence Erlbaum Associates.

3

Self-Explanation: Enriching a Situation Model or Repairing a Domain Model?

Nicholas deLeeuw
Vassar College

Michelene T. H. Chi
University of Pittsburgh

When people are reading a difficult text, one of the things they may do is talk themselves through the difficulty. That is, they might start explaining to themselves the parts they do understand, try to think of related knowledge that might help them understand the rest, and/or make an effort to problem-solve the gaps in their understanding. These efforts by readers to explain a text to themselves are what we call *self-explanation* (Chi & Bassok, 1989). Because self-explanation is directed toward a goal (understanding the text, or what the text describes), and requires conscious thought and effort, we think of it as an intentional strategy on the part of the reader. In this chapter, we consider the process of self-explanation in the context of two accounts of learning from a text, the Mental Model Revision view of Chi (2000) and the Construction–Integration model (Kintsch, 1998). Although there are some core similarities between these accounts of how readers combine old and new knowledge, they do yield some different predictions about intentional processes in general and self-explanation in particular. Some evidence that speaks to these differences is presented in the latter half of the chapter.

Many of the examples that follow are taken from deLeeuw (2000). In that study, 17 middle school students were instructed to self-explain after reading each paragraph of a textbook chapter on the human circulatory system (Towle, 1989). This choice of examples matches the focus in this chapter on directed self-explanation while reading a descriptive text.

WHAT IS SELF-EXPLANATION?

Self-explanation occurs whenever people explain a problem out loud as they solve it, or a text to themselves as they read it. It may occur spontaneously (e.g., Chi, Bassok, Lewis, Reimann, & Glaser, 1989; Pirolli & Recker, 1994), or in response to instructions (e.g., Bielaczyc, Pirolli, & Brown, 1995; Chi, deLeeuw, Chiu, & LaVancher, 1994; Coleman, Brown, & Rivkin, 1997). There are ample demonstrations that instructing students to self-explain while problem solving results in better solutions (Chi et al., 1989; Didierjean & Cauzinille-Marmeche, 1997; Mwangi & Sweller, 1998), and that having them self-explain while reading results in better understanding of the text (Chi et al., 1994; Coleman et al., 1997). The processes involved in self-explaining while reading and while problem solving may or may not be very similar. This chapter concerns itself with self-explanation while reading in response to instructions.

The general instruction to explain what one is reading (Chi et al., 1994; Coleman et al., 1997) results in a larger class of utterances than those we call self-explanations. Following Chi (2000), we refer to self-explanations as those statements that are concerned with the topic of the text. This excludes self-monitoring statements ("I'm having trouble understanding this"), text-monitoring statements ("This is confusing"), and other non-topic-oriented statements ("I'm thirsty"). Self-explanations also include summaries and paraphrases that in some way restate knowledge that is already in the text, although these are not the focus of our work. The subclass of self-explanations that is of most interest is what Chi (2000) called *Self-Explaining Inferences*, or SEIs. These are on-topic statements that go beyond the information presented in the text. Self-explanations, then, are a subset (the topic-relevant ones) of what people produce when asked to vocalize while reading, and SEIs are the subset of self-explanations that are more than restatements of information in the text. They are analogous to elaborations and inferences of the information in the text. Chi et al. (1994) showed that among subjects instructed to self-explain, those who produce more SEIs show the greatest increase in understanding.

Self-Explanation in the Context of Mental Model Revision

The mental model revision view (Chi, 2000) starts with the assumption that learners have an existing mental model of what they are going to read about, before they start reading. Thus if they are reading a chapter about the human circulatory system, the assumption is that they know something about the heart and the blood, veins, and arteries, before they ever start reading. This mental model of the text domain is referred to as a *do-*

main model, to distinguish it from other varieties of mental models. In our work with the circulatory system, for example (Chi et al., 1994), we encountered students who believe that the heart oxygenates blood, or that red blood cells carry nutrients, to give just a couple of examples. We also found students who could not describe how the lungs fit into the system, or who could not distinguish between veins and arteries. The domain model is therefore thought of as a mix of correct and incorrect knowledge, which may have large or small gaps of knowledge relative to a more expert description, such as that presented in a textbook.

The mental model revision view further assumes that not only do students often come into a learning situation with an existing, often incorrect domain model, but that their preexisting domain model is flawed in a coherent way (Chi & Roscoe, in press). By coherence we mean both that the flawed model is an internally consistent one, and that it embodies an identifiable set of alternative or incorrect assumptions. The coherence of a domain model can be assessed either empirically or analytically. Empirically, coherence in the internally consistent sense means that students can use their domain model to give predictable and systematic answers to questions, and do so consistently. For example, about half of the eighth-grade students tested in the Chi et al. (1994) study thought that the human circulatory system was organized as a "single loop," in which blood goes from the heart to the body and returns to the heart for oxygenation. On the basis of such a flawed model, one can predict that their answers to the question "Why does blood have to go to the heart?" would be "To get oxygen." The second sense of coherence, that models embody an identifiable set of alternative assumptions, can be determined analytically through an analysis of the domain. For the domain of the human circulatory system, we identified three fundamental assumptions that differentiate one of the flawed mental models, the "single loop" model, from the correct "double loop" model. For example, the single loop model differs from the correct double loop model in systematic ways, in their assumptions about the source of oxygen, the purpose of blood flowing to the lungs, and the number of loops. That is, all students with the single loop model assume that it is the heart (rather than the lungs) that provides oxygen; that blood goes to the lungs to deliver oxygen (rather than to exchange carbon dioxide and oxygen); and that there is just one loop rather than two (Chi & Roscoe, in press), even though there are variations among the single loop models that students hold.

In the mental model revision view, learning from a text is a process of repairing the existing domain model. This involves three kinds of processes: (a) insertions of information from the text into the domain model; (b) replacement of wrong knowledge in the domain model with correct information from the text; and (c) inferences of new knowledge that is not explicit in the text, but that specifically addresses flaws in the domain model. An example of a straight insertion would be the student who knows that arteries take blood away from the heart and that veins take blood to the heart, but does not know anything about the function of capillaries. That student could insert information about the role of capillaries, which is to take blood from the arteries to the veins, without any further revisions to his or her domain model. An example of replacement would be the student who believes that veins take blood away from the heart, but learns that arteries perform that function instead. The role of inferences is seen as especially important in tailoring what is learned from the text to the reader's existing domain model. For example, few texts, including the one we studied (Towle, 1989) specifically state that the heart does not oxygenate blood. They state what the heart and lungs do, but the reader who believes that the heart oxygenates blood must infer that this is wrong, thus making a crucial correction to their domain model.

In this context, self-explanation inferences are an observable manifestation of the process of repairing a flawed but coherent domain model. Readers reveal in these statements how it is that they resolve the differences between their domain model and the text, in order to produce a new and better domain model. For example, Chi (2000) analyzed a single subject's protocols in the context of the subject's existing flawed single loop domain model. Many of the explanations were meaningless unless they were interpreted from the perspective of attempts at repairing the student's flawed mental model. That is, the explanations this student produced were shown to be specifically directed toward the flaws in her domain model, and created a resolution of the conflict between her single loop domain model coming in, and the double loop described in the text. Thus, self-explanations appear to be overt manifestations of the processes of repairing one's existing flawed domain model.

Self-Explanation in the Context of Situation Model Building

Although the mental model revision approaches focus on how new knowledge can change the understanding of a domain, they do not attempt to explain how new knowledge is acquired from a text. This is the focus of comprehension models, including the construction–integration (CI) model (Kintsch, 1998; Kintsch & van Dijk, 1989). Self-explaining inferences can also be viewed as fitting into this framework. This framework provides an alternative hypothesis about the function of SEIs: instead of being called on in the service of repairs to an existing mental model, they may be called on to aid in the creation of a new mental model that is a representation of the text. In the next section, we briefly lay out a basic outline of this model, and then explain how SEIs can be seen in this context.

Comprehension Processes to Build a Situation Model. Comprehension processes in the CI model consist of building basically two levels of representation: a propositional text-based representation and a situation model (van Dijk & Kintsch, 1983). Because deep comprehension in the context of learning a scientific text is affected mostly by the quality of the situation model (Kintsch, 1986, 1994), we focus on the construction of the situation model in the CI model and its contrast to the repair of a domain model in self-explaining.

The basic assumption of the CI model is that comprehension is the building of an episodic representation of the situation described by the text. This episodic representation is referred to as the situation model, analogous to a mental model of the situation described by the text. The situation model is an integrated network that combines a propositional text-based representation (reflecting the microstructure and the macrostructure of the text) and prior background knowledge. However, because prior knowledge is activated on the basis of the nodes and links in a text-based representation, it seems that the situation model must be determined, to a large extent, by the text-based representation. That is, the situation model is an *enriched* and elaborated version of the text-based representation.

For example, suppose a student is reading the sentences: "When a baby has a septal defect, the blood cannot get rid of enough carbon dioxide through the lungs. Therefore, it looks purple." A text-based representation is built, consisting of a proposition network linking the nodes (baby; septic defect; blood; carbon dioxide; through the lungs) by relations (baby *has* a septal defect; blood *cannot get rid of* carbon dioxide), and relations among the linked nodes (baby has a septal defect *when* blood cannot get rid of carbon dioxide). The text-based representation consists of meanings with direct links to the words in the text. It encompasses the literal representation of the text, without elaboration or intrusions of knowledge. Assuming that there are no coherence omissions in the text, such as missing referents and argument overlap, all students are capable of constructing pretty much the same text-based representation of these two sentences. (Note that *coherence* is used here to refer to the text, not the mental model.)

However, in order to understand these two sentences, background knowledge about the circulatory system must be retrieved and incorporated into the network. For example, one might need to relate knowledge about the septum, that it usually separates the red blood (carrying oxygen) from the purple blood (carrying carbon dioxide), to the "septal" node in the text-based representation. Likewise, the node "through the lungs" will activate relevant knowledge such as "Blood gets rid of carbon dioxide through the lungs." Notice that the relevant knowledge that is retrieved and becomes integrated with the text-based representation is driven by local associations and activations (Kintsch, 1998), such as the association of "through the lungs" with the activated knowledge about "blood getting rid of carbon dioxide through the lungs." Aside from the details of how the CI model works (i.e., once all the relevant associations are formed, then spreading activation processes select those portions of the activated knowledge that are strongly interconnected and inhibit isolated elements), the resulting effect is that only contextually appropriate knowledge remains. Thus, the situation model consists of the correct text knowledge integrated with the relevant retrieved prior knowledge.

When Automatic Comprehension Processes Fail. As long as the largely automatic processes involved in construction and integration are successful at building a coherent situation model, there is no reason for readers to engage in anything as effortful as explaining the text to themselves. But readers sometimes get stuck, particularly when there are problems in the text itself. We divide problems in the text into two general kinds that we call *text-structure omissions and text-content omissions.* Either may result in the use of additional processes directed at resolving some incoherence in the emerging representation of the text.

Text-structure omissions are problems in the text that lead to difficulty in establishing a coherent text base. These may reflect, for instance, a failure of the text to sufficiently signal how the proposition related by a given sentence is connected to the propositions from previous sentences. Such connections are normally established by overlapping arguments and explicit connectives. For example the following two sentences from Towle (1989) are connected by argument overlap:

> *Each side of the heart is divided into an upper and lower chamber.*
>
> *Each upper chamber is called an atrium (AY-tree-uhm), and each lower chamber is called a ventricle (VEN-trih-kul).*

The upper and lower chambers are each explicitly referred to in each sentence. The following two adjacent sentences, on the other hand, are not explicitly connected:

> *In each side of the heart blood flows from the atrium to the ventricle.*
>
> *One-way valves separate these chambers and prevent blood from moving in the wrong direction.*

It is up to the reader to make a connection and realize that *these chambers* refer to the *atrium* and the *ventricle.* The reader may supply these connections on the basis of propositions from earlier sentences, or from background knowledge, or by inference. In the majority of cases, these types of inferences are effortless and are considered automatic. One type of these automatic inferences are bridging inferences, such as substituting the referent for a pronoun ("the heart" for "it"). The second variety of automatic inferences, automatic generation, is similarly "effortless." For example, connections may be induced based on overlapping arguments to propositions. A subject who reads that "Deoxygenated blood flows through capillaries that merge and form larger vessels called venules" (Towle, 1989) may automatically generate the unstated proposition that deoxygenated blood flows through venules. These automatic processes are not considered true inferences by Kintsch (1998) because they occur as a natural consequence of the construction and integration processes. Nor are they candidates for SEIs according to Chi (2000), again because they are automatic. Only occasionally, though, the reader may not supply a connection at all.

Text-structure omissions can cause difficulty in comprehension. For example, the potential difficulty that these omissions create has been demonstrated in studies that present alternate versions of the same text to different subjects. Britton, Van Dusen, Glynn, and Hemphill (1990) compared recall for four different versions of two texts about the Korean and Vietnam wars. A computer simulation of the Kintsch theory (1984) was used to determine which texts required more inferences to repair problems in argument overlap. The recall scores for these passages were negatively correlated with the number of inferences required, so the more coherent texts were more memorable. A similar finding comes from Britton and Gulgoz's (1991) study, which created a "principled" revision of a text about the Vietnam War, with principles derived from the Kintsch and van Dijk (1978) model. Again, more coherence at the text base level led to better memory for the text. McNamara and Kintsch (1996), using the same original text and principled revision, also found an advantage for the more coherent text in terms of recall and answering multiple-choice questions. These studies establish that text-structure omissions can create problems for readers, even though automatic inference and knowledge retrieval processes can bridge them in most cases. Nevertheless, we assume that such omissions can be readily supplied by readers, so long as the text is reasonably well written and appropriately targeted. We are more concerned with content-structure omissions.

Content-structure omissions occur when the text does not explicitly state how elements of the situation it is describing are connected to one another. Such omissions are typical, and even desirable. That is, it would be a very unusual (and boring) text that included *all* of the information needed to completely represent its topic. Texts generally leave out information that a typical reader could supply through background knowledge or inference, in order to avoid seeming redundant (Kintsch, 1998). Sometimes texts also omit information that the typical reader cannot supply, as analyses of real-world descriptive texts have shown (Beck, McKeown, Sinatra, & Loxterman, 1991; Britton & Gulgoz, 1991). For example, if a text states that "The septum divides the heart length wise into two sides," (Towle, 1989), but does not relate this to keeping oxygenated and deoxygenated blood separate, the reader may not be able to infer this function about the septum.

Not surprisingly, text revision studies establish that content-structure omissions may lead to problems. Beck and her colleagues (Beck et al., 1991) revised social studies texts aimed at elementary school students. Revisions to the texts included establishing causal connection between events, and were thus aimed at establishing connections between elements of the situation the text described (pre-Revolutionary American history). Readers of the revised, more coherent texts performed better on tests of recall and comprehension. Subsequent studies using similar styles of revision yielded mixed results. Sinatra, Beck, and McKeown (1993), using a text on whaling, did not find an influence of the text revision on recall. One possibility for this divergent result, they hypothesized, was that the subjects had more background knowledge on this subject than they did on the American Revolution, therefore they did not need the addition of causal relations in the revised text. This interpretation was later confirmed in a study by McNamara, Kintsch, Songer, and Kintsch (1996). They found that high-knowledge subjects improved their comprehension on a less coherent text, whereas low-knowledge subjects needed a more coherent text. These findings suggest that high-knowledge subjects might be engaged in more effortful processing by drawing on prior knowledge to substitute for what was missing in the text. Thus, self-explanation inferences are consistent with both the situation model building perspective (especially in the case of high-knowledge subjects) and the mental model revision perspective.

Intentional Controlled Processes in Situation Model Building and Mental Model Revision. Kintsch (1998) therefore allows that when the comprehension process does not go smoothly, some (nonautomatic) effortful controlled processes may be needed to create a coherent representation of the situation described by the text. These controlled processes encompass what are typically called inferences, and in the context of this volume, we call them intentional. SEIs would be observable examples of controlled processing, in this view.

In the situation model building view, intentional, or controlled, inferences may occur when a reader perceives a problem in his or her understanding of the situation described by the text. Consider the following sentence from Towle (1989): "When a person has an infection, the number of white blood cells can increase tenfold." Although they have just read (four sentences back) that white blood cells "defend the body against disease," readers may not automatically invoke a connection between infection and disease. And they may not see the connection between more white blood cells and fighting an infection. In these cases, readers may search for prior knowledge that resolves this content structure gap. For example, they may recall being taught that infections cause disease. They may also try to induce a solution to the problem by imagining a possible element of the situation and seeing how it integrates with the rest of the mental model. For example, they may postulate that more white blood cells allow the body to combat more infectious agents. Or the element of the model needed to solve the problem may be arrived at by a combination of retrieval and reasoning, such as considering a similar situation and reasoning by analogy. These intentional processes of retrieval, integration, and reasoning by analogy do encompass Chi's definition of SEIs. Thus, SEIs could fit into the CI framework as a form of controlled inferences that extend the normal comprehension process by bringing in both new (generated), and old (retrieved) knowledge.

However, there may be a subtle difference in that SEIs, as an intentional process, are brought to bear when the reader perceives not so much a content structure gap in the text, but a discrepancy or conflict between the content of the text and the content of one's domain model (Chi, 2000).

The Role of Prior Knowledge in Situation Model Construction for Novices and Experts

Comprehension in the CI model is a process of integrating information in the text with related prior knowledge in order to create a situation model. Whether that prior knowledge serves as background or foreground to the comprehension process is a matter of expertise. This distinction is important for understanding SEIs in situation model construction because it speaks to the role of prior knowledge in SEI production. For the novice, comprehension is dominated by the text, with background knowledge brought in piecemeal on the basis of the words in the text. Kintsch (1998) referred to this as *text base dominated comprehension*.

A domain expert, on the other hand, automatically links the information in the text to a wealth of other knowledge, so that the situation model that is created may be structured on the basis of existing schemas and knowledge, with new information just filling in slots in those structures. When prior knowledge is activated, it provides routes to retrieval of other prior knowledge. Therefore, the more expert the reader is in the domain, the more these pathways are quickly and automatically activated, and the more they are tightly linked. In situation-dominated comprehension, then, well organized and practiced prior knowledge tends to dominate comprehension. That is, the expert reader's existing model of the domain takes center stage in the comprehension process, even as he or she absorbs new information about the domain contained in the text being read. For example, if a circulatory system novice reads that "The heart pumps blood," and then, 20 sentences later, reads that "Blood enters the heart through the left atrium," the reader may not make a connection between the two (i.e., it is the same blood). A more expert reader, however, would have already activated some mental model of the blood's circulation, so that the latter sentence fits neatly into a structure already activated in working memory. Thus expertise, and the resulting situation-dominated comprehension, should enable readers to automatically resolve content-structure omissions, successfully creating a situation model without recourse to controlled processes, including SEIs.

COMPARING SITUATION MODEL CONSTRUCTION AND DOMAIN MODEL REPAIR

The mental model revision view and the situation model construction view differ in that the former treats the novices the same way as the latter treats the experts, in that both novices and experts come into the learning situation with prior mental models, but with the added twist that novices have flawed mental models whereas experts have largely correct mental models. Thus, the two views previously outlined are largely compatible, and we could even view them as complementary, with the exception that they address different issues. Because experts are likely to know the correct mental model, the issue of repairing their mental models does not exist for the situation model construction view. Moreover, the situation model construction view describes the comprehension process, and the mental model revision view describes the repair process, which is activity beyond comprehension that addresses problems in the situation model. Thus, the simplest way of combining these two views would be to assume that readers create a situation model, closely tied to the text, while reading, and then use that model as the basis for comparison and repair of the domain model. But there are several sticking points that suggest that the synthesis of these two approaches is not quite so simple.

In brief, the mental model revision view assumes an activation of one's existing mental model, even for a novice with a flawed domain model. This means that a flawed domain model is predicted to have a strong influence on learning and that intentional processes such as SEIs will be directed at that flawed model. In contrast, the situation model building view assumes activation of an existing domain model only for an expert; and the flawed models of novices therefore have little influence on the learning process; and intentional processes will be focused on repairs of problems in the text. Thus, the situation model building view basically describes two situations: the novice with low background knowledge and the expert with high background knowledge. The mental model revision view discusses a third option, cases in which novices have a coherent but flawed conception.

At a more general level, the difference between these two views boils down to what is in the foreground of the learning process and what is in the background. In a text-base dominated situation model construction process (in the case for novices), the text is the foreground of what is being learned, and prior knowledge is background knowledge. From the standpoint of mental model revision, however, this perspective is reversed. The existing domain model is the focus of the learning process, and the text is considered as it impacts that model. Putting the reader's domain model in the foreground of the comprehension process is actually not at all incompatible with the CI model. In Kintsch's (1998) terms, this is the case of situation-dominated comprehension, described earlier. The representation being constructed is dominated by the reader's well-organized knowledge of the text's topic. This is essentially equivalent to saying that the reader's domain model, not the text, guides the comprehension process. So put in the terms of the CI model, the mental model revision view claims that self-explanation reflects situation-dominated processing, despite a lack of expertise. This would predict activation of an existing domain model, a strong influence of flawed domain models, and a self-explanation process driven by the domain model and not the text. The remainder of this chapter addresses each of these points in more detail and considers some evidence that bears on these issues.

What Is Activated During Reading?

The mental model revision and situation model construction views make different assumptions about what prior knowledge is activated during reading. By activation we mean something akin to Ericsson & Kintsch's (1995) long-term working memory, knowledge that is readily available for incorporation into the mental model under construction. A central assumption of the mental model revision approach is that readers are working on their domain model as they read, and therefore must activate all or part of a coherent prior model, not just the minimum related information necessary for comprehension. That is, each activation is targeted at either the entire mental model or portions of it, so that the knowledge that is activated in reading successive sentences is coherent (and/or connected).

This activation of a coherent model is not based on expertise and is assumed even for the novice with a deeply flawed domain model. By contrast, the CI model predicts only targeted activation of prior relevant knowledge for the novice, based on close associations to the propositions underlying the text. This implies that the various associations activated with the reading of successive sentences need not be coherently connected. For the novice, comprehension should be text base dominated, that is, closely tied to the text and not to any prior domain model. Moreover, there should not be any coherence in the knowledge activated. For the experts, on the other hand, comprehension should be situation dominated, in that a coherent domain model can be activated. Thus, the situation model construction view for the experts is analogous to the mental model revision view for the novice, with the exception that novices may work with flawed models.

Both perspectives predict a strong influence of prior knowledge for more expert readers. The correctness and elaborateness of the resulting mental model should be highly dependent on background or prior knowledge, whether it is activated based on expertise or effort. Thus expertise studies cannot discriminate between these two views. For example, McNamara et al. (1996) gave middle school students with more or less background knowledge about the circulatory system a text on heart disease that was varied in both local and global coherence. Not surprisingly, the higher knowledge readers did better on tests of recall, on question answering, and on problem solving. But the extent of the advantage depended on the coherence of the text. Given a high-coherence text, there was only a slight advantage in free recall for the high-knowledge readers, but given a low-coherence text, the gap in recall between low- and high-knowledge readers widened substantially. These results confirm that having more domain knowledge leads to better comprehension, at least in part because the knowledge compensates for deficiencies in the text. But they do not discriminate whether a coherent domain model is activated or only relevant targeted associations are activated.

Both perspectives also predict that more effortful processing while reading has a payoff, especially for high-knowledge readers. McNamara et al. (1996) found a consistent pattern of improved recall for more coherent texts when they measured text-base-level memory, but the pattern was different for problem solving questions, designed to tap the situation model. Low-knowledge subjects still performed better on these tests when provided with texts that were more coherent. But the high-knowledge subjects actually did better with the baseline, minimally coherent text. Evidently the lack of connections in the text forced those readers to supply their own structure and content-filling knowledge, which resulted in a better situation model. Another study also provided evidence that greater activation of prior knowledge can be achieved through effort as opposed to expertise. Mannes and Kintsch (1987) provided readers with an outline of a short text's topic, which involved the industrial applications of bacteriology. The outline served as a manipulation of prior knowledge in this study. It was either based on and thus consistent with the text, or based on a related article from an encyclopedia and therefore inconsistent with the structure of the text. The information content of the two outlines was the same. Subjects given the inconsistent outline did better on reasoning tasks designed to rely on their situation models. Thus the inconsistencies between text and the structure of prior knowledge (from the outline) appeared to spur processes that created a more useful situation model. Chi (2000) also proposed that noticing conflicts between one's domain model and the text drives effortful intentional processes such as SEIs. These studies also support the assertion in the mental model revision view that greater activation of prior knowledge can be achieved through effort as opposed to expertise. However, they do not discriminate between a coherent model activation and a greater quantity of related knowledge activation, because the tests of knowledge were based on the normative, correct, model presented in the text.

Enforced self-explanation may serve a role similar to that of the inconsistent outline, or less coherent text, by also forcing readers to be more mindful of their existing domain knowledge (Chi & Bassok, 1989; Kintsch, 1994). Enforced production of self-explanations is certainly more effortful than not producing self-explanations, and the results (e.g. Chi et al., 1994) show greater gains in knowledge for students who self-explain. But again, gains in correct answers to questions do not tell us whether greater learning was achieved by more successfully incorporating the text into an existing domain model, or by injecting more of the domain-relevant knowledge into a situation model based on the text. The real test of whether students activate an existing mental model while self-explaining or whether they merely retrieve and incorporate relevant knowledge is what becomes of flawed domain models.

What Is the Influence of a Flawed Domain Model and Incorrect Prior Knowledge?

Flaws in the existing domain model play different roles in the mental model revision perspective and the situation model construction perspective. In the former case, a coherent domain model (or portions of it) is activated, even for a novice with a flawed model. Understanding is driven by the goal of assimilating new information with the existing domain model, flaws and all. If conflicts are noticed, then the domain model has to be repaired. Thus, the mental model revision perspective predicts that it is possible that the text information fails to successfully repair the prior flawed domain model, and that the resulting domain model continues to be flawed in a coherent way. This prediction is supported by evidence in Chi et al. (1994, Table 5). In that study, we found that more than half of the students (13 out of 24) continued to display flawed mental models in their understanding after reading the circulatory text, even though their flawed mental models were much improved.

In contrast, the situation model construction perspective views the text-based comprehension of the novice as driven by specific nodes and links of the text, with individual relevant pieces of background knowledge associated with the nodes and links, activated to enrich the text-base representation. Because the situation model arises from a piecemeal integration of relevant and related knowledge to the text-base representation, it is not clear how the resulting situation model, if incorrect, can be coherent. That is, if background knowledge is incorrect, then the resulting situation model is incorrect at places where the relevant background knowledge is incorrect. The implication of the CI processes is that the resulting misunderstanding cannot be "coherent" because incorrect background knowledge is brought to the text-base representation in a piecemeal way, depending on the nodes and relationships expressed in the text sentences.

For example, consider the student whose model of the circulatory system is based on a single loop. Blood goes from the heart to the lungs to get oxygen, then from the lungs to the body, where the oxygen is depleted, and then back to the heart. This model consists of a number of component functions (heart pumps blood to lungs, lungs oxygenate blood, blood travels from lungs to body, etc.) that are linked to each other (The heart pumps blood to the lungs SO THAT the lungs can oxygenate the blood, etc.) Although it is flawed, this model can be quite coherent in terms of its underlying assumptions that are used to make consistent predictions. Most of these specific nodes and links are correct and will be echoed by the text. Thus in the situation model view, a good deal of the students' existing knowledge is activated because it is closely linked to the text. However, the central organization feature of the model, the single loop, should not be activated. The text will also not mention a single loop, nor will it mention the blood traveling from the lungs to the body, because these are both wrong. Thus these incorrect nodes and links are not alike.

In the mental model revision perspective, however, the coherent but incorrect single loop model is activated, so that readers will essentially try to fit the correct information in the text into their incorrect organization. Much of what is in the text will be perfectly compatible with that flawed model, because most of the specific nodes and links in the model are correct. And the text will not mention the single loop, even to say that it is wrong. So the readers will either notice that specific functions in the text (e.g., the pulmonary artery carries blood from the heart to the lungs) contradict the global organization of their model, or they will fail to integrate those nodes into their domain model, thereby leaving the resulting domain model a still-coherent and somewhat enhanced version of a globally flawed model.

What Is the Goal of Intentional Processes?

Intentional processes, including SEIs, are distinct from automatic processes in comprehension in that they are directed at solving a problem. That problem might be in the text, in the form of text or content structure omissions, or it might be in the domain model, in the form of misinformation or a gap in knowledge. As we stated earlier, content-structure omissions consist of gaps in local coherence at the text-base level, and should not require any intentional processes to repair so long as there is adequate background knowledge to cover them. So in this section we consider whether self-explaining inferences are driven by content level problems within the text, or by flaws in the existing domain model.

Text Coherence and SEI Production. A situation-dominated comprehension or the mental model revision view would predict that self-explanations are driven by problems in the domain or situation model (in the sense that it conflicts with the text), rather than problems in the text. If self-explanations were driven by problems in the text, then in principle we would expect to see different readers self-explaining at the same troublesome points in the text, as readers would use self-explanations to resolve these difficulties. Moreover, if it is difficulty with the text itself that is driving self-explanation, there should be some consistency among different readers of the same text, especially readers with similar backgrounds. As we alluded to earlier, Chi (2000) reanalyzed data from both the Chi et al. (1994) and the Chi et al. (1989) studies, and found this was not the case. There was no consistent pattern of when self-explanations were produced across subjects. Instead, a very idiosyncratic pattern of self-explanations was produced by each student, suggesting that problems in the text are not the source self-explanation generation. This was the case despite the fact that all of the subjects read the same text under the same conditions. This pattern of individual differences in the idiosyncratic locations at which explanations were generated was obtained for both spontaneous explainers and enforced explainers.

Using the data from deLeeuw's (2000) dissertation, we were able to replicate this idiosyncratic pattern in a more systematic way. Subjects in this study were seventh graders, reading the same circulatory system chapter (Towle, 1989) as in Chi et al. (1994). In this study, however, there was a second version of the text created using an analysis of content-level incoherence or omissions. In places where the text failed to explicitly connect the function of one component to those of the others in a causal chain, or failed to explicitly place a component in a hierarchy of system parts, these details were added to the revised version of the text. The revised version was therefore more explicit in connecting all of the components of the circulatory system, both functionally and hierarchically. Thus, the revised version had all the content omissions filled. Students reading either version of the text were prompted to self-explain after each paragraph, 16 times in all. (An additional 18 students were not prompted to self-explain, but their results are not discussed here). The verbalizations they produced were later segmented into roughly sentence size, and each segment was classified in one of five categories. These were summaries, paraphrases, self-monitoring statements, elaborations that did not add information about the circulatory system, or self-explaining inferences (SEIs). SEIs contained information about the circulatory system not presented in the text (or not yet presented). The majority of utterances (80%) were summaries or paraphrases of the text. Only 5% of them were classified as SEIs.

The protocols for each student were combined to yield a count of how many SEIs were produced at each prompting location in the text. This would show if any problems in the text led to a higher number of SEIs for that portion of the text. However, no locations yielded significantly higher numbers of SEIs than any other, based on a one-way ANOVA with 16 levels, one for each prompt. The only difference that approached significance, F (15, 225) = 1.629, p = .0675, was entirely due to two prompts (10 and 14) that drew no SEIs from any subject. These passages concerned William Harvey's discovery that the circulatory system formed a closed double loop, and the composition of the blood. Although these two paragraphs drew fewer SEIs than others, no location drew significantly more SEIs, which would have been the indication that a lack of text coherence at particular location was the driving force behind SEI production. For these students and these texts, at least, it was not.

The same analysis revealed that overall text coherence also did not influence the production of SEIs. Because the revised text in this study explicitly provided functions and connections between functions that were lacking in the original, it had fewer content-structure omissions. If those omissions in the original text were an impetus to self-explain, we would expect that students assigned to read the original text would self-explain more, overall, than students reading the revised text. However, the number of SEIs produced in response to the original text (mean = 4.00) was no greater than the number produced in response to the revised text (mean = 4.22), F (1, 225) < 1, n.s. Subjects in this study were not producing SEIs in response to a lack of coherence in the text.

These results do not mean that students never produce SEIs, or use other intentional processes, in response to problems in the text. The McNamara et al (1996) study mentioned earlier suggested that they do. But the fact that SEIs were produced, and were not text driven, lends indirect support to the view that they were produced in response to domain model flaws. More direct support for this hypothesis is based on an analysis of the domain models subjects brought in to this study.

Domain Model Structure and SEI Production. If the production of SEIs did not reflect the structure of the text, did it reflect the structure of students' domain models? The mental model revision view predicts that it should reflect the structure of the domain model. In order to test whether SEIs are generated as a function of the structure of the domain model, we need to characterize the structure of a domain model.

In order to capture the structure of students' prior domain models, each of the students in the deLeeuw (2000) study underwent a detailed interview in which they responded to a series of prompts about each of 31 components of the circulatory system. Transcripts of these interviews were translated into a set of propositions concerning the functions of each component. These propositionalized representations were then further analyzed as described next.

Perhaps the most effective method to capture students' domain model is to analyze the transcripts in such a way as to depict the model, as was undertaken in Chi et al. (1994). In a multistep procedure, Chi et al. (1994) identified and classified students' mental models of the circulatory system according to the number of loops in the subject's model of blood flow, whether lungs played a role in oxygenating blood, whether the chambers of the heart were assigned appropriate functions, and similar features. The range of classifications was from a no-loop model in which blood was pumped from the heart and did not return, to a double loop model in which substantially all of the major features were correct. Also, it is not obvious how the production of SEIs should correspond to a specific prior model, although one could assume that the more flawed a mental model is, the more SEIs may be needed to repair that model. However, such direct correspondence does not take into account the fact that students often miss opportunities for repair (thereby not producing any SEIs) because they overlooked conflicts between their flawed domain model and the text information (Chi, 2000). Thus, a new method of assessing structure is needed. Here, we characterize the structure of a domain model by three properties: the amount of missing knowledge, the amount of wrong knowledge, and connectedness.

The domain model revision view predicts that SEIs will be produced in response to missing knowledge in a reader's domain model. However, missing knowledge was very unlikely to be filled in unless it was present in the text, so missing knowledge was defined as specific functions of circulatory system components that were mentioned in the text but not in the subject's pretest. The texts were analyzed in much the same way as student interviews, so that a set of propositions about the functions of the same 31 components covered in the interviews was created. The number of propositions explicitly laid out in the original text was 31. The amount of missing knowledge in a students' domain model was estimated by subtracting the number of functional propositions expressed in their pretest interview from that number. Students who expressed fewer functional propositions were rated as having more missing knowledge, and thus were expected to generate more SEIs.

The domain model revision view also predicts that SEIs will be produced when there are inconsistencies between the text and the reader's mental model. These are most likely to occur when the reader's knowledge is wrong. Wrong knowledge was assessed by counting the number of wrong arguments in the functional propositions. For example, if a student said that "the left side of the heart pumps deoxygenated blood" (pump [location [heart, left side] type [blood, deoxygenated]]), only a single argument (deoxygenated) was counted as wrong. However, if a the student said that "the heart oxygenates blood" (add [heart, oxygen, blood]), the entire proposition—all three arguments—was counted as wrong, because that function is not actually performed by that structure. Students with more wrong arguments were expected to generate more SEIs.

Another property of structured knowledge is its connectedness. More connections yield a richer knowledge structure, and a richer structure should provide both more routes to the retrieval of prior knowledge and more of a basis for knowledge generation. The connectedness of students' prior domain models was assessed by looking at enabling links from one function to another. Enabling links exist where the function of one component enables the function of another component. For example, the heart pumps oxygenated blood to arteries, which enables the arteries to deliver the oxygenated blood to the capillaries, which allows the capillaries to deliver oxygen to the body cells, and so on. The number of components (such as the heart, lungs, septum) with links to and/or from them was divided by the number of functional propositions to give a connectedness score.

These three aspects of students' domain models—the amount of missing knowledge, the amount of wrong knowledge, and the connectedness in terms of the number of enabling links—were analyzed together in a single multiple regression, with the number of SEIs as the dependent variable. The results of this regression show that students' prior mental mod-

TABLE 3.1
Multiple Regression to Predict the Number of Self-Explained Inferences (SEIs)

*Independent variables**	*Coefficient*	*F value*
Overall regression	$r^2 = .600$	**F (3, 13) = 6.505**
Missing functional propositions in pretest	**.422**	**F (1, 13) = 9.554**
Wrong arguments to propositions in pretest	**.480**	**F (1, 13) = 13.281**
Connectedness or links per proposition in pretest	**15.260**	**F (1, 13) = 15.557**
Text assignment (original / revised)	‡	F (1, 13) < 1
Intercept	**-17.993**	**F (1, 13) = 12.454**

Note. ‡Factor removed in stepwise procedure, $F < 4$.
*Reliable predictors ($p < .05$) are shown in **boldface**.

els did have a strong influence on how many SEIs they produced, in a pattern that is consistent with the mental model revision view. Table 3.1 presents the results of a multiple regression using the number of SEIs as the dependent measure. As predicted by the mental model revision view, missing, wrong, and connected knowledge in the pretest domain models had positive weights in the regression model and led to more SEIs. Thus, the overall structure of the domain model, as assessed by the amount of missing knowledge, wrong knowledge, and connectedness, was a strong predictor of how many SEIs were produced by each student.

Thus, in these data (deLeeuw, 2000), SEIs were associated with domain model problems and structure, but not with text problems. These results are consistent with the mental model revision view that a reader activates a coherent domain model while self-explaining, working on its flaws and depending on its structure. The goal of these SEIs appears to have been domain model repair.

SELF-EXPLANATION AND INCREMENTAL MENTAL MODEL CHANGE

Chi and her colleagues (Chi & Roscoe, in press; Chi, Slotta, & deLeeuw, 1994; Slotta, Chi, & Joram, 1995) made a distinction between two types of conceptual change required when learning science. These may be called radical conceptual change and ordinary, or incremental conceptual change.

Radical conceptual change involves completely replacing old concepts with new ones, because the target scientific concept is incompatible with the existing "folk" concept. (*Replacing* means to consider an alternative conception.) The radical conceptual change required to conceive of electricity as a kind of process as opposed to a kind of substance, for example, is a radical one. This requires a wholesale ontological shift from a matter-based concept to a process-based concept (Chi, 1997). This kind of radical conceptual change is probably not accomplished through self-explanation. Because the shift required essentially involves replacing (or learning to ignore) old concepts, and building up new ones, it cannot be accomplished through incremental changes to an existing mental model.

But many scientific concepts require only a more modest shift in understanding. We have used the circulatory system, at least at the level taught in middle school, as an example of a domain that requires only *incremental conceptual change*. There are often false beliefs that must be changed about the circulatory system, for example, the belief that the heart oxygenates blood. Ideally, this should be replaced with the correct understanding that the lungs oxygenate blood. However, both of these beliefs remain firmly in the realm of substances, so conceptual change requires only a simple replacement of one piece of knowledge for another. We contend that this more incremental conceptual change is not that difficult.

The finding that the production of SEIs is dominated by students' domain models suggests that SEIs should be associated with conceptual change of the "nonradical" sort. That is, if readers are processing the text with their existing domain model in mind, it should be reflected in incremental changes to that model. To assess incremental changes, recall that in this study, subjects' pretest interviews about the circulatory system were coded into propositions about functions of the various system components. The same was done for posttest interviews, yielding detailed before and after representations of their knowledge. The analysis that follows focuses on the number of functional propositions gained from pretest to posttest.

The key issue in this analysis is whether a gain in functional propositions (from the pretest to the posttest interviews) was related to the production of SEIs while learning. It is possible that these self-generated explanations about functions added knowledge to the students' mental models that was later reflected in their posttest interview. To address this possibility specifically, SEIs were divided according to the kind of knowledge they embodied. The category of most interest was functional SEIs, which included statements about functions of the circulatory system components not explicitly stated in the text. These represented 52% of the total number of SEIs. The other categories were hierarchical (11%), spatial (8%), and connective (28%). This last category was for explanations that tied one function to another. Because functional SEIs were logically the most closely tied to gains in functional propositions, this was the only category of SEIs used as an independent variable to predict gains.

What factors led to gains in these subjects' mental models? This analysis follows the same procedure as the multiple regression to predict the

TABLE 3.2
Influences on Gain in Functional Propositions.

	Stepwise Elimination Regression	*Multiple Regression of All Factors*
Independent variables*	Coefficient / F value	
Overall regression	r^2 = **.594**	r^2 = .660
	F (2, 14) = 10.243	**F (5, 11) = 4.275**
	p < .01	**p < .05**
Missing functional propositions in pre-test	‡	.131 F (1, 11) = .535
Wrong arguments to propositions in pre-test	‡	–.018 F (1, 11) = .011
Connectedness or links per proposition in pre-test	‡	–1.630 F (1, 11) = .098
Text assignment (original/ revised)	**3.540** **F(1, 14) = 9.235**	**3.508** **F (1, 11) = 8.048**
Number of SEIs about functions	**.732** **F(1, 14) = 10.872**	.684 F (1, 11) = 3.265
Intercept	**–2.056** **F(1, 14) = 4.494**	–1.578 F(1, 11) = .052

Note. ‡Factor removed in stepwise procedure, $F < 4$.
*Reliable predictors ($p < .05$) are shown in **boldface**.

number of SEIs (Table 3.2). Aspects of the subjects' pretest domain models (number of missing functions, number of wrong arguments, connections between functions) were used as predictors, along with the choice of original or enhanced texts and the number of functional SEIs. The results, presented in Table 3.2, show that both the number of functional SEIs and the choice of texts were reliable predictors of gains in functional propositions. (The results change only slightly if the total number of SEIs is substituted for functional SEIs.) Students benefited from reading the enhanced text, and also from explaining the text. The stepwise procedure eliminated all of the factors based on the pretest domain model, showing that the text and SEI production were more closely linked with gains than any of these.

However, Table 3.2 also shows the same regression run without the step-wise procedure, in effect treating the pretest factors as controls. The results for the text are similar, still showing a reliable effect of reading the enhanced version. The number of functional SEIs approaches significance in this case, $F(1, 11) = 3.265$, $p = .098$. This shows that the factors that predict SEIs overlap somewhat with the SEIs themselves in predicting gains. Subjects that were predisposed by their initial mental models to produce SEIs were also predisposed by these same factors to gain new functions from pretest to posttest. But SEIs also made a contribution to their gains, even after controlling for the differences in their pretest models.

Overall, these data point to two conclusions: that the enhanced text in deLeeuw (2000) was effective at helping students learn more about the functions of the circulatory system, and that producing SEIs also helped students learn more. In terms of mental model change, these two factors were the strongest predictors of proposition level additions to students' domain models.

DISCUSSION

In this chapter, we basically proposed three conjectures. First, we proposed that learning and understanding a (scientific) text may be viewed as a process of repairing a preexisting, coherent, but often flawed domain model, and not necessarily the building of a situation model. Second, we proposed that the role of self-explanations is to repair one's domain model, and not necessarily to resolve inconsistencies and discrepancies in a text. Third, we proposed that for some domains, understanding may often involve incremental mental model changes and not wholesale replacement of one mental model for another. Although our three conjectures may not be sharply differentiated from the alternative views, we posed them in such a contrastive way as a means of testing our ideas and predictions.

We presented some evidence to support our conjectures, although the evidence is by no means conclusive. It is merely suggestive that perhaps these conjectures might be true and worthy of further testing with more vigorous predictions. Moreover, we have not presented any evidence to directly contrast our conjectures and the alternative views. For example, to claim that a coherent preexisting mental model is activated while learning, one would have to show that the self-explanations, in composite, are coherent and are not merely a set of disjoint pieces of related knowledge.

We also did not fully address the question of what drives intentional processes. In the mental model view, intentional processes such as self-explaining are assumed to occur when the subjects perceive a conflict between the information in the text and their domain models. However, in order to notice such conflicts, the subjects must actively monitor what the text is saying and how it fits in with their mental model. Active monitoring can be enforced by asking subjects to self-explain. However, some subjects are perhaps more motivated to monitor their own comprehension even without such enforcement. However, we have no specific insights about the source of these individual differences.

There is one important caveat that should be pointed out. In the comprehension literature, there is a distinction between the topic that one is reading about (e.g., a disease such as septal defect), and the role of background knowledge (the circulatory system) on comprehension about such diseases. In the self-explanation literature, the domain model addressed is the one that the text topic addresses. That is, we looked at the way the students' domain model of the circulatory system changes as they read more about the circulatory system. It is not clear what the implication of such differences are for our conjectures.

In closing, we note that although Kintsch (1998) correctly conceived that "Comprehension is model building," we would add that learning is often model revision.

ACKNOWLEDGMENT

We are grateful for the comments provided by D. J. Bolger and Marguerite Roy.

REFERENCES

Beck, I. L., McKeown, M. G., Sinatra, G. M., & Loxterman, J. A. (1991). Revising social studies text from a text-processing perspective: Evidence of improved comprehensibility. *Reading Research Quarterly, 26*(3), 251–276.

Bielaczyc, K., Pirolli, P. L., & Brown, A. L. (1995). Training in self explanation and self regulation strategies: Investigating the effects of knowledge acquisition activities on problem solving. *Cognition and Instruction, 13*(2), 221–252.

Britton, B. K., Van Dusen, L., Glynn, S. M., & Hemphill, D. (1990). The impact of inferences on instructional text. In A. C. Graesser & G. . Bowers (Eds.), *The psychology of learning and motivation* (Vol. 25, pp. 53–70). San Diego, CA: Academic Press.

Britton, B. K., & Gulgoz, S. (1991). Using Kintsch's computational model to improve instructional text: Effects of repairing inference calls on recall and cognitive structures. *Journal of Educational Psychology, 83*(3), 329–345.

Britton, B. K., Van Dusen, L., Gulgoz, S., & Glynn, S. M. (1989). Instructional texts rewritten by five expert teams: Revisions and retention improvements. *Journal of Educational Psychology, 81*(2), 226–239.

Chi, M. T. H. (1997). Creativity: Shifting across ontological categories flexibly. In T. B. Ward, S. M. Smith, & J. Vaid (Eds.), *Conceptual structures and processes: Emergence, Discovery and Change* (pp. 209–234). Washington, DC: American Psychological Association.

Chi, M. T. H. (2000). Self-explaining expository texts: The dual processes of generating inferences and repairing mental models. In R. Glaser (Ed.), *Advances in Instructional Psychology* (pp. 161–237). Mahwah, NJ: Lawrence Erlbaum Associates.

Chi, M. T. H., & Bassok, M. (1989). Learning from examples via self explanations. In L. B. Resnick (Ed.), *Knowing, Learning, and Instruction: Essays in honor of Robert Glaser.* (pp. 251–282). Hillsdale, NJ: Lawrence Erlbaum Associates, Inc.

Chi, M. T. H., Bassok, M., Lewis, M. W., Reimann, P., & Glaser, R. (1989). Self explanations: How students study and use examples in learning to solve problems. *Cognitive Science, 13*(2), 145–182.

Chi, M. T. H., de Leeuw, N., Chiu, M. H., & LaVancher, C. (1994). Eliciting self explanations improves understanding. *Cognitive Science, 18*(3), 439–477.

Chi, M. T. H., & Roscoe, R. (in press). The processes and challenges of conceptual change. In M. Limon & L. Mason (Eds.), *Reframing the Processes of Conceptual Change: Integrating theory and practice.* Dordrecht, The Netherlands: Kluwer Academic Publishers.

Chi, M. T. H., & Slotta, J. D. (1993). The ontological coherence of intuitive physics. *Cognition and Instruction, 10*(2–3), 249–260.

Chi, M. T. H., Slotta, J. D., & de Leeuw, N. (1994). From things to processes: A theory of conceptual change for learning science concepts. *Learning and Instruction, 4*(1), 27–43.

Coleman, E. B., Brown, A. L., & Rivkin, I. D. (1997). The effect of instructional explanations on learning from scientific texts. *Journal of the Learning Sciences, 6*(4), 347–365.

de Leeuw, N. A. (2000). *How students construct knowledge from multiple sources.* Unpublished manuscript, Learning Research and Development Center, University of Pittsburgh.

Didierjean, A., & Cauzinille-Marmeche, E. (1997). Eliciting self explanations improves problem solving: What processes are involved? *Cahiers de Psychologie Cognitive/Current Psychology of Cognition, 16*(3), 325–351.

Ericsson, K. A., & Kintsch, W. (1995). Long-term working memory. *Psychological Review, 102,* 211–245.

Kintsch, W. (1986). Learning from text. *Cognition and Instruction, 3*(2), 87–108.

Kintsch, W. (1988). The role of knowledge in discourse comprehension: A construction–integration model. *Psychological Review, 95*(2), 163–182.

Kintsch, W. (1994). Text comprehension, memory, and learning. *American Psychologist, 49*(4), 294–303.

Kintsch, W. (1998). *Comprehension: A paradigm for cognition.* Cambridge: Cambridge University Press.

Kintsch, W., & van Dijk, T. A. (1978). Toward a model of text comprehension and production. *Psychological Review, 85*(5), 363–394.

Mannes, S. M., & Kintsch, W. (1987). Knowledge organization and text organization. *Cognition and Instruction, 4*(2), 91–115.

McNamara, D. S., & Kintsch, W. (1996). Learning from texts: Effects of prior knowledge and text coherence. *Discourse Processes, 22*(3), 247–288.

McNamara, D. S., Kintsch, E., Songer, N., & Kintsch, W. (1996) Are good texts always better? Interactions of text coherence, background knowledge, and levels of understanding in learning from text. *Cognition and Instruction, 14*(1), 1–43.

Mwangi, W., & Sweller, J. (1998). Learning to solve compare word problems: The effect of example format and generating self explanations. *Cognition and Instruction, 16*(2), 173–199.

Pirolli, P., & Recker, M. (1994). Learning strategies and transfer in the domain of programming. *Cognition and Instruction, 12*(3), 235–275.

Sinatra, G. M., Beck, I. L., & McKeown, M. (1993). How knowledge influenced two interventions designed to improve comprehension. *Reading Psychology: An International Quarterly, 14,* 141–163.

Slotta, J. D., Chi, M. T. H., & Joram, E. (1995). Assessing students' misclassifications of physics concepts: An ontological basis for conceptual change. *Cognition and Instruction, 13*(3), 373–400.

Towle, A. (1989). *Modern biology (teacher's edition).* Austin, TX: Holt, Rinehart & Winston.

van Dijk, T. A., & Kintsch, W. (1983). *Strategies of discourse comprehension.* New York: Academic Press.

4

Acupuncture, Incommensurability, and Conceptual Change

Paul Thagard
Jing Zhu
University of Waterloo

In November 1997, the U.S. National Institutes of Health conducted a consensus development conference on acupuncture. Like the previous 106 consensus conferences sponsored by NIH since 1977, the acupuncture conference consisted of presentations to a panel charged with making recommendations concerning medical practice. However, it was unusual in being the first cosponsored by the new NIH Office of Alternative Medicine and the first to consider therapies from outside the Western medical tradition. Acupuncture, involving the insertion of needles under the skin at prescribed positions, is a central component of the 2,500-year-old system of traditional Chinese medicine. This system of medicine employs a conceptual system very different from the one that evolved in Europe and America over the past century and a half. Allchin (1996) said that the contrasting traditional Chinese and Western views of acupuncture "offer a particularly deep version of Kuhnian incommensurability" (p. S107).

In the 1960s, philosophy of science was scandalized by the suggestion that competing theories might be incommensurable with each other (Feyerabend, 1981; Kuhn, 1970). If two conceptual systems such as those comprising the oxygen and phlogiston theories of combustion are radically different, then rational comparison and assessment of them becomes difficult if not impossible. Subsequent discussions showed that claims of radical incommensurability in the history of science were greatly exaggerated (e.g., Laudan, 1984; Nersessian, 1984; Thagard, 1992). Although competing scientific theories may indeed occupy very different conceptual systems, there is usually enough conceptual, linguistic, and evidential overlap that rational assessment of the comparative explanatory power of the two theories can take place. In Kuhn's most recent writings, incommensurability is no longer a dramatic impediment to the comparability of theories, but rather an unthreatening observation on difficulties of translation and communication (Kuhn, 1993).

Nevertheless, even if rationality-destroying incommensurability is rare within science, it would not be surprising if it occurred at the boundaries between science and nonscience. Contrast, for example, the cosmology of modern astrophysics with that of Australian aboriginals. The ontology, concepts, and linguistic context of these cosmologies are so radically different that explicit comparison and rational evaluation in terms of the standards of each is very difficult. Of course, from the empirical and theoretical perspective of Western science, the superiority of astrophysics over aboriginal cosmology is obvious, as are the advantages of the scientific perspective. Still, it is possible that radical incommensurability, of the sort that Kuhn and Feyerabend mistakenly attributed within Western science, may arise between science and alternative views of the world.

This chapter is an investigation of the degree of incommensurability between Western scientific medicine and traditional Chinese medicine, focusing on the practice and theory of acupuncture. In the next section, we very briefly sketch the conceptual and explanatory structure of modern medicine. We then provide a more detailed description of the structure of traditional Chinese medicine, oriented around such concepts as *yin*, *yang*, *qi*, and *xing*. It is then possible to discuss how the conceptual and explanatory differences between Western medicine and traditional Chinese medicine generate impediments to their comparison and evaluation. We outline linguistic, conceptual, referential, and explanatory difficulties that might be taken to imply that traditional ideas about acupuncture are incommensurable with Western medicine. We argue, however, that the difficulties can to a large extent be overcome, as they were at the NIH meeting in the service of the attempt to improve medical treatments. Our conclusion is that the dramatic differences between Western and traditional Chinese medicine do not provide insurmountable barriers to rational evaluation of acupuncture.

One positive contribution of this chapter is that its display of the conceptual and explanatory structure of traditional Chinese medicine provides an informative contrast that highlights aspects of the nature of Western science. We conclude with a discussion of how appreciation of different medical frameworks can require conceptual change that is both intentional and emotional. Thinkers are more likely to appreciate an alternative conceptual scheme if they have the goal of gaining such an appreci-

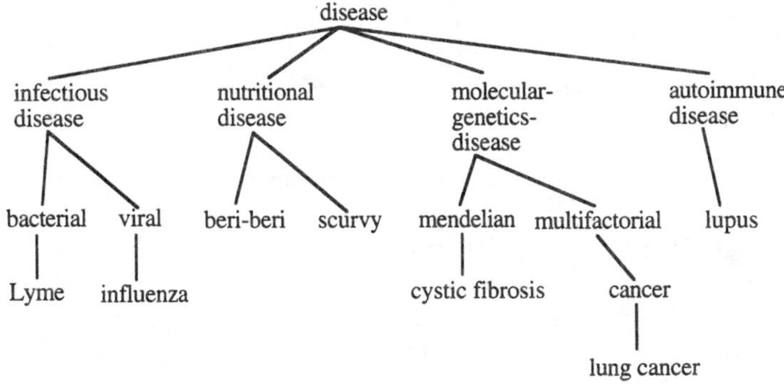

FIG. 4.1. Hierarchical organization of disease explanations, with examples of particular diseases. From Thagard (1999). Reprinted by permission.

ation, and acquiring the alternative scheme may involve changes in emotional attitudes as well as in concepts and beliefs.

WESTERN SCIENTIFIC MEDICINE

What is the structure of modern medicine? Biomedical theories are not naturally represented as formal axiom systems, but can naturally be characterized in terms of hierarchical cognitive structures (Schaffner, 1993; Thagard, 1996, 1999). Figure 4.1 depicts at a very general level the conceptual and explanatory structure of scientific medicine as it has evolved since Pasteur proposed the germ theory of disease in the 1860s. Diseases can be classified according to the bodily systems that they affect, for example into heart or skin diseases, but a deeper classification is based on the causes of disease. Modern medicine recognizes four kinds of causes of disease: infectious agents such as viruses, nutritional deficiencies such as lack of vitamin C, molecular-genetic disorders such as cancer, and autoimmune reactions such as the attack on the connective tissue that produces lupus erythematosus.

For each class of disease, there is an explanation schema that specifies a typical pattern of causal interaction.[1] Infectious diseases fall under the following explanation schema that became very successful in the 19th century:

[1]Explanation schemas and similar abstractions have been discussed in philosophy and cognitive science using varying terminology. See, for example, Darden and Cain (1989), Giere (1994), Kelley (1972), Kitcher (1981, 1989, 1993), Leake (1992), Schaffner (1993), Schank (1986), and Thagard (1988, 1992).

Germ Theory Explanation Schema:
Explanation target:
Why does a **patient** have a **disease** with **symptoms** such as fever?
Explanatory pattern:
The **patient** has been infected by a **microbe**.
The **microbe** produces the **disease** and **symptoms**.

To apply this schema to a particular disease, we need to replace the terms in boldface with specific examples or classes of examples. For example, influenza instantiates the schema by specification of symptoms such as fever, aches, and cough and by specification of the class of flu viruses that cause the symptoms. Figure 4.2 diagrams the causal structure of the germ theory of disease. Germs such as viruses and bacteria cause infections that produce symptoms that develop over time, constituting the course of the disease. Treatments such as antibiotics and vaccines can kill the germs or inhibit their growth, thereby stopping or preventing the infection that produces the symptoms.

Analogous explanation schemas for nutritional, molecular-genetic, and autoimmune diseases have been presented elsewhere (Thagard, 1996, 1999). Here, we have only presented enough of the conceptual and explanatory structure of modern medicine to provide a contrast with an alternative approach.

TRADITIONAL CHINESE MEDICINE

Traditional Chinese medicine developed for more than 2,500 years almost entirely free from Western influences. Its theories and practices of diagnosis and treatment are remarkably different from those of Western medicine. Some of its treatments such as herbal therapies and acupuncture are currently receiving increasing attention in the West as part of a rapidly growing interest in alternative and complementary medicine. As is described later, numerous experimental and clinical studies have confirmed that acupuncture treatments can relieve pain and reduce nausea. How-

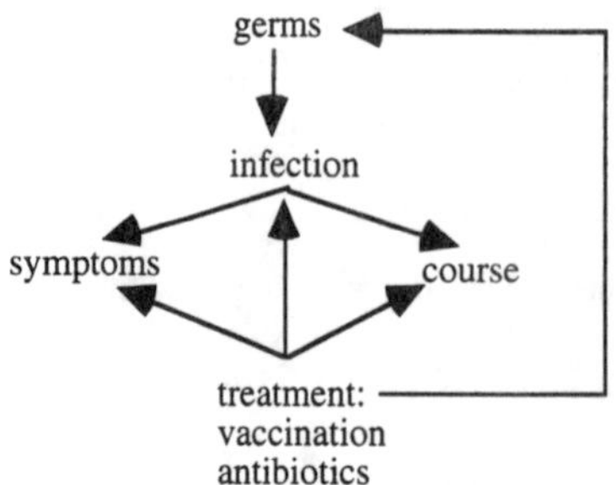

FIG. 4.2. Causal structure of the germ theory of disease. From Thagard (1999). Reprinted by permission.

ever, the theories of traditional Chinese medicine seem bizarre from the point of view of modern Western medicine. Even if some proponents of traditional Chinese medicine claim that Western and Chinese medicine should complement each other, they admit that Chinese medicine is organized on totally different principles (Porkert & Ullmann, 1988, p. 55). In this section, we try to display this organization and outline the conceptual and explanatory structure of traditional Chinese medicine.

The Balance of Yin and Yang

In ancient China, people believed that everything in the universe consists of two opposite but complementary aspects or forces, which combine to create a whole unit (Zhen, 1997). *Yin* and *yang* refer to the two basic categories of the universe, negative and positive respectively, and they are in constant flux. Every thing or event in the world is to be regarded as the interaction of an active and a conservative force, each of which has its own peculiar characteristics that determine the nature of the thing or event. According to *Yellow Emperor's Classic of Internal Medicine: Plain Questions* (chapter 5), one of the most important and original classics of traditional Chinese medicine, "The principle of *yin* and *yang* is the way by which heaven and earth run, the rule that everything subscribes, the parents of change, the source and start of life and death" (Guo, 1992).

The original meaning of the two words *yin* and *yang* in Chinese referred, respectively, to the side of a mountain that lies in shadow and the side that lies in sun. Yin could also refer to the shaded bank of a river, yang to the sunlit bank. But the terms are no longer strictly confined to their original meaning and have become basic and abstract categories in both Chinese philosophy and people's ordinary thinking. Typically, dynamic, positive, bright, warm, solid features are defined as yang, whereas static, negative, dark, cold, liquid, and inhibiting features are characterized as yin. Sunlight and fire are hot, whereas moonlight and water are cool, so that the sun and fire are yang whereas the moon and water are yin. Yin and yang are complementary to and interdependent on each other, even though they are opposites. For every individual thing, the yin and yang it contains do not remain in a static state, but are constantly in a dynamic equilibrium affected by the changing environment.

Like everything else, the human body and its functions are all governed by the principle of yin and yang. Remaining healthy and functioning properly require keeping the balance between the yin and yang in the body. Diseases arise when there is inequilibrium of yin and yang inside the body. This principle is central to traditional Chinese medicine, and its application dominates the diagnosis, treatment, and explanation of diseases. For example, a patient's high fever, restlessness, a flushed face, dry lips and a rapid pulse are yang symptoms. The diagnosis will be a yin de-

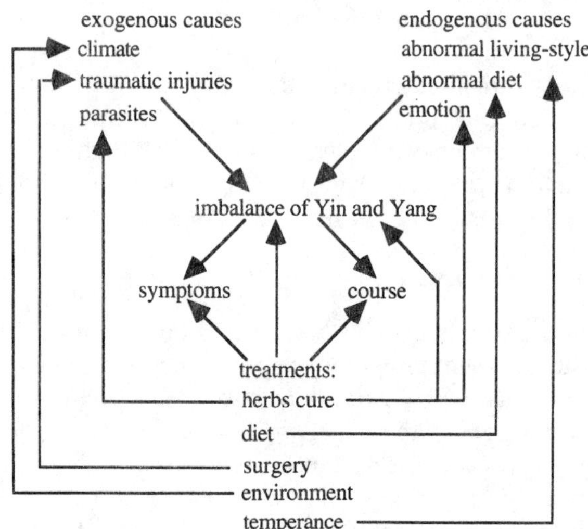

FIG. 4.3. Causal structure of disease concepts in the theory of *yin* and *yang* balance.

ficiency, or imbalance brought by an excess of yang over yin. Once the yin–yang character of a disease is assessed, treatment can restore the balance of yin and yang, for example by using yin-natured herbs to dampen and dissipate the internal heat and other yang symptoms. The imbalance of yin and yang can be caused by either exogenous factors, such as climate, traumatic injuries, and parasites, or endogenous factors, such as extreme emotional changes (anger, melancholy, anxiety, and so on), abnormal diet, intemperance in sexual activities, and fatigue. Figure 4.3 displays the structure of the causal network underlying the yin–yang explanation of disease. As with the germ theory of disease shown in Fig. 4.2, causes produce a set of symptoms and their course of development.

The way in which this causal structure explains disease can also be described by the following schema:

Yin and Yang Balance Theory Explanation Schema:
Explanation target:
Why does a **patient** have a **disease** with associated **symptoms**?
Explanatory pattern:
The **patient's** body is subject to exogenous and endogenous **factors.**
The **factors** produce an **imbalance** of **yin** and **yang**.
The **imbalance** of **yin** and **yang** produces the **disease** and **symptoms**.

This is the most general and fundamental pattern of disease explanation in traditional Chinese medicine, but there are also some more specific explanation schemas.

The Theory of the Five *Xing*

According to Aristotle and Hippocrates, everything in the world consists of four fundamental elements: earth, air, fire, and water. Similarly, the ancient Chinese considered metal, wood, water, fire, and earth to be fundamental. In Chinese, each of these is a *xing,* and the five collectively are called five-xing. There are two important differences between the theory of five-xing and the theory of four elements in ancient Greece. First, even though the five xings were considered as the basic components of the universe, the ancient Chinese did not use them to analyze the substantial constitution of particular things. Rather, the five xings are five basic categories that can be used to classify things according to their properties and relationships to other things. Second, the five xings are not independent of each other, but have significant relationships and laws of transformation among them. Hence instead of translating xing as "element," various commentators prefer to call the five xings the "Five Transformation Phases" or the "Five Phases of Change" (Porkert & Ullmann, 1988; Unschuld, 1985).

There are two basic kinds of relation or sequence among five xings: Mutual Promotion (Production) and Mutual Subjugation (Conquest). The principle of Mutual Promotion says that five xings may activate, generate, and support each other. It is through these promotions of the elements that five xings continue to survive, regenerate, and transform. The sequence of Mutual Promotion is as follows: wood promotes fire, fire promotes earth, earth promotes metal, metal promotes water, water promotes wood, and wood again promotes fire. The principle of Mutual Subjugation concerns relations such as restraining, controlling, and overcoming. Mutual restraint keeps the balance and harmony among the five xings: wood subdues earth, earth subdues water, water subdues fire, fire subdues metal, metal subdues wood, wood in its turn acts on earth. Figure 4.4 shows the Mutual Promotion and Mutual Subjugation relationship among five xings.

The meaning of the principles comes from experience. Fire is created when wood is burned. Ash (earth) is left after burning. All metals come from earth and liquefy on heating, while water is indispensable for growing trees and vegetation. These relations support the principle of Mutual Promotion (Production). On the other hand, the ancient Chinese noticed that trees grow on earth, impoverishing the soil. To prevent floods, dams and channels are built with earth. Water puts out fire, and metals can be softened and melted by fire. A sword or ax made of metal can be used to fell a tree. These relations are summarized in the principle of Mutual Subjugation (Conquest).

Most things in the world can be classified into one of the five basic categories according to their properties, function, and relations with others. For example, the liver is similar to wood with respect to its mild features,

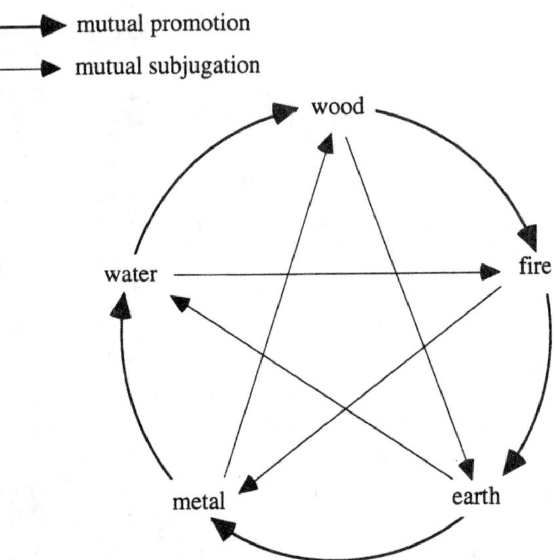

FIG. 4.4. Mutual Promotion and Mutual Subjugation relations among five *xings*. Adapted from Shen and Chen (1994), p. 17.

and the heart warms the whole body so it is analogous to fire. The spleen is responsible for assimilation of nutrients and corresponds to the earth. The lung is clear, analogous to metal. The kidney is similar to water by virtue of its responsibility of regulating fluids in the body.

In diagnosis and treatment, those things classified into the same kind are related to each other and have the same mutual relations with the objects in the neighboring categories. For example, a disease in the liver calls attention to the eyes, tendons, and the emotion of anger. Great anger is considered very harmful to the liver in traditional Chinese medicine. The liver pertains to wood, which flourishes in spring, so that liver diseases are prevalent in spring. The classification and correspondence in terms of five xings illustrate the mutual relationship between the human body, the seasons, climate factors, senses, and emotions. According to the principles of Mutual Promotion and Subjugation, the disease in one organ is not isolated from the other organs. A disease in the liver (wood) is probably due to the functional deficiency of the kidney (water), so the treatment should not only be aimed to the liver, but also enhance the function of the kidney as well as those of others. Thus the perspective of traditional Chinese medicine is more holistic than the Western perspective, which tends to look for the seat of a disease in a particular organ.

The theory of five xings specifies aspects of the more general theory of yin and yang balance. The improper function of an organ is originally caused by imbalance of yin and yang, and in turn influences the harmony between other organs, which can also be analyzed in relation to yin and yang. Here is the explanatory schema:

Five Xings Explanation Schema:

Explanation target:

Why does a **patient** get a **disease** with associated **symptoms**?

Explanation pattern:

The **imbalance** of ***yin*** and ***yang*** causes one or more organs, which belong to the corresponding **xing**, to **malfunction**.

The **malfunction** of one organ produces the **disorder** among all the organs, which are related between each other according to the rules of the theory of five xings.

The **disorder** among organs produces the **disease** and **symptoms.**

The Circulation of *Qi*

Another fundamental concept in traditional Chinese medicine is *qi,* which plays a central role in the theoretical background to such therapies as acupuncture, moxibustion, and massage. In the ordinary Chinese language, the term *qi* refers mostly to air or gas, and sometimes is also used to indicate a kind of emotion—anger. In the terminology of Chinese medicine, qi has a different meaning. First, qi is not a type of substance and has no fixed shape or constitution. Second, it is indispensable for life. Third, it is responsible for the resources of the function and operation of organs and the whole body. Qi has variously been interpreted in terms of the Greek pneuma, vital force, or energy (Lloyd, 1996; Lu & Needham, 1980). Qi cannot be observed directly, but with long and assiduous training and practice, a doctor can supposedly detect its flow and changes in a patient. A person can also detect the flow of qi and control its direction in some degree by exercises and meditation (Moyers, 1993).

There are basically two kinds of qi, *congenital qi* inherited from one's parents and vital for one's life, and the other type acquired after birth. We get the acquired qi from food and water, which is assimilated by the spleen and stomach, and from the air inhaled by the lungs. The acquired qi is constantly replenished and is fundamental to maintaining the life activities of the body. Because qi is dynamic, active, and warms the body, it falls under the yang category. Blood and body fluids, two kinds of fluids circulating inside the body, have the functions of nourishing and moistening. Therefore, they belong to the yin category. Qi is capable of producing and controlling blood, warming and nourishing the tissues, and activating the functions of organs.

Qi circulates along channels within the body called *meridians.* The system of meridians is unique to traditional Chinese medicine regarding the human body, and does not correspond to blood vessels or nerves. The resource of qi inside meridians comes from the internal organs, such as heart, spleen, lung, and stomach. As a unit, the system works to reinforce the coordination and balance of bodily functions.

Disease occurs when the circulation of qi is obstructed. Doctors need to identify where and why the flow of qi is blocked and carry out the proper treatment to restore the circulation of qi. Deficiency of qi can also cause illness, and the appropriate treatment is to replenish it. Figure 4.5 displays the causal structure of the theory of qi, and we can summarize disease explanations in the following schema:

Theory of Qi Explanation Schema:
Explanation target:
Why does a **patient** have a **disease** with associated **symptoms**?
Explanation pattern:
The body of the **patient** contains a meridian system which conducts the flow of *qi*.
An **obstruction occurs that blocks the flow of** *qi*.
The *qi* blockage produces the **disease** and **symptoms.**

Before proceeding to discuss philosophical issues concerning the relationship of Western and Chinese medicine, we should stress that both these traditions are concerned primarily with the treatment of patients, and that the development of explanatory theories of diseases has been driven largely by this practical aim.

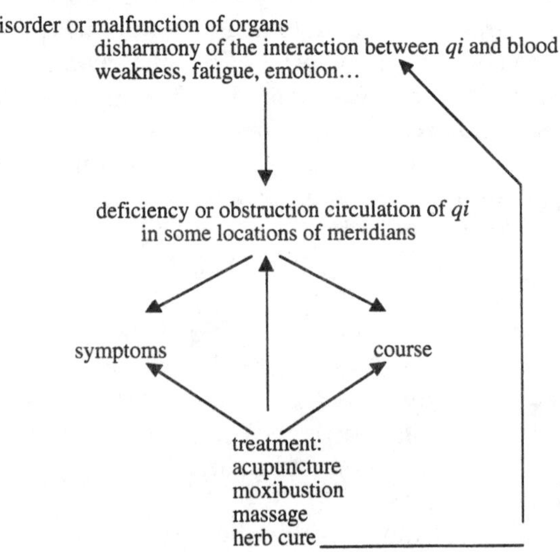

FIG. 4.5. Causal structure of diseases due to *qi* blockage.

INCOMMENSURABILITY

It is obvious from our brief review that the conceptual and explanatory structure of traditional Chinese medicine is very different from that of Western medicine, but are these differences so large that they cannot rationally be compared? This question is of considerable current practical importance because of controversies concerning the medical legitimacy of acupuncture and other traditional Chinese treatments. If traditional Chinese medicine and Western medicine are mutually unintelligible, then evaluation of one within the framework of the other would seem to be impossible. We now consider four potential impediments to mutual intelligibility: the linguistic differences between Chinese and Western languages, the differences in conceptual organization between Chinese and Western systems of thought, referential differences between Chinese and Western theories, and explanatory differences involving notions of causality and correspondence.

Our discussion distinguishes between *strong* and *weak* incommensurability. Two theories or conceptual schemes are strongly incommensurable if they are mutually unintelligible, so that someone operating within one conceptual scheme is incapable of comprehending the other. Weak incommensurability, however, does not imply mutual unintelligibility, but only that the two conceptual schemes cannot be translated into each other. If traditional Chinese medicine were strongly incommensurable with Western medicine, there would be no possibility of rational evaluation of Chinese medicine from the Western perspective. We argue, however, that the weak incommensurability that holds between the two medical traditions does not prevent rational evaluation of practices such as acupuncture.

Linguistic Differences

In both its spoken and written structure, the Chinese language is very different from European languages such as English, French, and German. Crucial terms from traditional Chinese medicine are not merely technical terminology, but are embedded in much broader linguistic usage. There are no terms in European languages that correspond even roughly to yin and yang, which are accordingly left untranslated. The term qi is often translated as "energy," but this translation is misleading if it generates an association with Western scientific concepts of electrical or mechanical energy, rather than with concepts such as breath, emotion, and force. Similarly, the translation of xing as "element" both adds and subtracts from the meaning of the Chinese term because it adds the association of element as a fundamental constituent of the world and loses the relational aspects of five-xing that are crucial to their explanatory roles.

The difficulty of translating Chinese medical terminology into European languages does not, however, show that Chinese and Western medicine are incommensurable. Even though there is no simple mapping of terms like yin, yang, xing, and qi into English, the fact that the linguistic divergence can be systematically described by writers such as Lloyd (1996), Porkert and Ullmann (1988), and Unschuld (1985) shows that comparison can proceed despite complexities of translation.

It is possible, however, that difficulties of translation run deeper than lack of corresponding terms for yin, yang, and so on. Bloom (1981) argued that the structure of the Chinese language is radically different from European languages in that it lacks distinct markings for counterfactual conditionals, which are if–then statements in which the if proposition is false. So it is not possible to make in Chinese such utterances as, "If the Chinese government were to pass a law requiring that all citizens make reports of their activities to the police hourly, then what would happen?" He claims that Chinese speakers tend to brand the counterfactual as in some sense "unChinese." Bloom's claim is an instantiation of the linguistic relativity hypothesis of Whorf (1956), according to which differences in language generate radically different patterns of thought. If Bloom is right that the Chinese language enforces a non-Western attitude toward counterfactual conditionals, this may signal differences in understanding of causality, inasmuch as causation involves counterfactual dependence between events (Lewis, 1986). It is possible, therefore, that the explanatory claims of Chinese medicine are untranslatable into European languages because they presuppose a very different conception of causality.

Bloom's linguistic claims have, however, been strongly challenged. Cheng (1985) argued that the psychological experiments that Bloom used to support his claim of linguistic divergence were methodologically flawed and used poorly translated materials; and his experiments did not replicate (Au, 1983). The Chinese language does in fact allow the statement of counterfactual conditionals, so there is no evidence of linguistic differences in the understanding of causality between Chinese and Western culture. Native speakers of Chinese, including the second author of this chapter, report that Chinese people can understand counterfactuals very well. In sum, the substantial linguistic differences between the Chinese and European languages do not generate insurmountable barriers to comprehension and translation, and therefore do not support claims of incommensurability between Chinese and Western medicine.

Conceptual Differences

The problem of comparing Western and Chinese medicine is not just that the terms are different, but that the concepts are different in their places in conceptual hierarchical organization. Much current work in cognitive science views concepts as being organized in terms of kind hierarchies and part hierarchies (Thagard, 1992). For example, a chicken is a kind of bird which is a kind of animal, and a beak is a part of a bird. There are problems, however, in placing Chinese concepts into the kind hierarchy of the Western system. Yin and yang do not seem to be kinds of anything familiar to Western thought. They are not things or substances or events or processes, and they involve a kind of abstraction not found in Western concepts. So the problem of translating Chinese terms for them into English is not just a matter of finding the right term, but also reflects the fact that they do not fit into the Western conceptual organization.

Similar problems arise with xing and qi. The standard translation "elements" suggests that five-xing are a kind of thing or substance, but this classification fits poorly with their crucial relations of promotion and subjugation. *Qi* would seem to be a kind of process, like energy, but its association with breath and force suggests that it is not a kind of process familiar to Western science or common sense. Thus the terms yin, yang, xing, and qi all represent concepts that do not fit naturally in the Western hierarchy of kinds. Moreover, the kind hierarchy for diseases in Chinese medicine tends to divide them into ones caused by too much yin, too much yang, or by blockage of qi, rather than according to the Western classification in terms of infectious, nutritional, molecular-genetic, and autoimmune causes. Thus the differences between Western and Chinese medicine are conceptual (mental) as well as linguistic (verbal).

Additional differences are found in the part hierarchies of the two systems. Traditional Chinese medicine did not permit autopsies and dissections, and so did not develop the detailed system of anatomy and physiology that evolved in Europe after the 16th century. According to Shen and Chen (1996), the term *zang-fu* refers to the five solid *zang* organs of the human body (heart, liver, spleen, lung, and kidney) and the six hollow viscera (gallbladder, stomach, small intestine, large intestine, bladder, and the *sanjiao*). The latter does not correspond to any part recognized in Western medicine, but consists of portions of the chest and abdomen that are thought to be important for the flow of qi. The function of other organs is sometimes described in ways similar to Western medicine, but is sometimes radically different; for example, the heart houses the mental faculties. Traditional Chinese medicine ignores some organs such as the pancreas that are viewed as medically important in Western medicine.

Although the kind hierarchies and part hierarchies of traditional Chinese medicine and Western medicine are obviously different, it would be an exaggeration to say that they are mutually unintelligible. Concepts such as qi and sanjiao are undoubtedly alien to Western medicine, but their meaning can be acquired contextually from works such as Shen and

Chen (1994). Conversely, practitioners of traditional Chinese medicine can acquire Western concepts such as *germ, virus,* and *pancreas.*

Buchwald and Smith (1997) presented a precise characterization of incommensurability that they reported as Kuhn's final thoughts on the subject:

> If two scientific schemes are *commensurable,* then their lexical structures can be fit together on one of the following two ways: (1) every kind, taxonomic or artefactual, in the one can be directly translated into a kind in the other, which means that the whole of one structure is isomorphic to some portion of the other; or (2) one structure can be grafted directly onto the other without otherwise disturbing the latter's existing relations. In the first case one scheme is subsumed by the other. In the second, a new scheme is formed out of the previous two, but it preserves intact all of the earlier relations among kinds. If neither case holds, the two systems are *incommensurable* (p. 374).

Our discussion so far makes it clear that traditional Chinese medicine does not fit with Western medicine in the first way, as there is no direct translation of yin, yang, and kinds of Chinese disease into Western terminology. The second way of fitting does not work either, because grafting the two schemes together would require diseases to be classified simultaneously in conflicting ways, for example as both infectious and caused by excessive yin. Thus on the characterization of Buchwald and Smith, Chinese and Western medicine are incommensurable, although the lack of fit does not imply that they are not comparable or mutually intelligible. This is weak incommensurability arising from untranslatability, and contrasts with the strong incommensurability discussed by Laudan (1990, p. 121), who said that two bodies of discourse are incommensurable if the assertions made in one body are unintelligible to those utilizing the other.

Referential Differences

The meaning of a concept is a matter of both its relation to other concepts and its relation to the world. So far, we have discussed linguistic and conceptual differences between Western and traditional Chinese medicine, but it is also clear that the two approaches make very different claims about the world. Not only are yin, yang, qi, and five-xing not part of the ontology of Western science, they are not even kinds of entities, properties, or processes that are part of that ontology. Conversely, traditional Chinese medicine does not even consider many of the referential claims of Western science, for example concerning such entities as disease-causing microbes. A Kuhnian would be tempted to say that Western physicians and traditional Chinese doctors live in different worlds.

There is, however, considerable overlap in the two ontologies. Both Western and traditional Chinese physicians examine peoples' bodies with similar perceptual systems, even if there are differences in some examination techniques. Pulse taking is different in the two cultures, in that traditional Chinese doctors aim to detect pulses with three different grades of force, but both Chinese and Western doctors grasp wrists and detect pulses. Despite their different beliefs about what exists, it would be an exaggeration to place the traditional Chinese and Western doctors in different worlds.

Explanatory Differences

In Western scientific medicine, explanations are based on causal relations. A disease explains symptoms because the disease causes the symptoms, and the treatment is judged to be effective only if the treatment causes the elimination of disease. Although much of Western medicine is still based on the clinical experience of physicians rather than on scientific experiments, there is increased pressure to evaluate treatments using randomized, blinded, controlled trials (Sackett, Rosenberg, Gray, Haynes, & Richardson, 1996). Carefully controlled experiments are needed to determine whether treatments are causally effective, because they rule out alternative causes such as expectations and biases in physicians and patients (Thagard, 1998).

According to Lloyd (1996), traditional Chinese medicine similarly is interested in identifying causal factors, but it also has an additional explanatory style based on "correspondences" (p. 113). Unschuld (1985, p. 52) described the role in ancient Chinese thought of concepts of magic correspondence and systematic correspondence, both of which are based on the principle that the phenomena of the visible and the invisible world stand in mutual dependence. Concepts like yin, yang, and qi are embedded in a system of correspondences that involve noncausal dependencies. For example, the movement of qi in the body is understood in part on the basis of the body having an upper half (yang) and a lower half (yin), and a left side (yang) and a right side (yin; Unschuld, 1985, p. 88).

Thus traditional Chinese medicine is closer to prescientific assumptions of homeopathic magic, which employs the principle that like corresponds to like, than it is to modern conceptions of causality. Thagard (1988, ch. 9) described how much prescientific and pseudoscientific thinking is based on resemblance rather than causality. The causal mode of explanation found in current scientific medicine has no room for explanations based on resemblance and mystical correspondences, so it is difficult to compare the two kinds of explanation head to head. Here the debate between traditional Chinese medicine and Western science has to move to a metalevel involving the efficacy of the different styles of explanation. Evaluating traditional Chinese herbal medicine is also very difficult from the perspective of Western, evidence-based medicine because prescribed herbal remedies often involve mixtures of numerous kinds of herbs suggested by correspondence-based ideas. Determining the causal effect of a single herb would be viewed as pointless within traditional Chinese medicine.

Even here, however, there is not complete breakdown of intelligibility, as traditional Chinese medicine does want to claim causal effectiveness for its treatments. Although it seems mysterious from the Western medical perspective why acupuncture places needles at certain points in the body that are thought to have the relevant correspondences, it is still possible to ask the question, common to both traditions, of whether the needling is causally effective. Hence the explanatory gap between traditional Chinese medicine and Western science is not so great as the gap, say, between Western science and fundamentalist religion, which claims that the primary source of evidence is a sacred text. Moreover, the gap between Western and Chinese medicine has shrunk over the centuries, in that the current explanatory role of systematic correspondences in Chinese medicine is much smaller than it was originally.

In sum, our discussion of the linguistic, conceptual, ontological, and explanatory differences between traditional Chinese medicine and traditional Western medicine has shown that the two approaches are not strongly incommensurable. Considerable mutual comprehension is possible, although it does not go so far as to permit translation of one conceptual system into the other; hence the two stems are weakly incommensurable. Let us now see how weak incommensurability affects the evaluation of acupuncture.

EVALUATING ACUPUNCTURE

In the last section, we saw that the linguistic, conceptual, referential, and explanatory differences between traditional Chinese medicine and Western medicine do not constitute insuperable barriers to their rational comparison, although the explanatory differences are more serious impediments. A Western researcher demanding that acupuncture and other therapeutic practices be evaluated with respect to their explanatory coherence as shown by randomized and blinded clinical trials would be stymied by a proponent of traditional Chinese medicine who said that all this was simply irrelevant. But traditional Chinese medicine is not a mystical religion; it is aimed at improving people's health, and its practitioners sincerely believe that it succeeds. Hence even for the most orthodox practitioners of traditional Chinese medicine, there is an empirical standard, not just a doctrinal one.

In a head-to-head clash between Western and traditional Chinese medicine, it would be necessary to choose one of the conceptual–explanatory systems as superior and reject the other. A skeptical Western physician, for example, could argue that Western medicine has incontrovertible successes and that the whole Chinese system can be dispensed with. There is no reason, however, why evaluation of traditional Chinese medicine needs to be this holistic. Some prescientific medical practices, such as the North American aboriginals chewing salicin-containing willow bark to relieve pain, have turned out to be medically effective even by modern standards. It is entirely possible, therefore, that some traditional Chinese therapies such as acupuncture and herbal remedies might have some efficacy.

Acupuncture is a family of procedures, the most familiar of which involves penetration of specific points on the skin by thin metallic needles. If acupuncture were only comprehensible within traditional Chinese medicine, then it might indeed be concluded that acupuncture is strongly incommensurable with the substantially different system of Western medicine. But acupuncture has in fact been evaluated from the perspective of Western medicine, most recently and publicly by the NIH Consensus Development Conference that took place in November, 1997. The operations of this conference are a striking example of evaluation occurring in the face of conceptual difficulties. Acupuncture would never have been invented within Western medical science, but that does not make it immune to scientific evaluation.

Like previous NIH Consensus Conferences, the acupuncture conference consisted of 1½ days of presentations followed the next morning by presentation of a consensus report. This report was prepared by a 12-member panel drawn from different backgrounds, including both acupuncture specialists and Western-trained medical experts. Panel members worked until 4 a.m. on the final day of the conference to reach agreement on a statement that was publicly released later that morning.[2] The panel concluded that "there is clear evidence that needle acupuncture is efficacious for adult post-operative and chemotherapy nausea and vomiting and probably for the nausea of pregnancy." It also found some evidence of efficacy for postoperative dental pain, and suggestive but not conclusive evidence for pain relief in other conditions such as menstrual cramps. Because acupuncture has minimal adverse effects, the panel stated that

[2]The consensus statement and press release, as well as the abstracts of presentations, are available on the World Wide Web at http://odp.od.nih.gov/consensus/cons/107/107_statement.htm. The statement will eventually be published in a medical journal. We are indebted to one of the panel members, Daniel Moerman, for information on the panel deliberations.

acupuncture may be a reasonable option for a number of clinical conditions such as stroke rehabilitation and osteoarthritis.

The panel reached its conclusions using the standards of Western medicine. Ideally, evaluation of medical effectiveness should be based on randomized, controlled, blinded clinical trials, but such trials have only been a part of medical research since World War II, and most Western medical practices are based on medical experience rather than rigorous tests. With a procedure as obvious as acupuncture, it is not easy to perform properly controlled experiments: unlike placebo pills, patients clearly know whether they have received acupuncture or not. Experiments using "sham" acupuncture, in which needles are inserted at nonstandard acupuncture points, have provided mixed results, often intermediate between orthodox acupuncture and nontreatment. The panel decided not to insist on the highest standards of medical efficacy based only on rigorously controlled experiments, but rather to evaluate acupuncture based on the more usual clinical standards of Western medicine. The panel concluded that acupuncture may well be effective for the treatment of nausea and pain, and recommended future high-quality, randomized, controlled clinical trials on its effects.

The panel's recommendations were based on a large body of printed information provided by NIH in advance of the conference, and on the presentations of 24 speakers on the first day and a half of the conference. Although a few of the talks presented acupuncture within the context of traditional Chinese medicine, the vast majority discussed its effectiveness from the Western evidential perspective. Several talks discussed the possible neurochemical basis of acupuncture, presenting evidence that acupuncture stimulates the production of endogenous opioids and affects the secretion of neurotransmitters and neurohormones. The panel report, however, remained open to the traditional Chinese medicine based on qi: "Although biochemical and physiologic studies have provided insight into some of the biologic effects of acupuncture, acupuncture practice is based on a very different model of energy balance. This theory may provide new insights to medical research that may further elucidate the basis for acupuncture." This statement is not an endorsement of traditional Chinese medicine, but it suggests that its theory as well as its practice may turn out to be useful in Western scientific medicine. The implication, however, is that the theory of *qi* would need to be evaluated according to scientific standards, not in accord with traditional Chinese texts or the doctrine of correspondences.

According to some sociologists, science is essentially a power play in which some researchers marshal resources to triumph over others (Latour, 1987). One interpretation of the NIH consensus conference would be that acupuncture proponents managed to dominate by assembling speakers and panel members to endorse their claims. Alternatively, the conference organizers could conceivably have assembled a panel of hard-line Western medical researchers who would have dismissed acupuncture as pseudoscientific trickery. Although consensus conferences undoubtedly have a political dimension, their operation is designed to encourage evidence evaluation rather than political manipulation. The 12 panel members were presented with a common body of information to evaluate, and most of them had no strong interest for or against acupuncture; only 2 of the 12 were practicing acupuncturists, and both had Western medical training. Some of the studies they looked at, particularly the well-done and replicated studies concerning the effects of acupuncture on postoperative nausea, were very impressive.

CONCEPTUAL CHANGE AS INTENTIONAL AND EMOTIONAL

We have argued that the substantial conceptual differences between traditional Chinese medicine and Western medicine can be overcome, but it would be rash to exaggerate the ease with which mutual understanding can be accomplished. Consider two people, one an expert on and a proponent of traditional Chinese medicine - C - and the other trained in Western medicine - W. Initially, C and W will scarcely be able to talk to each other, with the former using concepts like qi and the other using concepts like *germ* and *immune system.* Any degree of mutual comprehension that develops will depend not only on casual communication, which will be ineffective, but on the kind of intentional conceptual change that is discussed in this volume. C and W each must have the motivation to acquire enough of the other's conceptual system that comparison and evaluation becomes possible. Only then do C and W have the capability of changing their conceptual systems by adopting components of the alternative system and by revising their own concepts (see Thagard, 1992 for a taxonomy of conceptual changes).

People who undergo conceptual change, whether from the traditional Chinese system of medicine to the Western system or vice versa, must have a set of cognitive goals that directs their thinking. First, they must have the goal of understanding the alternative system, which requires becoming familiar with (but not necessarily endorsing) its concepts, hypotheses, and evidence. Accomplishing this goal may involve trying to translate the alternative system into more familiar terms, or understanding the system on its own terms. Second, they must have the goal of assessing the alternative systems with respect to explanatory coherence and practical efficacy. Third, they must be willing to recognize an alternative conceptual system as superior in important respects to their own and therefore worthy of replacing it, partially or totally. Thus the development of mutual understanding and the process of conceptual change depend in part on the intentions of people to take seriously conceptual systems that differ from the ones they currently hold.

The goal of understanding an alternative system may be most effectively accomplished by intentionally striving to appreciate the kinds of linguistic, conceptual, referential, and explanatory differences already discussed. Learning a second language is a challenging task that requires much motivation. Becoming aware of conceptual differences in organization of kind hierarchies can also benefit from having the goal of noticing such differences. Differences in reference and explanatory style are often so subtle that they are not noticed unless a thinker has the explicit goal of seeing how an alternative system makes claims about the world and explains occurrences in it.

One major impediment to conceptual change that has been largely ignored in psychological and philosophical discussions is the emotional attachment that people have to their own systems. Like all thinking, scientific cognition is in part an emotional process (Thagard, in press). People do not only hold and use their concepts and hypotheses, they also feel emotionally attached to them and respond with negative emotions to concepts and hypotheses that clash with them. For a proponent of traditional Chinese medicine, acupuncture may be a revered practice associated with happy outcomes, whereas for a Western physician it may seem like a ridiculous throwback to prescientific practices held in contempt. Conceptual change about different approaches to medicine involves changing not only concepts, hypotheses, and practices but also emotional attitudes toward those concepts, hypotheses, and practices. Having the intention to understand and evaluate alternative views can make the emotional component of conceptual change more easily realized.

Emotional conceptual change can be understood in terms of alteration in the positive or negative valence attached to a concept or other representation. Concepts such as *baby* and *ice cream* have positive valence for most people, whereas concepts such as *death* and *disease* have negative valence. Emotional conceptual change is change of valence from positive to negative or vice versa. Consider, for example, religious fundamentalists who encounter the Darwinian concept of evolution. Initially, this concept has negative valence because of its associations with scientific views that the fundamentalists see in conflict with their religious views, which have strong positive valence. For fundamentalists to accept the theory of evolution, they not only need to change their beliefs about concepts such as *human,* which is a kind of animal in the Darwinian scheme but not in the religious one, they also need to change the valence that they attach to concepts such as *evolu-*

tion. Conversely, biologists who attach positive valence to the concept of evolution because of its role in a powerful and successful scientific theory would require emotional conceptual change if they were to become fundamentalists and view evolution as not only false but otiose. Similarly, proponents of Western and traditional Chinese medicine start with different emotional valences for concepts such as *germ* and *qi,* and adoption of the alternative approach to medicine will involve changes to these valences as well as cognitive changes to beliefs and concepts.

What are the mental mechanisms for emotional conceptual change? First, a concept can acquire a valence through emotionally charged associations, for example a positive experience with ice cream or a negative one with sickness. Second, once a concept has a valence, new experiences can lead to different associations, as in someone who formerly disliked ice cream but grew to enjoy it. Third, and most dramatically, emotional conceptual change can be the result of emotional coherence, in which a whole network of representations is adjusted for both the acceptability and the emotional valences of the representations; see Thagard (2000) for an account of how emotional coherence can be computed. A dramatic shift in emotional coherence would be required for a fundamentalist to become a Darwinian or vice versa, and for an advocate of Western medicine to become a practitioner of traditional Chinese medicine or vice versa. Entrenched emotional attitudes may be a substantial barrier to such large-scale cognitive–emotional shifts.

This section discussed conceptual change at a more individual level than earlier ones, which compared whole communities of medical practitioners, but the issues are essentially the same. For a community to undergo conceptual change, the individuals in it must undergo conceptual change. Such change is a social process as well as an individual one, as it often requires interactions between individuals. For a discussion of the need to integrate social and psychological explanations of scientific change, see Thagard (1999).

CONCLUSION

We embarked on this study in order to examine a more extreme case of possible incommensurability than typically occurs in the history of Western science. The issue is important because questions about incommensurability raised by Kuhn and Feyerabend are often used to support relativist views that challenge the rationality of science (Laudan, 1990). Our examination showed that there are indeed linguistic, conceptual, referential, and explanatory differences that make mutual evaluation of traditional Chinese medicine and Western scientific medicine difficult. We also saw, however, that these difficulties can to a great extent be overcome by earnest, intentional attempts to learn alternative languages, conceptual schemes, and explanatory patterns. As the NIH consensus conferences showed, a therapeutic practice like acupuncture can be evaluated for its effectiveness without adopting the theoretical framework from which it arose. We do not need to have a grand, holistic clash of traditional Chinese medicine versus Western scientific medicine to conduct a useful piecemeal evaluation of particular treatments. The two systems of medicine are weakly incommensurable (mutually untranslatable), but they are not strongly incommensurable (mutually unintelligible). Despite the substantial barriers to complete translation that divide different systems of medicine, rational scientific evaluation of practices such as acupuncture is possible. But such evaluation requires earnest intentions to understand alternative systems sufficiently to make comparison with more familiar methods possible.

For future research, much more needs to be done concerning the nature of emotional conceptual change. Does it involve more complex emotional changes than simply a shift of positive and negative valences, for example ones involving full-fledged emotions such as love and disgust? Are the processes of emotional conceptual change that operate in science the same as ones that operate in other areas of life, for example in psychotherapy? To what extent can emotional conceptual change be intentionally controlled? How frequently are emotions impediments to evidence-based cognitive change, and what does it take to overcome such impediments? Are nonverbal representations such as visual images also subject to emotional change? Answers to such questions should contribute to a deeper understanding of conceptual change in medicine, science, and everyday life.

ACKNOWLEDGMENTS

We are grateful to Daniel Moerman, Cameron Shelley, and the editors of this volume for comments on an earlier draft, and to the Social Sciences and Humanities Research Council of Canada for financial support.

REFERENCES

Allchin, D. (1996). Points east and west: Acupuncture and comparative philosophy of science. *Philosophy of Science, 63*(supplement), S107–S115.

Au, T. K. (1983). Chinese and English counterfactuals: The Sapir–Whorf hypothesis revisited. *Cognition, 15*, 155–187.

Bloom, A. (1981). *The linguistic shaping of thought: A study of the impact of language on thinking in China and the West*. Hillsdale, NJ: Lawrence Erlbaum Associates.

Buchwald, J. Z., & Smith, G. E. (1997). Thomas S. Kuhn, 1922–1996. *Philosophy of Science, 64,* 361–376.

Cheng, P. W. (1985). Pictures of ghosts: A critique of Alfred Bloom's *The Linguistic Shaping of Thought. American Anthropologist, 87,* 917–922.

Darden, L., & Cain, J. (1989). Selection type theories. *Philosophy of Science, 56,* 106–129.

Feyerabend, P. K. (1981). *Realism, rationalism, and scientific method.* Cambridge: Cambridge University Press.

Giere, R. N. (1994). The cognitive structure of scientific theories. *Philosophy of Science, 61,* 276–296.

Guo, A. (Ed.). (1992). *Huang di nei jing su wen jiao zhu (Annotations on Yellow Emperor's classic of internal medicine: Plain questions, in Chinese).* Beijing: People's Medical Press.

Kelley, H. H. (1972). Causal schemata and the attribution process. In E. E. Jones, D. E. Kanouse, H. H. Kelley, R. E. Nisbett, S. Valins, & B. Weiner (Eds.), *Attribution: Perceiving the causes of behavior.* Morristown, NJ: General Learning Press.

Kitcher, P. (1981). Explanatory unification. *Philosophy of Science, 48,* 507–531.

Kitcher, P. (1989). Explanatory unification and the causal structure of the world. In P. Kitcher & W. C. Salmon (Eds.), *Scientific explanation* (pp. 410–505). Minneapolis: University of Minnesota Press.

Kitcher, P. (1993). *The advancement of science.* Oxford: Oxford University Press.

Kuhn, T. (1970). *Structure of scientific revolutions.* (2nd ed.). Chicago: University of Chicago Press.

Kuhn, T. S. (1993). Afterwords. In P. Horwich (Ed.), *World changes: Thomas Kuhn and the nature of science* (pp. 311–341). Cambridge, MA: MIT Press.

Latour, B. (1987). *Science in action: How to follow scientists and engineers through society.* Cambridge, MA: Harvard University Press.

Laudan, L. (1984). *Science and values.* Berkeley: University of California Press.

Laudan, L. (1990). *Science and relativism.* Chicago: University of Chicago Press.

Leake, D. B. (1992). *Evaluating explanations: A content theory.* Hillsdale, NJ: Lawrence Erlbaum Associates.

Lewis, D. (1986). *Philosophical papers.* Oxford: Oxford University Press.

Lloyd, G. E. R. (1996). *Adversaries and authorities.* Cambridge: Cambridge University Press.

Lu, G., & Needham, J. (1980). *Celestial lancets: A history and rationale of acupuncture and moxa.* Cambridge: Cambridge University Press.

Moyers, B. (1993). *Healing and the mind.* New York: Doubleday.

Nersessian, N. (1984). *Faraday to Einstein: Constructing meaning in scientific theories.* Dordrecht: Martinus Nijhoff.

Porkert, M., & Ullmann, C. (1988). *Chinese medicine* (M. Howson, Trans.). (1st U.S. ed.). New York: Morrow.

Sackett, D. L., Rosenberg, W. M. C., Gray, J. A. M., Haynes, R. B., & Richardson, W. S. (1996). Evidence-based medicine: What it is and what it isn't. *British Medical Journal, 312,* 71–72.

Schaffner, K. F. (1993). *Discovery and explanation in biology and medicine.* Chicago: University of Chicago Press.

Schank, R. C. (1986). *Explanation patterns: Understanding mechanically and creatively.* Hillsdale, NJ: Lawrence Erlbaum Associates.

Shen, Z., & Chen, Z. (1994). *The basis of traditional Chinese medicine.* Boston: Shambhala.

Thagard, P. (1988). *Computational philosophy of science.* Cambridge, MA: MIT Press/Bradford Books.

Thagard, P. (1992). *Conceptual revolutions.* Princeton: Princeton University Press.

Thagard, P. (1996). The concept of disease: Structure and change. *Communication and Cognition, 29,* 445–478.

Thagard, P. (1998). Explaining disease: Causes, correlations, and mechanisms. *Minds and Machines, 8,* 61–78.

Thagard, P. (1999). *How scientists explain disease.* Princeton, NJ: Princeton University Press.

Thagard, P. (2000). *Coherence in thought and action.* Cambridge, MA: MIT Press.

Thagard, P. (forthcoming). The passionate scientist: Emotion in scientific cognition. In P. Carruthers, S. Stich & M. Siegal (Eds.), *The cognitive basis of science.* Cambridge: Cambridge University Press.

Unschuld, P. U. (1985). *Medicine in China: A history of ideas.* Berkeley: University of California Press.

Whorf, B. (1956). *Language, thought, and reality.* Cambridge, MA: MIT Press.

Zhen, Z. (Ed.). (1997). *Zhong guo yi xue shi (History of Chinese medicine, in Chinese)* (2nd ed.). Shanghai: Shanghai Science and Technology Press.

5

Metacognitive Aspects of Students' Reflective Discourse: Implications for Intentional Conceptual Change Teaching and Learning

M. Gertrude Hennessey
St. Ann School

> *Tonya, an 11-year-old, sixth grade student crawled under the knee space of her computer station. She sat cross-legged, with her back against the wall, and hands cupped together as if holding something in the palm of her hands. She sat there for an extended period of time, gazing down at her hands, with a meditative expression on her face. Eventually, her classroom teacher approach Tonya, sat on the floor next to her, and asked her what she was thinking about: "Oh, I was just sitting here holding my thoughts in my hands. Not really, just pretending! I know I can't really hold my thoughts in my hands." As she raised her cupped hands toward her teacher, she continued. ". . . I am trying to find out more about my thoughts and how they help me understand things about science . . . I thought, if I could hold my ideas in my hands I could take a better look at them to see why my ideas are intelligible, plausible or fruitful for me." With that response, Tonya took her cupped hands, placed them on her head – as if returning her thoughts to her mind – and crawled out from under the computer station. As she crawled out, she continued to hold a conversation with her science teacher about the possibility of two active forces working on a book as it rests on the lab bench. The remainder of the conversation centered on Tonya's beliefs about the plausibility of her thinking and the need for a mechanistic or causal explanation for both forces before she could say for certain that her ideas were fruitful (Hennessey, 1991a, p. 1).*

The thoughts experienced by this 11-year-old student as she attempts to discern the status of her conceptions about a topic in physics can be described as *metacognitive* and her approach to learning may be described as *intentional*. What makes her thoughts metacognitive? What makes her approach to learning intentional? Descriptions of what constitutes metacognition and intentional learning are, at best, difficult to explicate. Flavell (1981) referred to metacognition as a "fuzzy concept." Descriptions of what constitutes intentionality in learning are, likewise, fuzzy. The general purpose of this chapter, however, is to cut through that fuzziness by describing characteristics of metacognition and intentionality that have emerged within the research community since Bereiter and Scardamalia (1989) argued that intentional learning should be a major goal of instruction.

Fundamental to the concept of metacognition is the notion of thinking about one's own thoughts (Flavell, 1976) or thinking processes (Brown, 1978). Fundamental to the concept of intentional learning is the notion that both cognitive and metacognitive processes are necessary if learning is to be a goal rather than an incidental outcome of instruction (Bereiter & Scardamalia, 1989). The central question addressed in this chapter is: What is the relationship between metacognition and intentional learning? To my mind, they are deeply interconnected. Throughout the course of this chapter, I intend to shed some light on this interconnectedness.

The specific goals of this chapter are twofold. First, the theory behind the constructs of interest—intentional learning, metacognition, and conceptual change—is examined, with special attention devoted to the relationship between metacognition and intentional learning. Second, I examine ways in which these constructs are exhibited within an educational setting. Thus, the focus of the chapter moves from theory to practice. I describe applications of theoretical models of metacognition, intentional learning, and conceptual change to educational situations, as well as a parallel effort to enhance our understanding of the theory through its application. More specifically, I describe the design features of an elementary educational setting that promotes metacognition and subsequent intentional learning. Factors such as the social and educational environments are explored to examine the role they play in promoting or constraining metacognition and intentional learning. Examples from students' discourse serve as illustrations of theory in operation within a classroom setting.

SHARED FRAMEWORK

Until recently, psychology was dominated by a philosophy of science known as *behaviorism*. Over the past several decades, however, a significant shift has taken place in the psychology community, away from behaviorism and toward a "cognitive" or "information-processing" view (Baars, 1986). This shift has been referred to as "the cognitive revolution in psychology" (Baars, 1986; Palermo, 1971; Reynolds, Sinatra, & Jetton, 1996). The reasons for this radical shift in perspective are complex and beyond the scope of this chapter. It suffices to say that the cognitive revolution experienced in psychology is not unlike the classical revolutions described by Kuhn (1962) in *The Structure of Scientific Revolutions*—a modern-day example of a "scientific revolution"—a radical paradigm shift in the viewpoints of research communities.

Many researchers working within the science education community have also experienced a "cognitive revolution" consistent with that of psychologists. Over time, the revolution or paradigm shift slowly changed their behaviorist views of learning toward a more constructivist epistemology. By *constructivist,* I mean a view that knowledge is not transmitted from teacher, text, or activity to the learner but rather constructed by the learner through a process of conceptual change. By *epistemology,* I mean an area of philosophy concerned with the nature and justification of human knowledge. A *constructivist epistemology,* therefore, is a philosophy in which learners are aware of the central role of ideas in the development of knowledge and of how ideas are revised through a process of conjecture, argument, and test (Smith, Maclin, Houghton, & Hennessey, 2000).

The shift from a behaviorist perspective of learning to a constructivist perspective has important practical implications, in the form of a constructivist pedagogy, that have only begun to inform practices within science education. By *constructivist pedagogy,* I mean a pedagogy in which learners actively develop, test, and revise their ideas about the phenomena under consideration through collaborative firsthand inquiry with their peers (Smith et al., 2000).

According to Sinatra (2000), we may be experiencing yet another "revolution" in our thinking about learners and the learning process. The current emerging framework is that learners are not only active in constructing meaning, but they can be *intentional.* The notion of intentionality includes key concepts such as cognitive goals, conscious control, and purposive use of knowledge (Bereiter & Scardamalia, 1989; Sinatra, 2000). Unlike many researchers working within the field of psychology, I do not test intentionality in a laboratory or a classroom setting. Tests of key constructs related to intentionality can be found in the reviews of research on metacognition (see Hacker, Dunlosky, & Graesser, 1998), self-regulation (see Boekaerts, Pintrich, & Zeidner, 2000; Zimmerman & Schunk, 1989), and conceptual change (see Schnotz, Vosniadou, & Carretero, 1999). Studies found in these collections examine how specific factors influence aspects of students' intentional thought. My goal is to look for these aspects in learning situations and describe those situations. In the following section, I describe the theoretical framework for the constructs of metacognition, conceptual change, and intentional learning that serve as a conceptual framework for my educational practice.

Intentional Learning

Intention is an intrinsic property of an individual person. Webster (1978) defined intention as a focus on "purpose" or "direction." According to Bereiter and Scardamalia (1989), however, both the "goal intention" and the "implementation of intention" are important when describing intentional learning. Sinatra and Pintrich (chapter 1, this volume) draw on Bereiter's (1990) characterization of intentional learning and describe the key features of intentional cognition as (a) internal initiation of thought, (b) goal-directed action, and (c) conscious control. Thus, for Sinatra (2000), intentional learners not only cognitively engage in the learning process, but also monitor and regulate their learning in a metacognitive manner, and are influenced by the motives, goals, beliefs, and emotions they bring to the learning process.

A look at the chapter-opening vignette illustrates multiple components of Sinatra's (2000) view of intentional learning. The use of intentional-level processing can be inferred in at least three parts of the vignette. The first occurs when Tonya moves away from the rest of the students to seek a place of solitude and relative quiet. Her use of this simple strategy may have been a unconscious automatic response acquired over years of learning experience, but it seems from the context more likely that it was the result of her conscious and deliberate choice to concentrate on her thinking. The second illustration occurs when Tonya cupped her hands, as if holding an object. In this instance, Tonya's actions were likely influenced by her intention to purposively monitor her existing knowledge. Third, Tonya reports she was "holding my thoughts" and "trying to find out more about my thoughts," a strong indication that she was engaged in the process of self-interrogation and introspection (Brown, 1978) and making judgments about what she knows or does not know. These actions were most likely initiated by her and under her conscious control. They were definitely not undertaken at the direction of her classroom teacher. Finally, the vignette illustrates that Tonya was highly engaged, conscious, and deliberate in thought about her own cognition. This brings us to the question: What exactly does it mean to regulate learning in a metacognitive manner?

Metacognition

In recent decades there has been a considerable rise in research on metacognition following the pioneering work of the 1970s (see Hacker et al., 1998). This research has grown from the early writings of Flavell (1976; 1979) and Brown (1978) to be widespread in areas such as problem solving, mathematics, writing, reading, science, and learning skills programs.

Reasons for the increased focus on metacognition include an upsurge in cognitive theories of learning (see Hacker et al., 1998) and the optimistic promise that interventions aimed at enhancing students' metacognition might lead to corresponding improvements in conceptual understanding of curricular content (Baird & Northfield, 1992; Hennessey, 1991a; White, 1988). Pintrich (1999) claimed such improvements in conceptual understanding are not surprising because learners are most successful when they have insights into their own capabilities and access to their learning repertoires.

The precise definition of metacognition is a subject of some debate (see Hacker et al., 1998). The stance adopted here is that metacognition refers to an "inner awareness or process, not an overt behaviour" (White, 1988, p. 73). This inner awareness can be about what one knows (content knowledge), one's learning process (knowledge construction), or one's current cognitive state (awareness of mental constructs). A key characteristic of metacognition is the ability to "think about an idea (proposition, concept, or theory) rather than merely think with it" (Kuhn, Amsel, & O'Loughlin, 1988, p. 7). In the later case, a person uses ideas or conceptions as a means of organizing and interpreting experiences without awareness. In other words, individuals are metacognitive when they make their own thoughts objects of cognition (Brown, 1978; Flavell, 1976). Furthermore, possessing the ability to be metacognitive does not guarantee that learners will engage in thoughtful application of that ability. Motivational aspects are also crucial in determining the development and application of metacognition (Gardner & Alexander, 1989; Pintrich, Marx, & Boyle, 1993).

Theorists' views of metacognition are varied and highly influenced by the disciplines that inspired them (Hacker et al., 1998). However, consistent across views are the following aspects: awareness of one's thinking; active monitoring of cognitive processes; regulation of cognitive processes; and application of heuristics to organize problem solving (Hennessey, 1999). Due to the multidimentional characterization of the term metacognition, it is imperative to clarify my view. I adopt a convention used by many researchers and reserve the term for conscious and deliberate thoughts that have ideas as their object.

This is not to say that other abilities are not important. Abilities such as execution of strategies (Dominowski, 1998; Sitko, 1998), employment of heuristics (Davidson & Sternberg, 1998), and regulation of behavior while performing a complex task (Hacker, 1998; Winne & Hadwin, 1998) are abilities that have the potential to lead to success on a given task. However desirable these competencies may be, they do not guarantee an awareness of one's own thoughts or an ability to contemplate the rational arguments used to support one's knowledge claims. Rather, they are the observable features of successful performance. As such, they merely reflect the use of appropriate strategies (i.e., knowing what to choose in terms of solution attainment and efficiency). This does not guarantee conscious *reflection* on potential or competing strategies, nor does it guarantee reflection on why the strategy was effective. To me, this distinction is analogous to that proposed by Sinatra and Pintrich (chapter 1, this volume). The ability to think *about* the significance of a specific strategy or heuristic is an intentional level process, whereas the automatic execution of a set of strategies or heuristics reflects algorithmic level processing. The awareness of one's own thinking should be helpful to students in their learning and conceptual change.

Conceptual Change

Conceptual change learning has its roots in two relatively independent research traditions: science education and cognitive development. In science education, the term conceptual change is closely tied to a group of educators and philosophers of science at Cornell University (Hewson, 1981, 1982; Posner, Strike, Hewson, & Gertzog, 1982; Strike & Posner, 1985, 1992). This approach to conceptual change is closely connected to instructional theories of learning. Hewson (1981) set the tone for thinking about conceptual change within the science education community when he described it as a theory about how to promote learning within the domain of science. In developmental psychology, on the other hand, conceptual change research is closely connected to the efforts of researchers to provide an alternative to the Piagetian explanation of cognitive development (Vosniadou, 1999). Research emanating from the various fields of psychology has produced important findings about the nature and process of conceptual change (see, for example, Carey, 1985a, 1985b, 1991; Wellman & Gelman, 1992; Metz, 1995).

My goal here is not to clarify the contributions of the two fields to our current understanding of conceptual change as this task has been succinctly accomplished by others (Guzzetti & Hynd, 1998; Schnotz et al., 1999; Sinatra & Pintrich, chapter 1, this volume). Rather, having acknowledged the two traditions, I discuss the science education view of conceptual change learning that was most influential in my research.

The most influential theory of conceptual change in science education was developed by Posner and his colleagues (1982) and elaborated in several articles (Hewson, 1981, 1982; Strike & Posner, 1985, 1992). Posner et al.'s (1982) Conceptual Change Model (CCM) described learning as an interaction between new and existing conceptions, with the outcome being dependent on the nature of the interaction. Two central concepts of the model are status and conceptual ecology. Hewson and Hewson (1992) succinctly described the central notion of status. They indicated that an idea's intelligibility (its comprehensibility), plausibility (its credibility), and fruitfulness (its usefulness) determine the status of an idea for an individual. The claim is that the greater the degree to which a person understands, accepts, and finds an idea useful, the higher its status. Existing conceptions with high status are well formed, have conceptual coherence, and achieve something of value for the individual holding them. A central prediction of the CCM is that conceptual change does not occur without concomitant changes in relative status. If a new conception conflicts with an existing conception of high status, the model predicts that the new conception will not be accepted until the status of the existing conception is lowered. This happens, according to the model, if the individual holding the conception becomes dissatisfied with his or her existing conception. Therefore, the more dissatisfied an individual becomes with his or her current conception, the more likely it is that a radical change will occur.

In conjunction with the notion of status, Posner et al. (1982) used the metaphor of a "conceptual ecology" to explain how current conceptions influence an individual's view of new information. There are multiple assertions implied by this metaphor. One is that individuals hold certain commitments and beliefs about the nature of knowledge, the nature of the physical phenomena under investigation, and what counts as reality or truth. In an effort to incorporate new experiences into an individual's conceptual ecology, the learner's epistemological and metaphysical beliefs and ontological commitments serve as a base for determining what counts as a valid explanation of a phenomena. A second assertion is that concepts exist in interrelated networks and that a change in one concept affects how the learner views other concepts. Last, there is the assumption that the learner's ideas may be competing for the same ecological niche. The ideas that survive, so to speak, are most likely to be the ideas that help the individual successfully resolve anomalies and conform with the individual's epistemological stance.

In the literature on conceptual change, the meaning of the term *change* is often not explicitly addressed. The notion of change as described in the CCM includes two senses of change: conceptual capture and conceptual exchange. That is, learning involves the addition of new knowledge to what is already known as well as change in conceptions. Hewson and Hewson (1992) argued that the word "change" has at least three different connotations. The first connotation is that of extinction. They use an example based on a fairy tale to explain the notion of extinction: A frog changes into a prince when the princess kisses the frog. In this case, there is one entity before (the frog) and a different entity after the change process (the prince). The second notion of change connotes an increase or decrease in amount. Here, Hewson and Hewson use the metaphor of a savings account: The balance grows when the money earns interest, the balance drops when the owner of the account spends money. Hewson (1981) referred to this type of change as *conceptual capture.* The third notion of change connotes an exchange of one entity for another. In a political election, when the incumbent loses the election to the challenger, there has been a change in individuals holding the office. Both politicians may continue to live in the same city, but only one individual holds the political office. Hewson (1981) referred to this type of change as *conceptual exchange.*

There is no consensus within the research community as to which of these conceptions of change best characterizes the change that goes on within the minds of students. For example, consider when a student changes his or her thinking about matter as being "continuous" to a view of matter as composed of small particles. Hewson and Hewson (1992) noted that the sense of change as extinction does not seem to be an appropriate characterization here because the student likely remembers both views. A better characterization would be the notion of exchange. The student exchanges one idea of the nature of matter for another. This type of change is best understood as a change in the *status* of a particular conception. The first notion (matter is continuous) loses status, whereas the second notion (matter is composed of small particles) gains in status. Studies on the issue of status show that is it possible for students as young as 11 or 12 to work with the notion of raising and lowering the status of their own conceptions (Hennessey, 1991b; Hewson & Hennessey, 1992).

While struggling to define change, researchers also struggled to characterize the factors that initiate the change process. Posner et al. (1982) identified dissatisfaction as the initiating agent. Dykstra (1992) implicated "disequilibration," and Scott, Asoko, and Driver (1992) described "cognitive conflict" as the initiating event. More recent developments, stemming from a constructivist approach, pointed to multiple factors that have the potential to play a role in conceptual change. For instance, Pintrich, Marx, and Boyle (1993) addressed the role of motivational beliefs and classroom contextual factors as contributors of change. Along similar lines, Dole and Sinatra (1998) claimed there are many factors that influence individuals to change their thinking. Clearly, there is no consensus on the initiating events of change.

Posner et al.'s (1982) CCM of learning continues to be widely cited and has served as a theoretical framework underpinning numerous studies. The description of the four conditions (dissatisfaction, intelligible, plausible, fruitful) necessary for conceptual change provides a sound model of how learners might come to understand their own beliefs while simultaneously changing the status of those beliefs (Hennessey, 1991a, 1991b; Hewson & Hennessey, 1992; Hewson & Hewson, 1992).

Pintrich et al. (1993) acknowledged the strength of the conceptual change model to provide an explanation of how learners might come to change their beliefs about academic subject matter, but at the same time they questioned the validity of some of the model's underlying assumptions. First, they questioned the assumption that students approach their classroom learning with a solely rational goal of making sense of the information and coordinating it with their prior conceptions. Second, they questioned whether students actually behave like scientists in that, when they become dissatisfied with an idea, they search out new constructs that will balance their general conceptual model. Third, they questioned how much students resemble the scientific community that sets and enforces the norm of commitment to understanding. In sum, they contended, there are serious theoretical difficulties in relying on an overly rational model of conceptual change.

During the past decade, the authors of the CCM have acknowledged the importance of considering both institutional and social factors that can support or impede the process of conceptual change. Strike and Posner (1992) revised their theory of conceptual ecology to acknowledge that:

> A wider range of factors needs to be taken into account in attempting to describe a learner's conceptual ecology. Motives and goals and the institutional and social sources of them need to be considered. The idea of a conceptual ecology thus needs to be larger than the epistemological factors suggested by the history and philosophy of science (p. 162).

Similarly, Hewson (1992) acknowledged the role of social interaction and intentionality in the conceptual change process:

> I see conceptual change as primarily a way of thinking about learning; i.e., it is something that a learner does as an *intentional act* (emphasis added), rather than something done by a teacher. There is, of course, much that a teacher can do to facilitate a student's learning, without any need to regard this as a mechanistic, causal process. Finally, it seems to me that the knowledge a learner gains only has validity in terms of, and is thus relative to, his or her conceptual ecology. Since a learner's conceptual ecology is a product of all the experiences and social interaction he or she has had, it will have many elements in common with those of other people (pp. 11–12).

Based on my experience working with the CCM in a classroom setting for more than 15 years, I concur with that analysis. The conceptual change model of learning can, at times, be viewed as an overly rational model of how learners come to change their conceptions. The authors of the CCM assume an active learner who selectively attends to information, activates prior conceptual knowledge, monitors comprehension, and assesses the status of the new information in relationship to prior conceptions while cognitively engaging in academic tasks. These cognitive processes require that learners be *willing* and able to recognize, evaluate, and, if necessary, reconstruct existing ideas and beliefs. Dissatisfaction with an existing conception and the perception of the fruitfulness of a new conception are possible only if the learner is willing and able. I argue that this level of cognitive processing is highly sophisticated and involves intentional level processing. It is precisely this highly sophisticated level of processing that separates *intentional conceptual change* from other types of conceptual change that may occur automatically. It might be helpful to return to Hewson and Hewson's (1992) characterizations of conceptual capture and conceptual exchange. Conceptual capture and conceptual exchange can take place without conscious awareness. However, it is precisely when the process of either conceptual capture or conceptual exchanges comes under conscious control (i.e., the learner is cognitively engaged in monitoring, assessing, and regulating his or her learning in a metacognitive manner) that the learning and subsequent change process becomes intentional.

Creating a classroom environment that facilitates the development of a community of intentional, motivated, and thoughtful learners that can support intentional conceptual change is not a simple, straightforward task. The design features of an elementary science curriculum that appear to support this type of learning are discussed next.

FROM THEORY TO PRACTICE: APPLICATION OF THEORIES AND MODELS TO AN EDUCATIONAL SETTING

The idea of intentional conceptual change is based on the assumption that the learner is capable of consciously controlling his or her learning process. Inherent in intentional conceptual change is the ability to recognize, evaluate, and reconstruct meaning. According to this view, learners must recognize the existence and nature of their current conceptions, decide whether or not to evaluate the utility and worth of their conceptions, and decide whether or not to reconstruct their conceptions. None of these conscious control processes are straightforward, and all carry sophisticated metacognitive demands. The ability to monitor and regulate learning is intimately connected with the notion of intentional conceptual change. To examine the interconnections in more detail, I draw on data from two distinct but conceptually related studies.

The Studies

Rather than summarize the findings from each study in turn, I introduce them here and then discuss several emerging themes that have implications for intentional conceptual change.

Status Study. The notion of status, as mentioned earlier, is central to the process of conceptual change (Hewson, 1981, 1982; Hewson & Hewson, 1992; Posner et al., 1982). This suggests that making the status of students' conceptions explicit should be part of a teacher's plan for conceptual change teaching and learning. In order to examine the feasibility of revealing and monitoring the status of students' conceptions as part of regular classroom practice, I designed a study to explicitly introduce the notion of status to a class of 20 sixth-grade students working on a unit on force and motion (Hennessey, 1991b).

Three major goals guided the design of the study. The first objective was to determine the feasibility of monitoring the status of students' ideas. The second was to use the technical language of the CCM with sufficient precision to allow differences in status to emerge. The third goal was to probe the changes in the status of students' conceptions. These goals constituted a test of Posner et al.'s (1982) CCM. It is important to note that determination of the status of students' ideas was based on their metacognitive reflections about the intelligibility, plausibility, and fruitfulness of their conceptions (Hennessey, 1991b; Hewson & Hennessey, 1992). Data from this study is labeled [*Status, 1991*].

Facets of Metacognition Study. Project META (Metacognitive Enhancing Teaching Activities) was a 3-year longitudinal study examining young students' (ages 6–12) metacognitive capabilities. Three major goals guided the study. The first goal was to describe the multifaceted nature of young students' metacognition; the second was to examine changes in students' metacognitive abilities over time; and the third was to examine the relationship between students' metacognitive ability and conceptual change learning (Hennessey, 1999; Hennessey & Beeth, 1993). Data from this study is labeled [META—followed by the year from which the data is drawn].

Key Features of the Studies. First, much of the research presented here should be considered exploratory in nature because of the "messy" character of the constructivist approach to teaching and learning applied in the educational setting. It is important to keep in mind that the teaching and learning activities employed within these research projects were consistent with the students' everyday practices and not implemented for the sole purpose of the research per se. Thus, the students were not given cards to sort, syllogisms to evaluate, specific problems to solve, or elements to encode for the purpose of data collection. Rather, the purpose of all teaching and learning activities utilized was to support students in their struggle toward understanding the science content under consideration.

Another important element to keep in mind is that the fundamental approach to instruction changed with the needs of each student. Because of the holistic character of the teaching and learning process, it is difficult if not impossible to single out one specific factor that may account for observed changes. Likewise, the "messy" context in which the research was conducted made it almost impossible to condense the reported results into measures that allowed for comparisons with traditional classrooms. Other features to keep in mind are that the studies have small sample sizes, lack control group comparisons, and have not been replicated.

With the aforementioned caveats in mind, the anecdotal records and gathered data reveal that the students in both studies displayed a sophisticated way of thinking and talking about the science content under consideration and about their own learning processes, helping themselves to become independent learners.

The reflective discourse emanating from the studies involved two different formats. The first format involved vigorous verbal interactions among students and among students and their teacher (either in small groups or in whole-class discussions). The second format involved either verbal or written self-reflections. Students worked individually for about a week to write essays (written self-reflections) or audio record (verbal self-reflections) their individual views about the topic at hand. Consequently, these verbal and written self-reflective discourses were more organized and coherent in nature than the verbal interactions.

There are a few other features to keep in mind about the classroom discourse: (a) it is focused on the details of the students' thinking rather than on the utterances of the classroom teacher; (b) it is highly reflective of the capabilities of most students at each grade level; and (c) it is reflective of students' canonical and noncanonical (or alternative) views of science.

The next sections discuss the "conceptual change supporting conditions" (Duit, 1999, p. 265) that support or hinder learning at the intentional level. I begin with the social and educational environment because they provide the contextual framework in which student's metacognitive abilities develop. I then describe relevant pedagogical practices.

Social and Educational Environmental Factors As Supporting Conditions or Conceptual Constraints for Intentional Learning

Although the studies described here were not designed to address the role of the educational environment and social context in learning, multiple researchers (Bereiter & Scardamalia, 1989; Pintrich, 2000; Shapiro & Schwartz, 2000) have identified these factors as supporting conditions that influence whether intentional learning will occur. For this reason, a brief description is provided of the learning environment and social context within which the studies were conducted.

Teaching and Learning: An Interactive Joint Process. The curricular approach underpinning the studies consisted of a sustained attempt to teach elementary science from a coherent, constructivist perspective. First, the approach consisted of teaching in three parallel strands—teaching for conceptual change, promoting students' metacognitive understandings, and engaging students with deep domain-specific issues in science (Beeth & Hewson, 1999a). Second, many interrelated pedagogical practices were part of the teaching and learning process: a focus on helping students understand, test, and revise their ideas; a stress on the function of the social community in the negotiation of meanings and the growth of knowledge; and an emphasis on increasing students' responsibility for directing important aspects of their own inquiry. Third, the role of the teacher, the student, the activities or tasks, and assessment were purposely integrated to support these objectives (Beeth, 1998; Beeth & Hewson, 1999b).

As a researcher and teacher, I used many of the conceptual change teaching strategies reported to be effective in the literature, including: (a) making students aware of their initial ideas; (b) encouraging students to engage in metacognitive discourse about ideas; (c) employing "bridging analogies" and "anchors" to help them consider and manipulate new ideas (Clement, 1993); (d) encouraging them to apply new understandings in different contexts; and (e) providing time for students to discuss the nature of learning and the nature of science (Carey, Evans, Honda, Jay, & Unger, 1989).

The students were encouraged to consciously engage in personal meaning making. Their roles included: (a) taking responsibility for representing their ideas; (b) working to develop their ideas; (c) monitoring the status (intelligibility, plausibility and fruitfulness) of their ideas; (d) considering the reasoning underlying specific beliefs; (e) deciding on ways to test specific beliefs; (f) assessing the consistency among their ideas; and (g) examining how well these ideas extend to new situations.

Both the students and I selected learning activities and tasks with the potential to make students aware of their own views, help them examine the reasoning that supported their views, and promote conceptual conflict or dissatisfaction with their views. Assessment was ongoing and multifaceted. Students were given many different options for communicating their understanding. Such communications involved presentations in oral, written, visual, or graphic form; questions raised about a topic or idea; application of their understanding to another context; or reflection on the growth of their understanding.

The students' and my roles changed as students progressed through the grade levels. For example, the goal for first-grade students was to state explicitly their own views and to begin to generate supporting reasons. Consequently, the aim for this group of students was to begin to differentiate "what" they thought from "why" they thought it. By fourth grade, the goal was for students to become aware of criteria by which their ideas were evaluated. By sixth grade, the goal was for students to not only monitor the status of their own thinking but also to monitor that of others (peers and science experts), consider the consistency of their thinking with other ideas, and consider whether their ideas fit with a pattern of evidence.

I consistently monitored the information supplied by the students about the status of their thinking to guide the direction of each class, introduce new ideas, challenge their thinking, and engage them in the process of conceptual change. As the curriculum progressed, students assumed more control of the topics studied, but maintained the emphasis on explanatory understanding and theory building. The students perceived their role to be one of clarifying, evaluating, and rearranging their thinking about the topic at hand, a task over which they had control.

Collegiality: Developing a Community of Learners. Another feature of the teaching and learning approach was the social structures that characterized the educational environment. The students and I strived to create a *community of learners* (Brown & Campione, 1994) where social dialogue and collaboration is an essential aspect of the learning environment. Students worked together in a variety of ways to plan and conduct investigations, negotiate the meaning of words, and learned to listen, share, and raise questions about each other's views. In such an environment, my role was often complex. Frequently, I served as a facilitator and scaffolder of student inquiry. At other times, I introduced the views of the members of the professional science community for students to consider. This kind of social interaction facilitated students' awareness of the diversity of viewpoints and the importance of seeking to fully understand the ideas of self and others. It also widened the range of ideas for students to consider, which often led them to develop more complex viewpoints. Moreover, the students themselves viewed these social interactions as vitally important to the learning and knowledge acquisition processes.

Pedagogical Practices. A variety of additional factors may have contributed to the effectiveness of the curriculum in bringing about a change in students' thinking. Involving students in authentic inquiry may be particularly important in promoting cognitive development. Students were given the responsibility for managing most aspects of their own inquiry. Generally, I began units by giving students a set of phenomena to explore. It was the students' tasks to record the questions they found problematic about the phenomena, to articulate and refine the questions they wanted to explore further, and to plan ways to pursue their investigations.

Students took the responsibility for representing their ideas in multiple ways. It is well documented in the conceptual change literature that making ideas public facilitates the process change (e.g., Hewson & Thorley, 1989). Students were encouraged to use a variety of means to make their ideas public including poster production, concepts maps, physical models, drawings of conceptual models, word processing to write out ideas, audiotapes to dictate ideas, and small-group and whole-group discussion to present ideas orally. Poster productions, audio recordings, video recording of group discussions, and written statement preserved a record of those ideas so that students could explicitly compare earlier and later ideas. Explicit representations not only helped students to clarify their ideas or discover aspects of their ideas that were not clear to them, it also helped them to concretize and systematize inherently complex and abstract ideas.

Finally, I selected problems that invited the students to consider issues of deep disciplinary significance. Units allowed students to explore phenomena by theorizing about the nature of matter, gravity, heat and temperature, force and motion, living things, heredity, and the origins of the universe. These topics involved areas where students' initial conceptions can be quite fuzzy and different from the ideas expressed by science experts. Consequently, in pursuing their investigations, students worked to clarify and understand their initial ideas. The day-to-day lessons were designed to allow students to experience the difficulties in coming to understand their ideas about the content under investigation, and to learn about the kind of mental work that goes into understanding and clarifying ideas. As a result, the students encountered anomalies that challenged their thinking and new ideas that contributed to the process of conceptual development.

Implications of the Supporting Conditions for Intentional Conceptual Change

The host of social and environmental factors just described provided a *shared framework* for students to define learning. I perceive this shared framework as analogous to the framework shared by members of a research community. For example, the social and environmental factors served as a "set of assumptions" that guided the students in thought, action, and communication. These assumptions, at times, were focally conscious as the students thought about specific problems or communicated with one another. Although the set of assumptions were not as sophisticated as those shared by the research community, it was an explicit goal of the curriculum and pedagogical practices to help students build increasingly sophisticated sets of assumptions about learning over a 6-year period.

The social and environmental factors, by design, challenged students to consider many sides of an issue and to engage in the cognitive process of high elaboration. By high elaboration, I mean deep processing of information, elaborate cognitive strategies of connecting and comparing existing conceptions with new information, and significant metacognitive reflection about what they were thinking and why. The thoughtful processing of ideas and information, through high elaboration, may lead students toward a restructuring of their thinking (Dole & Sinatra, 1998).

In what context does high elaboration occur? Bereiter's (1990) description of *intentional learners in inquiring classrooms* captures what I mean by high elaboration. Is there evidence that the social and environmental factors in my classroom supported students' ability to learn intentionally? The answer is yes. The intentional character of the students is evidenced by their conscious awareness and control of their learning. That is, they exhibited deep, analytic, critically reflective awareness and regulation of their thought processes. This is a form of high metacognitive engagement, to which I turn next.

DATA ANALYSIS: FACETS OF STUDENTS' METACOGNITIVE ABILITIES

There is a plethora of literature stemming from both cognitive psychology and science education that indicates that children can become aware of and manage their own thinking processes (for a series of articles on metacognition see Hacker et al., 1998). An analysis of protocol from Project META suggested that all six cohorts of students who participated in the project had little or no difficulty in becoming aware of their existing conceptions and frequently engaged in an evaluation of those conceptions. However, the purpose of the project was not to gather evidence that children, even young children, can be metacognitive. There is enough data available in the literature to support this claim. The purpose was to try to tease apart and categorize the types or range of metacognitive responses frequently encountered within a classroom setting. It was hypothesized that the students' metacognitive ability would be multifaceted in nature.

Minstrell (1992) introduced the term *facet* to mean a convenient unit of thought or reasoning used by students in addressing a particular situation. Students use language (reflective discourse) as they reveal or explain their thinking. Thus, a facet is an attempt to capture the intention of each expressed idea in one statement. A facet (a unit of thought) may reveal personal thinking about content, it may be strategic, or it may represent a generic bit of information. For example, *"I think there are two forces acting on the book as it rests on the table" [Status, 1991]*. In this unit of thought, the student has revealed her personal thinking about the number of the forces acting on a book "at rest." The comment would be categorized as a facet about conceptions. A facet may capture the reason used by the student to support his or her thinking (i.e., a facet about reasoning) or it may capture the implications or limitations of students' thinking (i.e., a facet about implications). Consider the following statement:

> "I spent a good bit of time thinking about the interaction between the book and the table on a macroscopic level. It wasn't until I shifted my perspective to a microscopic level that the idea of active force between the molecules of the book and the molecules of the table began to make sense to me" [*Status, 1991*].

In this complex unit of thought, the student commented on the implications of changing her perspective from focusing on macroscopic events to focusing on microscopic events. The conceptual shift resulted in a new level of understanding for this student. Facets may reveal key aspects of a student's thinking or learning process or the status of his or her thinking (i.e., explicitly commenting on the intelligibility, plausibility, or fruitfulness of the idea under consideration). Finally, a facet may refer to or reveal specific components of a student's conceptual ecology. It is important to keep in mind that facets are merely a convenient way of describing a unit of thought. In many instances a student's units of thought do not stand independent of one another. For example, an individual cannot consider the implications of his or her knowledge claims or the reasoning used to support those claims without first considering the content of his or her claims.

Data analysis involved reading the entire corpus of students' verbatim transcripts and assigning segments of student discourse to one or more of the following six categories: (a) conceptions (statements in which the student had engaged in the process of considering his or her current thinking); (b) reasoning (statements in which the student had referred to the reasoning used to support his or her thinking); (c) implications (statements in which the student had explicitly considered the implications or limitations of his or her thinking); (d) thinking processes (statements in which the student had explicitly considering his or her thinking or learning process as an object of cognition); (e) status (statements in which the student had commented on the status of his or her thinking); and (f) conceptual ecology (statements in which the student had referred to or specifically used any components of his or her conceptual ecology).

In developing these coding categories, I was responsive both to important issues raised in the literature on metacognition and to what emerged inductively from the data. Because the coding categories are not independent of one another, all the coding categories that applied were checked off. For example, an individual who was discussing the implications of his or her knowledge claims could conceivably reveal the reasoning used to support the claims. In this instance, the unit of thought would be checked off in both categories (implications and reasoning).

The main analysis focused on the type and level of metacognitive process engaged in by the students. The type of metacognitive process ranged from an ability to think about one's own ideas to a higher, more sophisticated ability to critique and analyze one's own ideas. Age differences appeared to be only minimal across the first three coding categories. Across the set of coding categories labeled *Thinking or Learning Process, Status, and Conceptual Ecology*, differences in the frequency at which the students engaged in these more sophisticated metacognitive processes were noted. For example, the students in Grades 4 through 6 (in addition to the metacognitive processes displayed by the younger students) displayed evidence of their ability to (a) temporarily bracket or set aside their own conceptions to consider the competing views of others, (b) reflect on the status of conceptions of self and others, and (c) evaluate the consistency and generalizability of a set of conceptions.

The following two vignettes illustrate the multifaceted nature of each student's metacognitive ability.

> During a classroom demonstration, a large transparent container of water was placed on an overhead projector. Students were asked to predict what they thought would happen when various objects were placed in the water. The objects in question were two stones—a small (2cm diameter) granite stone and a large (10cm diameter) pumice stone. The students did not have the opportunity to handle the stones. Brianna, a first-grade student, was engaged in a conversation with me about her predictions.
>
> T: Would anyone like to predict what he or she thinks will happen to these stones. Yes, Brianna.
>
> B: I think the both stones will sink because I know stones sink. I've seen lots of stones sink and every time I throw a rock into the water, like it always sinks, yeah, it always does.
>
> T: You look like you want to say something else.
>
> B: Yeah the water can't hold up rocks like it holds up boats and I know they'll [stones] sink.
>
> T: You sound so sure, let me try another object.
>
> B: No you gotta throw it in, you gotta test my idea first. [Small stone is placed in the tank; it sinks] See, I told you I knew it would sink. [Teacher places larger rock down and picks up another object.] No you've gotta test the big one too because if the little one sunk the big one's gotta sunk

> (sic). [Larger stone is placed in the tank—it floats.] [With emphases] No! No! That's not right! That doesn't go with my mind [student grabs hold of head] it just doesn't go with my mind (Hennessey & Beeth, 1993, p. 17).

First, the vignette illustrates that metacognition monitoring, on the part of this first grader, involved more than merely revealing her current conceptions. The student is involved in a form of self-interrogation and introspection and an interpretation of past and on-going experiences. These thoughts involve intentional level constructs. For example, consider the following units of thought: "*. . . I think the both stones will sink . . . I've seen lots of rocks sink and every time I throw a rock into the water . . . it always sinks.*" In this instance, the student has revealed her current thinking about the possible action of the stone when placed in the water. She then drew on her past experiences of stones in water to interpret current experiences. As Brianna continued the discussion, she began to reveal her metaphysical beliefs about the nature of water. She was using her beliefs about water to support her current views about stones. For example: "*. . . The water can't hold up rocks like it holds up boats…I know they [referring to stones] will sink.*" As the discussion continues, Brianna on two separate occasions insisted that I test her ideas. "*. . . You [got to] test my ideas first . . . no you've [got to] test the big one too because if the little one [sinks] the big one's [got to sink.]*" It is important to note that the student asked me to test *her ideas* and not merely asked to test the rock; that is, the student is consciously aware that her thinking is the object of the test. Brianna's final comments, coupled with her hand actions, indicated that she was aware of the anomalous event and that this anomaly was inconsistent with her current view of both water and rocks. "*No! No! That's not right! That doesn't go with my mind (student grabs her head) it just doesn't go with my mind.*"

The level of metacognitive monitoring, self-interrogation, and conscious introspection of ongoing experiences is more prominent and sophisticated when considering the discourse of sixth graders. Consider the following vignette:

> *Jill, a sixth-grade student, word-processed the follow essay as part of the assessment process in her physics class. I had specifically asked the students to focus on the element of change within their thinking. The following questions were posed to the students: Do you think your ideas about the force or forces, if any, acting on the various items in the circus have changed? If so, in what way have your ideas changed? Why do you think your ideas have changed? Jill responded: "In the past I thought for instance the BOOK ON THE TABLE had only 1 force, and that force was gravity."*

In this comment, the student merely revealed her past understanding of the instance.

"I couldn't see that something that wasn't living could push back. I thought that this push back force wasn't a real force but just an in the way 'force,' or an outside influence on the book."

Jill, in this instance, revealed her metaphysical beliefs about the nature of living and nonliving objects and to some extent the nature of forces. She continued:

"However, my ideas have changed since the beginning of this year. Sr. helped me to see the difference between the macroscopic level and the microscopic level, that was last year. But I never really thought about the difference very much."

The student explicitly stated that she was aware that her ideas had changed over time and she offered a causal explanation for the change in her thinking. She continued:

"This year, I began to think about the book on the table differently – then [last school year] I was thinking on the macroscopic level and not on the microscopic level. This year I wasn't looking at the table from the same perspective as last year. Last year I was looking at living being the important focus and now I am looking at the molecules as being the important focus."

Jill acknowledged that she was aware of a shift in the focus of her thinking as well as a change in her thinking.

"When I finally got my thoughts worked out, I could see things from a different perspective. I found out that I had no trouble thinking about two balanced forces instead of just gravity working on the book. It took me a whole YEAR to figure this concept out!!! Now I know it was worth THE YEAR to figure it out because now I can see balanced forces everywhere!"

Thorough self-interrogation and introspective monitoring, Jill was able to judge her past and current thinking; moreover, she acknowledged that the construction of her thinking took a significant amount of time. The remainder of the essay illustrates that Jill could generalize and apply her current understanding to new situations. The vignette also reveals Jill's metaphysical belief about the nature of molecules (they can cause an effect) and her epistemological belief about the nature of an explanation (some explanations are better and more important than others). Lastly, this 12-year-old student displayed an impressive understanding of the concept of velocity.

"Balanced forces are needed to produce constant velocity! The book on the table has a velocity of zero; that means it has a steady pace of zero. Why, Sr. asked, did my ideas change? I think my ideas changed because I have expanded my mind to more compli-

cated ideas! Like molecules in a table can have an effect on a book, that balanced forces and unbalanced forces are a better way of explaining the cause of motion, and that constant velocity and changing velocity are important things to look at when describing motion" (Hennessey & Beeth, 1993, p. 18).

Data drawn from the studies provide a wealth of examples that shed light on the nature and range of students' metacognitive abilities. This process, like cognitive engagement, is not an all-or-none phenomenon. The two examples given are representative of a continuum of engagement and elaboration: Brianna (a first grader) is a beginner to the process, whereas Jill (a sixth grader) demonstrates high metacognitive engagement.

Conclusions Based on Project META

Based on the data gathered from Project META, there is a significant amount of evidence to support the claim that the students who participated in the project (students in grades 1 through 6) provided extensive and varied examples of their ability to think about their thoughts as objects of cognition.

When assessing students' metacognitive ability, two key elements should be kept in mind. First, the metacognitive process is very subtle; a great deal of it rests on sensing states of mind and having a language to describe states of mind. The students' natural language contains a rich commonsense vocabulary for the phenomena of thought. At times, it is difficult for them to think of specific vocabulary to describe their states of mind without in some way utilizing metaphors drawn from the physical world. For example, students frequently spoke about *finding* support for an argument, *retrieving* a piece of information, or *linking* ideas together. Even these terms hardly do justice to the mental events the students wish to describe. Likewise, when describing mental events, the students frequently gave anthropomorphic attributes to the physical world (e.g., intention). With metacognitive sophistication, however, students began to articulate that the anthropomorphic attributes are language devices employed to describe their thoughts. For example:

A fourth-grade boy (age 9) was carrying on a discussion with the other members of his class. He was trying to explain what he does with his thoughts when he comes across new science ideas for the first time. In the following excerpt, Eamon tried to explain what goes on in his head. ". . . I try to look for a fit. Like if it doesn't fit with any [or all] of the ideas that I have in my head I just leave it and wait for other ideas to come in so that I can try to fit them together with my ideas. Maybe they will go with my ideas and then another idea will come in and I can fit it together with that idea and my understanding just keeps on enlarging. An idea usually does finally fit."

I asked Eamon for an explanation:

> *"What do you mean when you say you wait for an idea to come in? Do you think ideas come into your head?"*

Eamon continued with his explanation:

> *"It's just an analogy. Like Kelly's throw it away analogy. I don't think Kelly really means you can throw ideas away <Kelly: Right> and I really don't think ideas can like jump out of someone's head and into mine. I mean people talk and I hear what they say. You talk and I hear what you say. But I have to decide what to do with what you say. I have to see where it fits in with the ideas in my head. But sometimes I can't connect it. <T: Why?> Because I don't have enough pieces yet so I just hang on to the idea. Or sometimes what I hear isn't plausible to me then I don't try to connect it (Hennessey & Beeth, 1993, pp. 21–22).*

It is clear from this vignette that Eamon was aware that he was employing a language device [. . . *wait for other ideas to come in* . . .] to help clarify his thought. Although this 9-year old had misused the term *analogy* when describing a metaphor, it was still very clear from the rest of the discourse that he knew that he was using a language device.

A second key element to keep in mind when assessing students' metacognitive ability is that metacognitive thoughts are graded in the sense that some are much more prominent in the system than others. In fact, one can distinguish two levels of this grading or priority structure: a *representational level*—an inner awareness of one's own unobservable constructs (internal representations) made public through verbal discourse, writing, use of illustrations, or conceptual models (external representations); and an *evaluative level*—an ability to draw inferences about one's own unobservable constructs. For example, the evaluative level includes the ability to consider the implications or limitations inherent in personal knowledge claims, refer to thinking or learning processes, comment on status, or to refer to components of one's own conceptual ecology (specifically consistency and generalizability). All students (irrespective of grade level) consistently engaged in metacognitive processes at the representational level. Metacognitive processes at the evaluative level, however, were more prominent among the students in Grades 4 through 6.

Conclusions Based on Status Study

The data from the Status Study revealed that students in Grades 4 through 6 displayed a sophisticated ability to self-analyze the status of their conceptions. Hewson and Hewson (1992) described the different methods of status determination, depending on whether data is gathered in individual interviews or in classrooms, and whether or not the technical language (intelligible, plausible, and fruitful) of the conceptual change model is used. Determining status from normal classroom discourse is a complex, high-inference task. For example, when the technical language is not used, it is a challenge to recognize a particular segment of classroom talk as being status-related. Thorley (1990) devised a framework for categorizing particular segments of discourse as being about intelligibility, plausibility, or fruitfulness. According to Thorley, students' conceptions can be rendered intelligible through representational models such as language, images, analogies, exemplars, and others. Plausibility can be revealed by listening to the students talk about consistency with other knowledge or past experiences, causal mechanism, epistemological and metaphysical beliefs, and so on. On the other hand, the analysis of status when working with students in Grades 4 through 6 who know and can use the technical language is very different from the previous method. Status analysis becomes an easier task. The advantage of eliminating the time-consuming work of status analysis is obvious.

Certainly, there is a need to be cautious about accepting students' use of the technical terms. However, in this study, students spent several weeks developing meanings for these terms from the conceptual change model. They did this through a variety of activities involving small-group work to identify initial understandings of the terms, whole-class discussions of the contributions of the various groups, and building a consensus about a set of descriptors for each of these technical terms (see Hewson & Hennessey, 1992 for final set of these descriptors). In other words, I did not impose my meaning of the terms on the students. Also, keep in mind that it was common practice of the students to negotiate shared meanings for most of the concepts under consideration within their science classes.

Can students determine the status of their own conceptions? For the students who participated in the studies described here, I argue the answer is unequivocally yes. How does this status-determining ability interact with learning science content? When analyzing the "science talk" (i.e., students' conceptual understanding of the science content under consideration), there is a significant amount of data to suggest that the students developed an impressive qualitative understanding of the science content that is far beyond most students at their respective grade levels.

Metacognitive Factors: Implication for Intentional Conceptual Change

As mentioned previously, I see the process of intentional learning and intentional conceptual change as analogous. I also claim that metacognitive engagement and intentional conceptual change are highly interconnected.

It is important to keep in mind that the studies mentioned in this chapter were not specifically designed to probe the nature of this interconnectedness. The data, however, may shed some light on this relationship. There is ample evidence from these studies that elementary students have no difficulty engaging in metacognitive processes. The data support the claim that not all metacognitive thoughts take place at the same level; that is, metacognitive thoughts can take place at both the representational level and the evaluative level. It is this grading or priority structure, I believe, that may be the key to understanding the relationship between metacognition and intentional conceptual change.

Metacognitive processes at the representational level (an inner awareness of one's unobservable constructs made public through verbal discourse) may include an intentional component or it may not. The ability to merely externally represent one's internal constructs may take place at either the algorithmic level or the intentional level. The issue here is one of automaticity. Metacognitive processes at the evaluative level (the ability to draw inferences about one's unobservable constructs, consider the implications or limitations inherent in personal knowledge claims, refer to one's thinking or learning process, comment on the status of one's conceptions, or refer to components of one's conceptual ecology) are more likely to take place at the intentional level. The sophisticated nature of these processes makes it less likely that they are automatic. Both aspects of metacognitive ability are relevant to intentional conceptual change, however. The first relates to the moment-to-moment control of cognition that promotes students' ability to monitor and fine tune their thinking as they work toward a goal-directed task. The second relates to critiquing of cognition. This aspect of metacognition involves students' ability to engage in purposeful and evaluative thought over disconnected elements of knowledge to purposefully assemble or connect pieces of knowledge. In this sense, both levels of metacognition are necessary for the students to organize their mental efforts in the service of internally initiated, self-guided learning. Therefore, both should be fostered by instruction designed to support the development of metacogitive abilities underlying intentional conceptual change.

DISCUSSION

This chapter opened with a vignette of an 11-year-old student who was trying to determine the status of her conceptions about a physics topic. Her thinking process was described as metacognitive and her approach to learning was described as intentional. I discussed a number of issues related to the nature of metacognition, intentional learning, and intentional conceptual change throughout the chapter. Factors such as social and educational environment were discussed as well. Woven together, issues such as metacognitive ability, social and educational environment, epistemological stance, and intentional conceptual change create a complex and at times "messy" picture of everyday life in a constructivist classroom. As a classroom teacher with more than 25 years of teaching experience, the "messiness" is easily handled. As a researcher in science education, on the other hand, investigating the "messiness" or probing into the nature of the learning process taking place within this "messy" environment is much more difficult. For example, the ability to follow any one strand (i.e., metacognitive ability, or pedagogical practice, or social interaction) to the extent that that strand can be isolated and followed over a number of years, gives the reader a sense of the enormity of the task. Research in a living classroom is indeed messy!

The research literature mentioned in this chapter, broadly defined, encompasses many significant studies that focus on the fundamental question: Can metacogitive theory be applied to intentional conceptual change? For example, the researchers who contributed to the Hacker et al. (1998) text asked: Can instruction of metacognitive processes facilitate learning? Likewise, the researchers who contributed to Schnotz et al. text (1999) on conceptual change learning asked similar questions about the effects of conceptual change on classroom learning. This volume seeks to accomplish the same with regard to intentional conceptual change learning. The bottom line question is: Does it have an effect? Does it make a difference? My answer to these questions is a resounding "yes."

The various vignettes presented in this chapter provide the reader with a small window into a constructivist-based classroom. The "voices" of the older students, although limited due to space constraints, give the reader a sense of the students' thought processes after spending 6 years in an educational setting designed specifically to address students' understanding of science content. If the reader "listens" carefully to the students' voices about science content, the students display an in-depth understanding of the physics content. Likewise, if the reader "listens" carefully to the voices that reveal metacognitive ability, we learn that elementary school children are capable of engaging in more sophisticated levels of metacognition than many researchers have assumed.

The constructivist insights achieved by these students go well beyond the new insights of elementary school students that are commonly reported in the theory of mind literature (Montgomery, 1992; Sodian & Wimmer, 1987; Wellman, 1990). In light of this literature, it is significant that the students understood that knowledge grows out of and depends on their prior ideas, and that individuals have different perspectives that influence their sense-making efforts. Students were also deeply aware that collaboration and consensus building enhanced their knowledge-building efforts. Furthermore, in their classroom essays, the students' were able to identify the importance of being able to bracket the perspectives of self, others, and the science community, and to be actively engaged in thinking about how these different perspectives relate to each other. They also made a distinction between cognitive activities of memorizing and understanding. In all these ways, the students developed a more sophisticated, constructivist epistemology than has been previously reported for students of this age or than would be expected by those espousing the Piagetian hypothesis that elementary students are "concrete" thinkers.

The voices of the students are silent when it comes to intentional conceptual change learning. However, their ability to engage in sophisticated metacognitive processes, which is reflected in their voices, provides evidence, although indirect, that they are quite capable of engaging in intentional conceptual change learning.

In closing, it is true, as Kuhn (1962) observed, that any new paradigm always first appears as a rough draft. This chapter is but one attempt to apply a bit of sandpaper to a corner of that "rough draft" paradigm—the corner occupied by intentional conceptual change learning. I began with the boxes we have built for ourselves in our thinking about metacognition, conceptual change, social and education environments, and intentional learning. That is what a paradigm or framework is, of course: a set of boxes we, as a research culture, have put things into so that the world makes sense to us. What most of us tend to forget, however, is that the boxes are our own creation and get broken down and formed again every so often. The box we called *behaviorism* has broken down before our eyes, as an ever-increasing number of researchers sought to describe the nature of learners and the learning process. For decades now, researchers in psychology and education have tried to redefine learning. Libraries are full of our attempts to make sense of this complex human phenomenon. The new boxes, in this chapter, are being redrawn around the tenants of "constructivism," "metacognition," "social and educational environment," and "intentional conceptual change." Other chapters, of course, will draw other boxes, and rightly so. Care must be taken, however, not to try and reduce learning to some formula or recipe or set of principles. It is as if we think that we can find a sort of genetic or generic key that will unlock the whole mystery. Sometimes I have the feeling that we are searching with a microscope for something that can be grasped only in panorama. Perhaps learning is the natural expression of a fully integrated human being. And part of what that human being must integrate is the animated creative spirit within that is ultimately connected to a larger source of meaning beyond. The logic is simple: Of the literally hundreds of skills, competencies, traits, characteristics, and qualities used in the literature to define and describe learners and the process of learning, those that are most essential in the fluid world of today may in fact be the outer fruits of that inner metacognitive life.

ACKNOWLEDGMENT

I am grateful to Gale Sinatra and Paul Pintrich. Their skillful editing has helped bring this chapter together in a fabric more tightly woven that I could achieve on my own.

REFERENCES

Baars, B. (1986). *The cognitive revolution in psychology*. New York: Guilford Press.

Baird, J. R., & Northfield, J. R. (1992). *Learning from the PEEL experience*. Melbourne: Monash University.

Beeth, M. E. (1998). Teaching science in 5th grade: Instructional goals that support conceptual change. *Journal of Research in Science Teaching, 35*(10), 1091–1101.

Beeth, M. E., & Hewson, P. W. (1999a, March). *Facilitating learning of science content and scientific epistemology: Key elements in teaching for conceptual change*. Paper presented at the Annual Meeting of the National Association for Research in Science Teaching, Boston, MA.

Beeth, M. E., & Hewson, P. W. (1999b). Learning goals in an exemplary science teacher's practice: Cognitive and social factors in teaching for conceptual change. *Science Education, 83*, 738–760.

Bereiter, C. (1990). Aspects of an educational learning theory. *Review of Educational Research, 60*, 603–624.

Bereiter, C., & Scardamalia, M. (1989). Intentional learning as a goal of instruction. In L. B. Resnick (Ed.), *Knowing, learning, and remembering: Essays in honor of Robert Glaser* (pp. 361-392). Hillsdale, NJ: Lawrence Erlbaum Associates.

Boekaerts, M., Pintrich, P., & Zeidner, M. (Eds.). (2000). *Handbook of self-regulation*. New York: Academic Press.

Brown, A. L. (1978). Knowing when, where & how to remember: A problem of metacognition. In R. Glaser (Ed.), *Advances in instructional psychology*. (Vol. I, pp. 77–165). Hillsdale, NJ: Lawrence Erlbaum Associates.

Brown, A. L., & Campione, J. C. (1994). Guided discovery in a community of learners. In K. McGilly (Ed.), *Classroom lessons: Integrating cognitive theory and educational practice* (pp. 229–270). Cambridge, MA: MIT/ Bradford Press.

Carey, S. (1985a). Are children fundamentally different thinkers and learners from adults? In S. F. Chipman, J. W. Segal, & R. Glaser (Eds.), *Thinking and learning skills* (Vol. 2, pp. 485–517). Hillsdale, NJ: Lawrence Erlbaum Associates.

Carey, S. (1985b). *Conceptual change in childhood*. Cambridge, MA: MIT Press.

Carey, S. (1991). Knowledge acquisition: Enrichment or conceptual change? In S. Carey & R. Gelman (Eds.), *The epigenesis of mind: Essays on biology and cognition* (pp. 257–291). Hillsdale, NJ: Lawrence Erlbaum Associates.

Carey, S., Evans, R., Honda, M., Jay, E., & Unger, C. (1989). "An experiment is when you try it and see if it works:" A study of grade 7 students' understanding of the construction of scientific knowledge. *International Journal of Science Education, 11*, 514–529.

Clement, J. (1993). Using bridging analogies and anchoring intuitions to deal with students' preconceptions in physics. *Journal of Research in Science Teaching, 30*(10), 1241–1257.

Davidson, J. E., & Sternberg, R. J. (1998). Smart problem solving: How metacognition helps. In D. J. Hacker, J. Dunlosky, & A. C. Graesser (Eds.), *Metacognition in educational theory and practice* (pp. 47–68). Mahwah, NJ: Lawrence Erlbaum Associates.

Dole, J. A., & Sinatra, G. M. (1998). Reconceptualizing change in the cognitive construction of knowledge. *Educational Psychologist, 33*(2/3), 109–128.

Dominowski, R. L. (1998). Verbalization and problem solving. In D. J. Hacker, J. Dunlosky, & A. C. Graesser (Eds.), *Metacognition in educational theory and practice* (pp. 25–45). Mahwah, NJ: Lawrence Erlbaum Associates.

Duit, R. (1999). Conceptual change approaches in science education. In W. Schnotz, S. Vosniadou, & M. Carrettero (Eds.), *New perspectives on conceptual change* (pp. 263–282). New York: Pergamon.

Dykstra, D. (1992). Studying conceptual change: constructing new understandings. In R. Duit, F. Goldburg, & H. Niedderer (Eds.), *Research in physics learning: Theoretical issues and empirical studies* (pp. 40–57). Kiel, Germany: Institute for Science Education at the University of Kiel.

Flavell, J. H. (1976). Metacognitive aspects of problem solving. In L. B. Resnick (Ed.), *The nature of intelligence* (pp. 231–235). Hillsdale, NJ: Lawrence Erlbaum Associates.

Flavell, J. H. (1979). Metacognition and cognitive monitoring: A new era of cognitive development inquiry. *American Psychologist, 34*, 906–911.

Flavell, J. H. (1981). Cognitive monitoring. In W. P. Dickson (Ed.), *Children's oral communication skills* (pp. 35–60). New York: Academic.

Gardner, R., & Alexander, P. A. (1989). Metacognition: Answered and unanswered questions. *Educational Psychologist, 24*(2), 143–158.

Guzzetti, B., & Hynd C. (Eds.). (1998). *Perspectives on conceptual change: Multiple ways to understand knowing and learning a complex world.* Mahwah, NJ: Lawrence Erlbaum Associates.

Hacker, D. J. (1998). Self-regulated comprehension during normal reading. In D. J. Hacker, J. Dunlosky, & A. C. Graesser (Eds.), *Metacognition in educational theory and practice* (pp. 165–191). Mahwah, NJ: Lawrence Erlbaum Associates.

Hacker, D. J., Dunlosky, J., & Graesser, A. C. (Eds.). (1998). *Metacognition in educational theory and practice.* Mahwah, New Jersey: Lawrence Erlbaum Associates.

Hennessey, M. G. (1991a, April). *Analysis and use of the technical language of the conceptual change model for revealing status: 6th graders' conceptions of force and motion.* Paper presented at the Annual Meeting of the National Association for Research in Science Teaching, Fontana, WI.

Hennessey, M. G. (1991b, August) *Analysis of conceptual change and status change in sixth graders' conceptions of force and motion.* Unpublished doctoral dissertation, University of Wisconsin-Madison.

Hennessey, M. G. (1999, April). *Probing the dimensions of metacognition: Implications for conceptual change teaching–learning.* Paper presented at the Annual Meeting of the National Association for Research in Science Teaching, Boston, MA.

Hennessey, M. G., & Beeth, M. E. (1993, April). *Students' reflective thoughts about science content: A relationship to conceptual change learning.* Paper presented at the Annual Meeting of the American Educational Research Association, Atlanta, GA.

Hewson, P. W. (1981). A conceptual change approach to learning science. *European Journal of Science Education, 3*(4), 383–396.

Hewson, P. W. (1982). The case study of conceptual change in special relativity: The influence of prior knowledge in learning. *European Journal of Science Education, 4*(1), 61–78.

Hewson, P. W. (1992, June). *Conceptual change in science teaching and teacher education.* Paper presented at a meeting on "Research and Curriculum Development in Science Teaching" under the auspices of the National Center for Educational Research, Documentation, and Assessment, Ministry for Education and Science. Madrid, Spain.

Hewson, P. W., & Hennessey, M. G. (1992). Making status explicit: A case study of conceptual change. In R. Duit, F. Goldburg, & H. Niedderer (Eds.), *Research in physics learning: Theoretical issues and empirical studies* (pp. 176–187). Kiel, Germany: Institute for Science Education at the University of Kiel.

Hewson, P. W., & Hewson, M. G. (1992). The status of students' conceptions. In R. Duit, F. Goldburg, & H. Niedderer (Eds.), *Research in physics learning: Theoretical issues and empirical studies* (pp. 59–73). Kiel, Germany: Institute for Science Education at the University of Kiel.

Hewson, P. W., & Thorley, N. R. (1989). The conditions of conceptual change in the classroom. *International Journal of Science Education, 11*(5), 541–553.

Kuhn, D., Amsel, E., & O'Loughlin, M. (1988). *The development of scientific thinking skills*. San Diego, CA: Academic Press.

Kuhn, T. (1962). *The structure of scientific revolutions*. London: University of Chicago Press.

Metz, K. (1995). Reassessment of developmental constraints on children' science instruction. *Review of Educational Research, 65*(2), 93–127.

Minstrell, J. (1992). Facets of students' knowledge and relevant instruction. In R. Duit, F. Goldburg, & H. Niedderer (Eds.), *Research in physics learning: Theoretical issues and empirical studies* (pp. 110–128). Kiel, Germany: Institute for Science Education at the University of Kiel.

Montgomery, D. (1992). Young children's theory of knowing: The development of a folk epistemology. *Developmental Review, 12*, 410–430.

Palermo, D. (1971). Is a scientific revolution taking place in psychology? *Scientific Studies, 1*, 135–155.

Pintrich, P. R. (1999). Motivational beliefs as resources for and constraints on conceptual change. In W. Schnotz, S. Vosniadou, & M. Carretero (Eds.), *New perspectives on conceptual change* (pp. 33–50). New York: Pergamon.

Pintrich, P. R. (2000). The role of goal orientation in self-regulated learning. In M. Boekaerts, P. Pintrich, & M. Zeidner (Eds.), *Handbook of self-regulation* (pp. 451–502). New York: Academic Press.

Pintrich, P. R., Marx, R. W., & Boyle, R. A. (1993). Beyond cold conceptual change: The role of motivational beliefs and classroom contextual factors in the process of conceptual change. *Review of Educational Research, 63*(2), 167–199.

Posner, G. J., Strike, K. A., Hewson, P. W., & Gertzog, W. A. (1982). Accommodation of a scientific conception: Towards a theory of conceptual change. *Science Education, 66*(2), 211–227.

Reynolds, R. E., Sinatra, G. M., & Jetton, T. L. (1996). Views of knowledge acquisition and representation: A continuum from experience-centered to mind-centered. *Educational Psychologist, 31*(2), 93–104.

Schnotz, W., Vosniadou, S., & Carretero, M. (Eds.). (1999). *New perspectives on conceptual change*. New York: Pergamon.

Scott, P. H., Asoko, H. M., & Driver, R. H. (1992). Teaching for conceptual change: A review of strategies. In R. Duit, F. Goldburg, & H. Niedderer (Eds.), *Research in physics learning: Theoretical issues and empirical studies* (pp. 310–329). Kiel, Germany: Institute for Science Education at the University of Kiel.

Shapiro, S. L., & Schwartz, G. E. (2000). The role of intention in self-regulation. In M. Boekaerts, P. Pintrich, & M. Zeidner (Eds.), *Handbook of self-regulation* (pp. 253–273). New York: Academic Press.

Sinatra, G. M. (2000, April). From passive to active to intentional: Changing conceptions of the learner. In G. M. Sinatra (Chair), *What does it mean to be an intentional learner? Alterna-*

tive perspectives. Symposium presented at the American Educational Research Association Annual Meeting, New Orleans, LA.

Sitko, B. M. (1998). Knowing how to write: Metacognition and Writing Instruction. In D. J. Hacker, J. Dunlosky, & A. C. Graesser (Eds.), *Metacognition in educational theory and practice* (pp. 93–115). Mahwah, NJ: Lawrence Erlbaum Associates.

Smith, C. L., Maclin, D., Houghton, C., & Hennessey, M. G. (2000). Sixth-grade students' epistemologies of science: The impact of school science experiences on epistemological development. *Cognition and Instruction, 18*(3), 349–422.

Sodian, B., & Wimmer, H. (1987). Children's understanding of inference as a source of knowledge. *Child Development, 58*, 424–433.

Strike, K. A., & Posner, G. J. (1985). A conceptual change view of learning and understanding. In L. H. T. West & A. L. Pines (Eds.), *Cognitive structure and conceptual change*. Orlando, FL: Academic Press.

Strike, K. A., & Posner, G. J. (1992). A revisionist theory of conceptual change. In R. Duschl & R. Hamilton (Eds.), *Philosophy of science, cognitive science, and educational theory and practice* (pp. 147–176). Albany, NY: Academic Press.

Thorley, N. R. (1990, August). *The role of conceptual change model in the interpretation of classroom interactions*. Unpublished doctoral dissertation, University of Wisconsin-Madison.

Vosniadou, S. (1999). Conceptual change research: State of the art and future direction. In W. Schnotz, S. Vosniadou, & M. Carrettero (Eds.), *New perspectives on conceptual change*. New York: Pergamon.

Webster's new twentieth century dictionary of the English language. (1978). Unabridged, (2nd ed.). New York: Collins-World.

Wellman, H. M. (1990). *The child's theory of mind*. Cambridge, MA: MIT Press.

Wellman, H. M., & Gelman, S. A. (1992). Cognitive development. Foundational theories of core domains. *Annual Review of Psychology, 45*, 337–375.

White, R. T. (1988). Metacognition. In J. P. Keeves (Ed.), *Educational research, methodology, and measurement* (pp. 70–75). Oxford: Pergamon.

Winne, P. H., & Hadwin, A. F. (1998). Studying as self-regulated learning. In D. J. Hacker, J. Dunlosky, & A. C. Graesser (Eds.), *Metacognition in educational theory and practice* (pp. 277–304). Mahwah, NJ: Lawrence Erlbaum Associates.

Zimmerman, B. J., & Schunk, D. H. (Eds.). (1989). *Self-regulated learning and academic achievement: Theory, research, and practice*. New York: Springer-Verlag.

6

The Role of Domain-Specific Knowledge in Intentional Conceptual Change

Margarita Limón Luque
Universidad Autónoma de Madrid, Spain

> "*Attention with effort is all that any case of volition implies.* The essential achievement of the will, in short, when it is most "voluntary", is to ATTEND to a difficult object and hold it fast before the mind"
>
> (James, 1890, p. 561).

> "*. . . Belief means only a peculiar sort of occupancy of the mind, and relation to the self felt in the thing believed; and we know in the case of many beliefs how constant an effort of the attention is required to keep them in this situation and protect them from displacement by contradictory ideas*"
>
> (James, 1890, p. 562).

> "Effort of attention is thus the essential phenomenon of will . . . *What constitutes the difficulty for a man laboring under an unwise passion of acting as if the passion were unwise? Certainly there is no physical difficulty. . . .The difficulty is mental; it is that of getting the idea of the wise action to stay before our mind at all. When any strong emotional state whatever is upon us the tendency is for no images but such as are congruous with it to come up. . . . The cooling advice which we get from others when the fever-fit is on us is the most jarring and exasperating thing in life. Reply we cannot, so we get angry; for by a sort of self-preserving instinct which our passion has. . . . Such is the inevitable effect of reasonable ideas over others*—if they can once get a quiet hearing . . ."
>
> (James, 1890, pp. 562–563).

Although written more than a century ago, these passages from the *Principles of Psychology* by William James provide a good starting point for illustrating several issues discussed throughout this chapter. Over recent decades, one of the clearest results obtained in research on conceptual change concerned subjects' resistance to changing their prior ideas and beliefs. The explanation of this resistance and of why people do not take into account alternative ideas was one of the goals pursued by many researchers.

Models of conceptual change focused mainly on cognitive factors for its explanation (e.g., Chi, 1992; diSessa, 1993; Strike & Posner, 1985; 1992; Vosniadou, 1994; Vosniadou & Brewer, 1987). Nevertheless, as cognitive factors have shown themselves as clearly insufficient for such explanation, in the last years there has been growing interest in the literature in developing theoretical frameworks that include metacognitive, attitudinal, motivational and affective factors to explain conceptual change processes (e.g., Chinn & Brewer, 1993; Dole & Sinatra, 1998; Kuhn & Lao, 1998; Pintrich, Marx, & Boyle, 1993). Empirical results have suggested that, in many cases, such factors may be responsible for resistance to change.

The term *intentional conceptual change* brings together cognitive and metacognitive, motivational and affective factors, and underlines the need to explain how they interact to account for the mechanisms and processes involved in conceptual change. First, this chapter introduces what I mean by *intentional conceptual change.*

Intentional conceptual change clearly involves a volitional component: People *must* be willing to change. As James (1890) wrote with regard to will in his classic *Principles of Psychology,* volition involves "attention with effort" (p. 561) to a difficult object with the intent of holding it in mind. This idea illustrates a first requirement of intentional conceptual change: to focus learner's attention on the task and on what knowledge needs to be changed. The passage opening this chapter also highlights another important aspect of intentional conceptual change: It is voluntary. Therefore, it involves not only the will, but also awareness.

In the second chapter-opening quotation, James emphasized the close relationship between beliefs and volition. He stated in the same chapter that "will is a relation between the mind and its 'ideas' " and that:

> "*. . . The terminus of the psychological process in volition, the point to which will is directly applied, is always an idea... The only resistance which our will can possibly experience is the resistance which such an idea offers to being attended at all.* To attend to it is the volitional act, and the only inward volitional act which we ever perform" (p. 567).

Conceptual change often involves overcoming this resistance to review our beliefs and to attend to alternative ones. Thus, attending to alternative ideas that contradict ours entails a volitional act: the effort of being willing to attend to them. However, research findings on anomalous data and conceptual change have provided sound evidence of how often people of different ages and with different levels of domain-specific knowledge protect their ideas and beliefs from "contradictory" and alternative ones (e.g., Chan, Burtis, & Bereiter, 1997; Limón & Carretero, 1997, 1999; Mason, 2000).

Second, this chapter discusses and presents research examples to illustrate the interaction between cognitive, metacognitive, and motivational factors and how they may influence intentional conceptual change. Particularly, it focuses on the role of domain-specific knowledge in intentional conceptual change.

The third paragraph of the chapter-opening quotation illustrates the emotional aspects involved in intentional conceptual change. When we have ideas or beliefs we want to protect from others, "cognitive resistance" to change may have an emotional component that also obstructs change. In the example from James, individuals may even realize that the alternative idea is more reasonable, but they *want* to keep their original ideas. As they realize they cannot accept the alternative idea and maintain coherence, they can become angry! More recently, Sutherland (1992) described examples of this so-called "irrational behaviour." Throughout this chapter research examples are presented in the domain of history where emotional reactions may obstruct change.

In sum, my intent is to (a) present a conceptualization of intentional conceptual change, (b) illustrate, with examples from our own research, the role of domain-specific knowledge in satisfying the requirements necessary for intentional conceptual change, and (c) present some conclusions and implications of intentional conceptual change for learning and teaching practice.

WHAT IS INTENTIONAL CONCEPTUAL CHANGE?

Chi (1992) proposed an interesting difference between *processes* and *outcomes* of conceptual change. Outcomes of conceptual change are changes in an individual's knowledge that result as a consequence of the change process. Enrichment, reassignment of concepts, change in the framework theory, or a radical restructuring of prior knowledge are examples of possible outcomes of conceptual change. Processes of conceptual change are the mechanisms by which individuals achieve change in their prior knowledge. Intentional conceptual change is one answer—not the only one—to the question: How is the process of conceptual change achieved?

From my perspective, intentional conceptual change is a process that demands some prerequisites. Different outcomes may result from the process, but the prerequisites to initiate the process are the same. To date, the literature on conceptual change has focused more on describing possible outcomes of conceptual change than on describing processes. Moreover, the attempts to describe and explain the process of conceptual change have centered mainly on cognitive mechanisms. A virtue of intentional conceptual change is that it underscores the close relationship between cognitive mechanisms and metacognitive, motivational, and emotional factors.

Prerequisites for Intentional Conceptual Change

I argue that intentional conceptual change requires three prerequisites:

- Individuals need to be aware of the need to change and to be able to know what to change. I call this the metacognitive prerequisite of intentional conceptual change.
- Individuals must want to change. They must consider change as a personal goal, and not as something imposed by others. I refer to this as the volitional prerequisite of intentional conceptual change.
- Individuals must be able to self-regulate their process of change; that is, they must be able to plan, monitor, and evaluate their process of change. This is referred to as the self-regulation prerequisite of intentional conceptual change.

For intentional conceptual change to take place, the three prerequisites have to be fulfilled.

What Type of Conceptual Change Can Be Achieved Through Intentional Conceptual Change?

What outcomes of conceptual change should be expected from a process of intentional conceptual change? To answer this question, I briefly review the kinds of conceptual change and types of change described in the literature.

Carey (1985) established the classic distinction between weak and radical restructuring. Weak restructuring refers to change that occurs in the shift from novice to expert. This case does not involve change to the central core of the theory or require abandonment of certain beliefs or misconceptions. In this case, novices develop more relations among concepts. Their schemata can be changed or formed. When learners are faced with major anomalies that cannot be accounted for by their existing theories, a "new paradigm" is required, giving rise to a *radical restructuring*.

Vosniadou (1994) distinguished several types of conceptual change. According to her, the simplest form of conceptual change would be *enrichment*. This involves the addition of new information to the individual's existing knowledge. *Revision* would be another type of conceptual change, required when the information to be acquired is inconsistent with beliefs, presuppositions, or the structure of a theory. A third type of change involves revision of the framework theory. According to Vosniadou (1994), framework theories "represent relatively coherent systems of explanation, based on everyday experience and tied to years of confirmation" (p. 49). This third type of conceptual change, *to change a framework theory*, is rather difficult to achieve because it involves reviewing the theory's presuppositions that are based on everyday experience and supported by years of confirmation. Intentional conceptual change may be necessary for people to achieve a change of their framework theory.

Chi (1992) distinguished two main types of conceptual change: conceptual change that occurs within an ontological category, and conceptual change that occurs across ontological categories. This second type of conceptual change she called *radical conceptual change*. Radical conceptual change can be understood as the development or acquisition of new conceptions, with the initial conceptions remaining more or less intact.

Conceptual change within the same ontological category (same tree or branch in the individual's conceptual network) is not as difficult to achieve as radical conceptual change. Concepts can migrate within the tree, or develop, or add new attributes. Some attributes may become more salient. A reorganization of the tree occurs, but concepts do not change their basic meaning. In contrast, radical conceptual change involves a change in meaning. Concepts become incommensurable with those initially held.

White (1994) distinguished between *conceptual* and *conceptional* change. For him, "concept" has two possible meanings. The first refers to classification. People classify objects according to the definition accepted by the majority. Then, conceptual change can be understood as learning to classify objects. The second meaning refers to all the knowledge a person has and associates with that concept. According to this meaning of concept, every new piece of information added may change an individual's concept. In this case, conceptual change is understood as accretion.

Conceptions are systems of explanation. To change conceptions entails major shifts that are much more difficult to achieve than those required to change concepts. Conceptional change involves change to detailed explanations of phenomena. Conceptional change implies revision of knowledge, whereas conceptual change implies only an addition of knowledge.

Distributed encoding involves the reuse and integration of intuitive knowledge (p-prims) into the knowledge base. This is one of the main changes described by diSessa (1993) to explain the shift from naïve to expert physics understanding. Together with this change of function, there is a structural change in the individual's conceptual network. The change in depth, breadth, and integration of the expert's conceptual network is the major change from intuitive to expert physics.

Ivarsson, Schoultz, and Säljo (2002) supported a sociocultural approach of conceptual change. The mastering of mediational means, the appropriation of tools, and their use in an effective way according to cultural practices (Mayer, 2002) are the main outcomes of conceptual change.

Potentially, all of these outcomes can be achieved through intentional conceptual change. Nevertheless, some questions become especially relevant: Which of these types of conceptual change is intentional conceptual change best suited for? What type of outcome is intentional conceptual change inadequate for? When does an individual initiate intentional conceptual change?

Intentional conceptual change requires individuals to make a considerable effort to change. It demands that learners pay deliberate attention to change and consider it as a personal goal to be achieved. Therefore, those types of change that require greater restructuring of the individual's prior knowledge may be those that demand intentional conceptual change. Although this has yet to be established empirically, intentional conceptual change might be necessary for radical restructuring to be achieved.

Some of the outcomes described earlier involve partial or weak modifications of the individual's prior knowledge. Enrichment, perhaps one of the most common types of change our knowledge endures, involves the addition of new information. Often, we are not even aware that a change has occurred in our knowledge network. If our learning goal is to acquire information, but not necessarily to achieve a deep understanding of the topic, we do not necessarily activate an intentional conceptual change process. It may take too much time and effort for our purposes.

Consider an example from everyday experience. Imagine you are a driver with more than 15 years of driving experience, but you are not very familiar with cars other than your own. One day your car is broken and you decide to rent a car. When you try to put the car into reverse to exit the parking lot, you move the gear lever to the left and then push it forward as you usually do in your own car. However, the car moves forward instead of back. You stop and try to figure out how the gears work in this car. Finally, you notice a schematic picture of the lever that illustrates how to put the car into reverse gear. As a result of this experience, you may change your knowledge about cars and how to drive, particularly your knowledge about how gear levers work. It could be said that the result of this change is that you have enriched your knowledge. In such a situation, you may not have been aware of the change and you may not have paid too much attention to the problem because it was readily solved.

In a case like this, to fulfill the three requisites I defined for intentional conceptual change may not be necessary for your learning purposes. On one hand, it would be time demanding and effortful. On the other hand, you do not intend to have a deep understanding of how gear levers work in other cars and will not be interested in paying special attention to this change.

Imagine now a similar situation in a different context. The driver in this case is someone who is just going to pass his examination to get a driving license. A few minutes before the exam, the car he usually drives breaks down and he has to use a different one for the test. He has 5 minutes to get used to the new car. On attempting to leave the parking lot, he encounters the same problem with the gear level. In this context, if the driver can keep calm, he probably invests effort and attention to discover what is wrong. He is motivated, and, using his beliefs and prior knowledge about cars, he may develop some hypotheses and try to check them out following a plan made up on the spot. In this context, maybe intentional conceptual change would be useful if it can be carried out in the short period of time provided by the context. Nevertheless, the outcome of the process will more likely be enrichment, and will result in a weak change.

So, when does a learner activate an intentional conceptual change process? As the examples illustrate, the context may facilitate or obstruct intentional conceptual change. For instance, contexts with short time requirements make it more difficult to carry out intentional conceptual change. Contexts where reflection and self-regulation of knowledge are promoted may facilitate intentional conceptual change. Individual's learning purpose is a second variable that may influence whether or not individuals initiate intentional conceptual change. When the learner's purpose is to develop a deep understanding of the topic, intentional conceptual change may be necessary; when the learner's purpose is simply to accumulate information without any kind of organization or meaning (for him or her), intentional conceptual change is not only unnecessary, but inappropriate.

When individuals are presented a problem that challenges them and is personally relevant (so they easily would feel engaged in it), they may be more willing to activate an intentional conceptual change process. If the heuristics, usual strategies and automatic knowledge they apply prove inadequate to solve the problem, then intentional conceptual change is more likely to occur. Even so, the outcome of the process—the type of change achieved—may not necessarily be a radical restructuring. The characteristics of the task or problem presented—that is, the degree of personal relevance and challenge—are variables that may influence individuals to initiate intentional conceptual change. On the other hand, what is considered a problem and the degree of challenge may depend, among other factors, on the amount of domain-specific knowledge possessed by the individual; individuals' level of expertise may obstruct or facilitate the fulfillment of the three prerequisites for intentional conceptual change.

More variables may be needed to explain when intentional conceptual change is activated than those I identify. Further research and theoretical development are needed to explore the full range of variables involved. This chapter focuses on the influence of the level of domain-specific knowledge and how expertise may influence the prerequisites needed for successful intentional conceptual change.

PREREQUISITES OF INTENTIONAL CONCEPTUAL CHANGE AND DOMAIN-SPECIFIC KNOWLEDGE

Intentional conceptual change, as a type of mechanism by which conceptual change may be accomplished, may take place in any content domain. Thus, it is possible to talk about intentional conceptual change in history, science, mathematics, etc. In this sense, intentional conceptual change is a domain-general process, and the three prerequisites enumerated earlier would be necessary for such a process to occur, independently of the content of the task or problem presented. On the other hand, as I try to illustrate in this section, the level of domain-specific knowledge (level of expertise) individuals have is a relevant factor to determine whether these three prerequisites can be satisfied or not.

Metacognitive Prerequisite and Level of Expertise in the Domain

For intentional conceptual change to take place, individuals must first become aware of the need for change, and second, become aware of what needs to be changed. This latter depends on the type of change demanded, the outcomes individuals intend to accomplish, their goals, motivation and prior knowledge, among other factors. Sometimes, students need to notice the contradiction between their beliefs or ideas and alternative ones presented in a particular task. At other times, they need to realize that it is a particular epistemological belief that they need to change, or, that they may first need to change their motivation or their way of approaching the task.

Learners must be aware not only of the need for change, but they must notice in a particular context what they need to change. To do so, they must evaluate the type of change required and the outcome expected. They must evaluate the "available resources" (prior knowledge, epistemological beliefs, goals and motivation, problem-solving skills, etc.) that they may need to accomplish the change and to achieve the desired outcome. To do so, learners have to apply their metacognitive knowledge to evaluate what they know, what they lack, and where the obstacles may lie to accomplishing the required change. This may be a very hard task that likely needs to be trained and scaffolded.

For several years, my research has focused on the study of individuals' reaction to anomalous or contradictory data (e.g., Limón & Carretero, 1997, 1998, 1999, Limón, 2000, 2001, 2002). We were interested in the differences that might be found in relation to two variables: the domain studied and individuals' level of domain-specific knowledge.

A first step along the path to conceptual change is the awareness of contradiction. The second step is to realize the need for change. A further step would be for individuals to be aware of what needs to be changed. Awareness of contradiction means, first, realizing that alternative views may be possible, and second, finding them plausible to explain something your view cannot. However, even if individuals realize a contradiction exists and are aware of the need for change, this does not guarantee that they will be aware of what, in particular, needs to be changed.

Cognitive, motivational, and affective factors are involved in realizing contradictions and finding alternative views to be plausible candidates to build a better explanation. The following studies illustrate with some research examples how a high or low level of domain knowledge may influence such awareness.

The general plan of the studies was to present an open, ill-defined problem in the domain explored. As problems were ill-defined, different answers could be given and all of them were accepted. There was not a "correct" answer. Before presenting the problem, individuals' prior knowledge about the topic of the problem was evaluated. In all the studies, the same question was asked at different moments during the task: at the beginning, after new or contradictory information was given, and at the end. Thus, individuals' answers were evaluated throughout each stage of the task. Using this methodology, it was possible to register changes immediately after new or contradictory information was introduced and to compare individuals' initial and final answers to evaluate change.

In Limón and Carretero (1997), the problem chosen for the study was the origin of life: how the first organic molecule appeared on earth. The study was divided into two parts. Here I refer only to the procedures and results of Part II. Participants were 69 ninth graders (aged 14 to 15), 57 eleventh graders (aged 16 to 17) and 63 twelfth graders (aged 17 to 18). Their prior knowledge on the topic was rather low, although all had received instruction in it. Those who had received the most instruction on the topic were the twelfth graders. In the second part of this study, each group of subjects was divided into two conditions: condition A and condition A+B.

In condition A (only anomalous data presented), a fictitious situation was presented in a short text that described two research groups, one headed by Dr. Hamilton and the other headed by Dr. Smith. These groups maintained opposite hypotheses. The text explained that Dr. Hamilton's group maintained an hypothesis familiar to students from Part I of the study. This hypothesis, (Oparin's hypothesis about the origin of life), was chosen by most of the participants as the correct explanation of how organic life first appeared on Earth. Then, three statements made by Dr. Smith that clearly refuted Dr. Hamilton's hypothesis were presented. The statements referred to three key points in Oparin's hypothesis: the primeval atmosphere conditions, the requirement of liquid as the medium required for the appearance of organic compounds, and the energy source.

Then, students were asked if they thought Dr. Hamilton could maintain his hypothesis or not, and why. Finally, they were asked again to choose which hypothesis they considered the most adequate of the those presented in Part I, although they were not constrained to choose one of the original hypotheses presented. They could, instead, construct their own hypothesis, mix some of the ideas presented, or introduce new ones. They could also answer that none of the hypotheses were adequate. They were allowed to consult the text with the hypotheses and the summary table presented in Part I, as much as they wanted.

In condition A+B (confirmatory plus anomalous data were presented), the same fictitious situation was presented, but in this case, three counterarguments made by Dr. Hamilton defending his hypothesis were also introduced. Therefore, in this condition not only anomalous data but also confirmatory data were presented.

Finally, students were also asked to choose which hypothesis they considered the most adequate of those originally presented or to construct their own as in condition A. They could also consult the text and summary table as much as they wanted. Table 6.1 shows how many students became aware of contradictions and how many did not.

Chi-square analyses confirmed that there were significant differences among the three groups regarding their awareness of contradictions (χ^2 = 15.389, p = 0.0005). Almost all of the twelfth graders realized that the two research teams presented opposite hypotheses. The number of students that were not aware of the contradiction decreased dramatically from ninth grade to twelfth grade. As twelfth graders were those who had received the most instruction on the topic, this result could be interpreted as due to level of topic knowledge. The more knowledge students had, the less difficulty they had noticing the contradiction and realizing the need for change. Nevertheless, it cannot be discarded that developmental factors might have contributed to these differences.

TABLE 6.1
Students Who Were Aware and Not Aware of Contradiction Between Dr. Smith and Dr. Hamilton's Hypotheses (Frequencies and Percentage They Represent in the Total Number of Subjects of Each Group)

	Awareness of contradiction	
Grade	*Aware of contradiction (Category 1)*	*Not aware of contradiction (Category 2)*
9th grade	49	20
n = 69	(71%)	(29%)
11th grade	45	12
n = 57	(78.9%)	(21.1%)
12th grade	61	2
n = 63	(96.8%)	(3.2%)
TOTAL	155	34
N = 189	(82%)	(18%)

Note. From Limón and Carretero (1997).

When individuals have low domain-specific knowledge about the content of a problem, as was the case with the younger students in our study, they may have difficulties noticing contradictions and therefore, they may not be not aware of the need for change. This answer from one of the younger students in our study (ninth grader) illustrates this point. When she was asked if both research teams could maintain their hypotheses, she said yes, without being able to explain why. Then, when she was asked which one of the hypotheses presented best explained how the origin of life occurred, she answered:

> *"number 4 (a superior being who created the organic compounds and the conditions necessary for them to be synthesized) because as it is brief and simple I can understand it, and it is not necessary to explain any more"* (Participant 7, ninth grader, condition A+B).

This student was unable to understand the other hypotheses presented, and therefore, she could not evaluate them. Thus, she was unable to notice contradiction and to consider she needed to change something. Being aware of what needs to change was clearly much more difficult or perhaps even impossible for this student. A certain amount of domain-specific knowledge seems to be necessary to: (a) have a position regarding the topic, (b) be able to understand and to evaluate versions alternative to one's own, (c) realize contradictions, and (d) identify what knowledge needs to be changed.

Moreover, the domain of the problem presented might also influence students' awareness of contradiction. Recently, some findings seem to indicate that realizing contradictions may be easier in some domains than others (Limón, 2000).

In this study, participants were 290 seventh graders (aged 12 to 13) and 360 tenth graders (aged 15 to 16). They were presented with three tasks: one about a historical topic (the so-called "Discovery of America"), one about a science topic (the heating of the earth), and one about an ethics problem (a fictional situation involving the concept of friendship). Two alternative views were presented to students on each topic. Three arguments supporting the two views were also introduced. Participants were asked to rate how much they were in agreement with the arguments presented in support of each view. They were also asked a series of questions to determine whether they noticed the contradiction, if they could identify and differentiate the two opposite versions, and if they thought they could be reconciled.

In the case of contradiction, they were asked if both views were contradictory and if it would be possible to find people who may agree with either one. They had to mark their answers on a scale from 1 (totally disagree) to 5 (totally agree). A repeated-measures ANOVA with one between-subjects factor (*grade*, two levels: seventh- and tenth-graders) and one within-subjects factor (*domain*, with three levels: history, science, and ethics) was carried out. The dependent variable measured was the recognition of contradiction. Results revealed a significant main effect of the within-subjects factor, domain, $F(2,1296) = 62.852$, $p < .0001$; a significant effect of the *domain* X *grade* interaction, $F(2, 1296) = 9.239$, $p < .0001$; and no significant effect of the between-subjects factor. Table 6.2 shows the means and standard deviations of domain for the three tasks.

As Table 6.2 shows, students were more able to recognize contradictions in the history task than in the ethics or science task. In the case of history, even if students do not have high domain-specific knowledge, they may be more familiar with the problem. Science problems usually involve more technical concepts totally unfamiliar to students. Instead, history usually employs less technical terms, and many of them are often used in

TABLE 6.2
Means of Contradiction Recognizing
for the History, Science, and Ethics Tasks

	Grade 7th		*Grade 10th*		*Total*	
Domain	*M*	*SD*	*M*	*SD*	*M*	*SD*
History	11.434	.109	11.856	.098	11.645	.073
Ethics	11.238	.103	11.217	.092	11.227	.069
Science	10.897	.101	10.672	.091	10.784	.068

Note. Scores could range from 1 to 15. Tukey test indicated that there were significant differences between the three total means ($p < .0001$). From Limón (2000).

daily life. Students may have heard these terms and this can make history arguments more understandable, although they usually do not know their disciplinary meaning. On the other hand, because of the nature of historical knowledge, historical arguments may induce opinions more often than scientific arguments.

For instance, in our science task, one of the items said: "The heating of the atmosphere due to the increase of CO_2 expelled by cars and factories is the second factor responsible of the temperature increase on the Earth surface." The opposite argument explained that increases in the Earth's volcanic activity due to spontaneous heating of the Earth was the second factor responsible for the temperature increase on the Earth's surface. In contrast, in the history task, one argument said: "The Discovery of America involved the death of many native individuals, but not so many as is usally claimed. Many Spaniards also died. There were laws to avoid the exploitation of the natives. The Day of the Discovery has to be celebrated. It meant a lot of changes for both native and European people." The opposite argument was that no celebration should take place because the "Discovery" only meant the death and exploitation of many natives at the hands of conquerors.

History arguments such as these may be seen as more debatable. Even if students do not know much of the details of history, the issues seem more debatable than those in science. Scientific arguments seem to be less debatable and, in this particular case, more linked to specific knowledge of the effect of CO_2 or the volcanic activity of the Earth. As students' specific knowledge is low, they may not have enough knowledge to identify or support either of the two positions presented.

Also, epistemological beliefs about the domain and about teaching and learning in science and history may be, in part, the cause of these differences. Often science is presented to students as an unquestionable corpus of knowledge. This may explain why students develop beliefs that science and what scientists say is always true, reliable, and unquestionable. They may think that there is no space for opinions in science: theories work or do not work. They may believe that scientific results and theories are based on empirical testing and supported by the scientific method, otherwise they would not be scientific. When students study science and have to solve physics or chemistry problems, for example, their answers are evaluated as right or wrong. In their experience, there is always a scientific model that explains which answers are right and which are wrong.

If students hold these underlying beliefs about science and science learning, it is reasonable to expect them to show difficulties realizing contradictions in science tasks. To be presented two different views of scientific phenomena may be surprising for students who are used to considering there is only one right answer or theory.

In contrast, as illustrated earlier, in history the nature of arguments may seem more debatable than in the case of science, and less specific knowledge is necessary to develop an opinion. Nevertheless, similar to the case of science, students are usually presented only one view of history in lessons and textbooks and they may, therefore, believe there is only one "correct" view of history (as well as science) and it is the one presented in their textbook or by their teacher. But as less specific knowledge is required to develop an opinion and the nature of arguments is more debatable, even students who maintain positivist beliefs about history and its learning may be able to represent two sides of an argument. Issues of "identity" and affect may come into play as students position themselves as in favor of one or the other view. More of our students supported the "Spaniards view" than the "Latin American view" in our study. This might explain why students were able more to identify the two versions and recognize the contradiction in the history task than in the science one, even though they had more difficulty reconciling the two views in the history task because affective engagement was higher than in the science one. Domain differences may influence both students' recognition of contradiction and their reconciliation of opposing views.

Finally, the way anomalous data are presented may overload an individual's cognitive system and make it more difficult to notice contradictions. In the study by Limón and Carretero (1997), introduced briefly earlier, participants were divided into two conditions: A and A+B. Participants in condition A were presented only with anomalous data. Those in condition A+B were presented both anomalous and confirmatory data. Table 6.3 shows that younger students with the lowest level of knowledge about the origin of life were more influenced by the presentation of confirmatory data and anomalous data. When only conflicting data were presented (A condition), all groups noticed the contradiction. Instead, when both conflicting and confirmatory data were presented (A+B condition), younger students had more problems noticing contradictions. Thus, the presentation of both confirmatory and conflicting data affected younger students more. A possible explanation of these results may be that younger students' cognitive systems may be overloaded in the A+B condition, impeding their recognition of contradiction. However, older students seemed not to show this overloading effect, which might be due either to developmental differences or to their higher level of domain-specific knowledge about the task content.

Experts in a domain are likely able to deal with larger amounts of data without suffering an overloading effect. However, a study with history experts (Limón, 1995; Limón & Carretero, 1998, 1999) showed that confirmatory data were more salient for these individuals than conflicting data, and that history experts used only about 60% of the documents presented (no

TABLE 6.3
Students That Were and Were Not Aware of the Contradiction in the A+B and A Conditions (Frequencies and Percentage They Represented From the Total Number of Subjects in Each Group)

		Awareness of contradiction	
Grade	*Condition*	*Aware of contradiction (Category 1)*	*Not aware of contradiction (Category 2)*
9th grade n = 35	A+B	18 (51.4%)	17 (48.6%)
11th grade n = 28	A+B	19 (67.9%)	9 (32.1%)
12th grade n = 31	A+B	29 (93.5%)	2 (6.5%)
TOTAL N = 94	A+B	66 (70.2%)	28 (29.8%)
9th grade n = 34	A	31 (91.2%)	3 (8.8%)
11th grade n = 29	A	26 (89.7%)	3 (10.3%)
12th grade n = 32	A	32 (100%)	0 (0%)
TOTAL N = 95	A	89 (93.7%)	6 (6.3%)

Note. From Limón and Carretero (1997). Reproduced with permission.

significant differences between the two groups—historians and undergraduates—were found). This suggests that, possibly, when individuals feel quite sure of their knowledge, as in the case of experts, they may bias their reading and evaluation of data, not paying so much attention to the conflicting data, so that sometimes they are less likely to notice contradiction.

Regardless, becoming aware of contradiction is not sufficient to guarantee change. This point is illustrated with some excerpts taken from students' answers in the studies previously described. One seventh-grader (#245) was asked about the possibility of reconciling alternative views about the history task. In the task, participants were told that each view was taken from a different textbook. She answered:

> "No, it is impossible to reconcile these views. Nothing is the same! They're totally different. If these are real textbooks, what a mess the world is in!" (From Limón, 2000).

This student believes all textbooks should say exactly the same thing. History should always be "the same." No alternative or discrepant views are possible. Different views would mean something was wrong. She is perfectly aware of the contradiction, but instead of thinking something should be changed in her knowledge base, she attributes the contradiction to the "poor quality" of the textbooks that were incapable of telling the truth (or at least one of them was). If they do not say the truth, then how can one be sure of one's knowledge? This seems to be the question she is asking in her mind. This is why noticing contradiction leads some students to become confused and unsure of their knowledge. Consider these examples P. and his classmate (both tenth-graders) were discussing how to answer in the history task. After some minutes of discussion, P. raised his hand and said to the experimenter:

> "We are discussing our answers. We realize there are two versions, but we are confused. Please, tell us which one is true, because *only one* can be true, and *only one* answer will be correct" (From Limón, 2000).

> "I don't know which one is right. It's clear that one is telling the truth and the other is lying. I think everyone should maintain their hypothesis until somebody discovers which of the two hypotheses is actually true. In my opinion, this is not going to happen. I disagree with this hypothesis—number 5—because I think God is the creator of life" (From Limón & Carretero, 1997, eleventh-grader).

These students did not really notice the contradiction, because they do not accept the two versions as valid. They noticed there were two versions, but they did not realize the contradiction between the two. To realize that the two versions contradict, one would have to consider both versions to be viable explanations, but these students considered one version to be true and the other to be false. Both cannot be true because of their epistemological beliefs that there should be only one right answer. For them, there is no need to change anything at all. Rather, they just need to discover who is telling the truth and who is lying! The goal of the task became to find out which one was "correct."

Students are likely so used to solving well-defined problems, where only one solution exists, that they cannot conceive of problems or situations that may have more than one solution. This epistemological belief may be applied, as our examples illustrate, to either history or science.

General or domain-specific epistemological beliefs may impede individuals' awareness of the need to change their knowledge. However, epistemological beliefs may also facilitate the awareness of the need to change. For instance, scientists or historians considering knowledge as something dynamic and subjected to review are not surprised or confused about the possibility of finding alternative views to their own; rather, they expect as much.

Volitional Prerequisite and Domain-Specific Knowledge

I defined the volitional prerequisite of intentional conceptual change as willingness to change. This section discusses first what is necessary before there is willingness to change, and how the level of domain-specific knowledge may contribute or not to creating the right conditions, and second, why there is resistance from individuals to be willing to change.

What Is Necessary for Individuals to be Willing to Change Their Knowledge? Once more, on considering the conditions necessary for willingness to change, we must take into account cognitive, motivational, and emotional factors. As Strike and Posner (1985, 1992) pointed out, for individuals to be willing to make changes in their knowledge, the new theories or ideas have to be considered intelligible, plausible, and fruitful. In other words, they have to be "cognitively appealing."

On the other hand, for individuals to be willing to change, it is necessary to pay attention to the task or problem presented, and to be interested and engaged in the task. Brophy (1999) indicated that for this to happen, an optimal match between the individual's prior knowledge and experiences and the features of the learning domain or activity has to occur. Moreover, the domain has to be familiar enough to be of interest to the learner. So, for individuals to be willing to change, the problem or task has to be meaningful not only in the cognitive sense (enabling them to understand the content and to be able to notice what to change), but also in the motivational sense (enabling them to appreciate its value and find it relevant for their goals).

Eccles (1983) proposed three general interest or value beliefs: interest, utility, and importance of the task. *Interest* refers to an individual's intrinsic preference for a domain or task. *Utility* refers to the potential usefulness of the task or content for individuals to achieve some of their goals. *Importance* refers to the individual's perception of the salience or personal relevance of the task. It is more likely that an individual will be willing to change if he or she is intrinsically interested in the content or task, but overall he or she has to be able to see the change as potentially useful and personally relevant.

If individuals are interested in a domain or task and domain-specific knowledge is high, willingness to change is more likely than if their domain-specific knowledge is low. If domain-specific knowledge is low, individuals may have difficulty determining what to change and evaluating the relevance and utility of change. This was the case of some of the participants in the study on the origin of life described earlier (Limón & Carretero, 1997). One of them responded to the task as follows:

> "Well, I realize that the two [research] teams (Dr. Hamilton's and Dr. Smith's) are saying different things, but I don't know who is saying the right thing. I do not have enough knowledge to say who I agree with. I realize I should change my answer, but I have chosen hypothesis 5 [Oparin's hypothesis] because that is what I have studied, and it is the one I understand the best" (from Limón & Carretero, 1997, eleventh-grader).

When individuals are highly interested in the domain or task and have a high level of domain-specific knowledge, willingness to change is determined by the perception of the salience of change and the evaluation of the utility of change. As the next research data show, willingness to change does not come easy for experts. Only when the change is seen as useful and relevant to achieve certain goals does the willingness to change occur. Consider an expert scientist doing research in his or her field of specialization. Some empirical results may be found that do not fit with the dominant theory of the field. He or she will notice the contradiction between the new data and the theory, be very engaged and interested in explaining these data, but still may not change. Nevertheless, if the change is seen as very useful and important for supporting a new theory—which may be a goal—the scientist will likely be willing to change.

If individuals have low interest in a domain or a task, and their level of domain-specific knowledge is low, willingness to change is not likely at all. Finally, if individuals have high domain-specific knowledge but are not interested in the task, they may process the information in a shallow manner and willingness to change is not likely to appear. Nevertheless, if change is perceived as personally relevant and useful, individuals may be willing to change. In other words, there may be complex interactions between prior knowledge and interest that moderate the relation between prior knowledge and conceptual change. Figure 6.1 summarizes the interaction between the level of domain-specific knowledge, the level of interest in the domain or task, and an individual's perception of the utility and relevance of change.

Individual differences may also influence willingness to change. For instance, individuals who have a high need for cognition (Kardash & Scholes, 1996), a disposition toward actively open-minded thinking (Sà, West & Stanovich, 1999), a high ability to "decontextualize" their reasoning or separate their reasoning from their beliefs and goals. (Stanovich & West, 1997), have less need for closure (Kruglanski &Webster, 1996), and more relativistic epistemological beliefs (Hofer & Pintrich, 1997; Schommer, 1990, 1993) may be more willing to change than those who present the opposite characteristics.

Why Is It Difficult for Individuals to Be Willing to Change? Affective and emotional factors may be obstacles for individuals' willingness to change. This is quite frequent in history where personal values and cul-

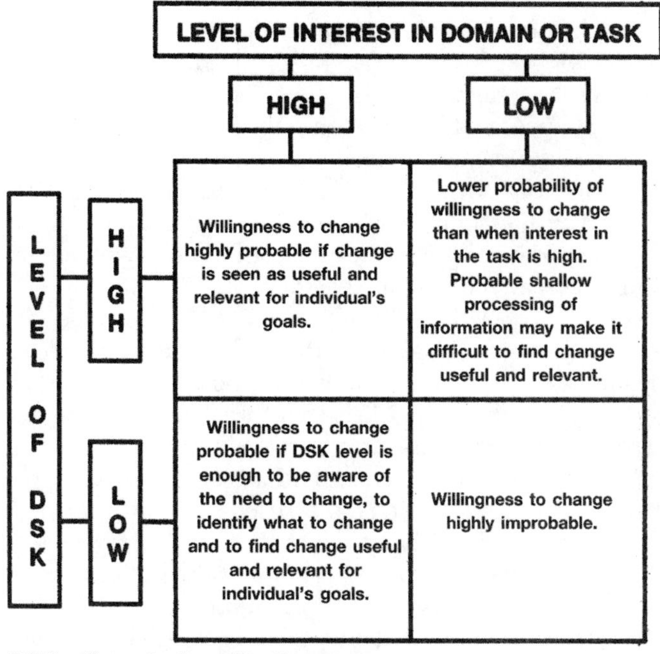

FIG. 6.1. Interaction of the level of domain specific knowledge and the level of interest for an individual to be willing to change.

tural and national identity are often reflected in the narrations of the past constructed by historians. For instance, now that Europeans are developing a European identity, clashes between national identity and European identity occur. For the British, it is difficult to accept the idea of substituting the pound with the euro, miles by kilometers, etc. These units have been used for centuries and are symbols of the UK. Even if British citizens agree there are advantages to the economical union from a cognitive point of view, there are still identity feelings with affective and emotional components that may obstruct change. The "cognitive appeal" of the anomalous data or conflicting information may be not enough to induce change. If the prior knowledge to be changed has an affective charge, it is more entrenched and consequently, it is more difficult to change. In such a circumstance, individuals may not want to change. In these cases, the second requisite of intentional conceptual change, willingness to change, is more difficult or even impossible to achieve.

The literature on biased reasoning has presented clear results consistent with this idea (e.g, Baron, Granato, Spranca, & Teubal, 1993; Ditto & López, 1992; Kardash & Scholes, 1996; Klaczynski, 1997; Klaczynski &

Gordon, 1996; Klaczynski, Gordon, & Fauth, 1997; Kunda, 1990; Sà et al., 1999; Stanovich & West, 1997). When information is pertinent to personal goals, theories, or beliefs, individuals apply a wide range of reasoning tactics to preserve the integrity of their ideas. Consequently, individuals are not objective processors of information. This may explain why often, as illustrated in the prior section, anomalous data may be not enough for individuals to notice contradictions. According to Klaczynski et al. (1997), individuals display the competence necessary for critical reasoning only when it is activated by certain contextual conditions (e.g., time constraints are relaxed, accuracy motivation provided).

The availability of both types of reasoning (everyday heuristics and critical reasoning principles) allows individuals to use sophisticated strategies when they are required to suit their purposes. When individuals are faced with goals, theories, or beliefs that threaten theirs, more sophisticated reasoning strategies are activated and information is processed more deeply. Alternatively, when individuals are faced with goals, theories, or beliefs that preserve theirs, they use less sophisticated strategies (Klaczynski & Fauth, 1997; Klaczynski et al., 1997; Kunda, 1990). In these cases, they reason according to the principle of "cognitive economy" and invoke only shallow processing of information.

Some of the results obtained in the studies with history experts (Limón, 1995; Limón & Carretero, 1997, 1998) illustrate how experts developed more sophisticated reasoning strategies when conflicting information was presented. Expert historians and final-year history undergraduates solved a microhistorical problem about the expulsion of the Morisco population from Spain in the XVII century.

Participants (15 in each group) were interviewed about the topic before being presented with any information. They were then posed the problem and asked who benefited from the expulsion of the Moriscos from the dukedom of Spain where a large number of them lived. Four answers were possible: the nobility (particularly the duke himself), a small oligarchy, both of these, or none of these. Five documents about different factors that might contribute to explaining who benefited from the expulsion were presented, and after the participants had read them, they were asked the same question again: Who benefited from the expulsion? Subsequently, another five documents about the same factors, complementary to the first five, were presented, and individuals were again asked the question. Each document contained data that could be interpreted as being in favor of or in opposition to each of the four possible answers. Finally, individuals were presented with a table (Table 6.4) showing arguments elaborated with data contained in the ten documents presented that were in opposition to the answer they had given after being presented with all the documents.

TABLE 6.4
Participants' Answers After Presenting Conflicting Information

	GROUP 1 (STUDENTS) (*n* = 15)		*GROUP 2 (PROFESSORS)* (*n* = 15)	
CATEGORY 1: Subjects who maintained their hypothesis.	S1, S2, S8, S9, S10	5 (33.33%)	S2, S3, S7, S9, S10, S15	6 (40%)
CATEGORY 2: Subjects who maintained their hypothesis, but slightly.	S3	1 (6.67%)	S1, S8	2 (13.3%)
CATEGORY 3: Subjects who moved back to H_0, but adding some confirming data.	S5, S6, S14, S15	4 (26.67%)		0 (0%)
CATEGORY 4: Subjects who extended their hypothesis to include the new data.	S4, S13	2 (13.33%)	S4, S5, S6, S11, S12, S13, S14	7 (46.67%)
CATEGORY 5: Subjects who changed their initial hypothesis partially.	S7, S12, S11	3 (20%)		0 (0%)

Note. From Limón and Carretero (1999). Reproduced with permission.

The relevant result for the point I want to illustrate was that historians showed more sophisticated reasoning strategies than undergraduates when they were presented with theory-threatening information in the final phase of the study. Although both groups of participants showed themselves to be "conservative," preserving their initial answer and previous beliefs and knowledge about the topic of the problem, there were qualitative differences in the way the historians justified their answers. Historians used their domain-specific knowledge about that period—and not only about the topic in question—to include conflicting data in their explanations, but to keep the core of their initial theories and beliefs, and not to change them. Their implicit purpose seemed to be to maintain their initial theories and beliefs (although, in order to include the conflicting data they knew they should include, they introduced some minor changes.) They seemed unwilling to change their core theories.

Why were the historians so resistant to change, even though they clearly noticed the contradiction and the need to change their hypothesis? Consider this example:

> Subject 6, Group 2 (Modern History specialists), in Phase 2 (after presentation of the last five documents):
>
> "Apparently, the oligarchy benefited, because they obtained lands and nobility titles, but the economic data does not show that the Duke benefited. However, this seems to me a contradiction, because it does not coincide with typical situations where there exist power networks. In these networks, if one benefits, everybody benefits. There is a demographic increase, according to Documents 4 and 9, and a comparison between Document 2 and Document 7 shows that the sugar cane crop was lost. Thus, the answer I consider to be the most correct is "B" (the oligarchy benefited)."
>
> In Phase 3, after seeing the table with the conflicting data, the same participant said:
>
> "In the short term the Duke does not benefit on an economic level, although perhaps he does so on a political level (he may obtain greater political control in Gandía, since the main offices were held by people belonging to his network—though it would be necessary to know more details, for instance, the family relationships between the Duke and members of the oligarchy). In the long term, there are political benefits for the Duke. With regard to the oligarchy, in the short term, particularly during the years immediately after the expulsion, they could lose out from an economic point of view, but in the medium term they benefited because they obtained lands and political power. In the long term they also benefited, because their social position improved, and they constituted a group with political–social power to face the Royal Court. Lands became an instrument for acquiring socio-political power, as was usual in that historical period."

In brief, her final answer was: in the short term and at an economic level, "D" (none of them); in the medium term, "B" (the oligarchy); and in the long term from an economic, social and political point of view, "C" (both of them).

She integrated some of her prior ideas: first, the expulsion was damaging at an economic level in the short term, but beneficial at a political and social level in the long term; second, in that period it was usual to find the establishment of networks of power motivated by a desire for social improvement (in the case of the oligarchy), and for the power of privileged groups to be maintained. She seemed to be using a kind of schema about how political and social power worked in that period, and trying to make the conflicting data fit that schema. And she was very sure of her knowledge and of this schema for explaining a problem she categorized as typical of that period. She did not see the need to change this schema, even though there were data she might have considered that would have forced her to do so. She made some changes in her explanation to adjust the data to her schema. She noticed the contradiction and the need to make some changes in her explanation, but she did not see the need to change a more general schema that she did not want to change, because she was highly confident. She had a wide experience of working with historical data from this period, and she relied absolutely on her core knowledge base.

So, experts may be more "unwilling" to change their core prior theories and beliefs because they have a high level of domain knowledge and feel sure of what they know. Literature on expertise (e.g., Boshuizen & Schmidt, 1992; Brammer, 1997; Custers, Boshuizen, & Schmidt, 1998; Norman, Brooks, Colle, & Hatala, 2000; O'Byrne & Goodyear, 1997; Patel, Kaufman, & Arocha, 2000; Rikers, Schmidt, & Boshuizen, 2000) has shown that experts often develop schemas that encapsulate domain knowledge, allowing them to work at a higher level of generality and in a heuristic way. These schemas are powerful explanatory tools in which experts feel very confident, because of their demonstrated efficacy.

At the same time, however, experts realized they should include the conflicting data presented, in contrast to the younger high school students in the other studies, who had low knowledge and were often not even aware of contradictions. The experts showed rather sophisticated strategies to fit the conflicting data to their core prior knowledge about the topic, introducing some limited changes in their answers. Further, they knew they were doing an experimental task for a psychologist, and a few of them seemed to believe they could not change their mind radically. They might be maintaining beliefs such as: "If I change my mind radically, I will not be considered an expert. Experts should show a consistent and stable behavior because their knowledge base is solidly rooted. They cannot change their mind two or three times in an hour and a half, and cannot show doubt, particularly when the problem is presented by a psychologist who wants to evaluate expert historians' reasoning."

In the last phase of the task, they were shown a table depicting opposing arguments supported by data contained in the documents they had reviewed earlier. They seemed to think that as experts, they should have noticed the conflicting data when the documents were presented initially. They seemed to feel their base knowledge and their reliability as experts were being questioned. They might have been trying to preserve their self-efficacy, or even to some extent their self-esteem, by preserving their core prior knowledge about the topic. This could also force them to develop more complex explanations to fit the conflicting data into their core prior knowledge about the topic avoiding a more radical change.

For individuals to develop and use sophisticated reasoning strategies to preserve their beliefs, theories, or goals, they should have a certain level of domain-specific knowledge. The higher the level, the better and more frequently these sophisticated reasoning strategies may be used. At least, this is what our research findings seem to support. In the study just described, only historians used these more sophisticated reasoning strategies and processed information more deeply when they were presented conflicting data. Undergraduates felt confused when they were presented the conflicting data. They noticed the conflict and a few of them changed their final answer, just accepting the conflicting data without building a new explanation, and they became very confused about what explanation could work to solve the problem. Most of the undergraduates noticed the contradiction, but they just seemed to prefer to put aside the conflicting data and to maintain their answer. They were unable to build a new explanation integrating the whole data. Also, historians were more aware than undergraduates of the threat conflicting data might involve for them, precisely because of their greater domain-specific knowledge.

Individuals with low or naïve domain-specific knowledge—even if they have adequate reasoning competence—may have difficulty in recognizing contradiction, evaluating conflicting data as threatening, applying their reasoning strategies and processing information deeply, precisely because of their lack of domain-specific knowledge.

Self-Regulation Prerequisite for Intentional Conceptual Change

The third prerequisite for intentional conceptual change consists of the application of self-regulation abilities to the process of change. Self-regulation abilities have been widely discussed (e.g., Boekaerts, Pintrich, & Zeidner, 2000; Pintrich, 2000; Schraw & Dennison, 1994; Schunk & Zimmerman, 1994; Winne, 1995).

Self-regulation has a metacognitive component. For instance, Hacker (1998) indicated there is general consensus that metacognition includes "knowledge of one's knowledge, processes, and cognitive and affective states; and the ability to consciously and deliberately monitor and regulate one's knowledge, processes, and cognitive and affective states" (p. 11).

Schraw (1998) distinguished two components of metacognition: knowledge of cognition and regulation of cognition. *Knowledge of cognition* refers to what individuals know about their cognition. It includes three kinds of metacognitive awareness: declarative, procedural, and conditional knowledge. *Regulation of cognition* refers to a set of activities individuals do to control their learning, such as regulating attentional resources and learning strategies or attending to comprehension breakdowns. These two components are correlated (Schraw & Dennison, 1994).

Similarly, these two components of cognition can also be distinguished for motivation and emotion. *Metamotivation* and *metaemotion* refer to knowledge and regulation of motivation and emotion. In general, regulation of cognition has received more attention by researchers than regulation of motivation and emotion (Boekaerts, 1995; Pintrich, 2000). As Alexander (1995) pointed out, self-regulation is at the intersection of motivation, cognition, and metacognition. However, each has its own definitional problems, making self-regulation a fuzzy concept. Nevertheless, there is consensus that self-regulation involves planning, monitoring, and evaluation abilities (Schraw, 1998). I consider self-regulation abilities to include cognition, motivation, and emotion. Although these areas can be distinguished theoretically, in practice they are highly interrelated.

Therefore, if this third prerequisite of intentional conceptual change is fulfilled, individuals should be able to plan, monitor, and evaluate their change process, not only in the cognitive area, but also in the motivational and emotional ones. Individuals who are able to self-regulate their change process should be aware of their own knowledge and beliefs and should be willing to change to achieve their goals. They should also be able to (a) identify the discrepancies between their own knowledge and alternative views, (b) identify the need for change, (c) identify what needs to be changed, (d) maintain engagement in the task in accordance with their goals and interest, (e) plan, monitor, and evaluate their motivation, emotions, interest, and strategic skills in order to achieve the goal of change, (f) plan and monitor activities that may help the change process, and (g) evaluate the results of the change process.

Is self-regulation of cognition, motivation, and emotion the only prerequisite for intentional conceptual change? My answer is no. Even if individuals are good self-regulators, they may find it difficult to apply their self-regulation skills if they do not have sufficient domain-specific knowledge.

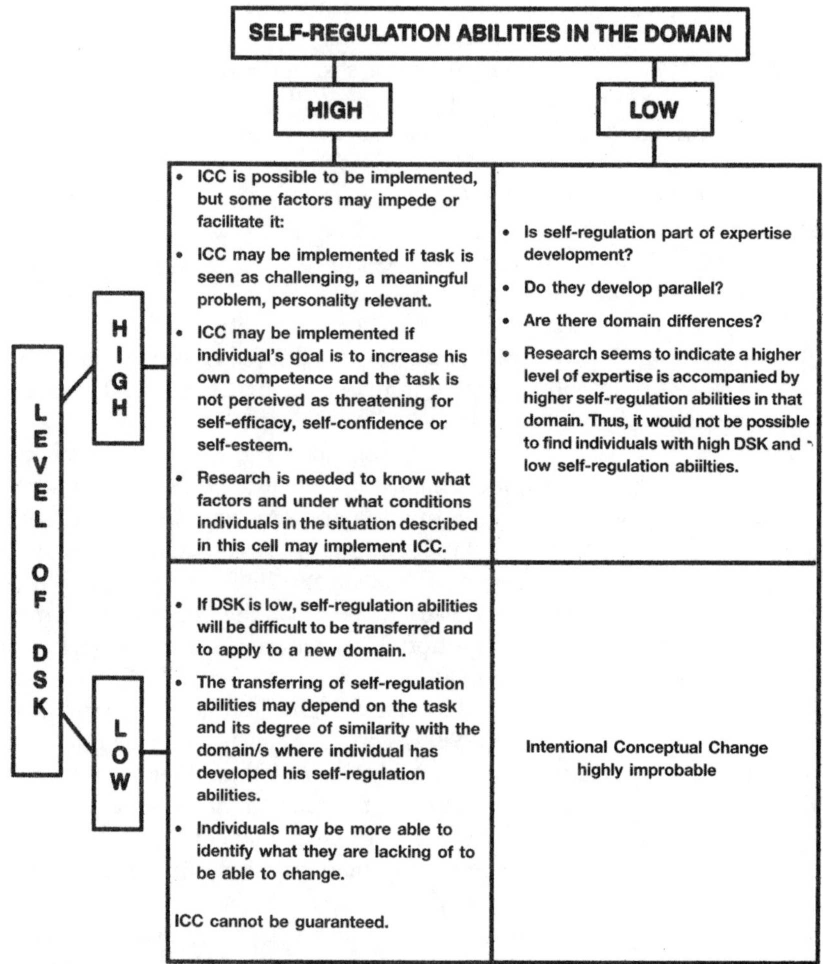

FIG. 6.2. Level of domain specific knowledge, self-regulation and intentional conceptual change.

Figure 6.2 displays the potential interactions between high and low domain knowledge and high and low self-regulatory abilities and their role in intentional conceptual change.

Regarding the second requisite of intentional conceptual change, volition, good self-regulators have abilities that may help to create favorable internal conditions for the process of change. They also have self-management skills that may help them regulate levels of arousal to handle stress, emotions, anxiety, and boredom. These skills undoubtedly facilitate individuals' willingness to change, but as was the case with some of our students when they were presented hypotheses about the origin of life, they may be willing to change but unable to have the arguments to support change. They know they have to change, they realize their hypotheses cannot explain some facts and results, but their low knowledge may obstruct a successful utilization of their self-regulation skills.

Good self-regulators are able to detect roadblocks to change and actions needed to achieve change. Even so, individuals may consciously decide they do not want to change. In the example about the euro as a new currency, good self-regulators may identify their feelings and why they are resistant to change, but they may decide they do not want to change. In this case, change is a goal to be avoided, not approached.

Low or biased prior knowledge on the topic or in the domain may contribute to "unwillingness" to change. This may vary with the domain; the phenomenon seems to be more frequent in history and social sciences, where issues are considered more debatable and more attached to emotional reactions, than in science. Good self-regulators may be more aware of their own biases, although this does not guarantee change. In the literature on the psychology of thinking and reasoning, it is well known that individuals try to protect their beliefs (Baron et al., 1993; Evans, 1989; Kardash & Scholes, 1996; Klaczynski, 1997; Klaczynski & Gordon, 1996; Klaczynski et al., 1997; Sà et al., 1999; Stanovich & West, 1997). Sometimes individuals are not aware of the desire to maintain their beliefs. Even for good self-regulators, it would require a great deal of effort to use their skills to change their knowledge and beliefs.

Self-regulation is necessary for intentional conceptual change. Willingness to change and to consider change as a personal goal are also necessary conditions for intentional conceptual change. The level of domain knowledge influences these factors. In the next section, I discuss briefly how the level of expertise may influence self-regulation and intentional conceptual change.

Domain-Specific Knowledge Level, Self-Regulation and Intentional Conceptual Change. Discussing the relationship between cognitive and metacognitive abilities and domain-specific knowledge, Schraw (1998) argued that cognitive skills are more encapsulated within the boundaries of the domain than metacognitive ones. He explained that both metacognitive knowledge of cognition and regulation of cognition improve as expertise within a domain improves. Therefore, metacognition and regulation of cognition would be domain-general in nature, although initially they may start out as domain- or task-specific.

In contrast, Boekaerts (1995) considered self-regulated learning to be domain-specific. Learning goals have a double trajectory: "learning how to" and "learning to monitor one's learning." At the initial states of learning, when instructions to monitor learning are given, students with a low level of domain knowledge are at a disadvantage.

In general, experts are more able to regulate their learning than novices, and according to those who agree with Schraw, they are also more able to transfer metacognitive knowledge and regulatory skills to new domains, even if they are not experts in those domains. Applying this to conceptual change, it could be said that transfer of these skills may facilitate the process of change, although conceptual change may be difficult to achieve if individuals do not have at least the minimum amount of domain-specific knowledge required by the task to understand it and thus be able to apply their metacognitive and self-regulation skills.

For example, consider a task that intends to promote weak conceptual change about a particular concept in physics. The task involves reading some texts to answer some questions. The texts refer to the results obtained by two different teams of researchers. Findings from the two groups contradict each other. Imagine the participants were a group of experts in literature, a group of experts in physics, and a group of students who are novices in both literature and physics. Experts in literature are likely to be expert readers. When presented a text in physics, they are able to transfer their metacognitive knowledge about reading to this text. They may plan how they are going to learn from the text. They may plan their reading process. For example, they know they need to extract the main ideas. They monitor and evaluate the process. However, as their prior knowledge on the text topic is very low, they will be unable to apply their reading skills to the text and their understanding of it will be likely rather limited. Thus, their performance in the task may be quite similar to that of novices. However, as experts in literature they may transfer their metacognitive and self-regulation skills; they may be more aware of the obstacles to be overcome to accomplish the task. They likely may know what they need to do to overcome these obstacles and how to do it. For instance, they may know that to extract the main ideas of the text, they need to know the meaning of technical words that appear in the text, and plan to look them up in a technical dictionary. In contrast, novices may not be aware of their potential problems understanding the text and the task itself and be unable to establish a plan to effectively remedy them. This is summarized by the bottom left cell in Fig. 6.2.

Experts in literature may be able to transfer a general strategy to solve their current problem. They may examine the goal of the task, evaluate their resources, and decide what they need to do to accomplish their goals. They will likely look for the goal and objectives of the task at the beginning of the text, according to what they are accustomed to doing when reading other texts. In contrast, novices may not be able to identify the type of text presented and its characteristics.

Thus, these metacognitive and self-regulation skills may help experts to be aware of what they know, what they need to know to accomplish the task, and where the difference lies between their current and desired knowledge states. Therefore, they may realize better than novices what they need to change. The identification of the differences between what they know and what they should know may also contribute to their greater willingness to change than novices in both literature and physics.

Good self-regulators, with low levels of domain-specific knowledge, as may be the case with literature experts reading outside their domain, are more likely to activate an intentional conceptual change process than naïve or novice self-regulators, as may be the case with students who are novices in both literature and physics.

If the task presented evaluates only individuals' performance in the conceptual change task by assessing their answers to some questions presented immediately after reading texts on physics, it is likely that both groups (experts in literature and novices in both literature and physics) will show similar outcomes. However, if the task introduced provides individuals time to reflect about what they are asked and what they need to do to accomplish the task, and allowed individuals to carry out their planning before their performance is evaluated, perhaps novices and good self-regulators (experts in literature in my example) would show better performance than novice self-regulators (student who are novices in both literature and physics in my example). For the latter, an intentional conceptual change process will be almost impossible to activate. This is represented by the bottom right cell in Fig. 6.2.

According to Boekaerts' Model of Adaptable Learning, students' continuously judge whether a learning situation is benign, neutral, or threatening for their well-being (Boekaerts, 1992, 1996; Boekaerts & Niemivirta, 2000). This "nonstop evaluation that results in emotion/action readiness of upcoming and ongoing learning activities" (Boekaerts & Niemivirta, 2000, p. 427) is what she defined as *appraisal.*

A central assumption of Boekaerts' model is that individuals self-regulate their behavior according to two basic priorities. First, individuals want to extend their knowledge and skills, in order to expand their personal resources. Second, individuals want to keep their available personal resources "to prevent loss, damage and distortions of well-being" (p. 428). Each learning situation triggers a network of specific connotations for each student. In her model, this is represented by links between the appraisal process and the contents of a dynamic working model. This working model has three components that feed it with information continuously. Each component constitutes a different source of information.

Component 1 is the perception of the learning situation. It includes the task, the instructions given by the teacher and the physical and social context. Component 2 includes knowledge relevant for the learning situation: activated domain-specific knowledge and skills, and cognitive and metacognitive strategies that were successful in the domain. Component 3 refers to aspects of individuals' self-system: goal hierarchy, values, and motivational beliefs related to the domain activated by the learning situation.

Appraisals triggered by each learning situation are unique because the information is different for every learning situation. Appraisals elicit positive or negative experiential states and specific behavioral intentions. Positive appraisals are evoked when the information in the dynamic working model is positive. This means that either relevant scripts are available (domain-specific knowledge) or the task to be performed is relevant for personal goals and gains. Negative appraisals occur either when no relevant scripts or domain-specific knowledge are available or when the learner is not disposed to be very engaged in the task.

Positive and negative appraisals lead learners to two different modes of processing information to learn. Positive appraisals direct individuals' learning intentions and behavior toward a *mastery mode* where "gains in resources" (to increase competence) is the main goal pursued. Negative appraisals, on the other hand, direct individuals' learning intentions and behavior toward a *coping mode,* where "prevention of loss of resources" is the goal pursued. The coping mode urges students to protect their egos or restore their well-being, so it is also called *ego-protective mode*. Along a particular learning situation, learners can switch from one mode of processing to the other.

Applying this model to self-regulation and intentional conceptual change, when individuals are presented with a conceptual change task such as the ones illustrated previously, if they have a very low level of domain knowledge or no domain knowledge at all, the task may trigger a negative appraisal. This may happen because no relevant knowledge can be activated (Component 2 of Boekaerts' model), and/or because individuals are not willing to become engaged in the task or are not interested in the domain of the task (Component 3). Moreover, the task may be perceived as too difficult. In this case, the coping mode of processing is likely to be activated, self-regulation skills are not activated, and an intentional conceptual change process does not take place (the bottom right cell in Fig. 6.2).

When individuals have a high level of domain knowledge (the top two cells in Fig. 6.2), whether the coping or the learning mode is activated depends more on the contributions of Components 1 and 3 to the dynamic internal model. If the task is perceived as challenging and individuals feel engaged and motivated, the activation of the learning mode to gain new knowledge is highly probable. Self-regulation abilities will be activated and an intentional conceptual change is more likely to take place, although it would also be necessary for the individual to be willing to change (information provided by Component 3 should indicate this) and to see the need for change (information provided by Components 1 and 2 should indicate this).

As earlier indicated, individuals may switch from one processing mode to another. Thus, it is possible that individuals who started to work mindfully on a task later switched from the mastery to the coping or ego-protective mode. For instance, students who lack metacognitive knowledge and skills usually find it difficult to interpret their failure in a task. Rather than trying to find out what the source of difficulty is, what metacognitive control they lack, they may opt to protect their ego. This may happen because they have lost confidence in their capacity to learn in that particular situation (Component 3) or because they do not have sufficient domain-specific knowledge (Component 2). This may also change their perception of the task (Component 1). They may consider it to be too difficult. This may happen to those learners that have low domain-specific knowledge and/or are low self-regulators when they are faced with a conceptual change task. Thus, the intentional conceptual change process that may have been already initiated will be aborted and learners will switch to the ego-protective or coping mode, withholding effort and putting obstacles in their performance path. This "self-handicapping" strategy has been reported in the literature (e.g., Boekaerts & Niemivirta, 2000; Covington, 1992; Jones & Berglas, 1978). The strategies that students may be activating might explain the poor results often obtained after implementing instructional programs to promote conceptual change (e.g., Tillema & Knol, 1997).

Switching from one mode to another and developing ego-protective strategies may also appear in the case of individuals with high domain-specific knowledge. For instance, some of the experts in history seemed to behave in such a way when they solved the Morisco problem described earlier. In the final phase of the task, when they were faced with contradictory information, instead of changing their initial schemas activated during the task (Component 2) that took more than 2 hours of work (the task was seen as effortful, Component 1), they seemed to switch from the mastery to the ego-protective mode. To prevent the loss of confidence in their knowledge and a possible loss of self-efficacy (Component 3), they seemed to show an ego-protective strategy. They protected their core prior theories from conflicting data, developing sophisticated explanations to include the conflicting data and avoid making dramatic changes in their answers. As they have high domain-specific knowledge, they possessed sufficient knowledge resources to build solid and plausible arguments to defend their knowledge and their self-efficacy. Undergraduates, with a lower level of domain knowledge, were unable to build such a strategy.

Contradictory information seemed to have changed some individuals' goals from pursuing learning goals to pursuing ego-protective goals, and this change would involve a change in their self-regulation strategies. Conflicting data may be seen as threatening to individuals' knowledge and self-confidence, thus it seems not surprising that coping or ego-protective strategies may be activated.

Further research is needed to discover which variables may facilitate or impede intentional conceptual change in individuals with a high level of domain knowledge, who are good self-regulators in their domain. The question of whether the development of self-regulation abilities occurs in parallel with domain-specific knowledge acquisition in all domains also merits research attention.

In summary, even if at the beginning of the process, individuals may activate an intentional conceptual change, while engaged in the task the information provided by the three sources may change the processing mode, and intentional conceptual change may be interrupted. The examples described here illustrated how either individuals with low or high domain-specific knowledge may use ego-protective strategies that block an intentional conceptual change process. Further research is needed to study these strategies carefully in relation to conceptual change processes. Figure 6.2 summarizes what was discussed in this section.

SOME CONCLUSIONS AND IMPLICATIONS OF INTENTIONAL CONCEPTUAL CHANGE FOR LEARNING AND TEACHING

Intentional conceptual change is, I believe, one means by which conceptual change can be achieved, but it is not the only one. Many outcomes of conceptual change (i.e., enrichment, revision, reassignment) can potentially be achieved through intentional conceptual change. However, due to the demands required for strong restructuring of learners' knowledge, it seems that intentional conceptual change might be more appropriate, and probably more successful, in promoting this type of outcome.

A strong restructuring of individuals' knowledge is effortful, time demanding, and requires individuals to be highly engaged in the task. It also requires individuals to consider change as relevant and useful. They must consider learning as a personal goal, and a certain amount of domain-specific knowledge is required.

According to my definition, intentional conceptual change demands three main prerequisites: awareness of the need to change and to identify what needs to be changed (the metacognitive prerequisite), willingness to change (volitional prerequisite), and the ability to self-regulate the change process (self-regulation prerequisite).

Therefore, for intentional conceptual change to take place, individuals must be interested and engaged in the task, to be aware and to perceive change as needed and personally relevant. Also, they have to perceive the task as challenging, but not too difficult so as to activate ego-protective goals to avoid self-esteem and self-confidence loss. The primary appraisal (Lazarus & Folkman, 1984) evoked by the task must be positive—the task must be perceived as nonthreatening for the learner's well-being. At the same time, individuals must be able to analyze what is required to handle the task, taking into account the conditions and context in which it is presented. This involves self-regulation abilities and a certain level of domain-specific knowledge. Learners should be oriented toward meaningful learning and increasing their competence through conceptual change.

A certain amount of domain-specific knowledge seems necessary, although not sufficient, for intentional conceptual change to occur. As some of the research examples illustrated, individuals with low or no domain-specific knowledge find it difficult to carry out a process of intentional conceptual change. Intentional conceptual change demands a high level of domain-specific metacognitive skill to plan, monitor, and evaluate the change process. Individuals with low levels of knowledge find it difficult to identify what needs to be changed and why. Moreover, even if they are interested in the domain, because of the difficulties associated with low domain knowledge, they may find the task too frustrating. So, from my perspective, it would be more useful to promote intentional conceptual change when individuals have an intermediate or high level of domain-specific knowledge. Research is needed to support this point and to determine what level of domain knowledge is optimal to carry out an intentional conceptual change and if there are domain differences in the process.

However, high levels of domain-specific knowledge do not guarantee intentional conceptual change. Experts may need to perceive the task as challenging. For them to be willing to activate an intentional conceptual change process, they should be faced with a task they perceive as a "problem," not as a routine task. It has been suggested that experts encapsulate domain knowledge allowing them to work at a higher level of generality (e.g., Boshuizen & Schmidt, 1992; Rikers et al., 2000; Zeitz, 1994). When they are faced with a routine task, they seem to use heuristics developed through acquiring expertise. These heuristics seem to be applied in a rather automatic way to domain tasks where they have expertise. Only when the task involves a *problem* for experts, do they seem to be challenged to invest more effort and face the task in a less automatic way. So, the goal of radical change in experts' knowledge may require a challenging problem so that heuristic problem solving is reduced. Experts also may need to consider the task to be personally relevant. As they are very sure of their knowledge and consider it reliable, sometimes it may be difficult for experts to accept conflicting data because they may perceive it as threatening to their self-confidence, self-efficacy, or even their self-esteem. They may develop conservative strategies to protect their knowledge and avoid radical changes. In some domains, as may be the case with history, individuals' values or beliefs may impede their willingness to change. Throughout this chapter I provided some examples; nevertheless, further research is needed to explore in detail how domain differences may affect intentional conceptual change. Further research is also needed to determine when and under what conditions (learner, task, and domain characteristics) intentional conceptual change is necessary to achieve the type of change pursued.

Regarding the implications for teaching and learning, first, intentional conceptual change should be promoted when students have a certain amount of domain-specific knowledge. Naïve students and those with low levels of domain knowledge encounter many difficulties implementing an intentional conceptual change.

Second, for intentional conceptual change to be implemented, individuals should be explicitly informed that this is the goal to be pursued, and what this goal involves: identification and self-regulation of their beliefs, knowledge, motivation, and emotions. This is demanding and effortful, and these abilities are not usually trained or evaluated as a learning goal by teachers and educational practices, so students will probably need to learn them. In this regard, it is important initially to adjust the tasks presented to learners' characteristics and abilities, in order to scaffold the development of the necessary skills.

Teachers and social contexts (parents, classmates, collaboration among teachers) may also contribute to provide students with the necessary support. For instance, parents and teachers could support students by explaining and emphasizing the importance of self-control and self-knowledge of their own learning process in classes or while helping students to do their homework. Intentional conceptual change may be an outstanding tool to develop intentional learners. Discussion among peers and work in teams may help some students to fulfill the prerequisites of intentional conceptual change.

Intentional conceptual change should be considered as a medium to long term objective, and therefore not recommended if the teacher's goal is to get quick results and quick changes. This feature of intentional conceptual change should not discourage teachers from trying to encourage it. On the contrary, it may provide an excellent opportunity to scaffold students' abilities to regulate their learning, including cognitive, metacognitive, motivational, and emotional aspects. It also provides students the opportunity to develop metacognitive knowledge—to reflect on their learning, their motivation and emotions.

Intentional conceptual change demands that learners pay attention to the process of change and how they control it at every stage. To promote successful intentional conceptual change, it is essential for teachers and researchers to evaluate the process of intentional conceptual change, not only the outcomes of the process.

ACKNOWLEDGMENTS

This chapter has benefited from a grant from the Spanish Ministry of Education (CIDE) to fund my research project on Motivation and Conceptual Change in History, Science, and Ethics (1998–2000). Very special thanks to Paul Pintrich and Gale Sinatra for their invitation to contribute in this volume, for their help to improve this chapter, and for their understanding of the special situation I had during the writing of this chapter. I really appreciate very much their patience, support, and help.

REFERENCES

Alexander, P. A. (1995). Superimposing a situation-specific and domain-specific perspective on an account of self-regulating learning. *Educational Psychologist, 30*(4), 189–194.

Baron, J., Granato, L., Spranca, M., & Teubal, E. (1993). Decision-making biases in children and early adolescence: Exploratory studies. *Merrill-Palmer Quarterly, 39,* 22–46.

Boekaerts, M. (1992). The adaptable learning process: Initiating and maintaining behavioural change. *Journal of Applied Psychology: An International Review, 41,* 377–397.

Boekaerts, M. (1995). Self-regulated learning: Bridging the gap between metacognitive and metamotivation theories. *Educational Psychologist, 30*(4), 195–200.

Boekaerts, M. (1996). Personality and the psychology of learning. *European Journal of Personality, 10,* 377–404.

Boekaerts, M., & Niemivirta, M. (2000). Self-regulated learning. Finding a balance between learning goals and ego-protective goals. In M. Boekaerts, P. R. Pintrich, & M. Zeidner (Eds.), *Handbook of self-regulation* (pp. 417–450). San Diego: Academic Press.

Boekaerts, M., Pintrich, P. R., & Zeidner, M. (Eds.). (2000). *Handbook of Self-regulation.* San Diego: Academic Press.

Boshuizen, H. P. A., & Schmidt, H. G. (1992). On the role of biomedical knowledge in clinical reasoning by experts, intermediates and novices. *Cognitive Science, 16,* 153–184.

Brammer, R. (1997). Case Conceptualization Strategies: The relationship between psychologists' experience levels, academic training, and mode of clinical inquiry. *Educational Psychology Review, 9*(4), 333–351.

Brophy, J. (1999). Toward a model of the value aspects of motivation in education: Developing appreciation for particular learning domains and activities. *Educational Psychologist, 34*(2), 75–85.

Carey, S. (1985). *Conceptual change in childhood.* Cambridge, MA: Bradford/MIT Press.

Chan, C., Burtis, J., & Bereiter, C. (1997). Knowledge building as a mediator of conflict in conceptual change. *Cognition and Instruction, 15*(1), 1–40.

Chi, M. T. H. (1992). Conceptual change within and across ontological categories: examples from learning and discovery in science. In R. Giere (Ed.), *Cognitive models of science: Minnesota studies in the philosophy of science* (pp. 129–186). Minneapolis, MN: University of Minnesota Press.

Chinn, C. A., & Brewer, W. F. (1993). The role of anomalous data in knowledge acquisition: a theoretical framework and implications for science education. *Review of Educational Research, 63*(1), 1–49.

Covington, M. V. (1992). *Making the grade. A self-worth perspective on motivation and school reform.* Cambridge, UK: Cambridge University Press.

Custers, J. F. M., Boshuizen, H. P. A., & Schmidt, H. G. (1998). The role of illness scripts in the development of medical diagnostic expertise: Results from an interview study. *Cognition and Instruction, 16*(4), 367–398.

diSessa, A. (1993). Towards an epistemology of physics. *Cognition and Instruction, 10*(2/3), 105–225.

Ditto, P. H., & López, D.F. (1992). Motivated skepticism: Use of differential decision criteria for preferred and nonpreferred conclusions. *Journal of Personality and Social Psychology, 63,* 568–584.

Dole, J. A., & Sinatra, G. M. (1998). Reconceptualizing change in the cognitive construction of knowledge. *Educational Psychologist, 33*(2/3), 109–128.

Eccles, J. S. (1983). Expectancies, values and academic behaviors. In J. T. Spence (Ed.), *Achievement and achievement motives* (pp. 75–146). San Francisco: Freeman.

Evans, J. St. B.T. (1989). *Bias in human reasoning. Causes and consequences.* Hillsdale, NJ : Lawrence Erlbaum Associates.

Hacker, D. (1998). Definitions and empirical foundations. In D. J. Hacker, J. Dunlosky, & A. C. Graesser (Eds.), *Metacognition in educational theory and practice* (pp. 1–23). Mahwah, NJ: Lawrence Erlbaum Associates.

Hofer, B. K., & Pintrich, P. R. (1997). The development of epistemological theories: Beliefs about knowledge and knowing and their relation to learning. *Review of Educational Research, 67*(1), 88–140.

Ivarsson, J., Schoultz, J., & Säljo, R. (2002). Map reading versus mind reading: Revisiting children's understanding of the shape of the earth. In M. Limón & L. Mason (Eds.), *Reconsidering conceptual change. Issues in theory and practice.* Dordrecht, the Netherlands: Kluwer Academic Press.

James, W. (1890). *The Principles of Psychology.* New York: Henry Holt & Co.

Jones, E. E., & Berglas, S. (1978). Control of attributions about the self through self-handicapping strategies: The appeal of alcohol and the role of underachievement. *Personality and Social Psychology Bulletin, 4,* 200–206.

Kardash, C. M., & Scholes, R. J. (1996). Effects of pre-existing beliefs, epistemological beliefs and need for cognition on interpretation of controversial issues. *Journal of Educational Psychology, 88,* 260–271.

Klaczynski, P. A. (1997). Bias in adolescents' everyday reasoning and its relationship with intellectual ability, personal theories, and self-serving motivation. *Developmental Psychology, 33*(2), 273–283.

Klaczynski, P. A., & Fauth, J. M. (1997). Developmental differences in memory-based intrusions and self-serving statistical reasoning biases. *Merrill-Palmer Quarterly, 43*(4), 539–566.

Klaczynski, P. A., & Gordon, D. H. (1996). Self-serving influences on adolescents' evaluations of belief-relevant evidence. *Journal of Experimental Child Psychology, 62,* 317–339.

Klaczynski, P. A., Gordon, D. H., & Fauth, J. M. (1997). Goal-oriented critical reasoning and individual differences in critical reasoning biases. *Journal of Educational Psychology, 89*(3), 470–485.

Kruglanski, A. W., & Webster, D. M. (1996). Motivated closing the mind: "Seizing" and "freezing." *Psychological Review, 103,* 263–283.

Kuhn, D., & Lao, J. (1998). Contemplation and conceptual change: integrating perspectives from social and cognitive psychology. *Developmental Review, 18*(2), 125–154.

Kunda, Z. (1990). The case for motivated reasoning. *Psychological Bulletin, 108*(3), 480–498.

Lazarus, R. S., & Folkman, S. (1984). *Stress appraisal and coping.* New York: Springer-Verlag.

Limón, M. (1995). *Procesos de razonamiento en la solución de problemas con contenido histórico* [Reasoning and problem solving in history]. Unpublished PhD Dissertation, Universidad Autónoma de Madrid, Madrid.

Limón, M. (2000). *Motivación y cambio conceptual: implicaciones para el aprendizaje y la enseñanza de las Ciencias Sociales y Naturales en la ESO.* [Motivation and conceptual change: Implications for learning and teaching science and social sciences in secondary school]. Final Research Report for the Spanish Ministry of Education (CIDE). Madrid: Universidad Autónoma de Madrid.

Limón, M. (2001). On the cognitive conflict as an instructional strategy for conceptual change: a critical appraisal. *Learning and Instruction, 11*(4/5), 357–380.

Limón, M. (2002). Conceptual change in history. In M. Limón & L. Mason (Eds.), *Reconsidering conceptual change. Issues in theory and practice* (pp. 259–289). Dordrecht, the Netherlands: Kluwer Academic Press.

Limón, M., & Carretero, M. (1997). Conceptual change and anomalous data: a case study in the domain of natural sciences. *European Journal of Psychology of Education, XII*(2), 213–230.

Limón, M., & Carretero, M. (1998). Evidence evaluation and reasoning abilities in the domain of history: An empirical study. In J. F. Voss & M. Carretero (Eds.), *Learning and reasoning in history* (pp. 252–271). London: The Woburn Press.

Limón, M., & Carretero, M. (1999). Conflicting data and conceptual change in history experts. In W. Schnotz, S. Vosniadou, & M. Carretero (Eds.), *New Perspectives on Conceptual Change* (pp. 137–160). Oxford: Elsevier.

Mason, L. (2000). Role of anomalous data and epistemological beliefs in middle school students' theory change about two controversial topics. *European Journal of Psychology of Education, 15*(2), 239–346.

Mayer, R. E. (2002). Understanding conceptual change. In M. Limón & L. Mason (Eds.), *Reconsidering conceptual change. Issues in theory and practice* (pp. 101–111). Dordrecht, the Netherlands: Kluwer Academic Press.

Norman, G. R., Brooks, L. R., Colle, C. L., & Hatala, R. M. (2000). The benefit of diagnostic hypotheses: Experimental study of an instructional intervention for forward and backward reasoning. *Cognition and Instruction, 17*(4), 433–448.

O'Byrne, K., & Goodyear, R. K. (1997). Client assessment by novice and expert psychologists: A comparison of strategies. *Educational Psychology Review, 9*(3), 267–278.

Patel, V. L., Kaufman, D. R., & Arocha, J. F. (2000). Conceptual change in the biomedical and health sciences domain. In R. Glaser (Ed.), *Advances in instructional psychology, educational design, and cognitive science* (pp. 329–392). Mahwah, NJ: Lawrence Erlbaum Associates.

Pintrich, P. R. (2000). The role of goal orientation in self-regulated learning. In M. Boekaerts, P.R. Pintrich, & M. Zeidner (Eds.), *Handbook of self-regulation* (pp. 452–502). San Diego: Academic Press.

Pintrich, P. R., Marx, R. W., & Boyle, R. A. (1993). Beyond cold conceptual change: the role of motivational beliefs and classroom contextual factors in the process of conceptual change. *Review of Educational Research, 63*(2), 167–200.

Rikers, R. M. J. P., Schmidt, H. G., & Boshuizen, H. P. A. (2000). Knowledge encapsulation and the intermediate effect. *Contemporary Educational Psychology, 25*, 150–166.

Sá, W. C., West, R. F., & Stanovich, K. E. (1999). The domain specificity and generality of belief bias: Searching for a generalizable critical thinking skill. *Journal of Educational Psychology, 91*(3), 497–510.

Schommer, M. (1990). Effects of beliefs about the nature of knowledge on comprehension. *Journal of Educational Psychology, 82*, 498–504.

Schommer, M. (1993). Epistemological Development and academic performance among secondary school students. *Journal of Educational Psychology, 85*(3), 406–411.

Schraw, G. (1998). Promoting general metacognitive awareness. *Instructional Science, 26*, 113–125.

Schraw, G., & Dennison, R. S. (1994). Assessing metacognitive awareness. *Contemporary Educational Psychology, 19*, 460–475.

Schunk, D. H., & Zimmerman, B. J. (Eds.). (1994). *Self-regulation of learning and performance: Issues on educational applications*. Hillsdale, NJ: Lawrence Erlbaum Associates.

Stanovich, K. E., & West, R. F. (1997). Reasoning independently if prior belief and individual differences in actively open-minded thinking. *Journal of Educational Psychology, 89*(2), 342–357.

Strike, K. A., & Posner, G. J. (1985). A conceptual change view of learning and understanding. In L. West & L. Pines (Eds.), *Cognitive structure and conceptual change* (pp. 211–231). New York: Academic Press.

Strike, K. A., & Posner, G. J. (1992). A revisionist theory of conceptual change. In R. A. Duschl & R. J. Hamilton (Eds.), *Philosophy of science, cognitive psychology, and educational theory and practice* (pp. 147–176). Albany: State University of New York Press.

Sutherland, N. S. (1992). *Irrationality: why we don't think straight!*. Sussex, UK: Constable Co. Also New Brunswick, NJ: Rutgers University Press.

Tillema, H. H., & Knol, W. E. (1997). Promoting student teacher learning through conceptual change or direct instruction. *Teaching and Teacher Education, 13*(6), 579–595.

Vosniadou, S. (1994). Capturing and modeling the process of conceptual change. *Learning and Instruction, 4*(1), 45–70.

Vosniadou, S., & Brewer, W. F. (1987). Theories of knowledge restructuring in development. *Review of Educational Research, 57*(1), 51–67.

White, R. T. (1994). Conceptual and conceptional change. *Learning and Instruction, 4*(1), 117–121.

Winne, P. H. (1995). Inherent details in self-regulated learning. *Educational Psychologist, 30*, 173–188.

Zeitz, C. M. (1994). Expert-novice differences in memory, abstraction, and reasoning in the domain of literature. *Cognition and Instruction, 12*(4), 277–312.

II

EPISTEMOLOGICAL AND SOCIAL/MOTIVATIONAL FACTORS IN INTENTIONAL CONCEPTUAL CHANGE

7

Interest, Epistemological Belief, and Intentional Conceptual Change

Thomas Andre
Iowa State University

Mark Windschitl
University of Washington

Research examining alternative conceptions and conceptual change has contributed importantly to our understanding of how learners construct scientific ideas. Extensions of this research have informed instructional approaches that facilitate conceptual change and have contributed to better understandings of how science, or any discipline, might be taught more effectively.

Certainly, considerable evidence demonstrates that instruction that challenges students' preexisting conceptions can facilitate conceptual change (Wandersee, Mintzes, & Novak, 1994). Similarly, computer-based simulations that challenge preconceptions also facilitate conceptual change (Andre, Hasselhuhn, Kreiter, Baldwin, Leo, Miller, Mroch, Duschen, Werner, & Akpan, 2000; Frederiksen, White, & Gutwill, 1999; Windschitl & Andre, 1998; Yang, Greenbowe, & Andre, 1999). In addition to text and simulations, the appropriate use of hands-on experience has been shown to help learners reconfigure their notions of science phenomena (McDermott, 1984).

Despite these successes, as the chapters in this book make clear, conceptual change is not simply a matter of rational decision making. Students often seem to resist changing their conceptions in a variety of ways (Chinn & Brewer, 1993). Conceptual change strategies seem to work effectively for some students, but not for others. This chapter discusses possible reasons for these puzzling reactions to instruction by exploring how noncognitive and motivational factors influence conceptual change. We explore two lines of our research that investigate how two not-strictly-cognitive factors, *subject matter interest* and *epistemological beliefs*, contribute to conceptual change.

These lines of research emerged serendipitously. In a series of studies, Chambers and Andre (1991, 1992, 1995, 1997) examined the use of conceptual change features in instructional text dealing with electrical circuits. Because Andre and Chambers believed subject matter interest and prior experience would relate to conceptual change, they assessed and used those variables as covariates to control variance. This chapter reports an important reanalysis of those data, examining subject-matter interest as an independent effect contributing to conceptual change. Regarding epistemological beliefs, a study by Windschitl and Andre (1998) compared traditional versus constructivist instructional uses of a computer simulation with biology students to effect conceptual change. In this study, epistemological beliefs turned out to have not only an influence on conceptual change but an interesting interaction with constructivist–objectivist modes of instruction as well. Windschitl has since initiated a line of research that examines epistemology in preservice teachers' conceptualizations of inquiry.

We have good reason to think that interest and epistemological beliefs play a role in intentional conceptual change. Intentional learning is framed as internally initiated action in the service of developing knowledge or skills (see Bereiter & Scardamalia, 1989; Sinatra & Pintrich, chapter 1, this volume). Interest in particular subject matter, then, seems a likely influence on how learners purposefully attend to various aspects of problems posed in that subject-matter area, how they consciously exert effort to gain knowledge and skills, and how they persist in their problem-solving efforts.

Intentional learning is also characterized by self-regulated, goal-directed activity. Intentional learning processes such as awareness and self-regulation allow learners to evaluate goal satisfaction and redirect attention to aspects of learning tasks as needed. Learners' epistemological beliefs—their beliefs about the nature of knowledge and knowing—contribute to their perceptions of what the goals of learning activities should be. If some learners, for example, believe that knowledge is simply the accumulation of a fixed body of factual knowledge delivered to them by authoritative sources, it is reasonable to assume that they will have different goals for learning than others who believe knowledge is a complex social and individual construction that is tentative and evolving. Similarly, these two groups of learners will likely regulate their own learning progress toward these goals very differently.

In this chapter, we provide evidence that interest is related to conceptual change and describe how epistemological beliefs influence conceptions and conceptual change. We summarize these two lines of research and draw implications for future investigations, theory, and educational practice.

The issue of what is meant by *conceptual change* is itself complex. Conceptual change refers to changes in grand theoretical or metatheoretical perspectives, as well as smaller scale changes in the concepts, principles, and models students use to interpret and predict what will happen in particular situations (Wandersee, Mintzes, & Novak, 1994). Initial descriptions of conceptual change seemed to imply that students had well-formed theories about physical phenomena that were inconsistent with the theories accepted by the communities of scientists. Such major changes in theories were thought about as parallel to the Zeitgeist shifts discussed by Kuhn (1970). The Wandersee et al. (1994) review makes clear that students most frequently have a set of intuitions or beliefs that do not constitute well-formed theories. An example would be the belief that heavy objects fall faster than lighter objects, blood flows from the heart to organs but does not return, or that electricity flows unidirectionally from a power source to an object. These intuitions or beliefs can be held by students independent of whether they fit consistently into an overall theory. Here, we use *conceptual change* mostly in this smaller sense. Students have beliefs about particular situations and these beliefs lead them to respond to questions about these situations in ways inconsistent with the way biologists or physicists would respond. We examined whether differences in instructional treatments lead students to change the way they answer those questions. In the work with electricity described in this chapter, for example, we developed the test situations based on an assessment of students' answers in those situations prior to instruction (Andre & Ding, 1991; Wang & Andre, 1991). We demonstrated that students receiving particular instructional treatments answer those questions differently from students receiving different instructional treatments (Wang and Andre) or untutored students (Andre and Ding). In this sense, students have changed their conceptions. The more recent work by Windschitl discussed later addresses broader scale conceptual change. Preservice teachers typically have reception learning models of how students learn. Windschitl's work concerns how students' epistemological systems need to change if they are to develop more constructivist models of learning.

INTEREST AND CONCEPTUAL CHANGE

In a series of studies on facilitating learners' understanding of electric current flow, Chambers and Andre (1991, 1992, 1995, 1997) embedded conceptual change features designed to challenge alternative conceptions and promote conceptual change in a traditional science text. The conceptual change features were based on Shipstone's (1984) description of students' alternative models of electric current flow. In Shipstone's *sink model*, students believe a single wire connection between a power source and a device can power the device. In his *clashing currents* model, students believe that positive and negative electricity leave their respective terminals of power supplies and clash at the device, thereby powering it. In the *weakening current* model, students believe that there is a circuit around which current flows, but that the current weakens as a result of powering each device. In the physically correct *constant current* model, current is unidirectional and constant around a circuit.

The conceptual change features created by Andre and Chambers consisted of diagrams of functional or nonfunctional electrical circuits (see Chambers & Andre, 1995, 1997 for examples). Students were asked to indicate if they believed the circuit would function and to indicate why. The text then presented several alternative answers based on the common alternative conceptions identified by Shipstone (1984). Next, the text presented reasons why incorrect alternative conceptions would not be tenable, an explanation of the scientifically accepted model, and the correct answer. These conceptual changes features were designed to induce disequilibrium (Piaget, 1929) or dissatisfaction (Posner, Strike, Hewson, & Gertzog, 1982) and offer a model that appeared plausible, thereby promoting conceptual change. Conceptual change features of text have also been called *refutational features* (Hynd & Alvermann, 1986).

Across Andre's and Chambers' studies, conceptual change text was compared to the standard traditional text or to an augmented traditional text to which additional explanatory diagrams were added. This augmented text was designed to control for the greater length of the conceptual change text as compared to the traditional text. The major difference in the augmented traditional text and the conceptual change text was in the kinds of processing the texts were designed to enhance. Consistent with the Posner et al. (1982) model, the diagrams and the added language in the conceptual change text were designed to activate existing conceptions and to challenge common misconceptions with evidence. The added diagrams and text in the augmented traditional text simply enhanced the traditional text with additional presentations of the scientifically accepted views. Across the studies, conceptual change texts consistently led to superior performance on a posttest assessing conceptual understanding. The posttest consisted of presenting electrical situations and asking students to indicate if they would function or not function and why. The finding that conceptual change text enhanced conceptual understanding is consistent with other work in this area (e.g., Guzzetti, Snyder, Glass, & Gamas, 1993; Hynd & Alvermann, 1986)

As noted, Andre and Chambers also assessed the students' interest and experience with physics and electricity as well as students' overall verbal ability. These variables were used as covariates in the analyses, but additional relationships were not explored. In this chapter, we present a series of reanalyses of these data to further explore the influence of interest and experience on conceptual change.

In Study 1, college students enrolled in introductory psychology classes read either a conceptual change or traditional text on electric circuits (Chambers & Andre, 1995). The text taught the concepts of electrical current, electrical potential (voltage), resistance, series and parallel circuits, and Ohm's law. The conceptual change text contained the features described above; the traditional text did not.[1] Before reading the texts, students completed a background questionnaire that contained seven items related to experience (e.g., How many semesters of physics did you take in high school?) and twelve items related to interest (e.g., As a child or adolescent, how interested were you in building electronic or electrical toys?). Another portion of the test assessed verbal ability.

In this reanalysis, we sought to determine whether interest influenced conceptual change independently of ability, experience, and experimental condition. To do so, we first explored whether interest, experience, or verbal ability were related to gender or experimental condition. There were no significant differences with respect to condition, nor did the genders differ in verbal ability. However, males displayed more interest, $F(1, 279) = 102.18$, $p < .0001$, and experience, $F(1, 279) = 168.13$, $p < .0001$, than did females. We computed correlations between the individual difference variables; as expected, interest and experience were correlated, $r = .65$, $p < .0001$, but verbal ability was not correlated with either interest or experience. We conducted preliminary regression analyses to determine if interest or experience would interact with the experimental conditions or with each other. They did not.

Our main analysis consisted of a two-stage regression in which posttest performance was the predicted variable and type of text (conceptual change or traditional), gender, and verbal ability score were entered in the first block, and interest and experience scores were added in the second block. Table 7.1 summarizes the regression results. When entered in the first stage of the regression, verbal ability, type of text, and gender related significantly to posttest performance. Students with higher verbal ability performed better than students with lower ability, males performed better than did females, and students who received conceptual change text did

[1]In addition to the conceptual change features, presence or absence of adjunct questions was also manipulated. This variable had no effect on the posttest in any of the studies and is not discussed further.

TABLE 7.1
Summary of Hierarchical Regression Analysis for Texttype, Gender, Verbal Ability, Interest, and Experience Predicting Posttest Performance in Study 1

Variable	*B*	*SE of B*	*Beta*	*t*	*Significance Level*	*Tolerance*
Step 1						
Texttype	3.79	1.21	.25	3.01	.03	.99
Gender	-1.35	1.20	-.50	-6.12	.02	.99
Verbal Ability	.68	.18	.30	3.65	.00	.99
Step 2						
Texttype	4.20	1.09	.28	3.86	.00	.97
Gender	-2.80	1.38	-.19	-2.03	.04	.59
Verbal Ability	.65	.17	.28	3.89	.00	.99
Interest	.08	.04	.22	2.38	.02	.62
Experience	.66	.19	.33	3.40	.00	.55

Note. Adj. R^2 = .36 for Step 1; Δ Adj. R^2 = .14 for Step 2 ($ps < .05$).

better than students who received traditional text. When interest and experience were added in the second stage, this pattern changed, primarily by reducing the influence of gender.[2] All of the variables displayed significant relationships with the posttest. But more importantly, interest and experience showed significant relationships with conceptual test performance that were independent of gender and verbal ability. These results suggested that the students' degree of interest in the subject matter positively influenced the degree to which they are able to construct conceptual understanding from instructional text regardless of whether traditional or conceptual change text was used.

A similar pattern of results was found in Study 2. This study involved five experimental conditions. Students read either traditional text, augmented traditional text, or conceptual change text. There were three conceptual change text conditions. In one condition, students simply read the conceptual change text. In the second condition, students read a similar text, but rather than telling students the correct answers and directly contradicting their alternative conceptions with text statements, the text directed students to a simulation program. The simulation program allowed students to build the depicted circuit and to test whether it would work. The third conceptual change condition was similar to the second condition, but students constructed the circuit from a kit containing necessary electrical components and then tested it. The posttest used was the same as in Study 1.

---

[2]A more detailed analysis of the relationships among gender, interest, and conceptual change can be found in Andre (1997).

In the first stage of the regression analysis, condition and gender were entered. In the second stage, verbal ability, experience, and interest were added. Table 7.2 summarizes the regression model and results. Gender and condition were significant when entered by themselves in the first stage; however, when verbal ability, experience, and interest were added in the second stage, gender was no longer significant. Verbal ability, experience, and interest each contributed significantly to posttest performance, as did condition. Preliminary analyses had revealed no significant interactions. Thus, in Study 2, as in Study 1, interest contributed independently and significantly to performance on a test of conceptual understanding of simple electrical circuits. In addition, differences between the genders in achievement in physical science may be due, at least partially, to differential interest (see Andre, 1997 for a more detailed discussion of this relationship).

One problem with the data in Study 1 and Study 2 is that there were no pretest measures of performance. Interest related to performance on a conceptual change posttest, but one might argue that interest influenced the posttest by influencing prior knowledge. Analysis of a third study was conducted to assess this possibility. Study 3 replicated the design of Study 1; students read either conceptual change text or traditional text and completed the same posttest used in Study 1. Study 3 differed from Study 1 in that students also completed a pretest that was similar in content to the posttest. This analysis of the Study 3 data was designed to better assess conceptual change from pretest to posttest and to assess the influence of interest on posttest performance independent of its influence on prior knowledge. If interest could be shown to influence performance on a conceptual posttest independently of prior knowledge, a claim that interest influences conceptual change would be strengthened.

TABLE 7.2
Summary of Regression Analysis for Condition, Gender, Verbal Ability, Interest, and Experience Predicting Posttest Performance in Study 2

Variable	*B*	*SE of B*	*Beta*	*t*	*Significance Level*	*Tolerance*
Step 1						
Condition	1.11	.45	–.22	–2.46	.02	.99
Gender	–4.34	1.27	–.31	–3.42	.00	.99
Step 2						
Condition	–.80	.39	–.16	–2.02	.05	.96
Gender	–.36	1.35	–.03	–.27	.79	.66
Verbal Ability	.55	.19	.23	2.94	.00	.98
Interest	.09	.04	.28	2.78	.01	.61
Experience	.56	.14	.36	3.96	.00	.77

Note. Adj. R^2 = for Step 1; Δ Adj. R^2 = .22 for Step 2 ($ps < .05$).

Preliminary analyses indicated no significant interactions between interest, experience, type of text, or gender. Students improved significantly in performance from pretest to posttest, demonstrating enhanced conceptual understanding on the posttest. The analysis of main interest here involved a path analysis that more clearly specified the relationships between interest, experience, gender, verbal ability, pretest performance, and performance on a posttest assessing conceptual understanding. To conduct the path analysis, we needed to describe the relationships we might plausibly expect between outcome performance on a test of conceptual understanding and gender, interest, experience, verbal ability, and pretest.

What should influence pretest performance in a given domain? Interest in a subject matter is correlated with learning that subject matter (Hidi & Harackiewicz, 2000; Pintrich & Schunk, 1996), and is plausibly related to experience and choices in that subject matter, such as vocational choices (Pintrich & Schunk, 1996). Interest in physical science also is correlated with gender (Andre, Whigham, Hendrikson, & Chambers, 1999); females show less interest in physical science than do males. Thus interest and gender can be considered to be correlated variables that directly influence experience. Interest and gender may directly influence pretest performance or may influence pretest performance only indirectly through their influence on experience. Verbal ability is likely to influence pretest performance, but would not be necessarily likely to influence experience with physics. Prior experience in a subject matter should relate to pretest performance in that subject matter.

What should influence posttest performance in a given subject domain? Clearly prior knowledge as assessed by pretest performance is likely to influence posttest performance. Degree of prior knowledge is one of the prime predictors of the degree to which individuals learn from educational experiences (Pressley & McCormick, 1995). If experience influences prior knowledge (pretest performance), then it does not seem likely that experience should independently influence posttest performance. Prior experience should increase prior knowledge and prior knowledge as measured by pretest performance should mediate the effect of prior experience on subsequent learning as reflected on a posttest. However, it seems plausible that interest would influence posttest performance independently of any effect on prior experience or pretest performance. Students with higher interest should be more motivated to engage in conceptual change that occurs after the influence of prior experience. It is known that students with higher interest are more likely to engage in deep processing of instructional materials (Pintrich, 1989; Schiefele, 1991). The path analyses we conducted were focused on examining these relationships. These predicted relationships are illustrated in Fig. 7.1.

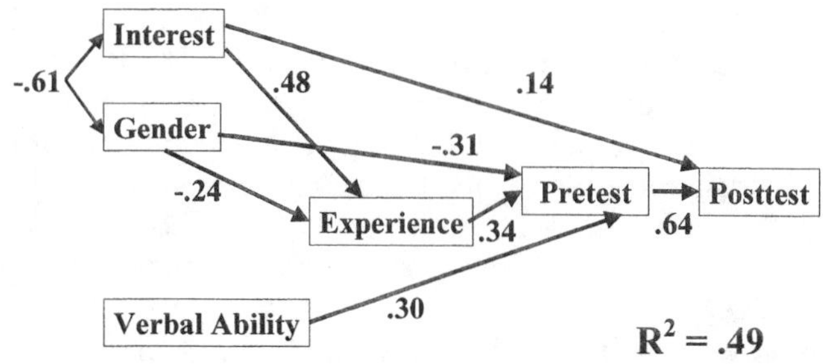

FIG. 7.1. Summary of path analysis for Study 3.

We first tested the complete model using the AMOS program distributed by SPSS, Inc. Interest, gender, and verbal ability were entered as endogenous variables predicting experience, pretest, and posttest. Experience, in turn, was used as a predictor of pretest and posttest performance. All possible paths were included. The paths between interest and pretest, interest and verbal ability, gender and verbal ability, gender and posttest, verbal ability and posttest, and experience and posttest were not significant. The remaining paths were significant and represent the relationships previously predicted and shown in Fig. 7.1. The nonsignificant paths were eliminated from the model and theoretically predicted paths were included. The resulting model is shown in Fig. 7.1. The χ^2s of the reduced model and the full model were both nonsignificant.

Figure 7.1 supports the following interpretation. Verbal ability predicts prior knowledge, but does not correlate with interest, gender, or prior experience. Gender predicts experience and also pretest performance. Interest influences prior experience, but does not directly influence pretest performance because its influence is mediated by prior experience. Experience directly predicts pretest performance, but does not directly influence posttest performance.[3] Most importantly for this discussion, interest exerts an effect on posttest performance independently of its effect on experience. This latter finding supports the contention that interest directly influences the processing necessary for conceptual change to occur.

Taken together, the results of these reanalyses of the data from Studies 1–3 support the claim that interest influences conceptual change. The assessments used in Studies 1–3 were shown to be sensitive to changes in conceptual understanding from pretest to posttest (Carlsen & Andre, 1992). Students in the population sampled typically display conceptions about electricity that differ from accepted scientific views (Andre & Ding,

---

[3]A two-stage regression, similar to those use for studies 1 and 2, was also conducted. The results yielded a similar pattern, interest significantly predicted posttest performance independently of experience, verbal ability, and pretest.

1991; Wang & Andre, 1991) and there were significant improvements in conceptual understanding from pretest to posttest in Study 3. These findings support the contention that posttest performance in these studies reflects improved conceptual understanding of electricity. In all three studies, interest was significantly related to posttest performance independent of prior experience, verbal ability, and treatment condition. And, in Study 3, interest was shown to facilitate posttest performance independent of prior knowledge.

How might interest influence conceptual change? Chinn and Brewer (1993, 1998) described typical actions students take when presented with anomalous data that provide a conceptual challenge to a preexisting belief or model. These responses included ignoring the data, rejecting the data, excluding the data from the domain of the theory, holding the data in abeyance, reinterpreting the anomalous data to remove the anomaly, peripherally changing the preexisting model, being uncertain about the validity of the data, or engaging in theory change. Chinn and Brewer (1993) also described characteristics that led to or interfered with theory or conceptual change. One characteristic that promotes theory change is deep processing of (careful reflection on) the presented data. They suggested, based on work by Petty and Cacioppo (1979, 1984), that the students' degree of involvement in the topic would relate to the probability of deep processing; interest in subject matter should be correlated with degree of involvement. Dole and Sinatra (1998) presented a similar model in which they argued that degree of engagement relates to learning. Thus, the Chinn and Brewer and Dole and Sinatra models predicted that students should engage in deeper processing of anomalous data when they have a higher degree of interest in the subject matter than when they do not. Chinn and Brewer (1993), however, did not directly explore interest in the subject matter in their work. The present results suggest that interest is likely to relate to the strategies students select when faced with anomalous data that challenges preexisting beliefs.

How does this work relate to intentional conceptual change? The decision to engage in deeper processing while studying requires an intention on the part of the learner. Learners make decisions about the cognitive and metacognitive activities in which they engage while learning. A model analogous to the Ajzen and Fishbein (1980) model of the influence of attitude on behavior would relate interest and intention. In the Ajzen and Fishbein model, behavior is directly influenced by the intention to engage in the behavior. Thus, intention mediates the influence of attitudes on behavior. Intention is influenced by attitude and by subjective norms (perceived social pressure related to the behavior) as well as by practical considerations. We propose that a model in which interest influences intention to engage in the cognitive processing necessary for conceptual change would explain the effects we observed. The details of such a model are beyond this chapter and our present thinking, however.

The important point made in this section of the chapter is that these three studies provide data that demonstrate a role for interest in conceptual change. Students more interested in a subject matter are more likely to demonstrate conceptual understanding on a posttest. The present research was based on what Pintrich and Schunk (1996), following Krapp, Hidi, and Renninger (1992), called *personal interest*. Personal interest refers to the student's preexisting degree of interest in a given subject matter conceptualized as a "relatively stable, enduring disposition of the individual" (Pintrich & Schunk, p. 301). Personal interest contrasts with situational interest or "interest . . . generated mainly by environmental conditions" (Pintrich & Schunk, p. 302). Although personal interest is not under the control of the teacher or instructional system, situational interest can be directly influenced. An interesting question is whether instructional interventions designed to increase situational interest would produce similar positive effects on conceptual change. Were they to do so, the previous finding would suggest that increasing interest would also help students engage in conceptual change.

PERSONAL EPISTEMOLOGIES AND CONCEPTUAL CHANGE

Conceptual change theories entail fundamental assumptions about *how* learners think, but such theories, based on the notion of "hot cognition," compel us to ask *why* learners might be inclined to change their ideas about the world. Why, for example, would a physics student draw on a variety of experiences to cultivate his or her own conceptualizations of force and motion when readily available "authoritative" sources such as teachers and textbooks offer clear explanations that are scientifically correct? Why would one biology student conclude that ideas about inheritance based on Mendelian principles are "wrong" in light of new findings in molecular genetics, whereas a classmate will struggle to reconcile the explanations that these two theories offer for the same phenomena? To begin answering such questions, or at least to begin asking better questions, we must explore the epistemological frameworks of learners. Epistemology is an area of philosophy concerned with the nature and justification of human knowledge. It poses questions about the character of individual and disciplinary knowledge, about how individuals come to know, about the theories and beliefs they hold about knowing, and more recently, about the manner in which such epistemological premises influence thinking in general.

Epistemological thinking has been described as a cognitive process, as in *epistemic cognition* (Kitchener, 1983), *epistemic reflection* (Baxter-Magolda, 1992), or, simply as *ways of knowing* (Belenky, Clinchy, Goldberger, & Tarule, 1986). These are assumed to be cognitive processes of a higher level than simple inductive reasoning or general critical thinking. Some researchers suggest that epistemological cognition is distinguishable from both cognition and metacognition, functioning as a third-order monitoring process of the epistemological nature of problems (Kitchener, 1983; Wilkinson & Schwartz, 1987).

Personal epistemological theories have multiple dimensions that can be grouped into two general categories: the nature of knowledge and the nature of knowing (Hofer & Pintrich, 1997). The dimensions comprising *nature of knowledge* are *certainty of knowledge* and *simplicity of knowledge* (these dimensions are typically named by the naïve or unsophisticated perspective). Certainty of knowledge is the degree to which one sees knowledge as fixed or fluid. From the naïve epistemological perspective, absolute truth exists with certainty; at more sophisticated epistemological levels, knowledge is tentative and evolving. King and Kitchener (1994) regarded openness to new interpretations of experience as a key indicator of this dimension. Similarly, Kuhn (1991) spoke of evaluative epistemologists as more open to the possibilities that their theories may be modified through dialogic exchanges with others. The second dimension, simplicity, is viewed on a continuum on which knowledge viewed as an accumulation of facts represents the less sophisticated pole, and knowledge viewed as a dynamic and meaningful interrelationships among relative, contingent, and context-dependent concepts represents the more sophisticated pole. Under the category of the *nature of knowing* are the two dimensions of *source of knowledge* and *justification for knowing*. From less epistemologically sophisticated perspectives, sources of knowledge originate outside one's self and reside in external authorities from whom they may be unproblematically transmitted. More epistemologically sophisticated individuals see themselves as knowers with the ability to construct knowledge in interaction with others. The second dimension, justification for knowing, focuses on how individuals evaluate their knowledge claims, including the use of evidence, the use they make of authority and expertise, and their evaluation of experts. As individuals learn to evaluate evidence to substantiate their beliefs, they (ideally) move through a continuum from dualistic beliefs, to the multiplistic acceptance of opinions, to reasoned justification for beliefs.

LOGICAL AND EMPIRICAL CONNECTIONS BETWEEN PERSONAL EPISTEMOLOGIES AND CONCEPTUAL CHANGE

There are convincing logical arguments why we should consider personal epistemologies a potentially significant influence on individuals' conceptual change. Consider the intellectual activities associated with conceptual change in classroom situations: Students make personal understandings explicit to themselves and others; they construct personal hypotheses or predictions about phenomena, then reconcile the outcomes of experiments with their predictions; they analyze the differences between competing conceptualizations of phenomena; they use evidence to construct arguments in support of particular explanations; and they engage in sense-making dialogue with others. Epistemologically unsophisticated individuals would find it difficult to fare well in such an instructional environment. These kinds of instructional approaches seem ill-suited for students who believe that knowledge is either right or wrong, that knowledge is an accretion of facts dispensed by authorities, and that this knowledge is not open to personal interpretation, let alone "negotiation" by a group of students. On the other hand, students, who believe that they construct meaning by interrelating ideas from the text, personal experience, and the ideas of others to create their own explanations for phenomena, seem much more likely to exercise these dispositions (under such classroom conditions) and undergo conceptual change. In reflecting on the relationship between epistemology and learning, Perry (1981) posed the simple question: "When students radically revise their notions of knowledge, would they not be likely to change their ways of going about getting it?" (p. 102). Similarly, Hofer and Pintrich (1997) argued, "If one believes knowledge is simple, there is no reason to attempt to use deeper processing strategies such as elaboration; simple memorization will suffice" (p. 128).

Over the past 20 years, researchers have pursued empirical evidence of the relationship between epistemology and learning. In a study of college undergraduates, Schommer (1990) asked students to complete a questionnaire on epistemological beliefs. Her instrument was based on four factors: belief in simple knowledge, certain knowledge, innate ability, or quick learning (all stated from the naïve perspective). Several weeks later, students were asked to read a passage from a text as if preparing for a test, supply a concluding paragraph to the text, rate their degree of confidence in comprehending the material, and complete a mastery test. Belief in quick learning predicted students' oversimplified conclusions, low test scores, and overconfidence. Students who believed in certain knowledge were likely to generate inappropriately absolute conclusions. In a second study on statistical comprehension (Schommer, Crouse, & Rhodes, 1992), belief in simple knowledge was negatively correlated with test performance. Perry (1970) and Ryan (1984) found that students' understanding of complex topics was affected by their beliefs about knowledge. According to self-reports in the Ryan (1984) study, dualists (individuals holding the conception of knowledge as right or wrong) were more likely to resort to low-level comprehension strategies such as recalling factual information from the text. In contrast, relativists (who believed knowledge must be judged only within the context in which it is claimed) tended to use high-level comprehension strategies such as integrating information from different sources.

More recent studies have specifically examined the relationships between personal epistemologies and conceptual change. In an investigation of 265 high school students who were studying refutational texts about Newtonian motion, Qian and Alvermann (1995) found that individuals who believed in knowledge as simple and certain had poorer conceptual change scores than students who believed that knowledge is complex, evolving, and dependent on context.

In our own work (Windschitl & Andre, 1998), we studied 250 undergraduates enrolled in an introductory biology class to determine if epistemological beliefs would predict conceptual change, and to ascertain whether instructional conditions would interact with epistemological sophistication to affect conceptual change. Students were given an adaptation of Schommer's (1990) epistemology questionnaire that assessed participants' beliefs about the nature of knowledge and knowing. Students were also given a 24-item multiple-choice instrument that assessed their understanding of core concepts associated with the human cardiovascular system, such as the pattern of blood flow through the body, movement of oxygen through the heart and lungs, and the effects of physical activity on blood flow. The students were then randomly assigned to one of two instructional conditions—confirmatory or exploratory. The confirmatory group was given a set of 12 problems to solve using a computer simulation of the human cardiovascular system. They were asked to follow directions to adjust certain variables within the simulation and generate the screen conditions to show a particular type of output for interpretation. The students had few options for exploration. This sequence eventually presented them with evidence that refuted commonly held misconceptions about the cardiovascular system. Over the next 2 weeks, these students attempted to resolve the 12 "cases." The exploratory groups, on the other hand, were prompted during an orientation period to consider how to construct simple hypotheses about the cardiovascular system's operation. They were shown how to test a sample hypothesis about the cardiovascular system using the simulation. They were then asked to test another sample hypothesis on their own, after which the class discussed the results. The students were then asked to resolve the same 12 cases that the confirmatory group investigated, but without being given further direction. Individuals in the exploratory group were required to explicitly state a prediction about certain phenomena within cases, formulate their own hypotheses about how to test their prediction with the simulation, and then find ways to test them.

After administering the posttest, we found that students' levels of epistemological sophistication were significant positive predictors of conceptual change scores. There was also an interaction between experimental group and epistemological belief. In the exploratory condition, we expected more epistemologically sophisticated participants to perform better than less epistemologically sophisticated participants. In the confirmatory condition, we expected either a neutral or negative relationship epistemologically. Precisely this result was found. Individuals with more sophisticated epistemological beliefs performed better when allowed to construct and test their own hypotheses, but individuals with less sophisticated beliefs did poorly when asked to do the same. In the confirmatory condition, the reverse was true. Given that epistemologically less mature students believed that knowledge is simple and certain, an instructional approach that provided highly prescribed instructions as to how to proceed and led students to specific conclusions would be consistent with these students' ideas about knowledge. Epistemologically unsophisticated students should find less compatible an approach that emphasized self-exploration and self-construction of knowledge. The reverse relationships should hold true for epistemologically more mature students. We also found that, overall, the exploratory experience produced greater conceptual change in participants than the confirmatory experience. This was interesting because the confirmatory group had only to follow directions for each of the 12 cases to be "presented with the correct answer" (e.g., that blood flow to the intestinal organs decreases during exercise, or that blood travels in a double loop through the circulatory system). By contrast, participants in the exploratory condition were *never guaranteed* of creating for themselves the conditions in the simulation that would refute commonly held alternative conceptions. The superior performance by students in the exploratory group may be a result of intentionally constructing new personal theories by developing hypotheses, testing them, and interpreting the results. This sense-making process highlights not only the "final answer" but the path of reasoning used to arrive at the conclusion. Such exploration may effectively challenge students' existing ideas and lead them to develop more robust conceptions.

GROUNDING STUDIES OF EPISTEMOLOGY AND CONCEPTUAL CHANGE IN AUTHENTIC CONTEXTS

From the preceding discussion, it appears that the epistemological beliefs of learners have strong associative links with conceptual change. These relationships, however, are not as straightforward as they seem. Most of the literature on epistemology presumes that individuals hold epistemological beliefs somewhere on a continuum between unsophisticated (naïve) and highly sophisticated beliefs, and that these beliefs are stable across contexts. Both of these have become contested notions.

Several studies have reported that individuals often hold incommensurable views on knowledge and knowing. In studies of individuals' perceptions of science, Songer and Linn (1991) described a "static" view of science as believing that knowledge is certain and unchanging, mostly facts to be memorized, versus a "dynamic" view of science as believing that knowledge stems from evidence, changes and expands, and relates to daily life. In response to survey questions, most secondary school students in their study (63%) could be characterized as having mixed beliefs, consisting of a combination of static and dynamic ideas and ideas that were difficult to classify.

In a study of physics students, Roth and Roychoudhury (1993) found that some students spoke about knowledge in constructivist terms, yet used metaphors for learning that derived from an objectivist epistemology. A student who indicated that he "wrote his own mindbook," a constructivist metaphor, held a view of knowledge incommensurable with the same position. The authors claimed:

> There seems to be evidence for the concurrent existence of beliefs and metaphors pertaining to different epistemologies in such a way that a clear identification of an individual with any one epistemology is impossible. Accordingly, situationally dependent referents determine the choice of a particular metaphor. This seems to suggest that it might be more appropriate to speak of epistemological positions only in specific contexts than as descriptors of an individual's views in general (p. 17).

Roth and Roychoudhury argued that these results can be interpreted as students' compartmentalizing their knowledge so that they can hold incommensurable views without realizing this conflict (Davis & Mason, 1989; Lederman & O'Malley, 1990).

To find alternative frameworks that help explain these consistencies, Hammer and Elby (2001) challenged some of the conventional conceptions of epistemology. They argued that, for the most part, researchers have presumed personal beliefs about knowledge as unitary components of essentially stable epistemologies—*unitary* meaning that each belief corresponds to a unit of cognitive structure, which an individual either does or does not possess. In response, they proposed a framework of *epistemological resources* at a finer grain size than such unitary beliefs, analogous to diSessa's (1993) account of phenomenological primitives at a finer grain size than unitary (mis)conceptions. They described these epistemological resources as smaller and more general than theories or traits. These resources can accommodate contextual dependence and provide an account of productive resources. Their framework includes general categories of epistemological resources. The first includes resources for understanding the general nature of knowledge and how it originates. In this category, individuals draw on various epistemological positions depending on the domain and context involved. Resources in this category include: knowledge as propagated, knowledge as free creation, knowledge as fabricated, knowledge as direct perception, and knowledge as inherent. The activation of any of these resources under certain conditions does not preclude the activation of other resources within that same category or from other categories. These resources are available from an early age for use, as needed, in various contexts. Other categories of resources are those for understanding epistemological activities, such as accumulation, forming rules, forming stories, guessing, brainstorming, checking, comparing, sorting, and naming (see Collins & Fergusen, 1993 for details), and, resources for understanding epistemological stances, such as belief and disbelief, doubting, understanding, puzzlement, and acceptance.

Regardless of how we conceptualize epistemology, there is a need to ground future research in authentic contexts for learners rather than ask learners to project about hypothetical circumstances. In addition, more in-depth ways of assessing epistemologies that are invoked in particular circumstances need to be developed. One such context in science education, for example, deals with teachers (as learners) and focuses on their *conceptions of inquiry*. Many teachers believe that inquiry is synonymous with the scientific method—an oversimplified and unproblematic view of science (Crawford, 1998; Flick, 1995; Fradd & Lee, 1999). Many also see inquiry as a way to arrive at "correct answers." Conceptions of inquiry vary dramatically among teachers and have profound implications for the design of learning experiences for their students (Tobin, Tippins, & Gallard, 1994; Wells, 1995).

In an attempt to address these issues, Windschitl (2000) conducted a series of studies with preservice secondary science teachers, using independent science activities as a context with which to monitor their epistemologies and their changing conceptions of classroom inquiry. For each of the past 3 years, students in a secondary science methods class were asked to engage in a 2-month independent inquiry on a topic of their choice. The students' inquiry activities focused on bird-feeding behaviors, the effects of air pollution on sunsets, the electrical conductivity of fruits, and dozens of other phenomena. To prompt reflection on their inquiries, the preservice teachers kept a journal in which they recorded the details of their inquiry. The journals typically included a range of written reflections including the straightforward reporting of hypothesis testing procedures, and also the frustrations, triumphs, second thoughts, and false starts associated with independent inquiry. Each time the students entered thoughts about their inquiry project, they also described how these experiences were influencing their thinking about organizing inquiry for their future students. In this sense, it was a "dual journal," intended to stimulate "pedagogical thinking" (Fieman-Nemser & Buchmann, 1995) by connecting episodes of personal inquiry experiences with how those experiences could translate into a framework for working with future students. The goal was to involve them in long-term experiences that would change their conceptions of inquiry from the oversimplified script of the scientific method to a more sophisticated understanding of inquiry as a way of knowing that is comprised of complex, interrelated phases and that results in knowledge that is neither certain nor fixed.

Analysis of preinquiry statements and journal entries revealed that participants had different characterizations of inquiry, and that these characterizations were linked to the way they approached their own inquiry project. About a third of the students conceived of inquiry as a linear process. They believed that hypothesis testing was a matter of stepwise movement from one phase to the next until the process was complete. One participant, Jonathon, commented:

> This inquiry project for me was a very linear process. I had to go through each step before I got to the next. I was not, with the experiment that I chose to do, allowed to try something else after I ran the experiment.

For such participants, the phases were discrete tasks, the requisites of which were shaped only by the details of the previous phase. These participants rarely projected how a phase might be procedurally or conceptually linked to an upcoming phase (e.g., the way a hypothesis is stated affects the analysis of the data).

In contrast, about a third of participants thought of inquiry as a process involving mutually interdependent considerations. Their remarks in both preinquiry statements and their journals reflected the belief that the phases of inquiry only make sense in relation to one another and that phases have to be considered simultaneously at the outset of the inquiry. For example, Amanda, who was studying sunsets, wrote that during the initial phases of inquiry, she had to consider multiple criteria simultaneously. Her journal entries, like those of other participants who had more complex conceptions of inquiry, provided evidence of goal-directed metacognition:

> [My] hypothesis was: The higher the pollution index rating for the day, the deeper red the sunset at night. So—more and more questions came up—What pieces of data test my hypothesis? What related directly to my question? By going back and forth between my hypothesis and data collection I was able to define how to collect data and reinforce what my hypothesis was.

Adapting Hammer and Elby's (2001) framework of epistemological resources, one could say that Jonathon and Amanda were invoking resources for understanding epistemological activity. Jonathon was activating a model of inquiry as script; Amanda, on the other hand, was using a model of inquiry as mutually interdependent considerations.

Before conducting their inquiry, students were asked to submit metaphors that they believed represented the nature of the inquiry process. Individuals who believed in inquiry as a simple, linear process suggested metaphors that were equally simple. These metaphors emphasized either the sequential nature of the hypothesis testing process (e.g., building a pyramid layer by layer, building a house from the foundation up, or walking up a set of stairs). Individuals who saw inquiry as a process of mutually interdependent considerations used metaphors that suggested inquiry was more complex, such as that of a detective who had to consider a range of possible hypotheses at the same time he examined a crime scene for evidence. Here again, the notion of epistemological resources can be used, specifically those of epistemological stances one can adopt. It is hard to envision how participants, who viewed inquiry as building a pyramid or walking up a set of stairs, would include epistemological stances of disbelief, doubting, or puzzlement in their repertoire of intellectual activity. Conversely, stances such as doubt and puzzlement seem to be part and parcel of inquiry modeled on the thinking of a detective.

Examining still other aspects of participants' data, those with oversimplified views of inquiry described fewer problems than other participants. Two individuals, in fact, claimed that they encountered no problems at all, and reported in their journals little more than what one would find in a laboratory notebook. The few problems that were cited by this group of participants were primarily concerns about the operationalizing of variables, the logistics of collecting data, and accuracy in recording data. Participants who had more sophisticated conceptualizations of inquiry wrote about problems in designing ways to collect and analyze data as well, but they also wrestled with questions about the relationships between inquiry phases. They asked themselves how well their data answered their original questions, or whether their hypothesis was affecting the way they observed phenomena.

All participants claimed that their experiences strongly influenced their thinking about conducting independent inquiry with high school students. Those participants with simple ideas about inquiry discussed how their own students might be helped to *complete* a successful inquiry activity, whereas participants who saw inquiry as more complex focused on how they could help students *understand* inquiry as a process. Specifically, these participants stated that they would give their own students opportunities for inquiry-oriented dialogue with each other as well as with the teacher.

With regard to conceptual changes that occurred as a result of these experiences, approximately two thirds of participants who saw inquiry as simple and unproblematic maintained satisfaction with their original metaphors and did not report changes in their conceptions of inquiry. Of those participants with the most sophisticated views of inquiry at the outset of the experience, about two thirds of them claimed that they did change their conceptions of inquiry, describing inquiry at the end of the experience as "more organic" than they originally believed. One of the participants, for example, reconceptualized the process as "navigating a web of information."

The results suggest that epistemology is an important theoretical construct with which to understand the novice teacher's beliefs about inquiry and about inquiry instruction. What is less clear, however, is how these independent inquiry experiences can be used to improve preservice teachers' understandings of inquiry and make these individuals better mentors for their future students. Simply providing them with their own independent inquiry experiences appears to be a half-measure.

It may be necessary in methods classes to explicitly address epistemological issues within the context of individuals' inquiries and to make clear how individuals' interpretations of inquiry may be shaped by unexamined beliefs about the certainty/tentativeness and simplicity/complexity of knowledge. If epistemological beliefs influence the goals of learning and how one monitors progress toward those goals, then it may be fair to say that these beliefs contribute to intentional conceptual change. However, if epistemological beliefs operate only at the implicit level during problem solving or conceptual change activities, they do not have as clear a place in the model of intentional conceptual change. A science methods class is an appropriate place to raise the consciousness of epistemological beliefs in individuals as they learn the craft of teaching. In this way, epistemological beliefs could play a key role in the purposeful examination of one's personal theories about inquiry. Epistemological beliefs in such a context would become both a mediator and an object of intentional intellectual activity.

IMPLICATIONS FOR THE DESIGN OF INSTRUCTION

The arguments in the preceding section suggest that interest in subject matter and epistemological beliefs are positively associated with conceptual change. If this is true, then it makes sense to design curriculum, employ strategies, and use assessments that foster interest and epistemological sophistication in learners.

One consideration for the design of curriculum is to base units of instruction on *essential questions* (also known as driving questions). Normally, teachers announce to students that they will be studying "volcanoes" or "plants." This usually generates little enthusiasm for the subject matter. However, essential questions can be used to frame the unit, such as: What would happen to us if Mt. Rainier erupted? or How could we grow plants on a space station? These types of questions generate interest because they can be relevant to students' lives and they involve authentic concerns. Fashioning a unit of instruction around answering such questions may also support deeper epistemological thinking on the part of students because the answers to essential questions are complex and cannot be found in textbooks. Answering these types of questions requires purposefully integrating different kinds of information from many different sources. For example, the question about growing plants on a space station requires students to understand the fundamentals of plant growth such as how light, water, and nutrients interact to support life. The context of growing plants in space can generate further questions that lead students into even deeper aspects of the topic such as: What kind of light do plants require? Can artificial lighting suffice? Do they need cycles of light to imitate day and night? What are the effects of gravity on seedlings and mature plants? Is soil necessary for plants?

What kinds of pedagogical strategies would cultivate interest or epistemological sophistication? In general, teachers should provide regular opportunities for "sense-making" during class. Sense-making, as opposed to unproblematically absorbing information, means that students have extended opportunities to work with phenomena rather than watch teacher demonstrations or read from a text. They also have access to multiple representations of phenomena (diagrams, animations, graphs, pictures, stories) and are allowed (where appropriate) to express their understanding of ideas using a variety of modes. They also have opportunities for dialogue with the teacher and with peers about the phenomena of interest. The discourse in the classroom is not only about creating or revising conceptions, but also about fashioning arguments that support one's positions as well as understanding "what counts" as a viable argument. Assessment criteria should be tied to the soundness of students' thinking as well as the correctness of their conceptions. This reinforces the thinking process in learners rather than exclusively privileging "right answers."

Many of these recommendations may sound familiar, and, indeed, they are all consistent with constructivist models for instruction. Constructivist instruction, also known as teaching for understanding, has other principles beyond those mentioned here. These features just mentioned, however, have the potential to generate student interest, foster more sophisticated approaches to learning, or both.

INTEREST, EPISTEMOLOGY, AND INTENTIONAL CONCEPTUAL CHANGE

On the face of it, the findings that interest and epistemology influence conceptual change are important, but not necessarily related. Moreover, how are these variables related to intentional conceptual change? Is it possible to create a theoretical model that integrates these apparently diverse findings? We believe that building a theoretical perspective that combines aspects of expectancy-value models of motivation (Eccles, 1983; Pintrich & Schunk, 1996) and the Ajzen and Fishbein (1980) model of attitude and behavior can relate these apparently diverse findings. Intrinsic interest values are included in expectancy-value models; high interest should increase task value and should positively influence motivation to engage in a task. Epistemological beliefs are likely to influence both one's perception of the nature of the task, perceptions of the task difficulty, and expectations for success in the task. Intention to engage in a task should be related to one's motivation for the task. The task, in the present context, is engaging in the cognitive processing necessary for conceptual change. We argue that the intention to engage in that processing is related to one's interest in the situation and to one's epistemological conceptions. Working out the details of such a model remains for the future, but our intuition is that these apparently diverse lines of research are both integral to an overall account of intentional conceptual change.

This chapter summarized evidence demonstrating that personal interest and epistemological beliefs influence the conceptual change process. Increased interest and more sophisticated epistemological beliefs facilitate conceptual change. We believe these variables influence intentional conceptual change by influencing how students perceived the nature of the learning task and by influencing motivation for and intention to engage in the cognitive processing necessary for conceptual change. In addition, research on how to facilitate change in students' epistemological beliefs and whether changes in situational interest would facilitate conceptual change also need to be done. One implication of this chapter is that context or situation is determined by the interaction of individual difference characteristics with the characteristics of the instructional situation and sociocultural context. Further exploration of such complex interactions represents a fruitful approach to subsequent research on conceptual change.

REFERENCES

Ajzen, I., & Fishbein. M. (1980). *Understanding attitudes and predicting social behavior.* Englewood Cliffs, NJ: Prentice-Hall.

Andre, T. (1997), Minds-on and hands-on activity: Improving instruction in science for all students. *Mid-Western Educational Researcher, 10,* 28–34.

Andre, T., & Ding, P. (1991). Student misconceptions, declarative knowledge, stimulus conditions and problem solving in basic electricity. *Contemporary Educational Psychology, 16,* 303–313.

Andre, T., Haselhuhn, C., Kreiter, K., Baldwin, W., Leo, C., Miller, T., Mroch, A., Duschen, A., Werner, B., & Akpan, J. (2000). *Mission Newton! And Thinker Tools: Using prior simulations to promote learning about motion.* Paper presented at the Annual Meeting of the Mathematics/Science Education Technology meeting, San Diego, CA.

Andre, T., Whigham, M., Hendrikson, A., & Chambers, S., (1999). Competencies beliefs, positive affect, and gender stereotypes of elementary students and their parents about science versus other school subjects. *Journal of Research in Science Teaching, 36,* 719–748.

Baxter-Magolda, M. B. (1992). *Knowing and reasoning in college: Gender related patterns in students' intellectual development.* San Francisco: Jossey Bass.

Belenky, M. F., Clinchy, B. M., Goldberger, N. R., & Tarule, J. M. (1986). Women's ways of knowing: *The development of self, voice, and mind.* New York: Basic Books.

Bereiter, C., & Scardamalia (1989). Intentional learning as a goal of instruction. In L. B. Resnick (Ed.), *Knowing, learning, and remembering: Essays in honor of Robert Glaser* (pp. 361-392). Hillsdale, NJ: Lawrence Erlbaum Associates.

Carlsen, D., & Andre. T. (1992). Use of a micro-computer simulation and conceptual change text to overcome student preconceptions about electric circuits. *The Journal of Computer-Based Instruction, 19,* 105–109.

Chambers, S. K., & Andre, T. (1991, December). *A text-based approach for facilitating conceptual change in learning science: The role of interest in evidence for long-term effects.* Paper presented at the meeting of the Iowa Educational Research and Evaluation Association, Cedar Rapids, IA.

Chambers, S. K., & Andre, T. (1992, April). *Learners' attention to and learning from scientific text as a function of conceptual change or didactically oriented text.* Paper presented at the annual meeting of the National Consortium for Instruction and Cognition, San Francisco, CA.

Chambers, S. K., & Andre, T. (1995). Are conceptual change approaches to learning science effective for everyone: Gender, prior subject matter interest, and learning about electricity. *Contemporary Educational Psychology, 20,* 377–391.

Chambers, S. K., & Andre, T. (1997). Gender, prior knowledge, interest, and experience in electricity and conceptual change text manipulations in learning about direct current. *Journal of Research in Science Teaching. 34,* 105–123.

Chinn, C. A., & Brewer, W. F., (1993). The role of anomalous data in knowledge acquisition: A theoretical framework and implications for science instruction. *Review of Educational Research, 63,* 1–49.

Chinn, C. A., & Brewer, W. F., (1998). An empirical test of a taxonomy of responses to anomalous data in science, *Journal of Research in Science Teaching, 35,* 623–654.

Collins, A. & Fergusen, W. (1993). Epistemic forms and epistemic games: Structures and strategies to guide inquiry. *Educational Psychologist, 28,* 25–42.

Crawford, B. A. (1998, April). *Creating and sustaining an inquiry-based classroom: A different view of teachers' work.* Paper presented at the annual meeting for the National Association of Research in Science Teaching, San Diego, CA.

Davis, P. J., & Mason, J. H. (1989). Notes on a radical constructivist epistemethodology applied to didactic situations. *Journal of Structural Learning, 10,* 157–176.

diSessa, A. (1993). Towards an epistemology of physics. *Cognition and Instruction, 10,* 105–225.

Dole, J. A., & Sinatra, G. M. (1998). Reconceptualizing change in the cognitive construction of knowledge. *Educational Psychologist, 33*(2/3), 109–128.

Eccles, J. (1983). Expectancies, values and academic behaviors. In J. T. Spence (Ed.), *Achievement and achievement motives* (pp. 75–146), San Francisco: Freeman.

Fieman-Nemser, S., & Buchmann, M. (1995). Pitfalls of experience in teacher preparation. *Teachers College Record, 87*, 53–65.

Flick, L. B. (1995). Navigating a sea of ideas: Teachers and students negotiate a course toward mutual relevance. *Journal of Research in Science Teaching, 32*, 1065–1082.

Fradd, S. H., & Lee, O. (1999). Teachers' roles in promoting science inquiry with students from diverse language backgrounds. *Educational Researcher, 28*(6), 14–20.

Frederickson, J. R., White, B. Y., & Gutwill, J., (1999), Dynamic mental models in learning science: The importance of constructing derivational linkages among models, *Journal of Research in Science Teaching, 36*, 806–836.

Guzzetti, B. J., Snyder, T. E., Glass, G. V., & Gamas, W. S. (1993). Promoting conceptual change in science: A comparative meta-analysis of instructional interventions from reading education and science education. *Reading Research Quarterly, 28*, 116–159.

Hammer, D., & Elby A. (2001), On the form of a personal epistemology. In B. K. Hofer & P. R. Pintrich (Eds.), *Personal epistemology: The psychology of beliefs about knowledge and knowing* (pp. 169–190). Mahwah, NJ: Lawrence Erlbaum Associates.

Hidi, S., & Harackiewicz, J. M., (2000). Motivating the academically unmotivated: A critical issue for the 21st century. *Review of Research in Education, 70*, 151–180.

Hofer, B., & Pintrich, P. (1997). The development of epistemological theories: Beliefs about knowledge and knowing and their relation to learning. *Review of Educational Research, 67*, 88–140.

Hynd, C., & Alvermann, D. (1986); The role of refutation text in overcoming difficulty with science concepts. *Journal of Reading, 29*, 440–446.

King, P. M., & Kitchener, K. S. (1994). *Developing reflective judgment: Understanding and promoting intellectual growth and critical thinking in adolescents and adults.* San Francisco: Jossey Bass.

Kitchener, K. S. (1983). Cognition, metacognition, and epistemic cognition. *Human Development, 26*, 222–232.

Krapp, A., Hidi, S., & Renninger, K. A. (1992). Interest, learning, and development. In K. A. Renninger, S. Hidi, & A. Krapp (Eds.), *The role of interest in learning and development* (pp. 3–25). Hillsdale, NJ: Lawrence Erlbaum Associates.

Kuhn, D. (1991). *The skills of argument.* Cambridge, England: Cambridge University Press.

Kuhn, T. S. (1970). *The structure of scientific revolutions.* Chicago: University of Chicago Press.

Lederman, N., & O'Malley, M. (1990). Students' perceptions of tentativeness in science: Development, use, and sources of change. *Science Education, 74*, 225–239.

McDermott, L. (1984). Research on conceptual understanding in mechanic. *Physics Today, 37*, 24–32.

Perry, W. G. (1970). *Forms of intellectual and ethical development in the college years: A scheme.* New York: Holt, Rinehart & Winston.

Perry, W. G. (1981). Cognitive and ethical growth: The making of meaning. In A. Chickering (Ed.), *The modern American college* (pp. 76–116). San Francisco: Jossey Bass.

Petty, R. E., & Cacioppo, J. T. (1979). Issue involvement can increase or decrease persuasion by enhancing message-relevant cognitive responses. *Journal of Personality and Social Psychology. 37*, 1915–1926.

Petty, R. E., & Cacioppo, J. T. (1984). The effects of involvement on responses to argument quantity and quality: Central and peripheral routes to persuasion. *Journal of Personality and Social Psychology, 46*, 69–81.

Piaget, J. (1929). *The child's conception of the world.* New York: Harcourt Brace.

Pintrich, P. R. (1989). The dynamic interplay of student motivation and cognition in the college classroom. In C. Ames & M. L. Maehr (Eds.), *Advances in motivation and achievement: Motivation enhancing environments* (Vol. 6, pp. 117–160). Greenwich, CT: JAI Press.

Pintrich, P. R., & Schunk, D. H., (1996). *Motivation in education: Theory, research and applications.* Englewood Cliffs, NJ: Prentice Hall.

Posner, G., Strike, K., Hewson, P., & Gertzog, W. (1982). Accommodation of a scientific conception: Toward a theory of conceptual change. *Science Education, 66,* 211–227.

Pressley, M., & McCormick, C. B., (1995). *Advanced Educational Psychology.* New York: HarperCollins.

Qian, G., & Alvermann, D. (1995). Role of epistemological beliefs and learned helplessness in secondary school students[1] learning science concepts from text. *Journal of Educational Psychology, 87,* 282–292.

Roth, W. M., & Roychoudhury, A. (1993). Physics students' epistemologies and views about knowing and learning. *Journal of Research in Science Teaching, 31,* 5–30.

Ryan, M. P. (1984). Monitoring text comprehension: Individual differences in epistemological standards. *Journal of Educational Psychology, 76,* 249–258.

Schiefele, U. (1991). Interest, learning, and motivation. *Educational Psychologist, 26,* 299–323.

Schommer, M. (1990). The effects of beliefs about the nature of knowledge incomprehension. *Journal of Educational Psychology, 82,* 498–504.

Schommer, M., Crouse, A., & Rhodes, N. (1992). Epistemological beliefs and mathematical text comprehension: Believing it is simple does not make it so. *Journal of Educational Psychology, 82,* 435–443.

Shipstone, D. (1984). A study of chilren's understanding of electricity in simple DC circuits. *European Journal of Science Education, 6,* 185–198.

Songer, N., & Linn, M. (1991). How do student's views of science influence knowledge integration? In M. C. Linn, N. B. Songer, & E. L. Lewis (Eds.), *Students' models and epistemologies of science. Journal of Research in Science Teaching, 28,* 761–784.

Tobin, K., Tippins, D., & Gallard, A. J. (1994). Research in instructional strategies for teaching science. In D. Gabel (Ed.), *Handbook of research on science teaching and learning* (pp. 43–93). New York: Macmillan.

Wandersee, J. H., Mintzes, J. J., & Novak, J. D., (1994). Research on alternative conceptions in science. In D. Gabel (Ed.), *Handbook of research on science teaching and learning* (pp. 177–210). New York: Macmillan.

Wang, T., & Andre, T. (1991). Conceptual change text versus traditional text and application questions versus no questions in learning about electricity. *Contemporary Educational Psychology, 16,* 103–116.

Wells, G. (1995). Language and the inquiry-oriented curriculum. *Curriculum Inquiry, 25,* 233–269.

Wilkinson, W. K., & Schwartz, N. H. (1987) The epistemological orientation of gifted adolescents: An empirical test of Perry's model. *Psychological Reports, 61,* 976–978.

Windschitl, M. (2000). *An analysis of preservice teachers' open inquiry experiences.* Paper presented at the annual meeting of the American Educational Research Association, New Orleans, LA.

Windschitl, M., & Andre, T. (1998). Using computer simulations to enhance conceptual change: The roles of constructivist instruction and student epistemological beliefs. *Journal of Research in Science Teaching, 35*(2), 145–160.

Yang, E. M., Greenbowe, T., & Andre, T. (1999). *Spatial ability and the impact of visualization/simulations software on learning electro-chemistry.* Paper presented at the annual Meeting of the National Association for Research on Science Teaching, Boston.

8

*Personal Epistemologies and Intentional Conceptual Change**

Lucia Mason
University of Padova, Italy

For some time psychological research has underlined how domain-specific knowledge, general strategic knowledge, and motivational factors such as goal orientation, interest, self-efficacy, and self-regulation all affect learning processes. Only relatively recently has research argued that an additional element, epistemological beliefs, also influences thinking and reasoning. The key point of this chapter is that beliefs about the nature of knowledge and knowing may facilitate or constrain intentional conceptual change. Sinatra (2000) defined the intentional learner as "one who uses knowledge and beliefs to engage in internally-initiated, goal-directed action, in the service of knowledge or skill acquisition" (p. 15). This chapter argues that personal epistemologies determine the organization of students' goals; that is, they determine students' goal orientation to deliberately change their conceptions.

The chapter first situates intentionality in cognition and underlines the meaning of *intentional learner* by reference to the literature that depicts learners in broader terms than simply "active constructors." This is followed by a review of research on beliefs about the nature and acquisition of knowledge that has flourished along two lines, one on the development of epistemological thinking and the other on their effects on learning in four fields of study: text comprehension and metacomprehension, problem-solving and transfer, science and mathematics, and conceptual change. This

---

*This chapter was written while the author was at the University of Lecce, Italy.

last topic becomes the main focus to argue how beliefs about the nature and acquisition of knowledge contribute to intentionality in learning. The few empirical studies on the influence of these beliefs on knowledge revision are introduced. In the subsequent sections, the need of intentionaliy to solve problems of knowledge is discussed, followed by an examination of the crucial link between personal epistemologies and intentional learning in the process of conceptual change. Data from research with elementary and middle school students illustrate how self-initiated and self-controlled conscious and goal-directed learning actions are essential to intentional conceptual change. In particular, excerpts from students' written and oral discourse document how epistemological beliefs may, or may not, guide their efforts toward the learning goal of knowledge revision. The chapter concludes with some suggestions for future research.

INTENTIONALITY AND COGNITION

In the 1970s and 1980s, psychological research underwent a cognitive revolution that led to a radical change in the conception of learners. The predominant behaviorist view of learners, as passive receivers of information from the environment, was abandoned in favor of a view of learners as active meaning producers (Reynolds, Sinatra, & Jetton, 1996). In cognitive psychology there has been ample investigation into how the structures of the individual's mind, such as schemata or mental models, intervene in the active process of knowledge construction. A large amount of literature on so-called "misconceptions," mainly in science domains, has shown that individuals construct mental representations of concepts that are alternative to those they are exposed to.

More recently, learners have been viewed not only as active, but also intentional. As reviewed clearly by Sinatra (2000), research in both cognitive and educational psychology began to describe what can influence learning, beyond prior knowledge and active processing of new information. It would be impossible to describe all examples that illustrate various aspects of intentionality in the literature of both research areas. Only some examples that are more pertinent to the core of the argument about how epistemological beliefs contribute to intentionality in conceptual change are described.

In his investigation of what it means to be rational, Stanovich (1999) used the label *thinking dispositions* to describe what affects problem-solving performance beyond prior knowledge and cognitive ability. In his conceptualization, they are viewed as intentional-level psychological attitudes because they play a role at a higher level of cognition than the algorithmic. Thinking dispositions refer to the individuals' goal organization, which accounts for the normative/descriptive gap manifested in many reasoning tasks, that is, individual differences at the intentional level of cognition. "They are telling us about the individual's goals and epistemic values—and they are indexing broad tendencies of pragmatic and epistemic self-regulation" (p. 158).

Significant relationships between constructs that reflect the intentional level of the psychological structure in problem solving and reasoning performance have been documented. For instance, in Stanovich and West's (1998) Study 2, a wide analysis of the association between cognitive ability, thinking dispositions, and performance in various tasks from the literature on heuristics and biases was carried out. The composite measure of thinking dispositions was an additive combination of several questionnaire subscales aimed at tapping epistemic self-regulation. For example, they assessed what Baron (1985) defined as the disposition to weigh new evidence that conflicts with a held belief, to spend a considerable amount of time on a problem before giving up, and to evaluate others' opinions in order to form one's own. They are dispositions toward open-minded thinking and have strong similarities with two epistemological dimensions about the nature of knowledge as defined by Schommer (1990, 1993), that is, belief in simple/complex knowledge and belief in certain/uncertain knowledge, which will be introduced later. The results show that thinking dispositions could predict individual differences in a variety of tasks. For example, a thinking disposition to suspend one's own conceptions when examining alternative points of view promotes more effective reasoning and critical thinking.

An emphasis on the intentional level of cognition can be found in the literature on metacognition (e.g. Hacker, Dunlosky, & Graesser, 1998). It refers to the characteristics that make individuals aware of their own knowledge and the agents of their thinking processes. It also allows them to monitor their cognitive functioning (Hennessey, chapter 5, this volume). Motivation, particularly its component goal orientation, can also facilitate or constrain intentional learning (Linnenbrink & Pintrich, chapter 12, this volume). Moreover, the notion of self-regulation (e.g., Boekaerts, Pintrich, & Zeidner, 2000), of which motivation is a key construct, is closely linked to intentionality (Ferrari & Elik, chapter 2, this volume).

Bereiter and Scardamalia (1989) used the expression *intentional learning* to indicate "cognitive processes that have learning as a goal rather than an incidental outcome" (p. 363). Whether intentional learning occurs may depend on situational factors—what the specific situation offers to goal-reaching—and on the individual's mental resources that are activated in the situation. Concerning learning conditions, the two authors introduced a distinction between learning *through* problem solving and learning *as* problem solving. In learning through problem solving, learning is the result of operations applied to knowledge states in order to attain a solution to the problem. In this case problem solving is a way of acquiring knowledge or ability. In mathematics, for instance, problem solving is seen as the best way to understand concepts. However, a student involved in problem solving may not understand a concept but rather simply apply a procedure or sequence of steps. In learning as problem solving, the goal itself is a learning goal. It is problematic to be reached, so all efforts should be directed toward it. In this case problem solving means solving the learning problem, that is, understanding a concept, not learning a procedure or routine. It essentially involves goals rather than strategies. The intentional learner is not only conscious and motivated, but also actively pursues learning as a goal that is not focused on schoolwork (activities, products). Instead it is focused on knowledge that is objectified, analyzed to detect fallacies and inadequacies, evaluated, accumulated, and restructured (Bereiter, 1990; Scardamalia, Bereiter, & Lamon, 1994).

Concerning the individual mental resources that may support or deter intentional learning, Bereiter and Scardamalia (1989) referred to learners' implicit theories of knowledge and learning, that is, their personal epistemologies that, in Stanovich's (1999) terms, are thinking dispositions that shape the individuals' goal organization, as stated earlier. To have a learning goal implies that a student prefigures a knowledge state that is not yet possessed. The student's beliefs about the nature and acquisition of knowledge are important to the learning process as they constrain the goal.

In the theoretical framework of this chapter, intentionality is characterized by internally initiating and controlling actions with learning as a goal (Sinatra, 2000). The argument to be developed is that personal epistemologies, as thinking dispositions, may guide or constrain the goal. This occurs because only certain beliefs about the nature of knowledge and knowing are a powerful resource for engaging in internally initiated, goal-directed actions in the service of knowledge revision.

EPISTEMOLOGICAL BELIEFS

Epistemological beliefs have been defined as "socially shared intuitions about the nature of knowledge and the nature of learning" (Jehng, Johnson, & Anderson, 1993, p. 24). An examination of the differences between knowledge and beliefs as underlined by research (Nespor, 1987; Pajares, 1992) or perceived by students and teachers (Alexander & Dochy, 1994, 1995; Alexander, Murphy, Guan, & Murphy, 1998) is not within the aims of this chapter; rather, the discourse focuses directly on these beliefs. As pointed out by Hofer and Pintrich (1997, 2002; Hofer, 2000), in the literature the content of the construct of epistemological beliefs varies in terms of what is included or excluded. In that definition, as well as in most of the literature in educational psychology, epistemological beliefs refer to the nature of knowledge, the nature of learning, and often include beliefs about intelligence. How knowledge is acquired is probably intertwined in a student's network of beliefs. Schommer, Mau, and Brookhart (1999) recently considered that beliefs about learning may be precursors to beliefs about knowledge. On the other hand, in most developmental psychology literature, the term *epistemic* or *epistemological* refers instead to knowledge, reasoning, and justification processes concerning knowledge only. In the next two paragraphs, the wider and narrower (in the purer epistemological sense) contents of the construct are evident.

Kitchener's (1983) described a three-level model of cognition that distinguishes epistemic cognition from cognitive and metacognitive. Cognition is involved, for instance, when computations are made to solve a problem, and metacognition when we choose, and know why, a strategy for computing, and monitor our own cognitive functioning in the task. On the other hand, epistemic cognition is involved when we reflect on the nature of problems and their possible solution. Epistemic cognition essentially refers to personal beliefs about the organization and sources of knowledge, their truth value, and justification criteria for assertions. It has been found to be particularly necessary in the solution of ill-structured problems (King & Kitchener, 1994; Schraw, Dunkle, & Bendixen, 1995). More recently, in delineating a model on the development of critical thinking, Kuhn (1999) also made a distinction between three kinds of thinking. The first is the metacognitive thinking that concerns declarative knowledge (to know what). The second is the metastrategic thinking that concerns procedural knowledge (to know why). The third, of interest here and that influences the first two, is epistemological thinking, which concerns a wider understanding of what knowledge and knowing are, both on the general (How does one come to know?) and personal (What do I know of what I know?) levels.

Research on personal epistemologies flourished in the last decade along two principal lines: The development of epistemological thinking and the effects of beliefs about the nature and acquisition of knowledge on different aspects of the learning process. Issues from the first line of research are briefly reviewed, whereas those from the second line, more pertinent to the overall argument, are introduced in greater detail (for a complete review, see Mason, 2001c).

Development of Epistemological Thinking

Developmental psychologists have focused on the nature and justification of knowledge and on the epistemic features of reasoning processes and perspectives. Forms of intellectual and ethical development (Perry, 1968), the development of women's ways of knowing (Belenky, Clinchy, Goldberger, & Tarule, 1986), epistemological reflection (Baxter Magolda, 1992), reflective judgment (King & Kitchener, 1994), relativistic thinking (e.g., Chandler, 1987; Chandler, Boyes, & Ball, 1990; Leadbeater, 1986), dialectical thinking (e.g., Benack & Basseches, 1989), and argumentative reasoning (Kuhn, 1991) have all been investigated. Despite differences in specifics and terminology used by the different theorists, a shared developmental sequence can be drawn from their works (Moshman, 1998).

From childhood to adolescence to early adulthood, individuals move from an objectivistic to a subjective relativistic to a rational constructivist view of knowledge and knowing, although at different individual rates. An objectivist individual believes that knowledge is absolute, certain, nonproblematic, right and wrong, and does not need to be justified because observations of reality or authorities are its sources. This belief characterizes, but is not confined to, epistemological thinking in childhood, and it can appear at later ages. A subjective relativistic believes that knowledge is ambiguous, idiosyncratic, and individuals have their own views and own truths. This belief is typical in adolescence. Rational constructivists have an epistemology that restrains them from both extreme views, the objectivist and relativistic, as it is grounded on the belief that there are shared norms of inquiry and knowing. Thus, some positions are reasonably more justified and sustainable than others. This more sophisticated perspective, which is implied by the development of a metacognitive type of rationality, develops well into adulthood. It leads to a mature understanding of the nature and justification of knowledge that requires active processes of reflection on the aim and the nature of reasoning. This ability makes it possible to define, explain, and justify standards for the evaluation of one's own and others' thinking. It also leads to understanding, in a self-reflective manner, the reasons underlying one's own beliefs and attitudes (Baron, 1991).

Carey and Smith (1993) criticized theorists (such as Kitchener, King, and Kuhn) who state that children and young adolescents only believe that knowledge is absolute and unproblematic, that it comes directly from sensory experiences, and that it includes certain facts. By referring to the theory of mind research, they pointed out that between the ages of 3 and 6, children begin to view the mind as more than a receptacle of facts (e.g., Astington, Harris, & Olson, 1988; Wellman, 1990). At about 6 years old, children begin to conceive knowledge as something that is constructed by the mind and begin to take into account the quality of the knowledge source (Montgomery, 1992). According to Carey and Smith (1993), the development of epistemological thinking is part of the domain of the development of theory of mind. Studying middle school students' epistemological views, for instance, means understanding to what degree they have developed their theory of mind from the process initiated in childhood. It should be pointed out that in the developmental psychology literature, the construct of epistemological beliefs is approached either as a cognitive developmental structure that features a general level or stage (e.g., King & Kitchener, 1994) or as a cognitive process (e.g., Boyes & Chandler, 1992; Perry, 1981). Discussing epistemological development implies a logically evolving sequence of structures as systems of coherent representations. In the educational psychology literature, the construct of epistemological beliefs is often considered a set of different beliefs that are not necessarily organized into cognitive structures and can even be orthogonal, as described later.

Epistemological Beliefs and Learning

The second line of research on personal epistemologies addresses the effects of beliefs about the nature and acquisition of knowledge on individuals' learning. Schommer (1990, 1993; Schommer, Crouse, & Rhodes, 1992) developed a research program that has been seminal to the study of the linkages between these beliefs, cognition, learning, and academic performance. She analyzed the components of epistemological beliefs and challenged the idea that they are unidimensional by proposing that a belief set is made up of five more or less independent dimensions that do not follow a stage or level sequence; learners may be sophisticated in some beliefs but not in others. The dimensions underlying personal epistemologies are hypothesized to be: structure, certainty and source of knowledge, and speed and control of learning. Schommer (1990) developed an instrument to assess epistemological beliefs that many researchers in the field have used or referred to. The first version of the Epistemological Questionnaire comprised 63 items to be rated on a Likert-type scale, divided into 12 subsets of items. Factor analyses of these subsets as variables in all empirical studies of the research program revealed four dimensions of epistemological beliefs, two on the nature of knowledge and two on the nature of learning. At the extremes of the continuum these are:

- Simple/complex knowledge: from the belief that knowledge is isolated, unambiguous items of information to the belief that it is a set of interconnected concepts;
- Certain/uncertain knowledge: from the belief that knowledge is absolute and stable to the belief that it continuously evolves;
- Quick/gradual learning: from the belief that learning occurs quickly or not all to the belief that it is slow and gradual;
- Fixed/malleable ability: from the belief that the ability to learn is a fixed non-modifiable entity to the belief that it can be improved through the experience of learning itself.

More recently, Schommer (1994a, 1994b) outlined the idea that the complexity of epistemological beliefs may be better represented as a frequency distribution rather than a single point along each continuum. For instance, learners with sophisticated views in the dimension of certainty of knowledge may believe that many things in the world are unknown or continuously evolving, some things are temporarily unknown, and few things are certain.

The next section outlines findings of empirical research on personal epistemologies that contribute to the learning process. Authors use different constructs to refer to the epistemological views, or name them differently. Figure 8.1 displays the different constructs used in the research reviewed next and their relations to one another.

Epistemological Beliefs, Text Comprehension, and Metacomprehension. By referring to Perry's pioneering work on intellectual and ethical developmental, Ryan (1984b) investigated college students' beliefs about the nature of knowledge in relation to their monitoring of text comprehension and academic performance. Perry (1968) identified nine epistemological "positions" that appear to be integrated structures developing along an invariant sequence. On the basis of the ratings of seven statements drawn from Perry, Ryan identified two students' epistemological positions: dualistic (fact-oriented), which corresponds to the "objectivistic" view described by Moshman (1998), mentioned earlier, or relativistic (context-oriented) with characteristics as already outlined in reviewing developmental psychology research. Students were asked to describe the criteria used to monitor whether or not they comprehended chapters of textbooks, producing a range of 15 different kinds of monitoring criteria. These were divided into two categories according to Bloom's taxonomy (Bloom, Engelhart, Furst, Hill, & Krathwohl, 1956): the first involved knowledge-monitoring criteria, the second concerned comprehension and application-monitoring criteria. Findings indicated that personal epistemologies may constrain the choice of monitoring criteria and the effectiveness of text-processing activities. Dualist students reported the use of criteria concerning the knowledge category more often. Relativist students, on the other hand, reported criteria related to higher levels in that taxonomy, the comprehension or application categories. The students who claimed they used the second category of monitoring criteria attained higher grades in the Fundamentals of Psychology course than those reporting the use of the first category. Moreover, students who reported the use of multiple monitoring criteria attained higher grades than those who relied on a single criterion.

Ryan (1984a) also examined the relationship between college students' epistemological beliefs and their conceptions of term paper coherence. Be-

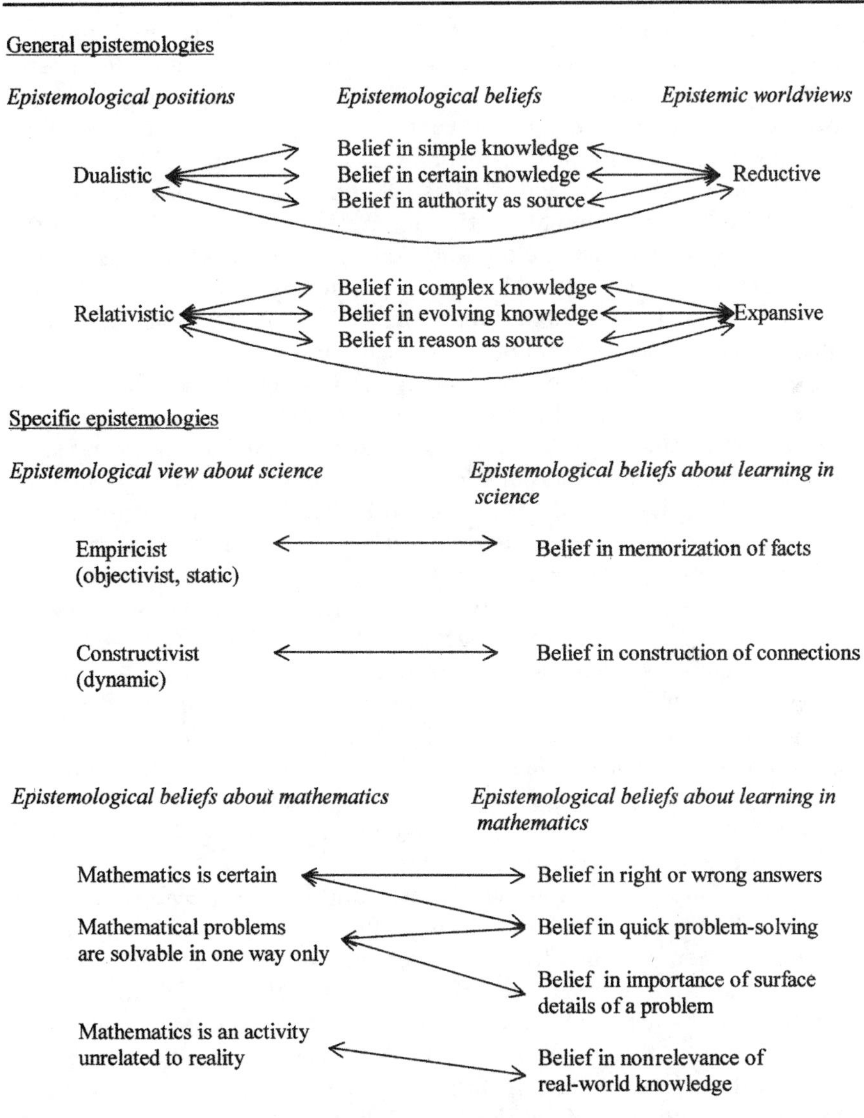

FIG. 8.1. Different constructs used in reviewed research on epistemological thinking and learning, and their relations to one another.

liefs were classified as immature when they did not refer to the quality of the relationship between various parts of a paper, but referred instead to the information contained in the text. They were considered mature when the conceptions appealed to the consequentiality and connectedness of different parts of the text. Students who held relativistic epistemological beliefs reported mature conceptions of prose coherence more often than students with dualistic stances. Moreover, essays produced by the former were more likely to be evaluated as coherent than those by the latter.

In the first of a systematic series of studies, Schommer (1990) focused on the influence of epistemological beliefs on reading comprehension. The construct of epistemological beliefs, as previously described, is intended as more or less independent dimensions that do not follow a stage or sequence. It includes beliefs about both the nature and acquisition of knowledge, assessed using the Epistemological Questionnaire. The students read a text, about either the social sciences or physical sciences, that presented controversial information on a topic and lacked a concluding paragraph. For instance, the social sciences passage introduced four different, but plausible, theories of aggression with the underlying issue that any resolution would require integration of aspects of all four theories. The students were asked to read the passage and write a tentative conclusion (or conclusions) on the basis of what was written. Results showed that the more students believed in quick learning, the more they wrote oversimplified conclusions suggesting the information was certain and absolute despite the hypothetical nature of the data introduced in the passage. Belief in quick learning was also a predictor of the ability to make a self-assessment of text comprehension, in that the students who scored higher on this dimension were more likely to overestimate their comprehension. In addition, belief in certain knowledge was a predictor of inappropriate absolute conclusions in the final paragraph.

Another study by Schommer, Crouse, and Rhodes (1992) on the relationship between the belief in simple knowledge and mathematical text comprehension, revealed that this belief influenced students' comprehension and metacomprehension. The less they believed in the simplicity of knowledge, the more they understood the introduced concepts and accurately assessed their comprehension. Kardash and Scholes (1996) addressed the effects of college students' beliefs about one of Schommer's four epistemological dimensions, that is, the certainty/uncertainty of knowledge (assessed using a modified version of Schommer's Epistemological Questionnaire), and the need for cognition in their interpretation of a controversial topic. The topic concerned the relationship between HIV and AIDS, where students could believe to different extents that HIV causes AIDS. As in Schommer's (1990) study, the students read a text presenting conflicting views on the topic and wrote a concluding paragraph.

The less the students believed in certain knowledge, the less their initial beliefs about the topic were radical, and the more they needed cognitive involvement, the more they wrote paragraphs taking into account the inconclusive nature of the controversial evidence read in the text. The effects of epistemological and topic-specific beliefs on students' cognitive and strategic processing when interpreting controversial information about the same topic, HIV–AIDS relationship, were investigated by Kardash and Howell (2000). It emerged that their beliefs about the speed and effort involved in learning influenced the overall number of cognitive processes that students manifested in comprehending and monitoring their comprehension of a dual-positional text. Undergraduates with more sophisticated beliefs about the nature of learning used more strategies overall than their peers with less sophisticated views in that dimension. This effect seemed to be more quantitative than qualitative. In addition, topic-specific beliefs produced a qualitative effect on comprehension and comprehension monitoring in that they affected the specific type of cognitive processing used by students.

Importance of belief in knowledge as an integrated system of ideas, rather than a collection of separate facts for understanding controversial texts (on the extinction of the dinosaurs), was examined by Rukavina and Daneman (1996). High school and college students read one of two text formats. The first described science as an inquiry and introduced the two competing theories about dinosaur extinction (catastrophic and gradual theories) as possible solutions to the ongoing scientific problem (integrated-text format). The second did not refer to the conflict between the two theories, which were presented successively in two separate texts (separate-text format). Students' epistemological beliefs were assessed by two subsets of items drawn from Schommer's Epistemological Questionnaire, those concerning simplicity and certainty of knowledge. Only students with less-advanced beliefs about the nature of knowledge benefited from reading the integrated-text format. However, this format helped all students on tasks requiring knowledge integration and a deeper understanding of the text.

As shown in Fig. 8.1, the dualistic and relativistic positions identified by Ryan can be seen in relation to Schommer's dimensions regarding the nature (simple and certain versus complex and evolving) and source (authority versus reason) of knowledge.

Epistemological Beliefs, Problem Solving, and Transfer. The relation between epistemological beliefs (intended as different dimensions in accordance with Schommer) and problem solving was investigated by Schraw et al. (1995). They hypothesized that beliefs about the nature and acquisition of knowledge would be related to solving ill-defined problems such as syllogisms, but would not be related to solving well-defined problems such as the question "Is truth unchanging?" University students' personal epistemologies were assessed by the Epistemic Beliefs Inventory, an instrument constructed with items drawn from Schommer's Epistemological Questionnaire and other new items specifically aimed at assessing beliefs about the source of knowledge. The authors expected that solving problems with only correct answers would not require assumptions about the nature of knowledge. Rather, they would be involved in answering the question about truth, a task that would involve epistemological assumptions, according to Kitchener's (1983) three-level model of cognitive processing. The results confirmed their expectations as student performance in a syllogism problem-solving task did not correlate with their performance in the essay written to solve the ill-defined problem (Is truth unchanging?). Moreover, the five dimensions underlying students' personal epistemologies explained a significant portion of performance variance in the ill-defined problem-solving only. Those who formulated a more relativistic answer to the dilemma about the stability of the truth held more sophisticated beliefs about the nature and source of knowledge.

The construct of epistemic worldviews was proposed by Spiro and his collaborators' (Spiro, Feltovich, & Coulson, 1996), who examined the relationship between different views on learning in complex domains. They developed the Cognitive Flexibility Inventory (CFI) as an assessment instrument aimed at identifying beliefs and preferences about learning as related to advanced knowledge acquisition in ill-structured domains. Through this instrument, two epistemic worldviews, defined as "prefigurative schemas," have been identified in medical students. They are prefigurative in that they constrain the individual's understanding of what knowledge is and how it can be acquired. They act as lenses that determine the kind of schemas an individual is more likely to produce. To exemplify, a student who believes that complex knowledge can first be decomposed into separate pieces and then recombined as a whole, in order to understand it better, has difficulty in reaching a deep understanding of conceptual material characterized by interaction and codetermination of its elements. The first epistemic worldview is a reductive one, and a learner who holds this kind of prefigurative schema has the following characteristics:

1. Seeks and relies on single, rather than multiple, representations of complex phenomena;
2. Decomposes systems into separate parts and then lists them to make a synthesis of components, thus neglecting interconnections among elements;
3. Expects regularity in knowledge structures as it is assumed that the world is essentially orderly;

4. Avoids complexity and ambiguity, seeks out simplicity and closure;
5. Retrieves and applies preexisting knowledge structures in rigid ways;
6. Does not recognize the experiential tone of ideas that are seen as abstract entities;
7. Tends to absorb knowledge passively, depends on authorities, and is concerned about being judged by others.

The second epistemic worldview is expansive, and the learner holding it has a set of beliefs directly opposed to those constituting the reductive worldview.

Relations can be found between the three constructs mentioned so far; that is, epistemological positions, epistemological beliefs, and epistemic worldviews (Fig. 8.1). For instance, the reductive prefigurative schema that a student may hold corresponds with the dualistic position and belief in simple, certain knowledge, and in authority as a source of knowledge.

A study by Jacobson & Spiro (1995), grounded theoretically on the framework of the cognitive flexibility theory (Spiro, Coulson, Feltovich, & Anderson, 1994), examined whether there are differences in learning between students with the expansive and reductive epistemic worldviews. In the experimental condition, the participants worked at the computer with a hypertext about science, technology, and society, whereas in the control condition participants had the same information in a traditional text characterized by linearity and chapter divisions. The findings show a significant difference in performance in a transfer task that required writing an essay about a topic that was not included in the material studied, but related to it. Experimental condition students who scored in the complex/flexible range of the CFI attained higher scores in the transfer measure than students in the same condition, but in the simple/rigid range of the CFI.

Epistemological Beliefs and Learning in Science and Mathematics. Epistemological beliefs have been investigated not only as general convictions about the nature and acquisition of knowledge, but also as convictions about knowing and learning in specific domains, mainly science and mathematics. This section is not aimed at comprehensively reviewing all existing research, but rather underlining some issues, concerning beliefs and learning about the two specific fields of knowledge most studied, that are relevant to the discourse developed in this chapter.

Concerning the scientific area, scholars have investigated the beliefs of students of various ages regarding the nature of science and its knowledge construction methods (e.g., Carey, Evans, Honda, Jay, & Unger,

1989; Désautels & Larochelle, 1998; Driver, Leach, Millar, & Scott, 1996; Lederman, 1992; Ryder, Leach, & Driver, 1999), beliefs about the modeling process and use of models in science (e.g., Grosslight, Unger, & Smith, 1991), and beliefs about the structure and learning of physics (e.g., Hammer, 1994; Roth & Roychoudhury, 1993, 1994).

Overall, it can be stated that students with naïve beliefs hold an empiricist or objectivist view of the nature of science and scientific enterprise that leads them to believe that scientists use pure facts about the world as indubitable empirical evidence. On the other hand, students with sophisticated beliefs hold a constructivist view of science that implies recognizing the role of scientists' theoretical frameworks, distinction, and coordination between theories and evidence.

The influence of personal scientific epistemologies on learning science knowledge was also investigated, albeit scantily. Songer and Linn (1991) found that only middle school students with a "dynamic" view of science—that is, it evolves and requires active construction of connections between concepts to be learned—integrated information while trying to understand the underlying explanatory principles of the thermodynamics phenomena examined. Similar findings were reported by Edmondson and Novak (1993) with university students. Schauble, Klopfer, and Raghavan (1991) studied specific beliefs about scientific experimentation and their effects on understanding causal relations to be taken into account when solving the given problems. Students had two types of models of experimentation. One was a scientific model that led to trying to understand the processes generating an effect. The other was an "engineering" model that led to manipulating variables to produce an effect. Only students who held the scientific model of experimentation were more likely to explore and select experimental data, interpret them in the light of their hypotheses, and pay more attention in excluding causal relations between variables and the effect studied. The relations between beliefs about science and beliefs about learning in science are shown in Fig. 8.1.

Concerning the mathematical area, it has been documented that student beliefs about mathematics and mathematics learning and problem solving affect their problem-solving performance. Through an intensive study of students in a high school geometry class, Schoenfeld (1988, 1989) clearly showed that although the discipline was taught in a way that would be evaluated as good teaching and the students scored well in typical achievement tests, their beliefs about the discipline and themselves as learners of mathematics were maladaptive to learning. For example, they believed that each mathematical problem could be solved in a few minutes and only in one way, and if it were not possible to solve it in a short time, it was not worth spending extra time thinking about it. Silver (1985) found the same beliefs identified by Schoenfeld and underlined how mathematical tasks are approached differently by students who believe that they should consider the structure underlying the problems to be solved and by students who believe they should consider surface details in texts. Also, Lampert (1990) pointed out that students' common view of mathematics is characterized in terms of certainty, and fast and correct answers that become true when accepted by the authority of a teacher.

Earlier, Lester and Garofalo (1982) also revealed beliefs about mathematics that were not adaptive to learning in third graders. They believed that the difficulty of a problem was due to the quantity and size of big numbers; that all problems could be solved by applying one operation, in rare cases two; that the operation to be carried out is determined by key words in the text, usually in the last sentence or question, thus it is not necessary to read all the text; only if there is time can the work be monitored and controlled.

Verschaffel, De Corte, and Lasure (1994, 1999) found in upper primary school students the belief that real-world knowledge is not relevant when mathematical word problems are to be solved. Interestingly, learners can be aware of a difference between the conventional answers given in a school mathematics test context—in which realistic considerations are not required according to their view—and answers given in real situations (Greer & Verschaffel, 1997). This belief turned out to be very entrenched and resistant to change. Belief in big numbers as an index of problem difficulty was found more frequently in elementary school poor mathematical problem-solvers than in good problem-solvers, who also manifested less metacognitive awareness (Lucangeli, Coi, & Bosco, 1997). The relations between beliefs about mathematics and beliefs about learning in mathematics are shown in Fig. 8.1.

Epistemological Beliefs and Conceptual Change Learning. In the previous sections, the importance and influence of personal epistemologies on different types of learning were elucidated. What has to be examined now, as the core focus of the chapter, is the relationship between beliefs about the nature of knowledge and knowing and conceptual change learning. The question is: To what extent do some beliefs facilitate and others impede knowledge restructuring?

Personal epistemologies are not foreign to the process by which individuals manage to revise their knowledge structures in order to meaningfully integrate new and preexisting knowledge. For instance, it can be speculated quite easily that to believe that knowledge is certain, absolute, simple, and comprising many isolated facts to be memorized, or to believe that knowledge is a complex system of interconnected elements that are continuously evolving and must be learned through integration of information, can make a difference in conceptual change learning. In their analysis of responses to anomalous data, Chinn and Brewer (1993, 1998) identified epistemological beliefs among the factors that may influence an individual's response to evidence conflicting with their personal theories about a phenomenon or event. Epistemological presuppositions appear in the model of conceptual change proposed by Vosniadou (1994, chap. 13, this volume) on the basis of systematic research on the development of concepts in astronomy, although they reflect more specific content, not general beliefs about knowledge. The *framework theories* (Wellman & Gelman, 1992) that constrain specific theories leading to the formation of mental models are made up of epistemological and ontological presuppositions. For instance, children's and lay adults' alternative mental models of heat, as well as the specific and framework theories underlying them, are based on the ontological presuppositions that objects have properties and "hot" and "cold" are properties of the object, along with many others. They are also grounded on the epistemological presuppositions that things are as they appear to be and that something exists only if perceptible to the senses. Changing the framework theory is a long and gradual process as it requires modification of entrenched presuppositions that are linked to years of observation and experience. However, it is a necessary condition for successfully integrating new information into a learner's conceptual structures without producing "synthetic models," that is, conceptual compromises between old and new knowledge, combined to avoid changing those presuppositions.

Before reviewing research on the influence of epistemological beliefs on conceptual change, it is necessary to clarify that in this and subsequent sections, the term *epistemological beliefs* basically refers to Schommer's (1994a) different dimensions that are not organized into stage-like structures and may vary within individuals. The components of the construct include beliefs about the nature of both knowledge and learning (see Table 8.1). According to Hofer and Pintrich (1997), the inclusion of beliefs about learning (i.e., belief in quick learning and in the fixed ability to learn) in the construct of epistemological beliefs is questionable because they do not deal explicitly with how knowledge is defined and justified, that is, with the traditional definition of the construct that psychological research has taken from philosophy. For a clear definition of the content, Hofer and Pintrich therefore proposed to limit it to beliefs about the nature of knowledge and the process of knowing, although they maintain that beliefs about learning (and teaching as well) and knowledge may be intertwined in an individual's network of beliefs. It should be noted that not all of the few studies carried out on the relationship between personal epistemologies and the revision of ideas in learning concepts, which will be reviewed in this section, have considered all the dimensions emerging from the use of Schommer's questionnaire (the instrument used in all four

TABLE 8.1
Dimensions of the Epistemological Belief Construct Used in Reviewed Research on Their Influence on Conceptual Change

Nature of Knowledge	*Nature of Learning*
Dimension of certain/uncertain knowledge: absolute and stable/tentative and evolving	Dimension of speed of learning: quick or not-at-all/gradual process
Dimension of simple/complex knowledge: isolated, unambiguous items/interconnected concepts	Dimension of control of learning: fixed ability to learn/malleable ability to learn
Dimension of source of knowledge: handed down by omniscient authority/derived from reason	

studies reviewed) in their analyses. As described shortly, only the dimension of certain/evolving knowledge, the most pertinent to examining the role of belief about the nature of knowledge in the revision of conceptions, was taken into account in two of the four reviewed studies (Mason, 2000, 2001b). This general epistemological dimension also includes belief in the source of knowledge, that is, belief in knowledge as delivered by an omniscient authority or derived from reason.

Qian and Alvermann (1995) investigated the role of beliefs on the nature of knowledge in learning concepts from reading a text. Students in Grades 9 through 12 read a refutational text on the Newtonian theory of motion, which directly compared alternative conceptions about motion. In particular it contradicted the pre-Newtonian impetus theory. Their epistemological beliefs were assessed by a shorter version of Schommer's Epistemological Questionnaire. The findings indicate the importance of epistemological beliefs in predicting conceptual change. Students with less sophisticated beliefs were less likely to abandon their naïve conceptions about motion. On the contrary, students with more advanced beliefs generated more change in their conceptual structures. In particular, two epistemological dimensions, beliefs in simple and certain knowledge and in quick learning, were important factors predicting knowledge restructuring.

The relationship between the learning environment and epistemological beliefs about conceptual change was studied by Windschitl and Andre (1998). University students enrolled in a human anatomy and physiological survey course were required to learn the cardiovascular system in two simulation conditions. In the confirmatory one, which reflected a more objectivist learning environment, they used simulation in prescribed steps, following written instructions that led to solving a number of problems. In the exploratory condition, which reflected a constructivist learning environment, the students were involved in formulating and testing hypotheses following a thematic instructional guide as possible solutions to the same questions given to the confirmatory group. Students' personal epistemologies were assessed by Schommer's Epistemological Questionnaire. The constructivist environment produced significantly greater conceptual change than the objectivist for two of six common alternative conceptions. In addition, the instruction interacted with students' epistemological beliefs. Those who held more sophisticated beliefs about the nature of knowledge and learning produced better results in terms of changing their own conceptions when they were allowed to explore the new conceptual material in the constructivist setting, rather than in the traditional instructional setting. The opposite occurred for the students with less advanced personal epistemologies. They produced more conceptual change when they followed the instructions given on how to use the simulation than in the constructivist situation. These students believed in simple and certain knowledge. An instructional context that showed them how to proceed step by step was consistent with their learning approach and was motivating. Students with more mature personal epistemologies believed in complex and continuously evolving knowledge and were more comfortable and motivated in a learning environment that called for their active construction of new knowledge. It corresponded more closely with their beliefs and attitudes toward knowledge and knowing.

Mason (2000) investigated epistemological beliefs in relation to anomalous data in theory change on two controversial topics. One was scientific, the extinction of dinosaurs in the Cretaceous era, and the other historical, the construction of the great pyramids in Giza (Egypt). Eighth graders were introduced to two theories for each topic, the first of which was familiar; that is, the meteor impact theory for dinosaur extinction and the classic theory for the construction of the pyramids. The second two were alternative theories, that volcanoes were responsible for the extinction of the dinosaurs and that a more ancient population may have built the pyramids. For both topics, the introduction of the alternative theory was preceded by presenting evidence supporting it, but conflicting with the familiar theory. The findings indicated that acceptance of anomalous data made the most significant contribution to theory change. Students' change in theory about the two controversial topics was, in fact, strongly mediated by their response to anomalous data: The more these were considered as valid and incoherent with the theory held, the more they accepted the alternative theories. Students who discounted anomalous data, either by evaluating them as invalid or consistent with their familiar theory, were more likely to refuse the alternative theories. Acceptance of anomalous data was, in turn, related to the dimension of students' belief about the stability (certain/evolving) and source (handed down by authority/derived from reason) of knowledge. This dimension, that includes both these aspects of the nature of knowledge, emerged from an exploratory factor analysis of the data gathered by administering Schommer's Epistemological Questionnaire. As mentioned before, it was the only dimension of students' beliefs network that was taken into account. Although not strongly, the relation between belief about knowledge and knowing and acceptance of anomalous data was greater for the scientific topic. Students who believed in the changing nature of knowledge tended to accept evidence conflicting with their entrenched conceptions and, consequently, to change their theory about the topic. On the other hand, students who believed in the static nature of knowledge tended to discount, in one way or another, anomalous data and remain attached to their current theory.

Students' beliefs in the stability/instability of knowledge mediated the acceptance of evidence conflicting with their prior knowledge, although this effect was not strong. With this regard, a small number of students who scored highest and lowest in the dimension of certain knowledge were interviewed individually. The purpose of the interviews was to analyze qualitatively the justifications of their ratings for two representative items of this epistemological dimension: Scientists can ultimately arrive at the truth, and today's truth may be tomorrow's fiction. Concerning the first item, the students who agreed with it appealed to the following reasons to justify their rating about scientists: (a) they are experts as they have studied a lot; (b) they are people with special abilities; (c) they use powerful instruments and procedures; (d) they put a lot of dedication into their work. The following examples of justifications illustrate these ideas:[1]

> Because they're studying, they've been looking for the truth and they'll continue to do so. They're people who study even more than teachers, they're the ones who go and find out things, perhaps about the Egyptians now. They're the ones who discovered the Pyramids. (Alice)

> Because they might feel an incredible passion for these things, so great that sometimes it leads them to find the truth about almost everything. Some subjects are more complicated, some less, but they get there in the end because of their passion. If they didn't have this passion, they wouldn't be as involved as they are, I think. (Martina)

Justifications given by the students who disagreed with the item were based on the following aspects of their representations of scientists: (a) some things are hard to discover; (b) new problems in knowledge will al-

[1]The students' sentences in interviews and written notes and texts have been translated trying to maintain the same "tone" as in the original Italian version.

ways arise; (c) they have their limitations, too; (d) some pieces of evidence will always be missing. What follows are examples of justifications given by students who referred to these different reasons:

> No, they can't because for each thing they discover there'll always be ten questions without an answer. How can they know about the whole world? Impossible. They can get to the truth for some things but not for everything. They can't arrive at everything. The more they move forward in knowing things, the more things they find that they can't understand. (Silvia)
>
> No, because they're ordinary people like us. I don't think they've got special abilities to discover the truth, the things that happened, perhaps a long time ago. I don't think scientists can reach . . . , I mean, they must have limitations because they're just like us, they can't. Yes, they can progress, but I think the human being has limitations which can't be overcome. (Jennifer)

Concerning the item on knowledge uncertainty, the students disagreeing with it appealed to the nature of knowledge as introduced in books or learned at school, which is certain and absolute:

> Because the truth is true, because when somebody tells the truth, it is the truth . . . What's in books isn't changed ever. Books become different, but the things written inside don't change. (Gianluca)
>
> A true thing can't change, if it's true it's true and that's that. It can't become false all of a sudden. Things you learn at school are true, you can be uncertain about friendship perhaps, not school things (Laura).

Students in agreement with the item referred to some events in the history of science they studied at school, which document the evolving nature of knowledge:

> Because truth can't always be the same. For example, what's true today, say a theory about some ancient populations, can change if other information is discovered. For example, once the Earth was thought to be at the center of the Universe with the stars revolving around it. Instead it's the opposite, it's the Earth that revolves. Truth has changed. (Alessandro)

The fact that more sophisticated beliefs about this aspect of the nature of knowledge contribute, although not strongly, to the acceptance of anomalous data, and then to theory change, highlights the importance of students' belief that theories change because what was once accepted as true may no longer be acceptable. This may occur both on the "distal" level of scientific community knowledge (professional science) and on the "proximal" level of one's own scientific understanding (Hogan, 2000).

A related study (Mason, 2001b) aimed at identifying the different reasons given by students for accepting or refusing evidence conflicting with their held theory, and seeing whether those reasons fit into the taxonomy of responses proposed by Chinn and Brewer (1998). A qualitative analysis was carried out on all written explanations the students were asked to provide in order to motivate their initial theory preference, anomalous data acceptance or rejection, and their final theory preference for both controversial topics. Written explanations were categorized on the basis of the reason types given by the learners. One of the reasons most cited in sustaining one's own point of view in all steps of the research procedure concerned the epistemological belief in the authoritative source of knowledge. For example, the reasons given by many students to justify their belief in the first theories introduced, the familiar ones, and their rejection of the second, alternative theories were expressed in this way:

> I am pretty sure this theory is true because of the many findings supporting it. In particular, one piece of evidence has impressed me. If the special element found, iridium, is very rare on Earth but, on the other hand, very common on asteroids, it is a clear sign in favor of the theory based on the meteor impact on the Earth. (Eleonora)

> I do not think this theory is true because it is the first time I have heard about it. I have never read it in books so I am not convinced. (Alice)

The work of scientists, as well as teachers and books, appeared as major sources of believable knowledge. Interestingly, students who accepted evidence that conflicted with their personal theories and those who rejected it, both referred to this epistemological dimension, but their beliefs were opposing (Mason, 2000, p. 339):

> The very clear evidence is based on long years of study carried out by qualified people using the most appropriate tools, so it should be considered as valid and acceptable. I realize that my initial belief in the meteor theory as the cause of dinosaur extinction is no longer right. (Riccardo)

> I think the data are not valid so they can be debated. I believe, in fact, that scientists cannot always be sure of what they do and say. They make mistakes, too. (Michela)

Riccardo's belief in scientists' authority as a source of believable knowledge caused to value the evidence that conflicted with his prior knowledge, that is, he accepted it as valid and recognized its inconsistency with what he already knew about the extinction of dinosaurs. This, in turn, led him to change his initial theory about the phenomenon. On the other hand, Michela's belief that scientists' authority as a source of certain knowledge is questionable led her to discount the believability of the data and it was functional to her not changing her initial theory about the phenomenon. The beliefs expressed by Riccardo and Michela are two examples of how assumptions about knowledge in general, or related to a specific field—in this case, scientists as an authoritative source of knowledge—influence individuals' responses to anomalous data, as pointed out by Chinn and Brewer (1993, 1998). Both epistemological beliefs intervened in students' process of dealing with different theories about a controversial topic, although the contribution was in opposing directions.

INTENTIONALITY AND PROBLEMS OF KNOWLEDGE

As stated earlier, self-initiated and self-controlled conscious and goal-directed actions define the core of intentionality in learning. In the process of conceptual change, intentionality requires that students should deal with problems of knowledge. This means that first they must notice that what they already know does not match a new conception or perceive the potential of new information that can lead to other knowledge. Once they have noticed or perceived that, they have to make the learning process into a problem-solving process in that "the goal itself is a learning goal and (that) there is something problematic about achieving this goal" (Bereiter & Scardamalia, 1989, p. 365). In other words, the students must invest their effort in solving problems that have to do with the state of their own understanding of phenomena or events. The result of such a learning process is a goal of knowledge that brings about the revision of prior knowledge and the attainment of higher levels of understanding.

To illustrate this issue I refer to the written production of elementary school students involved in a research project on instructional practices to promote and sustain conceptual change in science domains (Mason, 1998, 2001a; Mason & Boscolo, 2000). What follows are notes written by two fourth graders in a classroom in which writing was introduced as a learning tool in science classes, that is, to make explicit and communicate ideas, to reason and reflect on one's own and others' conceptions. A unit on the role of decomposers in the decay process, among them microorganisms, which was part of a wider curriculum on ecological concepts, was implemented in the classroom. This acted as a community of learning in which thinking, reasoning, arguing, and reflecting were greatly valued by the teacher to support conceptual change. In their notes the learners expressed what puzzled them after seeing the effects of yeast combined with sugar and mold on different food items (Mason, 2001a, p. 319):

> Now my new idea is that yeast is a living thing and that without sugar it cannot "grow." I understand this point thanks to the experiment and the discussion. However, not everything is clear yet. I still do not know how yeast is born and also how it dies. I have to understand this. (Giampiero)

> I have doubts about the fact that mold on food can be compared to a disease because I do know that mold comes from spores in the air which land on the food, that is from the outside like a disease which comes from a microbe getting into our body, but a disease can come also from our insides. I am struggling with this stuff. (Maria)

In these notes, the students' intentions to move toward a higher level of understanding and their personal learning goal of knowledge construction is quite evident.

Next is a written text produced by a fourth grader to reason on ideas stated in a group discussion on the crucial question of what is food for plants, during the implementation of a curriculum unit on photosynthesis (Mason & Boscolo, 2000). Its reflective nature is another relevant example of awareness of knowledge that is lacking. As pointed out by Bereiter and Scardamalia (1989), a vital part of intentional learning is knowing what one does not know and prefiguring a state of knowledge not currently possessed.

> Can plants stay alive only through water? This is the question. In my opinion they cannot live on water only because they also need sunlight and should be put outdoors. Yes, it is true that water contains many mineral salts but my idea is that plants need sunlight as it warms them and if they lived in the cold they would die. Jessica has said that she keeps a plant inside always. I think it is impossible for a plant to stay alive if it is always inside as it needs to stay in the air and capture sunlight, not the artificial light of a room. Every one of my neighbors' plants died because they did not have the true, natural, sunlight. I made a comparison with cactus. The cactus is a plant which lives in the desert. Yes, I think it needs water but above all warmth and sunlight; it is in the desert, in fact. Moreover, I made another comparison: Can a human being survive only on water and stay in the artificial light of lamps? No, I do not think so as humans need other food and to breathe fresh air. My conclusion is that plants need many things just like humans. So far I am not able to say what these things are (p. 213). (Alessia)

It is more likely that a student processes new information in greater depth when trying to compensate for a knowledge gap. An awareness of the need to revise knowledge is a necessary precondition for the conceptual change process. The successful integration of new and preexisting information, pursued intentionally, leads to awareness of the changes occurring in one's own conceptual structures. This appears in the following reflective text written by a fifth grader after a group discussion on food chains (Mason, 1998):

> Today we discussed the expression "food chain". In a previous class I completed some cards on food chains. At the end of the discussion I realized that I had maintained a totally different thing. In fact the plant is at the basis of a food chain as it is the only living thing which produces by itself its own food (producer). Instead on the cards I had put first the biggest animal that actually is the last in a chain. I believed that it was number one in a chain because it is the biggest and strongest and so it can eat everything else. Now I am aware that it is a consumer, which can be primary, secondary, tertiary, etc. according to the link of the chain. If plants did not exist, animals and human beings could not live because they produce oxygen and are the first link of the chain. In fact, if they did not exist, herbivores would die and, in turn, carnivores and omnivores as well since they eat the former (p. 375). (Valentina)

This kind of reflection shows that the learner experienced the changes of representation in her cognitive structures. She succeeded in self-regulating her learning because she intentionally pursued the goal of knowledge revision. She was able to express her initial conception and why she had it, as well as the conception she constructed in the scaffolded context of the group discussion and why she now had the new conception.

LINKING PERSONAL EPISTEMOLOGIES AND INTENTIONALITY IN THE PROCESS OF CONCEPTUAL CHANGE

To link conceptual change with personal epistemologies, it is necessary to explain how beliefs about the nature and acquisition of knowledge act as thinking dispositions to guide students' efforts toward the goal of knowledge revision. To give a clear sense of if, and how, personal epistemologies contribute to conscious and purposive learning actions directed at re-constructing one's own conceptions to solve problems of knowledge, I refer to two cases of eighth graders, Giuliana and Valerio, representative of opposite stances. Both participated in the studies mentioned earlier on the relationship between anomalous data and epistemological beliefs in theory change on controversial topics. Their oral and written discourse on the nature of knowledge, in particular on the two dimensions regarding its structure and certainty, is a good reflection of the different ways in which their personal epistemologies affected their learning actions producing, or not producing, knowledge revision.

The Case of Giuliana

Giuliana believed that scientists cannot reach the ultimate truth, as new problems of knowledge will always be raised. In the individual interview, she maintained:

> I think we'll never get to the truth, because, as we get into the future, there'll be more and more research, newer and newer findings, there'll be perhaps new machinery, that is new tools to certify the truth; but there won't be complete truth because we won't be there. O.K., they say that that civilization actually existed, but how can we be sure of that? I'm thinking of history. It's the same in the science domain. We're now studying what scientists used to think, Darwin's and Lamarck's theory of evolution for example, but nowadays new things have been discovered. For instance, now we don't know how to cure cancer, but there's research going on, and perhaps they'll find a way to cure it in future. However, people are dying of it now, in future they might not die anymore. Even if we're able to cure cancer, perhaps there'll be another incurable disease, because even if they succeed in curing one thing there'll always be something incurable. I don't think man knows everything or may ever be able to know everything. I don't think that's possible.

She was also strongly convinced of the uncertain nature of knowledge that continuously evolves:

> I think nothing is true. You can say about the Egyptians, for example, that once such and such was believed, but now there's another truth, we aren't sure of anything. We weren't there at the time of the Egyptians, and so we can only hypothesize about it. Historians rely on documents, studies, findings, but I really don't know how true it is what they say. We can say it's true now, but tomorrow another scientist may say "I've found another document that proves something else" and then we'll have two different things and we'll no longer know which is true and which is false. When the atom was discovered it was considered the smallest particle, but now the quark's been discovered. What we believed before, now we don't believe anymore because the quark is smaller. Perhaps in fifty years' time an even smaller particle will turn up and then we'll be told that what we believed in before was false. It's really something to do with progress.

In her epistemological perspective, the nature of knowledge is also not simple and unambiguous. She did not seek single answers. Also, she believed that thinking about problems that cannot have a single answer is not a waste of time:

> It's important to "waste time" on questions. It's right to search, think, understand by discussing what's still unknown as true. It's right to doubt it because we must discuss, and discussing about uncertain things is better. We

> can listen to others' opinions. We cannot come to a single answer, but this is never a waste of time. At least for me, a discussion's never time lost. Discussing's always fruitful to understand others' ideas or even as a pastime. Yes, it can be a pastime when you go to a meeting where they discuss. Discussing is important to a person culturally.

For both topics, she fully accepted the evidence conflicting with her held theories, recognizing its validity and inconsistency with her prior knowledge. Acceptance of the anomalous data made her value the alternative theories and accept them as new possible accounts of the phenomena examined. She wrote clearly that reflecting on evidence she had read led to discounting the familiar theories because empirical data supported the alternative ones. Aware of the cognitive conflict in her conceptual structures, she intentionally built on new knowledge to resolve it, showing self-regulated learning.

As a comment on her change in theory, on an epistemological plane, she wrote:

> It is not difficult for me to change a theory but it does not mean that I continuously "change my hat." To make me change my ideas there should be specific, detailed, valid evidence supporting a new theory, otherwise I do not change it.

She also wrote that to change theory about one topic was not as easy as the other:

> I think that it is easier to change your theory about dinosaurs because to change your theory about the Egyptian pyramids means changing knowledge about the history of humankind. To a person the history of humankind is more important than a theory on dinosaurs, that is, on their extinction by a meteor or volcano. Human history is the most important to a person because it documents the life of past peoples and it is also important not to make the same mistakes as made in the past.

Reflecting on the work she had done that resulted in conceptual change, when interviewed Giuliana maintained:

> There are those who're willing to change their mind and those who aren't. For these people what they had studied once is true and will be true for all their life. Instead, we need to be a bit elastic. Those who never change won't be willing, if they have cancer, to undergo new studies, new experiments as guinea-pigs. They won't be willing as they'll have a barrier in their minds. Probably I will. If they say that there's a new cure, those people will continue the traditional treatment because they believe that only that cure's the true cure. I'd rather have an open mind, be flexible, and if they tell me that

> the new cure could be better, I'd willingly try it out. If I were a terminal patient, I'd die. This means that it's better to undergo experiments. If doctors try new medicines out and then can say that they're effective as they have been experimented on my body, it means that other people will survive since I've been willing to be a guinea-pig. Later in time many people will live because I underwent the treatment. This is important.

Giuliana holds beliefs about the nature of knowledge and knowing that made her treat learning as inherently problematic (Bereiter & Scardamalia, 1989). By approaching it within a problem-solving framework, she elaborated and revised goals to be pursued in order to construct more advanced knowledge. Her learning was intentional learning within the framework of solving a conflict between two positions on a phenomenon by evaluating evidence supporting them. It resulted in theory change and metaconceptual awareness of successful knowledge revision.

The Case of Valerio

Valerio believed that scientists can arrive at the truth for everything as they possess special features, both cognitive and motivational:

> They're very interested in what they do. They aren't indifferent, they care about it. They want to discover things. Maybe they're cleverer than the other people, they get to understand more quickly than the others.

In his personal epistemology, knowledge is absolute, certain, and of the right/wrong type:

> What's true is true and that's all. What's right isn't wrong. That's all. What's true cannot become false, that is, change, more or less suddenly. What we now study, in history, for example, is true, we know that it's true. They can't say that it's false, never.

In addition, knowledge is believed to be simple and unambiguous as there is a single answer for each question:

> There couldn't be more hypotheses and theories on a problem because otherwise we couldn't know anything. About an archaeological find, for instance, there's only a theory otherwise we could not say what age or civilization it belongs to.

Consequently, in his epistemological framework to think on problems that do not have a clear, unique answer is meaningless:

> To know that a thing's right and remains as such is always much better. Language's a subjective thing, but science's objective, the things are certain and remain as they are . . . To think of some things, to talk about things that aren't clear's a waste of time. Things have to be known clearly.

For both topics, he discounted the evidence conflicting with his theories. He admitted that the evidence he had read about the extinction of dinosaurs could be valid but, at the same time, he evaluated it as not inconsistent with the theory he held on the phenomenon. He failed to recognize the conflict of information. One theory (the familiar) is catastrophic as it states that the extinction was rapid like the effect of the meteor on the earth's surface. The other (the alternative) is gradual as it stated that prolonged massive volcanic eruptions caused the extinction of dinosaurs. Valerio explained that the anomalous data (introduced to sustain the volcano theory) supported the meteor impact theory. Thus, his initial theory remained unchanged and it was justified by maintaining that the theory is proven to be true by all the empirical evidence found regarding the event.

He stated that the anomalous data about the construction of the pyramids could not be valid and justified his belief by referring to a personal reason:

> I like the Egyptians, I like this population. I prefer to believe that the pyramids were built by Egyptians and not by any another ancient population.

In addition, he evaluated the evidence conflicting with the familiar theory on the topic as consistent with it, as many things could still be discovered and at the moment the data supporting the alternative theory are not inconsistent with what he had learned at school. He only admitted that the pyramids might not have been built as tombs for the Pharaohs but for other reasons. Commenting on the ease or difficulty of changing conceptions on a topic, he wrote:

> It is very difficult for me to change a theory I believe in because I think it is better than many others. Even in the case it is wrong, I will not reject it because it is my theory.

In fact, Valerio did not change his theory, either about the extinction of dinosaurs or construction of the great pyramids. However, he admitted that to change his theory about the historical topic would have been easier than for the scientific one as we know less about the first.

Valerio held beliefs about the nature of knowledge and knowing that did not help him engage in a process of theory change. The belief that knowledge is certain, so that what was previously known should remain unaltered, acted as a constraint because knowledge revision was not his learning goal. He did not recognize any conflict of information so he did not act in a problem-solving framework with intellectual efforts directed at restructuring his conceptions. He carried out the learning activities but did not treat learning as problematic. Moreover, his affective attachment to the initial theories as "his" theories further constrained the process of conceptual change.

In the Cognitive Reconstruction of Knowledge Model, Dole and Sinatra (1998) used the term *engagement*, previously introduced for reading (Guthrie & Wigfield, 1997), to indicate a continuum in the processing of information. At one end of the continuum, individuals are engaged superficially and the level of elaboration is low. This may result in the assimilation of new information into existing knowledge structures without significantly changing conceptions held. At the other end, they are engaged in effortful, deep, critical elaborations that may result in conceptual change, although this is not guaranteed. The highest form of engagement implies not only comparing and connecting existing and new information, but also reflecting about what an individual is thinking and why, as illustrated in several examples reported here. Situated at the intentional level of cognition, the construct of engagement combines both cognitive and motivational aspects of learning. A student may engage in the use of elaborative strategies and in metacognitive reflection but with no motivation to change conceptions. In this regard, a significant aspect that emerged from the study previously mentioned (Mason, 2001b) was the affective involvement by some students with the meteor impact theory on dinosaur extinction. They could admit that scientists were not wrong in supporting the alternative theory with evidence, nevertheless they could not renounce their deep "attachment" to the theory held, as expressed in the following written justifications:

> The data are not sufficiently valid. In fact, the theory of volcanic eruptions does not convince me. However, if scientists have examined samples of the clay layer and come to the conclusion that it deposited over a very long period of time, this would be evidence of the truth of the volcano theory. But I believe that dinosaurs disappeared in a short period of time because of an asteroid which devastated the Earth. (Eleonora)

> I do not want to say that scientists are wrong, they might be right. I only mean to say that I am fully convinced of the meteor theory and I like it. (Michael)

In these cases, students' affective attachment to the idea of a meteor colliding with the Earth strongly contributed to them keeping their initial theory against evidence to the contrary. Compared with Valerio, they manifested a higher level of engagement that involved metaconceptual awareness (Vosniadou, chapter 13, this volume) that the data they had read conflicted with their entrenched theory and that acceptance of this evidence would imply theory change. In addition, their beliefs about scientists' work led them to accept the validity of the data. However, they did not pursue the goal of embracing a new theory as they were not motivated to abandon a familiar theory to which they were deeply committed. As highlighted (Pintrich, Marx, & Boyle, 1993), conceptual change is not a "cold" process but rather a process of evolving "hot" cognitions. Short but hard-hitting expressions such as "This theory is what I believe in! Nobody can make me change it!" reflect the degree to which a student's affective involvement may constrain it.

CONCLUSIONS AND FUTURE DIRECTIONS FOR RESEARCH

In this chapter I argued that epistemological beliefs—that is, beliefs about the nature and acquisition of knowledge—may facilitate or constrain intentional conceptual change. Intentionality has been described as conscious and purposive actions, initiated by the learner toward the goal of learning. After reviewing empirical research on the influence of epistemological beliefs on different aspects of learning, it has been considered how these beliefs can also affect knowledge revision processes. To be intentional learners pursuing the goal of changing conceptions, students should be engaged in problems of knowledge; that is, they should notice that they approach new information that does not fit into their conceptual structures, or perceive that new information could lead to other knowledge to be integrated with what is already known. Students' efforts must be invested in solving problems that have to do with the state of their own understanding of a phenomenon or event.

Successful integration of old and new information starts from an awareness of the need for revision of knowledge and ends with an awareness of the changes occurring in one's own conceptual structures. In this highly demanding process, both cognitively and motivationally, epistemological beliefs may or may not guide students' efforts toward the learning goal of knowledge revision. Several examples taken from research findings with elementary and middle school students documented how their oral and written discourse can reflect different moments in an intentional conceptual change process. Naïve beliefs about the nature of knowledge and knowing reflect thinking dispositions that are not conducive to developing the intention to change conceptions, whereas advanced or sophisticated beliefs direct and sustain learners' intellectual effort, whose components are both cognitive and motivational, in producing knowledge changes. Beliefs about the nature of knowledge and knowing contribute to determining the degree of engagement at the intentional level of cognition. A student who believes that knowledge is absolute and certain, made up of compartmentalized facts that must be memorized in order to learn them, and that what is known cannot change otherwise the truth would not exist, cannot engage in conceptual change processes to the same extent as a student who believes that knowledge is hypothetical and evolving, that what is true today may no longer be acceptable in the future, that learning means making connections between concepts and integrating them in a consistent whole. In the first case effort is more likely to be avoided, whereas in the second it is more likely to be activated and directed toward the goal of knowledge revision. This conceptual model of the role of epistemological beliefs in intentional conceptual change is summarized in Fig. 8.2.

Recent research on powerful novel learning environments implemented in real classrooms, in science (e.g., Smith, Maclin, Houghton, & Hennessey, 2000) and mathematics (e.g., De Corte, Verschaffel, & Op't Eynde, 2000) has begun to indicate that some educational interventions can produce positive effects on students' beliefs about knowledge and knowing in these domains. Helping learners to refine their general and specific personal epistemologies is not only important to attaining the highest levels in the development of their theory of mind but also to improving thinking dispositions crucial to sustaining intentional conceptual change (Mason, 2002). Notwithstanding this last positive conclusion, some major questions may act as directions for future research, both theoretical and empirical.

First, there is a need to investigate the consistency or inconsistency of epistemological beliefs between contexts. In the cases of Giuliana and Valerio reported earlier, like other students, consistency emerged in how they responded to the epistemological questionnaire and interview questions, and how they dealt with the controversial topics. However, based on their research on different aged students' epistemology of science, some authors (Leach & Lewis, 2002; Leach, Millar, Ryder, & Séré, 2000) recently argued that students manifest different beliefs in different situations, so these convictions should not be referred to in isolation from the contexts in which they are activated (see also diSessa, Elby, & Hammer, chapter 9, this volume). Can a student's epistemology be inductivist for some questions and constructivist for others, depending on the situation? Or does a student's epistemological stance indicate a consistent position that is reflected in his or her reasoning in a wide variety of situations? The answer to this question is of critical importance as it shapes our conception about the role of personal epistemologies in conceptual change.

Second, research should investigate in greater depth the interactive dynamics between epistemological thinking and learning concepts in the

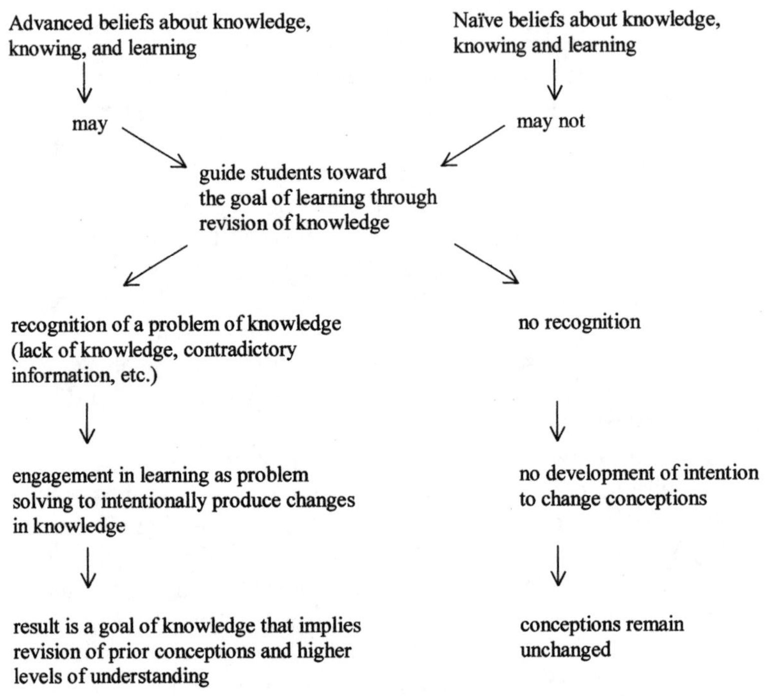

FIG. 8.2. A general conceptual model of epistemological beliefs in intentional conceptual change.

process of knowledge revision (Strike & Posner, 1993). If conceptual growth and change processes in science have been documented as affected by beliefs about the nature and acquisition of knowledge, can they be promoted and sustained by interventions aimed at refining these beliefs? If the construction of epistemological beliefs is affected by the ways concept learning is approached and assessed, can innovative educational interventions aimed at fostering and assessing deep conceptual understanding also be effective in refining students' personal epistemologies? In other words, to what extent can successful interventions in novel learning environments at school be effective in developing both personal knowledge structures and epistemologies, either general or specific, at the same time?

Third, the causal relation that links epistemological beliefs and conceptual change over time should be examined. The former are precursor to the latter and can facilitate or constrain it, as shown in the cases of Giuliana and Valerio. However, it could also be that students who engage in conceptual change first, are then motivated to change their epistemological beliefs. In other words, the students' change of conceptions about science or history content could lead them to a reexamination of more abstract beliefs about knowledge. For instance, if students are aware that they should revise their theory about the extinction of dinosaurs, this may cause them to question their general epistemological beliefs, not the other way around. Thus, could the line of development proceed from "concrete" to "abstract," that is, from changes of knowledge in a domain to changes of generalized beliefs about knowledge?

Fourth, volitional processes in conceptual change should be investigated, given that volition is what is intended as controlling and protecting intentions. Without them, even the best action plans are not necessarily successful (Corno, 1993). In what way(s) does volitional control mediate the effects of epistemological beliefs by highlighting the motivated persistent actions that feature intentional conceptual change? It is expected that thoughtful and reflective engagement in knowledge revision requires intent to learn by change of conceptions, decision to change, and maintenance of the intention until the learning goal is attained. As such, theoretical and empirical work should be carried out to further investigate the complex, but fascinating, topic of epistemological beliefs in intentional conceptual change.

REFERENCES

Alexander, P. A., & Dochy, F. J. R. C. (1994). Adults' views about knowing and believing. In R. Garner & P. A. Alexander (Eds.), *Beliefs about text and instruction with text* (pp. 223–244). Hillsdale, NJ: Lawrence Erlbaum Associates.

Alexander, P. A., & Dochy, F. J. R. C. (1995). Conceptions of knowledge and beliefs: A comparison across varying cultural and educational communities. *American Educational Research Journal, 32*, 413–442.

Alexander, P. A., Murphy, P. K., Guan J., & Murphy, P. A. (1998). How students and teachers in Singapore and the United States conceptualize knowledge and beliefs: Positioning learning within epistemological frameworks. *Learning and Instruction, 8*, 97–116.

Astington, J. W., Harris, P. L., & Olson, D. R. (1988). *Developing theories of mind.* Cambridge, UK: Cambridge University Press.

Baron, J. (1985). *Rationality and intelligence.* Cambridge, UK: Cambridge University Press.

Baron, J. (1991). Beliefs about thinking. In J. F. Voss, D. N. Perkins, & J. W. Segal (Eds.), *Informal reasoning and education* (pp. 169–186). Hillsdale: Lawrence Erlbaum Associates.

Baxter Magolda, M. B. (1992). *Knowing and reasoning in college. Gender-related patterns in students' intellectual development.* San Francisco, CA: Jossey-Bass.

Belenky, M. F., Clinchy, B. M., Goldberger, N. R., & Tarule, J. M. (1986). *Women' ways of knowing: The development of self, voice and mind.* New York: Basic Books.

Benack, S., & Basseches, M. A. (1989). Dialectical thinking and relativistic epistemology: Their relation to adult development. In M. L. Commonns, J. D. Sinnott, F. A. Richards, & C. Armon (Eds.), *Adult development*: Vol. 1. *Comparisons and applications of developmental models* (pp. 95–112). New York: Praeger.

Bereiter, C. (1990). Aspects of an educational learning theory. *Review of Educational Research, 60,* 603–624.

Bereiter, C., & Scardamalia, M. (1989). Intentional learning as a goal of instruction. In L. B. Resnick (Ed.), *Knowing, learning, and instruction: Essays in honor of Robert Glaser* (pp. 361-392). Hillsdale, NJ: Lawrence Erlbaum Associates.

Bloom, B. S., Engelhart, M. D., Furst, E. J., Hill, W. H., & Krathwohl, D. R. (1956). *Taxonomy of educational objectives. Handbook 1: Cognitive domain.* New York: McKay.

Boekaerts, M., Pintrich, P. R., & Zeidner, M. (2000). *Handbook of self-regulation.* San Diego, CA: Academic Press.

Boyes, M. C., & Chandler, M. (1992). Cognitive development, epistemic doubt, and identity formation in adolescence. *Journal of Youth and Adolescence, 21,* 277–303.

Carey, S., Evans, R., Honda, M., Jay, E., & Unger, C. (1989). "An experiment is when you try it and see if it works": a study of grade 7 students' understanding of the construction of scientific knowledge. *International Journal of Science Education, 11,* 514–529.

Carey, S., & Smith, C. L. (1993). On understanding the nature of scientific knowledge. *Educational Psychologist, 28,* 235–251.

Chandler, M. (1987). The Othello effect. Essays on the emergence and eclipse of skeptical doubt. *Human Development, 30,* 137–159.

Chandler, M., Boyes, M., & Ball, L. (1990). Relativism and stations of epistemic doubt. *Journal of Experimental Child Psychology, 50,* 370–395.

Chinn, C. A., & Brewer, W. F. (1993). The role of anomalous data in knowledge acquisition: A theoretical framework and implications for science education. *Review of Educational Research, 63,* 1–49.

Chinn, C. A., & Brewer, W. F. (1998). An empirical text of a taxonomy of responses to anomalous data in science. *Journal of Research in Science Teaching, 35,* 623–654.

Corno, L. (1993). The best-laid plans: Modern conceptions of volition and educational research. *Educational Researcher, 22*(2), 14–22.

De Corte, E., Verschaffel, L., & Op't Eynde, P. (2000). Self-regulation: A characteristic and a goal of mathematics education. In M. Boekaerts, P. R. Pintrich, & M. Zeidner (Eds.), *Handbook of self-regulation* (pp. 687–726). San Diego, CA: Academic Press.

Désautels, J., & Larochelle, M. (1998). The epistemology of students: the 'thingified' nature of scientific knowledge. In B. Frazer & K. Tobin (Eds.), *International handbook of science education, part 1* (pp. 115–126). Dordrecht, The Netherlands: Kluwer Academic Publishers.

Dole, J. A., & Sinatra, G. (1998). Reconceptualizing change in the cognitive construction of knowledge. *Educational Psychologist, 33*(2/3), 109–128.

Driver, R., Leach, J., Millar, R., & Scott, P. (1996). *Young people's images of science.* Buchingham, UK: Open University.

Edmondson, K. M., & Novak, J. D. (1993). The interplay of scientific epistemological views, learning strategies, and attitudes of college students. *Journal of Research in Science Teaching, 30,* 547–559.

Greer, B., & Verschaffel, L. (Eds.). (1997). Modeling reality in mathematics classroom [Special issue]. *Learning and Instruction, 7,* 293–397.

Grosslight, T. L., Unger, C., Jay, E., & Smith, C. L. (1991). Understanding models and their use in science: conceptions of middle and high school students and experts. *Journal of Research in Science Teaching, 28,* 799–822.

Guthrie, J. T., & Wigfield, A. (1997). *Reading engagement.* Newark, DE: International Reading Association.

Hacker, D. J., Dunlosky, J., & Graesser, A. C. (1998.). *Metacognition in educational theory and practice.* Mahwah, NJ: Lawrence Erlbaum Associates.

Hammer, D. (1994). Epistemological beliefs in introductory physics. *Cognition and Instruction, 12,* 151–183.

Hofer, B. K. (2000). Dimensionality and disciplinary differences in personal epistemology. *Contemporary Educational Psychology, 25,* 378–405.

Hofer, B. K., & Pintrich, P. R. (1997). The development of epistemological theories: Beliefs about knowledge and knowing and their relation to learning. *Review of Educational Research, 67,* 88–140.

Hofer, B. K., & Pintrich, P. R. (2002). *Personal epistemology: The psychology of beliefs about knowledge and knowing.* Mahwah, NJ: Lawrence Erlbaum Associates.

Hogan, K. (2000). Exploring a process view of students' knowledge about the nature of science. *Science Education, 84,* 51–70.

Jacobson, M. J., & Spiro, R. J. (1995). Hypertext learning environments, cognitive flexibility, and the transfer of complex knowledge: An empirical investigation. *Journal of Educational Computing Research, 12,* 301–333.

Jehng, J. J., Johnson, S. D., & Anderson, R. C. (1993). Schooling and students' epistemological beliefs about learning. *Contemporary Educational Psychology, 18,* 23–25.

Kardash, C. M., & Howell, K. L. (2000). Effects of epistemological beliefs and topic-specific beliefs on undergraduates' cognitive and strategic processing of dual-positional text. *Journal of Educational Psychology, 92,* 524–535.

Kardash, C. M., & Scholes, R. J. (1996). Effects of preexisting beliefs, epistemological beliefs, and need for cognition on interpretation of controversial issues. *Journal of Educational Psychology, 88,* 260–271.

King, P. M., & Kitchener, K. S. (1994). *Developing reflective judgement.* San Francisco, CA: Jossey-Bass.

Kitchener, K. S. (1983). Cognition, metacognition, and epistemic cognition. A three-level model of cognitive processing. *Human Development, 26,* 222–232.

Kuhn, D. (1991). *The skills of argument.* New York: Cambridge University Press.

Kuhn, D. (1999). A developmental model of critical thinking. *Educational Researcher, 28,* 16–26.

Lampert, M. (1990). When the problem is not the question and the solution is not the answer: Mathematical knowing and teaching. *American Educational Research Journal, 27,* 29–63.

Leach, J., & Lewis, J. (2002). The role of students' epistemological beliefs in the process of conceptual change in science. In M. Limón & L. Mason (Eds.), *Reconsidering conceptual change. Issues in theory and practice* (pp. 201–216). Dordrecht, The Netherlands: Kluwer Academic Publishers.

Leach, J., Millar, R., Ryder, J., & Séré, M.-G. (2000). Epistemological understanding in science learning: the consistency of representations across contexts. *Learning and Instruction, 10,* 497–527.

Leadbeater, B. (1986). The resolution of relativism in adult thinking: Subjective, objective, or conceptual? *Human Development, 29,* 291–300.

Lederman, N. G. (1992). Students' and teachers' conceptions of the nature of science: A review of the research. *Journal of Research in Science Teaching, 29,* 331–359.

Lester, F., & Garofalo, J. (1982, April). *Metacognitive aspects of elementary school students' performance on arithmetics tasks.* Paper presented at the American Educational Research Association Annual Meeting, New York.

Lucangeli, D., Coi, G., & Bosco, P. (1997). Metacognitive awareness in good and poor math problem solvers. *Learning Disabilities Research & Practice, 12,* 209–212.

Mason, L. (1998). Sharing cognition to construct scientific knowledge in school context: The role of oral and written discourse. *Instructional Science, 25,* 359–389.

Mason, L. (2000). Role of anomalous data and epistemological beliefs in middle students' theory change on two controversial topics. *European Journal of Psychology of Education, 15,* 329–346.

Mason, L. (2001a). Introducing talking and writing for conceptual change: A classroom study. In L. Mason (Ed.), Instructional practices for conceptual change in science domains [Special issue]. *Learning and Instruction, 11,* 305–329.

Mason, L. (2001b). Responses to anomalous data on controversial topics and theory change. *Learning and Instruction, 11,* 453–483.

Mason, L. (2001c). *Verità e certezze. Natura e sviluppo delle epistemologie ingenue* [Truth and certainty. Nature and development of naive epistemologies]. Rome, Italy: Carocci (in Italian).

Mason, L. (2002). Developing epistemological thinking to foster conceptual change in different domains. In M. Limón & L. Mason (Eds.), *Reconsidering conceptual change. Issues in theory and practice* (pp. 301–335). Dordrecht, The Netherlands: Kluwer Academic Publishers.

Mason, L., & Boscolo, P. (2000). Writing and conceptual change. What changes? *Instructional Science, 28,* 199–226.

Montgomery, D. E. (1992). Young children's theory of knowing: The development of a folk epistemology. *Developmental Review, 12,* 410–430.

Moshman, D. (1998). Cognitive development beyond childhood: Constraints on cognitive development and learning. In W. Damon (Series Ed.) & D. Kuhn & R. Siegler (Vol. Eds.), *Handbook of child psychology*: Vol. 2: *Cognition, language, and perception* (5th ed., pp. 947–978). New York: Wiley.

Nespor, J. (1987). The role of beliefs in the practice of teaching. *Journal of Curriculum Studies, 10,* 317–328.

Pajares, F. (1992). Teachers' beliefs and educational research: Cleaning up a messy construct. *Review of Educational Research, 62*(3), 307–332.

Perry, W. G. Jr. (1968). *Patterns of development in thought and values of students in a liberal arts college: A validation of a scheme.* Cambridge, MA: Bureau of Study Counsel, Harvard University (ERIC Document Reproduction Service No. ED 024315).

Perry, W. G. Jr. (1981). Cognitive and ethical growth: The making of meaning. In A. Chickering (Ed.), *The modern American college* (pp. 76–116). San Francisco, CA: Jossey-Bass.

Pintrich, P. R., Marx, R., & Boyle, R. (1993). Beyond cold conceptual change: The role of motivational beliefs and classroom contextual factors in the process of conceptual change. *Review of Educational Research, 63,* 167–199.

Qian, G., & Alvermann, D. (1995). Role of epistemological beliefs and learned helplessness in secondary school students' learning science concepts from text. *Journal of Educational Psychology, 87,* 282–292.

Reynolds, R. E., Sinatra, G. M., & Jetton, T. L. (1996). Views of knowledge acquisition and representation: A continuum from experience-centered to mind-centered. *Educational Psychologist, 31,* 93–104.

Roth, W.-M., & Roychoudhury, A. (1993). The nature of scientific knowledge, knowing and learning: the perspectives of four physics students. *International Journal of Science Education, 15,* 27–44.

Roth, W.-M., & Roychoudhury, A. (1994). Physics students' epistemologies and views about knowing and learning. *Journal of Research in Science Teaching, 31,* 5–30.

Rukavina, I., & Daneman, M. (1996). Integration and its effect on acquiring knowledge about competing scientific theories from text. *Journal of Educational Psychology, 88,* 272–287.

Ryan, M. P. (1984a). Conceptions of prose coherence: Individual differences in epistemological standards. *Journal of Educational Psychology, 76,* 1226–1238.

Ryan, M. P. (1984b). Monitoring text comprehension: Individual differences in epistemological standards. *Journal of Educational Psychology, 76,* 248–258.

Ryder, J., Leach, J., & Driver, R. (1999). Undergraduate science students' images of Science. *Journal of Research in Science Teaching, 36,* 201–219.

Scardamalia, M., Bereiter, C., & Lamon, M. (1994). The CSILE Project: Trying to bring the classroom into World 3. In K. McGilly (Ed.), *Classroom lessons. Integrating cognitive theory and classroom practice* (pp. 201–228). Cambridge, MA: Bradford/MIT Press.

Schauble, L., Klopfer, L. E., & Raghavan, K. (1991). Student's transition from an engineering model to a science model of experimentation. *Journal of Research in Science Teaching, 28,* 859–882.

Schoenfeld, A. H. (1988). When good teaching leads to bad results: The disasters of "well taught" mathematics classes. *Educational Psychologist, 23,* 145–166.

Schoenfeld, A. H. (1989). Explorations of students' mathematical beliefs and behavior. *Journal for Research in Mathematics Education, 20,* 338–355.

Schommer, M. (1990). Effects of beliefs about the nature of knowledge on comprehension. *Journal of Educational Psychology, 82,* 498–504.

Schommer, M. (1993). Epistemological development and academic performance among secondary students. *Journal of Educational Psychology, 85,* 406–411.

Schommer, M. (1994a). An emerging conceptualization of epistemological beliefs and their role in learning. In R. Garner & P. A. Alexander (Eds.), *Beliefs about text and instruction with text* (pp. 25–40). Hillsdale, NJ: Lawrence Erlbaum Associates.

Schommer, M. (1994b). Synthesizing epistemological belief research: Tentative understanding and provocative confusion. *Educational Psychology Review, 6,* 293–319.

Schommer, M., Crouse, A., & Rhodes, N. (1992). Epistemological beliefs and mathematical text comprehension: Believing it is simple does not make it so. *Journal of Educational Psychology, 84,* 435–443.

Schommer, M., Mau, W. C., & Brookhart, S. (1999, April). *Identifying the structure of middle school students' beliefs about knowledge and learning.* Paper presented at the American Educational Research Association Annual Meeting, Montreal, Canada.

Schraw, G., Dunkle, M. E., & Bendixen, L. D. (1995). Cognitive processes in well-defined and ill-defined problem solving. *Applied Cognitive Psychology, 9,* 523–538.

Silver, E. A. (1985). Research in teaching mathematical problem solving: Some underrepresented themes and directions. In E. A. Silver (Ed.), *Teaching and learning mathematical problem solving: Multiple research perspectives* (pp. 247–266). Hillsdale, NJ: Lawrence Erlbaum Associates.

Sinatra, G. (2000, April). *From passive to active to intentional: Changing conceptions of the learner.* In G. M. Sinatra (Chair), What does it mean to be an intentional learner? Alternative perspectives. Symposium presented at the American Educational Research Association Annual Meeting, New Orleans, LA.

Smith, C. L., Maclin, D., Houhgton, C., & Hennessey, M. G. (2000). Sixth-grade students' epistemologies of science: The impact of school science experiences on epistemological development. *Cognition and Instruction, 18,* 349–422.

Songer, N. B., & Linn, M. C. (1991). How do students views of science influence knowledge integration? *Journal of Research in Science Teaching, 28,* 761–784.

Spiro, R. J., Coulson, R. L., Feltovich, P. J., & Anderson, D. K. (1994). Cognitive flexibility theory: Advanced knowledge acquisition in ill-structured domains. In R. B. Ruddell & M. R. Ruddell (Eds.), *Theoretical models and processes of reading* (pp. 602–615). Newark, DE: International Reading Association.

Spiro, R. J., Feltovich, P. J., & Coulson, R. L. (1996). Two epistemic world-views: Prefigurative schemas and learning in complex domains. *Applied Cognitive Psychology, 10* [Special issue], S51–S61.

Stanovich, K. E. (1999). *Who is rational? Studies of individual differences in reasoning.* Mahwah, NJ: Lawrence Erlbaum Associates.

Stanovich, K. E., & West, R. F. (1998). Individual differences in rational thought. *Journal of Experimental Psychology: General, 127,* 161–188.

Strike, K. A., & Posner, G. J. (1993). A revisionist theory of conceptual change. In R. A. Duschl & R. J. Hamilton (Eds.), *Philosophy of science, cognitive psychology, and educational theory and practice* (pp. 147–176). New York: State University of New York Press.

Verschaffel, L., De Corte, E., & Lasure, S. (1994). Realistic considerations in mathematical modeling of school arithmetic words problems. *Learning and Instruction, 4,* 283–294.

Verschaffel, L., De Corte, E., & Lasure, S. (1999). Children's conceptions about the role of real-word knowledge in mathematical modeling of school word problems. In W. Schnotz, S. Vosniadou, & M. Carretero (Eds.), *New perspectives on conceptual change* (pp. 175–189). Amsterdam: Pergamon/Elsevier.

Vosniadou, S. (1994). Capturing and modeling the process of conceptual change. *Learning and Instruction, 4,* 45–69.

Wellman, H. M. (1990). *The child's theory of mind.* Cambridge, MA: Bradford/MIT Press.

Wellman, H. M., & Gelman, S. A. (1992). Cognitive development. Foundational theories of core domains. *Annual Review of Psychology, 43,* 337–375.

Windschitl, M., & Andre, T. (1998). Using computer simulations to enhance conceptual change: The roles of constructivist instruction and student epistemological beliefs. *Journal of Research in Science Teaching, 35,* 145–160.

9

J's Epistemological Stance and Strategies

Andrea A. diSessa
University of California, Berkeley

Andrew Elby
David Hammer
University of Maryland

INTRODUCTION

Theoretical Framework

The focus of this chapter might be described as "intuitive epistemology," what people know about knowledge, knowing, and learning, as acquired from their experiences in everyday life and in school. The study of students' epistemological ideas has become increasingly active in recent years (see Hofer & Pintrich, 1997). In general, this research validated the principle that students have ideas about knowledge that affect their learning in significant ways. We continue in that direction.

Our approach to intuitive epistemology, however, differs substantially from most prior studies. In particular, most prior research took what we describe as a *categorical*[1] approach. A prototypical categorical strategy is to attribute particular beliefs to students. "A student believes that knowledge is simple and unproblematic" (Schommer, Crouse, & Rhodes, 1992), or "Knowledge is always subject to questioning and change" (Linn & Songer, 1993). We describe these attributions of belief as categorical because they presume a consistent attribution to the student without attention to context, for example, that elements of the belief exist as coherent

[1]Hammer and Elby (2002) use the term *unitary* instead of *categorical*. The intended meaning is similar.

categories within the student's conceptual repertoire, and that the student behaves consistently with respect to the stated belief. Researchers usually recognize that there are often exceptional circumstances and difficulties in data. However, unless researchers explicitly take on the issue of context dependence, we describe the approach as categorical.

A categorical approach typically divides students into classes (e.g., those that have vs. those that do not have some belief); students within the class are assumed to behave similarly to one another, and the research program does not explicitly include the reasons for variation of behavior across people and across circumstances. More subtle and complex approaches may still be aptly described as categorical. For example, stage theories (King & Kitchener, 1994; Perry, 1970) are likely to be categorical at each point in time. Multidimensional frameworks (Hofer & Pintrich, 1997; Schommer, 1990) still may presume coherent belief-like attributions (most obviously at poles of the continua) and may not explicitly describe context dependence of the positioning of a subject between the poles.

In this chapter we examine categorical approaches to intuitive epistemology critically. In part, we are motivated by prior work on "intuitive physics," students' unschooled ideas about the physical world. diSessa (1993) argued that intuitive physics is best understood as made up of hundreds or thousands of fine-grained, context-sensitive knowledge elements. Views of intuitive physics that attribute to students a smaller number of more coherent structures—naïve theories, beliefs, or misconceptions—greatly underestimate the richness and generativity of students' reasoning about physical phenomena. Moreover, such views assume too much systematicity in intuitive thought. If many context-sensitive elements are at issue, then any description in localized form (e.g., as the possession of a theory or misconceived belief) almost certainly overestimates either the power of a single element to control thinking or the organization of multiple cognitive elements into a coherent whole. This is not to say that students' reasoning about physical phenomena always lacks coherence and systematicity. What we question are theoretical frameworks and attendant methodologies that *presume* such coherence and systematicity (or choose not to examine them explicitly), and as a result may overlook evidence in students' behavior of the context-sensitive activation of finer-grained knowledge elements.

We expect a similar state of affairs in the study of intuitive epistemology, that categorical approaches (a) underestimate richness and generativity and (b) presume too much systematicity. Our main purpose in this chapter is to probe the validity of categorical approaches in these respects against a case study of an individual student.

It may be helpful to lay out a rough model for scientific description of individual cognition (or, perhaps, of any focus of scientific inquiry). In general, we expect to find a level of description we could call "causal." A successful account at the causal level would explicate the details of action in context to explain a person's behavior in any instance. We might, for example, have a computer model that shows exactly which knowledge elements are activated and how they combine to produce the behavior observed. diSessa's (1993) account of phenomenological primitives is an example of a framework for formulating causal level descriptions of intuitive physics.

Causal level descriptions are very difficult to achieve, however, and we do not attempt one here.[2] At the opposite end of the spectrum from causal level descriptions, common sense tempts us to make phenomenological attributions, such as "He believes people are stupid" when someone seems systematically to disregard others' ideas. Between causal and phenomenological levels, we should expect levels that have the advantage of simplicity compared to causal descriptions, while still demanding more accountability to detailed specification and consistency than commonsense phenomenological descriptions. We make generalizations about individuals and groups based on critical analysis of their cogency and based on hypothesis checking across multiple circumstance; we expect these generalizations to be insightful for their relative breadth even if they do not hold in every instance. Categorical accounts lie in these intermediate levels of description. Our work here is, in part, to make exceptions to the application of categorical descriptions evident in order to assess more precisely what these accounts have traded off, mainly in terms of adequate specification of context dependency, for their relative simplicity.

To study the reasoning of an individual in detail is to work outside mainstream categorical methodology. Categorical work usually seeks correlations across large numbers of subjects rather than attempting analysis of specific cases of epistemologies in action. This lack of attention to detailed analysis is a critical omission, in our view, because theories of intuitive epistemology need—eventually—to provide accounts at the causal level. We need to assess how much we are missing at various higher, coarser-grained levels of analysis and to get a sense of the context-sensitive behavioral dynamics that causal-level models need to encompass.

Setting in This Book

This section briefly positions this chapter with respect to the main interests of the book, intentionality and conceptual change.

Conceptual change is, in our view, best defined phenomenologically. In widespread instruction, students demonstrably have great difficulty

---

[2]We discussed the needs and began to explore possibilities for such an account of intuitive epistemologies elsewhere (diSessa, 1985; Hammer & Elby, 2002).

with a few particular topics. Force and motion is one such topic, which we pursue here. Others include evolution, the nature of matter, and the distinction between heat and temperature. The fundamental questions are (a) what accounts for observed difficulties, and (b) how may they be overcome? We subscribe to the term *conceptual change* to indicate that we presume difficult topics are difficult because of a substantial change in existing knowledge that must take place. We do not, however, believe that "concepts" necessarily describes what changes, nor even that "what changes" necessarily characterizes the learning process. More directly, we believe that some conceptual accomplishment is difficult because of the huge amount of reorganization that must take place, and frequently because unusual kinds of systematicity are required of expert thought. (See diSessa, 1993, 1996; diSessa & Sherin, 1998.)

Because intentional learning means different things to different people, we describe our orientation here along several dimensions. These dimensions are drawn from the introductory chapter by Sinatra and Pintrich. First, intuitive epistemology may be classified as metacognitive in two senses: (a) It is knowledge about cognition, broadly speaking, and is likely to have arisen from the subjects' experiences of their own reasoning; and (b) it is likely to be involved in executive or control functions in thinking. For example, a student may judge that her knowledge is sufficient, and therefore cease studying. That judgment involves her sense of what constitutes sufficiency. Another person might have "higher standards," and continue working to try to understand better. In the study that follows, epistemological ideas exert obvious controlling influences.

The "intentional learner" in the sense of Bereiter and Scardamalia (1989) is not the same thing as the "epistemologically wise" learner. The intentional learner orients specifically toward learning goals; an epistemologically wise student knows what to do if she chooses learning goals. Epistemological knowledge may be more instrumental than directive. It is an open question which is more influential in learning: deliberately setting learning goals or easily being able to attain learning goals that arise spontaneously. If it turns out that one always learns best by focusing directly on learning, then a good intuitive epistemology might, in fact, involve being an intentional learner. But a categorical adherence to learning goals may, for example, limit experience and rely too heavily on limited knowledge subsystems (e.g., the ability to judge what one must do to learn). Being intentional may simply be impossible in certain circumstances in overcoming epistemological problems. We return to this issue later.

Perhaps most central to intentionality as discussed by Sinatra and Pintrich are two foci: goal formation and consciousness. As already mentioned, intuitive epistemology seems to play an important role in goal formation in learning and problem-solving tasks. Students "reflect on" their current knowledge state, make judgments, and take actions they feel are necessary. This notion of reflection may be misleading. At least some of this "reflective" knowledge is implicit and reactive (Schoenfeld, 1992) and so would not meet the high standards of conscious goal formation. To be sure, as our study affirms, some parts of epistemological thought appear in conscious and deliberate form, satisfying the strongest standards for intentionality. We caution, however, that even in these cases there is almost certainly a strong undercurrent of implicit knowledge involved in the process of "noticing," "judging," and a strategy's "coming to mind" that would not pass the consciousness test. We feel this is neither a limitation of intuitive epistemology nor evidence that intuitive epistemology is not related to intentionality. Instead, we believe it is a fact of life that the most conscious thoughts and actions rely on a critical and frequently invisible substrate of unconscious thought. That is, there is no account of "conscious goal setting" that does not depend critically on an unconscious and inarticulate substrate (see also diSessa, 1994).

In this chapter we deal with intentionality from the bottom up. That is, we look at an individual (J) and occasions where she appears to involve her intuitive epistemology. Then we try to characterize the relation between the student's behaviors and intentionality, including consciousness and goal formation. In particular, we try to assess the plausibility that a "belief" (conscious or unconscious) could account for her behaviors. Although the bottom-up approach certainly has limits and disadvantages, it meshes nicely with the more-detailed-than-usual way in which we propose to explore the nature of intuitive epistemology.

Nature of the Study and Its Conclusions

This chapter presents a case study of one individual. As such, it has obvious weaknesses, but also some important strengths. Most obviously, we cannot conclude that all people are like the subject, nor even that anyone else in the world has a similar epistemological orientation.[3] Beyond that, the study is exploratory and results in hypotheses (a) about this student, (b) about what epistemological knowledge people have and do not have, (c) about the form of epistemological knowledge (e.g., whether it is belief-like), and (d) about how epistemological knowledge works in learning and problem solving. None of the hypotheses are definitively established, although we feel many competing hypotheses can be ruled out by the facts of this case. Specifically, we believe we can rule out many categorical descriptions of the subject's epistemology as consisting of global beliefs and/or personal traits.

[3]In fact, the subject was selected precisely because she provided an especially clear case of the difficulties inherent in categorical attributions.

The strengths of case study methodology are several. Most strongly, we should see context-dependent richness in the details of a subject's actual reasoning, if such richness exists. Although individuals may behave quite differently from each other at this detailed level, still the degree of context dependence should be indicative. Observations of context dependency can challenge specific categorical characterizations and also the cogency of particular levels and types of description. Even more, we believe it is appropriate to look to the phenomenology of reasoning in order to generate hypotheses about the nature of epistemological thinking. Too much prior work on epistemology involves speculation about what might or should count as epistemological knowledge, without the hard test of looking at process data. A case study can show how epistemological knowledge actually affects the student's learning and reasoning; by contrast, categorical studies typically provide general evidence of the influence of epistemology on behavior in correlations across many subjects. Our strongest results are precisely here: Struggling with actual student reasoning, we develop an unusual set of hypotheses about the specific nature and dynamics of an individual's epistemological knowledge and how it affects learning.

THE CASE OF J

The subject of this case study, whom we call J, was a female freshman taking introductory university physics. She was interviewed in a series of seven roughly 1-hour one-on-one clinical sessions with the first author. The interviews spanned the second half of her first semester of physics and carried into the second semester. J had done well in high school physics and did not seem to be having particular difficulties in freshman physics. All of the interviews were videotaped and transcribed. The analyses that follow are based on repeated viewing of the video tapes and review of annotated transcriptions. Roughly speaking, we reviewed the data, looking for hypotheses about J's epistemological knowledge. Then we collected data, positive and negative, relevant to each hypothesis. Finally, we rejected hypotheses that were sufficiently undermined and refined those that passed the preliminary data test.

The interviews were not originally intended to probe epistemology; they were intended to study the local dynamics of conceptual change. In J's case, however, epistemology appeared to play a substantial role in those dynamics, and the interviews raised provocative questions with respect to the nature of her epistemology. For example, although J was unusually creative and prolific at formulating interpretations of physical phenomena, she appeared to reject the obligation to justify some of her interpretations. Despite a demonstrated ability to identify and think through contradictions (on occasion), she often did not seem to feel that what appeared to us as contradictory interpretations needed reconciling. Thus we initiated study of J's epistemological ideas precisely because some of her tendencies seemed more pronounced than what we have seen in other students. She seemed to be quite aware of epistemological issues, but took actions at odds with our instincts as physicists, and frequently at odds with what we thought a sophisticated physics learner would do.

Some simple hypotheses about J's epistemological orientation were fairly easy to rule out. J was clearly bright, reflective, articulate, and at least as engaged as most students whom we interviewed. She was articulately cognizant of the fact that learning requires changing prior ideas. Although early on we might have described her as careless or disengaged, a large amount of data convinced us that these are insufficient to characterize her on any global level. J often appeared to be seriously engaged in thinking about the problems posed and took extended self-directed paths to consider and check possibilities. Although her physics seemed rich in intuitive ideas, this, by itself, did not separate her from typical freshmen. In the end, we took on the task of characterizing those aspects of J's thinking that appeared epistemological and trying to fit them into an overall pattern.

Our analysis comes in three parts. First, we describe some of the interesting patterns of behavior we found repeatedly in the interviews, together with examples and evidence. Examples mainly take the form of fairly direct descriptions of what happened in the interviews, protocol citations, or both. We describe these as *behavioral phenomena*, and we intend them to be more data driven than theory driven. However, in clumping data into categories, naturally some interpretation is necessary. Second, we return for a more synthetic and interpretive look at the systematicities in J's epistemological behavior. This amounts to a second, coarser level of description. Finally, we argue that the evidence of richness and context-sensitivity undermines characterization of J's epistemological behavior in terms of global traits or systematic beliefs. In other words, we use J to argue that a categorical approach ignores details essential to a causal understanding of intuitive epistemology.

BEHAVIORAL PHENOMENOLOGY

Before entering into detailed analysis, we preview the epistemologically loaded behaviors that we noticed in J:

1. Shifting interpretations: J gives contradictory accounts of the same situation on different occasions.

2. Splitting concepts: Technical terms, most notably "force," are used in multiple situations in ways that imply different core meanings. It is as if J thinks there is a range of fundamentally different kinds of forces.
3. Migrating language: J uses alternative technical terms (force, momentum) in the same contexts as if the terms were interchangeable.
4. Weak commitment to principles: J denies or demotes known-to-be-sanctioned physical principles because she feels her context-specific understanding is adequate.
5. Discounting details in explanations: J does not appear to feel she is bound to justify the existence of elements in her explanations.
6. Hedging: J frequently and explicitly shows limited commitment to what she is saying, or she provides explicit notification of vague meaning.
7. Strong commitment to a view: J is, on occasion, capable of careful, conscious consideration leading to strong personal commitment to particular ideas.
8. Reflective about learning: J thinks about learning and has drawn many sensible lessons from her experience.

Although items 1 through 6 suggest that J has a weak or maladapted intuitive epistemology, items 7 and 8 are particularly important in qualifying that view. In particular, 7 and 8 define occasions when J violates many generalizations one might make about her with regard to the systematicity and weakness of her epistemological knowledge.

1. Shifting Interpretations

J sometimes provided multiple interpretations of the same events. This is not in itself surprising in students. J's shifting interpretations, however, especially in one instance, had several striking properties. First, J shifted her interpretations frequently. Sometimes she would reverse several times in a single session, and in a matter of seconds from one to another. Second, she sometimes did not converge on one interpretation, even after extended work on a problem. With more typical students, one or another interpretation generally becomes "standardized." Finally, J seemed not to notice or care about multiple interpretations that, to us, were blatantly contradictory. In the principal example that follows, concerning a ball tossed straight up into the air (after it leaves the thrower's hand), she first claimed there was only one force (gravity) acting on the ball, and then, seconds later, she claimed there were two interacting forces. (To a physicist, there is only one force on the ball, the force of gravity. Gravity at first slows the ball in its upward motion, then accelerates it downward. There is nothing particularly distinguished about the peak of the toss. Gravity does not change size or direction, no new force enters or leaves the situation, nor does gravity enter into some special relationship, such as balance, at the peak.)

The interviewer introduced the ball toss in J's third session. The following quotations are sequential, and nothing is left out between the introduction of the task, her first interpretation, and her revised interpretation. (In transcriptions, we denote breaks, abrupt halts, or interruptions by the other speaker by "//". Brackets enclose explanatory notes or parallel comments by the second speaker. Ellipses denote speech omitted from the transcript. Before each extended quotation, we denote its position in the corpus as [<*interview number*> <*hour*>:<*minutes*>:<*seconds*>].)

[3 0:2:23]

A: I want to ask you about tosses. So, um. Alright, so, I've got this thing and I just throw it up in the air [tossing a ball and catching it], and // would you describe for me in a physics kind of way what's happening when you do this?

J: In terms of forces, or energies, or both or whatever?

A: Forces.

In J's subsequent description, she twice proclaimed that, after the hand released the ball, there would only be one force on the ball. She produced a description of the toss that was, for all practical purposes, correct. Emphasis is added below to bring out her contrasting interpretations.

[3 0:2:30]

J: Not including your hand, like if you just let it go up and come down, *then the only force on that is gravity*. And so it starts off with the most speed when it leaves your hand, and the higher it goes, it slows down to the point where it stops. And then comes back down. And so, but *the whole time, the only force on that is the force of gravity*, except the force of your hand when you catch it. And, when it starts off, um, it has its highest speed, which is all kinetic energy, and when it stops, it has all potential energy—no kinetic energy. And then it comes back down, and it speeds up again.

A: Sounds like a textbook problem.

J: It's more just like the first thing you learn.

A: Do you remember how you thought gravity worked before you took physics?

J: Well I think on a ball it's pretty obvious how gravity works, but I don't remember how first I learned gravity works.

The interviewer then asked about the peak:

A: Could you describe what happens at the peak of the toss?

J: Um, well air resistance, when you're throwing it, when you throw the ball up, the air, it's going // I mean, it's not against air because air is going every way, but the air force gets stronger and stronger to the point where it stops. The *gravity pulling down and the force pulling up are equal*, so it's in like equilibrium for a second, so it's not going anywhere. And then, um, gravity pulls it back down. Like *when you throw it, you're giving it a force upward, but the force can only last so long* against air and against gravity—actually probably more against gravity than against air. But, um, so *you give this initial force, and it's going up just fine*, slower and slower because gravity is pulling on it and pulling on it. Um, then it gets to the point, to the top. And then, um, it's not getting any more energy to go up. You're not giving any more forces, so the only force it has on it is gravity and it comes right back down.

... [One of J's turns is omitted during which she explains that you are not giving the ball any more force at the top.]

A: So is it like balanced at the top?

J: Yeah. For a second.

A: What's balancing?

J: It's I mean // I guess you could say that it's balancing because *I guess the force of gravity is equal to* [brief pause] *I guess you'd say whatever is left of the force you gave it at the beginning* so that neither one is larger than the other for it to go anywhere. But that's only for like a second. But you can say it's in balance for a second.

diSessa (1996) provided an account of the intuitive physics underlying J's reasoning, focusing on what provoked J to add a second force to her description and on some of the details of the transition. The relevant point, with respect to J's intuitive epistemology, is not that she so easily changed her account but that she made no remark about it. It is hard to imagine she did not notice having changed, within seconds, from saying there is one force to saying there are two. More likely, she did not consider it worth noting, partly because she does not see the two interpretations as being different (see snippet [7 1:17:50] later). This suggests an epistemological judgment that a change in description (e.g., from a one-force explanation to a two-force explanation) does not actually represent a change in interpretation.

J continued to tell some version of this two-force story until some minutes later when the interviewer prompted her to think about acceleration. J then entered into a fairly extended reasoning chain, supported by occasional interviewer prompts. The final part of this exchange brought her to the "school" interpretation that gravity is the only force, and gravity accounts for the acceleration that reduces velocity.

[3 0:22:30]

J: If you took the ball and pushed it up, pushed it up, pushed it up // kept giving it these new forces, new forces, then it wouldn't be constantly accelerating because acceleration would be changing. You'd be going fast and then slow, fast and slow. But when you just throw it up and let it come back down, then *the only force on it is gravity* so the velocity is changing, but the acceleration is constant. And so I think that this [drawing of constant acceleration] is better because the acceleration is constant, but it's negative and the acceleration is still constant, which is [unintelligible] [nods head]

A: Now what you have is the force of gravity, and that's always the same amount.

J: Right.

J could not hold this interpretation stable. The interviewer pointed to a previous diagram where she had both gravity and the imparted force of the hand displayed, and, although apparently a bit surprised, she resumed the double force story.

[3 0:23:30]

A: So gravity's always pushing that way. Gravity's a constant. So if you have // okay, and you said that, going down, this upward force [pointing to the diagram] is all gone, is that right?

J: Right.

A: OK. So it [the second, upward force] just starts at some maximum and goes down to zero and just stays at zero. Is that what it does?

J: Oh, the force? Yeah. It like dissipates. It has a certain amount of energy at the beginning, and it slowly dies out, and it's gone.

The saga of the toss and its two interpretations is a truly extended one. In the next to last interview, J was given a computer-based instructional sequence designed to teach the one-force model of the toss. With barely a lapse, J progressed through the instructional sequence without invoking the upward force. The tutorial culminated in J providing a perfect and detailed single-force accounting of what happens during a toss.

As the final probe of the whole interview series, the interviewer switched off the computer that had apparently scaffolded a local stability for J's one-force conceptualization. He asked her again to describe what happens in a toss. At first, she gave the one-force story (mixed a bit with a correct account of energy changes in the toss), even emphasizing that there is only one force (italics). Prompted simply to remove the energy part of the story, J revised, and, without comment, resumed the two-force story.

[7 0:59:00]

A: Describe one more time what happens.

. . . [small interchange deleted]

J: Okay. You start off and you give the ball an initial velocity, and that comes from the force from your hand. And then, it travels with that momentum. And, once you let it go, *it has no outside forces. The only force it has on it is one force downward*, which is equal to *mg*, the mass of the ball times gravity. And, so, it goes up and as it goes up, its kinetic energy decreases because it's not getting any energy from any outside forces, until it gets to the point where velocity is zero for a split second. And that's where it has all potential energy and no kinetic energy 'cause it's not // doesn't have any more. And then comes back down. And then starts off slow and then picks up speed because of the force downward. And then you catch it again and stop it.

A: Okay. So, um, could you describe that just in terms of forces?

J: Okay, starting from when it leaves your hand. [Sure.] Okay, *initially, it has force up and a force down. And the force up is the force that you gave it*. And the force down is *mg*. And the force down stays the same all the whole time. . . . [omitted details] *The force up is what changes.* Because, it starts off big and as it goes up it gets smaller and smaller and smaller. So, it's just like *the forces are adding just like vectors*. And, so, *at the top, when it has no velocity, is the point where the vectors are the same for a second*. And then, *this force stays zero, and this force* [gravity] *overcomes it* and then goes back down.

A: What vectors are the same at the top?

J: [coyly] The up one and the down one.

A: The down one is what?

J: *Mg*. [OK.] And the up one is the external force that you gave it with your hand.

In Appendix A, we document another case of Shifting Interpretations having to do with what is happening in the case of constant speed motion. In this case, J shifted in and out of claiming an unbalanced force is required for motion. In order to keep the size of the chapter manageable, we leave details out of the main text.

Commentary. It should be expected that students will change interpretations of a problematic situation. J, however, seemed indifferent to two apparently radical changes: the number of forces acting on a tossed body, and whether unbalanced forces are needed for constant motion. She did not note or worry about these shifts, even over an extended set of encounters that, for example, included instruction on a one-force model of the toss. When asked point blank about her two different interpretations of the toss at the very end of the last interview, J replied that she did not really feel there was a difference between the two interpretations. It seemed a matter of language to her, and she had merely learned to "use the right words" in the one-force explanation. According to physicist standards, J is making inappropriate judgments about the compatibility of different descriptions, which we interpret as an epistemological issue.

[7 1:17:50]

J: It's funny though because I think that it would be easy for somebody watching that [the tape from her prior interview] to think that I didn't understand what was going on. And it's funny because I don't think that now [the one force model] I understand what's going on any better than I did then. But I can explain it to you in the right way.

A: In the physics way, probably.

J: Which is, kind of, not frustrating, but it's weird. . . . I can say, OK, I correctly said what was going on, but I don't think I understand any differently. Like maybe I'm getting words confused, but I don't think that I have this revelation "that's how it works." Because I still think I understood how it worked.

Notably, J acknowledged that "somebody watching" would think that she had changed her story; she accepted the fact that she had nominally changed her account. She thinks, however, that there was no change in her *understanding*, only in the *language*. We could not determine, based on this data alone, to what extent she was correct in this. However, two points are more definite. First, by the standards of physics, one cannot sustain both one- and two-force interpretations. They are different claims about a situation. Second, diSessa (1996) provided an interpretation of J's two descriptions that implicates specific conceptual changes, in particular, a shift in activation of specific p-prims. In net, we believe the most plausible interpretation is that she is genuinely thinking differently in the one-force and two-force cases, and that it is unusual that she does not feel any contradiction.

Our purpose here is to understand J's epistemological stance and strategies in these interviews.[4] How can we make sense of the ease with which she was willing to shift interpretations? One approach is to identify contexts in which her actions would not seem out of place. Everyday experience often involves feelings, thoughts, and ideas that are "hard to put into words" and that admit multiple, seemingly contradictory accounts, each trying to point toward the intangible from a different direction. J may have been applying such an epistemological stance to her reasoning about the toss, producing behavior that, to physicists, seems very strange. J's behavior, however, is not bizarre; it is just contextually inappropriate by the standards of physics.[5] Later, we have more to say about her stance toward language.

On a higher plane, the strategy of analysis we just used with J—noting a context in which the epistemological strategies she employs may be appropriate—goes to the heart of the difference between categorical approaches to intuitive epistemology and the contextual approach we advance here. Again, J is not doing something that is absolutely wrong. Instead, it is a contextual issue, her use of an otherwise productive strategy in an inappropriate context, that defines her epistemological orientation toward learning physics. As a bonus, understanding the contexts in which counterproductive physics-learning strategies correspond to sensible epistemological stances can help teachers map instructional pathways; teachers can help students adapt (and in some cases contextually limit) their naïve epistemological knowledge to construct a more sophisticated stance toward physics knowledge and learning.

Intentionality. What do we make of these situations and this pattern of behavior from the point of view of intentionality? First, it is difficult to see how J could even potentially formulate a goal that will help her di-

---

[4]We are not suggesting that J's behavior is entirely a matter of epistemology. Clearly J's intuitive physics plays a role here. So may her feelings in this moment about admitting having been wrong: J may be trying to cover herself. Still, her epistemology is implicated in that she considers saying that her accounts differed only in language, a plausible way to defend her earlier arguments.

[5]Reasoning in physics does often involve multiple accounts of the same phenomena. For instance, one may describe a toss in terms of forces or in terms of energy. However, these multiple accounts are expected to be rigorously and explicitly consistent with each other. One force cannot turn into two.

rectly in this context. Rather, (at least in the case of the toss) she apparently does not perceive sufficient difference between her interpretations to warrant any concern that would motivate a relevant action.

Furthermore, the most obvious beliefs one could formulate to explain her behavior, say, "You don't have to be careful of description," or "Any two descriptions are the same," simply do not make sense categorically. J knows that sometimes you need to be careful (as we show later), and that sometimes different words make a difference. Instead, following the earlier arguments, we propose that J's epistemological orientation is embedded in a *judgment in context*, which responds to the particulars of this situation (in what turns out to be an epistemologically unproductive way). In this case she judges that her different descriptions are not sufficiently different to worry about.[6]

2. Splitting Concepts

J acted as if she believed that the designation "force" could apply to different kinds of entities, without being constrained by common properties. By contrast, to a physicist, all exemplars of technical categories share a core set of properties. For example, all forces have a magnitude and a direction, and they all relate to motion in exactly the same way (as described by $F = ma$). As far as we could see, J neither expected nor searched for core common properties among different kinds of forces. Instead, she acted as if different forces merely had a family resemblance to one another, like the multiple senses of everyday words.

We give several examples. First, J essentially claimed that the force of air pressure can never enter into the physics of a situation (except as air resistance to motion). She said that pressure acts in all directions at once, and hence cancels out: (Again, emphasis is added to highlight focal statements.)

[2 0:43:30]

J: It's [air pressure is] just everywhere, you know. It's not moving in one way to make the book move, because the book's not going anywhere. *You could say there's air pressure on every point, but there's air pressure going the exact opposite way on every point too. So it all completely counteracts. And it doesn't play a part.*

[6]To be a bit more precise, we would see J's epistemology acting in two stages. At first, she either does not notice these different interpretations of the same situations, or she may, implicitly or explicitly, regard them as unproblematic variations. At the next stage, when the issue is raised explicitly with her, she is aware of and directly reports a judgment in context: "These differences don't matter."

Even when prompted by the interviewer's calculation of the amount of force on one surface of a book (14 lbs. per square inch times about 30 square inches of book surface area = about 450 lbs. of force, "So, there's quite a lot of pressure on this book."), J replied, "Not enough to make it move," as if 450 lbs. were a small force. She later explained, "But air pressure is every which way.... I can't think of air pressure as being this way [gestures pressing on a book]."

J also explained that friction is a special kind of force that could never actually move things. "The friction is just sitting there; it's just there and it's something that just resists, you know, *it doesn't actually like physically push.*" According to physicists, although friction forces come and go in unusual ways, when they act, they have identical core properties to other forces. They have direction and magnitude and can initiate motion as well as stop it (e.g., when a stationary box is dropped on a moving conveyor belt).

On other occasions, J treated gravity as having different possibilities with respect to motion compared to other forces, and she did the same for the "normal force" a table exerts to support a book lying on it.

Commentary. Some conceptual aspects of J's thinking are not unusual. Students often think of friction as acting only to resist motion, and they often believe some forces (e.g., normal forces) are special in some ways. However, our attention here is on extreme behaviors that we can interpret as expressions of J's epistemology. J seemed extreme in her willingness to split concepts, which is a counterproductive attitude toward physical concepts. Our judgment that J is extreme in particular ways (this one included), of course, relies on experience that is not documented here and is subject to further empirical scrutiny.

Shifting Interpretations is in a sense opposite to Splitting Concepts. In one case, J allows two descriptions of the same situation (e.g., two forces are involved, or only one), and in the other, she feels the same word ("force") may apply, yet the situations are different in important ways (air forces and friction forces do not actually push like other forces). In the case of Shifting Interpretations, she felt intuitively that each (different) description was appropriate, despite strong cues of contrast (e.g., asserting the existence of two forces in one case and one in the other). In the case of Splitting Concepts, she feels intuitively that descriptions need to be differentiated, despite cues of similarity (e.g., the use of the same technical term, force; only one version of $F = ma$ for all forces; and the fact that, presumably, her physics instructors and text never distinguished types of forces in their core, causal properties).

At the general level, J is not reading certain classes of cues about similarity and difference (i.e., similarity among exemplars and what constitutes a significant difference in description). In particular, it seems J does not draw a metaconceptual (possibly metalinguistic) distinction between everyday terms, exemplars of which may share only family resemblance, and technical terms, which require a core similarity between exemplars. J's behavior is sensible when applied to everyday terms such as "food." In various contexts of everyday use, it is often appropriate to split the general idea of food into a variety of related ideas that do not necessarily share common properties or a common definition. It is, for example, a simple matter to find exceptions in everyday use to definitions such as "something you eat" or to "something that provides nutrition." Depending on context, it may or may not be appropriate to consider salt, water, vitamins, or candy as food. The philosophically classic example of an everyday category whose members share no definitive properties is "game."

Intentionality. As with Shifting Interpretations, it is implausible that J could, on her own, formulate any obvious goal to help her out precisely here. Given her reading of situations and of her own descriptions of them, it would not be sensible to "try to unify these ('obviously' different) kinds of forces."[7] In this case, we do not have data on whether J could respond more appropriately if the issue were raised explicitly, as it was in the case of dual models of the toss.

Just as with Shifting Interpretations, it seems difficult to formulate a relevant categorical belief that might be driving J. Perhaps it is that "words have variable meanings"? Certainly J would believe this (or at least act consistently with this belief) in some contexts. The difficulty with the categorical attribution, however, is that she also believes the opposite (or acts consistently with the opposite belief) in other contexts, that "words have specific meanings." For example, she does decide that one should not use the term "force" for things more aptly described as "momentum" (see the immediately following section). Furthermore, J simply cannot believe that using particular words does not imply any constraints.[8] What is at issue is when the constraints are loose, when they are tight, and in what way are they tight. Once again, describing her epistemological knowledge as carrying out judgments in context (how different might things be and still be called by the same name?) seems more appropriate.

---

[7]This is an example of the limits we hypothesized for "intentional learners" – in this case, J is not in a position to recognize what she should learn (which we called "dependence on limited knowledge subsystems").

[8]If J held "words have variable meanings" as a categorical belief, she would have difficulty understanding questions such as whether a tomato is a *fruit*, whether Baltimore is the *capital* of Maryland, or whether an older sister can be a *legal guardian*.

3. Migrating Language

J would often switch among terms like force, momentum, and velocity as if they were interchangeable. On one occasion, J was asked to graph acceleration, and she graphed velocity (although she acknowledged this when queried). On another occasion, J glossed $F = ma$ as implicating a proportionality between force and acceleration. However, she illustrated this by showing a proportionality between force and velocity, saying "the more force you give, the faster it's gonna go."

Once again, J is not so unusual in this regard. Confusions between velocity and acceleration, and between speed and position, have been widely documented. However, J seemed persistent in Migrating Language, and surprisingly unconcerned when she, herself, uncovered an inconsistency. These, we hypothesize, are epistemological orientations, and they are especially prominent with J.

Recall that J frequently described a moving object as "having a force." At one point in discussing a puck moving on ice, J seemed spontaneously to notice that that is a different situation than when the puck is constantly being pushed by a force. The interviewer gently suggested that, perhaps, J's "force" in the moving-without-pushing situation should be described as momentum. J seems to pick this up quickly and firmly.

[5 0:9:55]

A: Okay. What if I suggested that, um, that maybe you should describe that [an object just moving along, not being pushed] as momentum rather than force.

J: Oh. I'd agree with you.

. . . [brief clarification]

J: Yeah. Definitely. Because I actually shouldn't have been calling it force the whole time, because momentum takes into consideration the velocity that it's moving and how much mass it has. Whereas, when you give something a force, I mean, if you give something a force, then it has momentum. It doesn't have a force ["on it," a physicist would add] the whole time. So I was using them, not interchangeably, but I was using it to mean [inaudible]. Momentum does describe it a lot better.

Yet, J continued in other circumstances to describe momentum as "force," as in "the force given to it by the hand." See the earlier quoted segment in session 7, where she reverts to talking about "the force that you gave it." J's own discovery of a case of Migrating Language didn't "take" as a warning to be careful.

Commentary. We can rehearse the same objections to categorical constructions of J's behaviors here as in previous cases. A proponent of categorical descriptions might say J's behavior in this section stems from a tendency "not to be careful with language" or from the belief that "words have many meanings." But these attributions cannot account for her willingness to distinguish, on occasion, between force and momentum. At minimum, we must admit a context-specific dependence to Migrating Language.

To emphasize the contextuality of Migrating Language, imagine a context in which it is sensible for language to migrate. In high school English class, many students learn the distinction between a simile and a metaphor. When preparing for a test, students generally learn the difference and use the words correctly, just as J, sometimes, distinguished force from momentum. But later that night, when discussing a flowery anonymous love note, the same students might use "simile" and "metaphor" interchangeably because the technical distinction does no work for them in the context of trying to explicate the meaning of the note. J may have been similarly contextual in her judgments about force and momentum. She may see the difference when prompted, and view the distinction as relevant in some contexts, but in other contexts feel the distinction is artificial and unnecessary to her goal of getting her meaning across.

It is worthwhile emphasizing the epistemological nature of J's behaviors, beyond, say, specific conceptual confusions. First, we claim that J is not sufficiently attuned to the nature of scientific, technical concepts in general. Of course, we could be wrong about this. However, if we are correct, this is an epistemological issue, not just a (specific) conceptual one. Secondly, the irregularity of J's behavior supports an epistemological interpretation. Mixing force with momentum may be conceptual, but failing to be careful about the distinction *after articulately noting it,* constitutes a failure to deal with a knowledge-related issue effectively.

Evidently there is some relation between Migrating Language and Shifting Interpretations. However, they are not the same. J did not merely substitute "force" for "momentum" in describing the two-force toss. She implicated an entirely different causal mechanism, involving the dying out of one force and a shifting balance of strength (contrasting with one constant force acting to change velocity). On the other hand, it is entirely possible these two behaviors come back to the same epistemological orientation, one that does not recognize patterns of language use or concept types in learning physics that differ from those appropriate to more everyday contexts.

Intentionality. The patterns in Migrating Language seem similar to the previous two behavioral phenomena. J simply does not notice some differences and similarities in description or fact. Or, if she notices them, they are judged unimportant. One novel feature in the case of migrating terms is that J, at least sometimes, recognized a "slip" she previously gave no signs of recognizing (that one should call the motion of an object "momentum," not "force") when it came up explicitly. In this case, it seems J could have formulated an appropriate goal—to stabilize the differences she "discovered." But she apparently had no inclination to do this. At least, she did not give any evidence of taking on this goal, and, indeed, her language continued to migrate. So, with respect to Migrating Language, but not with respect to Shifting Interpretations or Splitting Concepts, J might have been in a position where intentional learning could have helped her.

4. Weak Commitment to Principles

J showed only a weak, context-sensitive commitment to general principles, often treating them as "rules of thumb," heuristics rather than laws. She often self-consciously (unlike Shifting Interpretations) changed her way of thinking about a situation, abandoning a physical principle she professed to believe, because it seemed right to do so in the particular context.

Several examples of Weak Commitment to Principles occurred while examining the case of a book pushed at constant speed across a table. The interviewer introduced some new forces into the picture, in addition to the force of the hand on the book and the force of friction pushing backward on the book. These additional forces were "reaction" forces to the forces that J initially saw in the situation. He introduced the force of the book pushing back on the hand (reaction force to the force of the hand on the book). J initially accepted that force, and even declared it equal to the force of the hand on the book. This is correct physics according to Newton's third law, also known as the principle of "action and reaction." (To every action, there is an equal and opposite reaction.) However, J soon retracted the "equal" assertion because, if the force of the book on the hand were equal to the force of the hand on the book, it would cancel out (in her mind), and leave motion unexplained.[9]

What are the epistemological implications of this move? Here, J found a conflict between her understanding of Newton's third law and her intuition that motion requires an unbalanced force. Rather than try to reconcile this inconsistency, which could have led her to revise her misunder-

[9]As do many physics students, J was misunderstanding two points. First, the force of the hand on the book could not cancel the force of the book on the hand because these two forces act on different objects: One acts on the hand; the other acts on the book. Second, the condition of balanced forces acting on the book would be consistent with constant velocity: An unbalanced force would be needed to cause a change in velocity.

standings, she chose to abandon the third law, deciding that it must not apply in this situation. This abandonment would not implicate epistemology if J never really "believed in" Newton's third law as a general principle. But in discussing the necessity of revising one's intuitive ideas when learning physics, J specifically cites the third law as a principle she believes, even in cases where it initially seems intuitively problematic:

[2 0:46:0]

J: . . . I mean, it's hard to convince someone that right now the chair is pushing on me as hard as I'm pushing down—130 pounds . . . I think that's something that once you've taken physics, that's totally normal. But if you said it to someone off the street, I think they'd say, "What are you talking about? No it's not. You know, obviously it's not pushing; there's nothing to push it up." *But it is.* [emphasis added]

We now return to the pushed book example. After J retracted her claim that the forces exerted by the hand and book on each other are equal and opposite, the interviewer suggested considering the horizontal force exerted by the book on the table (the "reaction" force to the force of friction impeding the book's motion). J immediately rejected this second force.[10] The interviewer persisted by showing her that the book would drag along a piece of paper placed under it; he claimed that that showed the book was pushing on the paper.

[4 0:21:50]

J: I think it's just sliding, and I think it's [the book is] just bringing the paper with it. I mean, it's a really simple situation. I think you could start saying there's all these millions and trillions of forces. . . . Um, I think you just have to make it real simple and say these are the major forces. I mean, yeah, we're talking air and there's air on top of this, but if you said that the force of air is gonna play a part, and you start getting this book that's just sitting there and millions of forces, then you start setting up more complicated situations, like flying on a plane or something like that, and there's

---

[10]Note that we quote two instances in other places (among several in the corpus of data) where J affirms "action and reaction"—that if object *a* is pushing on object *b*, then *b* pushes on *a* with the same magnitude of force. Here, she denies that principle by acknowledging the table's frictional push backward on the book while denying the book's push forward on the table. J's version of "action and reaction" is quite contextually sensitive.

just zillions of forces on this object. So I would just say that it's sliding against the table and bringing the paper with it.

J seems to be saying two things. First, she says that you should not consider such forces, because, if you did, that would create a confusing world of "millions of forces." In this moment, J's epistemological orientation is toward simplicity of description, which she prioritizes here over consistency with principles. She justifies omitting these other forces by describing the forces she allows as "major," perhaps thinking of the strategies she has seen in class of neglecting small forces. Note, however, that the action and reaction principle she used at some times, but not at other times, guarantees that the force she dismisses, the force of the book on the table, is as large as one she included, friction.

Second, in this passage J just asserts, with no explicit justification at all, that the paper's motion requires no force. Forceless motion is an everyday experience, but if J were holding at this moment to her view that motion needs unbalanced forces, this would not be an adequate explanation for her. Apparently, she sees the book as "bringing the paper with it," and her epistemological judgment in this context has her complacent with respect to the principle she used a moment earlier, that motion needs unbalanced forces.[11] (A moment later, as we discuss later, she returns to that principle, explicitly choosing it over $F = ma$.)

Commentary. J's commitment to principles is weak and contextual. She sets them aside in particular situations when they make things confusing, or when she feels she has another sensible way to treat the situation. This epistemological stance is appropriate to decision making in everyday situations, when sensitivity to immediate circumstances often appropriately supercedes general principles. Individuals who would never tell a white lie to spare a friend embarrassment may sensibly be considered somewhat fanatical. Abandoning principles easily is not, however, a productive stance to take with respect to learning physics, when students should be working toward principled coherence in their understanding. In contrast to J's behavior, students who are committed to principled coherence treat moments of confusion as opportunities to identify and reconcile inconsistencies between general principles and specific in-

---

[11]Why did J deny the reaction force of the book on the table, while only "demoting" the reaction force of the hand on the book to a small, ignorable force? While it is not important for the analysis of this chapter, we note the following contextual issues: (a) J could not feel the second force, as she could the force of the book on her hand; (b) Friction is a special force (split concept), so it might not need to behave like other forces; and (c) J had specific intuitive excuses, "sliding," "sticking," or "carrying along," that explain the motion of the paper on which the book rested without the need of a force. See, for example, diSessa & Sherin (1998).

tuitions, pushing through their confusion to construct new understanding (Hammer, 1994).

Intentionality. J's deliberation concerning the applicability of Newton's laws provides another indictment of the formulation of epistemological knowledge as beliefs, and further support for the viability of "judgment in context" as an alternative formulation. At first glance, J's behavior appears to follow from a general belief such as "for every rule, there's an exception." However, as part of J's reflection on denying the relevance of $F = ma$ to pushing a book across a table (see Appendix A and the end of the section of protocol [4 0:38:20] in section 7), J asserts that she initially believed $F = ma$ to be always true, but inasmuch as she judged it could not apply to pushing a book, she was forced to revise her beliefs. Thus, a consciously avowed epistemological belief ("$F = ma$ is always true") not only fails to govern her behavior in the situation, but also gets modified because of a judgment specific to this situation. Of course, as in all other cases, we cannot guarantee that there is no reformulated view of what she does that does not follow from some as-yet unknown belief. However, it seems difficult to formulate such a belief, and even more difficult to remove some implicit contextual judgment balancing her avowed belief that $F = ma$ was general versus whatever countervailing belief J might have had that caused her to abandon her prior belief.

5. Discounting Details in Explanations

J went beyond not pursuing details. She sometimes (implicitly) denied that they were relevant to the task of judging the adequacy of an explanation. In particular, when faced with difficulties working out the details of an explanation, J often settled for an incomplete explanation instead of exploring the possibility that her difficulties stemmed from flaws in her understanding of the underlying principles.

To explicate this claim, and to explore how this behavior does and does not differ from that of physicists, we distinguish between two kinds of accountability to details in physics explanations. The first, we believe, is a commonsense accountability, that if you impute particular entities acting (such as a force), you should be able to justify the existence of those entities (say, as forces of known kinds, such as gravity, that occur in known circumstances). A second level of accountability may be more specific and learned in school. In physics, you must hold yourself accountable for what happens at each instant. At an instant, a force either exists or it does not.

In contrast, J seemed to see it as acceptable to make claims without being able to justify the elements in those claims. For example, to J, it was acceptable to say that there is balancing without being able to say what balances (see the second quotation in [3 0:24:20]). Similarly, J found it acceptable for a force to have two different magnitudes at the same instant in time.

In the toss situation, J said at one point that the upward force given to the ball by the hand balances gravity at its peak and then that the hand's force was zero at the peak. The following quotation is J's response to the interviewer's questioning her with respect to these conflicting claims. Note that halfway through, J acknowledges the logic underlying the contradiction: If a decreasing upward force balances a downward force at a given moment, the upward force cannot vanish until some time later. However, instead of taking this contradiction as cause to question her explanation, she grasps for a way to keep her two ideas intact, eventually using the fact that "it's such a short amount of time" to excuse the need for a detailed reconciliation. This is an example of evading the more subtle "moment-by-moment" accountability.

[3 0:24:20]

A: If it's gone though, how can it balance?

J: Well, at that second that it balances, which isn't very long, is when it's like it's on its last // You know, it's slowly, slowly dying out, and that one second is the one time when it's equal. So it's not gone at that second it's, obviously. Or else, if it would be, if it was gone that second, then it would have been falling earlier, and it would have been gone a little bit lower. But at that one, when it's at its peak, it's right before it's going to be gone.

A: OK. That's right before, so it's gone some time after it starts the downward //

J: Well, when it stopped is when they're equal. But obviously it dies at that exact point for the gravity to pull it back down. So I guess you can say that at that point it goes away. But when it was completely stationery, it was still there enough to have it not fall. But, it's such a short amount of time, you know, it's not like it goes up and hangs out there for a while and then, oh, it dies out and comes back down. It goes up and it comes right back down. So it's like a really short amount of time. Just dies out.

Much later, in the last interview, J again asserts both that the upward force cancels gravity and that the "force of the hand" is zero. Indeed, at very nearly the end of the interview, when she has once again been brought to the point of recognizing both that she has all along claimed (from time to time) that the force of the hand is zero at the top *and* that (from time to time) she has said there is only one force, gravity, during the entire toss, she still maintains that there is a balancing, even though she is unable to identify the canceling force. J does not explore the possibility that her interpretation is in error, but holds fast to her belief that there is balancing, even if she cannot identify the balancing force. This appears to be an example of the more blatant accountability for named entities in an explanation.

[7 1:01:30]

J: At the top, the force is equal to zero because it's stopped. But // I guess you can't say they're equal to each other. I guess you have to say that they cancel each other out.

A: Which two forces cancel each other?

J: I'm obviously wrong [laughs] about something. [Interpretation: The persistence of the interviewer suggests to J that she must be doing something wrong.]

A: I'm just trying to get all the details.

J: . . . When it's at the top, it only has one force on it. Downward. And //

A: So, what's canceling out?

J: Well, I guess nothing's canceling out. I guess it's just, uh [long pause] I still think forces are canceling out, but I don't know which one's they are. [Laughs]

Commentary. Can we account for J's behavior in this subsection by ascribing to her a belief such as "details don't matter" or a trait such as sloppiness of thought? The evidence suggests not. For instance, in section 1 J justifies her omission of air pressure by referring to the details of how it acts. Air pushes in all directions at once, which makes the air pressure force cancel out.[12] Similarly, section 7 provides an extended episode of J's using careful, detail-oriented reasoning to explore an apparent contradiction. So, once again, J's behavior is best described as arising from a judgment in context: If J is using conceptual resources that seem very sensible to her at a given moment (e.g., the "balancing" schematization), and she faces difficulty working out the explanatory details, then she is likely to settle for an explanation that violates the accountability conditions listed earlier rather than to question her conceptualizations. When faced with anomalous data, physicists often decide that their inability to account for details does not threaten the core principles underlying their reasoning. So, even in the context of aca-

---

[12]From a physicist's perspective, a version of this argument correctly explains why air-pressure forces do not appear in most force descriptions in introductory physics.

demic science, J's behavior is not completely inappropriate. From a physicist's perspective, however, J stops pursuing the details too quickly in favor of just feeling things must work out somehow.

Typical of case studies, we cannot be sure how common J's refusal of accountability to details is. We do not know whether students come regularly into physics class accepting both of these types of accountability (to justify the existence of entities used in explanation, and to account for such analyses at each instant of time), one of them, or neither. Based on data and argument we do not present here, it is our expectation that moment-by-moment accountability regularly requires physics-specific epistemological sophistication. In any case, both kinds of accountability constitute likely epistemological difficulties and targets for instruction, for at least some students.

Intentionality. J didn't spontaneously note her own lack of accountability to details. Probably, her judgment in context is that she is being sufficiently accountable. Even bringing the issue to conscious consideration does not provide enough impetus to consider that there might be a problem in her thinking that needs consideration. As with prior cases (with the exception of Migrating Language), J does not seem to be in a position where conscious reflection or intentional learning could be productive.

6. Hedging

J frequently hedged with linguistic tags of limited commitment. Hedging is an explicit linguistic strategy for softening a claim, which we distinguish from Weak Commitment to Principles, the inconsistent adherence to or abandonment of principles.

In addition to explicit forms such as "kind of like" or "sort of," J allowed multiple views (that appeared contradictory to us) with noncommittal statements like, "You could think of it that way." Sometimes J made weak statements without explicit hedges when much stronger statements might be made. One such move that struck us as particularly interesting occurred when she was in her bind concerning unbalanced force, constant-speed motion, and $F = ma$ (reviewed in detail in the next subsection). In examining the case of a falling body, she said, "Well, I guess if you applied a constant force, you *could* have constant acceleration," ([4 0:29:00], emphasis added). She did not suggest that the lesson was the obvious one from $F = ma$: You *must* get constant acceleration with a constant force.

Commentary. Hedging is sensible when one has a developing knowledge system. Appropriately tagging both lack of commitment and also rough descriptions can be quite useful. But Hedging also serves as a buffer when sharper descriptions can be made, when more commitment is implied in the rest of one's analysis, or when one knows that one needs to strive for better, less-qualified descriptions. The choice of when to hedge and when not to is an epistemological judgment on the amount of commitment and accountability one should have toward some statement. It is important to make such choices well to leverage reconsideration of weak, possibly context-specific ideas based on stronger ones. Students who perceive their own knowledge landscape as flat (no part of it more generally secure than any other part) have difficulty bootstrapping toward a well-organized, consistent knowledge base.[13]

A proponent of categorical descriptions might hypothesize that J could never take a strong position on anything. One might also believe she is unreflective, did not monitor her statements and did not think much about what learning physics was about. In what follows, we show that these generalizations do not hold. J ended up taking a very strong position with respect to the unbalanced forces–$F = ma$ dilemma. Moreover, she several times remarked how frequently in the interviews she had to change her mind upon reflection. J could engage in relatively elaborate argumentation around a single point (see the next section). Finally, she *did* reflect on physics learning, and knew, for example, that it frequently forces one to change one's intuitive schematizations of the world (again, see later examples).

Thus, these final two behaviors, in sections 7 and 8, play a different role in our analysis. They directly show contextual difficulties in categorical descriptions of J's epistemology. Based on sections 1 through 6, it would be easy to caricature J with categorical (negative) descriptions of her epistemology. As now argued, however, she often showed sophistication and behavior at odds with the patterns we have described to this point.

7. Strong Commitment to a View

In the episode just previewed, J claimed that unbalanced forces are necessary for any motion.[14] With some prompting, J saw that this conflicted with $F = ma$. In particular, objects that move at constant speed need unbalanced forces on them (according to J's intuitions), but $F = ma$ then would require acceleration. In this situation J (a) questioned her own analysis; (b) carefully reviewed the logic of her arguments, for example, checking that

---

[13]Of course, students may also guess wrong about what parts of their knowledge are reliable, to be built on.

[14]This claim contradicts several other things that J appeared to believe at other times. For example, it is in contradiction with the one-force model of the toss she occasionally espoused. It is in contradiction because if gravity is the only force, then it is in the wrong direction to explain the upward part of the toss.

the meaning of acceleration would really imply one should be able to see an object speeding up; (c) summarized her own reasoning and the broad implications of it concerning general properties of physics knowledge; and (d) used reasoning about different exemplar situations (one she introduced and another that was introduced by the interviewer) to elaborate her understanding.

Here are some quotations from critical portions of this 25-minute-long segment. After J identifies the two primary forces on the book (the hand pushing it and the friction resisting its motion) the interviewer asks:

[4 0:17:10]

A: So could you relate the amount of force that I'm applying to the friction?

. . . [Clarification omitted]

J: Well, if it's moving, then yours is going to be bigger than the frictional force. And that's why, when it's not moving, the frictional force is greater than your force.

At this point, the interviewer deliberately introduces some reaction forces, as described earlier. J clearly monitored the implications of her "equal and opposite" description of the force of the book on the hand pushing it. She sees that it is in conflict with her principle that unbalanced forces are required for motion. Further, she checks her belief that there is such a reaction force in the first place and concludes: "You know it is because you can feel it."

[4 0:18:00]

A: And, now I'm pushing on this book. What about the force that the book is exerting on my finger?

J: Umm [long pause] It's the same as the force you're exerting on the book.

A: You look a little dubious.

J: Well, I don't think actually that that's true because when you have a book on the table, the force of the table and the book is the same; it's not going anywhere. [A book does not move vertically, and has balanced forces up (the table) and down (gravity).] When you're pushing it, it's moving. So I suspect [note hedging: "I suspect"] if the force was the same, then it wouldn't be going anywhere. If the force that the book exerted on your finger was the same as the force your finger exerted on the book. Because if the sum of the forces are zero, then it's not going to be moving. Some force has to be greater than another. But if we said that the force of your hand is greater than friction, then I'm not sure how the book is exerting a force on your hand. I mean, you know it is because you can feel it.

At this point, the interviewer introduced the second reaction force, which initiated the segment where J denied that a force was needed to move a piece of paper, described in section 4, Weak Commitment to Principles.

Following on, J proceeds on a fairly systematic pursuit (supported by the interviewer) of what might be wrong with her analysis. For example, she checks at least twice that she is justified in assuming acceleration is zero when velocity is constant. She seems careful and reflective about what it would take to convince her that there is acceleration in this situation.

[4 0:29:30]

J: That doesn't look to me like the book is accelerating. At all.

A: No, it doesn't.

J: Maybe it's just accelerating at the same rate. It seems to me that, see, if it has constant acceleration, the velocity is still increasing. It's just increasing at a constant rate, right?

A: Say that again.

J: If it has constant acceleration, the velocity is increasing, but it's at the same rate.

A: Yeah, that's right.

J: So, if you're pushing this, [if] it has constant acceleration, it still has to be getting faster and faster and faster.

A bit later:

[4 0:31:00]

J: See, I would think that when you're pushing it, it was a constant velocity, not a constant acceleration. I can't imagine someone telling me something that would convince me otherwise. Because // It's like you see accelerations, you feel acceleration. It's not like this book is really accelerating, and we just don't see it.

A: I see. It's something in physics you can see.

J: Yeah.

After checking alternatives, checking that she really believes you need unbalanced forces to move, checking that acceleration really must be visible if it is happening, J is committed to a paradox. You need unbalanced forces, but $F = ma$ says unbalanced forces require acceleration, which, however, she knows is not present. The interviewer tries to offer an opening.

[4 0:32:00]

A: So you said, the hard question is why is it moving if the forces are canceling. Suppose I said that well, things don't need a reason to move, they just move.

J: That wouldn't fly well.

Note that if J systematically had very limited commitment to ideas, she could have solved her problem, "taken the easiest path," by just accepting this (ironically, correct) offering from the interviewer. Instead, she is true to her beliefs, and remains troubled.

J summarizes her perplexity:

[4 0:36:50]

J: No, I'm just thinking about if that's true, let's say that every time there's a force something's moving, then it's going to be accelerating, because anytime something moves the forces aren't equal. And to me it's going to be very mind boggling to think that every time something's moving, it's accelerating.

A: That just does not sound possible.

J: That just is not slightly possible.

J is not hedging here. In the final segment, J shows she believed $F = ma$ was a universal idea. But she has come to an impasse. Rather than abandon her unbalanced force idea, she demotes $F = ma$ to "one of those darn equations" that is not always true. She shows that she has reflected on her own prior conceptual change, but she does not take this as an occasion where her conceptions need to change. This is a judgment in context.

[4 0:38:20]

J: I want it to be true, but there's just no way it is, you know. Like to me you look at $F = ma$, and there's a force and that has to mean acceleration [no hedging here]. But then it's easy to say "that's true," but I mean there's no way it is. I guess you can just say that, you know, those darn equations aren't applicable to every single thing. They're not always true. You can't live by them. But, I just want // I was just trying to think of an explanation of why. I mean, it makes sense. You can see it happening. You know that's what's happening. I don't know why I just started doubting myself because that stupid force formula.

A: Yeah, you said before that you "wanted it to be true." . . . I didn't know what you meant by "it". Do you remember?

J: No. I'm sure it was just // I mean I want what seems logical to me to make sense with what I've learned and what you can, like, you know, like when we were talking about the formulas. I mean you learn these formulas and you apply them to all these problems. But when something that you know is true—I mean to me it makes so much sense that it's crazy to even debate it, that if you're pushing this with a constant force, and you see it moving, that it's not accelerating. But then, to think about something that you've learned and you've been applying for so long and have it not make sense. Then you start doubting what // I started doubting what makes complete sense to me.

A: Does that happen a lot in physics or classes generally?

J: Well, I mean it's really neat when you learn something that isn't what you would intuitively have thought, but it makes sense, you go, "God, I totally understand that. It's not what the everyday person on the street would know, but I understand." Rather than this when I'm saying, "OK, that's something that I've learned, but it doesn't seem like that could //" I mean I know that can't be right. And do I just discard it and say // Because, I mean, you learn these formulas in school and you can't // You know half the time they only apply to certain perfect models, especially like in chemistry, you know, certain situations. And you can't apply them to absolutely everything. You think, oh, plug it into the formula. But when you're in real life, I mean, so many things have so many different things going on that you can't always say // I just thought that $F = ma$ was one of those that was universal, you know, it wasn't like specific.

Commentary. In this long sequence, J shows she is not in any sense categorically careless or uninvolved. J is not docile in her learning. "I want what seems logical to me to make sense with what I've learned." She shows she sometimes takes strong stands, unlike what Hedging and Weak Commitment to Principles suggest. Once again, contextuality is clear. She is making a judgment in this particular context that her intuitive understanding is the way to view *this* situation. Here, she is making an unusually bold move in demoting $F = ma$, about which she had correctly gotten the impression that it was a very general principle, to "just one of those darn equations" that applies to "certain perfect models." She is reflective about the nature of the knowledge that has been provided to her ($F = ma$ is general; equations frequently apply only in particular situations).

From a physicist's standpoint, J made the wrong choice of commitment, to her principle of unbalanced forces rather than to $F = ma$. What is relevant to this section's analysis, however, is that she *made* a commitment, holding to her idea and explicitly accommodating $F = ma$ as only applying to certain, "perfect" situations.[15] Whereas Hedging and other patterns we discussed earlier might lead one to believe J was not capable of or generally inclined to commitment—we describe this later as a tendency toward accepting fragmented knowledge—this episode showed her invoking epistemological resources for such commitment. Instructionally, we would like to help students like J make commitments to general principles more systematically, and, of course, we need to provide help in understanding how to judge which commitments are best to make. Although it is inappropriate to go into details here, we believe there are many strategies and considerations to discuss with students to help them make productive choices.

Intentionality. In a sense, J was intentional here in "learning" that unbalanced forces are necessary for motion: She explicitly considers and then responds to a challenge to the idea, and, in the end, reaffirms her commitment to it. Of course, as we noted, she was intentional in the wrong direction, and this raises again the question of the relationship between intentionality and epistemology. Here as previously, intentional learning seems dependent on epistemological judgments in context.

8. Reflective about Learning and the Revision of Intuitive Ideas

The segment quoted last shows the result of prior reflections on her own learning and of reflections on the nature of the knowledge she is being taught. In addition, the segment is, itself, an instance where she is forming her epistemological ideas. It certainly does not look like it involves "a belief in the immutability of scientific ideas," or the formation of an "authoritarian" or "antiauthoritarian" stance. It looks like she is generatively bending and shifting the contextuality of her prior ideas specifically about $F = ma$ ("certain perfect situations" becomes a more relevant description of context) and, possibly, about the nature of equations as knowledge.

[15]In keeping with Discounting Details, J does not seem to consider it important to pursue this reconciliation in detail—what specifically determines whether a situation is "perfect" such that $F = ma$ would apply? Why might it be that pushing a book across a table is not "perfect"?

J gave many other indications that she reflected on her learning experiences, and, in particular, on her learning experiences in physics. She seemed quite conscious of the fact that physics changes the way one thinks about familiar events. In one episode, she recounted how difficult it would be for a person unschooled in physics to believe action and reaction. Note the subtlety in her thinking: People would know what is happening, but not how it works.

[2 0:46:0]

A: And you say you know the desk is pushing up because if it weren't, the book would just come down.

J: Right. And it's the same as like equal and opposite forces. I mean, this chair right now is pushing up on me and the chair is pushing up on you. And the ground is pushing up on your feet. And that's something that's hard to think about. [You're tempted to say:] "No it's not; I don't feel it; I'm not moving anywhere." But it is [pushing up].

A short time later:

J: I think it's hard to think in your mind, "Oh, this table's pushed up." It's easy to say the table's counteracting, the table's supporting. I think that's something anybody would know. . . . [But] I mean, it's hard to convince someone that right now the chair is pushing on me as hard as I'm pushing down—130 pounds. This chair's pushing up on me. I think that's something that once you've taken physics, that's totally normal. But if you said it to someone off the street, I think they'd say, "What are you talking about? No it's not. You know, obviously it's not pushing; there's nothing to push it up." But it is. So maybe it's like what is going on is common knowledge, but how it actually works maybe I learned.

Commentary. J is not unreflective. She is learning at the epistemological level while she is learning physics, and she has a lot of important epistemological ideas right, from a physicist's perspective. Learning physics sometimes requires changing ideas to the point where ideas previously judged to be absurd come to seem natural. A physicist might find many faults in J's epistemological stance and strategies. But these are not categorical gaps, and they do not necessarily stem from beliefs that are wrong so much as contextually inappropriate judgments and actions.

Intentionality. These latter episodes appear the most like conscious reflection and belief formation of any in the corpus. Yet, still, judgments in context seem implicated in the very possibility of sensibly initiating reflection and in the judgments that select which new beliefs will result.

SYNTHETIC INTERPRETATION

In what follows, we seek a simplified, coarser-grained view of J's intuitive epistemology that loses as little as possible of the detail and contextuality displayed previously. We make no claim to having found the best compromise of succinctness and coverage, although we tried to enfold as many of the behavioral phenomena as possible.

Two central tendencies stand out in J: (a) a systematic bias toward accepting fragmented knowledge, and (b) a tendency to view learning physics as sense making (as opposed to, say, memorizing information). We now discuss these two tendencies in more detail.

Bias Toward Fragmented Knowledge

J was not exceptional in the nature of her intuitive ideas; naïve physics, we claim (e.g., diSessa, 1993; Smith, diSessa, & Roschelle, 1993), is inherently fragmented. She was unusual, however, in her stance toward that fragmentation. Compared to most students we have encountered, J seemed more at ease in offering multiple interpretations that fail to converge and in using multiple explanatory frameworks that we would see in tension with each other, including frameworks that contradict explicit instructed principles. One manifestation of her acceptance of fragmentation is that she does not feel compelled to believe physical categories share core properties (Splitting Concepts). A common meaning to "force," for example, involves, to her, an implausible commonalty across diverse-feeling situations. Furthermore, no way of thinking about things seems privileged over other ways. Instead, she relies on her intuitive feelings of understanding in particular cases. When she feels confidence in an interpretation, she judges it to be valid even if it appears to contradict another analysis she has given (Shifting Interpretations). The fact that physics frequently ignores some things (like small forces) is just one more example to her that you just have to go with what seems right. For J, the world is complex and diverse, and she is comfortable providing different analyses at each turn.

Because of her unusual dependence on intuitive judgments (and hence, on piecemeal, largely inarticulate knowledge), articulation per se is often infeasible. She refuses certain kinds of accountability about the details of her pronouncements. She acts as if she does not think[16] that exercising linguistic precision and making strong predictions are necessarily good or even workable strategies for promoting her own conceptual development (Migrating Language, Hedging). Words may shift their meaning as she shifts her attention, but this is not something she systematically attends to or worries about.

J has enough confidence in her own intuitive schematizations of how the world works that she often chooses them over some of the most prominent principles of a physicist's world view—namely, her unbalanced forces schematization versus $F = ma$, and her analysis of a pushed book (and slipping paper) versus "action and reaction." In the same vein, if she feels that a line of reasoning is correct, she does not feel that she needs good, articulable reasons for abandoning a stated principle (Weak Commitment to Principles).

J does not have confidence that some of the standard modeling procedures of physics *need* to apply and should be expected to be decisive. For example, physics demands moment-by-moment accountability in its analyses. At every instant, one is accountable for identifying and justifying the existence of each component of the analysis—for example, which forces are present. J does not see this universal systematicity as a good idea, or even workable. For example, J refuses to drop "balancing" just because she cannot find forces to balance.

Plenty of evidence suggests, however, that J's attitude toward learning is not entirely naïve from a physicist's perspective. She is not unreflective. She monitors her thinking and corrects some of her own mistakes. She knows to review her own arguments carefully, especially when they draw problematic conclusions. She knows that physics requires revised conceptualization. From a physicist's standpoint, her problem is not a lack of commitment to reconceptualization, but rather, a lack of commitment to the right *kind* of reconceptualization, for example, that physics technical terms require a core commonality among exemplars. J explicitly states, for instance, that she would *like* to think laws such as $F = ma$ are universal, but she is unable to make that work because intuitive schematizations have such a high priority in her thinking. Despite the fact that she does not seem to have a view of physical knowledge that captures some of its core and unusual properties, a physicist would in some ways appreciate J's strong commitment to sense making, discussed next.

Commitment to Sense Making

To J, learning physics entails making sense of the material in her own terms, as opposed to simply accepting the physics as presented in her

[16] J does not seem to be conscious of these particular issues, nor articulate about them.

class. For example, because passive forces such as friction seem intuitively different from forces that "actually like physically push," J views friction as a special kind of force with different properties (Splitting Concepts).[17] In general, she does whatever it takes—abandoning Newton's third law of action and reaction, for instance—to reconcile the physics under discussion with her intuitive sense of mechanism (Weak Commitment to Principles). Sometimes, when a bit of physics such as $F = ma$ conflicts with her sense of mechanism, she is willing to commit strongly to her intuitive view, for example, by concluding that $F = ma$ is "one of those darn equations" that does not always apply. Along these same lines, when considering the ball at its peak, J switches from one story (no upward force) to another story (balancing forces) precisely when her intuitive sense of "balancing" kicks in (see diSessa, 1993, 1996); without realizing her shifting conceptualizations, she adds an upward force in order to express her intuitive sense of what is happening. To a physicist, providing two contradictory explanations seems inconsistent with sense making, but to J, accepting as she does the fragmentation of knowledge, the "competing" explanations each seem sensible enough, so they are judged compatible. Inasmuch as she has made sense of the material at a level of precision and consistency that she accepts, she ends up considering herself to understand the ball toss (with a one-force model), and also to have understood it before (with a two-force model).

[7 1:17:50]

J: It's funny though because I think that it would be easy for somebody watching that [the tape from her prior interview] to think that I didn't understand what was going on. And it's funny because I don't think that now [the one force model] I understand what's going on any better than I did then. But I can explain it to you in the right way.

A: In the physics way, probably.

J: Which is, kind of, not frustrating, but it's weird. . . . I can say, OK, I correctly said what was going on, but I don't think I understand any differently. Like maybe I'm getting words confused, but I don't think that I have this revelation "that's how it works." Because I still think I understood how it worked.

J is articulately aware of her bias toward sense making: "I want what seems logical to me to make sense with what I've learned." When reflect-

[17]A physicist, devoted to global coherence as well as to sense making, might try to understand in what sense friction and the normal force can be understood as "pushes." But J's systematic bias toward fragmented knowledge makes this move unlikely.

ing on her learning, she explicitly focuses on the need to reconceptualize her own intuitive ideas rather than just to absorb new information. On the other hand, just because she has some articulate awareness of her orientation toward sense making does not mean she is constantly aware of this, or even that, in a particular instance, sense-making behavior is driven by any conscious awareness. For example, it is likely, if not certain, that on many occasions she will persist in thinking about something (a good sense-making strategy) just because she perceives she has not achieved a feeling of understanding.

In summary, ascribing to J a systematic bias toward fragmented knowledge and a tendency to view learning as sense making summarizes the eight patterns of behavioral phenomenology described earlier. On the other hand, this higher level and more compact description cannot be understood in a categorical sense as global beliefs or traits. First, in the previous section, we made clear there were many contextualities even at the finer grain of more specific behaviors (e.g., when to hedge, and when not to), and we argued that most of these behaviors could not be viewed as corresponding to or stemming from generalized beliefs or traits. This contexuality is still unexplained at the higher level; because the individual behaviors cannot be understood categorically, neither can a generalization derived from those behaviors. Second, we have evidently lost some specificity. Our two general characteristics do not literally imply all of the eight behavioral phenomena. For example, as far as we know, we might be wrong in attributing an unusual degree of hedging to J, even if she is unusual with respect to Shifting Interpretations. The overall patterns (bias toward fragmented knowledge and tendency to view learning as sense making) are "soft" enough to allow this. Furthermore, other students who warrant the same high-level description might, nonetheless, show the behavioral patterns in different degrees from J, and might show other patterns J did not display. Instructionally, different students might warrant different emphases. We make the argument against categorical interpretation more fully and carefully in the next section.

THE CASE AGAINST A CATEGORICAL INTERPRETATION

Our analysis of J's reasoning, focusing on her strategies and decision making, finds systematic epistemological tendencies. In this respect, we replicate a substantial body of earlier work (Hammer, 1994; Perry, 1970; see Hofer & Pintrich, 1997, for review). The central issue we review here is whether intuitive epistemologies are appropriately described categorically in terms of coherent knowledge (beliefs or theories) and/or global traits (e.g., cognitive styles or stages of development).

Context Dependency and Coherence

Systematic answers or other behavior can arise in a variety of ways; they do not always reflect systematicity or even coherence in the underlying cognitive structures. For instance, consider a pattern, identified in diSessa's (1993) study of intuitive physics, that is directly relevant to J's toss analyses. Asked to identify the forces acting on a ball at the peak of a vertical toss, students systematically described a balance between an upward force, in the direction the ball had been moving, and a downward force of gravity. However, when students were asked to identify the forces acting on the ball on its way down, or on a ball dropped from rest, neither balancing nor even a force competing with gravity were likely to appear in subjects' accounts. Subjects do not describe the descent of the ball in the toss in terms of the downward gravitational force overcoming a lingering upward force. (The force must linger, inasmuch as it is still present at the top of the toss—a fact that most students, other than J, readily acknowledge.) So, subjects are systematic in attributing balancing forces to the ball at its peak. However, subjects do not typically notice the apparent contradiction in their reasoning (a force gradually dying away and strong enough to balance gravity, but that instantly disappears from the analysis past the peak[18]) unless the interviewer brings it up. These repeated inconsistencies in students' answers indicate that their reasoning is not driven by coherent and consistently used beliefs or theories. So, this example shows that systematicities in students' behavior (e.g., their answers to questions about a toss) can arise even when the underlying knowledge structures are not belief-like or theory-like.

Despite that example and others like it, we, as analysts, are prone to put ideas together because they seem logically to belong with one another. Yet, we need empirical warrants to impute such connections to subjects. For example, at one time the common "balancing and overcoming" explanation of the toss was believed to illustrate an intuitive theory of physics (McCloskey, 1983). Later analysis suggested that a number of independent knowledge elements—that, in fact, are rarely activated together—account for the "intuitive theory" (diSessa, 1996). These and other argu-

[18]Galileo, pursuing the same two-force "theory" of a toss as naïve subjects, in fact, tried to incorporate a continuing-to-fade force in his analysis past the peak. He also sought to involve a competing force even in the simple situation where an object is dropped from rest, where forces other than gravity are essentially never introduced by novices. (See sections 201 and 202 in Galileo, 1954.) Scientists pursue systematicity and coherence well beyond what naïve or novice subjects do.

ments and data suggest that systematicities in students' reasoning about physics often result from regular responses to particular contexts, not from broadly used individual mental constructs or integrated patterns that one might call "theories" or systematic "beliefs."

In general, there is no reason to believe that intuitive epistemological ideas behave differently from intuitive physical ideas. J's data, in particular, do not support claims of either pervasive beliefs or global traits. Indeed, we have taken pains to show data that contradict many obvious categorical claims one might make about J's epistemology. Of course, it is difficult to rule out the possibility that some small coherent set of beliefs or "theory" can account for all the contextual dependencies we see in J's data. But the mere documentation of the complexity of J's reactions makes this implausible. Furthermore, in the following subsections we explicitly take up the challenge of showing that prior categorical views of epistemology fail to account for J's patterns of behavior. Instead of categorical epistemological knowledge, we see in J characteristic tendencies that "go together." However, these tendencies not only show significant context dependency, but also seem, on the face of it, to involve a multiplicity of dispositions and strategies. We continue to make these arguments next, augmenting consideration to include the extent of articulate awareness.

Articulateness and Consistency

Researchers working within a categorical framework typically assume that students' epistemologies are (a) coherent, and therefore applied with a fairly high degree of consistency, and (b) accessible to conscious reflection and report, with the right kinds of probes. However, J's tendency toward fragmented knowledge was neither consistent nor articulate. Although J explicitly states her devotion toward sense making, she never, in 7 hours of interviews, articulates her acceptance of fragmented knowledge, and she seems unaware of the influence that this acceptance exerts on her reasoning. For instance, she views her decision to reject Newton's second law in favor of her unbalanced force schema not as a choice stemming from her beliefs about knowledge, but as something that any rational sense-making person would do:

[4 0:38:20]

J: I want it to be true, but there's just no way it is, you know . . . *I don't know why I just started doubting myself because that stupid force formula.*

A: Yeah, you said before that you "wanted it to be true." . . . I didn't know what you meant by "it". Do you remember?

J: No. I'm sure it was just // I mean I want what seems logical to me to make sense with what I've learned and what you can, like, you know, like when we were talking about the formulas. I mean you learn these formulas and you apply them to all these problems. But when something that you know is true—I mean to me it makes so much sense that it's crazy to even debate it, that if you're pushing this with a constant force, and you see it moving, that it's not accelerating. But then, to think about something that you've learned and you've been applying for so long and have it not make sense. Then you start doubting what // *I started doubting what makes complete sense to me.* [emphases added]

Again, J is consciously aware that sense making is her primary concern. She is upset at herself for letting a "stupid force formula" make her doubt her intuitions. She entertained those doubts, she says, because she was so used to applying $F = ma$ to many different problems. She shows no sign, however, of being aware that her bias toward fragmented knowledge affects her epistemological behavior.

Moreover, J's bias toward fragmented knowledge was only that—a bias, not a consistent stance she took within these interviews. For instance, only after extensive thought and double-checking of her reasoning does J reluctantly decide to consider $F = ma$ a case-specific formula. Reflecting on her reasoning, she explains that she (mistakenly) "just thought that $F = ma$ was one of those that was universal." If J possessed the categorical belief that physics knowledge is fragmented, then she would have no reason to expect $F = ma$ to apply universally. In brief, J's tendency toward fragmented knowledge reaches neither the degree of articulation nor the degree of consistency generally associated with beliefs.[19]

Importantly, we do not claim that J is completely inconsistent in her reasoning, nor that she lacks articulate beliefs about knowledge and knowing. The former would belie our claim that we have found systematicities in J's epistemological stance, her orientation toward sense making and toward fragmented knowledge. The latter is contradicted by our noting her explicit beliefs about the nature of conceptual change, for example how ideas that would seem implausible to a "person on the street" can come to make perfect sense. Our claim is simply that tendencies and articulable knowledge constitute only a partial description of J's epistemological stance and strategies.

---

[19]Of course, it is possible to assume beliefs are things that come and go, without taking on accountability for explaining when they come and when they go. Such a concept of belief is nearly worthless as a scientific construct.

J Defies Categorization Within Existing Systems

So far in this section, to support our claim that categorical approaches to intuitive epistemology are limited, we first offered general arguments (e.g., analogy to research in intuitive conceptions of physics) and then offered arguments based on particular data presented here (concerning the articulateness and consistency of J's epistemology). Here, we add a third line of argument. We show that some of the most successful categorical approaches of which we are aware fail when confronted with the details of J's case. As we pointed out before, one cannot rule out that some unknown categorical scheme might account for all the patterns of behavior and context dependencies we see in J's case. But we can make it more and more implausible by demonstrating complexity and contexuality and by the consistent failure of proposed categorical views.

In Schommer's analysis of epistemological beliefs, the most predictively useful factor (Schommer et al., 1992) is Simple Knowledge, a dimension bounded on one extreme by the tendency to view knowledge as simple and unambiguous and on the other extreme by the tendency to view knowledge as complex. The four major characteristics of people on the naïve end of this spectrum, as revealed by the subset of dimensions that load most strongly onto this factor, are the tendencies to (a) avoid ambiguity, (b) seek single answers, (c) avoid integration, and (d) depend on authority. J's tendency toward fragmented knowledge certainly entails the avoidance of integration. But emphatically she does *not* depend on authority, preferring her own ideas (e.g., unbalanced forces schematization) to the principles sanctioned by physics (e.g., $F = ma$). Nor does she seek single answers; she often offers multiple explanations of a given phenomenon, such as the ball tossed straight up, which was the backbone of our data concerning her bias toward fragmentation. So, with respect to Schommer's Simple Knowledge dimension, J's behavior is in some ways naïve and in some ways sophisticated. Categorizing J as either naïve or sophisticated with respect to Simple Knowledge does not adequately capture her behavior.[20]

Perhaps a more science-specific categorization scheme would work better. Hammer (1994) developed a framework made up of several dimensions that succeeded in characterizing six different students' epistemologies within the context of an introductory physics course. Unlike J's interviews, Hammer's interviews were designed to remain close to the physics

---

[20]Schommer's (1990) Epistemological Questionnaire might classify J as nearly midway between naïve and sophisticated with respect to Simple Knowledge. But this does not capture the richness of her behavior, such as the fact that she actively tries to construct her own understanding while (implicitly) rejecting global coherence as a goal.

course context, asking questions about the course and his subjects' work in it. His subjects were taking an earlier version of the same course that J was taking.

Like our work in the Synthetic Interpretation section, Hammer worked at an intermediate level of description, analyzing individual subjects' protocols for systematicities that could serve as evidence for the existence and relevance of intuitive epistemology. He developed a framework for coding indications, made up of categories of belief along three dimensions: *Formulas . . . Concepts, Pieces . . . Coherence*, and *Authority . . . Independence*. Coded by these categories, each subject's protocol showed clear systematicities. As with J, each subject showed inconsistencies from the central tendencies. Still, the framework allowed general characterization of each subject's epistemology in the context of the introductory physics course.

We argue that the same framework would not be useful in characterizing J's epistemology in these interviews. No position on the *Formulas . . . Concepts* dimension describes J's behavior, even roughly. It is clear that J usually relies on intuitive, qualitative reasoning, which would rule out *Formulas* and may suggest *Concepts*. But J did not behave in a manner consistent with *Concepts*, either: She switched points of view frequently without noticing, and she did not, in general, treat formulas as expressions of conceptual substance.

We might try to classify her as *Apparent Concepts*, Hammer's middle ground in the *Formulas . . . Concepts* spectrum. Like J, an *Apparent Concepts* person relies on superficial conceptual reasoning. But unlike J, an *Apparent Concepts* person thinks that these conceptual tidbits serve primarily as mnemonics for the formulas, with no general expectation that physics can be understood conceptually. By contrast, in these interviews J tries to understand almost everything conceptually, though not in terms of what physicists would call "concepts." So, neither *Formulas, Apparent Concepts*, nor *Concepts* adequately captures J's behavior.

Similarly, J does not fit anywhere on the *Pieces . . . Coherence* dimension. The central tendency we have identified, J's acceptance of fragmented knowledge, clearly rules out a characterization of *Coherence*. But *Pieces* also fails, for two related reasons. A *Pieces* person thinks that physics consists of separate pieces that do not necessarily fit into any kind of coherent whole. As Hammer (1994) wrote, for a *Pieces* person, "to know something is to remember it; one either knows a piece or does not." But J views knowing as a matter of constructing an explanation that makes sense to her, not of remembering her teacher's—or even her own—ideas. For J, it is possible to fill in a gap in her knowledge by inventing a new conceptualization (such as balancing forces in a toss), not just by remembering or absorbing a new piece of knowledge. Second, the shifting conceptualizations out of which she constructs her understanding are too ephemeral and too changeable to function as pieces of knowledge that can be remembered and applied to various scenarios. J does not view physics knowledge as being made of well-defined pieces.

The central point is that categories like Schommer's *Simple Knowledge* assume that a unified characteristic is displayed in several ways (e.g., the four subtendencies of *Simple Knowledge*). Cases like J can and do show some of those presenting forms, but not others, undermining claims of coherent categorical attributes. In a similar way, neither the polar categories, nor "compromise" in-between positions of Hammer's scheme can effectively summarize J's behavior.

On the Nature of Context and Contextuality

We have argued that it is important to test categorical attributions against the details of individuals. Hammer (1994) did just that, for six students in an introductory physics course, and found patterns in their epistemologies along categories in a framework. Why do those categories not capture J?

Our view of the contextual sensitivity of intuitive epistemologies provides a plausible answer. As noted, Hammer designed his interviews to remain close to the context of the course his subjects were taking, a very different approach from that of diSessa in his interviews of J. For example, the physics questions that arose in Hammer's interviews originated almost exclusively from the homework assignments, textbooks passages, and lectures in the course, which was a traditional, highly formal presentation. Hammer's dimension, *Formulas . . . Concepts*, arose from these conditions: What were the students' epistemological stances toward the formalism?

diSessa's questions to J, in contrast, were unlike those posed in her physics course, and the context of these interviews was quite different from the context of that course. Although we can only speculate what would have happened if J had participated in Hammer's study, it is plausible that Hammer's categories would have applied. Just as students systematically describe a balance when asked about forces at the peak of a toss, but behave differently in other contexts, we expect the systematicities in students' epistemologies to depend on the nature of the questions they are considering. Thus J's epistemological behavior in her introductory physics class might have differed substantially from her epistemological behavior in clinical interviews centered on qualitative physics questions. There is some evidence of this difference, discussed in Appendix B.

A fundamental issue in this chapter is how much one must say in order to successfully characterize an individual. At one extreme, one may believe that students can be characterized by a few beliefs or even a briefly stateable theory. At the other extreme, one may insist that a good characterization should consist of a detailed model at the causal level that predicts what the subject does in almost all situations. Such an ultimate model undoubtedly would include a huge list of knowledge elements and situational dependencies. Our position is two-fold. First, traditional categorical descriptions of epistemologies entail unrecognized assumptions about consistency[21] that are bound to fail. Short of producing a detailed causal model, which we emphatically are not presenting here, we feel a great deal of advantage is available by pushing toward "finer-grained" characterizations, such as our list of behavioral phenomena. Of course, there will be limits and contextual dependencies to these as well. We believe our characterizations of J's epistemology are insightful, but would expect exceptions and cases of epistemological behavior that we could not explain. Future, improved characterizations at this same level may limit exceptions and cover more behaviors. Moving away from more global, simple characterizations will provide significant increase in explanatory power for tolerable extra cost in saying more about any individual.

Our second, higher level of description of J exemplifies what one gives up by providing simpler descriptions. First, the higher level descriptions do not unify and make redundant the more specific behavior phenomena. We do not yet know exactly what these behaviors have in common and how much an individual who displays one will display another. In fact, our presumption is that these behaviors are independent or mildly correlated, not strongly correlated or tightly related analytically. In addition, in looking toward causal-level descriptions, each behavior provides a locus of analysis and clues to the yet more detailed descriptions that should explain specific context dependencies that we pointed out, but did not presume to explain.

Are our two high-level characterizations of J (as biased toward fragmentation and toward sense making) substitutes for other global schemes? The answer is that we believe these are relatively good characterizations of J's behavior in these clinical interviews, respecting their high level of abstractness. However, we do not advance them (or their negatives) necessarily as good global descriptions of other students, or even of J in other macrocontexts. We consider it likely that other students would have *some* helpful and similarly high-level characterizations, but we may have to turn to very different descriptive language to capture what is essential about other students. We do not claim to have identified the range of such characterizations that may be profitable in summarizing the behaviors of other individuals.

We believe that the simple, insightful characterizations of individuals that are possible may vary from context to context. In this case, "context"

[21]It may be more accurate, in some instances, to say that inconsistency may be recognized by researchers offering categorical description, but it is not analyzed or accounted for.

does not refer to microcontexts where a student might either split concepts or not. Instead, it refers to the macroconditions of thinking. The clinical interviewing atmosphere in which we see J express the characteristics we attribute to her undermines reliance on authority, encourages thoughtful considerations, and (arguably, because of the nature of questions asked) undermines reliance on equations. This differs strikingly from the conditions of most college instruction, including the course J was taking. As argued in Appendix B, J might display a different epistemology in her class behaviors. A question in the same category is how would we characterize J's epistemology outside of physics? Would J's dispositions as we described them from these interviews be at all similar, for example, in a literature class or in an everyday conversation? We make no pretensions whatsoever with respect to these contexts.

These considerations reflect on the judgments we make about Hammer's (e.g., Hammer, 1994) or Schommer's (e.g., Schommer, 1990; Schommer, Crouse, & Rhodes, 1992) epistemological characterizations. They can provide insight into students' epistemologies *in particular (macro) contexts*. However, we suggest that we have shown in this study a degree of complexity and context sensitivity that deserves respect and investigation. In general, we advocate that categorical claims about student epistemologies be put to the test provided by individual process data.

In this section, we refined our arguments that categorical frameworks for characterizing epistemologies do not adequately capture J's behavior. One, we argued in general terms that systematicities in behavior do not necessarily stem from belief-like or theory-like coherence in the underlying knowledge structures. Second, using specific data, we showed that J's epistemology lacked the articulateness and consistency characteristic of beliefs or general traits. Third, we argued that two carefully developed categorical frameworks (in the form of systems of dimensions)—a general one used by Schommer and a physics-class-specific one used by Hammer, both fail to capture J's behavior. Our bottom line is that students' epistemological orientations should be expected to be highly complex and sensitive to contextual details. High-level generalizations may be insightful, but they can be expected to be limited in precision, and, indeed, they may vary from (macro) context to context.

CONCLUSION

Many researchers of student epistemologies assume a categorical framework, according to which epistemologies consist of a small number of beliefs or can be specified by positions along a small number of linear dimensions. In questioning the validity of categorical frameworks, we do not deny that students display epistemological systematicities. Indeed, our own work in this chapter and elsewhere (Hammer, 1994) finds a fair degree of epistemological consistency in our subjects. A categorical framework may be problematic, however, if it (a) presumes too much systematicity, and (b) assumes that the systematicities reflect belief-like or trait-like coherence in the underlying epistemological knowledge structures. By contrast, in our contextual framework we assume that intuitive epistemologies are very complex at the causal level. Higher levels of more compact description are possible and insightful. Yet, they will undoubtedly miss details of microcontextuality, reflected in the microcontextual exceptions in J's protocol to the systematicities we identified, and similarly in microcontextual exceptions Hammer (1994) noted in his subjects. It is also possible we will have to change descriptions to afford good coverage in different macrocontexts, say, in moving from the course-centered interviews in Hammer's study to the more conceptually centered clinical interviews here. Categorical frameworks have no analytical place in studying microcontextuality. Partly because of usually hidden assumptions about macro- and microcontextual dependence, or lack of analysis respecting them, researchers working within a categorical framework tend to develop and validate their categorizations by gathering data from large numbers of students, ignoring the possible effects of context on subjects' responses.

This chapter, by contrast, presented a detailed case study of one student. For the most part, our analysis of J's epistemological stance focused not on her explicit statements about epistemology, but on her behavior, her epistemology-in-action as she tried to understand physics. We described eight patterns of behavior observed repeatedly during the interviews. These constitute a finer-than-usual look at the cause and effect of epistemological ideas.

1. Shifting interpretations: J gives causally different accounts of the same situation on different occasions. This characteristic is unusual (compared to other students) to the extent that it is more frequent, does not converge, ignores elements of contradiction that are normally easily read, and sometimes rejects contradictions as an issue when raised by the interviewer.

2. Splitting concepts: Technical terms are used in multiple situations, but in ways that imply different core meanings.

3. Migrating language: J uses alternative technical terms in the same (or similar) context, as if they were interchangeable.

4. Weak commitment to principles: J denies or demotes physical principles because she feels her context-specific understanding is adequate.

5. Discounting details in explanations: J does not appear to feel she is bound to articulately justify the existence of elements in her explanations.

6. Hedging: J frequently and explicitly shows limited commitment to what she is saying, or provides explicit notifications of vague meaning.

7. Strong commitment to a view: J is, on occasion, capable of careful, conscious consideration leading to strong personal commitment to particular ideas.

8. Reflective about learning: J thinks about learning and has drawn many sensible lessons from her experience.

The status of these behavioral patterns is important to review. First, they are only hypotheses about what epistemological stances and strategies might look like. We have no calibration from similarly detailed studies of other individuals. For example, most students may hedge as much as J, and we are not in a position to evaluate the extent to which Hedging contributes to J's unique profile. Follow-up studies using multiple methodologies should help settle such issues.

On the other hand, our behavioral phenomenology results from fine-grained, bottom-up, and data-based analysis. This means of generating hypotheses should provide important complementarity to more a priori methods of guessing what constitutes intuitive epistemologies, or to methods that impressionistically synthesize a wide range of data.

We went on to synthesize the behavioral patterns J exhibited into two broad epistemological orientations: (a) a bias toward fragmented knowledge, and (b) a tendency to view learning physics as sense making. This synthesis serves two rhetorical functions. First, we used it to demonstrate what is given up at higher (coarser-grained) levels of description, compared to lower (finer-grained) ones. One gives up even more ability to deal with variation across contexts, and one gives up more specific and detailed focus to continue investigation in the hope of moving toward the causal level. Second, we used the higher level patterns to introduce the possibility of macrocontextual dependencies, in addition to microcontextual ones. We argued that our own high-level description of J, although useful for understanding her behavior in the context of her clinical interview, should not be ascribed to J as globally held beliefs or traits. She might well behave differently in different contexts, such as "school as usual." In other words, not only do we reject categorical characterizations as representing the specifics of knowledge-in-action, but we are wary that different macrocontexts may evoke different systematicities.

The contrast of high-level characterizations to our lower level phenomena might have important instructional implications. Helping students, for example, not to split concepts might be much more effective because of its specificity than just urging less acceptance of fragmentation. Students who do not treat learning physics as sense making could learn a lot from J's many different ways of making sense.

Part of our argument against categorical approaches to epistemological knowledge involved showing that J did not fit into two previously validated and seemingly appropriate dimensional schemes. Overall, from multiple perspectives and employing a range of arguments and analytic strategies, we conclude that analyzing J's behavior within a contextual rather than a categorical framework provides a richer understanding of her epistemological stance while, at the same time, providing an analysis that is fairer to macro- and microcontextual issues that we do not yet understand.

With respect to intentional conceptual change, our study has somewhat complicated conclusions. We frequently found that "beliefs" (explicit or implicit) seemed unable to carry the burden of explaining J's behaviors. Instead, we offered the idea of *judgment in context*, which provides a first pass at a replacement for the idea of "exercising beliefs" with respect to what is happening on occasions when epistemological knowledge becomes active. Judgment in context serves to label why J might make one epistemological move in one context (say, split a concept), and another move in another context (say, remain accountable to a core meaning across different exemplars of a concept).

We argued that, on many occasions, J's actions were evidently implicit and unconscious. Indeed, even when difficulties were raised explicitly, J often did not see problems in the way she treated physics knowledge. Thus, part of the time, she appears not to have enough conceptual or epistemological resources that intentionally bootstrapping her own learning is at all plausible. If one just does not see any difference between two analyses, why should one pose any task relevant to learning to discriminate them? Of course, J might intentionally formulate other learning goals on other occasions that would address the same issues. We did not see any examples of this, and consider it too speculative to pursue.

On the other hand, J sometimes expressed articulate beliefs about physics knowledge. She knew that it involved conceptual change and concomitant revisions of "what seems sensible." She even "knew" that $F = ma$ was supposed to be very general, before a judgment in context made her change her mind. J's original belief in the generality of $F = ma$ caused her to devote a great deal of effort in trying to find out what might be wrong with her own view of the situation. And yet, in the end, her belief in the generality of the principle was unstable, yielding to her judgment in context concerning how to think about an object pushed at constant speed.

ACKNOWLEDGEMENTS

Some of the work represented here was accomplished in the Local Dynamics of Conceptual Change Group, including Ming Ming Chiu, Andrea diSessa, David Hammer, Bruce Sherin, and Reed Stevens. Comments on a draft of the manuscript by Gale Sinatra and Paul Pintrich were helpful in pointing out areas where our arguments were unclear, and by asking important questions that we have tried to answer. This work was supported by a grant from the Spencer Foundation to A. diSessa. Andrew Elby's and David Hammer's work on this chapter was supported in part by a grant from the National Science Foundation (REC: 0087519). The opinions expressed are those of the authors and do not necessarily reflect the views of either foundation.

REFERENCES

Bereiter, C., & Scardamalia, M. (1989). Intentional learning as a goal of instruction. In L. B. Resnick (Ed.), *Knowing, learning, and remembering: Essays in honor of Robert Glaser* (pp. 361–392). Hillsdale, NJ: Lawrence Erlbaum Associates.

diSessa, A. A. (1985). Learning about knowing. In E. Klein (Ed.), *Children and computers* (pp. 97–124). New Directions for Child Development No. 28. San Francisco: Jossey-Bass.

diSessa, A. A. (1993). Toward an epistemology of physics. *Cognition and Instruction, 10*(2–3), 105–225.

diSessa, A. A. (1994). Speculations on the foundations of knowledge and intelligence. In D. Tirosh (Ed.), *Implicit and explicit knowledge: An educational approach* (pp. 1–54). Norwood, NJ: Ablex.

diSessa, A. A. (1996). What do "just plain folk" know about physics? In D. R. Olson & N. Torrance (Eds.), *The handbook of education and human development: New models of learning, teaching, and schooling* (pp. 709–730). Oxford, UK: Blackwell Publishers, Ltd.

diSessa, A. A., & Sherin, B. (1998). What changes in conceptual change? *International Journal of Science Education, 20*(10), 1155–1191.

Elby, A. (1999). Another reason that students learn by rote. *Physics Education Research:* A supplement to the *American Journal of Physics, 67*(7), S53–S60.

Galileo (1954). *Dialogs concerning two new sciences.* (H. Crew & A. deSalvio, Trans.) New York: Dover.

Hammer, D. (1989). Two approaches to learning physics. *The Physics Teacher, 27*(9), 664–670.

Hammer, D. (1994). Epistemological beliefs in introductory physics. *Cognition and Instruction, 12*(2), 151–183.

Hammer, D., & Elby, A. (2002). On the form of personal epistemology. In B. K. Hofer & P. R. Pintrich (Eds.), *Personal epistemology: The psychology of beliefs about knowledge and knowing* (pp. 169–190). Mahwah, NJ: Lawrence Erlbaum Associates.

Hofer, B. K., & Pintrich, P. R. (1997). The development of epistemological theories: Beliefs about knowledge and knowing and their relation to learning. *Review of Educational Research, 67*(1), 88–140.

King, P. M., & Kitchener, K. S. (1994). *Developing reflective judgment: Understanding and promoting intellectual growth and critical thinking in adolescents and adults.* San Francisco: Jossey-Bass.

Linn, M. C., & Songer, N. B. (1993). How do students make sense of science? *Merrill Palmer Quarterly, 39*(1), 47–73.

McCloskey, M. (1983). Naïve theories of motion. In D. Gentner & A. Stevens (Eds.), *Mental models* (pp. 299–313). Mahwah, NJ: Lawrence Erlbaum Associates.

Perry, W. B. (1970). *Forms of intellectual and ethical development in the college years: A scheme.* New York: Holt, Rinehart and Winston.

Schoenfeld, A. H. (1992). Learning to think mathematically: Problem solving, metacognition, and sense making in mathematics. In D. Grouws (Ed.), *Handbook for research on mathematics teaching and learning*. New York: Macmillan.

Schommer, M. (1990). The effects of beliefs about the nature of knowledge in comprehension. *Journal of Educational Psychology, 82*(3), 498–504.

Schommer, M., Crouse, A., & Rhodes, N. (1992). Epistemological beliefs and mathematical text comprehension: Believing it is simple does not make it so. *Journal of Educational Psychology, 84*, 435–443.

Smith, J. P., diSessa, A. A., & Roschelle, J. (1993). Misconceptions reconceived: A constructivist analysis of knowledge in transition. *Journal of the Learning Sciences, 3*(2), 115–163.

APPENDIX A: SHIFTING INTERPRETATIONS IN THE CASE OF CONSTANT MOTION

J exhibited two contradictory models of what is happening when an object is moving at constant speed. The first model entails the claim, discussed in the main text, that any motion requires unbalanced forces. In interview 4 (see Weak Commitment to Principles for details), J considers the case of a book moving at constant speed in being pushed across a table. She initially asserts that any motion implies unbalanced forces. But this brings her into conflict with $F = ma$, which says that if forces are unbalanced, there must be an acceleration, not constant speed. J's conclusion, after extended consideration, is that $F = ma$ cannot apply to this situation. In that exchange, her principle that motion requires unbalanced forces trumped $F = ma$.

In contrast, in the context of the computer-supported tutorial, J seemed completely comfortable with the idea that an object can move at constant speed with no forces. For example, at one point during a simulation of a toss, the interviewer intervened by turning off gravity. At that point in the simulation, the ball had passed from the hand, and the simulation showed that there was no force from the hand, either.

[6 0:56:30]

A: Now what's going to happen if I continue to let it run?
J: Well, it's going to keep going and it's never going to stop and come back down.

After showing that the simulation confirmed J's prediction, the interviewer continues:

A: So velocity just //
J: stays the same.
A: It stays the same. I turned off gravity.

J: All the forces. Right.

A: So does that make sense to you?

J: Yes. As long as you don't have air resistance.

Of course, J might well have learned during the tutorial. Still, it is striking that she did not comment that this interpretation of constant motion was counter to a principle she had considered so carefully and eventually endorsed as "obvious," that things need an unbalanced force to move. Again, see Weak Commitment to Principles for details on her prior consideration and personal commitment to this principle.

APPENDIX B: J'S EPISTEMOLOGY DEPENDS RICHLY ON CONTEXT

Much of this case study displayed microcontext sensitivities within the clinical macrocontext. Here, we consider the possibility—indeed, we believe the plausibility—that the relatively simple characterizations of J's epistemology that we produced apply only in a macrocontext that supports sense making. In particular, we believe J's predilection toward sense making might not appear as strongly in other macrocontexts.

Specifically, we argue that J's epistemological behavior *in her introductory physics class* might have differed substantially from her epistemological behavior *in clinical interviews centered on qualitative physics questions.* Unlike Hammer (1994), J's interviews neither centered on her physics course nor mimicked the tenor of that context. Although we have only limited data about J in the "physics class" context, we put together what we know about J and about that other context to argue that J might well appear epistemologically quite different in that context. In addition, we also have case studies of students who tried, successfully and unsuccessfully, to learn introductory physics by reconciling physical laws with their own intuition and experiences (e.g., Hammer, 1989, 1994). Triangulating among these different data sources allows us to sketch the following plausibility argument.

To begin, there is direct evidence that J found the clinical context unusual and different from her experience in physics class. She complained, at the beginning, when the interviewer did not offer evaluations of her answers, and, instead, insisted that she evaluate them herself.

[1 0:17:0]

J: But, but see, I can't give you an answer to the question we want to answer unless I know I'm on the right track. Because if I'm totally wrong, everything I say is wrong.

She also specifically remarked that problems posed were unusual, not like "pulleys and masses." A bit later, J troubled to characterize how she felt about the interviewing process, and she implicated sense making as unusual, but something she found enjoyable.

[1 55]

J: I like it [talking about physics in this way] because it's problem solving. In a way, it's weird to feel like I have to give an answer right away, so I'm saying some things that later I am realizing didn't really make that much sense, you know? Because, for me, I can think through things when I bounce things off each other instead of like thinking through the whole thing and saying, "okay here's the answer." I have to say this happens and this happens and maybe this will happen. So it makes me think, and here I am trying to figure something out, and I realize it is wrong, so I try to figure something else out and I think about it. I like that.

J goes on to assert that school makes you feel like you have to give correct answers immediately. "I just have to get over, personally, thinking that if I say all these wrong things this person's looking at me thinking I'm a total idiot . . . That's something school does to you."

At the time J took introductory physics at Berkeley, those courses proceeded at a very fast pace and emphasized quantitative problem solving.[22] In this environment, a student can learn what she needs to learn by trying to make sense of the material, reconciling physics concepts with her intuitions and experiences—but only if she is adept at doing so. Otherwise, doing well on tests requires the student to accept a fair amount of material, and to learn certain problem-solving techniques, without making sense of it all.[23] J, we know from her interviews, is *not* efficient at reconciling her intuitive sense of mechanism with canonical physics. Still, she earned a B in the course. To do so, she must have learned certain concepts and problem-solving techniques without making sense of it all. As compared to her sense making during the clinical interviews, J's sense making in her physics class must have been less pervasive and different in charac-

[22]When J took first-semester introductory physics in the early 1990s, the course covered kinematics, forces, energy, momentum, angular motion (including angular momentum), statics, gravitation, oscillations, waves, and fluid dynamics.

[23]From Hammer (1994) and Hammer (1989), compare Tony, whose sophisticated epistemological stance helped him pursue an integrated understanding of physics and who earned an A, with Ellen, who started off the semester trying to reconcile the physics with her ideas and experiences, but who quickly became overwhelmed by the pace of the course and reverted to rote learning in order to get through the assignments and exams.

ter. Specifically, in her physics class, J likely did not systematically trust her intuitive schematizations over the sanctioned laws of physics, treat friction as fundamentally different from other forces (Splitting Concepts), or resist thinking in physics-sanctioned ways. Had she done so, it is unlikely, we assert, she could have earned a high grade.

A critic could accept our conclusion about J's behavior in physics class while denying that it reflects a context-sensitive shift in her epistemology. Perhaps J, like Ellen from Hammer (1989), retained her epistemological bias toward sense making while consciously making concessions in order to survive. Elby (1999) showed that this kind of behavior is common. We lack direct evidence to the contrary. Again, however, we can offer a plausibility argument: J gives us reason to believe that she did not perceive herself as compromising her epistemological values in her physics class. For instance, she speaks often enough of liking her physics course and of feeling that she gets conceptual satisfaction out of it. Consider her comment on the realization that her chair pushes up on her as hard as she pushes down on it:

> **J:** This chair's pushing up on me. I think that's something that once you've taken physics, that's totally normal. But if you said it to someone off the street, I think they'd say, "What are you talking about? No it's not. You know, obviously it's not pushing; there's nothing to push it up." But it is. So maybe it's like what is going on is common knowledge, *but how it actually works maybe I learned*. [emphasis added]

She perceives revising her intuitive ideas in pursuit of sense making as an enjoyable part of physics class:

> **J:** Well, I mean it's *really neat* when you learn something that isn't what you would intuitively have thought, *but it makes sense*, you go, "God, I totally understand that. It's not what the everyday person on the street would know, but I understand." [emphasis added]

These reflections about physics class do not sound as if they come from someone who has consciously—and presumably, unhappily—renounced her favored learning strategy. Nowhere in 7 hours of interviews does J hint that she knowingly made epistemological concessions. Instead, J sounds as if she perceives sense making to have been part of her experience in the class.

We are arguing that J did not—could not—do nearly as much sense making in her class as she did in the clinical context, and yet she did not notice this fact. How could this be? Because some of J's epistemological knowledge is tacit, as argued earlier, J could have slipped into a different epistemological mode without being aware of it, just as she slipped into different interpretations of a situation without noticing (or without considering the changes to be significant). Our point is that a real shift in J's epistemology-in-action, not just a conscious adoption of epistemologically unfavored survival strategies, could well account for differences in J's epistemologically driven behavior in the two different contexts.

In summary, a plausibility argument suggests that J's epistemological behavior in her introductory physics class might well have differed from her epistemological behavior during the clinical interviews. This is not really so difficult to imagine. During the interviews, the interviewer's interest in J's thinking and the nature of the questions he asked, combined with the on-line pedagogical materials, probably created an environment friendly toward sense making. By contrast, as Ellen (Hammer, 1989) discovered, the introductory physics courses at Berkeley were not a friendly environment for sense making, except for students particularly adept at doing so.

The important general point of this argument is that we believe high-level characterizations of students' epistemologies are subject to macrocontextual effects. One of the consequences is that students, despite years of tuning their epistemologies toward contexts unfriendly to sense making, may have the epistemological resources needed to function well in more friendly sense-making environments.

10

Conceptual Change in Response to Persuasive Messages

Cynthia Hynd
University of Illinois, Chicago

In recent years, our understanding of conceptual change has undergone an evolution, now including aspects of cognition such as motivation, metacognition, attitude, and reflectivity. Pintrich, Marx, & Boyle (1993) signaled the attention to these processes in discussing the idea that conceptual shifts did not occur in a vacuum merely as an unconscious response to outside influences such as text and instruction; rather, these shifts represent motivated responses to such influences. Dole and Sinatra (1998) extended our understanding of conceptual change by positing the Cognitive Reconstruction of Knowledge Model (CRKM), in which change is an outcome of an interaction between message and learner characteristics, including motivation, leading to engagement in persuasive messages.

In this volume, conceptual shifts are treated as intentional; that is, individuals are aware that they are changing their ideas and do so partly because of attributes such as will, beliefs, attitudes, goals, motivations, self-explanations, and reflection. Thus, by *intentional* conceptual change, I mean change that is a result of motivated metacognitive effort. In one scenario of intentional conceptual change, individuals recognize that there are differences between their prior beliefs and their new beliefs, and they recognize that the change occurred because of positive evaluations of the new belief and discounts of the previous ones. It requires reflectivity on the part of individuals who undergo change. Indeed, Strike and Posner (1992), and Dole and Sinatra (1998) described the importance of cognitive conflict as a motivating factor for change. That is, in order for change to occur, individuals must reflect on their existing knowledge, notice the difference between their existing knowledge and the new message, feel discomfort at the difference, and evaluate the two in order to decide which to believe. If the new knowledge is clear and unambiguous, plausible, and potentially fruitful, and if the existing knowledge is weak, incoherent, and/or only loosely tied to one's conception of the world, then change is a likely outcome. But the process requires a motivated, reflective response.

This chapter discusses the relationship between cognitive, metacognitive, and affective responses to persuasive messages, or messages that elicit intentional change. First, I define the constructs of persuasion, conceptual change, belief change, and attitude as used in this chapter. Then I review the literature from educational psychology, social psychology, and communication on the cognitive, metacognitive, and affective dimensions of attitude, concept, and belief change and persuasion. After that, I draw on the research my colleagues and I conducted in history and physics classes that underlie these theories. Finally, I discuss the implications of this research.

DEFINING PERSUASION AND ITS RELATED CONSTRUCTS

Persuasive messages use argument, reasoning, and entreaty. The intent of the author of such messages is to convince individuals of the viability of an argument or to convince them to strengthen or change their beliefs or concepts. However, the impetus for being persuaded exists not only in the persuasive message itself, but also in one's perception of the message's credibility and in one's inner disposition to be persuaded.

In addition, a reaction to persuasion implies intentionality. Persuaded individuals are likely to be cognizant of the attempt to persuade; a shift in belief is the result of a reflective assessment of the message, requiring motivation. Thus, shifts represent motivated, intentional responses.

When an individual has been persuaded, it is often the result that the individual has undergone *conceptual change* rather than a mere strengthening or greater understanding of an existing idea. Conceptual change as I refer to it involves the rejection of a prior understanding in favor of a new one. It is akin to what Piaget (1973) referred to as accommodation, and is in line with Chi (1992), and Thagard's (1992) notion of conceptual change as a radical reorganization of knowledge structures. If a student knew Christopher Columbus was commissioned by Spain to find the New World, then learned more details about that arrangement, I would not consider the addition of that new knowledge to be conceptual change; the original premise is still believed, albeit broadened. However, if a student believed that Christopher Columbus was Spanish, then found out he was Italian, I would consider that new understanding to be conceptual change.

I do not mean to say that, in conceptual change, one idea is merely replaced by another and the original premise is immediately banished from one's thinking. My own changes in concepts have made it clear that the old idea often remains and, indeed, must be intentionally inhibited. What changes is the level of belief that is placed in the old idea. So, although I do not use the term conceptual change to describe evolutionary models of change (Vosniadou & Brewer, 1987), I do acknowledge that, in practice, individuals may hold several competing ideas in mind at once. They may choose adaptively among those various ideas based on how persuaded they are that one idea is more fruitful than others, in line with Smith, diSessa, and Roschelle (1993) and Siegler's (1996) notion of the way that changes occur.

Individuals can be surprisingly resistant to changing their concepts. If their concepts seem intuitively reasonable or are otherwise closely tied to the way they view themselves and the world, that is, crystallized, coherent, and firmly entrenched, then change is difficult (Dole & Sinatra, 1998; Hynd, Alvermann, & Qian, 1993; Posner, Strike, Hewson, & Gertzog, 1982). For example, students who intuitively think that gravity pulls harder on heavier objects think that way because it is a reasonable although erroneous understanding often derived from their real-world observations of objects falling. Failing to see the effects of air resistance, they attribute different rates of fall to the influence of weight. Thus, they resist the scientific notion that gravity acts on all objects equally, and ignore or discount the new notion in favor of their intuitive idea.

This chapter also refers to cognitive beliefs, cognitions, and beliefs interchangeably, so that conceptual change can mean a change in belief as well as a change in conceptual knowledge. There is some controversy about whether or not beliefs are the same as concepts. It is reasonable that someone can understand a concept without believing it. For example, an individual may understand a religious tenet without believing that it is true. However, the controversy becomes somewhat clearer if one separates belief and understanding. Understanding refers to something that may be comprehended but not necessarily accepted as true. Thus, *belief change* will be used interchangeably with *conceptual change* and will mean a change in knowledge that is not only understood but accepted.

Is there a difference between conceptual change and belief change? Often, we refer to belief changes when discussing changes in belief about topics in social science or ill-structured domains—topics about which there may be several viable opinions, each with evidence to support them. We refer to cognitive changes when discussing changes in belief about topics in scientific or well-structured domains where there is generally an accepted view. The assumption is that it is more difficult to change beliefs about ill-structured topics than to change beliefs about well-structured topics because beliefs about ill-structured topics are more tied to an individual's inner dispositions and experts do not always agree. However, the two beliefs could probably be thought of as on a continuum rather than as qualitatively different. Whereas it does seem to be true that ideas that are firmly tied to one's view of the world are more difficult to change than more tentative ideas, tentative and entrenched ideas can exist in any domain.

Conceptual change is similar to what social scientists refer to as *attitude change*. A three-component model of attitudes says that attitudes are made up of cognitive beliefs, affect or feelings, and conation or actions. Thus, cognitive beliefs are a subset of attitudes; attitudes also include the negative and positive feelings associated with cognitive beliefs (including motivation) and the willingness to act on those beliefs. Belief, affect, and conation are interdependent and mutually influential (Sheth, Mittal, & Newman, 1999). To illustrate, consider a girl who believes that heavier objects fall faster than lighter objects. That cognition or belief (belief because the cognition is accepted as true) is accompanied by an affective sense of self-efficacy, in that the student feels sure about her ability to act on the basis of the belief. She is sure, for instance, that if her mother dropped her a key and a book out the upstairs bedroom window at the same time, she should get ready to catch the book first. Heading for the book would be her conative response. If that scene were to actually take place, however, she would find, to her dismay, that the key and the book would need to be caught at the same moment. That realization might lead to a revision of her belief about falling objects and might also affect her sense of self-efficacy. If it did so, it would be considered an attitude change *and* a conceptual change. That is, as long as one assumes that conceptual changes include affective and conative responses, then they can be considered to be similar to attitude changes. This chapter makes that assumption.

Intentional conceptual change, then, as perceived in this chapter, represents a shift in what one believes about the concepts that one understands. The change is brought about by a metacognitive response to persuasive information and is accompanied by changes in activity.

ATTITUDE CHANGE AND PERSUASION

For decades, social psychologists studied attitude change in response to persuasive messages. According to learning theories of attitude change (Hovland, Janis, & Kelley, 1953), if you learn something, actions will follow. The direction of change is from believing to acting. Consistency theories of attitude, on the other hand, (e.g., Festinger, 1957; Kinder, 1978) suggested that a change in behavior can trigger a change in cognitive belief. Thus, the change would proceed in the opposite direction. Festinger and Carlsmith (1959), for example, found that the smaller the inducement needed to persuade an individual to advocate a public position that violates a private belief, the more likely a shift in the privately held belief. They theorized that the difference between the behavior (the public advocacy) and the belief caused discomfort (both a metacognitive and an affective response); participants changed their belief to reduce the discomfort. If the inducement had been large, then the inducement would be the reason for the public statement, not the belief. Since the inducement was small, however, it was not a large factor in the public statement and the individuals then were left to resolve the conflict between what they said and what they believed in order to rid themselves of discomfort. A behavior (the public statement) led to a belief.

Self-Perception Theory (Bem, 1967) suggests that no discomfort need occur. In cases of low involvement, individuals may not be strongly committed to their beliefs until they have behaved in certain ways. Thus, the participants would have reasoned that, because they made the public statement with only a small inducement, they must have believed what they said rather than what they previously thought they believed. There are two important aspects of this theory: (a) It puts affect at the forefront. Low involvement and high involvement (affective responses) determine beliefs and behaviors differentially; and (b) It highlights the role of metacognition and, thus, intentionality. Indeed, both consistency theories and self-perception theories discuss the notion that individuals are active participants in belief change. Either they actively notice and resolve their discomfort, or they actively determine their reasons for belief changes. That active determination is intentional conceptual change.

Conceptual/belief/attitude change is a more complicated process than learning information that was not known before. In conceptual change, individuals must inhibit an existing cognition to accept a new, competing one. That inhibition requires intentional effort. Thus, in conceptual change, intentionality and affect play a central role. To change a belief, one needs to have the disposition to change and to make a concerted effort to inhibit previous beliefs. That effort involves a motivated response or intentionality that may not be a part of initial learning.

Cognitive Dissonance

Social psychologists have identified a number of conditions leading to cognitive dissonance, a state thought to be necessary for conceptual change that is a metacognitive response to a mismatch between existing beliefs and new information. The main conditions for cognitive dissonance and resulting conceptual change and decisive action are minimum incentives, perceived choice, commitment, the presence of foreseeable consequences, personal responsibility for those consequences, and effort. A physics student I interviewed, for instance, was going to be an engineer and, so, was committed to understanding physics principles. She knew that each principle would help her in the future, so that it had foreseeable consequences. She got good grades, but was learning physics for other reasons, indicating that she needed minimal incentives. She also knew that it was important that she be responsible for learning, because she had to truly understand the information to use it. Thus, she sometimes stayed after class and clarified confusions with her instructor; she put effort into understanding. So, she was a good candidate for cognitive dissonance, and, indeed, when she learned about gravity, she experienced a great deal of discomfort knowing that her current beliefs were contradicted by her science teacher. She read several different textbooks on her own, discussed gravity with her father, and came in early the next day to talk to her teacher. Not all students exhibit her characteristics, however, and students may opt for *selective exposure* (Frey, 1986). That is, students may avoid information that contradicts existing cognitions, thereby eliminating dissonance. Even under the influence of persuasion that overtly encourages dissonance, students may hold to their existing beliefs if they are not predisposed to change, that is, if they feel little responsibility, the challenge is minimal, they see little value in changing, they are minimally involved, they have publicly committed to an alternative belief, their self-esteem is involved, etc. In other words, affect is central in determining whether or not dissonance occurs and conceptual change takes place, even when students are subject to persuasive messages.

In thinking about intentional conceptual change, I am unconvinced that selective exposure is always intentional. To avoid the conflict requires little involvement in the ideas. In some cases, however, students may actively disavow new information.

One of the students we studied exemplified that observation. Barry (Guzzetti & Hynd, 1998) was a student who was not very interested in physics, by his own admission during interviews. His self-esteem became involved, however, and involvement had an effect on his ability to change his concepts. Students were planning an experiment where they timed the fall of eggs in elaborate cartons dropped out of their second story window. Barry had come in that morning bragging that his egg carton would fall faster because he had put weights in the bottom of it. Things did not go as planned. His egg did not even come close to having the fastest time, and he could not believe it (dissonance occurred). He rejected a theory change, however, even when students told him that objects fall at the same rate and kidded him about his naïvete. They reminded him of Newton's theories and Neil Armstrong's demonstration of gravity with a hammer and a feather on the moon. He told them he did not care; he still did not believe it. He wrote this conclusion on his lab paper: "Heavier objects fall faster than lighter ones." Thus, even though he experienced dissonance between behavior and belief, his self-esteem and public commitment may have prevented a change in beliefs to match the behavior. Later, however, after reading refutational text, we observed him telling another student that ("don't you know . . . ?") objects fall at the same rate regardless of weight.

The Elaboration Likelihood Model

The most pervasive theory relevant to conceptual change is the Elaboration Likelihood Model or Heuristic Systematic Processing Model (Chaiken, 1980, 1987; Dole & Sinatra, 1998; Petty & Cacioppo, 1986). It hypothesizes two routes to persuasion—the central route and the peripheral route. The central route to persuasion involves systematic processing of arguments. The peripheral route involves heuristic processing and includes "variables peripheral to the message content" (Dole & Sinatra, 1998); that is, features not directly related to message content such as message type, friendliness of the speaker, or a compelling social context. Social psychologists agree that central processing of an argument is superior to peripheral processing, leading to higher levels of engagement in the ideas and thus to deeper levels of conceptual change than peripheral processing. This stands to reason because an individual must *understand* an argument if his belief is to be deeply held, and central processing evokes understanding.

On the other hand, individuals might use both routes under different circumstances. They might even use both at the same. In one study, Chaiken and Maheswaran (1994) found that even students who engaged in central processing of a persuasive message, evidenced by their superior understanding and recall of that message, paid attention to peripheral cues such as the expertise of the message author as a source of persuasion. And, at least in the case of expert historians reading unfamiliar historical texts, it appears that the use of both types of processing may lead to a more sophisticated reading of persuasive messages and possibly to deeper levels of commitment to a conceptual change. However, this supposition runs contrary to current thinking. Dole & Sinatra (1998) acknowledged that peripheral cues such as an attractive, credible, or trustworthy source can serve as "an impetus toward high elaboration, which may lead to central change and strong beliefs" (p. 118). However, that scenario is not likely, in their view. I argue, however, that, in cases where individuals have high domain knowledge as well as high involvement, the processing of messages is not an either–or event; rather, individuals use all available clues to decide if they will believe the persuasive message. In that case, the use of both central and peripheral processing is superior to using central processing alone. In some cases, an individual might use peripheral processes to screen which messages should be processed centrally. This screening might be adaptive and economical in the processing of texts under certain conditions and harmful under other conditions. For example, an individual might be wise to change the hotel he decided to stay at while visiting a Caribbean island based on credible advice from well-known travel guides and trustworthy friends, but unwise to pay attention to advice from those who stand to make a profit based on his choice of hotel. On the other hand, it might be disadvantageous to screen out central arguments you do not believe are credible if you know that you will have to present all sides of an argument for a test.

In a study of the way historians process historical documents compared to the way students process them, Wineburg (1991) asked historians to discuss the ways in which they read a group of documents about a topic in history outside of their areas of expertise. He asked high school students to do the same, except that those students had more topic knowledge. He found that the students and the historians used different reading strategies. The students engaged in central processing, in that they perceived they were to learn the facts. They read the documents for factual information. The historians, however, looked at the various historical documents as arguments, or as attempts to persuade readers to adopt a particular historical interpretation of an event. Therefore, they processed the documents as if they were persuasive texts about a topic in which they had little knowledge. What did they do? Apart from engaging in central processing of the arguments, they engaged in three strategies. First, they looked at the sources of information. That is, they evaluated the credibility of the author, the type of document (editorial, newspaper article, interview, etc.), and the credibility of the publisher. Second, they thought about the context of the writing (what was going on politically, socially, and economically at the time of the writing). Third, they looked for corroboration across sources. They noted whether the authors of the various documents agreed or disagreed. In their use of sourcing and context, they used peripheral sources to evaluate the texts and decide what to believe.

It could be said that, in the case of historians and other domain experts, cues such as source and context are not truly peripheral, but are, indeed, a part of the message quality itself. For example, experts in educational psychology recognize that an article in the *Journal of Educational Psychology* has undergone a rigorous review process and, thus, the arguments are likely to be of high quality. However, the key feature of a peripheral cue is whether or not it can be separated from a central one. I argue that all domain experts at one time or another have read faulty arguments in respected, refereed journals, and they have read brilliant arguments in less-respected or nonrefereed sources. Likewise, experts can be led to believe an argument because a source seems credible, even if the argument later turns out to be wrong. Thus, the source and the argument are independent.

Although *understanding* of a viewpoint is a necessary condition for radical, long-lasting conceptual change, it may not be optimally sufficient. If one's purpose is learning what the message said, then central processing probably is enough. However, if one's purpose is to decide what to believe, then central processing of arguments is enhanced by a belief that those arguments are credible. Perception of credibility is an important variable in one's decision to undergo conceptual change and, thus, even though it is peripheral to the message itself, it plays an important role in intentional conceptual change. Chinn and Brewer (1993), who described the characteristics of anomalous data that elicit their acceptance, believed that the data must be credible, unambiguous, and exist in multiple forms. Thus, although central processing is necessary for intentional conceptual change, peripheral processing enhances the possibility that change will take place.

Those who have done research on the processing of persuasive messages have found that central or systematic processing of arguments relies on both message characteristics and individual characteristics. Messages that are strong (Petty & Cacioppo, 1986), repeated (Cacioppo & Petty, 1979), use multiple communicators (Harkins & Petty, 1981), use rhetorical questions and arguments (Burnkrant & Howard, 1984), and are written (Chaiken & Eagly, 1976) are more likely to be persuasive. Consider a series of texts about Christopher Columbus. If one text (written) asks how the reader would characterize him (rhetorical question) before stating *strongly* that Christopher Columbus was foolhardy, greedy, stupid, and cruel, and then the message was corroborated by another (repeated by multiple communicators), the ideas in those texts are likely to be persuasive.

Interestingly, and as Dole and Sinatra (1998) suggested is possible, several of the cues just listed appear to be peripheral ones that induce individuals to pay more attention to the central arguments. For example, the persuasive value of the written word may be based on two factors: (a) students are conditioned to believe that what is written is true; and (b) students have the opportunity to review the arguments. Only the second reason is actually a function of the message; the first is a peripheral cue. If individuals believe that credibility is enhanced by multiple communicators who repeat arguments, they are likewise relying on peripheral cues. In addition, rhetorical questions may cause one to pay more attention to what follows, but are not part of the message itself—they just cause one to think about the message; thus they are peripheral cues as well.

Who is more likely to engage in central processing? Researchers have found that individuals who have beliefs that are moderately discrepant with the message (Eagly & Telaak, 1972), who find the information personally relevant (Sherif & Cantrell, 1947), who have a high need for cognition (Cacioppo, Petty, & Kao, 1984), and who have high topic knowledge are more likely to process the central arguments. As for moderate discrepancy, it makes sense that if one's views are too close to the views of the message, then that person may not notice a need to be persuaded, and thus, would not pay attention to the arguments. On the other hand, if one's views are too discrepant, then one might block out the message. Thus, moderate discrepancy is optimal. For example, if one already believes that tighter gun control is necessary, one would not really have to pay attention to the nuances of an argument for that position, especially if the purveyor of the information was a respected individual. One would believe it because it agreed with one's existing view, not because it was a good argument.

Less clear is the role of high topic knowledge. It seems intuitive that someone who did not perceive they knew very much about a topic would be easier to persuade to adopt a particular view, but these individuals did not pay attention to the arguments. Perhaps high topic knowledge allows one to *understand* message arguments better, and so they engage more in central processing, whereas individuals who have little knowledge may rely on peripheral cues to help them make up their minds.

Why did the historians described by Wineburg (1991) engage in peripheral processing as well as central processing of the texts? They had low topic knowledge, but high disciplinary knowledge. That is, they knew their field enough to understand the way in which documents are used in research, the way historians construct text, and the ways in which authors of historical texts gain expertise and credibility. And because they had low topic knowledge, they knew they must rely on their disciplinary knowledge. Second, their engagement in the activity was high. Processing of historical documents is central to their livelihoods as historians. Thus, they probably found the activity personally relevant and tied to their experiences. The theory suggests that personal relevance and closeness to experience would elicit central processing. But it is likely that the high need to understand the arguments led to the use of peripheral cues as well. Why? They may have perceived that their topic knowledge was low and knew that they had to rely on other cues in addition to central ones. In this instance, a high level of disciplinary knowledge was useful to them because it allowed the historians to evaluate the peripheral cues at a more sophisticated level than might be likely given less knowledge. Thus, their reading of the texts was sparked by affective as well as metacognitive responses: a motivation to understand (high need for cognition), a sense of self-efficacy in their ability to process historical texts, and a feeling that the activity was closely tied to their personal goals and experiences likely coexisted with a cognitive assessment of the types of knowledge that could be brought to bear to help them decide what to believe.

According to the theory, peripheral processing that does not lead to central processing is more likely when motivation and personal relevance are absent, there is a low need for cognition, or the individual knows little about a topic. Peripheral processors use cues such as the likability of the source, the length of the message, and the number of arguments to decide whether an argument is valid or not and do not use the strength of the argument itself.

Barry, the physics student described earlier, was probably a peripheral processor. By the end of a unit on gravity, Barry was able to explain gravity to another student. During the course of the unit, he experienced a moderate amount of dissonance, read a strong argument, and experienced various sources of information (his classmates, the experiment, and the teacher's explanations) that converged on the scientific explanation. Even under those conditions, however, his understanding of gravity was not entirely in line with the text explanation. Although he was finally convinced that heavier and lighter objects fall at the same rate, he had difficulty at posttest explaining the reasons for that belief. If the ideas lacked personal relevance, as we suspect in Barry's case, and the focus was on response involvement (how Barry looked to friends, which we also suspect), then peripheral rather than central processing of the message is likely. With central processing, involvement in the issue is necessary; for peripheral processing, response involvement can be a determining factor (Leippe & Elkin, 1987). That is, if a response will receive public scrutiny, individuals attend less to the arguments (and, presumably, more to what they think people want them to say). Response involvement distracted Barry from the message and led to less thorough learning of the physics principle.

In conclusion, processors of persuasive messages can use central processing solely, peripheral processing solely, or a combination of central and peripheral. Central processing is necessary for a deep understanding of the arguments: using central processing makes conceptual change a possibility, albeit not a sure thing. If peripheral processors screen out the arguments, thus do not engage in central processing, then only weak conceptual change is likely, as Dole and Sinatra (1998) pointed out. However, if individuals engage in both peripheral and central processing, arguments that are perceived as credible are most likely to be believed, and, so, conceptual change is likely.

What does the previous discussion have to do with *intentional* conceptual change? As previously discussed, intentionality is assumed when one is persuaded to adopt a view different from a preexisting one. The persuaded individual, because he thinks that the new message is more believable than his previous belief, must inhibit that response in favor of the new message. In using both peripheral and central cues to come to a decision about what message to believe, an individual is most likely intentional. Even Barry's response to the gravity lesson was guided by an initial overt rejection of Newton's principals. That overtness implies intentionality.

Message-Sidedness. One question social psychologists ask is whether one-sided or two-sided arguments are more persuasive. Karlins & Abelson (1970) said that, when an audience already has a positive view of the message, when only one message will be provided, or when only temporary change is sought, the one-sided arguments are more persuasive. If the audience initially disagrees with the author, however, or when it is probable that the audience will hear the other side from someone else, both sides of the argument should be presented. Two-sided messages may also be more effective when involvement in the topic is low.

One-sided arguments may result in less engagement in central processing for receptive individuals. But, then, the receptive individuals do not go through conceptual change. If the audience is not receptive to the message, then one-sided arguments encourage counterarguments. The audience is engaged in the text because they are committed to producing arguments to show that the text is not true. In such instances, only those who are engaged in the topic but who hold an opposite view would engage in central processing of the message. These individuals believe that the information is personally relevant, have a high need for cognition, or are otherwise motivated to process the text carefully in order to argue against it.

Two-sided arguments favor systematic processing. But whereas two-sided messages may be persuasive (lead to more conceptual change), the direction of persuasion is not clear-cut. Buehl, Alexander, Murphy, and Sperl (2001), for example, found that two-sided nonrefutational text was effective at changing students' ideas about the V-chip, but the direction of change was variable. Even though the author's opinion was clear to the researchers, it may not have been to the students, who often changed their opinions to match the side of the argument that the author meant to be the weaker side, believing that they had agreed with the author. Buehl et al. suggested that students in their study had difficulty determining the author's viewpoint in the two-sided nonrefutational message. My colleagues and I had similar experiences in a study of history texts. One of the texts was a two-sided, nonrefutational text about the controversial Tonkin Gulf incident of the Vietnam conflict. The author initially stated that the incident did happen, despite evidence that it may not have, and the United States responded responsibly. Then, he presented arguments for the other side, followed by arguments for his side. He ended with a restatement of his belief. But about one fourth of the students who read the text believed that the author's view was that of his detractors—presented before he discussed his side. That finding suggests that students do not automatically pay close attention to arguments in text. It may also be, however, that they were not paying attention to the peripheral cues of a two-sided message. In constructing such a message, authors traditionally present the favored view *after* the nonfavored view. So the position of the message within the text, a peripheral cue, could have helped students understand the message had they been aware of that cue. Another possibility is that the two-sided non-refutation allowed students to engage in selective exposure. That is, they may have believed that the message the author wanted them to believe was the one they believed themselves.

Message-sidedness is also important when considering the education level and background information of individuals. Highly educated individuals prefer two-sidedness in a message, because they feel the credibility of the source is enhanced. Further, message-sidedness is an important factor when there are differences in the positive or negative valence of attitudes and beliefs. A planned social change model (Sheth, Mittal, & Newman, (1999) suggested that, for individuals who already are positive about an idea involving social change (e.g., they agree that recycling is a good idea) and are engaging in behaviors consonant with the idea (they already recycle), reinforcement is all that is necessary (a one-sided message telling of the benefits of the position is a type of reinforcement). However, if the individual is negative and is not engaged (he does not believe recycling is feasible and he does not recycle), then a confrontation strategy is necessary. In that case, conceptual change is the goal. Either the discordant behavior is blocked, or the negative ideas are confronted (a two-sided refutational text confronts a person's beliefs). So, for conceptual change to take place, marketers agree that refutation is effectively persuasive. Refutation elicits discomfort, which motivates readers to change their beliefs and behaviors. The discomfort is an impetus for metacognitive activity, and so the result is intentionality.

The idea of inoculation is also relevant to intentional conceptual change. Inoculation is, as suggested by the term, a resistance to future arguments that is developed when one goes through a deep-seated conceptual change. Two-sided messages are more effective at inoculation, especially if those two-sided messages are refutational (Lumsdaine & Janis, 1953). In refutation, the counterarguments are provided to the reader and then shown to be wrong. So if individuals hear those counterarguments in the future, they are inoculated from backsliding, or returning to their previous ideas. For example, physics students who changed their intuitive ideas about gravity to be more in line with scientific thinking might not return to those ideas when other students espouse them. In fact, because the weaknesses in those ideas had been explained to them, they might be able to persuade the other students that *their* intuitive ideas need to be changed.

In the processing of two-sided arguments, individuals make reasoned assumptions about their credibility. The reason they use requires metacognition, and thus, individuals are engaging in intentional behavior. If their concepts change because of their assessments of the message, then intentional conceptual change has taken place.

Rhetoric and Conceptual Change

The field of communication embraces the sociopsychological research already discussed. The difference is that they also include the study of rhetoric. Rhetoricians assume that persuasion is the goal of communication. Aristotle believed that arguments were persuasive if they were logical, credible, and struck a responsive emotional chord (anger or mildness, love or hatred, fear or confidence, etc.). Kenneth Burke believed that identification with the audience was the most salient characteristic to persuasion. These rhetoricians and others, then, understand that persuasion is a function of the interaction between a message and the characteristics of the individuals to be persuaded. Only those messages that in some way are connected with individuals were likely to be persuasive.

CONCEPTUAL CHANGE IN PHYSICS

Elements of Belief Change as a Result of Reading Refutational Text

In research my colleagues and I conducted, we used persuasion to encourage students in physics classes to change their intuitive but nonscientific beliefs about the motion of objects. A key element in that persuasion was the use of refutational texts, texts that present commonly held beliefs, refute them, and then present scientifically viable beliefs as alternatives. Here is an example:

> The horizontal (forward) component of motion for a projectile is no more complicated than the horizontal motion of a bowling ball rolling freely along a level bowling alley. If the floor did not produce friction to slow the bowling ball, it would continue to move forward down the alley at a constant speed. *Despite the fact that many people think that a ball will slow or stop on its own, this will not happen.* Moving objects will keep moving at a constant rate unless they are slowed or stopped or their direction is changed because

of an *outside* force such as friction (author-created refutational text adapted from Hewitt, 1987).

If the text in that example were continued, it would argue that the second theory (Newton's) explains phenomena more completely than the commonly held theory and would provide evidence that the alternative theory is, indeed, more explanatory. The text is one of three types of persuasive arguments mentioned before: one-sided arguments, two-sided nonrefutational arguments, and two-sided refutational arguments.

The refutational text in the extract is different from the rhetorical form of refutation taught in writing courses only in the sense that its goal is that students learn information, whereas the goal of refutational essays is usually to change someone's opinion about a social issue. However, the difficult part in writing the scientific kind of refutation is to anticipate the thinking of readers in order to refute it, much the same as it might be when writing a persuasive essay.

My colleagues and I have spent years studying conceptual change learning in science and have come to at least one fairly stable conclusion: students change their intuitive but nonscientific conceptions to more scientific ones by reading refutational text (Alvermann & Hynd, 1989; Guzzetti, Snyder, Glass, & Gamas, 1993; Hynd, Alvermann, & Qian, 1993; Hynd, McWhorter, Phares, & Suttles, 1994) more than after reading straight informational texts. Not only is there experimental evidence that students move in the direction of scientific theory after reading refutation (Guzzetti et al., 1993), but there is also evidence from interviews and observations that change occurs and that students prefer refutation over other forms of science text dealing with the same topic (e.g., Guzzetti, Hynd, Skeels, & Williams, 1995). Refutation's power is somewhat mitigated in classrooms where instruction is ongoing and multifaceted (Hynd, Guzzetti, Fowler, Williams, & Seward, unpublished manuscript). In a study in classrooms where instruction about the principles of gravity was on-going, students in both advanced physics and regular physical science classes were affected by the refutational structure of a text on gravity. In the advanced classes, refutational text helped students explain the answer to an application problem (the application posttest). In the regular physical science class, students who read the refutational text prior to instruction did better on the true–false posttest. In addition, reading a refutational text either before or after other instruction helped them, as it did the advanced class, explain the answer to an application problem. Evidence from students' laboratory assignments additionally suggests that, for these students, having read the refutational text initially helped them interpret lab findings more scientifically. These data point to the conclusion that refutational text is beneficial to some students even when numerous other avenues for learning are available.

The significant point is that students change their ideas. The students who read these texts held nonscientific, intuitive ideas before reading. These ideas may not have been consciously determined but were firmly entrenched, nonetheless, because they represented notions that came from their sensory perceptions of the world and their interpretation of those perceptions. Therefore, we see refutation as being a persuasive form of argument rather than a mere description of information.

Why is refutation powerful? I have previously focused on two theories in conceptual change to explain it. One theory is that of Posner, Strike, Hewson, and Gertzog (1982), who posited four conditions necessary for conceptual change in science. First, students must be dissatisfied with their current ideas (experience dissonance). Second, students must understand the new scientific explanation. Third, they must find the scientific explanation believable, and finally, they must see the benefit in using the explanation in future settings.

The refutational texts we developed attempted to elicit dissatisfaction by pointing out the differences between an individual's explanation and the scientific one. In one study (Hynd et al., unpublished manuscript), we had 29 high school physics students comment on a number of texts. After reading them, they rated them on scales of clarity, credibility, usefulness, and interest. They then explained why they rated the texts that way. We categorized those comments. Their comments attest to the idea that students noted the differences between their own ideas and the text ideas. Therefore, we concluded that our texts elicited dissonance.

Second, our texts explained the scientific theory. Students mentioned clarity and in-depth information as being important in their evaluation of the refutational texts. Third, our texts used examples that were believable. Finally, our texts showed the explanatory usefulness the scientific theory would provide. Table 10.1 shows examples of comments that students made in the previous categories. In that study, students read narrative refutational, expository refutational, and nonrefutational informational texts on the same topic of projectile motion. The refutational texts were seen as the clearest, the most informative, the most reasonable, the most useful, and the most believable. They were consistently rated higher than the nonrefutational texts students read.

Another theory I have used to explain the power of refutation is that of Chinn and Brewer (1993), who described the characteristics of anomalous data that elicit their acceptance. Anomalous data are data that go against one's current conception. Chinn and Brewer believed that the data must be credible, unambiguous, and exist in multiple forms. Many students, for example, may consider a text's arguments because they believe in its credibility, whereas they may doubt the credibility of their classmates. Even

TABLE 10.1
Categories of Comments

Dissonance	There's a contrast between common people and physics.
	While it was saying the wrong ideas, they fit how I believed.
	It shows common ideas you can identify with but explains why they're wrong.
	It makes you think twice about what you think you know.
	If I thought about what it said, it would help me change my mind.
Clarity/Depth	It gets its points across
	. . . clearer than a text that beats around the bush.
	Talks about how gravity really works.
	It was good. It had a lot of information.
	A lot of detail of vertical and horizontal motion.
	Little questions. Everything I needed to know was there.
Believability	The text gave everyday life examples.
	It has a lot to do with everyday life. The things you do have to do with physics.
	It was half-realistic. Most people don't think of physics when an orange rolls or think of why the soda cup kept moving when he stopped.
Usefulness	It was dealing with things we could really do. It told us you can use it for the rest of your life.
	Because you could explain something to somebody by reading it.
	This information could be used in everyday life to better understand how objects react to forces.
Reinforcement	We did it in class. Most stuff I read says this will happen.
	. . . the information was believable because it was from other sources.
	It fits what I've learned.
Credibility	It's a text, right?
	I have no reason not to believe this. It's in a science book.
	It doesn't seem right to be, but because it's a text, it has to be true.
	I believe what I read.
Identification	It was like it was talking to me.
	You don't think you're stupid.
	While it was saying the wrong ideas, they fit how I believed.
	It explained what I believed in. It's not just me.
	It's good to know that people have different theories. At least my theory was there.
	It's just like me.
	The story was interesting. I could identify.
	It has a lot to do with everyday life, the things you do have to do with physics.

credible data must be unambiguous. If ambiguous, students are likely to reinterpret them as support for their existing theories; they are less likely to reinterpret the data if they are clear and observable. For example, it is hard to deny the theory that a coin and feather fall at the same rate, except for air resistance, when one sees the experiment performed in a vacuum. In our study, the refutational texts we used seemed credible and unambiguous (clear, as shown in the comments in Table 10.1). They also provided reinforcement for other forms of instruction aimed at changing the same ideas (multiple forms).

The theories helped explain why the refutational texts were persuasive. In addition to these explanations, however, the theories from social psychology and rhetoric further help us understand refutation's power. For example, note in Table 10.1 the use of both central and peripheral processes. Comments about clarity and usefulness are evidence of central processing, but students also used peripheral cues. With some of the students, we felt that their reliance on peripheral cues was based on the way they interpreted the task of learning. They seemed to perceive that it was their job to learn any fact presented in text, a less sophisticated view than that exhibited by the historians, but central to their perception of themselves as students, and, thus, tied up with their feelings of self-efficacy. So, even though the text they read went against their intuitive beliefs, students made comments about the text's credibility. Furthermore, they seemed to identify with the texts, thus showing that the arguments were persuasive in the way that rhetoricians describe. By tapping into students' intuitive beliefs before refuting them, the texts cause students to identify with the message. This may have engaged students' feelings that the ideas were personally relevant, encouraging central processing. Therefore, the affective feelings inspired by the texts helped students attend to the arguments and thoughtfully change their current conceptions.

In summary, students who are exposed to refutational texts have a variety of reactions that can be articulated and their reactions to those texts seem intentional. The refutational texts we used aroused dissonance, and, when individuals experience the discomfort of having their beliefs confronted, they become aware of the aspects of the message that cause the dissonance and actively seek to resolve the discomfort. Besides arousing dissonance, the texts were understandable, provided strong, logical arguments, fostered identification and feelings of personal relevance, were written, echoed similar information students were learning in their classrooms, explained the utility of the information, and were unambiguous. These features of the texts likely elicited central processing. They also seemed credible. This feature likely elicited peripheral processing. In addition, the style of refutation may have inoculated students against future intuitive explanations of the ideas from others. Consistency theories, self-perception theories, the Elaboration Likelihood Model, and ideas from rhetoric all are pertinent in explaining individuals' cognitive, metacognitive, and affective reactions to persuasion in the form of refutational text. Hence, the texts elicited intentional conceptual change.

Physics Classes and Conceptual Change

In the years that my colleagues and I have worked with physics students, we have come to appreciate the motivational and intentional aspects of conceptual change. Hynd, Holschuh, and Nist (2000) found that students in high school physics classes who changed their concepts after reading refutational texts ($N = 18$) rated their motivations slightly higher than students who did not learn the counterintuitive information, but, rather, maintained their original ideas ($N = 29$). On a 10-point scale with 1 being low and 10 being high, their average ratings were 7.64 and 6.55 respectively. The students who learned also rated their interests slightly higher than students who did not learn (7.86 and 6.02, respectively). Those overall motivation and interest ratings, however, do not tell the whole story. From our interviews, we found that students were motivated by several influences.

First, students wished to live up to the expectations they had set for themselves and that others had set for them. They often said things like, "I want to do the best I can do," stated like a mantra. Often they said their parents had instilled that desire in them. In other cases, they said they would feel that way whether or not their parents expected it of them. With some students, the desire to be the best they could be seemed to exist as a stable construct not limited to performance in physics classes. For example, Meredith said, "I want to do good in every, you know, I want to make good grades in, like, all of my classes just so that, I don't want to be, I don't want to be an average student. I mean, I want to be a better than average student."

Students also said they were motivated by the chance to meet their future goals. Doing well in physics would help them get into college, become a physicist, or get a scholarship. In fact, 56% of the students who underwent conceptual change about the targeted physics concepts said they wanted good grades because those grades would help them meet their future goals, whereas only a few students who did not change their concepts said that was why they wanted grades. Rather, they said things like, "I'm just doing it for the grades." Grades for the better students were more than just extrinsic motivators, then, but were tied to students' perceptions of themselves.

Other important motivations for these students were interest, understanding, and usefulness. If students were not interested or did not understand, they often ended up not undergoing conceptual change. For example, Charles said, "Well, when I don't understand something, I get frustrated, and I don't really want to learn. It's more, I have to. I can't understand the book, so if you don't pick it up in class and you go back and try learning in the book, and it doesn't make sense . . . And my parents can't help me cause they don't have no idea." On the other hand, if students were interested, they were more likely to go through the effort to understand information and, thus, were more likely to change their concepts. Lindsey said, for example, "Um, I am bored occasionally, but I still learn because, I mean, I still enjoy it. . . . Um, just for basic understanding, you know, about how things work. I don't know if I'd actually try to find out how long it's going to take a wave to hit a cliff, but knowing how to do it and the way to do it is pretty simple, that's nice to know." Students who learned the targeted physics principles often commented, when asked about the usefulness of information, that they thought physics was useful for helping them to understand everyday life (48% of the comments), rather than to help them with their careers (31%) or other classes (17%). Only one person commented that he did not think physics was useful. Students who did not undergo conceptual change, on the other hand, made comments that were more evenly distributed between career (27%), everyday life (26%), classes (26%), and not being useful (20%).

A final motivation that students mentioned was a need for self-efficacy. Mary, who did learn the counterintuitive physics principles, said, ". . . because it, it's not really easy. . . . you have to study, and you have to do everything, and I'm not really good at, like, just doing things." Charles complained, "I'm just not that good in it. I like history better." He discussed his frustration at not being able to learn material in physics on several different occasions. That sense of failure no doubt contributed to his lack of motivation.

We would expect students who were motivated to learn would be more likely to engage in deep learning strategies, exemplifying their intentions to carry through with behaviors consonant with those motivations, and in keeping with the idea that students who undergo conceptual change will engage in central processing of messages that is accompanied by conation. We asked students what strategies they used to learn counter-intuitive science concepts, and we coded their answers into three types of strategies we called social, cognitive, and strategic. Social strategies were those in which students relied on other individuals to help them understand concepts. Cognitive strategies were strategies that required mental activity like using logic, paying attention and listening, relating the information to something else, or trying to fit the principles into everyday situations. Some students discussed procedures that they followed like note taking, re-reading, and doing their homework. These responses were coded as strategic. Overall, only 12% of the students mentioned social processes as being important to learning. Furthermore, students who were able to change concepts mentioned cognitive effort (53%) more than they mentioned strategies they employed (33%), whereas students who did not change their concepts mentioned strategies (55%) more than they mentioned employing cognitive effort (33%). This finding is telling. Students who were able to change their concepts were more motivated by the usefulness of the information they were going to learn, saw learning as meeting important future goals, and engaged in more cognitive effort in learning. Students' existing attitudes and interests in the subject matter allowed them to think more deeply about the ideas in the texts, so that they were likely engaged in central processing of the information. That engagement made it more likely that they would experience dissonance between their existing beliefs and the information in the texts, that they would not opt for selective exposure, and that they would undergo conceptual change. Because of the overt effort implied, that conceptual change is seen as intentional.

CONCEPTUAL CHANGE IN A HISTORY CLASS

In a Hynd, Stahl, Montgomery, and McClain (1997) study, students changed their ideas about Christopher Columbus as a result of reading three conflicting texts. One text presented a traditional view of Columbus, close to the view that the students held about him, that he was brave, adventurous, and smart. It did, however, dispel some of the students' misconceptions about him, in that it clarified that he was not Spanish, that he did not land on the North American continent but on an island near Cuba, and that he was not the first man to believe that the earth was round. Another text was a revisionist view of Columbus. In this text, Columbus' exploits were described from a native "Indian's" perspective, and it depicted Columbus as cruel and greedy. The third was a postrevisionist text written in refutational style; it depicted Columbus as having a balance of good and bad qualities. After reading the texts, students' attitudes about Columbus changed to become more negative, and their misconceptions about him lessened. The postrevisionist refutational text had the greatest impact on students in that it produced more negative attitudes and lessened more misconceptions than the other texts. The revisionist text with the most overly negative tone about Columbus had the least impact. When we asked students what caused their change in attitudes, they mentioned that they liked the way the balanced postrevisionist text covered Columbus' life and found the style of the text made it clear that they had believed wrong information about Columbus previously. What does this study show? First, it is likely that students were affected by some of the peripheral features of the texts (their tone, their style). If they liked those features, they were more likely to engage in central processing. If they engaged in central processing, then they had a higher chance of intentionally changing their existing conceptions.

CONCLUSION

This chapter discussed several theories of attitude, concept, and belief change in response to persuasion. These theories are unique in that they emphasize an integration of belief, affect, and action. It also provided examples of the integration of these and other elements from the research my colleagues and I have done in both science and history. One thing seems clear; affect and intention are central to conceptual change. There are some characteristics of individuals that make it more likely that they will undergo conceptual change when confronted with information that goes against their existing beliefs. Students who are interested in the topic, have a high degree of knowledge, feel that the information is personally relevant and that it will be useful to them are more likely to undergo conceptual change. I suggest that the process, when using refutational text, goes something like this: A student who is interested in the subject of a text and believes the information will be useful to him begins to read. He may initially pay attention to peripheral cues in the text such as the tone, the style, and the credibility of the author. If he is impressed favorably with these features, he may be drawn to pay attention to the arguments. As he does, he comes across information that contradicts what he previously believed. This confrontation causes discomfort, and his first reaction is to argue to defend his position. That is not easy, however, because, every time he tries to argue a point, the text refutes it, removing his ability to counterargue. The text also presents a reasoned, cogent argument for the alternative idea. So the reader understands it and believes it. He then acts on the knowledge by participating in an experiment. His knowledge allows him to make a prediction about the outcome of the experiment. He has undergone conceptual change. Note the interaction between the message and receiver and the interplay among individual and textual elements. Also note the intentionality of the student's behavior. The student is an active participant in the processing of changing concepts, and his response is a motivated one. That intentionality is at the heart of conceptual change.

After reviewing Dole and Sinatra's (1998) Cognitive Reconstruction of Knowledge Model (CRKM), I suggest a revision to allow for the possibility that central and peripheral processes can be engaged in simultaneously, and that, in the case of conceptual change rather than mere learning, such simultaneous processing is optimal and even likely in cases of high involvement and disciplinary knowledge. Research is needed to provide evidence for that contention, however. In addition, I believe that research should be aimed at teasing out the possible differences in individual characteristics and message characteristics and their influences on individuals when they intentionally change their minds in response to multiple texts with conflicting messages. In cases where several texts disagree, it seems as if the reasons why people decide to believe some information and not others would become clearer.

REFERENCES

Alvermann, D. E., & Hynd, C. R. (1989). Effects of prior knowledge activation modes and text structure on nonscience majors' comprehension of physics. *Journal of Educational Research, 83*, 97–102.

Bem, D. J. (1967). Self-perception: An alternative interpretation of cognitive dissonance phenomena. *Psychological Review, 74*, 183–200.

Buehl, M. M., Alexander, P. A., Murphy, P. K., & Sperl, C. T. (2001). Profiling persuasion: The role of beliefs, knowledge, and interest in the processing of persuasive texts that vary by argument structure. *Journal of Literacy Research, 33*, 269–301

Burnkrant, R. E., & Howard, D. J. (1984). Effects of the use of introductory rhetorical questions versus statements on information processing. *Journal of Personality and Social Psychology, 47*, 1218–1230.

Cacioppo, J. T., & Petty, R. E. (1979). Effects of message repetition and position on cognitive response, recall, and persuasion. *Journal of Personality and Social Psychology, 37*, 97–109.

Cacioppo, J. T., Petty, R. E., & Kao, C. (1984). The efficient assessment of need for cognition. *Journal of Personality and Assessment, 48*, 306–307.

Chaiken, S. (1980). Heuristic versus systematic information processing and the use of source versus message cues in persuasion. *Journal of Personality and Social Psychology, 39*, 752–766.

Chaiken, S. (1987). The heuristic model of persuasion. In M. P. Zanna, J. M. Olson, & C. P. Herman (Eds.), *Social influence: The Ontario symposium* (Vol. 5, pp. 3–39). Hillsdale, NJ: Lawrence Erlbaum Associates.

Chaiken, S., & Eagly, A. H. (1976). Communication modality as a determinant of message persuasiveness and message comprehensibility. *Journal of Personality and Social Psychology, 34*, 605–614.

Chaiken, S., & Maheswaren, D. (1994). Heuristic processing can bias systematic processing: Effects of source credibility, argument ambiguity, and task importance on attitude judgment. *Journal of Personality and Social Psychology, 66*, 460–475.

Chi, M. T. H. (1992). Conceptual change within and across ontological categories: Examples from learning and discovery in science. In R. N. Giere (Ed.), *Minnesota studies in the philosophy of science (Vol. XV), Cognitive models of science* (pp. 129–186). Minneapolis: University of Minnesota Press.

Chinn, C. A., & Brewer, W. F. (1993). The role of anomalous data in knowledge acquisition: A theoretical framework and implications for science instruction. *Review of Educational Research, 63*(1), 1–49.

Dole, J. A., & Sinatra, G. M. (1998). Reconceptualizing change in the cognitive construction of knowledge. *Educational Psychologist, 33*(2/3), 109–128.

Eagly, A. H., & Telaak, K. (1972). Width of the latitude of acceptance as a determinant of attitude change. *Journal of Personality and Social Psychology, 23*, 388–397.

Festinger, L. (1957). *A theory of cognitive dissonance*. Stanford, CA: Stanford University Press.

Festinger, L., & Carlsmith, J. M. (1959). Cognitive consequences of forced compliance. *Journal of Abnormal and Social Psychology, 58*, 203–210.

Frey, D. (1986). Recent research on selective exposure to information. *Advances in Experimental Social Psychology, 19*, 41–80.

Guzzetti, B., & Hynd, C. (1998). *Perspectives on conceptual change: Multiple ways to understand knowing and learning in a complex world*. Mahwah, NJ: Lawrence Erlbaum Associates.

Guzzetti, B., Hynd, C., Skeels, S., & Williams, W. (1995). Improving physics exts: Students speak out. *Journal of Reading, 38*(8), 656–665.

Guzzetti, B. J., Snyder, T. E., Glass, G. V., & Gamas, W. S. (1993). Meta-analysis of instructional interventions from reading education and science education to promote conceptual change in science. *Reading Research Quarterly, 28*, 116–161.

Harkins, S. G., & Petty, R. (1981). The effects of source magnification of cognitive effort on attitudes: An information-processing view. *Journal of Personality and Social Psychology, 40*, 401–413.

Hewitt, P. G. (1987). *Conceptual physics*. Menlo Park, CA: Addison Wesley.

Hovland, C., Janis, I., & Kelley, H. H. (1953). *Communication and persuasion*. New Haven, CT: Yale University Press.

Hynd, C., Alvermann, D. E., & Qian, G. (1993). *Prospective teachers' comprehension and teaching of a complex science concept* (Reading Research Report No. 4). Athens, GA: National Reading Research Center, Universities of Georgia and Maryland.

Hynd, C., Guzzetti, B., Fowler, P., Williams, W., & Seward, A. (2002). *Text in physics class: The contribution of reading to learning counter-intuitive physics principles*. Unpublished manuscript, University of Georgia, Athens, GA.

Hynd, C., Holschuh, J., & Nist, S. (2000). Learning complex, scientific information: Motivation theory and its relation to student perceptions. *Reading and Writing Quarterly: Overcoming Learning Difficulties, 36*(1), 23–58.

Hynd, C., McWhorter, Y., Phares, V., & Suttles, W. (1994). The role of instructional variables in conceptual change in high school physics topics. *Journal of Research in Science Teaching, 31*, 933–946.

Karlins, M., & Abelson, H. I. (1970). *How opinions and attitudes are changed* (2nd ed.). New York: Springer.

Kinder, D. R. (1978). Political person perception: The asymmetrical influence of sentiment and choice on perceptions of political candidates. *Journal of Personality and Social Psychology, 36*, 859–871.

Leippe, M. R., & Elkin, R. A. (1987). When motives clash: Issue involvement and response involvement as determinants of persuasion. *Journal of Personality and Social Psychology, 52*, 269–278.

Lumsdaine, A., & Janis, I. (1953). Resistance to counter-propaganda produced by a one-sided versus a two-sided propaganda presentation. *Public Opinion Quarterly, 17*, 311–318.

Petty, R. E., & Cacioppo, J. T. (1986). *Communication and persuasion: Central and peripheral routes to attitude change*. New York: Springer-Verlag.

Piaget, J. (1973). *To understand is to invent: The future of education*. New York: Grossman.

Pintrich, P. R., Marx, R. W., & Boyle, R. (1993). Beyond cold conceptual change. *Review of Educational Research, 63*(2), 167–199.

Posner, G. J., Strike, K. A., Hewson, P. W., & Gertzog, W. A. (1982). Accommodation of a scientific conception: Toward a theory of conceptual change. *Science Education, 66*, 211–227.

Sherif, M., & Cantrell, H. (1947). *The psychology of ego-involvements*. New York: Wiley.

Sheth, J. N., Mittal, B., & Newman, B. I. (1999). *Customer behavior: Consumer behavior and beyond*. Fort Worth: The Dryden Press.

Siegler, R. S. (1996). *Emerging minds: The process of change in children's thinking*. New York: Oxford University Press.

Smith, J. P., diSessa, A. A., & Roschelle, J. (1993). Misconceptions reconceived: A constructivist analysis of knowledge in transition. *The Journal of the Learning Sciences, 3*, 115–163.

Stahl, S. A., Hynd, C., Montgomery, T., & McClain, V. (1997). *In fourteen hundred and ninety-two, Columbus sailed the ocean blue: The effects of multiple document readings on student atti-*

tudes and misconceptions (Reading Research Report No. 82). National Reading Research Center, University of Georgia.

Strike, K. A., & Posner, G. J. (1992). A revisionist theory of conceptual change. In R. Duschl & R. Hamilton (Eds.), *Philosophy of science, cognitive psychology, and educational theory and practice* (pp. 174–176). Albany, NY: State University of New York.

Thagard, P. (1992). *Conceptual revolutions.* Princeton, NJ: Princeton University Press.

Vosniadou, S., & Brewer, W. F. (1987). Theories of knowledge restructuring in development. *Review of Educational Research, (57)*, 51–67.

Wineburg, S. S. (1991). Historical problem solving: A study of the cognitive processes used in the evaluation of documentary and pictorial evidence. *Journal of Educational Psychology, 83*, 7–87.

11

Learning About Biological Evolution: A Special Case of Intentional Conceptual Change

Sherry A. Southerland
University of Utah

Gale M. Sinatra
University of Nevada, Las Vegas

It is a scenario familiar to many high school biology teachers. The students in Ms. Galloway's general biology class are having difficulties understanding a unit on natural selection. Despite explicit readings, activities, and problem sets, the students don't seem to be grasping the fundamental concepts that she is trying to teach. What could account for the difficulty? Natural selection can be a complex process to grasp, and Ms. Galloway realizes that there are a number of misconceptions that might be hindering her students, i.e., the idea that a species' "needs" allow them to adapt in order to survive, the idea that an entire population changes instead of individuals within that population, etc. However, Ms. Galloway has overheard her students murmuring in the hallway before class; she realizes that some of them consider the broader issues often associated with evolutionary theory to be contrary to their religious upbringing. Because of this, her students' discomfort with the topic is a palpable feeling in the classroom. Yet, she is puzzled: Is their difficulty due to the inherent complexity of natural selection? Is it due to students' perception of the conflict between science and religion? Is it due to some combination of the two?

It could be argued that learning about biological evolution may be significantly different from learning about many other topics in high school biology. For many topics, students may be able to simply incorporate new ideas into their existing knowledge structures. This type of learning has been called *assimilation, accretion, addition,* or *weak restructuring* (Chi, 1992; Rumelhart & Norman, 1981; Vosniadou & Brewer, 1987). As an example, students may readily add new knowledge about osmosis into their existing knowledge about water and membranes without much struggle.

As depicted in the scenario, however, new concepts presented in the classroom often conflict with conceptions that students already hold. In such cases of conflict, the process of learning is not a simple one, as students cannot easily assimilate the new information into what they already know. They may be hesitant to consider the new ideas, they may distort them, or reject them altogether (Chinn & Brewer, 1993). The process of knowledge restructuring in this case has been described *as radical restructuring* (Vosniadou & Brewer, 1987), *radical conceptual change* (Chi, 1992), or *conceptual revolution* (Thagard, 1992). By whatever name, the accommodation process that characterizes knowledge change is quite different from assimilation learning. To achieve such a change, students must juxtapose their existing conceptions against new ideas, they must weigh the similarities and differences, and then question their personal views (see for example, Chan & Bereiter, 1992; Dole & Sinatra, 1998; Posner, Strike, Hewson, & Gertzog, 1982). It is no wonder that radical change is difficult to achieve. Indeed, changing a conception has been found to be a far less likely occurrence than several other alternatives when a learner is faced with conflicting information (Chinn & Brewer, 1993).

Conceptual change regarding any concept is a difficult proposition, as anyone confronted with changing a long-held idea will attest. However, we argue that learning about biological evolution presents unique difficulties. To understand these difficulties, it is necessary to cover some theoretical ground. First, we must consider the relation between beliefs and knowledge when learning about biological evolution. Can students understand the mechanisms of biological evolution in general and yet, not believe that organisms evolve? Is there a different relation between beliefs and knowledge if humans are the species in question? Further, can students accept the validity of a theory of biological evolution if they feel it conflicts with their beliefs? What is the relation between acceptance and belief? Are these the same constructs?

With these issues as a backdrop, we argue that the unique difficulties inherent in learning about biological evolution make it a special case for *intentional conceptual change*. Through argument and empirical evidence, we show that students' knowledge about evolution, their personal epistemological beliefs about the nature of science (NOS), and their willingness to question ideas play a unique role in learning about evolution, particularly human evolution. Finally, we present an instructional approach to promote conceptual change about biological evolution through a process of heightening students' awareness of current conceptions of NOS as well as their own epistemological beliefs.

BELIEF, ACCEPTANCE, AND KNOWLEDGE OF EVOLUTION

In one respect, this chapter centers on the relationship between a learner's knowledge and her belief in evolution. Before one begins to discuss this relationship and its influencing constructs, it is necessary to clarify the terms we use and explain their derivation. The first pair of terms is *knowledge* and *belief,* and we employ a common distinction. We use knowledge to refer to a justified "true" belief (Siegel, 1998). That is, to qualify as knowledge, a proposition must be thought to be a true reflection of reality, it must have some sort of correspondence to reality, and the learner must have valid reasons that justify her acceptance of that proposition (justifications such as an objective, rational appraisal of supporting claims). In contrast, *beliefs* are understood to be a subjective way of knowing and are thought to be personal truths as opposed to truths about the world (Smith, Siegel, & McInerney, 1995). They are considered to be inherently subjective, so they are not held to the same epistemic criteria as knowledge. Beliefs are understood to be extrarational; that is, they are not based on evaluation of evidence, they are subjective, and they are often intertwined with affect.

The second distinction that must be drawn for the sake of the discussion is that between *acceptance* and *belief.* It is common within the community of evolution educators to draw a tight distinction between *acceptance* of a construct and *belief* in that construct—a distinction that is rarely made outside of this community (National Academy of Science, 1998; Smith, 1994; Smith et al., 1995; Smith & Scharmann, 1999). Smith and others explained that acceptance is dependent on a systematic evaluation of evidence. On the other hand, *belief* is based on personal convictions, opinions, and degree of congruence with other belief systems. Thus, it is inaccurate to explain that a scientist "believes" in the theory of evolution, as the use of believe implies that the judgment of the validity of the theory is based on subjective criteria, and this statement blurs the distinctions between scientific knowledge and religious belief. Instead, a scientist is said to *accept* evolutionary theory based on a systematic evaluation of available evidence. By using *acceptance,* one is implying that the individual's recognition of validity is based on something more than simply opinion, thus recognizing a crucial aspect of the nature of scientific knowledge and its distinction from other knowledge frameworks.

Given the distinction drawn between acceptance and belief, what is the relation between acceptance and knowledge of a concept such as biological evolution? There are a variety of suggestions of a relationship in the literature, some based on commonsense reasoning (as in our opening case) and others with a more empirical basis. A common suggestion is that students cannot come to accept evolutionary theory unless they develop some understanding of it. In support of this argument, Lawson and Worsnop (1992) provided one of the first empirical descriptions of the way learners' prior knowledge of evolution serves as a useful predictor of change of belief as a result of instruction. In their analysis of high school students enrolled in a biology course, they focused on the impact of students' reasoning abilities on belief [authors' phrasing] and understanding. They found that less-skilled reasoners were more likely to hold nonscientific beliefs initially, were less likely to be strongly committed to evolutionary statements, and were less likely to change their beliefs during instruction. But more importantly, the authors describe that prior knowledge and reflective reasoning skills were the only two variables that accounted for a significant portion of the knowledge gain—belief did not. The only significant predictor of pre to posttest change of belief was found to be students' prior knowledge of evolution. The authors concluded that reflective reasoning skills operate in the "acquisition of domain-specific knowledge, and that knowledge determines what one believes" (Lawson & Worsnop, 1992, p. 165). Thus according to Lawson and Worsnop (1992), it is knowledge that serves as a barrier to acceptance.

Others suggest the relation between acceptance and understanding operates in the other direction. Many researchers and teachers hold that failure to accept a scientific construct precludes developing an understanding of it (Smith, 1994). Members of this group argue that when teaching evolution, learners' acceptance of the idea must be addressed before they can come to understand the topic. Thus, a learner's rejection of evolutionary theory can prevent them from "hearing what [instructors] say" (Smith, 1994, p. 596) so that acceptance can serve as a barrier to developing a scientific understanding of the construct (Cobern, 1994; Jackson, 2000; Meadows, Doster, & Jackson, 2000; Scharmann, 1990; Smith, 1994).

In contrast to both of these positions (knowledge allowing for acceptance or acceptance allowing for the development of knowledge), a number of empirical studies show a different relation. In three primarily quantitative studies, Bishop and Anderson (1990), Demastes-Southerland, Settlage, and Good (1995), and Lord and Morino (1993) found no relation between students' stated acceptance and their understanding of biological evolution. A qualitative study by Demastes-Southerland, Good, and Peebles (1995, 1996) supports this assertion. They described how a student with creationist views constructed a scientifically sophisticated understanding of evolutionary theory during a year of coursework. This learner stands in contrast to another student who had a stated acceptance of evolution but who constructed only superficial understanding of the topic. In support of this position, Dole, Sinatra, and Reynolds (1991) found no relation between students' stated belief in creationism and their ability to comprehend a text on evolution. Taken together, the findings from these studies suggest that knowledge and acceptance may not be as viscerally tied as many have suggested. This argument has support in other domains. For instance, Brewer and Chinn (1991) described how undergraduate students, when presented texts that contradicted some of their personal conceptions related to the domains of special relativity and quantum mechanics, understood the new theories, but failed to accept them. Clearly there is evidence to suggest a dissociation of knowledge and acceptance—a position that fails to receive a great deal of commonplace or intuitive acceptance.

INTENTIONAL CONSTRUCTS AND UNDERSTANDING EVOLUTION

The research just reviewed details a more complicated picture than has previously been portrayed. Rather than a simplistic, unidirectional relation between acceptance and knowledge—or a lack of relation—we contend that intentional constructs play a central, mediating role in the interaction of knowledge and acceptance when learning about biological evolution. What do we mean by intentional constructs? Recently, there has been a theoretical shift in our perception of learning that suggests that learners are not only active constructors of understanding, they can be intentional toward learning (Bereiter, 1990).

To appreciate intentional level cognition, one must first understand a fundamental idea from cognitive science—that the cognitive processing system has a differentiated architecture (see for example, Anderson, 1990; Newell, 1990). Given the resource limitations of the human information processing system, cognitive scientists assume that cognition is organized in hierarchical levels in which information is processed and represented in qualitatively different ways. By performing different tasks and operating in different manners, these levels allow for efficient execution of various cognitive functions. For example, the algorithmic level of cognitive function contains perceptual and procedural representations that perform computations necessary for carrying out cognitive tasks (Stanovich, 1999). Processing at this level often occurs automatically, that is, quickly, accurately, and almost effortlessly (Speelman, 1998). In contrast, intentional level processing is goal-directed and, thus, is under the learner's conscious control. According to Stanovich (1999), this level "is concerned with action selection based on expected goal attainment in light of current beliefs" (p. 10). He went on to explain that intentional cognition involves essentially three elements: a set of beliefs (or knowledge base), a set of desires or goals, and a mechanism that determines actions based on consideration of both knowledge and goals (p. 12).

Each of the three categories identified by Stanovich (1999)—beliefs, goals, and mechanisms (which take both beliefs and goals into consideration)—are relevant to knowledge acquisition and change in the domain of biological evolution. Specially, we argue that epistemological beliefs, learning goals, and dispositions toward active and open-minded thinking are particularly relevant.

When learning about evolution, several beliefs come into play: beliefs about human origins, beliefs about what counts as evidence of evolutionary change, and beliefs about the nature of knowledge itself (known as epistemological beliefs). There are several reasons implicating epistemological beliefs as likely candidates for affecting conceptual acquisition as well as conceptual change in learning about evolutionary biology. First, evidence suggests that epistemological beliefs are related to general academic performance (e.g., Hofer & Pintrich, 1997; Schommer, 1994), and particularly to tasks that involve problem solving (King & Kitchener, 1994) and reasoning (Bendixen, Schraw, & Dunkle, 1998). Evolution is a difficult concept and requires a high level of reasoning and problem-solving skills for its comprehension (Fisher, 1992). Second, evolution is a theory that the general public perceives to be in a great state of uncertainty and constantly changing. Thus, it is reasonable to posit that one's epistemological degree of comfort with uncertainty is likely to impact knowledge acquisition and change in learning about this topic. Third, the teaching and learning of evolutionary theory has endured a long history of controversy, particularly within the United States, dating well back to before the Scopes trial. The controversy likely stems from and continues to influence the perception of many lay people that evolution conflicts with their religious convictions.

There is evidence to suggest that when considering controversial issues, learners are particularly likely to evoke epistemological beliefs. For example, Kardash and Scholes (1996) examined the impact of epistemological beliefs on the interpretation of controversial topics. They found that students who understood knowledge to be tentative were more likely to conclude that the mixed evidence they were provided about the relation of HIV and AIDS was indeed inconclusive, regardless of their original viewpoint on the issue. In contrast, students who viewed knowledge as certain tended to claim that the contradictory evidence they read was conclusive in the direction of their original beliefs. Thus, students' epistemological beliefs affected their evaluation of a science construct, suggesting that beliefs about knowledge can influence conceptual change.

Finally, there is evidence to suggest that students hold different epistemological standards for "hard" versus "soft" sciences (Buehl & Alexander, 2001; Hofer, 2000). This finding may be relevant to learning about evolution. For example, Hofer (2000) found that students considered knowledge in the natural sciences to be more certain than the knowledge base in disciplines based in the social sciences. Students also viewed experts as the source of scientific knowledge and considered truth as more obtainable in natural sciences than in social sciences such as psychology.

Such differences suggest that students have the mistaken notion that theories are particularly unreliable pieces of scientific knowledge—a suggestion that is supported by a great deal of research in the area (McComas, 1998; Smith et al., 1995). This misconception of theories is compounded by the controversial status of evolution to result in the layperson's conception of evolutionary theory as being particularly unreliable and questionable. Thus, the interaction of the complexity of the content, the controversial nature of evolutionary theory, and students' epistemological demand for greater certainty in the sciences may serve to inhibit their acceptance of this topic.

The second intentional level construct identified by Stanovich (1999) that likely impacts learning in evolution is goals. Pintrich (2000a) showed that achievement goals, particularly mastery goals, are associated with positive learning outcomes. Linnenbrink and Pintrich (2002) argued that mastery goals should be particularly influential in promoting conceptual change. They explained that "mastery oriented students would likely see new information as a way to meet their goal of learning and further their understanding of the topic: They may therefore be more open to changing their ideas about the phenomena, thus facilitating the conceptual change process" (p. 2). It seems likely that having a mastery goal to learn content in biological evolution would be an intentional level impetus for knowledge restructuring.

Finally, a third intentional level construct, dispositions, may be influential in determining how students use their knowledge and beliefs to achieve goals in learning about evolution. Stanovich (1999) defined dispositions as "relatively stable psychological mechanisms and strategies that tend to generate characteristic behavioral tendencies and tactics" (p. 157). One can think of dispositions as tendencies toward learning and thinking. According to Stanovich (1999), dispositions "index individual differences at the intentional level" (p. 158), perhaps because they drive actions by considering both beliefs and goals. Indeed, he described them as "broad tendencies of pragmatic and epistemic self-regulation" (p. 158).

Dispositions can account for differences in problem solving and reasoning even when algorithmic level differences (such as cognitive capacity) are taken into account (Stanovich, 1999). For example, Stanovich and his colleagues demonstrated that the tendency to think in an open-minded fashion and to weigh new evidence against a personal belief—

both considered to be dispositions—account for significant differences in reasoning performance (Sa, West, & Stanovich, 1999; Stanovich, 1999; Stanovich & West, 1997, 1998).

Considering that evolution is a complex topic, perceived to be controversial, potentially challenging to one's beliefs, and a theory in some degree of flux (as are all scientific theories), several dispositions may be invoked when learning about the topic. First, the challenge posed by the content itself suggests the relevance of the disposition to engage in effortful thinking. The Need for Cognition Scale developed by Cacioppo, Petty, Feinstein, & Jarvis (1996) measures this tendency using items such as, *The notion of abstract thinking is appealing to me*. Second, the controversial nature of the topic suggests that the disposition toward Actively Open-Minded Thinking, measured by a scale developed by Stanovich and West (1997), may also be relevant to learning about evolution. This scale assesses the tendency to be open to ideas that may conflict with one's own. It asks individuals to consider the degree to which they agree with statements such as, *People should always take into consideration evidence that goes against their beliefs*.

Conceptual change in general requires individuals to compare their personal conceptions against those of the scientific community. In learning about evolution, many of these ideas may be perceived as conflicting with strongly held beliefs, similar to what Chinn and Brewer (1993) referred to as "deeply entrenched beliefs" (p. 14). Thus, the degree to which someone values and identifies with their beliefs may be especially relevant in this domain. Two scales, the Belief Identification Scale (Sa et al., 1999; Stanovich & West, 1997) and the Values Scale (Costa & McCrae, 1992), measure the degree to which individuals hold fast to their beliefs by using statements such as, *Certain beliefs are just too important to abandon no matter how good a case can be made against them*, and *I believe that loyalty to one's ideals and principles is more important than "open-mindedness."* Finally, the degree of uncertainty and theory change in evolution requires a certain willingness to consider ideas flexibly. Therefore, two other dispositional measures that assess rigidity of thought/inflexible thinking may be relevant: Absolutism (Erwin, 1983), which includes items such as, *Right and wrong never change*, and Dogmatism (Troldahl & Powell, 1965), which includes items such as, *No one can talk me out of something I know is right*. These scales measure the tendencies to think in absolutist and dogmatic ways, which would likely impede the consideration of ideas as abstract, controversial, and difficult to observe as biological evolution.

To understand how intentional level constructs of beliefs, goals, and dispositions may promote or inhibit conceptual change in evolution, consider a student learning about adaptation who understands that "need" is a mechanism of biological change (in that organisms are thought to acquire a particular characteristic because they need it), a common misconception documented in the literature (Bishop & Anderson, 1990; Demastes-Southerland et al., 1995). Earlier we echoed the argument that conceptual change requires that students juxtapose their existing conceptions against new ideas (Chan & Bereiter, 1992; Dole & Sinatra, 1998; Posner et al., 1982; Strike & Posner, 1992). Such a comparison necessitates that our learner be aware of her conception that organisms such as giraffes "need" to reach leaves on high tree branches and so developed long necks, and our learner must have a goal of learning the new information about adaptation. This is important because our learner would only engage in the deliberate comparison of these two views if she had the goal of understanding the scientific view of change in a population. Next, our student must have the disposition to consciously question the validity of her conceptions about the origin of variations in the animal world and the flexibility of thought and nondogmatic views to find them lacking in explanatory power (Demastes-Southerland et al., 1995). In this case, the learner must be able to see the shortcomings of her views when presented with contradictory evidence and recognize that need plays no role in the production of variation in a population. Finally, our learner must explicitly compare her conception to that of the scientific explanation of natural variation in neck length in a population of giraffes and recognize that her explanation and the scientific explanation conflict. Such a comparison requires a willingness to engage in effortful thinking. The act of comparing these rival views may cause the learner to ask: How was the knowledge about variations in the neck length of giraffes discovered? On what assumptions is the theory of adaptation developed? Thus, it is only through an evaluation of one's conception (requiring a disposition to consciously question, flexibility of thought, and nondogmatic views) and a conscious comparison of rival explanations (requiring a willingness to engage in effortful thinking) that a prior conception can be restructured to accommodate the scientific alternative.

Now consider a potentially more difficult topic in evolutionary biology, the origin of humans. Conceptual change typically involves the process of evaluating the validity of a concept or set of conceptions. But, in the domain of human evolution, one may have to compare scientific explanations of biological diversity and one's personally held religious views on the origin of human life. For some individuals, the latter notion has a great deal of evidentiary support (although the evidence may not meet scientific epistemic standards), it has broad explanatory power, and it satisfies strong personal and societal goals. Thus, the change of such an entrenched belief may require a willingness to question one's beliefs. In such an instance, conceptual change may require the ability to question the very basis of one's worldview, and this requires a valuing of belief change.

We argued that intentional level constructs are implicated in learning about evolution. However, it should be acknowledged that for learners to use their epistemological beliefs, goals, and dispositions productively toward learning and thinking, they must be aware of these beliefs and tendencies when learning. Yet, learners are often not aware of their epistemological beliefs and are often not in control of their dispositions toward engaging with information. When learners are not aware of their beliefs or goals, they cannot and do not act intentionally in that their action is not determined by their beliefs or goals. Despite our subjective experience that we spend a considerable portion of our day in deliberate thought and action, it has been argued that much, if not most, of cognitive processing occurs at the algorithmic or unconscious level (Bargh & Chartrand, 1999). However, when beliefs, knowledge, and goals are brought into conscious attention, they can be used intentionally to achieve learning outcomes. Herein lies the promise of intentional constructs for learning about biological evolution.

Researchers extending theoretical accounts and empirical investigations of conceptual change have begun to explore how intentional constructs play a significant role in the knowledge reconstruction process. We propose that the consideration of intentional level constructs allow for a reconceptualization of the conceptual change process. Researchers using this orientation are moving away from the view that the impetus for change comes solely from external forces (such as materials, instruction, or teachers) toward the perspective that change can be initiated and controlled by the learner. For example, conceptual change researchers are now exploring how conscious beliefs, attitudes, goals, motivations, dispositions, etc. can contribute to (and sometimes impede) the change process (see for example, Pintrich, 2000; Pintrich, Marx, & Boyle, 1993; Venville & Treagust, 1998).

It is our contention that intentional constructs help to explain the complex relation between beliefs, knowledge, and acceptance when learning about an issue like biological evolution. Moreover, we contend that the failure to take such intentional constructs into account may explain why researchers have given contradictory accounts of whether knowledge or acceptance serves as the barrier to learning about biological evolution.

The difficulties associated with comparing scientific and religious constructs lead us to argue that to engage in conceptual change about evolution (particularly human evolution) may demand more intentional processing than knowledge restructuring in other domains. Intentional constructs that may need to be invoked include (but are not limited to) learners' general epistemological beliefs, specific epistemological beliefs about the nature of science, learning goals, personal dispositions toward engaging with cognitively complex ideas, and the willingness to be open-minded toward change.

Sorting out the complex interaction between intentional constructs, knowledge, and acceptance in learning evolution is a challenging research endeavor. As an initial attempt, we draw on our own empirical work and related literatures. As learners' goals have been the subject of intensive study elsewhere (Pintrich, 2000b, 2000c), we have focused our own investigation on the interactions of a set of epistemological beliefs and dispositions on acceptance and understanding of evolution. In the following section, we describe what is known in the literature about individual facets of these interactions, focusing first on the interaction of students' conceptions of the nature of science and their acceptance and/or understanding of evolution.

NOS, ACCEPTANCE, AND UNDERSTANDING EVOLUTION

The association of nature of science (NOS) conceptions, acceptance, and understanding of evolutionary theory is firmly argued in the philosophical science education literature (Lawson, 1999; National Academy of Sciences, 1998; Smith & Scharmann, 1999; Southerland, 2000), but it is less well established in the empirical literature. Because this research tradition stems more from the philosophical literature on the nature of science than from a psychological approach to understanding learning, little careful description of the action of specific constructs such as epistemology, acceptance, and understanding have been attempted. That which has been completed focused on a subset of the broader construct of epistemology—that is, nature of science conceptions. NOS deals with questions such as: What is scientific knowledge? How does it differ from knowledge produced through other frameworks? What is scientific evidence? How is scientific knowledge created and produced? Previous research demonstrated that students who develop a more sophisticated understanding of the nature of science are also more prone to accept evolutionary theory, as described by Johnson and Peebles (1987), Scharmann (1990), and Scharmann and Harris (1991). Although a number of studies lend support to the position that a firm understanding of the nature of science allows for greater acceptance of evolution, only one (Scharmann & Harris, 1991) successfully provided evidence to support the corresponding relationship between understanding NOS and understanding evolutionary theory. (However, it must be noted that this is the only study we located that focused specifically on this issue, so the limited number in support of a relationship between NOS and understanding evolution is more indicative of research attention to this area than of a weakness in this relationship).

Although philosophical arguments and previous research suggests relationships between NOS and acceptance of evolution, as well as NOS and understanding of evolution, what is the basis of these relationships? The interaction of NOS and understanding and acceptance of evolution may best be illustrated by examining how traditional science instruction goes awry when teaching evolution. Typically, teachers work to minimize explicit conflict in their classrooms. One way to do this is to completely avoid the topic of evolution. This may be effective in minimizing conflict but severely undermines the integrity of biology as a mature science. In the second common approach, the teacher presents "just the facts" of evolution without explicitly describing how science arrived at these facts or providing any justification for this knowledge.

The facts-only approach, which has been characterized as "scientistic" (Duschl, 1988; Southerland, 2000), serves to stress the declarative content of the discipline of evolution, as the facts are assumed to represent the "truth." Within the scientistic classroom, there is no explicit acknowledgment that these facts may contradict some aspects of the students' worldviews or cultural knowledge, as the only knowledge that has import is that of science. Students know implicitly or are told explicitly not to question or critically examine the facts of science within the confines of such a classroom. The scientistic approach may allow for a quiet classroom; however, it leaves the negotiation of the conflict between scientific knowledge and cultural beliefs systems to the unprepared student. Not only is the student left ignorant of how scientific knowledge is produced, he or she is also given no aid through instruction as to how to compare differing knowledge frameworks. The student is left on his or her own to ask, "Which one of these is right? Which one of these is wrong?" Unfortunately, however, neither of these questions may be helpful in understanding the basis of the contrasting worldviews. In addition, these questions may raise affective barriers that could prohibit subsequent engagement with the concepts. If the student's emotional and intellectual upheaval remains unrecognized, the learning that ensues is likely to be scattered and piecemeal. In a scientistic classroom, because a student's understanding of the nature of science remains undeveloped, the student's understanding and acceptance of evolution remains limited.

It has been argued that a useful alternative to these traditional approaches is to help students understand the very epistemic nature of science (NOS), that is, its presuppositions, methodological assumptions, goals, and boundaries. In teaching about the NOS, instructors emphasize the conventions underlying the practice of and knowledge produced through science (Poole, 1996; Smith & Scharmann, 1999). Thus, students are allowed to understand the difference between a scientific concept and a nonscientific concept; what science can legitimately comment on (i.e.,

What are the characteristics of a "living" thing?) and what it cannot (i.e., What is the meaning of life?).

Such an approach to teaching science is considered "nonscientistic" (Southerland, 2000) because it portrays science as a powerful, but bounded, human enterprise. Through such an approach, scientific knowledge is described as useful but tentative, as representing the best of what is known given its particular focus and methodological assumptions. Students come to understand that other endeavors have different foci and operate from different methodological and epistemological assumptions. It has been argued that a robust understanding of the NOS allows students to understand how and why knowledge produced through science is different from their religious beliefs. Such comparisons are precisely the type of deliberate juxtaposition of ideas required for intentional conceptual change. In a nonscientistic classroom, a student develops a firm understanding of the nature of science—an understanding that allows for the cognitive and emotional "room" to come to understand and/or accept evolutionary theory.

It is important to note that the NOS conceptions targeted in the science education literature and the focus of nonscientistic teaching have strong ties to the more general epistemological beliefs of interest to educational psychology. Clearly, the consideration of the epistemic criteria of scientific knowledge that would be the subject of discussion in a nonscientistic classroom would lead to a greater recognition and development of a learner's more general beliefs about the nature of knowledge. In our own work, we choose to focus on a learner's more general epistemological beliefs (understanding that they are heavily intertwined with a learner's NOS conceptions) simply because epistemological beliefs had a stronger and richer history in the literature to draw on and to inform.

Using the findings of both the educational psychology and science education, we mapped the interactions of what we thought to be the most promising constructs: acceptance, knowledge, epistemological beliefs, and learning dispositions.

OUR WORK ON EPISTEMOLOGICAL BELIEFS, DISPOSITIONS, ACCEPTANCE, AND UNDERSTANDING

Based on previous research, we posited that students' dispositions toward their beliefs and the degree to which they are willing to do the effortful work of weighing those beliefs against alternative points of view may be directly engaged when students are learning about a topic as potentially controversial as biological evolution. As noted, evolution is often perceived by the public to be in a state of great uncertainty, to be constantly changing, and to directly conflict with their religious convictions. Thus, we posited a degree of willingness to examine one's beliefs and entertain alternative points of view as a key factor in developing an understanding of scientific concepts in evolution.

We focused on the relation between understanding two biological constructs (one controversial—evolution, and one noncontroversial—photosynthesis), acceptance of these constructs, and students' epistemological beliefs and cognitive dispositions (Sinatra, Southerland, McConaughy, & Demastes, 2001). Using a sample of 93 undergraduate college students who had little if any college science exposure, we administered a set of surveys to ascertain students' (a) epistemological beliefs (Schommer, 1990), (b) cognitive dispositions, including Stanovich's (1999) Actively Open-Minded Thinking (Sá et al., 1999), the Need for Cognition Scale (Cacioppo et al., 1996), Absolutism (Erwin, 1983), and Dogmatism (Troldahl & Powell, 1965), (c) personal evaluation of the validity of photosynthetic theory and evolutionary theory (as it applies to humans as well as nonhumans), and (d) content knowledge for photosynthesis (Haslam & Treagust, 1987) and evolution (Settlage & Jensen, 1996).

Research Hypotheses

We hypothesized that there should be a relation between epistemological beliefs, dispositions towards open-mindedness and critical thought, and students' acceptance of evolutionary theory (both animal and human evolution). More pointedly, we hypothesized that those students who viewed knowledge as uncertain and changing and were disposed toward open-minded thinking would be more likely to accept the scientific explanation of evolution. We reasoned this would be so due to the commonly held perception that evolution is a theory in great flux. We also hypothesized that this relation would be magnified when the species under consideration was *Homo sapiens*. Conversely, we hypothesized that students who viewed knowledge as certain and fixed and were less open-minded would be less likely to accept evolution because it is "just a theory." We anticipated that, again, this negative relation would be magnified when human evolution was the construct in question. We also hypothesized that epistemological beliefs and dispositions would not be related to the acceptance of a scientific explanation such as photosynthesis, as this is a theory that is perceived by the public to be more certain and not in flux. Figure 11.1a depicts these hypothesized relationships. The square box in the diagram represents a student who is open-minded and views knowledge as changing. According to our hypotheses, this student would be more likely to accept evolution, but not

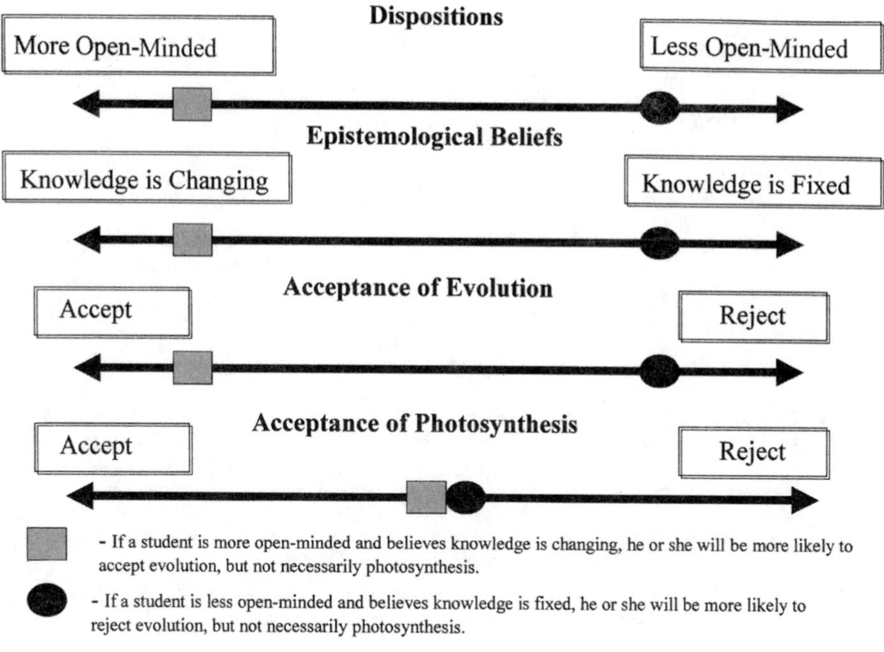

FIG. 11.1a. Hypothesized relation between dispositions, beliefs, and acceptance.

necessarily photosynthesis. The circle shows the converse situation of a student who is less open-minded and views knowledge as fixed. We hypothesized that this student would be more likely to reject evolution, but not necessarily photosynthesis.

Further, we hypothesized that there should be a positive relation between epistemological beliefs, dispositions toward open-mindedness, and students' understanding of evolutionary theory, using the rationale that students who are more epistemologically sophisticated and more open-minded would be more prone to have constructed an appropriate understanding of this perceived controversial theory. Alternatively, we did not expect the same relation for photosynthesis, as it is not typically perceived to be controversial. Figure 11.1b depicts our hypotheses regarding the relationship between dispositions, beliefs, and understanding.

Finally, with regard to understanding and acceptance of evolution, we hypothesized that there should be a relation between students' understanding of evolutionary theory and their acceptance of it, as seen in previous research. We anticipated that this relation would exist for both animal and human evolution. In contrast, we did not expect a relation between understanding and acceptance of photosynthesis, as this topic is not considered to be a controversial topic by the general public.

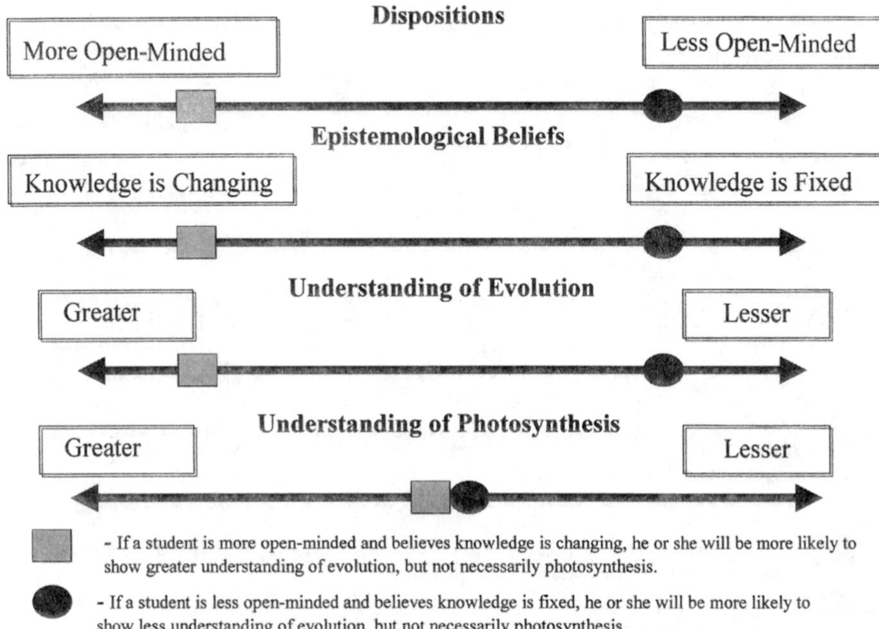

FIG. 11.1b. Hypothesized relation between dispositions, beliefs, and understanding.

Findings

As hypothesized, we found that students' epistemological beliefs and cognitive dispositions related to their degree of acceptance of *human* evolution ($r = -.23$, $p < .05$). These findings were in the expected direction. That is, students who have more sophisticated epistemological beliefs were more likely to accept human evolution. Similarly, students who enjoy critical, open-minded thinking were also more likely to accept human evolution. Conversely, students with less sophisticated epistemological beliefs, those who reported less interest in critical thought, and those who perceived there to be absolute right and wrong answers for questions were less likely to accept human evolution (see Table 11.1).

Regression analyses revealed a similar pattern. Using the acceptance measures as dependent variables and the measure of epistemological sophistication as a predictor in separate analyses revealed that there was no significant predictive relation between epistemological sophistication and acceptance of photosynthesis or animal evolution. However, the analysis predicting acceptance of human evolution approached significance, $F(1, 76) = 3.47$, $p = .06$.

TABLE 11.1
Intercorrelations Among Measures of Epistemological Sophistication (ES), Dispositions, Knowledge, and Acceptance

Measure	*1*	*2*	*3*	*4*	*5*	*6*	*7*
1. ES[a]	1.0	—					
2. Dispositions[b]	−.69*	1.0	—				
3. Photo. Knowledge	.01	−.01	1.0	—			
4. Evo. Knowledge	−.21	.09	−.02	1.0	—		
5. Photo. Acceptance	−.05	.06	.29*	.07	1.0	—	
6. Animal Evo. Accept.	−.16	.20	.10	−.14	.32*	1.0	—
7. Human Evo. Accept.	−.23*	.32*	.08	−.09	.10	.21	1.0

Note. All correlations based on $n = 74$.
[a]Scores based on sum of epistemological beliefs items.
[b]Based on a composite of disposition measures.
*$p < .05$.

In examining these relations for the other two content areas, we found no significant relation between students' epistemological beliefs, cognitive dispositions, and their *acceptance* of either animal evolution or photosynthesis (see Table 11.1). This finding is readily understandable for photosynthesis, as this theory is perceived to be a stable item of scientific knowledge. However, the lack of a significant relation for animal evolution was unexpected. This pattern of findings indicates that the relation between epistemology, dispositions, and acceptance differs when the construct under question is more controversial and more tied to students' entrenched beliefs. Thus, the relation between acceptance, epistemology, and dispositions seems to vary with the degree of controversy of the construct in question and the degree to which students' beliefs about the topic are more firmly entrenched. Our data supports this interpretation in that the correlations between acceptance and dispositions for photosynthesis, animal evolution, and human evolution ranged from low, to higher, to significant, respectively.

Also contrary to our hypothesis, we found no relation between students' general epistemological beliefs and their *understanding* of evolution or photosynthesis (see Table 11.1). However, when the subscales were analyzed separately, we found a very strong relation between students' Ambiguous Information scores (a subscale of the epistemology questionnaire using items such as *I dislike working on problems that have no clear-cut answers*) and their understanding of evolution ($r = -.31, p < .05$). That is, students who are uncomfortable with ambiguity were less likely to understand evolutionary theory. This same relation was not significant for photosynthesis. The findings suggest that while epistemological beliefs may not be closely related to understanding of all scientific topics, for controversial or ambiguous topics, students' comfort level with ambiguity may be a factor.

The findings for dispositions and understanding were similar to those regarding epistemological beliefs and understanding. That is, the only significant relation between cognitive dispositions and understanding was a very strong relation between understanding evolution and one of the dispositional scales when the scales were analyzed separately ($r = -.26$, $p < .05$). Belief Identification (the degree to which one is disposed to hold on strongly to one's beliefs, measured by items such as *One should disregard evidence that conflicts with one's established beliefs*) was found to have a very strong relation to knowledge of evolution. However, no relation was found between ratings on this scale and knowledge of photosynthesis. As was the case for the specific epistemological construct of ambiguity, the relation between understanding and depositions may vary with the perceived degree of ambiguity of the concept in question.

In terms of the relation between understanding and acceptance, our findings do not support the position that lack of knowledge serves as a barrier to acceptance of human evolution or that lack of acceptance prevents development of evolutionary knowledge. Indeed, we found no significant relation between knowledge of evolution and degree of acceptance, for either human or animal evolution. This suggests that students can have an understanding of evolutionary theory without accepting its validity, or, alternatively, they can accept the validity of the construct based on a very poor understanding of it. In a surprising contrast, a positive relation between understanding and acceptance was found for photosynthesis. This finding is interesting as it indicates that understanding may be related to acceptance, but only in certain instances. In our data, when the content is not related to firmly entrenched beliefs, when it is not perceived as controversial or ambiguous (as is the case of photosynthesis), there is a relationship between acceptance and understanding. But, when the content is related to students' entrenched beliefs and is perceived as controversial and ambiguous, epistemological beliefs and cognitive dispositions play the significant role in acceptance—not knowledge.

Our findings failed to support those of Lawson and Worsnop (1992) regarding the relation between acceptance and knowledge for controversial topics such as evolution. In our study, we found the strongest predictor of students' acceptance of evolutionary theory to be not students' knowledge (as suggested by Lawson & Worsnop, 1992), but students' epistemological beliefs about the certainty of knowledge and their dispositions toward critical thought about the ideas surrounding the controversial issue of human evolution.

In a like manner, our data suggest that the critical component to constructing an understanding of evolution was not belief, as might be expected from the wealth of arguments and some research in this area. Rather, one of the dispositional scales, Beliefs Identification (the degree to which one is disposed to hold on strongly to one's beliefs), showed a very strong relation to knowledge of evolution. This relation coupled with the lack of relation between acceptance and understanding of evolution, suggest that one's willingness to question beliefs may be more important in learning about human evolution than the content of those beliefs. That is, students who are capable of analyzing and questioning their beliefs, even if they do not accept the validity of evolutionary theory, can come to understand the construct. This has some empirical support from more qualitative investigators (Demastes-Southerland et al., 1995; Meadows et al., 2000). Thus, what becomes important in learning evolution is not simply accepting or rejecting evolution; rather, it is a learner's ability to examine and evaluate his or her beliefs.

What is important about our findings is how they contrast to the argument made by Lawson and Worsnop (1992). Indeed, we assert that the actual content of one's beliefs may not be as important when learning about evolution as one's dispositions toward those beliefs. Are students willing to examine what they believe? Do they consider change of beliefs to be favorable? Or do they understand beliefs as ideally fixed entities to be preserved in the face of contradictory information? Our data suggest that students' dispositions toward beliefs as measured directly by the Belief Identification Scale play a more fundamental role in learning about evolution than the actual content of students' beliefs about the construct.

GENERALITY TO OUR FINDINGS TO OTHER DOMAINS

Our findings reveal that the relation between intentional level constructs and understanding varies with the content in question (see Fig. 11.2). Recall that the epistemological construct of comfort with ambiguity and the disposition toward identification with one's beliefs were strongly related to understanding human evolution, but not to photosynthesis or animal evolution. Other research also suggests that epistemological beliefs are evoked more strongly when learning in some domains than others (see Buehl and Alexander, 2001; Hofer, 2000).

Bendixen et al. (1998) and Stanovich (1999) showed that epistemological beliefs and dispositions relate to reasoning about ill-structured problems, and Kardash and Scholes (1996) demonstrated that epistemological beliefs impact the interpretation of controversial topics. Thus, the degree of task complexity and controversy may determine the influence of intentional level cognition on conceptual change. Well-structured problems, with simple noncontroversial answers, may be solved though nonintentional, algo-

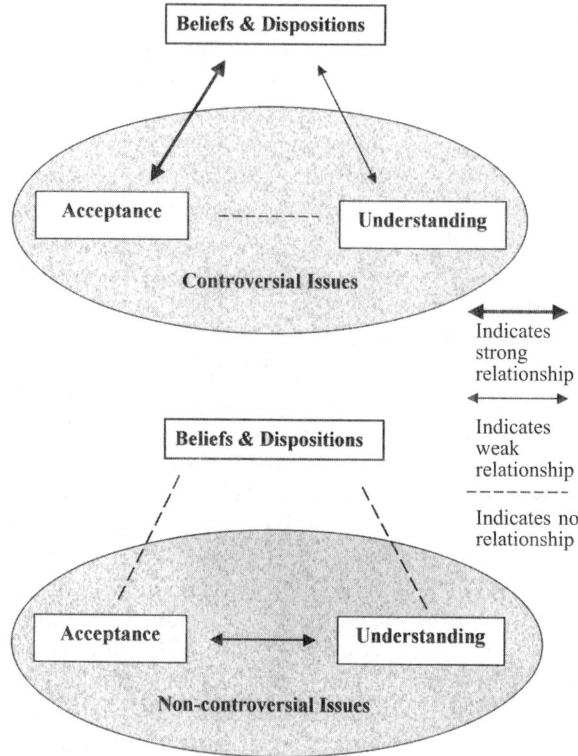

FIG. 11.2. Comparison of construct interactions found for controversial versus noncontroversial issues.

rithmic strategies, such as the automatic activation of background knowledge. When converting from miles to kilometers, intentional level cognition need not come into play if the conversion factor is known.

In contrast, when problems cannot be solved or content cannot be learned though the simple and straightforward application of basic cognitive processes, intentional constructs may be evoked to aid problem solving and learning. Evolution is a complex topic that is inherently difficult to learn even when one's personal beliefs do not conflict with the content. The situation becomes even more complex when firmly held religious beliefs are perceived to be in direct conflict with the scientific explanations of evolution in general, and heightened for explanations of human origins. Thus, the difficulty and controversy surrounding this topic may increase the likelihood that intentional constructs are invoked.

Thus, whether intentional constructs come into play when learning new scientific concepts may depend on the complexity of the topic, the degree to which the content is perceived to be in opposition to the learner's prior conceptions, and the perceived conflict with the learners' broad, culturally-based belief systems. If the content is more well-defined, less controversial, or if the learner does not hold an alternative conception or counter belief system, intentional constructs may not play as important a role in conceptual change. Alternatively, the learning of ill-defined, complex, or controversial topics that conflict with belief systems (such as human evolution) may require that intentional level constructs be evoked if learning and change are to occur.

WHAT IS THE ROLE OF INTENTIONAL CONSTRUCTS IN LEARNING EVOLUTION?

Taken together, our findings and that of the broader literatures paint a portrait of a complex interplay of intentional level constructs when learning about biological evolution. (Figure 11.3 graphically depicts this relationship.) Students' epistemological beliefs, dispositions, and goals are likely to be engaged when learning about controversial topics. Because of the nature of controversial topics, students may need to recognize that knowledge is not fixed, and they may need to be disposed toward open-minded thinking and belief change in order to construct a scientific understanding of evolutionary theory. We argue that intentional level cognitive processes are essential for students to be able to do the deep processing necessary to compare rival knowledge and belief systems, to weigh the explanatory power of each, and to be able to choose which explanation for biological change they will accept. Thus, intentional learning can play an essential role in conceptual change about evolution, although based on our own data it may be that such intentional level constructs are far more influential in terms of shaping a learner's acceptance of evolution. This last assertion is offered hesitantly, as the weak relationship we documented may be due to the methodological difficulties of measuring epistemological beliefs, so our data may not adequately portray underlying relationships. On the other hand, intentional level constructs may have a weaker impact on understanding simply due to the cognitive complexity of evolutionary theory, and so many other factors (such as a learner's background knowledge, reasoning abilities) also play an important role in shaping the learning that occurs.

Note that although our empirical work did not address the role of affect in learning about evolution, this construct is included in our model. Much of the previous philosophical and pedagogical literature on evolution education focused on the role negative affect plays in learning about evolution, and the role of affect has been acknowledged by many conceptual change theorists as we as a community have come to understand that con-

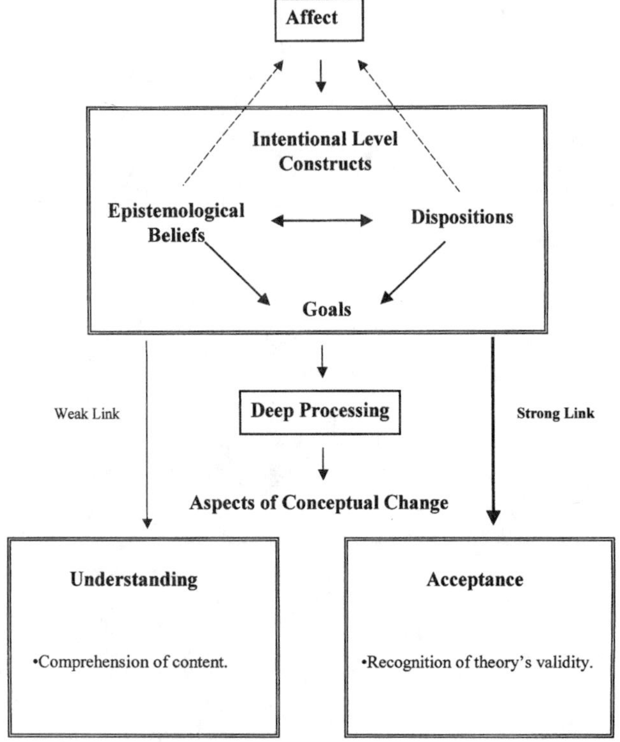

FIG. 11.3. Model of the role of intentional level constructs in learning controversial topics.

ceptual change is not a "cold process" (Dole & Sinatra, 1998; Pintrich et al., 1993; Demastes-Southerland et al., 1995). We do understand affect to play a mediating role in the conceptual change process, having a recursive relationship with the constructs of epistemology and dispositions, and allowing for or inhibiting the invocation of intentional level constructs and subsequent processing of information. More research is needed, however, before we can fully explicate that role.

HELPING STUDENTS BECOME INTENTIONAL LEARNERS: TEACHING ABOUT THE NATURE OF SCIENCE AND EVOLUTION

We argued that intentional level constructs are essential in learning about a controversial topic such as biological evolution. If conceptual change requires that students compare rival explanations, then such comparisons require a relatively sophisticated epistemological view, particularly in terms of students' scientific epistemologies, awareness of these views, and relatively open-minded, nonabsolutist personal dispositions. But how can such intentional learning be fostered in a science classroom? We argue that the most productive avenue for allowing students who might hold opposing religious views to come to understand evolutionary theory is to explicitly focus on their epistemological views and learning dispositions. The instruction described in this section, although it was developed through a series of authors not necessarily mindful of the role of intentionality in learning, can indeed allow for the development of evolutionary knowledge because of its initial development of a learner's intentional level cognition.

Scharmann (1990), in his description of a diversified instructional approach to the teaching of evolution, addressed two aspects of our model of intentional learning—the role of emotions and epistemology. The basis of Scharmann's proposal is that students need "a place to stand between two extremes" (p. 98) when learning about evolution. Scharmann explained that students need to be aware that consideration of evolutionary theory does not require that they turn away from long-held, firmly entrenched religious beliefs. Such a "place to stand" ensures that students' emotional reactions to instruction do not prevent them from further engaging with the material.

But how does a teacher create such a place in the classroom? Scharmann suggested that a diversified instructional strategy that targets not only evolutionary constructs, but also focuses on students' understandings of the nature of scientific knowledge, allows for students to consider scientific concepts without forcing them to turn away from culturally-based understandings. This need to ensure that students understand that science cannot and should not replace students' cultural knowledge is echoed by Southerland (2000) and NRC (1998), who emphasized the importance of detailing the limits of scientific knowledge. Teaching about evolution requires that students become familiar with the methodological principles of scientific knowledge (i.e., a realist ontology, rejection of metaphysical explanations, premium placed on parsimonious explanations) that by their very nature set boundaries on what science can address. As was described by Poole (1996):

> Science is the study of the world of nature. Religion includes questions about whether there is anything *other than* nature (e.g., God) to which nature owes its existence. As a matter of logic it is no use pointing to science, the study of nature to find out whether there is anything other than nature. . . . There are certain questions which science, as the study of physical observables, is unable to address (p. 165).

Thus, through such a nonscientistic, diversified instructional approach, students' epistemological views are developed to a point that they can begin to consider rival explanations, as emotionally they are not prevented from such a consideration.

Although such an understanding of the nature of science seems to be an overly ambitious goal for science instruction, a variety of educators offer specific suggestions for achieving this goal. Duveen and Soloman (1994) argued that the intersection of science and social concerns could be taught through role plays of the evolution–creation controversy. Although such discussions allow students to recognize the limits of various forms of knowledge claims, the National Academy of Sciences (1998) describes how the history of the development of a specific scientific theory is useful for demonstrating the tentative nature of scientific knowledge, the process of how a theory is challenged, what counts as scientific evidence, and how the cultural context influences a theory and its refinement. This instruction, therefore, would target the intentional level construct of students' disposition toward ambiguity. As scientific knowledge is portrayed as realistically and ideally tentative, constantly open to change and revision, this knowledge may allows students to gain some degree of comfort with ambiguity, thus allowing for closer and more serious consideration of evolutionary theory.

Scharmann (1990) also offered an account of how explicit deliberation of the methods and assumptions of science, as well as an explicit exploration of areas in which science conflicts with religious beliefs, are essential in allowing students to develop a more contemporary understanding of the nature of science. Through the use of controversial readings in natural history, small-group peer discussion about these readings, and reflective writings, students explore and develop their conceptions of the nature of science. Scharmann argued that an explicit understanding of the tentative, contextual, powerful nature of science, one that is bounded in terms of the topics it can address, is essential to students. We argue that such activities are essential because they allow for the development of students' intentional level constructs of epistemological views on the role of beliefs and the learning disposition to be comfortable with ambiguity—both of which we have found to be linked to the development of students' evolutionary knowledge. Because these constructs are the explicit focus of instruction, as they are developed, they are brought into conscious attention, and so they can be used intentionally to achieve learning outcomes, thus allowing for a greater understanding of evolutionary theory.

It is important to note, here, that the goal of such instruction is not to change students' religious beliefs or persuade them to accept evolutionary theory (although we must acknowledge that both sophisticated epistemological beliefs and dispositions do have a strong bearing on a learner's acceptance of evolution). Instead, the goal of such instruction is to help students understand how science does not provide the only answers important in their lives. This, in turn, decreases potential aversion to concepts and may help to avoid the negative emotions that can impede instruction related to evolution, allowing for intentional level constructs to be invoked. Then, through deep processing (Chinn & Brewer, 1993) or what Dole and Sinatra (1998) called *high engagement*, required by activities such as conducting inquiries, writing personal reflection, and justifying one's reasoning, the learner can examine his or her own conceptions and compare them to the content of evolution. Thus, intentional level constructs have the potential to allow for a deeper understanding of evolution.

At this point, let us return to Ms. Galloway's classroom and paint a picture of how instruction could have made a place for students to stand in the situation described earlier:

> *Throughout the school year, Ms. Galloway engaged her students in analyzing the nature of science during her biology class. From the outset, her students explored the boundaries of scientific knowledge, its presuppositions, and the ways it intersected other ways of understanding the world. Students were used to comparing scientific knowledge with knowledge produced through other inquiries, such as the arts and religion. Because of this familiarity with current conceptions of the nature of science—but more importantly, because of their anticipation that their ideas and counter viewpoints would be acknowledged in the classroom, students came anxious to contribute from the outset of the unit on evolution. Many came with specific questions about how the ideas they understood science to be asserting conflicted with their own religious ideas. Expectedly, Ms. Galloway began the unit asking: "What do you know about evolutionary theory—both conceptually and emotionally? Where does this theory intersect with your own ideas about change in a species?" After identifying students' reservations and reminding them both of the boundaries of scientific knowledge and the distinction between understanding and accepting a concept, Ms. Galloway began more traditional instruction. In this she emphasized not only the conceptual content of evolution, but also the process of how scientists came to know this content. While not all the students accepted these assertions, and not all the students formed scientific conceptions about this content, the emotional atmosphere of the classroom was open, enhancing students' degree of engagement with the material. As a result, many of her students developed their understanding of evolutionary theory.*

REFERENCES

Anderson, J. R. (1990). *The adaptive character of thought*. Hillsdale, NJ: Lawrence Erlbaum Associates.

Bargh, J. A., & Chartrand, T. L. (1999). The unbearable automaticity of being. *American Psychologist, 54*(7), 462–479.

Bendixen, L. D., Schraw, G., & Dunkle, M. E. (1998). Epistemic beliefs and moral reasoning. *Journal of Psychology, 132*(2), 187–200.

Bereiter, C. (1990). Aspects of an educational learning theory. *Review of Educational Research, 60*, 603–624.

Bishop, B. A., & Anderson, C. W. (1990). Student conceptions of natural selection and its role in evolution. *Journal of Research in Science Teaching, 27*, 415–427.

Brewer, W. F., & Chinn, C. A. (1991). Entrenched beliefs, inconsistent information, and knowledge change. In L. Birnbaum (Ed.), *The International Journal of the Learning Sciences: Proceedings of the 1991 Conference* (pp. 67–73). Charlottesville, NC: Association for the Advancement of Computing in Education.

Buehl, M. M., & Alexander, P. A. (2001). Beliefs about academic knowledge. *Educational Psychology Review, 13*(4), 385–418.

Cacioppo, J. T., Petty, R. E., Feinstein, J., & Jarvis, W. (1996). Dispositional differences in cognitive motivation: The life and times of individuals varying in need for cognition. *Psychological Bulletin, 119*, 197–253.

Chan, C., & Bereiter, C. (1992, April). *Effects of conflict and knowledge-processing strategy on conceptual change.* Paper presented at the Annual Meeting of the American Educational Research Association, San Francisco, CA.

Chi, M. T. H. (1992). Conceptual change within and across ontological categories: Examples from learning and discovery in science. In R. N. Giere (Ed.), *Minnesota studies in the philosophy of science: Vol. XV. Cognitive models of science* (pp. 129–186). Minneapolis, MN: University of Minnesota Press.

Chinn, C. A., & Brewer, W. F. (1993). The role of anomalous data in knowledge acquisition: A theoretical framework and implications for science instruction. *Review of Educational Research, 63*(10), 1–49.

Cobern, W. W. (1994). Belief, understanding, and the teaching of evolution. *Journal for Research in Science Teaching, 31*(5), 583–590.

Costa, P. T., & McCrae, R. R. (1992). Normal Personality Assessment in Clinical Practice: The NEO Personality Inventory. *Psychological Assessment, 4*(1), 5–13.

Demastes, S., Settlage, J., & Good, R. (1995). Students' conceptions of natural selection and its role in evolution: Cases of replication and comparison. *Journal of Research in Science Teaching, 32*(5), 535–550.

Demastes-Southerland, S., Good, R., & Peebles, P. (1995). Students' conceptual ecologies and the process of conceptual change in evolution. *Science Education, 79*(6), 637–666.

Demastes-Southerland, S., Good, R., & Peebles, P. (1996). Patterns of conceptual change in evolution. *Journal of Research in Science Teaching, 33*(4), 407–431.

Dole, J. A., & Sinatra, G. M. (1998). Reconceptualizing change in the cognitive construction of knowledge. *Educational Psychologist, 33*(2/3), 109–128.

Dole, J. A., Sinatra, G. M., & Reynolds, R. E. (1991, December). *The effects of strong beliefs on text processing: The case of evolution and creationism.* Paper presented at the National Reading Conference Annual Meeting, Palm Springs, CA.

Duschl, R. (1988). Abandoning the scientistic legacy of science education. *Science Education, 72*, 51–62.

Duveen, J., & Soloman, J. (1994). The great evolution trial: Use of role-play in the classroom. *Journal of Research in Science Teaching, 31*(5), 575–582.

Erwin, T. D. (1983). The scale of intellectual development: Measuring Perry's scheme. *Journal of College Student Personnel, 24*, 6–12.

Fisher, K. M. (1992). Teaching of evolution. In R. Good, J. Wandersee, M. Hafner, J. Trowbridge, & S. Demastes (Eds.), *Proceedings of the 1992 Evolution Education Research Conference* (pp. 103–108). Baton Rouge, LA: Louisiana State University Education Conference.

Haslam, F., & Treagust, D. F. (1987). Diagnosing secondary students' misconceptions of photosynthesis and respiration in plants using a two-tier multiple choice instrument. *Journal of Biological Education, 21*(3), 203–211.

Hofer, B. (2000). Dimensionality and disciplinary differences in personal epistemology. *Contemporary Educational Psychology, 25*, 378–405.

Hofer, B. K., & Pintrich, P. R. (1997). The development of epistemological theories: Beliefs about knowledge and knowing and their relation to learning. *Review of Educational Research, 67*(1), 88–140.

Jackson, D. F. (2000). *Shifting the relationship between personal and professional beliefs and practices in regards to evolution.* A paper presented at the annual meeting of the National Association of Research in Science Teaching, New Orleans, LA.

Johnson, R. L., & Peebles, E. E. (1987). The role of scientific understanding in college: Student acceptance of evolution. *American Biology Teacher, 49*(2), 93–98.

Kardash, C. M., & Scholes, R. J. (1996). Effects of preexisting beliefs, epistemological beliefs, and need for cognition on interpretation of controversial issues. *Journal of Educational Psychology, 88*(2), 260–271.

King, P. M., & Kitchener, K. S. (1994). *Developing reflective judgment: Understanding and promoting intellectual growth an critical thinking in adolescents and adults.* San Francisco: Jossey-Bass.

Lawson, A. E. (1999). A scientific approach to teaching about evolution and special creation. *American Biology Teacher, 61*(4), 266–274.

Lawson, A. E., & Worsnop, W. A. (1992). Learning about evolution and rejecting a belief in special creation: Effects of reflective reasoning skill, prior knowledge, prior belief, and religious commitment. *Journal of Research in Science Teaching, 29*(2), 143–166.

Linnenbrink, E. A., & Pintrich, P. R. (2002). The role of motivational beliefs in conceptual change. In M. Limón & L. Mason (Eds.), *Reconsidering conceptual change: Issues in theory and practice* (pp. 115–135). Dordrecht, The Netherlands: Kluwer Academic Publishers.

Lord, T., & Marino, S. (1993). How university students view the theory of evolution. *Journal of College Science Teaching, XXII*(6), 353–357.

McComas, W. F. (1998). The principal elements of the nature of science: Dispelling the myths. In W. F. McComas (Ed.), *The nature of science in science education* (pp. 53–70). Netherlands: Kluwer.

Meadows, L., Doster, E., & Jackson, D. F. (2000). Managing the conflict between evolution and religion. *The American Biology Teacher, 62*(2), 102–107.

National Academy of Sciences (1998). *Teaching about evolution and the nature of science.* Washington, DC: National Academy Press.

Newell, A. (1990). *Unified theories of cognition.* Cambridge, MA: Harvard University Press.

Pintrich, P. R. (2000a). The role of goal-orientation in self-regulated learning. In M. Boekaerts, P. R. Pintrich, & M. Zeidner (Eds.), *Handbook of self-regulated learning.* New York: Academic Press.

Pintrich, P. R. (2000b). An achievement goal theory perspective on issues in motivation terminology, theory, and research. *Contemporary Educational Psychology, 25*, 92–104.

Pintrich, P. R. (2000c). Multiple goals, multiple pathways: The role of goal orientation in learning and achievement. *Journal of Educational Psychology, 92*, 544–555.

Pintrich, P., Marx, R., & Boyle, R. (1993). Beyond cold conceptual change: The role of motivational beliefs and classroom contextual factors in the process of conceptual change. *Review of Educational Research, 63*(2), 167–199.

Poole, M. (1996). "... for more and better religious education." *Science and Education, 5*, 165–174.

Posner, G. J., Strike, K. A., Hewson, P. W., & Gertzog, W. A. (1982). Accommodation of a scientific conception: Towards a theory of conceptual change. *Science Education, 67*(4), 489–508.

Rumelhart, D. E., & Norman, D. A. (1981). Accretion, tuning, and restructuring: Three modes of learning. In J. W. Cotton & R. Klatzky (Eds.), *Semantic factors in cognition* (pp. 37–90). Hillsdale, NJ: Lawrence Erlbaum Associates.

Sa, W., West, R. F., & Stanovich, K. E. (1999). The domain specificity and generality of belief bias in reasoning and judgement. *Journal of Educational Psychology, 91*(3), 497–510.

Scharmann, L. C. (1990). Enhancing an understanding of the premises of evolutionary theory: The influence of a diversified instructional strategy. *School Science and Mathematics, 90*(2), 91–100.

Scharmann, L. C., & Harris, W. H. (1991). *Teaching evolution: Understanding, concerns, and instructional approaches.* Paper presented at the annual meeting of the National Association for Research in Science Teaching, Fontana, WS.

Schommer, M. (1990). Effects of beliefs about the nature of knowledge on comprehension. *Journal of Educational Psychology, 82*, 498–504.

Schommer, M. (1994). Synthesizing epistemological belief research: Tentative understandings and provocative confusions. *Educational Psychology Review, 6*, 293–319.

Settlage, J., & Jensen, M. (1996). Investigating the inconsistencies in college student responses to natural selection test questions. *Electronic Journal of Science Education* [On-line]. Available: http://unr.edu/homepage/jcannon/euse/settlage.html.

Siegel, H. (1998). Knowledge, truth, and education. In D. Carr (Ed.), *Education, knowledge and truth: Beyond the postmodern impasse* (pp. 19–36). London: Routledge.

Sinatra, G. M., Southerland, S., McConaughy, F., & Demastes, J. (2001, April). The Role of Intentions, Beliefs, and Knowledge in Learning about Evolution. In L. D. Bendixen (Chair), *Epistemological beliefs and learning: What do we know and how do we know it?* Symposium presented at the American Educational Research Association Annual Meeting, Seattle, WA.

Smith, M. U. (1994). Counterpoint: Belief, understanding, and the teaching of evolution. *Journal for Research in Science Teaching, 31*(5), 591–597.

Smith, M. U., Siegel, H., & McInerney, J. D. (1995). Foundational issues in evolution education. *Science & Education, 4*, 23–46.

Smith, M. U., & Scharmann, L. C. (1999). Defining versus describing the nature of science: A pragmatic analysis for classroom teachers and science educators. *Journal for Research in Science Teaching, 83*, 493–509.

Southerland, S. A. (2000). Epistemic universalism and the shortcomings of curricular multicultural science education. *Science & Education, 9*(3), 289–307.

Speelman, C. (1998). The automaticity of discourse comprehension. In K. Kirsner, C. Speelman, M. Maybery, A. O'Brien-Malone, M. Anderson, & C. Macleod (Eds.), *Implicit and explicit mental processes.* Mahwah, NJ: Lawrence Erlbaum Associates.

Stanovich, K. E. (1999). *Who is rational? Studies of individual differences in reasoning.* Mahwah, NJ: Lawrence Erlbaum Associates.

Stanovich, K. E., & West, R. F. (1997). Reasoning independently of prior belief and individual differences in actively open-minded thinking. *Journal of Educational Psychology, 89*, 342–357.

Stanovich, K. E., & West, R. F. (1998). Individual differences in rational thought. *Journal of Experimental Psychology: General, 127*, 161–188.

Strike, K. A., & Posner, G. J. (1992). A revisionist theory of conceptual change. In R. A. Dushl & R. J. Hamilton (Eds.), *Philosophy of science, cognitive psychology, and educational theory and practice* (pp. 147–176). Albany, NY: State University of New York Press.

Thagard, P. (1992). *Conceptual revolutions.* Princeton, NJ: Princeton University Press.

Troldahl, V., & Powell, F. (1965). A short-form dogmatism scale for use in field studies. *Social Forces, 44*, 211–215.

Venville, G., & Treagust, D. (1998). Exploring conceptual change in genetics using a multidimensional interpretive framework. *Journal of Research in Science Teaching, 35*(9), 1031–1055.

Vosniadou, S., & Brewer, W. F. (1987). Theories of knowledge restructuring in development. *Review of Educational Research, 57*(1), 51–67.

12

Achievement Goals and Intentional Conceptual Change

Elizabeth A. Linnenbrink
Paul R. Pintrich
The University of Michigan

Much of the work on conceptual change emphasizes the importance of considering students' prior knowledge as either a facilitating or constraining factor in the development of new understandings (Strike & Posner, 1992). That is, in order to understand the emergence of a refined conceptual understanding, researchers and educators must consider not only the context in which the new information is learned, but also what the learner "brings" to the situation. What is largely missing from this account, however, is the motivational orientation of the learner (Pintrich, Marx, & Boyle, 1993). The consideration of students' prior conceptions as well as their motivational orientation seems key to understanding when and why conceptual change occurs. Indeed, a number of researchers studying conceptual change have pointed to students' beliefs about their competence as well as their attitudes toward learning as important for understanding conceptual change processes (e.g., Pintrich, 1999; Pintrich et al., 1993; Sinatra & Dole, 1998; Strike & Posner, 1992). In this chapter, we consider the role of motivation in the conceptual change process, focusing specifically on how achievement goals relate to intentional conceptual change. Before we begin a detailed discussion of the relationship of achievement goals to intentional conceptual change, we first discuss what we mean by intentional conceptual change as well as how we define student motivation in terms of achievement goals.

INTENTIONAL CONCEPTUAL CHANGE

There are many models of conceptual change; in this chapter, we focus on two general categories or perspectives. The first general perspective is what we call the cognitive–developmental perspective on conceptual change; we label the second category the cognitive–contextual perspective. A key issue for both perspectives is what develops or what changes with conceptual understanding. In the cognitive–developmental model, given its roots in Piagetian and general organismic models, the nature of change is defined by the transition in internal cognitive structures, often called student theories or mental models (e.g., Vosniadou & Brewer, 1992, 1994; Vosniadou, chapter 13, this volume). According to this perspective, conceptual change is defined in terms of a change from using naïve theories or misconceptions to the use of more sophisticated theories and more scientifically accurate conceptions. The important idea is that these theories, models, or conceptions are internally organized in a coherent and explanatory fashion such that the nature of change involves changing the theory or model (Wellman & Gelman, 1998; Vosniadou, chapter 13, this volume). Of course, this change usually happens very gradually with experience over time, but development involves a change in the underlying domain-specific conceptual structure, theory, framework, or model.

In contrast, the cognitive–contextual perspective suggests that what changes is not an organized and structural theory or model, but rather the use of different ideas or different "bits of knowledge" or p-prims (e.g., diSessa, 1993; diSessa, Elby, & Hammer, chapter 9, this volume; Smith, diSessa, & Roschelle, 1993). Although cognitive–contextual models posit that there are some internal representations of knowledge that change over time, they do not assume that these ideas are organized in more coherent explanatory models or theories, especially in young children or naïve learners. In addition, these models place a stronger emphasis on the situated nature of cognition and how the use of ideas and concepts is activated, encouraged, supported, or constrained by the local context. In this case, what changes over time is the use of the different bits of knowledge in context. The models assume that individuals become more sophisticated in their use of these ideas and are better able to use the ideas in scientifically appropriate ways, depending on the context. Although the cognitive–developmental model also includes an important role for contextual factors, it tends to stress the internal organization and change in student theories or models.

Of course, there are other "strong" situated cognition perspectives on conceptual change that do not assume any internal representations of knowledge and instead focus on language use and discourse. However, given our focus on the cognitive and motivational psychological factors in conceptual change, we do not discuss these perspectives in this chapter.

We focus our discussion on how the issues of motivation and intentionality might play a role in the cognitive–developmental and cognitive–contextual perspectives on conceptual change. We now turn to the issue of intentionality and conceptual change.

The general issue of intentionality has a long and problematic history in both philosophy and psychology (see Brandtstadter, 1998; Dennett, 1996; Ferrari & Elik, chapter 2, this volume; Searle, 1998). In this chapter we do not dwell on many of these problems, but rather adopt a more pragmatic and psychological approach that focuses on the role of goals as well as individuals' purposeful attempts to attain those goals. This perspective emphasizes the guiding and directing function of goals as well as the various strategies that individuals might use to attain those goals (Brandtstadter, 1998; Pintrich, 2000c). Of course, this general intentional and self-regulatory perspective has been used to describe a great number of psychological systems and behavioral actions (Bandura, 1997; Boekaerts, Pintrich, & Zeidner, 2000; Brandtstadter, 1998), but it is not often applied to conceptual change. In this chapter, we attempt to integrate the intentional and regulatory perspective with models of conceptual change.

Although there are important differences in the cognitive–developmental and cognitive–contextual perspectives on conceptual change, both of them are concerned with how students come to change their conceptual understanding. If we then apply the intentional perspective to this problem (Ferrari & Elik, chapter 2, this volume), there seem to be three important core aspects of intentional conceptual change. First, there must be a goal the individual is actively pursuing, and the goal content must have something to do with changing one's prior knowledge or conceptual system. For example, the student must be pursuing a goal such as "I want to understand how X works," with the X being some common topic such as heat and temperature, motion and gravity, photosynthesis, etc. This type of understanding goal is different from other goals students might adopt in the classroom such as just getting good grades, doing the least amount of work, or staying out of trouble.

The second key aspect is that the individual should be aware or conscious at some level that he or she is pursuing this goal of conceptual understanding. For example, this would be reflected in the student who says, "I don't seem to understand this, my ideas about heat don't seem to match others. I need to think about this and maybe do something different to learn it better." This assumption does not mean that implicit or unconscious processes do not play a role; they are obviously important in conceptual change. It just means that there is metacognitive awareness of one's goal and one's progress towards this goal. Most models of conceptual change include metaconceptual or metacognitive awareness as an important aspect of change (see Vosniadou, chapter 13, this volume), so this second assumption is probably the least controversial of the three core aspects of intentional conceptual change.

Finally, a third core aspect of the intentional perspective is that there must be some type of agency, control, volition, or self-regulation on the individual's part as he or she uses various strategies to obtain this goal of conceptual understanding. That is, one should actively try to change one's understanding through one's own efforts at controlling one's own learning and thinking. For example, a student who wants to understand some phenomenon may try to use particular strategies to learn more about the topic, to check his or her understanding as he or she progresses, to spend more time at learning about the topic, etc. Of course, the student may be directed to use these strategies by the teacher or others, or by the press of the context, but in this case, the student would be assumed to be "other-regulated," not self-regulated. The important assumption is that the individual, to some extent, actually controls his or her own learning in an intentional and active manner. At the same time, the intentional perspective does not discount contextual factors or the important role that other regulation processes can play in conceptual change. It just argues for the possibility that students can take some control over their own learning (Pintrich, 2000c).

In addition, we hasten to add that we are not proposing that all conceptual change is intentional. There are clearly occasions when none of these three assumptions apply, and yet children do advance in their conceptual understandings. In particular, we assume that there are strong developmental differences in intentional conceptual change with very young children, who are less able to set goals and develop strategies, and who are less metacognitive in general, being unlikely to engage in intentional conceptual change. However, young children clearly do change their framework theories and conceptual understandings (Wellman & Gelman, 1998). Accordingly, we do not assume that intentional conceptual change is the whole story; in fact, it may only be a small part of the story of conceptual change, but it may be an important part. Given the importance of intentionality for conceptual change, the remainder of this chapter discusses the role of achievement goals and how they may help to guide and direct student efforts at intentional conceptual change. In other words, we address how achievement goals relate to the three criteria of intentional conceptual change.

ACHIEVEMENT GOAL THEORY

Before continuing with the discussion of the relation of motivation to intentional conceptual change, it is important to discuss our theoretical framework for understanding students' motivation and to provide some justification for the use of this framework. Over the years, researchers studying students' motivational processes have considered a variety of different theories including attribution theory, self-determination theory, expectancy-value theory, self-efficacy theory, and achievement goal theory, to name a few. In this chapter, we use achievement goal theory as a basis for understanding students' motivation in relation to conceptual change. We focus on achievement goal theory as this is a predominant theory among motivational theories today (Weiner, 1990). Furthermore, because achievement goals are situated, can be altered by the context, and are not based solely on individual differences, as is the case for a number of motivational constructs, achievement goal theory lends itself to applications in educational settings. That is, specific recommendations can be made to educators regarding how to promote mastery versus performance goals in classrooms. Finally, and most importantly, given our assumptions about intentional conceptual change and the importance of goals in intentional conceptual change, achievement goal theory is especially relevant in that it explicitly addresses the role of goals in motivation and learning.

Achievement goal theory suggests that students' goals for learning frame the way that they interpret and react to events (Dweck & Leggett, 1988). There are two main goals that serve as the basis for much of the research on achievement goal theory: *mastery goals*, where the focus is on learning and understanding, and *performance goals*, where the focus is demonstrating one's ability in comparison to others. Before describing these goals in detail, it is important to distinguish achievement goals from more specific *target goals* and more general *purpose goals*.

Target goals are specific goals for a situation such as getting 90% of the questions correct on an exam or finishing 10 pages on the paper you are writing (Harackiewicz & Sansone, 1991). In contrast, purpose goals are more general goals representing one's overall goals for life or the reasons why a person engages in various target goals (Ford, 1992). These goals are broad in that they have applications for all areas of life. Achievement goals represent a middle ground between purpose and target goals. That is, achievement goals are more general than target goals; they represent a general orientation toward achievement activities rather than a specific goal for a specific task. However, they are more specific than purpose goals in that they are only applicable in achievement situations and reflect why a person is engaging in a particular achievement task.

A student with a mastery goal orientation engages in achievement activities in order to learn, improve, and better understand what is being taught. These goals have alternatively been called learning goals (Dweck & Leggett, 1988), because students with these goals are most concerned with learning the information presented, or task goals (Maehr & Midgley,

1991; Nicholls, 1984), given the focus of attention on the task. In contrast, a student with a performance goal orientation is taking part in the activity in order to demonstrate his or her ability, often in comparison to others; a student with a performance goal will report that he tried to do well so that he would look smart or would do better than the other students in his class. Performance goals have also been referred to as ego-goals (Nicholls, 1984), which reflect the focus of performance goals on the self. That is, a basic premise behind a performance goal orientation is that one is trying to demonstrate the quality of one's ability and self-worth. Students with this goal are much more focused on these aspects of the self rather than the task to be learned (Maehr & Kaplan, 2000). It is important to note that these two achievement goals are thought to be orthogonal. Thus, it is possible for students to report endorsing high levels of both goals simultaneously (Pintrich, 2000b).

One of the promising aspects of applying achievement goals to classroom situations is that the context in which students work is thought to shape their achievement goals (Ames, 1992). Mastery goals are promoted in contexts where teachers emphasize learning and create situations in which students are able to make choices and feel autonomous. Evaluating and recognizing students for improvement can also help promote the adoption of mastery goals. In contrast, performance goals are promoted in contexts where teachers use normative grading practices and recognize students for their performance relative to others. Thus, unlike other motivational theories, which often consider individual differences as the sole predictors of motivation, achievement goal theory suggests that students' goal orientations can be influenced by the context in which the activity occurs.

Given the importance of goals and the role they play in intentional conceptual change, it is also important to consider how these two achievement goals, mastery and performance goals, relate to goals as we defined them in terms of intentionality. As noted earlier, one important aspect of intentional conceptual change is that a student must have a goal relating to changing his or her prior knowledge or altering his or her understanding of a concept. It is clear that students with mastery goals meet this criterion. Students with mastery goals are likely to report goals such as "I wanted to understand the material" or "I focused on improving my understanding of the concepts being taught." In contrast, it is not clear whether or not a performance goal meets this criterion. For instance, one performance-oriented student may report that he was focused on changing his understanding of a particular concept in order to be the best student in the class. Alternatively, it seems just as likely, and perhaps more likely, that another performance-oriented student would report that she was focused on trying to do better than others and make no mention of trying to understand the material or alter her prior understandings about the topic. In the first instance, the goal seems to meet the first criterion for intentional conceptual change, that students pursue a goal related to changing their prior knowledge. In the second instance, the goal does not meet this criterion

In terms of how achievement goals relate to learning in classroom settings, research examining the role of achievement goals on a variety of academic outcomes suggests that, overall, mastery goals are adaptive for learning situations. In particular, mastery goals are associated with increased persistence and engagement (Elliott & Dweck, 1988) as well as in-depth processing (Graham & Golan, 1991) and self-regulation (Pintrich, 2000b). So, students with mastery goals become more involved in various activities and this involvement is often of very high quality. In addition to the cognitive and behavioral benefits of mastery goals, mastery goals have also been associated with increased interest (Harackiewicz, Barron, & Elliot, 1998), higher positive affect (Roeser, Midgley, & Urdan, 1996), and reduced negative affect (Linnenbrink, Ryan, & Pintrich, 1999). Given this positive relation to self-regulation and in-depth processing, it seems likely that students with mastery goals also meet the other two criteria for intentional conceptual change. That is, mastery-oriented students are likely to be aware of their progress toward their goals and will employ self-regulatory strategies to meet these goals.

Traditionally, goal theorists have linked performance goals to a variety of maladaptive outcomes including decreased persistence, increased negative affect, use of more superficial rather than deep cognitive processing, and decreased self-regulation (Dweck & Leggett, 1988; Elliott & Dweck, 1988; Pintrich, 2000c). More recently, however, several studies found that performance goals can be adaptive in certain situations. For example, Harackiewicz and her colleagues found that students who adopted performance goals often received higher grades in introductory psychology classes (Harackiewicz, Barron, Carter, Lehto, & Elliot, 1997, Harackiewicz et al., 1998). Others suggested that performance goals may be adaptive when adopted in conjunction with mastery goals (Pintrich, 2000b, 2000c). However, the exact conditions under which performance goals are adaptive have not yet been clearly defined. Given the mixed findings relating performance goals to self-regulation and strategy use, it is unclear whether or not performance-oriented students will meet the second and third criteria for intentional conceptual change (i.e., metacognitive awareness of their goal and self-regulation or agency in pursuing this goal). Nevertheless, we do see different patterns for learning based on students' adoption of mastery versus performance goals; therefore, it seems logical to suggest that achievement goals may help to explain why some students, but not others, undergo conceptual reconfigurations even when they are presented with the same material.

ACHIEVEMENT GOALS AND INTENTIONAL CONCEPTUAL CHANGE

As is apparent from this discussion, students' motivation is not an all-or-none phenomenon. That is, it is not enough to consider *whether* students are motivated, we must also consider *what* motivates them—whether they are focused on learning or demonstrating their ability or both. Making this distinction seems essential to furthering our understanding of the role of motivational processes in conceptual change. For instance, a recent book on conceptual change edited by Guzzetti and Hynd (1998) began by describing several different examples of students' conceptual change. In one example, Moje and Shepardson (1998) described four students working in a group to learn about electrical circuits. These four students all interacted with each other and the task in very different ways. One student was focused on trying to solve the problem of describing a closed circuit. He seemed intent on learning about the circuit to the point of annoying the other students. Another student was so concerned about completing the worksheet assigned by the teacher and demonstrating his ability to the other students that he did not really care whether he, or the other group members, understood how to form a closed circuit. The third student at times seemed concerned about demonstrating her competence and at other times seemed to disengage. The fourth student seemed fairly uninterested and unmotivated to learn the task.

What is apparent from this example is that students in the same classroom working on the same task may interact with the same materials in very different ways. And, although the first and second students both seemed "motivated," their engagement in the activity was quite different. One explanation for these very different types of engagement is that these students had different achievement goals. The first student seemed to have adopted a mastery goal, whereas the second and third students acted in ways suggesting that they endorsed performance goals. The fourth student did not really seem to have any type of motivational goal at all. Considering achievement goals in this instance may not only help us to understand why the various students did not gain the same conceptual understanding from working on the same activity, but also help us to understand what we can do in classrooms to promote the engagement of all students.

The idea of considering students' achievement goals when studying conceptual change is not new. Indeed, Pintrich has written several key articles regarding the potential importance of achievement goals and other motivational processes for conceptual change (i.e., Pintrich, 1999; Pintrich et al., 1993). However, these articles focused primarily on the potential relation of motivational processes to conceptual change via depth of processing. This contribution has played an important role in urging conceptual change theorists and researchers to consider motivational and affective components of conceptual change. There is, however, a need to go beyond indirect relations of achievement goals to conceptual change. Therefore, a central focus of the remainder of this chapter is to explain *why* achievement goals may change the focus of the students and may directly impact the degree of conceptual change that can occur.

We begin by reviewing the existing, although very limited, empirical research on achievement goals and conceptual change. Using this research as a guide for how achievement goals relate to conceptual change, we then discuss, theoretically, *why* achievement goals relate to conceptual change. In this theoretical discussion, we consider how achievement goals may relate to conceptual change from both a cognitive–developmental perspective and a cognitive–contextual perspective. We then address possible mediators in the relation between achievement goals and conceptual change, still keeping in mind that this process may differ depending on one's theoretical perspective of conceptual change. Throughout this discussion, we focus on intentional conceptual change rather than conceptual change that occurs without some level of conscious awareness or goal for change.

Limited Empirical Evidence on the Relations Between Achievement Goals and Conceptual Change

The limited research available regarding the relation of mastery goals to conceptual change suggests that a mastery orientation promotes conceptual change (Lee & Anderson, 1993; Linnenbrink & Pintrich, 2002). In particular, Lee and Anderson (1993) conducted a qualitative study examining 12 students in two sixth-grade classrooms. They observed these students over the course of 40 lessons designed to teach students about matter and kinetic molecular theory. The authors interviewed students prior to the lessons to assess their motivation, attitudes, and understanding of the science concepts. They then observed the students during the lessons and interviewed them afterwards. The results suggested that students who reported a focus on understanding as their primary goal orientation (mastery goals) showed the greatest gains in conceptual understanding. These students were actively engaged in the learning activities and had an improved understanding of the concepts after the lesson.

At the University of Michigan, we also have documented the positive relation of mastery goals to conceptual change. In particular, we conducted two studies examining the change in college students' understanding of Newtonian physics after reading a passage designed to induce conceptual change. Using self-report measures of goals, we found that students who endorsed a mastery goal orientation showed a greater gain in their understanding of Newtonian physics than those students who did not endorse mastery goals (Linnenbrink & Pintrich, 2002). The first study also suggested that mastery goals were especially adaptive for students with low levels of prior knowledge. In the second study, we found that both a decrease in negative affect and an increase in elaborative strategy use associated with mastery goals mediated the positive relation of mastery goals to improved physics understanding.

The relation of performance goals to conceptual change is less clear. Lee and Anderson (1993) found that students who reported espousing performance goals as their primary goal and also did not endorse mastery goals showed little or no improvement in their conceptual understanding after the lesson. This suggested that performance goals hindered the conceptual change process. That is, even after instruction, these students were not advancing in their conceptual understanding of matter and kinetic molecular theory. In our laboratory studies using self-reported goals, we found that self-reported performance goals were unrelated to conceptual change (Linnenbrink & Pintrich, 2002). So for the college students we studied, performance goals were neither beneficial nor detrimental to conceptual change.

Hynd (1998) reported a case study of one high school student, Barry, who was very motivated by performance goals. For example, as students worked on an egg drop task to understand aspects of gravity, Barry said to a group of students, "I'm going to beat you. I'm going to put rocks in mine. Mine's going to weigh more than yours. I bet you mine weighs more. I'm going to go home and make mine weigh more. I'm going to put weights in the bottom so it falls faster. I'm going to tape (holds up two heavy strips of cardboard) these to the bottom of my box. It's going to weigh more. I'm going to make it weigh more. If my egg breaks, it don't matter" (Hynd, 1998, p. 33). This is a clear statement of performance goals where Barry was focused on trying to beat others, although it was misguided because adding weight will not make the box fall faster. In fact, when Barry was confronted with the anomalous data that his box did not fall faster than others, he attributed the data to measurement error in timing by other students. Hynd (1998) noted that Barry did show some conceptual change over time, although at the end of the unit he was still confused about why light and heavy objects fall at the same rate. It seems clear that the performance goal helped to engage Barry in the task and subsequently change some of his beliefs about gravity; however, he did not necessarily reach a coherent or systematic understanding of gravity.

In sum, the limited empirical evidence regarding the relation of achievement goals to conceptual change suggests that mastery goals are adaptive for the conceptual change process. The role of performance goals is less clear. Performance goals may be detrimental or they may not be directly related to conceptual change. However, the case study by Hynd (1998) suggested that they could be related indirectly if they lead to more cognitive or behavioral engagement in the task. It is clear that we need more theoretical and empirical work on the role of performance goals in conceptual change.

Given the scarcity of empirical evidence regarding the relation of achievement goals to conceptual change, it is also important to consider the theoretical distinctions between the two goals. In particular, we consider how the theoretical distinction between mastery and performance goals might further our understanding of the role of goals in conceptual change. Therefore, in the next section, we turn to a more theoretical discussion of these empirical findings.

Direct Relations of Achievement Goals to Intentional Conceptual Change: A Theoretical Analysis

We expect that achievement goals relate differently to conceptual change because mastery and performance goals differentially influence the focus of attention, the degree to which students are willing to alter prior concepts, and their specific goals for the activity. The way in which the focus of attention and willingness to alter prior concepts may impact conceptual change differs depending on the perspective one takes regarding the conceptual change process. Therefore, we discuss how achievement goals relate to conceptual change from both a cognitive–developmental and cognitive–contextual perspective. We begin with the cognitive–developmental framework.

Recall that with the cognitive–developmental framework, conceptual change involves the eventual replacement or reconstruction of naïve theories or understandings with more scientific explanations. This process is thought to occur as children are faced with contradictory evidence and begin to reorganize their frameworks for understanding the world. That is, under this model, children are thought to develop their own naïve theories to explain the world; conceptual change involves the modification and transformation of these theories to account for new evidence. When interpreting conceptual change through this framework, both focus of attention and altering prior theories are important in understanding why mastery versus performance goals differentially relate to conceptual change. Focus of attention is key for conceptual change in that students must attend to new information in order to detect discrepancies between what they are learning and their own theories about the phenomena. In this way, focus of attention can be linked to both the second and third criteria for intentional conceptual change. That is, if students focus on the task at hand, they should be more aware of their progress toward their goal of understanding. This reflects a metacognitive awareness of one's goal and one's progress toward one's goal, reflecting the second criterion for intentional conceptual change, metacognitive awareness. In addition, focus of attention can also be associated with increased self-regulatory strategy use, especially in linking what one already knows or believes to what one is learning. In this way, focus of attention can also be associated with the third criterion for intentional conceptual change, self-regulation and strategy use. Although a willingness to alter naïve theories does not directly tie into the three criteria for intentional conceptual change, it is also important for conceptual change, especially from a cognitive–developmental perspective.

With regard to the focus of attention, mastery goals should be more adaptive than performance goals inasmuch as mastery-oriented students would likely be more attuned to new information, allowing them to detect that their current conceptions are not consistent with the new information they are acquiring. That is, with a mastery orientation comes a focus on the task at hand; this focus on the information as opposed to the self (as is the case with a performance orientation) should allow mastery-oriented students to more readily detect a discrepancy between their current understanding and the information they are learning. Furthermore, the focus on learning associated with mastery goals should make mastery-oriented students more likely to try to connect what they are learning to their prior knowledge. The connection of new information to prior conceptions should further promote the detection of a discrepancy between what students are currently learning and their prior understandings, thus promoting conceptual change. Finally, work on self-regulation (Pintrich, 1999; 2000c) showed that mastery-oriented students are more likely to use cognitive and metacognitive strategies for learning. The use of these self-regulatory strategies should also help students develop revised concepts or theories. Although there is a cost to using these regulatory strategies in terms of effort and time, mastery-oriented students seem to accept these costs in pursuit of their goal of understanding and learning.

In contrast, performance-oriented students are focused on demonstrating their competence. With this goal comes a focus on the self and the self compared to others, which can decrease one's capacity to focus on new information. This change in the focus of attention may make it more difficult for performance-oriented students to detect that their current understanding does not match the new information they are learning. Because conceptual change is more likely to occur if students are dissatisfied with their current conceptions, the decreased attention of performance-oriented students to new information would likely be detrimental for conceptual change.

In addition to differences based on the goals one adopts in terms of recognizing the need for changing one's conception, achievement goals should also relate to how readily students are willing to alter their prior conceptions or theories. In particular, performance-oriented students may have trouble disentangling their sense of self from their conceptions. Performance-oriented students may feel threatened by the new information being presented because in order to accept the newly presented way of thinking, they first need to admit that they were incorrect in their prior understanding. By admitting that they were incorrect, these students would need to acknowledge that they were probably not better than others at the topic being studied. If students do not accept the new information as being valid, they need not admit that they were not successful in their goal of outperforming others. This conflict between demonstrating competence and conceptual change is clearly illustrated in the example of Barry presented earlier. Recall that Barry was so focused on winning the competition that he did not attend to the lesson about gravity. For mastery-oriented students, their sense of competence comes from learning; therefore, they do not have difficulty relinquishing prior conceptions if they feel that a new concept will advance them in their pursuit of understanding.

Finally, as discussed earlier, students' achievement goal orientations should also relate differently to the types of specific goals they have for the task. Mastery-oriented students are more likely to adopt a goal focusing on changing their understanding. Furthermore, mastery goals are generally associated with metacognitive awareness and self-regulatory strategies. Therefore, it seems quite likely that mastery-oriented students engage in learning in such a way that meets all three criteria put forth for intentional conceptual change. In contrast, it is unclear whether or not performance-oriented students will adopt a goal involving a focus on changing their understanding. That is, performance-oriented students may adopt goals to change their understanding in order to demonstrate their competence or they may simply focus on trying to outperform others. Furthermore, the evidence is mixed regarding the relation between performance goal adoption and metacognitive awareness and self-regulatory strategy use. Thus, although it is possible that performance-oriented students engage in learning in a way that meets the three criteria for intentional conceptual change, it seems equally likely that they are not intentional in their learning.

In addition to the linear relation of mastery and performance goals to conceptual change, it is also important to consider the interactive effect of mastery and performance goals on conceptual change, or the role of multiple goals. As discussed earlier, the two achievement goals are independent of one another. Therefore, a student may have high levels of both goals, high levels of mastery but not performance goals, high levels of performance but not mastery goals, or low levels of both goals. The role of multiple goals is especially important in this instance given the emerging evidence that adopting both goals is adaptive for cognitive and motivational variables (Pintrich, 2000b). That is, it seems plausible that having both goals may lead to very adaptive patterns of learning in a typical classroom context where students must engage in a variety of activities. For instance, a student who wants to learn about physics may benefit from also adopting performance goals in that he or she may try harder to memorize the various laws that will help him or her learn physics. On the other hand, a student with mastery goals but not performance goals may not see the benefits of memorizing the laws because it may not be clear to him or her that knowing these laws will help him or her learn. In terms of conceptual change, however, we have stressed the detriments of performance goals, especially in terms of an unwillingness to alter naïve theories. Therefore, although performance goals can sometimes be useful, it is unlikely that the adoption of both performance and mastery goals when conceptual change is necessary would be adaptive under a cognitive-developmental model of conceptual change. In this situation, students with performance goals would likely continue to endorse their prior conceptions and theories, thus inhibiting the conceptual change process.

The benefits of mastery goals and detriments of performance goals for conceptual change can also be interpreted using a cognitive–contextual model. Considering the role of achievement goals for conceptual change using a different model is important because the developmental and contextual models treat the representation of prior knowledge in very different ways. That is, the cognitive–contextual model suggests that naïve understandings of the world consist of p-prims, or small, disconnected pieces of information rather than as theories, as was purported by cognitive–developmental models of conceptual change. An important difference here is that the p-prims themselves do not need to be changed for conceptual change to occur. Rather, the conceptual change process involves the use of these p-prims in a more organized, consistent, and scientifically meaningful manner. Of course, there is still some restructuring required, but less than in the cognitive–developmental model. From this perspective, focus of attention is still important for conceptual change in that students must attend to the new information to begin to use their knowledge in more meaningful ways. However, willingness to alter prior beliefs is not as central to the conceptual change process. Therefore, we primarily discuss the role of attentional focus for cognitive–contextual models of conceptual change. As noted earlier, focus of attention is closely tied to the second and third criteria for intentional conceptual change (i.e., metacognitive awareness through the focus on the task and increased strategy use).

Similar to the cognitive–developmental model, we expect that mastery-oriented students would be more likely to focus on the new information they are learning (i.e., focus on the task at hand) than would students with performance goals. This focus on learning and the task should be useful when students attempt to use their prior knowledge and beliefs to account for a particular phenomenon. One particular aspect of mastery goals that may enhance conceptual development is that mastery-oriented students may be more likely to question the information presented and think carefully about why a certain organization and use of p-prims makes sense. This should help them engage in the types of deep processing and elaboration necessary for long-term understanding to occur. That is, mastery-oriented students are not likely to readily accept information given to them about how to use and organize various pieces of knowledge; instead, their focus on understanding should lead them to critically analyze the information and make sense of it before adopting it as a plausible explanation. Furthermore, the nature of mastery goals makes it likely that mastery-oriented students will engage in learning in an intentional manner, thus promoting conceptual change.

We still expect performance goals to relate negatively or be unrelated to conceptual change under a cognitive–contextual model of conceptual change; however, the reasons why performance goals may hinder the conceptual change process differ from those suggested for the developmental models of conceptual change. Recall that in the developmental model, we suggested that students who were performance-oriented would continue to endorse prior conceptions, thus making conceptual change difficult. Under current cognitive–contextual models, however, students need not alter prior conceptions. Instead, their ideas about when certain facets must be used or applied needs to be altered. As changing when to apply an idea is much less threatening to one's notion of one's self, performance goals should not interfere as much with the change process.

However, it is still conceivable that performance goals would not enhance conceptual change. First, as noted earlier, it is not clear whether performance-oriented students adopt goals that meet the first criterion for intentional conceptual change. Second, in terms of focus of attention, performance-oriented students focus on demonstrating their ability rather than on what they are learning. Therefore, they may not attend to the task in a way that allows them to gain a complex understanding of what they are learning. This focus away from the goal of learning makes it unlikely that performance-oriented students meet the second criterion for intentional conceptual change. Furthermore, because performance-oriented students are concerned with demonstrating their ability, it is likely that they may too quickly accept the notion that a certain facet, p-prim, or idea should be applied in a given situation inasmuch as adopting the theory being taught would help them demonstrate their ability (i.e., do better than others on a test or in a class discussion). In this way, performance-oriented students may initially appear to be undergoing conceptual change. Indeed, on a simple recall test occurring in relative close proximity to the learning session, performance-oriented students are likely to do well. However, a quick acceptance of the situation under which a certain idea is appropriate does not require an understanding of the phenomenon. Therefore, it may be that performance-oriented students do not really understand why a given facet is appropriate for a given situation. Such superficial processing should not lead to long-term recall of the information or substantial, long-term conceptual change in the use of the facets. The use of superficial rather than higher order strategies fails to meet the third criterion for intentional conceptual change.

In contrast to our hypotheses regarding the role of multiple goals in cognitive–developmental conceptual change models, adopting both mastery and performance goals may be adaptive if one is using a cognitive–contextual model of conceptual change. In particular, we suggested earlier that when students adopted both performance and mastery goals simultaneously, performance goals would still negatively impact the conceptual change process by preventing students from altering prior conceptions. Under a cognitive–contextual model of conceptual change, however, this does not pose a problem because it is not necessary for students to alter prior beliefs. Rather, students must change the way that they use and apply smaller bits of knowledge. Furthermore, our concern with performance goals under the cognitive–contextual model was the lack of attention to the task and the ready acceptance of new ideas. However, combined with a mastery goal, this should not be as much of an issue as the mastery goal should help students focus more on the task and may aid them in questioning the relevance of new information being presented. Finally, because mastery goals should promote the adoption of learning goals, monitoring, and self-regulatory strategy use in line with what we suggested was necessary for intentional conceptual change, and because it was unclear if performance goals helped students engage in intentional learning, the presence of a mastery goal should encourage students to engage in learning in an intentional manner, thus promoting intentional conceptual change. Therefore, the benefits of the performance goals in terms of initial engagement and the benefits of the mastery goals in terms of the focus on learning may be most adaptive for conceptual change under a cognitive–contextual perspective.

Potential Mediators of the Achievement Goals and Conceptual Change Relations

Thus far, we have discussed theoretically why achievement goals might differentially relate to conceptual change. However, it is also plausible that achievement goals may have their effects on conceptual change through various mediators (see Fig. 12.1). In this section, we examine how achievement goals relate to other motivational processes, which in turn relate to cognitive and behavioral engagement. We also explore how achievement goals relate directly to cognitive and behavioral engagement and why engagement is important for conceptual change.

Other Motivational Processes. A good deal of research has been conducted regarding the relation of achievement goals to other motivational processes and the relation of other motivational processes to various cognitive and behavioral outcomes. We focus here on efficacy, interest, and affect, as these seem important in terms of students' cognitive processing and engagement. Given that these other motivational processes are distinct from achievement goals, it is possible to examine how achievement goals predict these other types of motivational processes.

Self-efficacy can be defined as confidence in one's ability to perform a given task. Although much of the research on self-efficacy is independent from achievement goals (e.g., Bandura, 1997), a number of studies have examined how achievement goals relate to self-efficacy. In general, correlational research on the relation of achievement goals to self-efficacy suggests that mastery goals are related positively to self-efficacy (Pintrich & De Groot, 1990; Wolters, Yu, & Pintrich, 1996). Students who report that they focus on learning and understanding are also more likely to report that they feel confident in their ability to do the work at hand. In contrast, the relation of performance goals to self-efficacy is not as clear, with some research reporting no relation (Middleton & Midgley, 1997), others reporting a positive relation (Elliot & Church, 1997; Wolters et al., 1996), and still others reporting a negative relation (Anderman & Young, 1994).

It seems plausible that self-efficacy has both direct effects on conceptual change and indirect effects via behavioral and cognitive engagement. In terms of conceptual change, Pintrich (1999) suggested that the value of self-efficacy for conceptual change might vary depending on how self-efficacy is conceptualized and operationalized. If self-efficacy is defined as one's confidence in one's knowledge about what is being learned, self-efficacy may be detrimental to conceptual change processes because students might have such confidence in their prior beliefs that they are unwilling to change them. We expect this would be particularly problematic under a cognitive–developmental model of conceptual change because students may believe strongly in their naïve theories and therefore would not attend to information that contradicts their theories.

An alternative view is that self-efficacy reflects a confidence in one's ability to learn (Pintrich, 1999). From this perspective, high self-efficacy should enhance conceptual change in that students will feel confident that they can alter their prior theories or construct theories based on prior

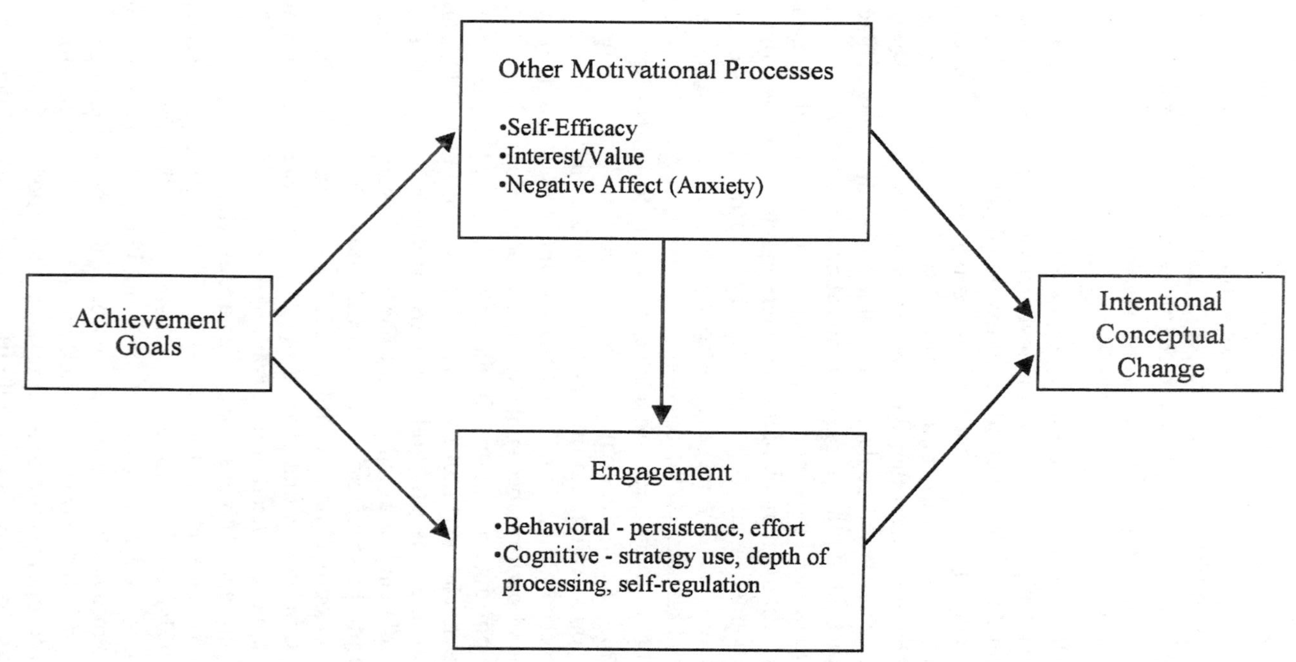

FIG. 12.1. Achievement goals and intentional conceptual change.

ideas or p-prims. There is some evidence to suggest that both these perspectives on self-efficacy play a role in conceptual change. In particular, a case study of one student suggested that the student's confidence in her knowledge initially limited how much she changed; however, over time, the student's confidence in being able to learn helped her develop a much more sophisticated view of gravity (Maria, 1998). Moje and Shepardson (1998) also presented data of four children working together on a science task that shows how the students' self-efficacy for doing the task mediated their interactions and what they eventually learned from the task.

This second perspective on self-efficacy, as efficacy for learning new ideas, may also fit better with our thinking about the relation of mastery goals to self-efficacy. That is, one reason why mastery goals are thought to relate to higher self-efficacy is that mastery-oriented students are focused on learning and understanding, and their success in improving over time may strengthen their beliefs about their ability to learn. Because the focus of mastery goals is on learning, it is likely that their efficacy beliefs will be in relation to their ability to learn, rather than their understanding for a particular content area or theory. Therefore, the positive relation of mastery goals to self-efficacy would be adaptive for conceptual change.

In addition to a direct relation to conceptual change, self-efficacy may also influence conceptual change via cognitive and behavioral engagement. Research regarding the relation of efficacy to persistence and effort suggests that high levels of efficacy are associated with increased persistence and effort, whereas low levels of efficacy are related to decreased persistence and effort, especially when a difficult task is presented (Schunk, 1991). Furthermore, self-efficacy has been associated with the increased use of cognitive and metacognitive strategies (Pintrich & Garcia, 1991). Overall, we expect that self-efficacy mediates the positive relation of mastery goals to conceptual change. It is unlikely that self-efficacy mediates the relation of performance goals given that there is no clear relation of performance goals to self-efficacy beliefs or conceptual change.

Students' interest and value are also important mediators to consider in the relation of achievement goals to conceptual change. A number of studies have linked mastery goals with increased personal interest (Harackiewicz et al., 1998; Pintrich & Schunk, 1996). This increase in interest is likely a result of students' progress in learning the task. That is, students who feel that they are learning are likely to become increasingly interested in the topic. This increase in personal interest may also be related to their increase in competence associated with mastery goals. In general, research on the relation of performance goals to interest in classroom settings suggests that performance goals are unrelated to interest (Elliot & Church, 1997; Harackiewicz et al., 1997). Although some laboratory studies suggested that performance goals may lead to increased interest via an increase in efficacy and involvement in the task (Elliot & Harackiewicz, 1996; Harackiewicz & Elliot, 1998), these results have not been replicated in the classroom.

In general, research on the role of motivational processes in conceptual change is relatively scarce; however, a few studies have examined the role of interest in the conceptual change process (e.g., Andre & Windschitl, chapter 7, this volume; Venville & Treagust, 1998). In particular, Andre and Windschitl (this volume) reported on data from three studies investigating college students' learning about electrical circuits. Their results suggest that interest enhances conceptual change. More specifically, they found both a direct effect and indirect effect of personal interest on students' change in their understanding of circuits. The indirect effect suggested that students who were interested in the topic also had more experience with the topic. This experience was related to an increase in prior knowledge, which in turn predicted posttest knowledge. The direct effect suggested that personal interest enhanced the conceptual change process even after controlling for prior experience and prior knowledge.

Venville and Treagust (1998) used interview data to examine high school students' understanding of genetics. They reported that although high school students who achieved high levels of conceptual change also reported being interested in the subject, there were also a number of students who reported high levels of interest with relatively small amounts of conceptual change. The authors noted, however, that students tended to be interested in the human heredity rather than the microscopic aspects of genetics. In this way, although the students showed interest in the topic generally, they were not interested in the aspects of the topic that were more likely to facilitate conceptual change. This may explain why Venville and Treagust (1998) did not report the same relation of personal interest to conceptual change as did Andre and Windschitl (this volume).

These somewhat contradictory empirical results suggest that further research is necessary in order to clearly understand the role of interest in the conceptual change process. However, there is also theoretical and indirect empirical evidence to suggest that interest relates to conceptual change. In particular, research relating interest to cognitive processing suggests that interest is linked to deeper processing of information including the use of elaborative strategies (Schiefele, 1991). Given the increase in depth of processing associated with interest, we would expect interest to enhance conceptual change. Of course, as noted by Venville and Treagust (1998), the focus of students' interest to particular aspects of the topic may be important in determining whether interest enhances conceptual change. Furthermore, it is also possible that an increase in interest may be beneficial for cognitive processing, but may be detrimental for conceptual change more generally in that interest may make it more difficult for students to relinquish prior beliefs (Dole & Sinatra, 1998). That is, as suggested by Andre and Windschitl (this volume), interest relates to greater prior experience with the topic and enhanced prior knowledge. This enhanced prior knowledge may mean that students have more elaborated theories, making it less likely for them to shift in their theoretical understanding of the topic. In this sense, situational interest (interest generated by the situation) may be a better predictor of conceptual change than is personal interest (individual difference in interest) because situational interest should not be linked with prior knowledge or experience. Of course, Andre and Windschitl (this volume) also found a direct effect of interest and found that prior knowledge was a positive predictor of posttest knowledge, suggesting that personal interest still plays an important role in conceptual change.

In summary, there is some preliminary evidence to suggest that interest mediates the relation between mastery goals and conceptual change. However, the way that interest relates to conceptual change may be more complex than a simple direct relation. Future research needs to carefully consider personal versus situational interest as well as the particular aspects of the topic that students find interesting.

Finally, the relation of achievement goals to negative affect may be important in understanding how goals relate to conceptual change. Although goal theorists have begun to consider the relation of achievement goals to both positive and negative affect, we focus here on negative affect, particularly anxiety, as this seems most likely to affect conceptual change. In general, mastery goals are either related negatively to negative affect (e.g., Elliott & Dweck, 1988) or are unrelated (e.g., Middleton & Midgley, 1997). Similarly, for performance goals, the results are mixed, but the majority of evidence indicates that performance goals are related to higher levels of anxiety (e.g., Elliot & McGregor, 1999; Middleton & Midgley, 1997).

Although conceptual change researchers have not examined the role of negative affect on conceptual change, a study conducted in our laboratory suggested that negative affect mediated the positive relation of mastery goals to conceptual change (Linnenbrink & Pintrich, 2002). Theoretically, it seems plausible that negative affect, particularly anxiety, may lead to students' continued endorsement of prior notions and may make it less likely that students change their thinking about various phenomena. That is, a student feeling anxious may feel threatened in a way that causes him or her to hold on to his or her prior understanding. It is likely that an anxious student will do all he or she can to reduce anxiety; therefore, the student would be less likely to consider new information because the uncertainty in his or her own understanding would increase anxiety rather than reduce it. This continued endorsement of prior beliefs seems especially problematic from a cognitive–developmental view of conceptual change because naïve theories must be altered for conceptual change to occur. Although negative affect should be less problematic from a cognitive–contextual perspective, given that conceptual change involves building on one's initial ideas, it is still plausible that a student's anxiety may narrow his or her view, thus limiting the amount of new information he or she absorbs. This narrowing of attention could also be detrimental for conceptual change.

In terms of cognitive strategies, negative affect may also be debilitating. Although people with negative affect are generally thought to focus on detailed information (Schwarz, 1990), this focus on details may overwhelm working memory capacities, making it more difficult to engage in self-regulatory processes. Working memory is important for self-regulatory processes in that self-regulation requires monitoring of one's progress, understanding, and strategy use. Limited working memory functioning would reduce the capacity to monitor, thus inhibiting self-regulatory processes. The decrease in self-regulatory processes should be detrimental to the conceptual change process in that self-regulation of one's goal pursuit is an essential component of intentional conceptual change. In support of this view, a study conducted in our laboratory suggested that negative affect reduced working memory functioning (Linnenbrink et al., 1999). Furthermore, this study showed that negative affect mediated the positive relation of mastery goals to working memory. Therefore, it seems plausible that negative affect may mediate the positive relation of mastery goals to conceptual change. Furthermore, an increase in negative affect associated with performance goals may help to explain why performance goals are, at worst, detrimental or, at best, unrelated to conceptual change.

Cognitive and Behavioral Engagement. We have suggested that self-efficacy, interest, and anxiety may mediate the relation of achievement goals to both behavioral and cognitive engagement. In addition, research on achievement goals suggests that mastery and performance goals are directly related to engagement (Pintrich & Schrauben, 1992). In this section, we focus on two types of engagement: behavioral and cognitive. *Behavioral engagement* refers to students' involvement in the activity in terms of their effort and persistence. *Cognitive engagement* refers to the types of strategies students use, the degree to which they elaborate on the information they are learning, the depth of processing of the information learned, and their self-regulation. Both types of engagement should be important to the conceptual change process.

In terms of behavioral engagement, studies have demonstrated that mastery and performance goals have direct effects on persistence and effort. In particular, mastery goals are related to high levels of effort and persistence (Ames, 1992; Elliott & Dweck, 1988). The relation of performance goals to effort and persistence is mixed (Ames, 1992; Elliott & Dweck, 1988) and may be dependent on students' level of efficacy as well as their perception of their progress toward their goal. When students have high feelings of efficacy, they may persist and exert effort because they see that as fruitful in reaching their goal of outperforming others. Similarly, performance-oriented students are generally likely to persist as long as they are successful. It is when performance-oriented students are faced with a challenge or fail at a task that they are less likely to continue to engage in the situation. In settings requiring conceptual change, it seems probable that students will encounter situations where their prior understanding results in failure or they are challenged by the new information they are learning; therefore, mastery goals, but not performance goals, should be most adaptive for learning situations requiring conceptual change.

Persistence and effort may be necessary but not sufficient factors for conceptual change to occur. That is, persistence and effort may help students attend to the new information and notice the necessity of altering prior theories (in the case of a cognitive–developmental model of conceptual change) or elaborate on their understanding of situations in which certain ideas are applicable (in the case of a cognitive–contextual perspective on conceptual change). However, the mere acknowledgement of a discrepancy and a need for change are not sufficient for change to occur; these ideas must be elaborated on and integrated with prior knowledge. Therefore, persistence and effort may help to start the conceptual change process, but it is unlikely that persistence and effort alone will result in any long-term conceptual change. Rather, as noted in our earlier discussion of intentional conceptual change, higher order cognitive processing is necessary for conceptual change to occur.

There is also a great deal of research investigating the relation of achievement goals to higher order cognitive processing. For instance, Graham and Golan (1991) demonstrated that mastery goals were associated with more in-depth processing of information than were performance goals. Furthermore, mastery goals have been linked to increased use of self-regulatory strategies and elaboration (Pintrich, 2000c). The work on performance goals and strategy use is mixed (Pintrich, 2000c). However, recent studies suggested that performance goals, at least in combination with mastery goals, may result in adaptive types of cognitive processing (Pintrich, 2000b). A study conducted in our laboratory lends support to the idea that cognitive engagement mediates the relation of achievement goals to conceptual change (Linnenbrink & Pintrich, 2002). Recall that we found that elaborative strategy use helped to explain why mastery goals were positively related to conceptual change.

It seems clear, regardless of one's perspective on conceptual change, that higher order cognitive strategies are essential for long-term conceptual change. For instance, Dole and Sinatra's (1998) Cognitive Reconstruction of Knowledge Model (CRKM) suggested that high cognitive engagement, conceptualized as deep processing, elaboration, and metacognitive strategy use, are essential components for strong, long-term conceptual change. They suggested that short-term change may occur through superficial engagement, but that long-term change occurs when individuals are actively engaged in learning the material and use high-level strategies to monitor their understanding. Of course, the way that higher order cognitive processing relates to conceptual change may vary depending on one's perspective.

From a cognitive–developmental perspective, elaboration and metacognitive strategy use are needed for students first to recognize the discrepancy between existing beliefs and new information and then to alter their beliefs to fit the new information. For the recategorization or transformation of one's prior conceptions to occur, an individual must be highly engaged in the learning process. One must carefully consider new evidence, consider how this relates to what one already believes or knows, conclude that one's prior understanding does not adequately account for the new information, and construct a new system to account for the contradictory information.

From a cognitive–contextual perspective, elaboration on ideas is essential for students to understand when various p-prims or facets are applicable (Hunt & Minstrell, 1994). As students learn the various situations where a certain p-prim is applied, they must be able to understand why the p-prim is applicable for long-term retention of this information to occur. So, rather than using high-level strategies to help transform an existing theory or belief system, as was the case for conceptual change under a cognitive–developmental model, students must use high-level strategies to consider where their existing pieces of knowledge are applicable. With low levels of engagement and superficial strategy use, students may "memorize" various situations where their existing ideas can be applied, but it is unlikely that they will retain these ideas over the long term.

CONCLUSION

Based on both direct and indirect effects, it seems clear that mastery goals are adaptive for intentional conceptual change, whereas performance goals may be detrimental or, at best, simply unrelated to conceptual change. In terms of a direct relation, both the empirical evidence as well as theoretical reasoning suggest that students with mastery goals are more likely to alter their understanding of a particular topic and engage in learning in an intentional manner. Although the explanations for why and how this occurs may differ based on one's perspective on conceptual change (i.e., cognitive–developmental vs. cognitive–contextual), mastery goals should have a direct effect on the conceptual change process.

In contrast, the relation of performance goals to conceptual change is less clear. It may be that performance goals do not enhance conceptual change, regardless of the definition of conceptual change under either a cognitive–developmental or cognitive–contextual perspective. The degree to which performance goals are detrimental to the conceptual change process, however, differs based on these two perspectives. From a cognitive–developmental perspective, performance goals should be detrimental for conceptual change as students with performance goals should be less likely to alter prior conceptions. As altering prior concepts is not central to the cognitive–contextual model, the detrimental effects of performance goals should not be as strong. Nevertheless, our analysis of performance goals in terms of the factors needed to promote intentional conceptual change suggests that performance goals do not consistently promote the type of engagement necessary to facilitate conceptual change.

In addition to the direct effects, the relation of achievement goals to conceptual change may be mediated by both motivational and cognitive mediators. In terms of motivational mediators, mastery goals are related to increased self-efficacy and decreased anxiety and negative affect, all of which should mediate the positive relation between mastery goals and conceptual change. In contrast, the increase in anxiety associated with performance goals should be detrimental to conceptual change, especially under a cognitive–developmental perspective. It seems likely that interest mediates the relation between mastery goals and conceptual change; however, the exact nature of this relation is unclear. Future research that considers personal and situational interest as well as the particular aspects of the topic that students find interesting may shed some light on this issue. Finally, mastery goals should be indirectly related to conceptual change via enhanced behavioral and cognitive engagement. As there is no clear relation between performance goals and engagement as well as performance goals and conceptual change, it is difficult to make claims regarding the relation between performance goals and conceptual change via behavioral and cognitive engagement.

In summary, it seems clear that considering students' motivational orientations is important for understanding why some students undergo radical conceptual change whereas others do not alter their existing conceptions intentionally. Future research should focus on clarifying how performance goals impact intentional learning in settings requiring conceptual change. In addition, empirically investigating the proposed motivational and cognitive mediators should provide us with a more nuanced understanding of how and why achievement goals influence intentional conceptual change processes.

REFERENCES

Ames, C. (1992). Classrooms: Goals, structures, and student motivation. *Journal of Educational Psychology, 84,* 261–271.

Anderman, E., & Young, A. (1994). Motivation and strategy use in science: Individual differences and classroom effects. *Journal of Educational Psychology, 80,* 260–267.

Bandura, A. (1997). *Self-efficacy: The exercise of control.* New York: Freeman.

Boekaerts, M., Pintrich, P., & Zeidner, M. (2000). *Handbook of self-regulation.* San Diego, CA: Academic Press.

Brandtstadter, J. (1998). Action perspectives on human development. In W. Damon (Series Ed.) and R. Lerner (Vol. Ed.), *Handbook of child psychology: Vol. 1. Theoretical models of human development* (5th ed., pp. 807–863). New York: Wiley.

Dennett, D. C. (1996). *Kinds of minds: Toward an understanding of consciousness.* New York, NY: Basic Books.

diSessa, A. (1993). Towards an epistemology of physics. *Cognition and Instruction, 10,* 105–225.

Dole, J., & Sinatra, G. (1998). Reconceptualizing change in the cognitive construction of knowledge. *Educational Psychologist, 33,* 109–128.

Dweck, C., & Leggett, E. (1988). A social cognitive approach to motivation and personality. *Psychological Review, 95,* 256–273.

Elliot, A., & Church, M. (1997). A hierarchical model of approach and avoidance achievement motivation. *Journal of Personality and Social Psychology, 72,* 218–232.

Elliot, A., & Harackiewicz, J. (1996). Approach and avoidance achievement goals and intrinsic motivation: A mediational analysis. *Journal of Personality and Social Psychology, 70,* 968–980.

Elliot, A., & McGregor, H. (1999). Test anxiety and the hierarchical model of approach and avoidance achievement motivation. *Journal of Personality and Social Psychology, 76,* 628–644.

Elliott, E., & Dweck, C. (1988). Goals: An approach to motivation and achievement. *Journal of Personality and Social Psychology, 54,* 5–12.

Ford, M. (1992). *Motivating humans: Goals, emotions, and personal agency beliefs.* Newbury Park, CA: Sage.

Graham, S., & Golan, S. (1991). Motivational influences on cognition: Task involvement, ego involvement, and depth of information processing. *Journal of Educational Psychology, 83,* 187–194.

Guzzetti, B., & Hynd, C. (1998). *Perspectives on conceptual change: Multiple ways to understand knowing and learning in a complex world.* Mahwah, NJ: Lawrence Erlbaum Associates.

Harackiewicz, J., Barron, K. E., Carter, S., Lehto, A., & Elliot, A. (1997). Predictors and consequences of achievement goals in the college classroom: Maintaining interest and making the grade. *Journal of Personality and Social Psychology, 73,* 1284–1295.

Harackiewicz, J., Barron, K. E., & Elliot, A. J. (1998). Rethinking achievement goals: When are they adaptive for college students and why? *Educational Psychologist, 33,* 1–21.

Harackiewicz, J., & Elliot, A. (1998). The joint effects of target and purpose goals on intrinsic motivation: A mediational analysis. *Personality and Social Psychology Bulletin, 24,* 675–689.

Harackiewicz, J., & Sansone, C. (1991). Goals and intrinsic motivation: You *can* get there from here. In M. L. Maehr & P. R. Pintrich (Eds.), *Advances in motivation and achievement* (Vol. 7., pp. 21–49). Greenwich, CT: JAI Press.

Hunt, E., & Minstrell, J. (1994). A cognitive approach to the teaching of physics. In K. McGilly (Ed.), *Classroom lessons: Integrating cognitive theory and classroom practice* (pp. 51–74). Cambridge, MA: The MIT Press.

Hynd, C. (1998). Conceptual change in a high school physics class. In B. Guzzetti & C. Hynd (Eds.), *Perspectives on conceptual change* (pp. 27–36). Mahwah, NJ: Lawrence Erlbaum Associates.

Lee, O., & Anderson, C. W. (1993). Task engagement and conceptual change in middle school science classrooms. *American Educational Research Journal, 30*, 585–610.

Linnenbrink, E. A., & Pintrich, P. R. (2002). The role of motivational beliefs in conceptual change. In M. Limón & L. Mason (Eds.), *Reconsidering conceptual change: Issues in theory and practice* (pp. 115–135). Dordrecht, The Netherlands: Kluwer Academic Publishers.

Linnenbrink, E. A., Ryan, A. M., & Pintrich, P. R. (1999). The role of goals and affect in working memory functioning. *Learning and Individual Differences, 11*, 213–230.

Maehr, M. L., & Kaplan, A. (2000, April). *It might be all about self: Self-consciousness as an organizing scheme for integrating understandings from self-determination theory and achievement goal theory*. Paper presented at the Annual Meeting of the American Educational Research Association, New Orleans, LA.

Maehr, M. L., & Midgley, C. (1991). Enhancing student motivation: A schoolwide approach. *Educational Psychologist, 26*, 399–427.

Maria, K. (1998). Self-confidence and the process of conceptual change. In B. Guzzetti & C. Hynd (Eds.), *Perspectives on conceptual change* (pp. 7–16). Mahwah, NJ: Lawrence Erlbaum Associates.

Middleton, M., & Midgley, C. (1997). Avoiding the demonstration of lack of ability: An underexplored aspect of goal theory. *Journal of Educational Psychology, 89*, 710–718.

Moje, E., & Shepardson, D. (1998). Social interactions and children's changing understanding of electrical circuits. In B. Guzzetti & C. Hynd (Eds.), *Perspectives on conceptual change* (pp. 17–26). Mahwah, NJ: Lawrence Erlbaum Associates.

Nicholls, J. (1984). Achievement motivation: Conceptions of ability, subjective experience, task choice, and performance. *Psychological Review, 91*, 328–346.

Pintrich, P. R. (1999). Motivational beliefs as resources for and constraints on conceptual change. In W. Schnotz, S. Vosniadou, & M. Carretero (Eds.), *New perspectives on conceptual change* (pp. 33–50). Amsterdam, The Netherlands: Pergamon.

Pintrich, P. R. (2000a). An achievement goal theory perspective on issues in motivation terminology, theory, and research. *Contemporary Educational Psychology, 25*, 92–104.

Pintrich, P. R. (2000b). Multiple goals, multiple pathways: The role of goal orientation in learning and achievement. *Journal of Educational Psychology, 92*, 544–555.

Pintrich, P. R. (2000c). The role of goal orientation in self-regulated learning. In M. Boekaerts, P. R. Pintrich, & M. Zeidner (Eds.), *Handbook of self-regulation* (pp. 451–502). San Diego, CA: Academic Press.

Pintrich, P. R., & De Groot, E. (1990). Motivational and self-regulated learning components of classroom academic performance. *Journal of Educational Psychology, 82*, 33–40.

Pintrich, P. R., & Garcia, T. (1991). Student goal orientation and self-regulation in the college classroom. In M. L. Maehr & P. R. Pintrich (Eds.), *Advances in motivation and achievement: Goals and self-regulatory processes* (Vol. 7, pp. 371–402). Greenwich, CT: JAI Press.

Pintrich, P. R., Marx, R. W., & Boyle, R. B. (1993). Beyond cold conceptual change: The role of motivational beliefs and classroom contextual factors in the process of conceptual change. *Review of Educational Research, 63*, 167–199.

Pintrich, P., & Schrauben, B. (1992). Students' motivational beliefs and their cognitive engagement in the classroom academic tasks. In D. Schunk & J. Meece (Eds.), *Student perceptions in the classroom* (pp. 149–183). Hillsdale, NJ: Lawrence Erlbaum Associates.

Pintrich, P. R., & Schunk, D. H. (1996). *Motivation in education: Theory, research, and applications.* Englewood Cliffs, NJ: Prentice Hall Merrill.

Roeser, R., Midgley, C., & Urdan, T. (1996). Perceptions of the school psychological environment and early adolescents' psychological and behavioral functioning in school: The mediating role of goals and belonging. *Journal of Educational Psychology, 88,* 408–422.

Schiefele, U. (1991). Interest, learning, and motivation. *Educational Psychologist, 26,* 299–323.

Schunk, D. H. (1991). Self-efficacy and academic motivation. *Educational Psychologist, 26,* 207–231.

Schwarz, N. (1990). Feelings as information: Informational and motivational functions of affective states. In E. T. Higgins & R. M. Sorrentino (Eds.), *Handbook of motivation and cognition: Foundations of social behavior* (Vol. 2, pp. 528–561). New York: The Guilford Press.

Searle, J. R. (1998). *Mind, language, and society: Philosophy in the real world.* New York: Basic Books.

Sinatra, G. M., & Dole, J. A. (1998). Case studies in conceptual change: A social psychological perspective. In B. Guzzetti & C. Hynd (Eds.), *Perspectives on conceptual change: Multiple ways to understand knowing and learning in a complex world* (pp. 39–53). Mahwah, NJ: Lawrence Erlbaum Associates.

Smith, J. P., diSessa, A. A., & Roschelle, J. (1993). Misconceptions reconceived: A constructivist analysis of knowledge in transition. *The Journal of the Learning Sciences, 3*(2), 115–163.

Strike, K. A., & Posner, G. J. (1992). A revisionist theory of conceptual change. In R. A. Duschl & R. J. Hamilton (Eds.), *Philosophy of science, cognitive psychology, and educational theory and practice* (pp. 147–176). Albany, NY: State University of New York Press.

Venville, G. J., & Treagust, D. F. (1998). Exploring conceptual change in genetics using a multidimensional interpretive framework. *Journal of Research in Science Teaching, 35,* 1031–1055.

Vosniadou, S., & Brewer, W. F. (1992). Mental models of the earth: A study of conceptual change in childhood. *Cognitive Psychology, 24,* 535–585.

Vosniadou, S., & Brewer, W. F. (1994). Mental models of the day/night cycle. *Cognitive Science, 18,* 123–183.

Weiner, B. (1990). History of motivational research in education. *Journal of Educational Psychology, 82,* 616–622.

Wellman, H. M., & Gelman, S. A. (1998). Knowledge acquisition in foundational domains. In W. Damon (Series Ed.) and D. Kuhn & R. S. Siegler (Vol. Eds.), *Handbook of child psychology: Vol. 2. Cognition, perception, and language* (5th ed., pp. 523–573). New York: Wiley.

Wolters, C. A., Yu, S. L., & Pintrich, P. R. (1996). The relation between goal orientation and students' motivational beliefs and self-regulated learning. *Learning and Individual Differences, 6,* 211–238.

III

PROSPECTS AND PROBLEMS FOR MODELS OF INTENTIONAL CONCEPTUAL CHANGE

13

Exploring the Relationships Between Conceptual Change and Intentional Learning

Stella Vosniadou
University of Athens, Greece

At the time when systematic science instruction starts, most children have already constructed a naïve theory of physics that makes it possible for them to interpret phenomena in the physical world. *Theory* is used here to denote a relational, explanatory structure, and not an explicit, well-formed, and socially-shared scientific theory. This naïve theory is based on everyday experience and information coming from lay culture and is very different in its structure, in the phenomena it explains, and its individual concepts, from the scientific theories to which children are exposed in school. Learning science requires the fundamental restructuring of the naïve theory, a restructuring that can be referred to as *theory change*. More specifically, *conceptual change* can be defined as the outcome of a complex cognitive as well as social process whereby an initial framework theory is restructured. Studies of conceptual change have shown that this is a slow and gradual affair often accompanied by misconceptions, inert knowledge, internal inconsistencies, and lack of critical thinking.

This chapter argues that it is possible for conceptual change to take place without intentional learning, but that this type of conceptual change is less than adequate. The new conceptions are unstable, often marked by internal inconsistencies, and not under the full conscious control of the learner. Intentional learning can greatly facilitate conceptual change not only by making the monitoring of information more efficient, but also by making learners have greater metaconceptual awareness of their underlying beliefs and presuppositions and access to greater and more efficient mechanisms for the acquisition of knowledge.

Intentional learning is defined here as the pursuit of understanding over and above the requirements of school tasks. In order to achieve this kind of learning, children must be purposeful and planful and able to monitor and regulate their learning in a metacognitive manner. It is assumed that intentional learning is something that develops and can be cultivated by instruction. Cognitive–developmental research shows that the process of conceptual change proceeds through the incorporation of scientific information into existing knowledge structures and the creation of synthetic models. Although these processes may not be under the conscious control of the learner, they may nevertheless move children in the direction of the desired conceptual change, suggesting that conceptual change can happen without intentional learning. Although intentional learning may not be absolutely necessary for conceptual change to occur, it is by no means irrelevant to the issue of conceptual change. Indeed, it is difficult to imagine how students can understand the most difficult and counterintuitive concepts of modern science by simply assimilating new information into existing knowledge structures and without being intentional. I argue here that intentional learning can greatly promote conceptual change.

Conceptual change does not happen only in learning science. It can be observed in mathematics, in history, in psychology, etc. I refer mostly to science concepts in this chapter because this is the area covered by my research.

WHAT IS INTENTIONAL LEARNING?

Sinatra (2000) recently defined *intentional learning* as the kind of learning that is goal directed and deliberate, internally initiated rather than initiated by the environment, and under the conscious control of the learner, who can initiate, redirect, or cease learning at will. "The intentional learner is one who uses knowledge or belief in internally initiated, goal directed action in the service of knowledge and skill acquisition" (p. 15). The construct of intentional learning is related in educational psychology with the constructs of metacognition, self-regulation, engagement, and critical thinking.

Sinatra (2000) argued that our conceptions of the learner have changed over the years from that of a passive receiver of information to an active constructor of knowledge, and more recently from an active constructor to that of an intentional learner as well. She claimed that researchers now realize that "learners have much more control over their learning than previously thought" (p. 29), and that "researchers in both cognitive and educational psychology now appreciate that learners play a self-initiated, goal-directed, purposive role in the learning process" (pp. 35–36).

I agree with Sinatra on the definition of intentional learning, and this is the definition I use. There is one area of possible disagreement, however, which has to do with whether we would like to believe that intentional learning is something that develops spontaneously with age, or as Bereiter and Scardamalia (1989) claimed, that "intentional learning is an achievement, not an automatic consequence of human intelligence," and "that it is not even encouraged and promoted by school-type tasks" (p. 366). Bereiter and Scardamalia (1989) argued that students develop strategies to meet the short-term goals of school tasks in ways that economize on mental effort and thus lack the more effortful moves that may lead to the development of intentional learning. "Children have little conception of learning as a goal directed process so that, when they try to direct their learning, they can do little except assign themselves some kind of school-like work" (p. 377). Bereiter and Scardamalia (1989) gave many examples in their chapter, based on their studies of learning in the school context, to support the conclusion that "school work does not produce intentional learning." Although we do not yet have the necessary evidence to draw educated conclusions, my tendency is to agree more with Bereiter and Scardamalia's pessimistic conclusions on this point. In other words, I think that although learners have the potential to become intentional, they do not all achieve this potential. Thus, I consider intentional learning not as an automatic characteristic of all learners, but as something that develops with age and is affected by schooling, although not necessarily by the nature of instruction that goes on in many schools.

To conclude, the definition of intentional learning used in this chapter is the deliberate and purposeful learning initiated by intrinsically motivated learners under their full conscious control. It is assumed that intentional learning is not an automatic characteristic of learners, but rather something that develops with age and expertise and can be facilitated by schooling. This chapter's purpose is to investigate the relationship between intentional learning and conceptual change. To do that, we need to better define what is meant by *conceptual change*. This is done next.

A THEORETICAL FRAMEWORK FOR UNDERSTANDING CONCEPTUAL CHANGE

The proposal that the learning of science involves conceptual change has its roots in the work of science educators like Novak (1977), Driver and Easley (1978), and Viennot (1979), who were among the first to pay attention to the fact that students bring to the science learning task alternative frameworks, preconceptions, or misconceptions, that are robust and difficult to extinguish through teaching. Posner, Strike, Hewson, and Gertzog (1982) drew an analogy between Piaget's concepts of assimilation and accommodation and the concepts of "normal science" and "scientific revolution" offered by philosophers of science such as Kuhn (1970), and derived from this analogy an instructional theory to promote "accommodation" in students' learning of science. The work of Posner et al. (1982) became the leading paradigm that guided research and practice in science education for many years. Recently, a number of researches called for a broader perspective on conceptual change, one that takes into consideration motivational and affective factors, does not treat children like rational scientists, and recognizes that science is socially constructed and validated (e.g., Caravita & Halden, 1994; Pintrich, 2000).

At present, most researchers agree that conceptual change is not something that takes place solely in individual minds, but a process that can be facilitated (or hindered) by sociocultural factors and educational settings. In order to fully understand conceptual change, we therefore have to investigate how individuals learn in social contexts. More specifically, a full theory of conceptual change needs to provide information about the following four variables:

1. Individual cognitive changes, such as changes in beliefs, in reasoning processes, and in strategies adopted during the process of conceptual change.

2. Individual motivational and affective variables, such as students' beliefs and attitudes about science, their motivation to engage in academic work, their beliefs about themselves as learners, and their epistemological beliefs about learning, their goals, interests, etc.

3. The educational settings in which science instruction takes place. It is important to examine whether these educational settings emphasize memorization or understanding, inquiry or learning by authority, allow students some degree of control over their learning or not, support a constructivist view of knowledge, foster metacognition, self-awareness, and intentional learning, etc.

4. The broader social and cultural environments in which students live and learn. Do they live in an environment of scientifically literate adults with high degrees of science knowledge or not? Is science knowledge something to be expected and demonstrated in everyday discourse, or do they live in a society where science knowledge is not appreciated?

Having described the broader framework within which we need to consider conceptual change, I consider in greater detail only one of the aforementioned perspectives, namely, the cognitive–developmental one. As a cognitive–developmental psychologist, I have studied most closely the cognitive changes that take place in the process of learning science. I do not consider this approach to be contradictory to an approach that emphasizes individual motivational/affective factors or an approach that focuses on sociocultural aspects of conceptual change. I believe that all these approaches are necessary for a complete analysis of the problem and provide complementary rather than contradictory kinds of information. Indeed, the point that both individual and social perspectives on learning are necessary was also made in a recent article by Anderson, Greeno, Reder, and Simon (2000).

The cognitive-developmental approach can provide information about the organization of conceptual structures and a description of how they change. It can also provide information about the mechanisms that may be responsible for bringing about these changes as well as about students' reasoning and strategies. These types of information are essential in order to understand how conceptual change takes place and about how motivational and social factors can best promote conceptual change. We cannot say much about the motivational and social variables that can influence conceptual change if we do not know exactly how conceptual change happens.

Indeed, most studies that discuss the motivational and social factors that may influence conceptual change are descriptive and do not propose a theory to explain why and how the proposed motivational and social factors influence conceptual change (for a beginning attempt, see Dole and Sinatra, 1998). The mechanism usually considered is the likelihood that students will engage in deeper processing of information. There is no doubt that deeper processing is a variable that can influence conceptual change. It is a reasonable assumption to make that students who process material more deeply are more likely to change their conceptions that those who do not. But we need to analyze further what "deeper processing" involves and how it happens. We need to understand the more specific processes that make deeper processing instrumental in bringing about conceptual change. The more successful we are in doing so, the better we will understand the motivational and sociocultural factors that can bring about conceptual change (see also Pintrich, 1999 on this point).

Having said that, I now outline a cognitive-developmental approach to conceptual change, paying particular attention to the possible mechanisms that may be involved.

A COGNITIVE-DEVELOPMENTAL APPROACH TO CONCEPTUAL CHANGE

The conceptual change approach described in this section is based on cognitive-developmental research and attempts to provide a framework for understanding how students learn science. This approach can be broadly characterized on the basis of the following five propositions:

1. The human mind has developed, through evolution, specialized mechanisms to pick up information from the physical and social world. The human child is a complex biological organism capable of engaging in quick and efficient learning immediately after birth. Some things are easy to learn, not because what is learned is less complex, but because human beings are prepared through evolution for this kind of learning. This seems to apply to the learning of language and to naïve physics. Naïve physics is the knowledge about the physical world that develops early in infancy and allows children to function in the physical environment.

2. Naïve physics is not a collection of unrelated pieces of knowledge. It provides a narrow but nevertheless coherent explanatory framework for conceptualizing the physical world. I argued previously (Vosniadou, 1994b) that naïve physics is organized in a framework theory that constrains the process of acquiring further knowledge about the physical world. I do not assume that this framework is anything like a scientific theory, but rather that it consists of narrow but nevertheless internally consistent explanations that attempt to organize the multiplicity of sensory experiences children have in the everyday world as well as the information they receive from the culture.

3. Naïve physics can stand in the way of learning science. This happens because scientific explanations of physical phenomena often violate fundamental principles of naïve physics, constantly confirmed by our everyday experience in the context of lay culture. After all, the currently accepted scientific explanations are the product of a long historical development of science, characterized by revolutionary theory changes that restructured our representations of the physical world.

4. Conceptual change is required to learn many science concepts. This is because the initial explanations of the physical world in naïve physics are not fragmented observations but form a coherent whole. Because of this, the learning of science requires acquiring a different theory about the physical world.

5. Conceptual change is a slow and gradual process that proceeds through the gradual replacement of the beliefs and presuppositions of naïve physics. Many so-called misconceptions can be explained as synthetic models formed by learners in their effort to assimilate new information into the existing framework theory. The change of the framework theory is difficult because it forms a coherent explanatory system based on everyday experience and is tied to years of confirmation.

The conceptual change approach described here is very different from the empiricist approach that many researchers and science educators take to characterize the process of learning science. Many science educators believe that there is little or no predisposition for learning. Knowledge acquisition is based on experience and develops in a continuous manner, enriching the knowledge already existing in memory. Some researchers, such as diSessa (1988, 1993), argued that intuitive physics is based on superficial and fragmented interpretations of physical reality that he called *p-prims* (phenomenological primitives). According to this view, learning science is basically a process of organizing p-prims into more complex and systematic knowledge structures governed by the laws and principles of physics (diSessa, 1993, 2000). I believe that diSessa (2000) uses the term *phenomenological primitives* to refer to the thousands of sensory experiences that form the background of our experiential knowledge of the physical world. My position is that children from early on organize at least some of these experiences in narrow but relatively coherent explanatory frameworks in their attempt to make sense out of the physical world (see also Vosniadou, 2002).

Based on an empiricist approach, many science educators think that science learning is difficult because students have limited experiences and/or because they do not know how to interpret the limited experiences they have. They claim that children do not (a) know how to test hypotheses, (b) accept explanations that should be rejected on the basis of the available evidence, (c) base their explanations on what they perceive through their senses and not on the logic of things, or (d) even see the need to explain why things happen. Instruction, according to this approach, should basically provide children with more experiences and opportunities to understand the process of doing science.

I find a great deal of truth in these explanations. There is no doubt that students base their explanations on everyday experiences that are by definition limited, that they need to develop better procedures for testing and evaluating hypotheses, and that the thinking of the expert is more coherent, more systematic, and more closely linked to the laws and principles of physics. On the other hand, children's thinking does not appear to be quite as limited as previously suggested. Vosniadou and Brewer (1994) found that 38 out of 60 elementary school children they examined provided well-defined explanations of the day–night cycle. These explanations were empirically accurate, in the sense of agreeing with the empirical evidence expected to be within their range. In addition to being sensitive to issues of empirical adequacy, the children seemed to show sensitivity to issues of logical consistency and of simplicity in their explanations.

Limitations in experiences and in logical thinking cannot fully explain the phenomena of misconceptions and of inert knowledge that are observed not only in elementary school students but in high school and college students as well. In order to explain these phenomena, we need a theory of learning not only as a process of enriching existing knowledge, but also as conceptual change, as described earlier.

A different but also widely known approach to learning and development is based on Piaget's theory. Piaget (e.g., 1970) also gave a great deal of attention to experience, but he claimed that the process of developing more abstract conceptual structures depends on the constructive activity of the learner. He chose to provide a structural account of the intellect in terms of a mathematical model. According to this model, the process of intellectual development proceeds through a series of stages, each characterized by a different psychological structure. In infancy, intellectual structures take the form of concrete action schemas. During the preschool years, these structures acquire representational status and later develop into concrete operations (described in terms of groupings based on the mathematical notion of sets and their combinations). The last stage of intellectual development, formal operational thought, is characterized by the ability to engage in prepositional reasoning, to entertain and systematically evaluate hypotheses, etc.

The process of cognitive development described by Piaget has been characterized as "global restructuring" (Carey, 1985) and is considered to be the product of the natural, spontaneous process of intellectual development and not of explicit learning. The implications of this approach for instruction are that not only should we provide students with rich experiences, we should also encourage the constructive activities of the learner so that these experiences are best utilized for knowledge acquisition. According to Piagetian theory, experiences may be interpreted differently at different stages, depending on the logical nature of the underlying conceptual structures. The understanding of science concepts is not really possible, according to Piaget, until the stage of formal operations that develops during adolescence.

Piaget was instrumental in introducing individual, psychological constructivism (as opposed to social constructivism) to learning research. The importance of prior knowledge and the mechanisms of assimilation, accommodation, and equilibration in the context of constructivism are important contributions of Piagetian theory to learning and instruction. Although I agree with the aforementioned aspects of Piagetian theory, the conceptual change approach described here differs in at least three areas from Piaget's views.

The first has to do with the importance of social, cultural, and instructional influences on learning. We place far greater importance on those factors than Piaget did. The second has to do with the emphasis on knowledge acquisition in specific subject-matter areas and the notion of domain-specific as opposed to global restructuring. The present approach focuses on knowledge acquisition in specific subject-matter areas and describes the learning of science concepts as a process that requires the significant reorganization of existing domain-specific knowledge structures. This type of knowledge reorganization is also known in the literature as *domain-specific restructuring*, as opposed to Piagetian *global restructuring* (see also Carey, 1985). The notion of restructuring is, of course, different from empiricist approaches that consider learning as knowledge enrichment. Finally, a third area of difference concerns the relative importance of biological factors on cognitive development. Without considering ourselves in the strong rationalist camp, we believe that there is greater biological predisposition to learning than Piaget has acknowledged in his work (see Pillatelli-Palmarini, 1979).

An example of the knowledge acquisition process in observational astronomy is provided next.

AN EXAMPLE OF CONCEPTUAL CHANGE: THE CASE OF THE EARTH CONCEPT

Our research revealed several representations that elementary school children form regarding the shape of the earth and explanations of the day–night cycle (Vosniadou & Brewer, 1992, 1994) that can be seen as "misconceptions." Figure 13.1 shows the range of representations of the shape of the earth obtained by elementary school children in a study conducted in the United States. Some children believe that the earth is shaped like a flat rectangle or a disc, is supported by ground below, and covered by sky above its top. Other children think that the earth is a hollow sphere, with people living on flat ground deep inside it, or a flattened sphere with people living on its flat top and bottom. Some other children form the interesting model of a dual earth, according to which there are two earths: a flat one on which people live, and a spherical one that is a planet up in the sky. These representations of the earth are not rare. In fact, only 23 of the 60 children that participated in this study (mostly fifth graders) had formed the culturally accepted model of the spherical earth. This finding has been confirmed by a series of cross-cultural studies that investigated the concept of the earth in children from India, Greece, and Samoa (Vosniadou, 1994a).

Why do elementary school children construct such misrepresentations of the earth? Even very young children are now exposed to considerable information regarding the spherical shape of the earth through children's books, TV programs, discussions with parents, globes, etc. In our studies in the United States (e.g., Vosniadou, 1994b; Vosniadou & Brewer, 1992), we had to go as far as testing 3-year-olds to find children who had not been exposed to this information. Many 4-year-old children already knew something about the spherical shape of the earth. It is therefore difficult to claim that children's misconceptions about the shape of the earth result

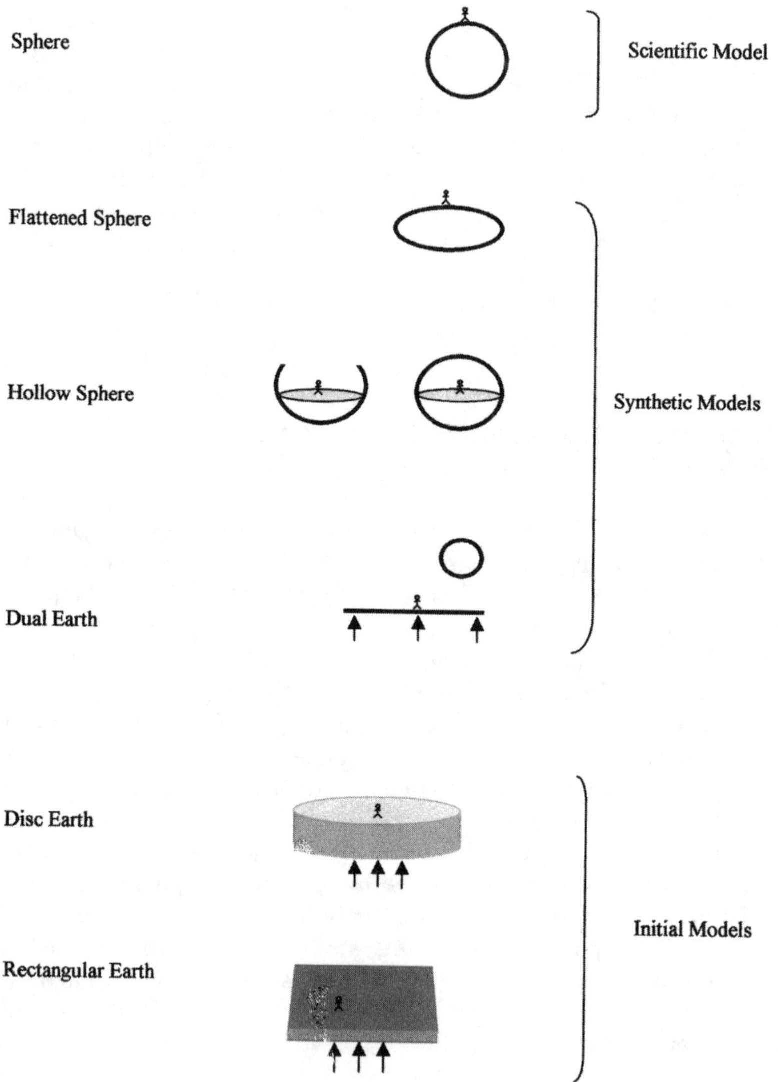

FIG. 13.1. Mental models of the earth.

from limited experiences. The explanation of misconceptions we propose is that they are caused by students' attempts to reconcile incompatible pieces of information, some of them stemming from everyday experience and some coming from the surrounding culture, often in the form of science instruction in the schools. Often the surrounding culture is inconsistent in the kind of information it provides. For example, we talk about the sun setting and rising, the sun going behind the mountains, etc. And although in the case of the earth shape and day–night cycle most individuals may be aware of the scientific explanations, this is not the case when we move to explanations of the seasons or the phases of the moon, or in areas of physics such as mechanics or thermodynamics.

If we look carefully at the misconceptions of the earth presented in Fig. 13.1, we see that in all cases they are attempts to solve the problem of how it is possible for the earth to be spherical and flat at the same time and how it is possible for people to live on this flat earth without falling. For example, the children who form the model of the hollow sphere seem to understand that the shape of the earth is spherical, but they believe that people live on flat ground inside the earth. On the other hand, the children who form the model of the flattened sphere think that the earth is spherical but also a little flat on the top and maybe the bottom where the people live. The children who form the dual earth model think that there are two earths: a round one up in the sky and a flat one on which people actually live!

All misconceptions regarding the shape of the earth encountered in the American sample, as well as the Indian, Greek, and Samoan samples in our studies (see Vosniadou, 1994b), can be explained as attempts on the part of the children to synthesize two inconsistent pieces of information: the information they receive from instruction according to which the earth is a sphere, and the information they receive from their everyday experiences and culture that the earth is flat and gravity operates in an up–down fashion. It appears that children from early on (6 to 7 months of age) organize space in terms of the directions of up and down and understand that physical objects fall down when they are not supported (see Baillargeon, 1990; Spelke, 1991).

Now, we can all understand how children may form an initial representation of the earth as a flat, physical object supported by ground below, with people living on its flat surface and with solar objects located above its top. Our studies of preschool children's ideas about the earth do indeed confirm the hypothesis that children start with this simple representation of the earth. The interesting question is why children do not change their flat earth representation to that of a spherical earth when they are exposed to the relevant information.

My answer is that the representation of the earth as a flat, physical object, is a complex construction supported by a whole system of observations, beliefs, and presuppositions that form a relatively coherent and systematic explanatory system. Figure 13.2 shows some of the observations, beliefs, and presuppositions of the specific and framework theories that underlie the representation of a flat, supported earth, which we assume to be the first representation of the earth that children form.

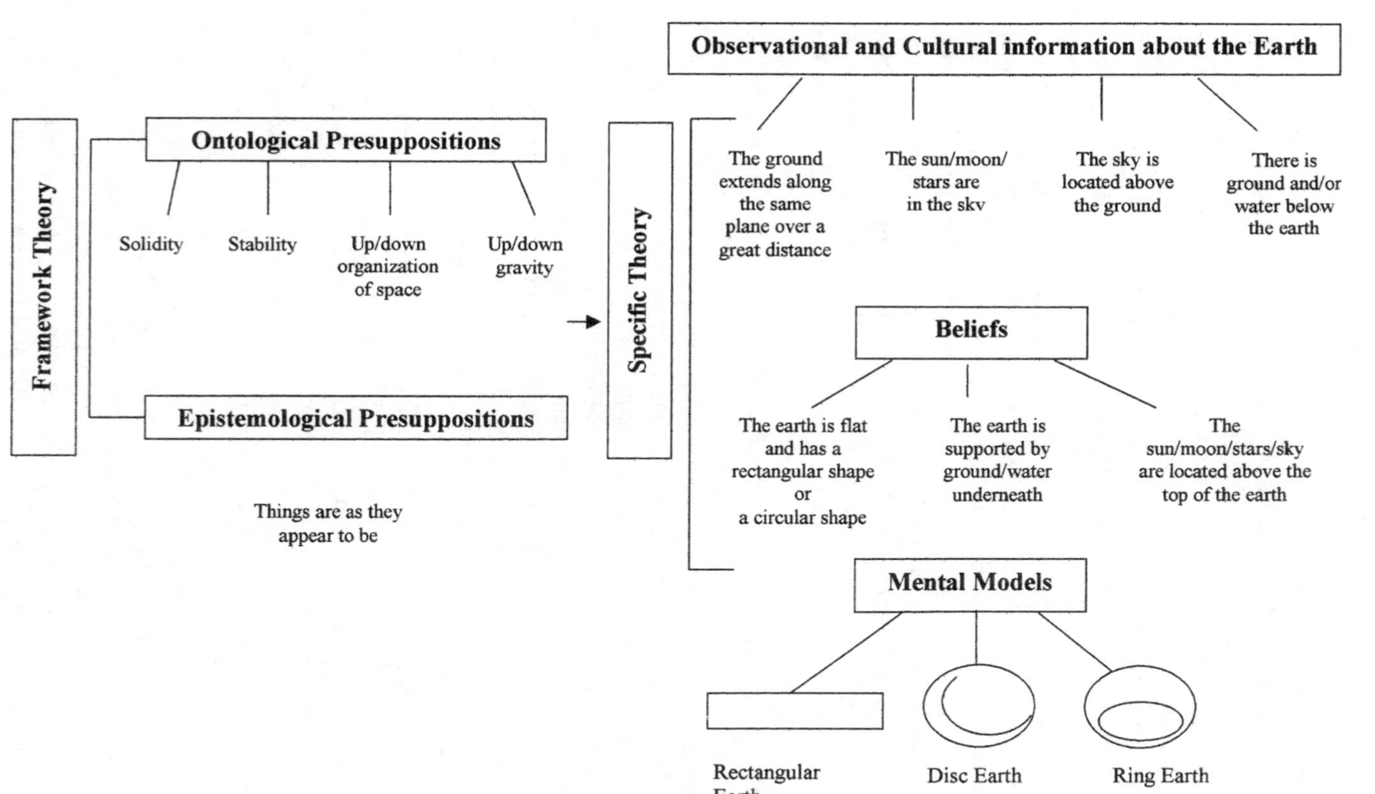

FIG. 13.2. Hypothetical conceptual structure underlying children's mental models of the earth.

I cannot go into detail here about this explanatory system (see Vosniadou, 1994b; Vosniadou & Ioannides, 1998). The important point to make here for our purpose is that the representation of a flat earth is based on the categorization of the earth as a physical and not an astronomical body. If the earth is categorized as a physical body, then it should be constrained by all the presuppositions that apply to physical bodies in general. As shown in Fig. 13.2, some of these presuppositions are that the earth is a solid, stable physical body, supported by ground or water; that space is organized in terms of the directions of up and down; and that unsupported objects fall "down."

Such presuppositions stand in the way of understanding the spherical shape of the earth and are not addressed by science instruction. An examination of the science curricula used to teach astronomy to elementary school children in the United States and in Greece shows that students are not provided with explanations of how it is possible for the earth to be round and flat at the same time or how it is possible for people to live on the "sides" or "bottom" of this globe without falling "down." It seems particularly important to teach children something about gravity in order for them to understand how people can live on a spherical, rotating earth.

The mechanism of adding information into an existing knowledge base can produce a misconception if the two pieces of information belong to two incompatible explanatory frameworks, as is the case in the shape of the earth. In these situations, the understanding of a scientific explanation requires a more fundamental restructuring of the knowledge base—the revision of fundamental presuppositions and beliefs—before the additive mechanisms can work. This is what we mean by conceptual change.

The aforementioned analysis is supported by empirical evidence not only in the case of astronomy, but in many other areas of physics. Our studies of conceptual change in mechanics and thermal physics (Ioannides & Vosniadou, in press; Vosniadou & Kempner, 1993), as well as other studies in biology, chemistry, and geology (Ioannidou & Vosniadou, 2000; Kyrkos & Vosniadou, 1997; Kouka, Vosniadou, & Tsaparlis, 2001), show that students form synthetic models in their attempts to incorporate the information they receive from instruction into a fundamentally different explanatory framework.

For example, in mechanics, children construct an initial concept of force as a property of objects that feel heavy. This internal force appears to represent the potential these objects have to react to other objects with which they come in contact. It is also central in explaining the motion of inanimate objects. In the ontology of the young child, the natural state of inanimate objects is that of rest, and their motion is a phenomenon that needs to be explained, usually in terms of a causal agent. This causal agent is the force of another object.

The initial concept of force is very different from the way the linguistic term *force* is currently interpreted by the scientific community. In Newtonian physics, force is not an internal property of physical objects but a process that explains changes in their kinetic state.

It appears that the process of understanding the scientific concept of force is slow and gradual, and likely to give rise to misconceptions. Students gradually differentiate the concept of weight from the concept of force and replace the notion of an internal force (force is a property of all objects that are heavy or have weight) with the notion of an acquired force (force is an acquired property of the objects that move). Despite important changes in the concept of force that occur with development, certain entrenched presuppositions of the framework theory, such as that force is a property of objects and that the motion of inanimate objects requires an explanation, continue to remain in place in the conceptual system of high school or even university students, who have been exposed to systematic instruction in Newtonian mechanics for at least 2 years (Ioannides & Vosniadou, in press).

IS INTENTIONAL LEARNING NECESSARY FOR CONCEPTUAL CHANGE?

The previous section argued that the process of conceptual change is slow and gradual and that it proceeds through the gradual replacement of the beliefs and presuppositions of intuitive physics. Some of mechanisms that seem to characterize this process are the addition and/or deletion of beliefs and presuppositions with the subsequent reorganization of the specific and framework theories within which these beliefs and presuppositions are embedded. In Fig. 13.2, I presented the kinds of presuppositions and beliefs that may give rise to the initial models of a rectangular earth, disc earth, or ring earth (observed in our studies of Samoan children and also of Greek children described in Vosniadou, 1994a). The possible change from a rectangular model of the earth to a disc model could be accomplished through a simple change in the belief regarding the shape of the earth (from rectangular to circular), which belongs to the specific theory of the earth.

A more fundamental change in beliefs would be required for the formation of the hollow sphere model—the earth is like a hollow sphere with people living on flat ground inside it. This model would require not only a change in the belief regarding the shape of the earth (from rectangular or circular to spherical), but also a change in the belief that the earth is supported by ground or water. Notice that the beliefs regarding the sky and solar objects located above the top of the earth could remain the same (thus, giving rise to the variant of the hollow sphere model in which the sky and solar objects are included in the top part of the sphere), or they could change, (thus, giving rise to the model of the hollow sphere in which the sky and solar objects surround the earth, as shown in Fig. 13.1).

The creation of the scientific model of the spherical earth would, however, require more than changes in the beliefs of the scientific theory. It would require fundamental changes in the ontological and epistemological presuppositions of the framework theory. It would require changes in the presuppositions regarding stability, up–down organization of space, and up–down gravity. These changes would amount to the realization that the earth cannot be categorized as a physical object but belongs to the category of astronomical objects instead.

This type of change is similar to the change in ontological categories described by Chi (1992), as well as to the kind of change observed in the history of science and described as "tree jumping" in Thagard (1992). According to Thagard (1992), one of the characteristics of the theory change that accompanied the move from the cosmological system espoused by Ptolemy to that espoused by Copernicus was a change in the categorization of the earth from a physical body to that of a planet, just like the other planets in the solar system (see Fig. 13.3). We could argue that something similar happens to children as they move from a simple distinction between the earth as a physical object and astronomical objects (objects in the sky, such as the sun, the moon, the various planets and starts), to a more complex categorization of major bodies into suns, planets, and satellites, etc, as shown in Fig. 13.3.

There is no doubt that conceptual change is a constructive process that requires the active engagement of the learner. The learner must be actively involved in incorporating incoming information, checking its consistency with existing knowledge, replacing beliefs and presuppositions, differentiating concepts, and creating new ontological categories when needed. As mentioned earlier, the cognitive system is highly adaptive and biologically prepared to pick up and organize certain types of information from the physical world, allowing efficient and quick learning to develop. One would argue that such a system is by nature "purposeful," but this notion of purposefulness does not include deliberateness and conscious control. I interpret intentionality to include deliberate purposefulness and conscious control of the learner. The question is: Is this kind of intentional learning necessary for conceptual change to occur? Can students engage in the kinds of conceptual change processes described here, without being fully aware of what they are doing and without being deliberately purposeful? One way to answer this question is to look for evidence that suggests lack of intentional learning while engaging in processes leading toward conceptual change. What would be the kind of evidence that would suggest lack of intentional learning?

(A) From Ptolemy to Copernicus

(B) From Grade 1 to Grade 5

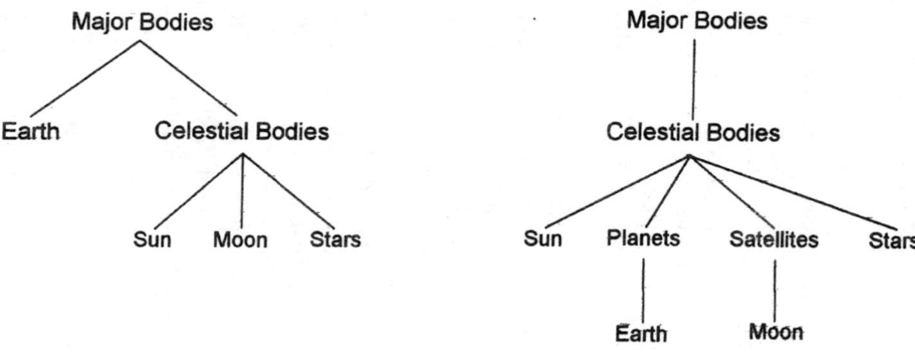

FIG. 13.3. Conceptual change in astronomy.

Internal Inconsistencies

One kind of evidence may be the existence of internal inconsistencies. To the extent that a purposeful and intentional learner checks for and corrects the conceptual system for consistency, the presence of inconsistencies is an indication for lack of intentional learning. The presence of inconsistencies is, of course, a common phenomenon in conceptual change research. Indeed, many researchers claim that in the process of conceptual change, students are fundamentally inconsistent.

In science education research, inconsistency is usually considered to be any instance where an individual subject uses the scientific concept correctly in some instances and incorrectly in others. I argue that this is not a good way to measure inconsistency because a student may appear to be inconsistent in his or her use of a scientific concept, but may hold instead an internally consistent alternative (synthetic) model. This is a more liberal notion of consistency (see Vosniadou, 2002). The studies in our lab that do not penalize students for holding alternate beliefs if they make consistent use of them show that between 80% and 85% of the students exhibit some internal consistency. This shows that 15% to 20% of the students are not able to incorporate the new information into logically consistent conceptual structures. As the complexity of the subject-matter area increases, this number may become larger.

One might object here that the presence of internal inconsistencies may not be related to intentionality in the sense that it is possible to have intentional learners who are goal-directed and motivated but unaware that pieces of their existing knowledge are in conflict.[1] It is indeed possible to have intentionality without full awareness; however, I think it is still fair to argue that students who are metacognitive and intentional should exhibit fewer internal inconsistencies in their thinking, and, that in this respect, intentionality should be negatively related to the presence of inconsistencies.

Lack of Explanatory Coherence

Another phenomenon we observe in conceptual change research that could be used as evidence for lack of intentional learning is lack of coherence. In other words, as students are exposed to scientific information, the coherence of the initial explanatory framework starts being destroyed. Instead of being restructured, the initial theory is replaced by a mixture of unconnected explanations tied to specific contexts of use, some of which are based on the initial theory and some on the scientific one (see Ioan-

[1]I am indebted to Gale Sinatra for drawing my attention to this possibility.

nides and Vosniadou, in press, for examples). Lack of coherence is different from lack of consistency. Coherence characterizes a theoretical structure that can be used to explain a number of diverse phenomena, but this can be done with greater or lesser internal consistency. Our studies of the concept of force have shown that as many as 53% of the 15-year-old students appealed to different kinds of forces in different contexts (see Ioannides & Vosniadou, in press). For example, some students think of the force of gravity when they deal with falling objects, but do not think that the force of gravity applies to stationary objects. Lack of coherence is related to the phenomenon of inert knowledge (Bransford, Franks, Vye, & Sherwood, 1989). Inert knowledge is knowledge used in limited contexts and does not generalize to other situations where it could also apply.

Noncritical Belief Change

Even when students appear to be successful in understanding the scientific information to which they have been exposed, they may be doing so without engaging in intentional learning. This can be the case if conceptual change (as judged by the adoption of the scientific model) has been achieved through noncritical belief change. In the pages that follow, I try to describe how something like this is possible.

The first time I became sensitized to issues having to do with lack of metaconceptual awareness and intentionality in conceptual change was in the context of a large classroom intervention that took place in a Greek elementary school. Based on the results of our studies in observational astronomy, my colleagues and I designed a detailed curriculum and instructional interventions for an 8-week course about the earth and the solar system for fifth-grade students (see Vosniadou, Ioannides, Dimitrakopoulou, and Papademitriou, 2001). This course included a unit on the relative sizes of the earth, the sun, and the moon. We wanted to teach the children about the relationship between the apparent size and distance of the sun and moon, and to show to them that the sun is actually much bigger than the moon, despite the fact that their size appears to be almost the same.

Before starting the instruction, we asked the children to make drawings of the sun and the moon depicting their relative sizes. As we had expected, most of the children thought either that the sun and moon had approximately the same size or that the sun was a little larger than the moon. After that, we proceeded with a series of instructional interventions in which the children read books about the sun and the moon that described their actual and relative sizes, saw videos, participated in discussions, and were exposed to demonstrations using real balloons of different sizes seen from different distances. Our goal was to make the students sensitive to the relationship between apparent size and distance. We wanted the children to understand that two objects that are very different in size may appear to be about the same if the smaller object is much closer to the observer than the larger. And, of course, we wanted them to relate these differences to the sun and the moon.

A week after the intervention, we asked the children to make a drawing depicting the relative sizes of the sun and the moon again. Practically all the children drew the sun much bigger than the moon this time—an important difference compared to their drawings prior to the intervention. If we had not pursued this issue further, we would have been convinced that our intervention had the desired effect.

After they finished with the drawing, however, we asked the children to answer the following question: Explain why the sun appears to be about the same size as the moon when in reality it is much bigger. The results were very interesting. Instead of providing explanations of the difference in apparent versus real size of the sun and the moon in terms of their size–distance relations, as we expected, the children denied that this difference ever existed. They gave answers such as these: The sun is always much bigger than the moon, but we cannot see the difference very well because clouds block the sun, or because the sun is very bright during the day and we cannot actually see how big it is, etc.

How do we interpret these results? I believe that they suggest that although children's representations of the sun and the moon had changed, the children were not metaconceptually aware of this change. The original representation was replaced by another, which happened to be more scientifically correct, but the memory of the first representation had faded. The children were not in a position to compare their previous representation to the present one and did not seem to understand the difference between appearance and reality.[2]

Because we know on the basis of developmental research that much younger children are able to distinguish appearance from reality (e.g. Flavell, 1988; Perner, 1991), it does not appear likely that our students (who were between 10 and 11 years of age) were not competent enough to distinguish appearance from reality. A more suitable interpretation of this finding is that the children were not thinking of the relative size of the sun and the moon in terms of an appearance/reality distinction, but rather in terms of what is the "correct" fact. Once the correct fact was registered,

---

[2]It may appear here that I am arguing for a replacement theory of conceptual change. There is a debate in the literature as to whether conceptual change involves the replacement of earlier concepts or the ability of the learner to entertain multiple perspectives. I think that findings such as the ones reported earlier suggest that both are possible, depending on the status of the learner's beliefs and his or her purposes of learning. If learners are not fully aware of their beliefs and do not think that they are involved in theory testing, then replacement is possible.

there was no need to remember much more. This is consistent with the findings that show that children do not make the explicit distinction between theory and evidence, do not understand how theories guide the hypothesis testing process, and do not treat their beliefs about the physical world as hypotheses subject to experimentation but as facts. If these facts happen to be proven wrong, they should be changed (Carey & Smith, 1993; Kuhn, Amsel, & O'Laughlin, 1988).

In order to investigate this question further, Kyriakopoulou and I designed a series of experiments to investigate whether the students who were able to construct the scientific models of the shape of the earth, the day–night cycle, the relative size of the sun, moon and earth, and the solar system, understood the difference between the scientific and phenomenal representations (Kyriakopoulou, 2001). If students decide to adopt the scientific explanation intentionally, they should be well aware of the differences and similarities between the scientific explanation and the phenomenal one and the advantages of one over the other. If, however, they were only trying to incorporate incoming information into existing conceptual structures without metaconceptual awareness, the differences and similarities between the scientific explanation and the appearance of things would not be apparent.

All the experiments were conducted with elementary school students from Grades 1, 3, and 5. The students were asked questions regarding (a) the shape of the earth, (b) the shape of the earth and gravity, (c) the relative size of the sun and the moon, (d) the relative size of the sun and the earth, and (e) the day–night cycle, and (f) the planetary system.

In experiment l, the children were shown four different cards depicting, for example, different representations of the relative size of the sun and the moon, two being more consistent with the scientific representation and two being more consistent with the phenomenal representation. In experiment 2, the children were shown only two alternative models, one closer to the phenomenal and the other closer to the scientific model. These models appeared this time on the screen of a computer and were dynamic instead of static (i.e., the earth was shown to rotate around its axis and to revolve around the sun, or the sun and moon moved up and down behind mountains, etc.). In the third experiment, the students constructed their own representations using a set of primitives (i.e., different possible depictions of the sun, moon, earth, etc.) again in a computer environment. The results of the three experiments were very similar with respect to the hypothesis being investigated. This chapter briefly discusses the results of the second experiment. The materials of the second experiment appear in Fig. 13.4.

At the beginning of the experiment, the children were given the following instructions: *As you know, the objects around us are sometimes different in*

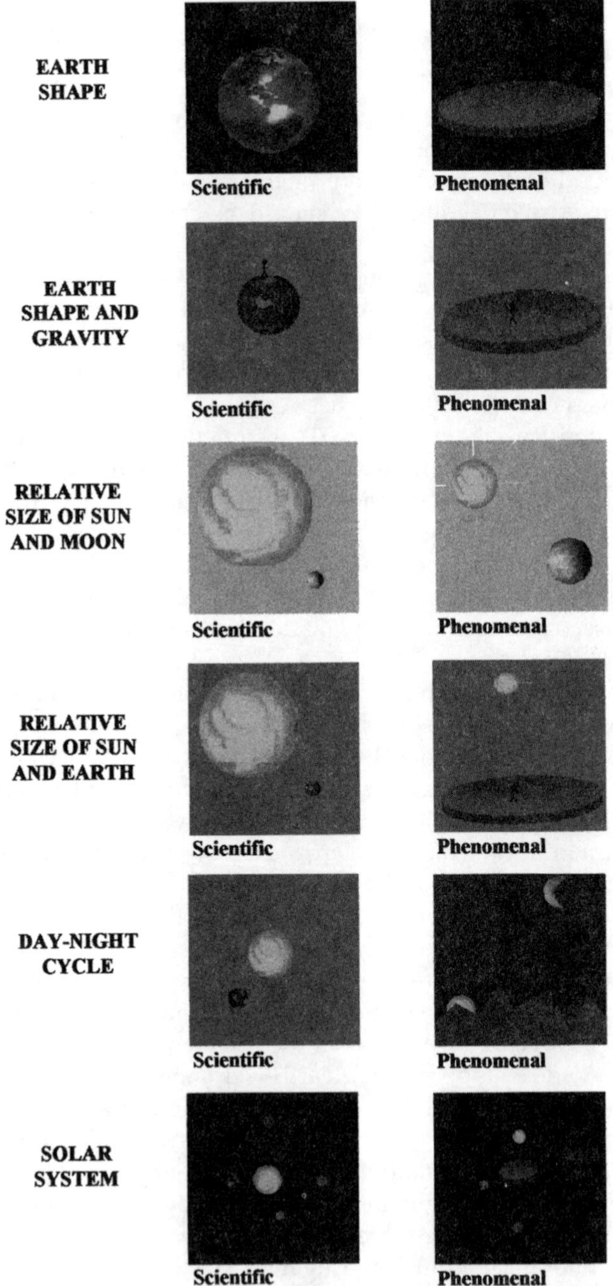

FIG. 13.4. Computer animations used to investigate students' ability to distinguish phenomenal from scientific representations in observational astronomy.

reality from what they appear to be. For example, look at this piece of paper (the child was shown a white piece of paper). *What is the real color of this paper?* (the child should say "white). The experimenter then placed the white piece of paper under a red plastic filter which made the white paper appear red. *What is the color that this paper appear to have now?* (the child should say red). *What is the real color of this paper* (the child should say white). If the child passed this pretest the experimenter proceeded. If not, the experiment stopped there.

The children who passed the pretest were shown the computer animation appearing in Fig. 13.4. They were told that the animations depicted different models of, for example, the shape of the earth, and they were told to choose from these the model that they thought was closer to the "real" shape of the earth and the model that was closer to the earth "as it appears to our eyes." They were reminded that sometimes what is real and what appears to our eyes is the same thing, and were asked to put their choices under a card that read: "As it is in reality" or "As it appears to our eyes." These cards were placed underneath the white paper and the white paper under a red plastic cover, shown earlier.

Table 13.1 shows children's categorizations following the instructions as a function of grade. The first category, in each grade column, represents the choices that were only phenomenal (phenomenal/phenomenal). In other words, the children selected only phenomenal models for both "reality" and "appearance." Table 13.1 shows that there were only a few responses of this kind for the earth shape and gravity, but more for the other questions. Obviously, the children who made these categorizations did not know the scientific representations. The third category in each grade column (scientific/phenomenal) shows the children who knew the scientific model and who made the correct categorizations—that is, they put the models closer to the scientific one under "reality" and the model closer to the phenomenal under "appearance." Many of the fifth-grade children were placed in this category, with lower percentages for Grades 3 and 1. The percent of correct categorization was lower for the solar system and for the relative size of the sun or moon, indicating that the children were not familiar with the scientific representations in these cases.

Of particular interest for our purposes are the two categories that represented only scientific choices (scientific/scientific) or reversed phenomenal/scientific. In other words, the children in these categories either selected the scientific model only or selected the scientific model for "appearance" and the phenomenal for "reality." As shown in Table 13.1, there were quite a number of children in this category. These children appeared to be mixed up as to which representation is closer to the phenomenal and which is closer to the scientific.

The results confirm our hypothesis that as children become exposed to representations closer to the scientific ones, their previous phenomenal

TABLE 13.1
Percent of Children's Responses in the Appearance/Reality Task as a Function of Grade

	Categories of Response								
	First grade			*Third grade*			*Fifth grade*		
Computer Animations	*Phenomenal/ Phenomenal*	*Phenomenal/ Scientific & Scientific/ Scientific*	*Scientific/ Phenomenal*	*Phenomenal/ Phenomenal*	*Phenomenal/ Scientific & Scientific/ Scientific*	*Scientific/ Phenomenal*	*Phenomenal/ Phenomenal*	*Phenomenal/ Scientific & Scientific/ Scientific*	*Scientific/ Phenomenal*
Earth Shape	10%	40%	50%	0%	35%	65%	0%	35%	65%
Earth Shape & Gravity	10%	40%	50%	10%	20%	70%	10%	0%	90%
Relative size of Sun & Moon	40%	45%	15%	10%	20%	70%	15%	35%	50%
Relative size of Sun and Earth	15%	35%	50%	0%	20%	80%	0%	10%	90%
Day/Night Cycle	30%	45%	25%	5%	15%	80%	20%	0%	80%
Solar System	20%	45%	35%	10%	40%	50%	15%	40%	45%

representations fade away in the background. The results, which were replicated in the other two experiments, suggest that children acquire the scientific representations as facts and incorporate them in their previous conceptual structures. As children become older and achieve a higher percentage of scientific representations, they also seem to become less inclined to mix phenomenal with scientific representations.

HOW CAN INTENTIONAL LEARNING FACILITATE CONCEPTUAL CHANGE?

Earlier I argued that cognitive–developmental studies of children's physical knowledge suggest that some conceptual change can take place without intentional learning. The lack of intentional learning was inferred from the finding that change from a "phenomenal" representation to a "scientific" one can come about without full metaconceptual awareness.

If this is indeed the case—and I admit a lot more needs to be done in order to investigate this phenomenon—why should we be bothered by this state of affairs? We need to be bothered only if we believe that intentional learning can facilitate conceptual change in some ways. Is there such a possibility? What is the extra value that intentional learning could bring to conceptual change? Next I discuss five hypotheses as to how intentional learning can facilitate conceptual change: (a) monitoring of learning, (b) metaconceptual awareness, (c) ability to entertain multiple representations, (d) epistemological views of science, and (e) more efficient mechanisms for conceptual change.

Monitoring of Learning

One kind of facilitating effect of intentional learning that researchers usually mention has to do with improvements in students' ability to monitor their learning, to capture failures in understanding, and to correct internal inconsistencies. Pintrich (1999) made a distinction between two kinds of metacognitive controls that are relevant to conceptual change instruction. One is the "tactical, moment-to-moment control of cognition" (p. 46), and the other is the strategic control of learning that has to do with students' abilities to control and guide their learning over long periods of time, to serve long terms effects.

Metaconceptual Awareness

In addition to the cognitive monitoring and strategic aspects of learning, there is another aspect of intentional learning that has to do with metaconceptual awareness. Here we are referring to students' awareness of their beliefs and presuppositions, their understanding of changes in these beliefs, and their ability to relate these changes to issues that have to do with the explanatory adequacy of beliefs. As mentioned earlier, cognitive–developmental research suggests that students are not always metaconceptually aware. They do not know exactly what they believe and do not understand the hypothetical nature of their beliefs.

This phenomenon could be related to the kind of instruction that goes on in most schools. Conceptual change in school settings is often associated not to reasoned change but to compliance to the authority of the teacher or the textbook. Often the reasons behind the proposed change are unclear. In many classrooms, science instruction follows such a path. It does not provide the open environment, the discussions with peers, and the inquiry processes that would allow students to examine their beliefs and question their explanatory adequacy. Certainly these types of classroom environments do not promote intentional learning.

The added value of intentional learning in this case is learning that is less fragile and vulnerable. In other words, we assume that the students who are aware that they have changed their beliefs and can justify this change on grounds such as greater explanatory adequacy, should be more capable of defending their beliefs from criticism and thus their learning should be less fragile.

Ability to Entertain Multiple Representations

Intentional learning may be related to the ability to entertain multiple representations. As mentioned earlier, the findings of cognitive–developmental research suggest that it is not always easy for students to hold more than one representation. It is interesting to note here that students' difficulty in holding multiple representations is not usually recognized. For example, Driver, Asoko, Leach, Mortimer, and Scott, (1994) criticized the individual (as opposed to the social) constructivist approach on the grounds that it does not consider the possibility that individuals can simultaneously entertain multiple representations or multiple conceptual schemas, "each appropriate to its specific, social setting. (Scientists after all, understand perfectly well what is meant when they are told 'shut the door and keep the cold out' or 'please feed the plants')" (p. 7). I believe that Driver et al. are correct in pointing out that conceptual change research has focused too much on the notion of "change" and has ignored the fact that we would like students to be able to entertain multiple representations (see also Vosniadou, 1999, for a discussion of this issue). However, I believe that they are wrong in their assumption that students are spontaneously able to entertain multiple representations in a reasoned fashion.

Sometimes the researchers who talk about multiple representations fail to see the difference between the flexible cognitive systems of scientifically literate adults (who are able to entertain simultaneously many representations and consider different points of view) from the inert knowledge of students. It is a common phenomenon in science instruction for students to learn to use scientific representations in the instructed contexts, usually of school science, but to continue to use their phenomenal representations in the everyday world. These students are not using multiple representations in a reasoned fashion because they do not understand how the two representations are related. I assume that this is not what Driver et al. (1994) referred to when they mentioned the need to develop learners who are capable of entertaining multiple representations.

Epistemological Views of Science

Driver et al. (1994) made another criticism of individual constructivist approaches that I think confuses the distinction between what students can do and the kinds of skills and attitudes that we would like science instruction to help them develop. This had to do with whether students see their beliefs or the explanations of science as providing a true picture of the physical world or think of them as a socially-based construction. Cognitive-developmental research, such as discussed here, suggests that students approach science learning with the view that their explanations of physical phenomena (as well as those of science) represent the true state of affairs about the world and do not understand their theoretical, hypothetical nature. Intentional learning could be related to the acquisition of more sophisticated epistemologies of science (Smith, Maclin, Houghton, & Hennessey, 2000).

More Efficient Mechanisms for Conceptual Change

Finally, another added value of intentional learning could be found in the use of more efficient mechanisms to achieve conceptual change. I argued before that our developmental studies show that the mechanisms that students tend to use to achieve conceptual change are mainly the addition and/or replacement of beliefs. These are not the most efficient types of mechanisms to use for conceptual change. They can cause synthetic models and are very difficult to use to produce restructuring. Clearly, such mechanisms are not adequate to bring about conceptual change when dealing with complex concepts, such as concepts in mechanics or in thermodynamics, where we need major conceptual reorganizations, the creation of new ontological categories, new forms of causality, etc. Indeed, this may be the reason why most students do not achieve conceptual change in these areas, even though they may be more successful with simpler concepts like the concept of the earth and explanations of the day-night cycle.

It is my impression that addition and replacement of beliefs are the mechanisms that characterize nonintentional conceptual change. The use of more sophisticated mechanisms—for example, the explicit use of analogies, abstractions, or models, the use of mathematics and thought experiments, that one finds in studies of how scientists think (Nerserssian, 1992)—seems to require intentional learning. The use of such mechanisms would make it less likely to create synthetic models and would make restructuring easier. The use of such mechanisms can only come from intentional learners who are fully aware of their beliefs and who can understand the differences between the new information that is presented to them and what they already know. As mentioned earlier, such mechanisms are used by scientists who are engaged in research for scientific discovery and who, of course, are highly intentional.

Whereas conceptual change in school settings does not involve scientific discovery but rather the understanding of the accepted scientific point of view, in both cases, significant reorganizations of existing structures must take place within a short period of time. Scientists must be ready to reexamine their hypotheses at all times in the light of new evidence, and if they do not do it as individuals, the scientific community challenges their findings for them and forces them to reexamine them. In classrooms where science teaching is more open, follows an inquiry model, and elicits a lot of discussions and debates, students are more likely to become intentional learners capable of using a variety of sophisticated mechanisms to produce conceptual change.

CONCLUSIONS

I have argued that intentional learning, namely, the purposeful pursuit of learning accompanied by awareness of one's beliefs and one's goals, is not necessary for some kinds of conceptual change to occur. Indeed, many students who are not intentional learners nevertheless achieve minor reorganizations of prior knowledge in the process of learning science in school settings. Intentional learning can, however, greatly facilitate conceptual change and it is probably necessary for understanding some of the more complex and difficult concepts of modern science. Finally, it appears that the kinds of instruction that are necessary to improve the learning of science are not different from the kinds of instruction that are required to develop intentional learning. In both cases, particular attention should be paid to issues that have to do with metacognitive control and metaconceptual awareness.

REFERENCES

Anderson, J. R., Greeno, J. G., Reder, L. M., & Simon, H. A. (2000). Perspectives on learning, thinking, and activity. *Educational Researcher, 29*(4), 11–13.

Baillargeon, R. (1990). *The development of young infant's intuition about support.* Paper presented at the Seventh International Conference on Infant Studies, Montreal, Canada.

Bereiter, C., & Scardamalia, M. (1989). Intentional learning as a goal of instruction. In L. B. Resnick (Ed.), *Knowing, learning and instruction: Essays in honour of Robert Glaser* (pp. 361–392). Hillsdale, NJ: Lawrence Erlbaum Associates.

Bransford, J. D., Franks, J. J., Vye, N. J., & Sherwood, R. D. (1989). New approaches to instruction: because wisdom can't be told. In S. Vosniadou & A. Ortony (Eds.), *Similarity and analogical reasoning* (pp. 470–497). New York: Cambridge University Press.

Caravita, S., & Hallden, O. (1994). Re-framing the problem of conceptual change. *Learning and Instruction, 4*, 89–111.

Carey, S. (1985). *Conceptual change in childhood.* Cambridge, MA: MIT Press.

Carey, S., & Smith, C. (1993). On understanding the nature of scientific knowledge. *Educational Psychologist, 28*, 235–251.

Chi, M. T. H. (1992). Conceptual change within and across ontological categories: Examples from learning and discovery in science. In R. N. Giere (Ed.), *Cognitive models in science.* Minneapolis: University of Minnesota Press.

diSessa, A. A. (1988). Knowledge in pieces. In G. Forman, & P. B. Puffal (Eds.), *Constructivism in the computer age* (pp. 49–70). Hillsdale, NJ: Lawrence Erlbaum Associates.

diSessa, A. A. (1993). Toward an epistemology of physics. *Cognition and Instruction, 10*, 105–225.

diSessa, A. A. (2000). *Changing minds.* Cambridge, MA: MIT Press.

Dole, J. A., & Sinatra, G. M. (1998). Reconceptualizing change in the cognitive construction of knowledge. *Educational Psychologist, 33*(2/3), 109–128.

Driver, R., Asoko, H., Leach, J., Mortimer, E., & Scott, P. (1994). Constructing scientific knowledge in the classroom. *Educational Researcher, 23*(7), 5–12.

Driver, R., & Easley, J. (1978). Pupils and paradigms: A review of literature related to concept development in adolescent science students. *Studies in Science Education, 5*, 61–84.

Flavell, J. (1988). The development of children's knowledge about the mind: From cognitive connections to mental representation. In J. Astington, P. Harris, & D. Olson (Eds.), *Developing theories of mind* (pp. 244–270). Cambridge: Cambridge University Press.

Ioannidou, I., & Vosniadou, S. (in press). The development of knowledge about the composition and layering of the earth's interior. *Paidagogiki Epitheorisi*, 31 (in Greek).

Ioannides, C., & Vosniadou, S. (2000). The changing meanings of force. *Cognitive Science Quarterly.*

Kouka, A., Vosniadou, S., & Tsaparlis, G. (August, 2001). The development of students' understanding of water as a solvent. Paper presented at the biennial meeting of the European Science Education Association, Thessaloniki, Greece.

Kuhn, D., Amsel, E., & O'Laughlin, M. (1988). *The development of scientific thinking skills.* California: Academic Press.

Kuhn, T. (1970). *The structure of scientific revolutions* (2nd ed). Chicago: University of Chicago Press.

Kyriakopoulou, N. (2001). *An experimental investigation of the distinction between phenomenal and scientific models in the area of observational astronomy.* Unpublished Master's Thesis, Program in Basic and Applied Cognitive Science, University of Athens.

Kyrkos, C., & Vosniadou, S. (1997). *Mental models of plant nutrition.* Poster presented at the Seventh European Conference for Research on Learning and Instruction, Athens, Greece

Nerserssian, N. (1992). How scientists think? Capturing the dynamis of conceptual change in science. In R. Giere (Ed.), *Cognitive Models of Science* (pp. 3–44). Minneapolis: University of Minnesota Press.

Novak, J. D. (1977). An alternative to Piagetian psychology for science and mathematics education. *Science Education, 61,* 453–77.

Perner, J. (1991). *Understanding the representational mind.* MIT Press.

Piaget, J. (1970). *Genetic epistemology.* New York: Columbia University Press.

Pillatelli-Palmarini, M. (Ed.). (1979). *Language and learning: The debate between Jean Piaget and Noam Chomsky.* Cambridge, MA: Harvard University Press.

Pintrich, P. R. (1999). Motivational beliefs as responses for and constraints on conceptual change. In W. Schnotz, S. Vosniadou, & M. Carretero (Eds.), *New perpectives on conceptual change* (pp. 33–50). Kidlington, Oxford: Elsevier Science Ltd.

Posner, G. J., Strike, K. A., Hewson, P. W., & Gertzog, W. A. (1982). Accomodation of a scientific conception: Toward a theory of conceptual change. *Science Education, 66,* 211–227.

Sinatra, G. M. (2000). From passive to active to intentional: Changing conceptions of the learner. In G. M. Sinatra (Chair), *What does it mean to be an intentional learner? Alternative perspectives.* Symposium presented at the American Educational Research Association Annual Meeting, New Orleans.

Smith, C. L., Maclin, D., Houghton, C., & Hennessey, M. G. (2000). Sixth-grade students' epistemologies of science: The impact of school science experiences on epistemological development. *Cognition and Instruction, 18*(3), 349–422.

Spelke, E., (1991). Physical knowledge in infancy: Reflections on Piaget's theory. In S. Carey & R. Gelman (Eds.), *Epigenesis of mind* (pp. 133–170). Hillsdale, NJ: Lawrence Erlbaum Associates.

Thagard, P. (1992). *Conceptual revolutions.* Princeton, NJ: Princeton University Press.

Viennot, L. (1979). Spontaneous reasoning in elementary dynamis. *European Journal of Science Education, 1,* 205–221.

Vosniadou, S. (1994a). Universal and culture specific properties of children models of the earth. In L. A. Hirschfield & S. A. Gelman (Eds.), *Mapping the mind* (pp. 412–430). New York: Cambridge University Press.

Vosniadou, S. (1994b). Capturing and modelling the process of conceptual change. *Learning and Instruction, 4,* 45–69.

Vosniadou, S. (1999). Conceptual change research: State of the art and future directions. In W. Schnotz, S. Vosniadou, & M. Carretero (Eds.), *New perspectives on conceptual change* (pp. 3-14). Kidlington, Oxford: Elsevier Science.

Vosniadou, S. (2002). On the nature of naive physics. In M. Limon & L. Mason (Eds.), *Reframing the process of conceptual change* (pp. 61–76). Kluwer Academic Publishers.

Vosniadou, S., & Brewer, W. F. (1992). Mental models of the earth: A study of conceptual change in childhood. *Cognitive Psychology, 24,* 535–585.

Vosniadou, S., & Brewer, W. F. (1994). Mental models of the day/night cycle. *Cognitive Science, 18,* 123–183.

Vosniadou, S., & Ioannides, C. (1998). From conceptual development to science education: A psychological point of view. *International Journal of Science Education, 20*(10), 1213–1230.

Vosniadou, S., Ioannides, C., Dimitrakopoulou, A., & Papademitriou, E. (2001). Designing learning environments to promote conceptual change in science. *Learning and Instruction, 11,* 381–419.

Vosniadou, S., & Kempner, L. (1993, April). *Mental models of heat.* Paper presented at the biennial meeting of the Society for Research in Child Development, New Orleans, LA.

14

When Is Conceptual Change Intended? A Cognitive–Sociocultural View

Giyoo Hatano
Keio University, Tokyo

Kayoko Inagaki
Chiba University, Chiba

Many investigators in cognition and instruction agree that knowledge is acquired by construction; it is not acquired by transmission alone (e.g., Resnick, 1987). Humans acquire knowledge richer than the knowledge they are presented with, or even invent knowledge that has never been presented, often as a byproduct of such cognitive activities as problem solving (a persistent endeavor to induce desired changes in the world) and comprehension activity (a systematic attempt to offer a coherent interpretation of what the world is like). This claim is self-evident when there is no teacher or when the teacher cannot verbalize the target knowledge. However, knowledge must be constructed, at least partially, even when the teacher gives learners the target knowledge in a verbalized form, or when the teacher carefully monitors learners so that their behavior can come to approximate the model behavior. Transmitted knowledge becomes usable in a variety of tasks involving problem solving and comprehension only after it is reconstructed; that is, interpreted, enriched, and connected to the prior knowledge of the learner. Thus, learners must be active and constructive.

Some investigators proceed a step further from that notion of active and constructive learners to assert that, at least in school, learners should be the agents of their own learning. For example, Brown and Campione (1994) claimed, "It is a fundamental tenet of our theory that students have a right to understand, evaluate, and orchestrate their own learning" (p. 270). Likewise, Bransford, Brown, and Cocking (1999) indicated, "Children need to understand what it means to learn, who they are as learners, and how to go about planning, monitoring, and revising, to reflect upon their learning and that of others, and to learn to determine for themselves if they understand. These skills of metacognition provide strategic competencies for learning" (p. xv).

We are quite sympathetic with this ambitious idea of learners to be agential, intentional, or metacognitively conscious, as proposed by the aforementioned investigators. Unlike the everyday learning that is embedded in the practice of achieving socially significant goals, school learning can be effective only when the learners possess and monitor their own learning goals. However, can we assume that learners are agential in the revision of knowledge as well as in its acquisition? Are learners, among others, willing to reorganize knowledge that has proven to be effective for years? As the title of this volume suggests, the editors consider it likely that learners intentionally change their conceptual knowledge (see also Sinatra, 2000).

We are somewhat skeptical of the idea that individual learners spontaneously revise their conceptual knowledge extensively in school. We are afraid that expecting such "epistemic" learners is unrealistic, although we, too, think learners' intentions, goals, agency, etc. are important in instruction-based conceptual change. We assume, instead, that conceptual change in school subjects, or instruction-based conceptual change, is induced through "comprehension activity" (Hatano, 1998; Hatano & Inagaki, 1987) led by a teacher and supported by peers. In other words, although such conceptual change occurs in the individual student's mind, it is induced socioculturally. Therefore, we need a sociocultural as well as cognitive formulation for intentional conceptual change.

There are a few reasons for this "modest" assumption that humans are willing to engage in laborious enterprise of achieving deep comprehension and changing conceptual knowledge only when socially supported (Hatano, 1998; Hatano & Inagaki, 1987). We offer three reasons why we believe that isolated, individual learners are rather unlikely to intentionally reorganize their knowledge system.

The first is concerned with why students are not always willing to engage in comprehension activity that may lead to instruction-based conceptual change. Comprehension activity involves investigating an interpretation and monitoring its plausibility carefully. As exemplified by scientific inquiry, it is necessarily a time- and effort-consuming process. Students may be satisfied with a set of procedural knowledge that is often quite sufficient to deal with problems that they frequently encounter. Even when they seek understanding, they may do so just by applying a causal schema, without suspecting that the initial idea may be false. That is, students are prone to understand events and phenomena by applying one of the available schemas, and they are very good at it.

The second and the third reasons concern why students often fail to revise extensively an old set of beliefs or to successfully replace it with a new, plausible idea. The second reason is that the necessity of revising one's conceptual knowledge extensively is seldom evident. There have been many social-psychological studies since Festinger (1957) that reveal a human tendency to preserve one's prior knowledge through biased collection and interpretation of new pieces of information. It seems reasonable to assume that students are motivated to revise conceptual knowledge on a fairly large scale only when the presented information is clearly discrepant with prior knowledge and hard to ignore, as pointed out by Chinn and Brewer (1993).

Third, learners may not know how their beliefs should be revised or where to search for promising alternative ideas. As Kuhn (1989) aptly pointed out, young children as well as lay adults often possess mental models of the objects they deal with repeatedly, but they are not very good at modifying the models based on newly offered evidence. Even scientists may stick to old ideas that have proven to be untenable, unless they can find promising alternative ideas (Dunbar, 1995). It is likely for students to try to mitigate the incoherence in the knowledge system by a variety of local repairs (Chinn & Brewer, 1993) if they do not know how to modify their core conceptual knowledge.

An important implication of this discussion is that, to induce conceptual change, it is not enough for a teacher to provide students with experience that shows the inadequacy of their conceptual knowledge (e.g., presenting "anomalous data," see Chinn & Brewer, 1993). Such experience may induce cognitive or "epistemic" motivation among students to check or even change their prior knowledge, but the motivation may not be strong enough to bring about enduring comprehension activity. To amplify the motivation, a teacher has to create and maintain a sociocultural environment that favors comprehension activity. Moreover, the teacher may have to provide students with the cognitive scaffold that may help them find promising alternative ideas. In other words, although seeking understanding is basic to human nature, it is still the responsibility of the teacher to motivate students to gain deep understanding, providing them with some sociocultural and cognitive support.

In this chapter, we discuss how instruction-based conceptual change can be induced by comprehension activity, and how a teacher arranges sociocultural factors so that such comprehension activity can occur. We also examine how a teacher helps learners to revise their conceptual knowledge, by organizing patterns of social interaction that enhance enduring comprehension activity, and by presenting a conceptual peg or a placeholder belief that cannot be thought of by students themselves but can be incorporated meaningfully by them. In short, we emphasize the sociocultural nature of intentional conceptual change; that is, one's attempt to revise the target conceptual knowledge, which is apparently just cognitive and personal.

WHEN DOES ONE ENGAGE IN PERSISTENT COMPREHENSION ACTIVITY?

Unlike spontaneous conceptual change that occurs naturally as children accumulate and enrich experiences in everyday situations (e.g., Carey, 1985; Inagaki & Hatano, in press; Wellman, 1990), instruction-based conceptual change takes place as products of systematic intervention, that is, specific science instruction (Vosniadou & Ioannides, 1998). In instruction-based conceptual change, students are expected to reorganize their knowledge system by acquiring new beliefs including conceptual devices or "scientific concepts" that are difficult for them to acquire through everyday experience. Many of these conceptual devices are counterintuitive, as represented by the concept of photosynthesis, the Darwinian conception of evolution, Newtonian concepts of movement, and so on. Thus, instruction-based conceptual change is a conscious belief revision (elimination of recognized inconsistencies by rejecting an old belief and/or incorporating a new belief), which often requires an effortful and laborious process. We believe such conceptual change is induced by enduring comprehension activity. In what follows, we discuss the circumstances in which students engage in comprehension activity. More specifically, we discuss (a) what motivates them to seek understanding, (b) how the motivation leads to various forms of comprehension activity, the outcomes of which include conceptual change, and (c) by what kind of instructional strategies motivation for comprehension is likely to be elicited and amplified.

Motivational States for Seeking Understanding

We proposed elsewhere (Hatano & Inagaki, 1987) a theory of motivation for comprehension or understanding (we use these terms interchangeably). When people recognize and feel that their comprehension is inadequate, they are motivated to pursue subjectively adequate comprehension or satisfactory explanations, and thus may engage in enduring comprehension activity by seeking further information from the outside, retrieving another piece of prior knowledge, generating new inferences, examining the compatibility of inferences more closely, and so forth. We call the state where people recognize the inadequacy of their understanding *cognitive incongruity*. We use this term rather than *cognitive conflict*, which traditionally has been used by a number of psychologists, to include a state where one recognizes that the available pieces of information are not well coordinated, as well as a state that has been recognized as cognitive conflict between newly arriving information and the existing knowledge system.

Three types of cognitive incongruity are distinguished: surprise, perplexity, and discoordination. The first two come from Berlyne (1965) and have been termed by many psychologists as *cognitive conflict*. The third type of cognitive incongruity was added by Hatano and Inagaki (1987). *Surprise* is often induced when people encounter an event or information that contradicts their prior knowledge. They will be motivated to understand what is wrong with and how to repair the knowledge by incorporating the new information. The comprehension activity induced by surprise is basically the same as what Ackerman (1984) called *comprehension repair*.

Perplexity is induced when people are aware of equally plausible but competing ideas related to the target object or procedure. People will seek further information not only to choose one of the alternatives with confidence, but also to find a justification for that choice. This form of comprehension activity might be called *plausibility comparison*, that is, two or more competing sets of beliefs are compared in terms of their plausibility.

When people recognize that available pieces of information are not well connected, or that other pieces of related information cannot be generated by transforming the existing ones, they have *discoordination*, and engage in a form of comprehension activity that can be called *conceptual coordination*, an attempt to make the target piece of information more convincing by connecting it to other pieces of knowledge. Part of conceptual coordination may be verbalized as self-explanation (Chi, Bassock, Lewis, Reimann, & Glaser, 1989), an inference that adds some knowledge to the piece of information available to learners. Discoordination is often experienced when one tries to use a concept or another piece of conceptual knowledge that is learned as a "placeholder," as well as to explain, clarify, or justify one's idea.

Needless to say, objectively identical situations may or may not arouse cognitive incongruity, because incongruity is induced only when people recognize and feel that their comprehension is inadequate. In other words, whether cognitive incongruity is experienced depends on one's ability for comprehension monitoring (e.g., Markman, 1979) or calibration of comprehension (e.g., Glenberg & Epstein, 1985). In addition, although experiencing cognitive incongruity is the necessary condition for engaging in comprehension activity, it is not a sufficient condition. There are two important, mediating factors between the experience of cognitive incongruity and engagement in comprehension activity. One is the existence of positive and favorable metacognitive beliefs about comprehension. Individuals have their own "domains of interest," in which they believe they are able to comprehend and also of which comprehension is valuable.

They are willing to engage in prolonged comprehension activity in those domains, but not outside the domains, even when they experience cognitive incongruity. Thus, it is necessary that students themselves recognize the target problem is important in instruction situations.

The other factor is the freedom from any urgent extrinsic reward at the moment. Here, studies on the so-called undermining effects of extrinsic rewards (e.g., Deci, Koestner, & Ryan, 1999; Lepper & Green, 1978; Sansone & Harackiewicz, 2000) are relevant. They suggest, although indirectly, the possibility that extrinsic rewards inhibit the motivation for comprehension. It changes the goal of the ongoing cognitive activity from comprehension to obtaining rewards. The expectation of external evaluation (e.g., a grade based on a test score) or of the authorized right answer to follow immediately may have similar undermining effects.

The Core Process of Comprehension Activity

How does comprehension activity induced by cognitive incongruity operate? According to which of the three types of incongruity—surprise, perplexity, or discoordination—is experienced, comprehension activity takes slightly different forms, as described earlier. More specifically, whereas perplexity leads to a comparison between two or more competing sets of beliefs in terms of plausibility, surprise induces an attempt to modify the current set of beliefs so that it can incorporate the presented data that are apparently incompatible. In the case of discoordination, the activity focuses on making a given set of beliefs that is tentatively taken as correct better connected to related beliefs and thus more convincing. However, it always involves as the core process the plausibility estimation of a possible interpretation, a set of beliefs sometimes constituting a model or a theory. The plausibility estimation process is one of collecting and evaluating various pieces of information relevant to the target interpretation.

Although comprehension activity involves the process of deriving an interpretation based on prior knowledge including schemas, it includes something more. First, a number of competing interpretations may be offered and held simultaneously, and their tenabilities are carefully monitored, through the plausibility estimation, by the comprehender, as typically seen among experienced scientists (e.g., Dunbar, 1995). In other words, in comprehension activity, it is supposed that the first interpretation to come to mind does not suppress other possible interpretations. Second, the selection of interpretations to be considered is constrained by their consistency with other interpretations and conceptual requirements (e.g., Collins, Brown, & Larkin, 1980). This is because the goal of comprehension activity is to achieve a coherent and convincing set of beliefs, in others words, to build, revise, or elaborate a model or a theory. Sometimes the activity leads to the reorganization of conceptual knowledge by excluding an old belief and/or including a new belief. Third, comprehension activity includes active tests of predictions derived from those interpretations. To put it differently, the activity not only tries to find an interpretation compatible with a given set of observations but also examines whether the target interpretation can generate testable predictions and whether these predictions are confirmed.

The plausibility estimation process may be prolonged, if it is not endless, because there can be quite varied pieces of information that are relevant to the target interpretation. Human beings are satisfied with an interim result of the plausibility estimation, however, because of their preferences for a particular interpretation. Therefore, prolonged comprehension activity often occurs among group members who favor or are committed to different interpretations. In other words, comprehension activity may take collective forms, in which the entire activity is partitioned spontaneously or deliberately. Those who favor a given interpretation tend naturally to collect, and probably assign importance to, pieces of information that support the interpretation. In contrast, those who favor another interpretation tend to pay attention to pieces of information that do not support the initial interpretation. In this sense, deep understanding does often occur in the interactions between individuals, as will be shown next. This social nature of comprehension activity is not surprising, especially considering that comprehension means to find a subjectively satisfactory explanation and that explanation is often provided in dialogical contexts.

Instructional Strategies for Inducing Comprehension Activity

The construction or revision of conceptual knowledge is based on motivation to understand a given set of observations better; therefore, strategies for arousing cognitive incongruity and inducing comprehension activity are also strategies that enhance instruction-based conceptual change. Four such strategies are proposed from the theory of motivation for comprehension. The first two are concerned primarily with the arousal and amplification of cognitive incongruity, and the last two with the elicitation of committed and persistent comprehension activity in response to induced incongruity.

The first strategy is to make students recognize the inadequacy of their understanding, for example, by confronting a phenomenon that does not confirm their prediction based on the prior knowledge (surprise), by posing a question that has multiple plausible answer alternatives (perplexity), or by inquiring about relationships among the target and related pieces of conceptual knowledge including a presented conceptual peg or placeholder concept (discoordination). This strategy must be applied with great care, because students are not always open-minded. For example, students tend to interpret new observations or anomalous data in biased ways so that they can be harmonious with their prior knowledge. Hence, in order to induce incongruity, teachers have to bring about distinctly novel or disconfirming phenomena, drawing students' attention to them and posing questions about these and related phenomena. A good example of this first strategy is to present a phenomenon that disconfirms students' predictions based on their misconception after they state their predictions in public, because the students cannot ignore the cognitive incongruity, or inconsistent relationships between new and stored pieces of knowledge, in such a social situation.

The second strategy is encouraging students to participate in dialogical interaction, such as discussion or reciprocal teaching, in the learning activities. Why can this strategy create or amplify motivation for comprehension? Four reasons can be offered. First, dialogical interaction invites a person to "commit" to some ideas by requiring the person to state the ideas to others, thereby placing the issue in question in the domains of interest. This helps one recognize the inadequacy of his or her comprehension (which otherwise is likely to be ignored) and thus arouse cognitive incongruity. Second, one has to make explicit what has been known only implicitly in the process of trying to convince or teach others. This leads one to examine one's own comprehension in detail and thus to become aware of any thus far unnoticed inadequacies in understanding. Third, because persuasion or teaching requires the orderly presentation of ideas, one has to organize better intraindividually what has been known. This will make one realize one's inadequacies of comprehension. Fourth, for effective argumentation or teaching, one must incorporate opposing ideas—that is, coordinate different points of view interindividually between proponents and opponents or between tutors and learners. This may also induce cognitive incongruity. Miyake (1986) presented a good example of how dialogical interaction motivates persons to engage in enduring comprehension activity that would not be induced without a partner, and to produce jointly a detailed mental model of an artifact.

The third strategy is freeing students from the pressure to conform to the externally set standards or to obtain sanctions from the external authorities. In other words, students should not be blocked from pursuing comprehension by material rewards, positive evaluations, or authorized correct answers. If students perform a procedure to obtain rewards, they refrain from being involved in comprehension activity even when incongruity is induced. They are certainly reluctant to risk varying the procedure, because they usually believe that safety lies in relying on the conventional version. Thus, deeper understanding by continuous experimentation is often made impossible by external rewards.

In fact, Inagaki and Hatano (1984) provided evidence to support the last assertion. They asked college students majoring in foreign language to translate English letters into Japanese, either under the expectation of external evaluation for their translation performance (evaluation condition) or under no such expectation (no-evaluation condition). It was found that the students in the evaluation condition looked up words in dictionaries more often than the students in the no-evaluation condition, but the former students' understanding of the text was shallower than those in the no-evaluation condition in terms of giving elaborated explanations for ambiguous expressions embedded in these letters. In other words, the students in the evaluation condition seemed to adopt the "safety strategy," which was oriented to avoid errors, even minor ones, and pay little attention to what was really "meant" in the text, resulting in shallow understanding of the content. This strongly suggests that the expectation of external evaluation prevents students from going beyond the imposed task into deep understanding.

The fourth strategy is to ensure that understanding is valued by reference group members. The encouragement of comprehension by reference group members will lead an individual to form metacognitive beliefs that emphasize the significance and capability of comprehension (at least in the domain in which expertise is acquired). This will make comprehension activity likely to occur when cognitive incongruity is induced. In a reference group that values comprehension, students are often required to explain the appropriateness of the procedure or the solution, largely in relation to others, but sometimes to themselves. Individuals may try to construct and revise mental models (or other forms of conceptual knowledge) of the target as the basis for explanation.

INSTRUCTION-BASED CONCEPTUAL CHANGE: TWO ILLUSTRATIVE STUDIES

To support these theoretical claims regarding the processes and strategies for students' engagement in comprehension activity, we present two exemplary studies in this section. The first study, which was a one-shot experiment, shows how presenting a question with plausible but mutually incompatible answer alternatives and inviting the whole class to discuss the question induces and amplifies cognitive incongruity and elicits comprehension activity, which takes a collective form. The second study is presented to show that, through prolonged comprehension activity induced by discoordination, even elementary school children can intentionally change their conception of what constitutes entities—more specifically, acquire an atomistic model of solid objects, fluid, and gas. Both studies dealt with lessons taught by a Japanese science education method called *Hypothesis-Experiment-Instruction* (Itakura, 1962), originally devised by Itakura and used primarily in science classes in elementary and junior high schools.

Whole Class Discussion as Collective Comprehension Activity

Before discussing two exemplary studies, we describe characteristics of Hypothesis-Experiment-Instruction (HEI) in relation to motivation for comprehension and collective comprehension activity. Its ingenious design—that is, first presenting to students a multiple-choice problem with conflicting alternatives and then inviting them to discuss the problem—induces and amplifies motivation for comprehension, which often leads to collective comprehension activity. To put it differently, enduring comprehension activity is initiated primarily by *perplexity*, by being presented a problem with several answer alternatives, some of which represent common misconceptions held by students, and this cognitive incongruity is amplified through discussion. The following procedure is usually adopted with this method:

1. Pupils are presented with a problem having three or four answer alternatives. The alternatives take a form of directly testable predictions, but they represent naïve interpretations, models, or theories that pupils tend to possess. The problem specifies how to confirm which alternative is right.
2. Pupils are asked to choose one answer by themselves.
3. Pupils' responses, counted by a show of hands, are tabulated on the blackboard.
4. Pupils are encouraged to explain and discuss their choices with one another.
5. Pupils are asked to choose an alternative once again. They may change their choices.
6. Pupils are allowed to test their predictions by observing an experiment or reading a given passage.

A teacher, after presenting the problem, serves as a chairperson or moderator who tries to stay neutral during students' discussion. Thus, although the teacher has control over what kinds of activities students engage in, she is not regarded as the source of knowledge as far as the topic of discussion is concerned. Because none of the discussion participants is considered as more capable or expert by status than any other, students are motivated to offer convincing arguments themselves. Thus, in step 4, students are often engaged in lively and prolonged discussions in large groups of 40 to 45. Typically, several students express their opinions often, but a majority of them tend to participate vicariously in the discussion, nodding or shaking their heads or making brief remarks. There is empirical confirmation in step 6 that can demonstrate clearly which answer alternative is correct. Therefore, students speak not only to offer plausible explanations but also to connect these explanations to their chosen prediction.

Students in the whole-class discussion are expected to acquire knowledge because this method is for learning basic concepts and principles in science. However, unlike participants in many psychological experiments on understanding, they are not explicitly asked to achieve comprehension as a final task outcome. They are encouraged only to discuss which alternative is correct.

Whole-Class Discussion on Conservation of Weight. We performed a number of experimental studies to examine the effects of whole-class discussion in HEI on children's acquisition of scientific concepts or revision of concepts acquired in everyday life. In one such study (see Hatano & Inagaki, 1991a), fourth graders received a science lesson concerning the conservation of weight when sugar is dissolved into water. Students were randomly divided into experimental and control groups (44 and 43 students, respectively) based on their performance on the target task in a pretest. Two thirds of the members in each group were nonconservers. Students in both conditions were given a problem with three answer alternatives: Suppose that two lumps of sugar and a glass of water on one tray and the weight on the other are balanced on a scale. The two lumps of sugar are put into the glass of water and dissolved completely after stirring. Now, does the glass of water with dissolved sugar (a) become heavier than the weight, (b) become lighter than the weight, or (c) remain the same weight?

In the experimental condition, all of the 6 steps of HEI were followed in groups of about 20 students each, whereas in the control condition, steps 3, 4, and 5 were omitted. Thus the difference between the conditions was in the extent of the exchange of ideas among the students, more specifically, of the information about who (or how many students) supported each of the alternatives and how they justified their choices, not in the amount of authoritative information given. Immediately before step 6, the students in both conditions were asked to rate their interest in observing the experiment using a balance scale on a four-point scale (from very eager to see the experiment to not eager to do so). After step 6, both groups of students were given a posttest consisting of the conservation of weight of sugar and other substances.

Processes of Whole-Class Discussion. Using audiotapes and relying on informal observations, we obtained group protocols of whole-class discussion, that is, transcribed sequences of members' utterances (with salient nonverbal behaviors recorded). Analyses of these group protocols suggest at least two components of a collective attempt to acquire or revise conceptual knowledge.

First, students' enduring comprehension activity was pushed forward by their social, more specifically "partisan," motivation as well as cognitive or "epistemic" motivation. In other words, their collective attempt was not a "pure" comprehension activity but aimed at winning an academic competition as well as comprehension. As soon as the whole group was divided (psychologically, not spatially or socially) into three according to their choice of answer alternatives, the students seemed to be motivated to work for the party they belonged to, that is, to collect more supporters and eventually win the argument by persuading all others. Most of the utterances were arguments against other parties that ranged from pointing out errors in reasoning to noting overlooked facts that they thought were critical. For example, the supporters of alternative (b) emphasized against the supporters of (c) the fact that sugar was dissolved completely into water and invisible, insisting, "The weight of the glass of water with dissolved sugar must decrease because completely dissolved sugar loses its weight." On the other hand, the supporters of the alternative (c) defended, saying, "The weight does not change because the sugar is only loosened in water." Speakers often gave signs of solidarity to supporters who had chosen the same alternative, and the supporters returned signs of agreement. When their prediction proved to be correct, they were quite excited and again exchanged signs of companionship. When it turned out to be wrong, they were greatly disappointed but tried to console each other.

This is not to say that the whole-class discussion was driven solely by the competitive desire to be academic winners. Cognitive motivation, the desire to know and understand, remained strong and underlay all the partisanship because the students were well aware that science lessons were situations in which they were to learn and acquire knowledge. In addition, the freedom to change one's prediction and, thus, affiliation to a party, and also the agreed reliance on experiment as the means for confirming or disconfirming predictions, seemed to enhance this motivation.

Thus the students were all seeking to share better comprehension as well as competing between parties.

The second element that the protocols suggest is that this partisanship made students' comprehension activity more effective because it served to divide the task into several manageable parts. It is hard for any individual to make plausibility estimations of multiple hypotheses—to collect arguments both for and against each alternative and to assess them impartially. In the HEI-induced collective comprehension activity, participants do not have to do this. Supporters of one alternative have only to try to defend it (offer arguments "for") by elaborating justifications because supporters of other alternatives naturally try to criticize them (propose arguments "against"). Thus, in response to other parties' criticisms, committed supporters could often think of more plausible and sophisticated explanations than they had at the beginning, while maintaining a more or less consistent standpoint. Moreover, assessing the strength of each argument, which would have been very hard if it had to be done on a purely cognitive basis, was helped by social cues. How good one's own or a comrade's argument was could be judged by whether it made opponents silent and/or attracted more supporters. Here, reactions of the third party would also be considered, because their attitudes could be changed more easily than those of the proponents or opponents.

Division of labor was also possible within a party. Because those students belonging to the same party shared many relevant opinions, they could easily add to or elaborate what had been said by their comrades. For example, defending the argument offered by the same party, the students used a sentence beginning with "I'd like to add to what [student's name] said." The students could make their explanation increasingly clearer, more persuasive, and more detailed in the course of discussion, although each of the individual contributors added only a little.

Our experimental study showed that cognitive motivation was amplified through the discussion. The students in the experimental condition showed greater interest in observing the experiment using a balance scale after the discussion (and immediately before the experiment) than those in the control condition.

Better Understanding as Products of Whole-Class Discussion. At the posttest given immediately after observing the experiment, almost all the students in both conditions acquired conservation responses to the target sugar-and-water task. However, the control students could not give reasonable explanations for why the dissolved sugar conserved its weight in water, whereas a majority of the experimental students gave adequate explanations. For example, more than one fourth of the experimental students gave atomistic or quasiatomistic explanations such as, "Sugar remains in water in particles that are too tiny for us to see," whereas none of the control students gave such reasons. About half of the control students could not give any explanation; they just described the observed result, such as "The weight of sugar and water is the same as the weight after the sugar is dissolved." Moreover, the experimental students showed greater progress in applying the principle of weight conservation to a variety of situations (e.g., when corn kernels are made into popcorn). These results suggest that collective comprehension activity induced through whole-class discussion enhanced individual students' comprehension.

Similar results were found in studies using other topics, such as the characteristics of monkeys in relation to their lives in trees (Inagaki & Hatano, 1989). Moreover, studies dealing with group discussions other than the HEI also report that group discussion, especially discussion within a group consisting of members with differing initial ideas, facilitated the understanding of topics such as of inheritance (Williams & Tolmie, 2000) and heating and cooling (Howe, Tolmie, Greer, & Mackenzie, 1995). These authors emphasized the importance of "sociocognitive conflict" in enhancing understanding.

It should be noted that what students in the HEI learn depends on what was discussed, especially what explanations were offered by proponents of the correct alternative. Thus, the effects of group discussion must vary from class to class because the content of the discussion necessarily varies. For example, a majority of the atomistic reasons given at the posttest were found in one class in which one of the students had justified his prediction of the conservation of weight by relying on atomism (i.e., a lump of sugar consisted of a large number of very small particles, and these particles still existed in water). It is reasonably clear that explanations offered in group discussion could be assimilated, or more accurately, reconstructed, when the students were given external feedback informing them which alternative was correct. In other words, through collective comprehension activity, the students were able to share a set of possibly correct explanations despite apparent opposition. Many of them not only understood why the weight was conserved but also developed a scientifically plausible model of the change in the sugar when it was dissolved. This development might be called a conceptual change, because it was an extensive revision of the model of lumps of sugar, or substance in general; more specifically, the students began to conceptualize a solid body as consisting of very small particles that continued to exist even when the original form was dissolved. However, it should be emphasized that the students "assimilate" the explanations proposed in the group discussion, not through mere imitative learning, but through reconstruction processes, and thus the explanations offered by them were often edited and expressed differently from student to student. Perret-Clermont (1980) also provided evidence for the constructive nature of group discussion and decision making.

To generalize, the whole-class discussion over the target phenomenon, represented by the HEI method, often enhances students' understanding and probably conceptual change. The analysis of group protocols strongly suggests that its effectiveness derives primarily from social amplification of individual motivation for comprehension and also from the division of labor created by group discussion. To put it differently, the whole-class discussion as collective comprehension activity is enhanced by partisan as well as cognitive motivation (Hatano & Inagaki, 1991b). This partisanship makes pupils' comprehension activity more effective, because it serves to divide the task into several manageable parts.

How a Conceptual Peg Operates

As the second example, we report a case of a long-term, successive revision of the concept of molecules by a group of elementary school children who were taught using the HEI method (Obara, 1971). In this case the teacher gave the scientific term as a conceptual peg or a placeholder for the core concept in the atomistic understanding of a solid object, fluid, and gas. The teacher indicated that everything consists of tiny, tiny particles called molecules or atoms, when the children discussed whether the weight of a piece of clay would stay the same when it was transformed.

As the first example indicates, amplifying the motivation to understand by requiring students to discuss the problem with a few alternative solutions seems an effective strategy for facilitating comprehension activity and resultant conceptual change. However, this strategy cannot induce conceptual change unless students are cognitively prepared; more specifically, they must be able to readily access a set of constituent beliefs that is to replace the old one. A number of previous studies in science education have shown that presenting an unexpected, surprising, or anomalous piece of information is not effective in inducing conceptual change (Vosniadou & Ioannides, 1998).

How can a teacher help students find an alternative concept, conception, or conceptualization, without giving up her constructivist orientation? We propose to give a conceptual peg or placeholder in a verbal form in the discursive context, as the HEI method sometimes adopts such an instructional procedure.

What words or concepts can serve as a placeholder? We do not think that every word or concept can be a placeholder. Only those words or concepts that are already in the zone of proximal development can serve as placeholders. Specifically, we assume that a word or concept can be a placeholder only if (a) it is useful in discursive context; (b) it is coherent with prior knowledge of learners that is relevant to the situation in question; and (c) its label is easy to pronounce and memorize. Equally important in introducing a placeholder word or concept is that learners are provided ample opportunities to use it in further problem-solving and comprehension activity. The word or concept must be reconstructed in learners' minds before it can serve as a conceptual device through which they see the world differently, in other words, it induces conceptual change.

The Data. Let us return to the case of a long-term revision of the conceptual knowledge about molecules. Five fifth graders jointly wrote an essay reflecting on and summarizing how their ideas about molecules had evolved mainly through participating in HEI. They had had a series of HEI lessons over the preceding three years on topics concerning solid bodies and their weight (including an experiment on the conservation of weight in the dissolution of sugar mentioned earlier), dissolution, and crystallization, and felt that the essay would be useful for new classmates who had not participated in those lessons. We could reasonably assume that they had been committed students in the HEI, shared metacognitive beliefs favoring comprehension, and were relatively free from such external rewards as grading. The essay clearly shows that, even under very good teaching, the conceptual change—to acquire a naïve molecular theoretic idea as a conceptual device through which the world is viewed—took years. At the same time, however, the essay reveals that, even among elementary school children, comprehension activity could be extended over a few years.

The essay indicates that these students learned the notion of molecules for the first time during lessons on solid objects and their weight; they were given a piece of information by their teacher, as a hint for considering the conservation of weight of solid objects (e.g., a clay ball transformed into a sausage), that every object consists of tiny, tiny particles called atoms or molecules. They then learned that, when water and alcohol are mixed, although the mixed liquid has less volume than the two volumes added, its weight equals the sum. They learned that this was because the size of alcohol molecules is different from the size of water molecules. They confessed, however, that it was very difficult for them to view liquid as consisting of tiny particles. They wrote:

> We could not imagine at all that water consists of particles. One of us said that water might consist of particles because drops of water were water. . . . Others said one after another, "How are particles connected?" "I wonder if something like drops of water rise up from the surface of water when clouds that are going to rain are produced," "After cookies are broken into very, very small pieces, these pieces are not connected, but water is connected on the glass even after it becomes fog." . . . We discussed how water might be

> made of particles among ourselves using arguments that seem strange from our present perspective, and we could not understand the idea of molecules of water at all (Obara, 1971, pp. 108–109).

According to the essay, these students understood the notion of tiny particles or molecules better when they learned about dissolution. They first thought that water with sugar dissolved in it would taste sweeter near the bottom of the glass than near the top, but found this was not true. They realized that water consists of molecules that are moving. This realization was reinforced by the fact that, even when we leave a lump of sugar in the bottom of a glass without stirring it, it eventually dissolves.

However, the students were still not convinced that water is made of particles. Their ideas about molecular theory advanced when they were exposed to lessons on crystallization, in which they constructed a model of a crystal by using a set of glass marbles, and tried to simulate molecular movement by themselves. The students wrote that many of their questions were suddenly dispelled by this exercise and they were very excited. In the following regular science lessons on ice, water, and steam, they were able to use their ideas about molecular theory freely.

The essay continues to trace the further development of their ideas, and also their insight that some mysterious phenomena could be understood by extending their comprehension of molecular theory. To summarize, this case illustrates how the term *molecules*, which was initially given as just a placeholder, was gradually enriched and became a core concept in the reorganized body of knowledge.

SUMMARY AND CONCLUSION: TOWARD A THEORY OF INSTRUCTION-BASED CONCEPTUAL CHANGE

Before concluding this chapter, we summarize here the previous discussion, focusing on how conceptual change is induced by instruction. How shall we conceptualize instruction-based conceptual change in the first place? We proposed elsewhere (Inagaki & Hatano, 2003) two contrasting mechanisms for conceptual change: one is local and bottom-up; the other, goal-directed and top-down. More specifically, the former is realized as the spreading of the truth–value alteration (spreading and recurring effects of new incongruous inputs) and the latter, through the conscious and deliberate revision of beliefs (a new set of beliefs replaces an old one based on the plausibility estimation of each of them). We assume that instruction-based conceptual change usually takes the latter form, and is thus induced through comprehension activity (Hatano, 1998).

Therefore, the critical processes through which instruction-based conceptual change is induced are those that arouse cognitive incongruity, those in which incongruity induces enduring comprehension activity, and those by which comprehension activity leads to belief revision. We propose that when students recognize their comprehension is inadequate (and cognitive incongruity is felt), they are motivated to pursue understanding, and the motivation for comprehension can be amplified socially, for instance, through peer interaction. We also propose, taking the constructivist position, to give a placeholder or conceptual peg, the meaning of which students can grasp only partially at the beginning when they are not accessible to alternative ideas. We believe that giving a carefully chosen placeholder when needed is perfectly acceptable to constructivists if students are given ample opportunities later to reconstruct the placeholder concept by using it in a variety of situations. Although not mentioned in this chapter, suggesting an analogy, which enables students to think of an alternative idea, is also a constructivistic strategy to induce conceptual change through comprehension activity. Using hinted analogies, students can map their knowledge about the source to the present new case (target) so that they can not only make a coherent interpretation of the set of observations for the target but also build a tentative model or theory.

Although understanding or conceptual change itself occurs in individual heads, it is far from an individual enterprise. This holds true for students as well as for scientists (Dunbar, 1995). We need to go beyond not only cold conceptual change (Pintrich, Marx, & Boyle, 1993) but also individualistic conceptual change. We emphasize that dialogical interactions, support for enduring comprehension activity by the reference group members, and the cognitive scaffold given by teachers are all indispensable sociocultural contexts of the elaboration and revision of conceptual knowledge. Therefore, a teacher's long-term endeavor to shape the classroom into a community of learners sharing the goal of understanding serves as important groundwork for the success of strategies for inducing prolonged comprehension activity and conceptual change.

We believe that we can induce instruction-based conceptual change only when students themselves are willing to revise their conceptual knowledge. We may impose a few pieces of knowledge as being scientifically correct, but in that case students accept this knowledge only because they have to, not because they are convinced that the new idea is more plausible than their earlier understanding. In fact, they most likely use the imposed piece of knowledge only when they are tested in school. In this sense, we agree with the notion of intentional conceptual change. We believe, however, we need its sociocultural formulations.

Researchers who are interested in instruction-based conceptual change in science have almost unanimously found that conceptual change requires intensive and systematic teaching, and even with good teaching, only a limited portion of older children and adults may successfully revise their prior conceptual knowledge (e.g., Clement, 1982). Immediate reactions to this recognition that inducing conceptual change is difficult may be various forms of explicit teaching, such as explaining where the old theory is wrong, providing a scientifically correct external model, and so on. However, we instead propose to maintain the constructivist orientation and enrich it with a few sociocultural ideas, that is, organizing peer interaction that enhances motivation for comprehension, hinting an alternative idea that is readily usable by children, and providing opportunities to use the idea in meaningful contexts.

We must admit, however, what we offer in this chapter is just a theoretical framework that connects conceptual change to comprehension activity, with an episode of a long-term conceptual change; we have conducted some experimental studies on comprehension activity but not those directly on conceptual change. We thus need future studies that demonstrate conceptual change can in fact be induced effectively by combining cognitive and sociocultural approaches.

REFERENCES

Ackerman, B. P (1984). The effects of storage and processing complexity on comprehension repair in children and adults. *Journal of Experimental Child Psychology, 37,* 303–334.

Berlyne, D. E. (1965). Curiosity and education. In J. D. Krumboltz (Ed.), *Learning and the educational process* (pp. 67–89). Chicago: Rand McNally.

Bransford, J. D., Brown, A. L., & Cocking, R. R. (1999). *How people learn: Brain, mind, experience, and school.* Washington, DC: National Academy Press.

Brown, A. L., & Campione, J. C. (1994). Guided discovery in a community of learners. In K. McGilly (Ed.), *Classroom lesson: Integrating cognitive theory and classroom practice* (pp. 229–270). Cambridge, MA: MIT Press.

Carey, S. (1985). *Conceptual change in childhood.* Cambridge, MA: MIT Press.

Chi, M. T. H., Bassok, M., Lewis, M., Reimann, P., & Glaser, R (1989). Self-explanations: How students study and use examples in learning to solve problems. *Cognitive Science, 13,* 145–182.

Chinn, C. A., & Brewer, W. F. (1993). The role of anomalous data in knowledge acquisition: A theoretical framework and implications for science instruction. *Review of Educational Research, 63,* 1–49.

Clement, J. (1982). Students' preconceptions in introductory mechanics. *American Journal of Physics, 50,* 66–71.

Collins, A., Brown, J. S., & Larkin, K. M. (1980). Inference in text understanding. In R. J. Spiro, B. C. Bruce, & W. F. Brewer (Eds.), *Theoretical issues in reading comprehension: Perspectives from cognitive psychology, linguistics, artificial intelligence and education.* Hillsdale, NJ: Lawrence Erlbaum Associates.

Deci, E. L., Koestner, R., & Ryan, R. M. (1999). A meta-analytic review of experiments examining the effects of extrinsic rewards on intrinsic motivation. *Psychological Bulletin, 125,* 627–668.

Dunbar, K. (1995). How scientists really reason: Scientific reasoning in real-world laboratories. In R. J. Sternberg & J. E. Davidson (Eds.), *The nature of insight* (pp. 365–395). Cambridge, MA: MIT Press.

Festinger, L. (1957). *A theory of cognitive dissonance.* Evanston, Ill: Row, Peterson.

Glenberg, A. M., & Epstein, W. (1985). Calibration of comprehension. *Journal of Experimental Psychology: Learning, Memory, and Cognition, 11,* 702–718.

Hatano, G. (1998). Comprehension activity in individuals and groups. In M. Sabourin, F. Craik, & M. Robert (Eds.), *Advances in psychological science. Vol. 2: Biological and cognitive aspects* (pp. 399–418). Hove, UK: Psychology Press.

Hatano, G., & Inagaki, K. (1987). A theory of motivation for comprehension and its application to mathematics instruction. In T. A. Romberg & D. M. Stewart (Eds.), *The monitoring of school mathematics: Background papers. Vol. 2: Implications from psychology; outcomes of instruction.* (Program Report 87-2, pp. 27–46). Madison: Wisconsin Center for Education Research.

Hatano, G., & Inagaki, K. (1991a). Sharing cognition through collective comprehension activity. In L. B. Resnick, J. M. Levine, & S. D. Teasley (Eds.), *Perspectives on socially shared cognition* (pp. 331–348). Washington, DC: American Psychological Association.

Hatano, G., & Inagaki, K. (1991b). *Motivation for collective comprehension activity in Japanese classrooms.* Paper presented at the meeting of American Educational Research Association, Chicago.

Howe, C. J., Tolmie, A., Greer, K., & Mackenzie, M. (1995). Peer collaboratin and conceptual growth in physics: Task influences on children's understanding of heating and cooling. *Cognition and Instruction, 13,* 483–503.

Inagaki, K., & Hatano, G. (1984). *Effects of external evaluation on reading comprehension and intrinsic interest.* Paper presented at the American Educational Research Association Annual Meeting, New Orleans.

Inagaki, K., & Hatano, G. (1989). *Learning histories of vocal and silent participants in group discussion.* Paper presented at the 53rd Annual Meeting of Japanese Psychological Association, Tsukuba, Japan. (in Japanese)

Inagaki, K., & Hatano, G. (2002). *Young children's naïve thinking about the biological world.* New York: Psychology Press.

Itakura, K. (1962). Instruction and learning of concept force in static based on Kasetsu-Jikken-Jugyo (Hypothesis-Experiment-Instruction): A new method of science teaching. *Bulletin of National Institute for Educational Research, 52,* 1–121. (in Japanese)

Kuhn, D. (1989). Children and adults as intuitive scientists. *Psychological Review, 96,* 674–689.

Lepper, M. R., & Greene, D. (Eds.). (1978). *The hidden cost of reward: New perspectives on the psychology of human motivation.* Hillsdale, NJ: Lawrence Erlbaum Associates.

Markman, E. (1979). Realizing that you don't understand: Elementary school children's awareness of inconsistencies. *Child Development, 50,* 643–655.

Miyake, N. (1986). Constructive interaction and the iterative process of understanding. *Cognitive Science, 10,* 151–177.

Obara, T. (1971). Children's naive molecular theoretic ideas. *Kagaku-kyouiku-kenkyuu (Studies in Science Education),* No. 3, 99–110. (in Japanese).

Perret-Clermont, A. (1980). *Social interaction and cognitive development in children.* New York: Academic Press.

Pintrich, P. R., Marx, R. W., & Boyle, R. A. (1993). Beyond cold conceptual change: The role of motivational beliefs and classroom contextual factors in the process of conceptual change. *Review of Educational Research, 63,* 167–199.

Resnick, L. B. (1987). Constructing knowledge in school. In L. S. Liben (Ed.), *Development and learning: Conflict or congruence?* (pp. 19–50). Hillsdale, NJ: Lawrence Erlbaum Associates.

Sansone, C., & Harackiewicz, J. M. (Eds.). (2000). *Intrinsic and extrinsic motivation: The search for optimal motivation and performance.* New York: Academic Press.

Sinatra, G. M. (2000). From passive to active to intentional: Changing conceptions of the learner. In G. M. Sinatra (Chair), *What does it mean to be an intentional learner? Alternative perspectives.* Symposium presented at the American Educational Research Association Annual Meeting, New Orleans.

Vosniadou, S., & Ioannides, C. (1998). From conceptual development to science education: A psychological point of view. *International Journal of Science Education, 20,* 1213–1230.

Wellman, H. M. (1990). *The child's theory of mind.* Cambridge, MA: MIT Press.

Williams, J. M., & Tolmie, A. (2000). Conceptual change in biology: Group interaction and the understanding of inheritance. *British Journal of Developmental Psychology, 18,* 625–649.

15

Future Directions for Theory and Research on Intentional Conceptual Change

Paul R. Pintrich
The University of Michigan

Gale M. Sinatra
University of Nevada, Las Vegas

The chapters in this volume comprise one of the first formal attempts to grapple with the issues of intentional learning and apply this perspective to our understanding of conceptual change. Needless to say, there is a great deal of theoretical and empirical work that remains to be done in order to make the general idea of intentional conceptual change a viable and useful one for our psychological models and educational practice. However, the chapters in this volume do mark the beginning of a program of research on intentional conceptual change, and we hope that this volume spurs on others to continue and extend this line of research.

There are a number of issues that need to be clarified and studied for this research area to be fruitful. The purpose of this final chapter is to raise some of these issues and suggest future directions for theory and research. We address seven general issues that are raised by the chapters in this volume: (a) clarifying our definition and models of intentional conceptual change; (b) specifying the structures and processes involved in intentional conceptual change; (c) conceptualizing the nature of potential domain differences; (d) addressing the possibility of developmental differences; (e) measuring intentional conceptual change; (f) clarifying the role of contextual factors; and (g) developing design principles for instruction to facilitate intentional conceptual change.

CLARIFYING OUR DEFINITION AND MODELS OF INTENTIONAL CONCEPTUAL CHANGE

There are a number of different definitions and models of intentional conceptual change presented in these chapters. There are two aspects to this issue. First, there is not necessarily agreement on the nature of conceptual change, regardless of the role of intentionality. For example, as was pointed out in the first chapter and as Linnenbrink and Pintrich also note, there are models of conceptual change that focus on the nature of change in internal cognitive structures, such as the change in children's theories about natural phenomena, or the change in their ontological commitments, or simply the change in their domain-specific concepts and category systems. These cognitive–developmental models often use a metaphor of change that involves the replacement or revision of the internal psychological structures of theories, knowledge, concepts, or category systems. As noted throughout this volume, these models discuss the distinction between radical conceptual change, which involves dramatic and large changes in mental models or frameworks, and conceptual change that involves more fine-tuning or revision of a mental model through addition and integration of new information. In contrast, more contextual models focus on change in the use of different tools to understand phenomena, such as change in the use of p-prims, change in the language used to describe and explain different phenomena, or changes in the ways in which the individual participates in a community of discourse. The differences in these base models of conceptual change make it difficult to refer to one "normative" model of conceptual change that is accepted by the field.

Moreover, once the idea of intentionality is added to the mix of conceptual change models, the complexity and diversity increases greatly. Accordingly, there are different models and definitions of intentionality that are then applied to different base models of conceptual change, resulting in a multiplicity of definitions and models of intentionality and conceptual change. In trying to bring some coherence to this diversity, it seems to us that there are three important assumptions or characteristics of intentional conceptual change that are developed in the chapters in this volume:

- Intentional conceptual change is a goal-directed activity with the goal being a change in conceptual understanding.
- Intentional conceptual changes involves some metacognitive or metaconceptual awareness or consciousness by individuals that they need to change their understanding or that they have a goal of understanding.

- Intentional conceptual change involves some internal agency, volitional control, or self-regulation on the part of individuals as they strive toward this goal of changed understanding.

In terms of the first characteristic, not all chapters adopt the assumption of a goal directed at learning or changing conceptual understanding, but many do include this feature. For example, Ferrari and Elik suggest that individuals do engage in conceptual change when they have a goal of changing their internal representations in order to have a better "mind-to-world fit." Thagard and Zhu explicitly argue that individuals must have a set of cognitive goals that directs their thinking, in particular, a goal of understanding an alternative system that differs from their own. Linnenbrink and Pintrich also note the importance of a goal orientation that is focused on learning and understanding as crucial in focusing an individual on intentional conceptual change.

Given that motivation is defined as the instigation and pursuit of goal-directed activity (Pintrich & Schunk, 2002), many of the other chapters also mention various motivational factors as important in intentional conceptual change. For example, Andre and Windschitl discuss the positive role of interest in conceptual change. Limón also notes that when value beliefs such as interest, importance, and utility are high, then students may be more likely to engage in conceptual change. Hynd discusses the social psychological motivators of attitude and belief change as facilitating or interfering with conceptual change. Related, but conceptually distinct, epistemological beliefs also are suggested as potential facilitators or constraints on conceptual change (e.g., Andre & Windschitl; diSessa, Elby, & Hammer; Mason; Southerland & Sinatra).

Given the generally positive relations among various motivational beliefs such as goals for understanding and value beliefs such as interest, utility, and importance, it is not surprising that these are all invoked as aspects of intentional conceptual change. At the same time, it is not clear if all these different motivational beliefs are necessary for intentional conceptual change. It seems that a goal of understanding or changing one's understanding would be necessary, albeit not sufficient for conceptual change. However, it is not clear if interest, importance, and utility are necessary for intentional conceptual change, or just correlates of motivated learning processes. The same question can be raised about the necessary role of attitudinal and epistemological constructs. This is a clear direction for future research in terms of distinguishing the role of motivational, attitudinal, and epistemological beliefs in the process of conceptual change in general, as well as in intentional conceptual change in particular.

The second assumption concerns the role of metacognitive awareness or becoming conscious of a need to change one's understanding. All the chapters in this volume endorse this assumption in one way or another. For example, Vosniadou highlights the role of metaconceptual awareness of internal inconsistencies in a belief system or theory. Hennessey demonstrates the importance of reflecting on and becoming metacognitively aware of differences between one's own beliefs or theories and representations reflected by teachers, peers, or text materials. Hynd defines intentional conceptual change as a "motivated metacognitive effort." Hatano and Inagaki note that individuals as well as groups of students have to recognize and become aware of the need to change their understanding. Ferrari and Elik claim intentional conceptual change requires what they call metaconsciousness, a special case of metacognition that requires "interpreting and mastering one's intentions in light of deeply held beliefs and values."

The descriptions of the role of metacognition in conceptual change described in these chapters are consistent with the traditional model of conceptual change from science education (e.g., Posner, Strike, Hewson, & Gertzog, 1982). Posner et al. posited the importance of becoming dissatisfied with one's current conceptions and becoming consciously aware of the need to change or revise one's thinking, events requiring a metacognitive or metaconscious awareness. In addition, many other models of conceptual change make this same assumption about the importance of metacognitive awareness (see Schnotz, Vosniadou, & Carretero, 1999).

However, if traditional models of conceptual change make this assumption of metacognitive awareness, then what is new about the idea of intentional conceptual change? We suggest that the assumption of metacognitive awareness alone is not sufficient for intentional conceptual change. Only when combined with the other two proposed characteristics of goal-directed and intentional action does metacognitive awareness become an aspect of intentional conceptual change. Of course, this assumption needs to be tested empirically in future research, but it is one way to distinguish conceptual change that can occur with metacognitive awareness from intentional conceptual change that involves all three assumptions of intentionality. This distinction allows for the fact that not all conceptual change is intentional. In fact, we agree with several contributors to this volume (Hatano & Inagaki; Ferrari & Elik; Vosniadou) that there may be many more occasions when conceptual change is not intentional, albeit it may involve metacognitive awareness.

The third and final assumption of intentional conceptual change is that individuals are agentic learners who take volitional and willful control of their own learning and, through the use of various self-regulatory strategies, come to change their own understandings. In one sense, the second and third assumptions reflect different aspects of metacognition. The second assumption refers to metacognitive awareness and knowledge, whereas the third assumption involves metacognitive control and regulation of learning (e.g., Brown, Bransford, Ferrara, & Campione, 1983; Pintrich, Wolters, & Baxter, 2000). At the same time, the third assumption expands the control and regulation processes to include not just control of cognition, but also control and regulation of motivation, affect, beliefs, and behavior to reflect more current models of self-regulated learning (Pintrich, 2000). For example, Linnenbrink and Pintrich discuss how students might use different cognitive or metacognitive strategies to control their learning in the service of goals of understanding. Vosniadou notes how metaconceptual or metacognitive awareness may not be enough for conceptual change, that conceptual change also requires the active monitoring and control of cognition. de Leeuw and Chi also note how intentional acts such as self-explanation are important intentional strategies undertaken by learners to attain their goal of conceptual understanding. Finally, Ferrari and Elik discuss how self-regulation can vary in quality and argue that intentional conceptual change requires highly effective self-regulation abilities. Clearly, there is a need for more research on the many different types of strategies that individuals may use to control their own learning and how and why these strategies actually result in a change in conceptual understanding.

SPECIFYING THE STRUCTURES AND PROCESSES INVOLVED IN INTENTIONAL CONCEPTUAL CHANGE

If the first issue concerns the "what" or definition of intentional conceptual change, the second issue reflects a focus on the "how" or the operation of intentional conceptual change. Individuals may intentionally use cognitive and metacognitive strategies in their learning (e.g., Linnenbrink & Pintrich; Vosniadou), but exactly how do these strategies result in conceptual restructuring? One explanation provided by de Leeuw and Chi suggests that the intentional strategy of self-explanation reflects students' attempts to correct their own flawed understandings by generating inferences designed to repair their conceptions. They describe how one student's self-explanations "were shown to be specially directed toward the flaws in her domain model, and created a resolution of the conflict between her ... model ... and the [model] described in the text." Further research along these lines is needed to more clearly specify the mechanisms underlying the interaction of intentional strategies and knowledge structures.

Another issue that a number of chapters discuss is the role of epistemological theories or beliefs in intentional conceptual change (e.g., Andre & Windschitl; diSessa et al.; Mason; Southerland & Sinatra). In most of these chapters, the basic idea is that certain types of epistemological beliefs can facilitate intentional conceptual change and that other types of epistemological beliefs can constrain it. However, it is still not clear exactly how these beliefs operate to facilitate or constrain conceptual understanding. Is it a direct mechanism such that different epistemological beliefs give rise to different levels of conceptual understanding? On the other hand, as some of the chapters suggest, epistemological beliefs may exert their influence indirectly such that they allow for the formation of goals of understanding and motivate the use of more thoughtful or deeper or intentional processing. Then, in turn, these processes may exert the more direct influence on conceptual change (Mason; Southerland & Sinatra). Again, there is a need for more research on these different possibilities for how epistemological thinking operates to influence intentional conceptual change.

The same questions about mechanisms or processes can be raised about other motivational constructs as well as social psychological constructs such as attitudes and beliefs. Southerland and Sinatra point out how beliefs and knowledge may have different roles to play in conceptual change, raising the possibility that students may often change their knowledge system and come to understand scientific theories like evolution, but still not accept the theory in terms of their beliefs about the concept. This is an important distinction and suggests a need for more research on how knowledge and belief processes operate in other topics besides evolutionary theory. Other chapters also raise questions about the role of motivational constructs like interest and value (e.g., Andre & Windschitl; Limón) and how these motivational beliefs may facilitate or constrain conceptual change. Most of these chapters suggest that positive motivational beliefs like high levels of interest or value for the topic increase the probability that students will attend to the material to be learned and persist at trying to change their understanding. At the same time, it is not exactly clear how these beliefs relate to intentional processes or to knowledge systems. There is a great need for theory and research to suggest more specific ways in which these motivational beliefs work with knowledge structures and other intentional processes.

CONCEPTUALIZING THE NATURE OF POTENTIAL DOMAIN DIFFERENCES

Southerland and Sinatra note the importance of domain differences in how intentional processes may interact with the nature of the topic. They show that the processes may vary depending on whether the topic is a controversial one, such as evolution, or a less controversial one. Although research on conceptual change has explored the nature of understanding in a myriad of topics in science, history, mathematics, etc., there has been little discussion about the potential for different processes to operate depending on the domain or topic. The nascent research on intentionality and motivation in conceptual change has paid even less attention to the possibility of substantive domain differences in the processes of conceptual change.

Many of the models of metacognition, self-regulation, and motivation are rather domain-general models and assume that the processes will operate in similar ways across domains. However, this may not be the case. The chapter by Limón shows how domain-specific knowledge enables the use of more sophisticated reasoning and thinking in a domain. In fact, she suggests that students low in domain knowledge may not even be aware of how their own knowledge differs from more sophisticated understandings. It also may be that different levels of domain-specific knowledge enable the generation of different goals as well as different types of intentional regulatory strategies. That is, beyond the possibility of general domain differences due to the nature of the content (e.g., Limón), there may be personal or individual differences in how knowledge, goals, and regulation interact to facilitate or constrain conceptual change. Similarly, Hynd illustrates in her chapter how motivational beliefs affected the processing of persuasive history texts by historians with low topic knowledge but high disciplinary knowledge. There is a need for more research on the nature of these interactions and how they relate to intentional conceptual change.

ADDRESSING THE POSSIBILITY OF DEVELOPMENTAL DIFFERENCES

Of course, given that intentional conceptual change includes various metacognitive or self-regulatory processes, there are likely to be developmental differences. Metacognitive control and self-regulation are relatively late-developing processes, often not developing until later childhood and adolescence (Brown et al, 1983; Schneider & Pressley, 1997). Of course, there are different aspects of self-regulation (e.g., emotional regulation) that play a role in early childhood, but in academic learning contexts, younger students often struggle with regulating their own learning (Pintrich & Zusho, 2002). Hennessey describes how elementary school children can be metacognitive, but still have difficulty translating their metacognitive awareness into strategies for regulating and changing their own understandings. This general developmental trend suggests that intentional conceptual change may be less likely to occur in younger children due to developmental constraints.

Interestingly, there is some developmental work that suggests that younger children may be more likely than older children to adopt a general mastery goal orientation (Dweck & Leggett, 1988; Pintrich & Zusho, 2002). It is expected that a general mastery goal orientation should lead to more self-regulation and conceptual change (Linnenbrink & Pintrich; Pintrich, 1999; Pintrich, Marx, & Boyle, 1993). If this is the case, then there is the paradoxical prediction that younger children who are more mastery-oriented would be more likely to engage in self-regulation and conceptual change. However, this paradox highlights the importance of considering both motivational and cognitive systems in understanding developmental change. Although it may be that younger children are more likely to be mastery-oriented, if they do not have the requisite metacognitive and self-regulatory strategies available to them, they may still have difficulty in conceptual understanding. Besides the importance of considering the developmental differences in motivation and cognition, this point highlights the need to consider how all three aspects of intentional conceptual change—goals, awareness, and self-regulation—work together developmentally to produce conceptual understanding.

MEASURING INTENTIONAL CONCEPTUAL CHANGE

As noted in this chapter, there are theoretical and substantive difficulties that must be resolved in order for research on intentional conceptual change to progress. At the same time, as in most scientific research, advances in theory go hand-in-hand with new developments in measurement and ways of conducting empirical research on the construct. The chapters in this volume represent some diversity in their methods for assessing intentional conceptual change, and the differences in methods raise some important questions about the future of empirical research on intentional conceptual change.

Many of the chapters use self-report questionnaire methods (e.g., Andre & Windschitl; Southerland & Sinatra) that have the advantage of providing clear operationalizations of the different constructs as well as being very pragmatic and easy to use with larger samples. There are direct measures of the different constructs, and the relations among the different constructs are easily indexed. This provides important information not only about the relations among the different constructs, but also about the potential processes of how intentional conceptual change operates. At the same time, self-report questionnaires tend to abstract the construct from the context and do not allow for fine-grained analysis of how the constructs might operate in different contexts. In addition, they tend to reify the boundaries between constructs, limiting the ways in which a researcher can really examine how the different constructs interact in a dynamic fashion. For example, if there are three general aspects of intentional conceptual change, self-reports could generate three different measures of goals, awareness, and self-regulation. However, these measures would be rather static indicators and would not necessarily permit an analysis of how goals serve to direct self-regulation of understanding as it actually happens in the context.

In contrast, interviews are somewhat better at capturing how different aspects of intentional conceptual change facilitate and constrain one another, mutually interacting within the context. For example, diSessa et al. show how one student's goals for understanding related to her epistemological thinking as well as her actual understanding of physics concepts. de Leeuw and Chi's methodology involves asking students to generate explanations while problem solving or thinking aloud. The examples given in these chapters show how dynamic the processes and interactions are between goals, content knowledge, and thinking in context. It is very difficult for self-report questionnaires to capture these dynamic and contextual relations. At the same time, interview data are limited in terms of the clear specification of the explanatory structures and processes that are operating. They provide excellent descriptions and can generate hypotheses, but need to be complemented with other methods.

Observations were less represented in this book, although Hennessey reports on children's statements as they engaged in instruction designed to foster conceptual change. Hatano and Inagaki also discuss children's behaviors and actions as they worked in small groups and classrooms focused on conceptual change. These types of data provide excellent examples of how the nature of the context can facilitate and constrain goals, metacognitive awareness, intentional strategy use, and ultimately conceptual understanding. They highlight the power of the context and the need for contextualizing our models of intentional conceptual change.

At the same time, if we assume that at least some aspect of intentional conceptual change is internally motivated and regulated, then there is also a need for data on the internal processes that are on-going as students work in these classrooms. This type of data can be supplied by self-reports, interviews, or stimulated recall from videos of the classroom (a method not discussed in this volume). It seems likely that in order to capture aspects of both individual internal processes and the role of context, there is a great need for studies that use multiple methods. This has been rare in most studies of intentional conceptual change, but should be a hallmark of future research.

CLARIFYING THE ROLE OF CONTEXTUAL FACTORS

Beyond issues of assessing the role of context, there are questions regarding the general role of contextual factors. As outlined in this chapter and in many of the chapters in this volume, intentional conceptual change is directed by individual personal goals and regulated by an individual's strategies and actions. This suggests a fairly individual and internal psychological model of intentional conceptual change. At the same time, it seems clear that contextual factors cannot be ignored in our models. Hatano and Inagaki make a strong case that intentional conceptual change is not motivated or supported strictly by individual goals or strategies. They propose that it must be induced socioculturally through the design of classroom activities (e.g., conceptual pegs, introduction of incongruities) that actively support, encourage, guide, and direct students to engage in the various individual goal-directed and intentional activities that should lead to conceptual understanding. Ferrari and Elik also describe intentional conceptual change within groups and broader cultural institutions.

These authors suggest that not only are the teacher's actions important, but that peer groups and peer behavior are also crucial. For example, peer groups that work together to resolve inconsistencies or incongruities provide support to one another to continue the deeper level analysis and thoughtfulness that are necessary for conceptual understanding to take place. Hatano and Inagaki suggest that this type of contextual support is necessary for intentional conceptual change and that without the contextual support, it is not likely that individuals will engage in intentional conceptual change. This is a clear direction for future research in terms of the relative roles of the individual and contextual factors. However, at this point in the development of the field, it is probably not fruitful or useful to continue to pit these two general factors against one another to see which one determines or exerts the greater influence on conceptual change. It is clear that both individual and contextual factors play a role, and the important questions for future research concern how they operate and interact together to produce intentional conceptual change.

DEVELOPING DESIGN PRINCIPLES FOR INSTRUCTION

Finally, the chapters in this volume do suggest some principles that could be useful in the design of instruction to facilitate intentional conceptual change. In some ways, intentional conceptual change relies on the individual and internal psychological processes, as do many models of self-regulation more generally (Pintrich, 2000). However, it is clear that contextual factors play an important role in motivating, instigating, and guiding an individual's self-regulation, so they also should play an important role in intentional conceptual change. Of course, there is much research to be done on the instructional implications of intentional conceptual change, but the following principles may be useful in designing instructional interventions to help test the different ideas proposed in this volume.

First, instruction should attempt to foster a goal of conceptual understanding or mastery in students. There are many ways to do this, including fostering interest in course content (Andre & Windschitl), aiding students' development of epistemological awareness and sophistication (Andre & Windschitl; Southerland & Sinatra), and focusing classroom discourse on understanding (Hennessey; Hatano & Inagaki), to name only a few. Basically, this design principle focuses on the first aspect of intentional conceptual change—goals directed toward learning and understanding.

Second, instruction should attempt to make students aware of the gaps or problems in their conceptual understanding. This principle invokes the general metacognitive or metaconceptual awareness assumption of intentional conceptual change as well as conceptual change models more generally (Vosniadou). There are many suggestions for how to highlight for students the incongruity (Hatano & Inagaki) or flaws (deLeeuw & Chi) in their conceptions. Hynd describes how refutational texts create dissonance that can spark processing similar to that evoked by self-explanations. She explains that on reading persuasive refutation texts, students "become aware of the aspects of the message that cause the dissonance and actively seek to resolve the discomfort." Many teachers already use the strategy of creating dissonance in their instruction, but this does not always result in students adopting a goal of restructuring their understanding. More research is needed to examine the interaction of contextual and individual factors to better explain how and why some individuals not only realize discrepancies but also take the action necessary to restructure their knowledge.

Third, instruction should offer or teach students different strategies for regulating and controlling their own cognition in order to foster deeper conceptual understanding. For example, instruction in self-explanation (de Leeuw & Chi) would be a strategy that most students could learn and it could be helpful to them in reaching a deeper understanding. Modeling or teaching other types of self-questioning or metacognitive strategies also would be helpful in fostering conceptual change (Linnenbrink & Pintrich).

As pointed out by several chapters in this volume, conceptual change is not always "cold" and may involve emotional commitments to ideas (Thagard & Zhu; Limón) or epistemological beliefs (diSessa et al.; Mason) that can hinder conceptual understanding. Thagard and Zhu explain that "having the intention to understand and evaluate alternative views can make the emotional component of conceptual change more easily realized." It would be helpful for teachers to model and teach students strategies for coping with emotional attachments or strategies for "setting aside" prior epistemological commitments and being open to new ideas (Thagard & Zhu; Southerland & Sinatra).

Last, both Hatano and Inagaki as well as Hennessey note the importance of building a classroom context that supports conceptual understanding. In many ways, this suggestion is in line with the general design principle of "building a community of learners" (Bransford, Brown, & Cocking, 1999) where students and teachers support one another in their quest for understanding. In these contexts, norms and expectations are developed that encourage all students to question their knowledge, become aware of their own knowledge and strengths and weaknesses, and work together to learn and understand. In addition, the nature of the tasks, the instructional practices, and the assessment tools used all help to focus and support conceptual understanding.

Our goals for this volume were to inspire researchers to more carefully consider the role of the learner in the conceptual change process, to balance internal and external factors in change models, and to contribute to the development of a more effective conceptual change pedagogy. The chapters included here do not satisfy these goals; rather, they represent only a beginning. We hope the researchers included here continue to pursue these productive lines of research, and we invite other researchers to explore the potential of intentional conceptual change.

REFERENCES

Bransford, J., Brown, A., & Cocking, R. (1999). *How people learn: Brain, mind, experience, and school.* Washington, DC: National Academy Press.

Brown, A., Bransford, J., Ferrara, R., & Campione, J. (1983). Learning, remembering, and understanding. In P. H. Mussen (Series Ed.) & J. Flavell & E. Markman (Vol. Eds.), *Handbook of child psychology: Vol. 3. Cognitive development* (4th ed., pp. 77–166). New York: Wiley.

Dweck, C., & Leggett, E. (1988). A social-cognitive approach to motivation and personality. *Psychological Review, 95,* 256–273.

Pintrich, P. R. (1999). The role of motivation in promoting and sustaining self-regulated learning. *International Journal of Educational Research, 31,* 459–470.

Pintrich, P. R. (2000). The role of goal orientation in self-regulated learning. In M. Boekaerts, P. R. Pintrich, & M. Zeidner (Eds.), *Handbook of self-regulation* (pp. 451–502). San Diego, CA: Academic Press.

Pintrich, P. R., Marx, R., & Boyle, R. (1993). Beyond "cold" conceptual change: The role of motivational beliefs and classroom contextual factors in the process of conceptual change. *Review of Educational Research, 63,* 167–199.

Pintrich, P. R., & Schunk, D. H. (2002). *Motivation in education: Theory, research, and applications.* Englewood Cliffs, NJ: Merrill Prentice Hall.

Pintrich, P. R., Wolters, C., & Baxter, G. (2000). Assessing metacognition and self-regulated learning. In G. Schraw & J. Impara (Eds.), *Issues in the measurement of metacognition* (pp. 43–97). Lincoln, NE: Buros Institute of Mental Measurements.

Pintrich, P. R., & Zusho, A. (2002). The development of academic self-regulation: The role of cognitive and motivational factors. In A. Wigfield & J. Eccles (Eds.), *The development of achievement motivation* (pp. 249–284). San Diego, CA: Academic Press.

Posner, G., Strike, K., Hewson, P., & Gertzog, W. (1982). Accommodation of a scientific conception: Toward a theory of conceptual change. *Science Education, 66,* 211–227.

Schneider, W., & Pressley, M. (1997). *Memory development between two and twenty*. Mahwah, NJ: Lawrence Erlbaum Associates.

Schnotz, W., Vosniadou, S., & Carretero, M. (1999). *New perspectives on conceptual change*. Amsterdam: Pergamon Elsevier Science.

Author Index

A

B

C

G

H

M

N

S

Subject Index

B

D

E

F

G

H

I

N

O

P

S

T

U

X

Y

Z